MW00615338

ANCIENT
Ocean Crossings

ANCIENT
Ocean Crossings

Reconsidering the Case for Contacts
with the Pre-Columbian Americas

STEPHEN C. JETT

The University of Alabama Press
Tuscaloosa

The University of Alabama Press
Tuscaloosa, Alabama 35487-0380
uapress.ua.edu

Typeface: Scala and Scala Sans

Manufactured in the United States of America
Cover image: Japanese woodcut of a nine-bamboo sailing-raft from Tai-tung, Formosa
(Taiwan), 1803, from S. N. Hata, *A Voyage to the Island of Chi-po-ran*
Cover design: Erin Bradley Dangar/Dangar Design

Cataloging-in-Publication data is available from the Library of Congress.
ISBN: 978-0-8173-1939-7
E-ISBN: 978-0-8173-9075-4

To all those living academics courageous enough to have continued pursuing their convictions concerning ancient contacts in the face of a highly negative intellectual climate, and who, despite the professional risks, have managed to make great contributions to building the study of transoceanic interinfluences into a serious and respectable endeavor. These and their departed predecessors are the giants on whose shoulders I stand.

Contents

Illustrations

Preface

In 1955, when I was entering my senior year in high school, unbeknownst to me the American Museum of Natural History archaeologist Gordon F. Ekholm wrote the following: "For many years it has been tacitly accepted as one of the basic tenets of Americanist [archaeological] studies that everything above the level of the simpler cultures such as could have existed at an early time in the subarctic regions of Siberia and Alaska was independently invented or developed in the New World. We have proceeded to study American Indian history with this as a basic assumption and have trained our students to look no further. . . . We often read that archaeological researches in the Americas have an especial value because they deal with an example of culture history isolated from the main stream of culture history in the Old World."[1] But—again, unknown to me—during the 1950s Ekholm and a few others were putting a major dent in the assumption of interhemispheric independence between the time that Ice Age hunters crossed the then-dry Bering Strait into America and the moment that Christopher Columbus arrived in the Bahamas in 1492. Little did I imagine that I was to become a major player in the study of the then (and still) much-reviled notion that a long history of pre-1492 transoceanic voyaging to many of the pre-Columbian societies of the Americas had resulted in increments, that such increments may even have been a primary stimulus for the emergence of true civilizations in the Western Hemisphere, and that these transoceanic contacts may have had consequential reciprocal effects on the history of the Eastern Hemisphere.

As an undergraduate majoring in geology at Princeton University in the late 1950s, I heard about a German meteorologist named Alfred Wegener, who in 1912 had proposed a theory that he called "continental drift." He had noticed that the coasts of the continents on either side of the Atlantic seemed roughly parallel, so that if those landmasses could be pushed together, the parts would fit more or less snugly against one another. Wegener's and others' investigations indicated that the sequences of rock strata at certain spots on opposite sides, as well as the fossils in those strata, were identical, and that the distributions of certain families of wild plants seemed inexplicable except on the basis of the continents' once having been joined. Accordingly, Wegener concluded that (long, long before the advent of humans on the planet) there had existed a supercontinent, which he called Pangaea, that subsequently broke up, its pieces then floating about over the ages and ultimately reaching their present positions.

Geologists of Wegener's time derided such ideas as "pseudoscience" and the "delirious ravings" of a mere meteorologist. And, as my geology professors said forty-five years later, in the interim virtually no reputable scientist had accepted the theory of continental drift. This was because no plausible mechanism had ever been proposed that could account for the continents' plowing through thousands of miles of solid oceanic crust, a phenomenon that had never been observed. Geologists' initial rejection of drift theory had not altered much over the years, even in light of the post-Wegener finding that the alignment of magnetic minerals (whose orientations indicate the directions of Earth's magnetic poles at the time of the formation of the rocks) were everywhere consistent in very late rocks but became increasingly more divergent among the continents the farther back in time one went. I couldn't believe what I was hearing. There seemed to be no way in which all of these independent phenomena could be accounted for *other* than by the continents' having split and moved. There *had* to be a mechanism—the evidence showed that—we just hadn't identified it yet. What was wrong with these doubting geologists?

As it turned out, the chairman of our own department, Harry H. Hess, was, along with his colleagues, in the process of developing a hypothesis about a possible mechanism of movement: convection currents in Earth's plastically deformable subsurface mantle that, as they diverged at the tops of their rising plumes, split overlying continents apart and, like snail-paced conveyor belts, carried the resulting pieces slowly in opposite directions. This concept, which came to be called "sea-floor spreading," supplied the missing mechanism for continental movement. It galvanized geologists around the globe and set the stage for the novel concept of "plate tectonics." This new paradigm accounted plausibly for a host of otherwise inexplicable phenomena, from island arcs to mountain building, from the geographical distribution of earthquakes and volcanism to that of metallic mineral deposits. As the geologist Kenneth Deffreyes said around 1970, "Ninety-nine per cent of the profession have had to admit they were wrong, including a great many who were in print saying continental migration couldn't possibly happen."[2] Wegener—with some modification and much amplification—was redeemed. As the physicist Thomas Gold put it, "A person who thought that continents or parts of continents might have moved in the past was ridiculed before 1960, despite the existence of good evidence from magnetic rock measurements. After 1965 anyone who did not believe in such movement was again a subject of ridicule."[3] Here we have a classic demonstration of the dictum that all truth passes through three stages: initial ridicule, subsequent violent opposition, and ultimate acceptance as self-evident fact.

In my schooling, I seemed to be destined to encounter questions of intercontinental connections. When I interviewed for admission to the PhD program in geography at Johns Hopkins University, I talked with Professor George F. Carter, a one-time graduate student of the renowned cultural geographer Carl Ortwin Sauer at the University of California, Berkeley. Carter spoke to me of his interest in the question of ancient transoceanic Old World cultural influences on certain Native American societies. Except for some vague notion concerning jade, my education had been conventional regarding this matter, and my reaction was a bit incredulous: "Aren't the cultures of the two hemispheres generally considered to be independent?," I asked. I thought to myself, If there really *were* something to this notion, wouldn't I have heard about it? Carter spoke of all sorts of evidence of interhemispheric contacts, especially the pre-Columbian sharing of a number of cultivated-plant species. I was polite but remained highly skeptical.

I "knew" that until around the time of Christopher Columbus, everyone had thought that the earth was flat, ending with an edge that one risked falling over; that marine architecture wasn't capable of creating ocean-crossing ships; and that the absence of the magnetic compass had prevented ships from safely sailing far out of sight of land. So I wondered if Carter was "all there" intellectually. I'm sorry to say that my perception's analogy to the resistance to Wegener's ideas that I had decried in geology escaped me at the time: the notion that cultural similarities across the seas, no matter how detailed, had to be independent, because no means of contact—neither adequate watercraft nor navigational techniques—were known to exist in pre-Columbian times.

While still at Princeton, I had taken the university's one (short-lived) anthropology course, with the sociologist Melvin Tumin and the social anthropologist Paul Bohannon, and had audited a course in linguistics. I had received intensive training in history in high school. And although I had been a geology major, my first aim as an undergraduate had been the acquisition of a *breadth* of knowledge. Accordingly, I had enrolled in many courses in what could collectively be called "culture history": the natures and histories of art and architecture, music, world religions, and philosophy—including a course in the philosophy of science with Carl Hempel, one of the two philosophers most often invoked by those who wished to make the social sciences, including anthropology, "scientific" (the other being Karl Popper). Thus when at Johns Hopkins I took Professor Carter's advanced cultural geography course, I found that I was intellectually "preadapted" to his history-of-culture approach.

Carl Sauer and his Berkeley colleague (and neighbor), the preeminent anthropologist Alfred Louis Kroeber, had greatly influenced each other, and Carter assigned Kroeber's geographically oriented 1948 *Anthropology* as the textbook for his class. I was dazzled by the book's breadth, information, and ideas. This was what I was *really* interested in, I discovered, but hadn't previously known about as an organized approach to knowledge. My new focus, then, was what is best termed "culture-historical geography": the study of the spatial aspects of the origins, spreads, distributions, and artifactual and landscape manifestations of cultural phenomena as they have developed and changed through time.

Some of Carter's ideas—widely considered radical, and widely dismissed—were certainly astounding, but I found those relating to transoceanic influences on the Americas to be increasingly persuasive as a whole. Carter permitted me to browse in his personal library of books and offprints of articles. Most riveting to me was Thor Heyerdahl's 1953 *American Indians in the Pacific*. My parents had read Heyerdahl's 1950 *Kon-Tiki* aloud to me as a boy, and I had found the adventure intriguing. But here, in *American Indians*, was an incredibly massive collection of multifarious lines of evidence bearing on the question of ancient pan-Pacific connections—what the 1947 *Kon-Tiki* experimental raft voyage had really been about: an attempt to demonstrate that means of ocean voyaging had been available to the ancients. Night after night, I stayed up late devouring this material, which included plant evidence, physical-anthropological comparisons, and cultural indicators.

We graduate students were required to produce research papers for Carter's courses. One paper I wrote was on the discovery and settlement of the Polynesian islands, in connection with which I read many works other than Heyerdahl's. One such book was Harold Gatty's 1958 *Nature Is Your Guide*, which as an undergraduate had introduced me to way-finding at sea (I must also acknowledge that C. S. Forester's Horatio Hornblower novels, which I read as a teenager, initially sparked my fascination for things nautical). Another work was the New Zealand historian Andrew Sharp's 1957 *Ancient Voyagers in the Pacific*, which argued for the west–east accidental settlement of the islands rather than intentional maritime migrations from the Americas as per Heyerdahl. I found that I concurred with some of both of these authors' ideas and dissented with others. A second term paper was inspired by Erland Nordenskiöld's 1931 *Origin of the Indian Civilizations in South America*. This paper eventually led to my writing articles delineating the many close similarities between ancient Indonesians and tropical Native Americans, particularly their shared weapon, the blowgun.

My general training in geography—"the spatial science," in which diffusion and distribution are integral concepts—conditioned me to thinking in terms of movement in geographic space and gave me background in earth-sun relationships, climatology, oceanography, and other matters relevant to ocean voyaging and navigation. Although I have worked on questions of transoceanic contact on and off over the years since my graduate school days, I have also done intensive cultural and historical work on the Navajo (Diné) of the American Southwest. This has provided me with an in-depth view of one particular people with which to balance the necessarily much shallower, generalist approach needed to make global culture-historical comparisons, giving me some perspective on how particular cultures actually operate over time.[4]

This book explores the general notion of pre-Columbian—and mostly pre-Norse—contacts between the Eastern and Western Hemispheres—with an emphasis on evidence for interaction rather than on the unanswerable question as to what individual or society was the "first" to "discover" America via the open oceans.

My main long-term goal in this area of investigation is simple. Negatively, my aim is to avoid my interpretations' being conditioned by any social or political idealism—not so easy in this values-charged area of investigation. Also eschewed is any attempt to "explain" cultural similarities solely by describing their respective cultural and ecological functions and relationships or by leaning on untested deductions as to how specific cultural similarities in distantly separated areas "must" have arisen according to evolutionary theory—that is, being in some sense deterministically elicited by preexisting cultural structures or by physical-environmental, psychological, societal, economic, and demographic considerations. Positively, my ambition is to begin with detailed empirical investigation and analysis and to proceed from there to applying, to the data obtained, carefully formulated evaluative criteria intended to ascertain, to the extent feasible, both what was possible and what actually happened in the past—whether significant transoceanic interaction really did take place—with a future target of attempting to distinguish between those interhemispheric cultural similarities best accounted for on the basis of contact and influence, and those more likely to be of independent origin.

That endeavor, in addition to providing some history of the controversy surrounding it, is what this book is largely about. Despite my remarks concerning the avoidance of theoretical assumptions, the approach is not atheoretical, and my future goal is to examine the general implications of the revised view of culture history that emerges—that is, what all of this may mean in terms of our understanding of how and under what conditions humans innovate, and how and why their cultures change, and elaborate or remain relatively static. The question of transoceanic contacts may or may not have as much potential for producing a paradigm shift as did the issues that Wegener addressed. However, my postulation that the hemispheres' more complex pre-Columbian cultures to some significant extent participated in what I call a "global ecumene" does have far-reaching implications for better comprehending humankind, its operations, and its history.

Although I give a number of examples of the myriad commonalities between various cultures of the Old World and the New, the present book is not intended to survey or explain them. Still, these commonalities do give much cause to question the notion of complete cultural independence between the hemispheres, as well as an incentive to investigate how such contacts could have occurred and whether they did in fact occur. It is the latter of these broad questions—rather than the issues as to precisely who may have gone where, and when, with what cultural baggage to transfer, and with what consequences—that is the focus of the present work.

Despite the publication of many books and articles since Thor Heyerdahl's best-selling 1950 volume *Kon-Tiki*, no one has attempted an organized, rigorous effort to provide an inclusive review of the many important scholarly considerations bearing upon the question of early transoceanic contacts; the subject is too vast to be encompassed within the pages of a single work. Much striking evidence, in a multiplicity of disciplines, has appeared rather recently. As detailed in the introduction, the present volume considers the physical-geographic, nautical, and navigational issues; possible motives for ocean crossings; and the physical and biological evidence of contacts having occurred. Cultural comparisons and their theoretical implications—along with discussion of subjective reasons for widespread opposition to the notion of long-distance diffusion—await a second book.

It is a truly daunting task to tackle such an enormous and heatedly debated topic, but the time seems ripe for reconsideration of these issues, and investigation has been enormously facilitated by a major research tool, John L. Sorenson and Martin H. Raish's monumental *Pre-Columbian Contacts with the Americas across the Oceans: An Annotated Bibliography* (1990, 1996; in both print and searchable diskette form), and its continuation in *Pre-Columbiana: A Journal of Long-Distance Contacts*, of which I am the editor. Another highly useful annotated bibliography of less global scope is Nicholas J. Goetzfridt's 1992 *Indigenous Navigation and Voyaging in the Pacific: A Reference Guide*. The reader is also directed to a succinct but pithy and well-balanced historiography of the transoceanic contacts controversy, Eugene R. Fingerhut's 1994 *Explorers of Pre-Columbian America? The Diffusionist-Inventionist Controversy*. One may also mention Jordan E. Kerber's 1991 *Coastal and Maritime Archaeology: A Bibliography* and take note of the ongoing Bibliographia Maritima in *Pre-Columbiana*.

Let us set sail, then, on a metaphorical voyage of discovery across the ancient global ocean.

Acknowledgments

The first acknowledgment must go to the late George F. Carter (1912–2004), whose influences were formative and fundamental, and whose early enthusiasm about this book project was gratifying. In addition to inspiring me with his publications, the late Thor Heyerdahl also made one or two observations on my early work. Stimulus came, too, from the many other individuals alluded to in this book's dedication. In addition, the writings of the late Stephen Jay Gould provided wonderful inspiration in the form of insights, erudition, and grace of expression.

The critical stimulation of presentations and discussions at various scholarly conferences should be mentioned. In that connection, I acknowledge specifically the late Douglas Fraser, the late Thor Heyerdahl, Carol L. Riley, the late J. Charles Kelley, Campbell W. Pennington, the late Robert L. Rands, Paul Shao, the late William McGlone, Phillip M. Leonard, the late James P. Whittall Jr., the late Rollin W. Gillespie, Helen K. Crotty, the late Jon Polansky, John J. White III, James Leslie, Roslyn Strong, the late Joseph B. Mahan Jr., William and Nancy Yaw Davis, and Alison T. Stenger.

I would like to thank Donald E. Vermeer for getting me involved as the Association of American Geographers representative to the Anthropology section of the American Association for the Advancement of Science, at whose 1995 conference the idea for this book began; the editor William Frucht for catalyzing the project; Alice Beck Kehoe (who recommended the University of Alabama Press), Carl L. Johannessen, John L. Sorenson, and the late David H. Kelley for ideas, corrections, and strong intellectual support over the years; and my wife and fellow geographer Lisa Roberts Jett for forbearance and general support. Phil Hailes's enthusiastic encouragement and helpful editorial suggestions are also appreciated, as are efforts on the part of Jeneen "Lucky" Becket; thanks, too, to Gunnar Thompson and Celia Heil. The late Louis Winkler made helpful observations concerning astronomy, as did Jarew Manning concerning microbiology. Don Eckler alerted me to some useful maps, and a number of others drew my attention to relevant references. I thank Gillett G. Griffin, Frank Norick, and the late Daniel J. Crowley for their friendly but keen challenges to some of my diffusionist observations. James L. Guthrie suggested (and created) several sources and generally provided intellectual stimulation.

Discussions with other cultural geographers not involved in transoceanic contact studies, including Frederick J. Simoons, the late Terry L. Jordan, the late Philip L. Wagner, and Charles F. Gritzner, were important stimulants as well, as were exchanges with myriad anthropologists/archaeologists, historians, art historians, botanists, human geneticists, oceanographers, and others, including laypeople. Among those from whom I learned much were my University of California, Davis, colleagues in anthropology and their graduate students—perhaps most from Dan Crowley and his student Katherine Brenda Branstetter—with whom my Department of Geography shared a floor during my early years there.

I thank the personnel of the multifarious libraries, particularly those of the Davis, Berkeley, and San Diego campuses of the University of California; and those of Emory University, the University of Georgia, Case Western Reserve University, the Cleveland Public Library, the Library of Congress, East Tennessee State University, and the Washington County (Virginia) Public Library. The private library of my stepfather the late John Ashbel Greene of Cleveland, Ohio, was most helpful regarding modern small-boat voyaging.

Versions of portions of the text have appeared in earlier publications (acknowledged in the text) and are used herein with permission of the Conference of Latin Americanist Geographers, Odyssey Verlag Wien, and *Pre-Columbiana*. Acknowledged with thanks, too, are the various entities and individuals who accorded permission to reproduce illustrations. Dean Barr provided photo services. Initial editing was done by Tim Yohn, followed by copyediting on the part of Anna Painter under the supervision of Paul Farrell. The interest and encouragement of Joseph B. Powell, then of the University of Alabama Press, and the enthusiasm of the thoughtful reviewers Kent Mathewson and Daniel W. Gade, resulted in acquisition of the manuscript by the press. In addition, the work has benefited from the editorial and other efforts of Daniel Waterman, editor in chief, and the helpful direct editorial oversight of the press's Wendi Schnaufer. Dawn Hall served as my meticulous copyeditor and Bonny McLaughlin as indexing coordinator.

Robert and Sharon Wilson kindly provided a generous subvention toward production costs.

ANCIENT
Ocean Crossings

Figure I.1. "The Knowledge of the Islands Newly Found by the King of Spain" through Christopher Columbus. Woodcut by Giuliano Dati, Florence, Italy, 1493.

Introduction

The [1492] discovery of America, and that of a passage to the East Indies by the Cape of Good Hope [in 1497], are the two greatest and most important events recorded in the history of mankind.
—Adam Smith, *Wealth of Nations*, 1776

Columbus and Consequences

On the morning of October 12, 1492—some half a century after Johannes Gutenberg had published the first book printed with moveable type, and thirty-nine years after the Turks had taken Constantinople and thus ended the last political vestige of the Roman Empire, and the same number of years after the Battle of Castillon at which the cannons of the French had decisively ended the supremacy of the English longbow—three ships commanded by Christopher Columbus landed on a speck of land in the Bahamas, one the admiral took to be an offshore isle of Asia.[1]

The European Middle Ages had already largely given way to the Renaissance, helped along by expanded learning and the widening use of gunpowder, and the Great Age of Discovery was in progress. The ultimate legacy of Columbus's landfall, accomplished on behalf of the Castilian crown, was a world changed in revolutionary ways, and the year 1492 signaled the commencement of unprecedented far-flung extrahemispheric conquests and colonizations on the part of several emerging European nation-states.

Migrations of Europeans to the "New World" (a world not recognized as "new" by Columbus himself) grew from the ensuing trickle of the 1490s into an ever-increasing tide. Natives of the Americas—and those of Australia and the Pacific islands—came to be decimated, displaced, and deculturated. Surviving populations underwent various degrees of miscegenation and were subjected to Latin- and German-derived languages and to Roman Catholic and, later, Protestant Christianity. At the same time, the interlopers introduced to the natives crops that these indigenes had not previously known, such as wheat, barley, and rice, as well as Eurasian domesticated animals: sheep, goats, cattle, horses, donkeys, and hogs. The harvests, cuisines, and demography of the Old World were forever, if slowly, altered as well by the bringing back of potatoes, manioc (cassava), and so forth.

More insidiously, diseases of the Old World were transmitted to the non-immune native peoples of the New, with devastating results—the Native American population crashed from perhaps 44 million to a mere two or three million in less than a century. Too, these seemingly ocean-isolated peoples and their continents—mentioned by neither Aristotle nor the Bible—created a crisis in European thought concerning an unthinkable separate creation. In brief, the greatest demographic and cultural collapses and most massive migrations and cultural and biological transfers of human history, as well as the transformation of traditional perceptions on both sides of the seas, had commenced, and the modern era had truly begun. Western civilization, and then much of the rest of the world, was to be metamorphosed from cultures based almost entirely on tradition into ones founded on innovation; from religion-driven ways of life to a significantly secular emphasis; and from essentially rural populations to mostly urban ones. Earth was to become definitively interlinked in a transportational, economic, and political network.

The Rutgers sociologist Eviatar Zerubavel has written, "only from Europe's standpoint was America discovered by Columbus. Only from an extremely narrow Eurocentric perspective can October 12, 1492, be seen as a beginning."[2] But "discovery" is not the main point of 1492; that year symbolizes the initiation of the unprecedented era of continuing European overseas exploration, exploitation, and colonization, of the development of a truly global modern "world system," and of the massive so-called Columbian exchange of people, animals, plants, and pestilences.

Despite Columbus's status in this regard, it is now agreed that he had a handful of Norse predecessors, as far as Europeans actually reaching the New World and establishing (temporary) settlement there are concerned. These known pre-Columbian sojourners in North America beyond Greenland, first sailing under the command of the Icelander Leif Eiríksson (Erikson)—now of Greenland—reached what is presently eastern Canada around AD 1000 and overwintered, with Leif's kinsman and successor Thorfinn Karlsefni establishing a short-lived settlement in this "Vínland" in about 1008.[3] However, this Norse feat is usually not accorded great cultural importance, because the lasting impacts of the brief European presence in Norse Vínland and environs are usually perceived of as having been negligible in both hemispheres (a perception that has been changing slightly in recent years).

Either/Or: Diffusionism versus Independent-Inventionism

Conventional thinking has long taken it as given that before the era of Leif Eiríksson the two hemispheres were entirely or essentially cut off from each other; that subsequent to initial settlement of the Americas by overland, foot-powered migration via the Bering Strait region during lowered-sea-level periods of the Late Pleistocene epoch (an "ice age" ending some 11,000 years ago), the post-Pleistocene meltwater-fed rising oceans formed effectively impermeable barriers to further interhemispheric communication. As Gabriel Haslip-Viera, Bernard Ortiz de Montellano, and Warren Barbour put it—ignoring the Norse—it is "the view of the profession that Old World explorers did *not* come to the Americas before Columbus."[4] The implication of this view is, then, that the cultures of the Old World and those of the Americas developed essentially independently of one another, and this remains the prevailing opinion. Here is a late twentieth-century (and extreme) restatement of the position, by a prominent historian of maritime cartography: "Each emergent civilization as it came to consciousness—in Mesopotamia, China, or America—was aware only of its own immediate environment. For thousands of years of human history this pattern was maintained, of multiple civilizations developing in isolation and ignorance of each other. This isolation was a natural product of physical geography, the impassible barriers of ocean, desert and mountain."[5]

This perception of the wholly separate evolutions of Earth's early civilizations, especially those of the Old World vis-à-vis those of the New, is a hoary one.[6] It originated in part from the general ignorance of the existence of the Americas on the part of Renaissance Europeans, who were astonished by what the explorations of Columbus and his successors had revealed. If *we* knew nothing of this new world, was the thought, then neither could our predecessors have known of it, much less Asians or Africans, they being less advanced and more distant. Importantly, too, the idea of culture-historical separateness derives from the mid-nineteenth-century emergence of Darwinian evolutionary theory. Darwin's concept of natural selection seemed to provide a mechanism to account for a regular repetition, in various places, of the process of civilization-building. The American attorney Lewis Henry Morgan was the most influential of the nineteenth-century founders of anthropology—the political theorists Karl Marx and Friedrich Engels adopted many of his ideas—and he was the quintessential evolutionist. In Berlin, the ethnographer Adolf Bastian had formulated the concept that humans' innate mental qualities were everywhere the same, providing a foundation for assuming that similar cultural developments spontaneously took place under similar stimuli wherever they occurred.

Despite these early evolutionist orientations, interest in the historical geographic movements of peoples and cultures was also widespread in the developing field, especially in Europe. But the 1920s and 1930s saw the rise of essentially ahistorical approaches. The Oxford anthropologist A. R. Radcliffe-Brown had a sociological view of culture and stressed the seeking of universal laws regulating human cultural behaviors, as opposed to stressing the historical particulars leading up to those behaviors. The prominent Polish-born British functionalist anthropologist Bronislaw Malinowski thought in terms of individual cultures' operating as essentially closed systems comprised of various parts, each of which could be understood in terms of its function in the "machine" as a whole. With regard to nonliterate peoples, any attempt to work out the individual histories of these parts (including possible outside origins) was seen as valueless speculation with no evidentiary foundation.

The tacit or explicit collective opinion of these scholars and their followers was that it was unnecessary to look outside of cultures themselves for explanations of how they worked and why, and that it was idle to consider the possibility of significant influences from afar via undocumented migration or via cultural diffusion (the group-to-group spread of ideas). The historical dissemination of culture traits (including overseas) nevertheless continued for years to engage the attention of many archaeologists, anthropologists, and geographers, especially in England, in German-speaking Europe, and in California. But the post–World War II rise of logical-positivist social science, as practiced in the United States by Lewis Binford in archaeology and Marvin Harris in cultural anthropology (among many others), reinforced the idea of local evolution of cultures without major exogenous inputs. Spatial cultural dissemination over time was deemed an inappropriate subject to consider, and proposals of transoceanic influences were looked upon with particular distaste. Even more limited studies of cultural spreading largely disappeared from the mainstream, and "diffusion" became the "d word," avoided in almost all serious academic discourse. If the process was mentioned at all, euphemisms such as "spread," "dispersal," and "transfer" would be used. As one historian put it, the "establishment charges that diffusionists are but a rabble of undisciplined intellectual guerillas intent on archaeological anarchy."[7]

Still, all along, a contrary if minority view continued to exist: that cultural spread had been vitally consequential in human history and that there had been, in reality, significant interhemispheric contacts by sea, probably many, not only before Columbus and Eiríksson but also, in some cases, millennia earlier; and, further, that these contacts had resulted in highly important cultural and biological exchanges between the peoples of the two hemispheres. This point of view is commonly called "diffusionism."

Although the great nineteenth-century German explorer and naturalist Alexander von Humboldt prefigured them, the nearest equivalents to continental drift's Alfred Wegener in the history of diffusionism were: (1) Sir Grafton Elliot Smith, founder of the British "Heliolithic School," centered in Manchester and, later, in London and including, especially, William James Perry; and (2) Father Wilhelm Schmidt of the University of Vienna, leading light of Austria's *Kulturkreis* historical ethnology school (along with his followers Wilhelm Koppers and Martin Gusinde).[8]

The German-Austrian culture historical school, in turn, had roots in German historicism (as practiced by the nineteenth-century pioneer of cultural geography Friedrich Ratzel,[9] among others, who, however, attributed intersocietal similarities to a shared primeval culture), especially by way of Fritz Graebner of the Berlin Museum of Ethnology and E. Foy of the Cologne Museum. The journal *Anthropos*—still being published—was initiated by the Viennese adherents. The term *Kulturkreis* (culture circle) was coined by Ratzel's student

Leo Frobenius to mean the entire content encompassed in a cultural manifestation. Whereas Graebner thought of cultural complexes as spreading from
their areas of origin more or less as wholes and occupying discrete geographical areas, Schmidt used the term *Kulturkreis* to refer to both the culture area
and the content of the culture, and he felt that individual culture traits were divisible and capable of spreading independently of one another. These scholars'
interests were largely Afroeurasian.

The third-generation standard-bearer of the German-Austrian school was the
Viennese art historian Robert von Heine-Geldern, a major champion of the notion of transpacific influences and usually classed by dissenters as a hyperdiffu-
sionist. As of the mid-twentieth century, the anthropologist Melville J. Herskovitz said, the mode of thought of the Germans and Austrians "has become one
of the leading schools of anthropological thought on the continent of Europe,
but has never achieved any degree of acceptance in English-speaking anthropological circles."[10]

The British school (which departed from the comparatively mild diffusionism of earlier Britishers such as E. B. Tylor and Augustus Lane-Fox Pitt Rivers) was the target of a great deal of criticism for its Egyptocentric stance and
other perceived shortcomings. Flawed though their knowledge and thinking
may often have been, members of the British school did, in fact, make some
quite important observations. In the view of George Carter, Elliot "Smith and
his school were half a century ahead of their time and have been most unfairly
lampooned."[11]

The principal inspiration for the minority diffusionist view has been the
multifarious and detailed cultural commonalities between geographically separated societies, especially the more elaborated ones, of the two hemispheres.
These congruencies—which are not usually across-the-board ones but tend to
be concentrated in certain sectors of culture—for example, religious—include
not only general resemblances such as subsisting on farming, living in aggre-
gated settlements, hierarchical social structure, and the like, but, evidentially far
more tellingly, likenesses in complex technologies and in certain arbitrary details of culture. Is it plausible that cultures could have independently originated
all the technical complexities of weaving and dyeing that are shared between
southern Asia and the Central Andean region of South America, for instance?
Are stepped temple pyramids that are oriented to the cardinal directions in both
Mesoamerica and Cambodia fortuitous convergences—especially in light of a
multiplicity of shared iconographies such as balustrades in the form of serpent
monsters—or do such pyramids reflect historical contact and interinfluence?
What is to be made of the old belief, in both China and Mesoamerica, that raw
jade can be discovered in nature owing to "exhalations" coming from the stone,
that a worthy person has a "heart of jade," that jade has medicinal powers, that
upon death, a person should have a piece of red-painted jade (sometimes in
the form of a cicada) plus grain placed in his mouth, and that "jade" is a word
for "precious" and is associated with iridescent feathers (kingfisher in China,

quetzal in Mesoamerica). The sharing of the technology to work this highly re-calcitrant stone is striking in itself (see also chapter 26).[12]

Who Must Shoulder the Burden of Proof?

As mentioned, the notion that pre-Columbian transoceanic (or "pelagic") con-tacts not only occurred but also resulted in important interhemispheric inter-influences is distinctly the minority opinion among historians, archaeologists, art historians, and scholars of other disciplines—even among cultural geogra-phers. In his 1993 "Voyages of the Imagination," for example, the American historian Frank J. Frost wrote, "Few fields have been so thoroughly dominated by lunatic logic as the history of exploration. Consider the feverish speculation about the possibility of Precolumbian visitors to the Americas, from both Eu-rope and Asia."[13] When there is a prevailing paradigm—in this case, that of the essentially independent cultural evolution of the two hemispheres following ini-tial settling of the New World more than 14,000 years ago—as a *practical* mat-ter it is incumbent upon those who differ with that paradigm to shoulder the burden of proof.

Still, the question of who, *theoretically*, is obliged to assume that burden has generated considerable discussion. In the nineteenth century, Adolf Bastian set the stage for assuming independence unless diffusion be demonstrated, whereas (a short time afterward) Fritz Graebner championed the contrasting assumption, that historical connections best explained correspondences. Many years later, Gordon Ekholm expressed his feeling that in the real world, "The burden of proof appears to rest with unfair weight upon the person who would postulate the diffusion of traits [even] from one subarea to another."[14] Years after that, the American anthropologist Harold E. Driver observed that it was the case that, "Nearly every ethnologist today believes that the burden of proof rests on the diffusionist."[15]

One of the reasons that interhemispheric independence is typically taken as a given is that it seems to cultural isolationists—"independent-inventionists"—unlikely in the extreme that humans could have traversed the vast, trackless oceans, at least in numbers adequate to have had notable overseas cultural im-pacts. At the same time, it is supposed—with Bastian—that humans everywhere are intrinsically pretty much alike and that the challenges they face are similar, so that if people could have invented something in one place, so too could they have done so in another. Further, isolationists feel that there is an absence of evidence of the kinds that *would* be present had such contacts really occurred.

Strictly speaking, cultural diffusion is the process of an innovation's spread-ing outward over time from a place of origin or "hearth," by means of person-to-person and group-to-adjacent-group contacts ("expansion diffusion"); it can also involve ideas being carried and introduced to a distant spot and then spread-ing outward from this secondary center. Because it is analogous to the spread of disease, this sort of dissemination is sometimes termed "contagious diffusion." The term *diffusion* is also employed more loosely and in a broader sense to include carriage of culture by migration ending in resettlement ("relocation diffusion," "demic diffusion") as well as by contagion.[16] A "diffusionist," then, is someone who tends to feel that human movements, contacts, and cultural exchanges—diffusion in the broad sense—are more often the source of at least detailed similarities between cultures, including cultures geographically very distant from one other, than is local evolution.

The historian J. H. Parry, in his 1981 *The Discovery of the Sea*, spoke for most scholars when he stated: "There are many tales of discoverers before Columbus; none is impossible, but [except for some involving Norse remains in Newfoundland,] no shred of evidence supports any of them."[17] In the following pages, we shall see whether this kind of contention is, in fact, supportable. Inventionists sometimes accuse diffusionists of presenting only favorable evidence and ignoring contrary data. Accordingly, we begin this reexamination of the question of transoceanic contacts by looking first at the not-unreasonable intellectual objections to the notion and by seriously assessing those reservations.

Cutting One's Self with Occam's Razor: The Principle of Parsimony, and Its Perils

A basic tenet of scientific investigation is the principle of parsimony: that, given the existence of more than one hypothesis capable of explaining all of the known facts about a phenomenon, the simplest (most "economical" or "elegant") of these hypotheses (subject to testing) is the one most likely to be correct. Application of this principle is often called using Occam's razor, after the fourteenth-century English philosopher Friar William of Occam (Ockham), who reputedly said, *Entia non sunt multiplicanda praeter necessitatem* (No more things should be presumed to exist than are absolutely necessary). This principle is applicable to the primary question at hand: whether specific arbitrary and complex conformities between cultures of the two hemispheres reflect primarily independent invention or historical diffusion.

Although the human mind yearns for simple answers, caution in applying the principle of parsimony is required, owing to the fact that in matters as complex as those of human affairs, simple explanations seldom suffice; how many relatively fully known historical explanations *are*, in fact, simple?[18]

Erich Kahler, author of *The Meaning of History*, wrote: "[It is] impossible to set apart, and add up, single causes of the final event. Not only are they innumerable, but they pass into one another, act upon each other, and, in scrutinizing the elements of this whole assemblage of pre-conditions, we are carried farther and farther, through an unending genealogy of processes, into the most diverse, spatially and temporally remote scenes of happenings."[19]

These thoughts may be compared with complexity theory, nonlinear dynamics (multiple causalities), and even chaos theory, in the physical and biological sciences.

Any acceptable explanation must truly account for *all* the known facts and be in conflict with none. In any event, even if the least complex hypothesis may be considered the most probable one, other explanations (including, perhaps, the true one), may still be quite possible and may, in fact, be little less probable than the most parsimonious one, which in any case should be seen only as a working hypothesis, to be tested to the extent possible.

The bottom line is, it is pretty safe to assert that the most economical initial hypothesis concerning some happening or another of human culture history will not, in the long run, turn out to provide the wholly (or even partly) correct explanation; causes usually turn out to have been significantly more complex than originally supposed. As the influential American cultural anthropologist Clifford Geertz observed, "Elegance remains, I suppose, a general scientific ideal; but in the social sciences, it is very often in departures from that ideal that truly creative developments occur. Scientific advancement commonly consists in a progressive complication of what once seemed a beautifully simple set of notions but now seems an unbearably simplistic one."[20]

I assign the last word here on this point to the first person recorded as having expressed such thoughts—and that, nearly two and a half millennia ago: Aristotle wrote, "according to Agathon: It is part of probability that many improbable things will happen."[21]

Scholars debating the independent-inventionist versus diffusionist points of view often have seen things very differently from one another. The Hong Kong archaeologist William Meacham expressed a commonly held opinion, that regardless of comparative congruencies, "Until [more economical local-evolution] hypotheses and interpretations have manifestly failed to accommodate the data, speculative reconstructions positing significant diffusion or migration into an area cannot be other than ill-founded."[22] Inventionists assert, more particularly, that it is more parsimonious to hypothesize independent evolution than it is to posit a long sea voyage (for which there may be no direct evidence) followed by cultural influence. Here is one statement relating to parsimony and migration (and one could as easily say diffusion): "migration theories are rarely parsimonious explanations because they presuppose [that] it is not enough to know what is going on within a system; you must know what is happening outside of it. Therefore, it can be argued that explanations for observed similarities and differences among people[s] should be sought first in conditions and events within the populations. . . . In short, in the interests of parsimony, do not invoke migrations beyond necessity."[23]

One problem with the approach that the American archaeologist John Terrell describes above is that it begins with the familiar presumption of cultures being largely closed systems, developing in isolation from one another and usually without much external influence, especially influence from afar. Although such independence may have been the case in the instances of a few human groups, generally speaking individual societies have in fact always been subject to a variety of outside contacts and influences and their cultures have always owed the bulks of their contents to diffusion (including via migration), not to internal evolution in situ. Naturally, each case needs to be examined individually and as empirically as possible. However, the overall observation may be made that, at least if contact can be established as having occurred, diffusion is the simpler of the two competing hypotheses regarding the origin of specific counterparts. This is because it is far easier to emulate than it is to invent,[24] as well as because different physical environments and different cultural and historical contexts are unlikely to produce closely similar evolutionary outcomes.

In light of the fact that the hypothesis of a single invention is simpler than the hypothesis of multiple inventions, the noted Cambridge historian of science Joseph Needham stated: "In all . . . fields of science and technology the onus of proof lies upon those who wish to maintain fully independent invention, and the longer the period elapsing between the successive appearances of a discovery or invention in two or more cultures concerned, the heavier that onus generally is," owing to greater time during which transmission could have occurred.[25] To rule out cultural transmission only because of geographic separation introduces an extra assumption—impossibility of contact—and could thus be considered less parsimonious.

Accordingly, in contrast to some writers' contention that positing transoceanic voyages to account for conformities is less economical than assuming independent invention, the most prominent archaeologist of Island Southeast Asia and the Pacific, the Australian Peter Bellwood, in contradistinction to Terrell, has maintained that "migrations can, in fact, be quite parsimonious explanations for patterns of human variation. . . . Fortunately, few archaeologists today take the strong antimigrationist stance that dominated the discipline in the early 1980s."[26] Indeed, migration may be seen as a more elegant explanation than not only independent invention but also contagious diffusion, since migration does not require multiple or even single transmissions from group to group.

Regardless of whether a culture trait is locally invented or is accepted from the outside, the essential process of adoption is the same: members of the society must perceive the new item as having some kind of appeal—utilitarian, religious, social, prestige, aesthetic, entertainment, novelty, or other value—and then must change their behaviors to admit and integrate the novelty into the existing structure of their culture. Adoption of either an invention or an introduction requires the society's overcoming initial reluctance to adopt—simple cultural inertia and/or active resistance of any of several possible origins—but it is always going to require less imagination and effort to copy something that has been presented to one than to think up and develop that same thing de novo.

Motive, Means, Opportunity

The approach that we are taking to the evidence in the transoceanic contacts controversy is analogous to that conventionally associated with criminal investigation, as laid out by the eighteenth-century German Joachim Georg Darjes:

Quis? Quid? Ubi? Quibus auxiliis? Cur? Quomodo? Quando?
What was the crime? Who did it?
When was it done and where?
How done and with what motive?
Who in the deed did share?[27]

In this book we endeavor to identify possible *motive(s)* for committing the deed, the *means* by which the deed might have been done and who had those means (which we look at first), and the *opportunity* of committing the deed, that is, being in the right place at the right time with the required equipment—the alleged "deed" being the pre-Columbian transfer of culture between the hemispheres via transoceanic contacts.

The idea of ancient voyaging across the great oceans *is* so controversial, however, that many people are not prepared even to contemplate the question of transoceanic influences until the physical possibility of contact has been established. Because of this resistance, it is well to commence our investigation by considering and addressing the principal scholarly reasons why the majority of researchers discount the feasibility of important interhemispheric interactions having occurred in the distant past (keeping in mind that there are also subjective factors favoring denial). That is what this book's part I endeavors to do.

In further service of this goal, in part II we examine closely the question of means—specifically, the watercraft, sailing rigs, and navigational methods available to various peoples long before 1492. In so doing, we consider, one by one, contentions as to why the "deed" could not have been committed—thus presenting the case for the isolationist "defense" first, followed by the diffusionist "prosecution's" critical comment on that defense.

Having discussed the means for potential transoceanic contacts, in part III we turn to a second of that trio of investigative questions: motive. Many may wonder what rewards could possibly have been worth months, perhaps years, of privation, discomfort, and, at times, mortal danger out on a trackless ocean and in alien lands—even if anyone actually supposed that land might exist across the seas. Beyond situations involving involuntary drift voyaging, might there have existed any motive or combination of motives that could have led to deliberate and repeated transoceanic crossings? That is a basic question that many skeptics pose concerning early voyaging of this kind, one that we shall endeavor to answer, at least provisionally.

Motive, means, and opportunity: of these three, in part IV we consider the last, though it is the most important since the first two prove nothing in themselves about whether the "deed" really was done. We investigate, therefore, whether data exist that may show that at least some such voyages in fact took place and had identifiable impacts. In other words, we ask: "Is there a corpus delicti, a 'body of the crime'?"

The showing that contacts did occur, using evidence other than purely cultural resemblances, is critical in view of isolationists' attitude that the burden of proof is on the diffusionist. If actual transfers can be demonstrated, then the principle of *ab esse ad posse* applies: "from 'it is' to 'it is possible,'" that is, "*if* it happened, it *can* have happened," no matter how implausible on the face of it, thus definitively refuting critics' claims of impossibility (and confirming that means did indeed exist, whether directly identifiable or not).

What is meant here by the question of "opportunity" is, then: Was there unequivocal occasion for cultural interinfluences to have occurred across the oceans before Columbus and Eiríksson, "hard" evidence that irrefutably demonstrates that significant seaborne human contacts between the hemispheres took place? If the answer is positive, if consequential contact can be shown, then opportunity for cultural exchange has been demonstrated and interhemispheric similarities can never again legitimately simply be assumed to be independent. Thus the thrust of part IV is to present some of the more concrete and compelling noncultural indicators of the occurrence of pre-Columbian transoceanic exchanges. In light of such exchanges, the principle of parsimony suggests that diffusion is indeed the more economical explanation for relevant cultural similarities.

I

Intellectual Obstacles to the Notion of Early Transoceanic Contacts

Things are seldom what they seem.
　　　　　—Sir W. S. Gilbert, 1878

In 2010, the maverick archaeologist Alice Beck Kehoe wrote, frustratedly, "For mainstream archaeologists, pre-Columbian contacts have been a dead issue. Primitive people couldn't cross oceans, that settles it." As a more conventional archaeologist expressed this attitude: "I find it more difficult to accept claims of diffusion when the alleged recipient culture is separated from the donor culture by a wide ocean."[1] An evidentiary double standard is being applied. The view, that pre-1492 sailors were incapable of crossing the Atlantic—not to mention the Pacific—before the Middle Ages, rests on a number of well-embedded myths. Part I of this book examines and refutes these misconceptions, beginning in chapter 1 by comparing the world's realities to people's misperceptions, past and present, of that world.

I

The Myth of the Oceans as Uncrossable Barriers

Where we taste
The pleasure of believing what we see
Is boundless as we wish our souls to be:
And such was this wide ocean.
                    —Percy Bysshe Shelley, 1818

Geographical Misperceptions

It is not surprising that many have questioned whether it is reasonable to suppose that pre-Columbian humans, voluntarily or by accident, crossed up to 12,500 miles of uncharted, storm-wracked open ocean, in numbers sufficient to have had demographic, cultural, or historical impacts of any importance. Most scholars would reply with a resounding "No way." However, this view of the oceans as having been essentially uncrossable barriers is, to a considerable degree, based on incorrect preconceptions.

First there is a perceptual issue. People tend to think of premodern Europe as one domain, populated by whites, and the pre-Columbian Americas, populated by Amerinds, as a completely different domain. In writing of gaps between socially distinct areas of space, the American sociologist Eviatar Zerubavel observed, "we often perceive even short distances across them as considerably greater than much longer distances between points located within what we consider to be one and the same chunk [of space]."[1] For instance, no one quarrels with the fact that ancient sailors of the Indian Ocean routinely made open-sea crossings of up to 2,000 miles,[2] while almost everyone protests at the suggestion that seafaring humans could have crossed comparable distances on the other oceans, say, in the Atlantic between West Africa and Brazil. If Indonesians reached East Africa and Madagascar (as they did some two millennia ago, possibly continuing on to West Africa), why could they not have sailed an equal distance in the other direction, to America?

Then there is the matter of terminology. The label "New World" was first used in 1494 by Peter Martyr—Pietro Martire d'Anghiera, an Italian humanist at the Spanish court—although he agreed with Columbus's insistence that where he had been was outlying parts of Asia. Even though the America-as-Asia idea persisted for decades in some circles, the ultimately conventional use of the terms "Old World" and "New World" implied to people's perceptions that the two "worlds" were entirely separate realms, not parts of a single global system. The terms "Eastern Hemisphere" and "Western Hemisphere"—also coined by Peter Martyr—are somewhat better, but the implication is still there that the twain never met before 1492. Matters were not improved by the introduction of the name "America" by the German geographer Martin Waldseemüller, in recognition of the Florentine explorer-cosmographer Amerigo Vespucci, who had also written in 1502 of a "new land" and who was the first to refer to that land as a "continent" equivalent to Africa, Europe, and Asia, as Waldseemüller thus showed it on his influential map of 1507.

Metageography

Our thinking about the world is affected by what has been called "metageography," described by the Stanford geographer Martin W. Lewis and historian Kären Wigen as "the set of spatial structures through which people order their knowledge of the world: the often unconscious frameworks that organize studies of history, sociology, anthropology, economics, political science, or even natural history."[3] Prevailing perceptions of the world's geography are strongly conditioned by the kinds of maps to which people have routinely been exposed. The Harvard historian of technology George A. L. Sarton observed, "We are so deeply map conscious that we can hardly understand mapless travels," and we view the world through the filter of our maps.[4] We may even find it difficult to absorb that humans could travel long distances in the days before decent maps were available.

The east–west axis of any standard present-day world map is the equator, and such maps terminate at either end along a north–south divide in the mid-Pacific, one-half of that ocean appearing at the right-hand end of the map, the other half at the left-hand end. This layout reinforces the notion of the pre-1492 Pacific as an insuperable barrier rather than as an entity connecting the lands of the two hemispheres. In *Terra Cognita*, which traces post-Columbian European conceptions of the world as shown by the history of cartography, Zerubavel wrote,

> By placing America on the far left side of their world maps (thereby establishing a lasting cartographic convention that has in fact prevailed to this day), early sixteenth-century mapmakers clearly helped promote in Europe's mind the absolute separation of the New World from the Orient.
> . . . [America's] placement on the far left rather than the far right side of world maps—totally separated visually from Asia—from the very beginning mentally lumped America together with (in fact, as an extension of) Europe into what later came to be known as "the West" and kept it from being perceived, as it very well could have been at least until 1522, as an extension of the Orient.[5]

To the extent that the ancient Greeks, who founded Western geography, thought in terms of continents, they recognized that those known to them—Europe, Asia, and Africa—were physically joined. But the Renaissance (re)discovery of the Americas changed people's perceptions. As Lewis and Wigen wrote, "By the late seventeenth century . . . [in Europe] the notion of a unitary human terrain [oikoumenē] . . . was disassembled into its constituent continents, whose relative isolation was now ironically converted into their defining feature."[6] This conception continues to influence our views.

The Matter of Mendacious Maps

Any flat map of our planet is necessarily a distorted compromise, because it attempts the partially impossible: accurately depicting Earth's curved surface on a planar surface. In practice, the surface of our orb is very commonly displayed on world maps via a Mercator's (conformal cylindrical) projection (for an example, see figure 3.1). With Lewis Carroll, we might well ask, "What's the good of Mercator's North Poles and Equators, Tropics, Zones, and Meridian Lines?"[7]

The sixteenth-century Flemish cartographer Gerardus Mercator designed his projection to permit the use of loxodromes (rhumb lines), that is, depiction of the route between any two points along any unchanging azimuth (compass direction) as a straight line, with correct angles between all such rhumb lines and all meridians of longitude and parallels of latitude (which also appear as straight). However, as a result of achieving this navigationally highly convenient property that facilitates the plotting of courses, the Mercator's projection suffers from distortions with respect to its other properties (feature shape, consistency of map distance, and area). These distortions are so great that contemporary geographers consider the projection to be unsuitable for general use, yet it continues to be almost standard in many settings.

For one thing, on a Mercator's map non-equator and non-meridian great-circle routes or orthodromes (for example, across the North Pacific), which continually change azimuth, appear as curved lines, giving the impression that they are much longer than they really are, especially those connecting east–west points away from the tropics; in actual fact, any great-circle route is a spherical straight line, that is, the shortest surface path between any two points on an orb. The significance of this is underlined when one plots on a globe (as by employing a taut string) the great-circle route from Tokyo to San Francisco via Aleutian waters. The route as seen from directly above is a straight line and is, in fact, a good deal shorter than a route running due eastward from Japan to California.

In addition, to create a flat, oblong map the curved surface of the globe away from the equator is, in effect, stretched out in an east–west direction, and the meridians of longitude on a Mercator's map run straight up and down and parallel rather than converging toward the poles as they do on a globe. Consequently, the farther from the equator a land area of a particular real size is, the greater are its apparent east–west dimension and its areal extent. This is increasingly so as one goes poleward. In addition, the farther poleward, the farther apart the parallels of latitude are shown, yielding a north–south exaggeration as well. Thus on a Mercator map the island of Greenland, for instance, is shown as larger than South America, when, in fact, it is but one-twelfth that continent's size. The farthest-poleward areas are omitted altogether on such a map, and what *is* shown in the higher latitudes is so stretched that it gives an extremely poor representation of distance and area.

As the poleward land areas look exaggeratedly wide, so do the water areas. For instance, the water gaps between Norway, Iceland, Greenland, Baffin Island, and Labrador are depicted as being much broader than they really are in comparison to equal true distances at low latitudes.

As an alternative to Mercator's projection, some modern world maps deal with lateral distortion by cutting the more poleward areas into separated gores (tapering, meridian-bounded lobes joined toward the equator). However, this approach breaks up the east–west continuity of the maps and makes the proximities and connections of the more poleward areas anything but obvious. This is true, for instance, of the widely used Goode's interrupted homolosine equal-area projection (introduced in 1925). This map greatly reduces poleward dimensional distortion, but gaps bite into the map from north and south—widening toward the poles—gaps that, not surprisingly, are placed in the Pacific and the Atlantic, further exaggerating the magnitude of oceanic separation. As normally drawn, Goode's projection is land focused, not ocean basin focused, and is less than ideally useful for considerations of possible transoceanic connections (although if the gaps between gores were placed in the continents rather than in the seas, this projection *could* be employed to depict the oceans more realistically).

How Separate Are the Hemispheres?

In contrast to standard maps, a simple polar cartographic projection, which is like an aerial photograph taken from directly over the North Pole, makes obvious the minimal water gaps in the northern parts of both the Atlantic and the Pacific (the gaps between Russia, Iceland, Greenland, and Canada, as well as between Siberia and Alaska have been, in fact, sometimes entirely closed by winter sea ice). Figures 1.1 and 1.2 show this proximity in an imaginative and useful fashion.

The shortest sea distance between Norway and Greenland is only about 1,150 statute miles, and geographically Greenland is part of North America. There are, of course, intermediate potential stepping-stones as well. The Shetland Islands, less than 50 miles northeastward from the Orkney Islands off the Scottish mainland (with Fair Isle in between), lie a mere 190 miles from Bergen, Norway. The Faroe Islands, farther out in the Atlantic, lie only 310 miles from Bergen, 180 miles from the Shetlands, and some 200 miles from Scotland's Hebrides Islands. Being mountainous, the Faroes are visible from

Figure 1.1. Map of the North Atlantic Ocean, showing the short sea distances between Europe and the North American mainland via the Orkneys, Shetlands, Faroes, Iceland, Greenland, and Baffin Island. The greatest uninterrupted sea distance is 240 miles. Presumed itineraries of the Norse voyages of circa AD 1000 are indicated by arrows. From Ivar T. Sanderson, *Follow the Whale*, 1956, p. 87. Reprinted by permission of Collier Associates, PO Box 20149, West Palm Beach, FL 33416 USA.

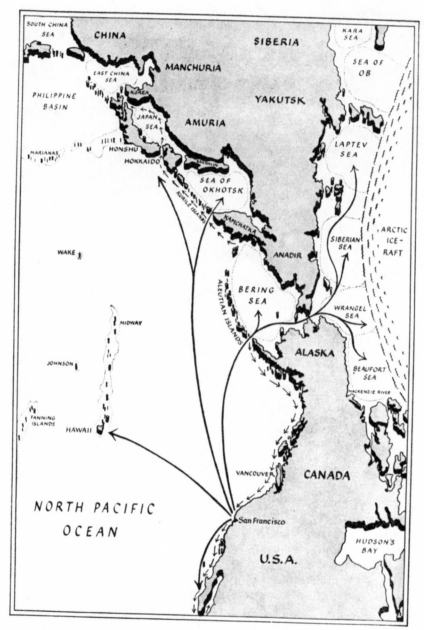

Figure 1.2. Map of the North Pacific, showing that the continuity of the coastlines of Asia and America is broken only by the 54-mile Bering Strait. The Kamchatka to Commander/Aleutian Islands distance is 225 miles. Short arrows indicate gray whale migration routes. From Ivar T. Sanderson, *Follow the Whale*, 1956, p. 255. Reprinted by permission of Collier Associates, P.O. Box 20149, West Palm Beach, FL 33416 USA.

40 to 50 miles out to sea and served as route markers even for ships that did not call there. Iceland is but 240 miles to the west of the Faroes. On any bearing between 30 and 80 degrees west of north, a ship would find itself in Iceland's soundings on the third day out from the Faroes. In good weather, Iceland's 6,952-foot Mount Öraefajökull would be visible after some 140 miles of sailing. From Iceland, it is just 178 miles to Greenland, and one need go only a third of the way to catch direct sight of that great island. On clear days, both lands are visible from the halfway point. Greenland is but 16 miles from Canada's Ellesmere Island (a day or two's walk on winter ice) and only 230 direct miles from Baffin Island; in clear weather, light-loom (see chapter 22) sometimes creates intervisibility. From Greenland straight to Labrador is about 525 miles. Thus, in crossing the North Atlantic one need never be more than 120 miles from land or more than about 70 miles out of sight of land. Further, this island-to-island route lies almost along a great circle, that is, the shortest possible overall transatlantic route.

To gain some idea of what these distances meant in terms of sailing times, we may turn to the writings of the scholarly Irish monk Dicuil (about AD 825) and to the medieval Norse sagas. Dicuil put the Faroes less than two days' sail from "the northernmost islands" of Scotland, and Iceland two days beyond that. According to the Icelandic *Landnámabók* and *Hauksbók*, it took seven days to sail nonstop from southern Norway straight to Iceland (632 statute miles at 3.2 knots). To get from Iceland to the southern tip of Greenland, normally only four days at 4.2 knots were required to cover the 460 miles of the usual route. Sailing directly from Norway to Greenland's Eastern Settlement necessitated twelve days to cover the 1,955 miles. Ireland, 632 miles away, was only five days' sail (three, according to *Landnámabók*) from Iceland, and circa 1,800 miles and eighteen days from Greenland.[8]

The aforementioned voyages are hardly of daunting durations, and they make one ponder whether there was any great reason that earlier, perhaps much earlier, peoples could not have crossed the North Atlantic with relative ease, even without sail. Such distances elsewhere were, in fact, being traversed 40,000 or more years ago (see chapter 15).

In the Pacific, one can travel by boat from Korea, on the Asian mainland, to Japan, up the admittedly foggy and inhospitable Kuril Islands chain (alongside which gray whales migrate) to the Kamchatka Peninsula,[9] along the northeastern Asian Coast, and across the 56-mile Bering Strait with the Diomede Islands in the middle; the Chukotka (easternmost Siberia) to Alaska water distance involved is exceeded by straits traversed by humans in near Oceania by at least as early as 37,100 years ago. In historic times there was much native interaction between Alaska and Chukotka, both over water and over winter pack ice. Alternatively, rather than go up the Asian mainland coast from the Kamchatka Peninsula into the Arctic, one could travel along the Commander Islands and the Aleutian Islands to mainland Alaska, the widest water gap being about 225 miles—"easily covered by the most primitive craft," in the opinion of the historian Gordon Speck, and a route signaled by migrating shorebirds and whales.[10] In fact, a core and blade stone tool industry from 6000 BC on Anagula in the Aleutians relates to that of Kamchatka (although so far no such sites are known on Russia's intervening Commander Islands).[11]

In high latitudes, there occurs an occasional atmospheric phenomenon known as the "arctic mirage," in which cold, dense air (as over ice) creates a lens that refracts light over the horizon. This allows land to be seen over 300 miles away, facilitating discovery. Under such conditions, the mountains of eastern Greenland, rising to as much as 12,139 feet, could be seen from 4,744-foot Snaefells Glacier behind Iceland's west coast. The highest part of Baffin Island is 240 miles beyond and just out of normal sight from the top of a peak in Greenland north of the Norse Western Settlement. Even without a mirage, on a sunny day ice-blink—the simple diffraction loom of glaciers' brightness—can be seen far beyond the horizon.[12]

Likewise, volcanic eruptions, as on Iceland (apparently witnessed by the early medieval Irish voyager Brendan of Clonfert) and in the Aleutians, could also greatly extend land visibility. For example, the 2009 eruption of Alaska's Mount Redoubt sent ash a dozen miles into the air; the ash plume of the 1996 eruption of New Zealand's Mount Ruapehu rose 18 miles into the sky; and the height of Vesuvius's cloud in AD 79 is estimated to have been 20.5 miles. Even quiescent volcanoes (for example, on Tonga's Tofoa Island) can put out plumes of steam visible from far away. Vegetation fires on land also send up high columns of smoke.

In short, people living or pausing on of any of the northern Atlantic and Pacific islands would inevitably have become aware of neighboring lands, which, if sought successively, would have led ultimately to the other side of the sea.

As well, the Atlantic is not exceedingly wide even at lower latitudes, especially between Brazil and West Africa. In fact, that latter distance, some 1,750 miles, is no greater than that which South Asians and Indonesians, for centuries before Columbus, commonly sailed between the southern tip of India and the Horn of Africa—and is some 765 miles shorter than the length of the Mediterranean Sea (the Romans' *mare nostrum*) and some 1,220 miles less than the length of the Mediterranean plus the Marmora and Black Seas (note that Phoenicians regularly sailed from one end of the Mediterranean to the other and beyond, and that such a voyage took longer and was more difficult and dangerous than would have been sailing the Canary Current with the trade winds across the Atlantic to America).

Again, in the North Atlantic the Azores—to which ancient Carthaginians almost surely sailed—break up the transoceanic distance, extending a third of the way across, and lie just over 1,300 miles from Newfoundland—a distance of about the same length as that of the Classical Mediterranean grain route from Egypt to Rome. Although owing to wind and current directions the position of the Azores is not favorable for sailing westward to the same latitude in the Americas, those islands are a feasible staging point for travel northwestward to

Canada, travel of the sort that the Portuguese engaged in beginning in the latter 1400s. These islands are also a potential stopping place on the return from the Caribbean region, as Columbus established on his first voyage.

As for the Pacific, which covers a third of the globe, its middle is some 12,425 statute miles across, a formidable distance indeed if the intervening islands are ignored. Most people's conception conforms to that expressed by the Harvard maritime historian J. H. Parry: "The [Pacific] Islands . . . are crumbs of land in an immensity of sea; they are easily missed."[13] However, although some enormous expanses of ocean are island-free, the usually linear South Pacific archipelagos are disposed in such a way that, according to the accomplished New Zealand sailor David Lewis, "It is possible to sail to almost all the inhabited islands of Oceania from Southeast Asia without once making a sea crossing longer than 310 [nautical] miles. The only exceptions are Easter Island, Hawaii, and New Zealand. . . . Such isolated lands apart, the majority of gaps between islands and even archipelagos are . . . usually in the 50- to 100-[nautical-]mile range."[14]

Although the uninterrupted distances to Easter, Hawaii, and New Zealand are much greater, they are not as enormous as might at first appear. From once-inhabited Pitcairn to Easter (Rapa Nui) is 1,128 miles, the distance broken (at about 134 miles) by uninhabited Ducie Island. The incremental distance from eastern Polynesia to Chile is not dauntingly great, either. From the Marquesas to South America is some 3,500 miles. From Easter, it is only 2,301 miles, a distance broken by a number of uninhabited islands; the widest water gap is only about 1,500 miles. In the latitude of Easter, prevailing westerly winds and east-setting currents may be encountered, at least seasonally.

These distances to South America are to be compared with the distance Polynesians once commonly traveled between the Society and Hawaiian Islands. Sailing southward from Hawaii, the nearest island is uninhabited Palmyra, about 1,000 statute miles away across currents and winds. From Hawaii to the first *inhabited* island to the south, Nukuhiva in the Marquesas, was a total 1,885 miles, an approximately 13.4 days' voyage. From Tahiti to Hawaii involved a distance of 2,242 miles and some 16 days' travel. From Tahiti to New Zealand is 2,073 miles, requiring about 17.3 days voyaging. The Easter to South America distance is only about half of that once regularly sailed by fellow Austronesians between Indonesia and Madagascar/East Africa (probably usually with a stop in the Maldives).

The Polynesian-seafaring expert Edward Dodd estimated that a canoe could average about 70 to 80 miles per day, which would mean that five and a half months would be required to take such a craft across the very widest part of the Pacific. But Dodd was thinking in terms of paddling canoes against the wind. With-the-wind sailing would have been very much faster; G. H. Heyen suggested 94 miles a day. The New Zealand archaeologist Geoffrey Irwin reckoned that, under good conditions, a Polynesian sailing-canoe could maintain a speed of 8 knots and could average 100 to 150 sea miles in twenty-four hours (150 miles, thought Captain Cook).[15] At the lower of these daily rates, which

Irwin felt could be maintained for a month or more, the very widest part of the Pacific could be traversed in only 83 days. At the higher rate, a mere 55.2 days would be needed. Of course, uninterrupted fair winds are unlikely to endure for so long a period, so real voyages would have taken substantially longer than the theoretically possible optimum. Crossing the ocean at less wide points could reduce the time.

The average velocity of a Phoenician merchantman is conservatively estimated to have been between 2 and 3 knots but may in fact have been nearer to 5, yielding an ordinary ten-hour day's voyage of some 50 nautical miles. Ancient descriptions of voyage lengths tell us that Mediterranean and Indian Ocean ships of Classical times sailed at about 3.42 to 7 knots, averaging perhaps 5.2 knots, on long-distance voyages with fair winds. When winds were foul, effective speed was likely reduced to about 2 to 2.5 knots.[16] At 5.2 knots, a ship could travel 125 nautical miles in twenty-four hours. The 1,750-mile Atlantic crossing from West Africa to Brazil would, at that speed, take but fourteen days! Under ideal conditions (admittedly, unlikely to be sustained), a traverse of the widest part of the Pacific in such craft would require just under 100 days. Known ancient maritime trading expeditions in Asian waters commonly lasted as much as two or three years. In that context, transoceanic sailing times would hardly have been prohibitive from a time-expenditure point of view.

An Ancient Narrow Atlantic Conception

If our contemporary perceptions regarding the widths of the oceans are conditioned by the maps we use, we may assume that the perceptions of the more educated among the ancients were similarly affected as well. For instance, maps from the time of Marinus and Ptolemy up to the early Renaissance show the Indian Ocean as completely landlocked, with southern Africa swinging around and joining East Asia, the ocean being erroneously illustrated as only about four times the size of the Mediterranean/Black Sea, a depiction that undoubtedly conditioned many ancient Western mariners' perceptions of that ocean's extent and hazardousness.

A broken Babylonian *mappa mundi* (world map) of the Persian period circa 600 BC depicts a very narrow, flowing cosmic ocean surrounding the world continent. Beyond it are shown five (originally eight) large "regions" or "islands," including a northern one "where the Sun is not seen," that is, the Arctic. Inscriptions indicate that Gilgamesh and other legendary heroes reached these territories. Thus, belief in overseas lands and their accessibility existed in Mesopotamia. Although early Greek thinkers otherwise influenced by Mesopotamian maps seem not to have fully shared this concept, subsequent ones did.[17]

Later Greek savants favored the spherical-earth concept, and some of them rather accurately estimated the planet's circumference (see chapter 2). Others, such as Poseidonios of Apameia and the supremely influential Ptolemy of Alexandria (second century AD), seem to have underestimated that distance by at least 5,000 miles, or some 20 percent, or more. Greek astronomers, geographers, and other scholars generally believed that India and West Africa were not far apart across the Atlantic and that one could sail westward to Asia, a view that seems likely to have encouraged westward voyaging on the part of the ancients (see chapter 12) as it did on the part of a classics-inspired Columbus a millennium and a half later.

In the fourth century BC, for example, Aristotle thought the Atlantic to be not very wide, although he nevertheless considered it impassable. Eudoxus of Cnidus (also fourth century BC), who had studied in Egypt, subscribed to the notion of a relatively narrow Ocean westward from Spain to India. In his *Geography* of about 200 BC, Eratosthenes of Cyrene much overestimated the eastward extent of Asia. He and Poseidonios (circa 100 BC) therefore also believed that India could be reached by sailing to the west. The concept of sailing westward to India was repeated by Ptolemy, and the first-century AD philosopher Seneca the Younger thought Spain and India to be but a few days' sail apart (*paucissimorum dierum spatium*), with the relevant route just waiting to be discovered.

One particular and initially rather aberrant ancient Greek conception of the earth was that of Krates of Mallos, the second-century BC royal librarian at Pergamon in Asia Minor. Krates's orb, influenced by earlier Pythagorean notions, showed two pairs of east-west-running continents separated by a tropical east–west ocean. A north–south strip of ocean separated Europe and Africa from the postulated continental masses to the west, but if the conjectural reconstruction of Krates's orb (figure 1.3) is at all accurate, this strip was not even as wide as the greatest north–south width of the Mediterranean Sea. Krates's notion was reinforced by the renowned Roman philosopher and politician Marcus Tullius Cicero (106–43 BC) and, about AD 430, by the Roman philosopher Macrobius. Krates's belief in overseas lands "became pervasive."[18]

About the first century AD, in *On the Cosmos*, a pseudo-Aristotelian writer expressed the belief that there might be, "at the other end of a ferry voyage," other *oikoumenēs* (inhabited worlds) than Afroeurasia, "separated from ours by a sea that we must cross to reach them, some larger and others smaller than it, but all, save our own, invisible to us."[19] Although believing that the Atlantic "cannot be navigated because of its vastness and desolation," the first-century AD Greek-speaking Roman historian and geographer Strabo of Pontus likewise believed that there existed a *Terra Occidentalis*, a western continent, on the globe's opposite side. "It may be," he opined, "that in this same temperate zone there are actually two inhabited worlds, or even more, and particularly in the vicinity of the parallel through Athens that is drawn across the Atlantic Sea."[20]

With such conceptions, people could well have supposed that land was not all that far offshore to the west of Europe and Africa, and on the basis of that supposition could have sailed in search of it and, under reasonably favorable conditions, succeeded in finding it, even if they were obliged to sail farther than anticipated, as was Columbus. If there is no recognized record of such success, that could reflect loss of such records (see chapter 11), post-voyage secrecy, or

Figure 1.3. Conjectural reconstruction of the globe as conceived by Krates of Mallos, second century BC. Note that the Atlantic Ocean is perceived as narrower than parts of the Mediterranean. From J. Oliver Thomson, *A History of Ancient Geography*, 1965, p. 203. Reprinted with permission of Cambridge University Press.

one-way journeys. The last of these would leave in the homeland no historical record of discovery, but absence of such a record would not necessarily mean that no impacts took place in the areas of disembarkation.

Thus, unlike many modern scholars, a goodly number of the ancients believed that there was a reachable world across the Atlantic Ocean. Perhaps some individuals acted on that belief.

2

Before Columbus, the Earth Was "Flat"?

Flat Wrong

We shall assume that the earth is spheroidal. The evidence of the senses and common observation are alone requisite.
—Strabo, *Geography*, AD 18–19

Most of us were told in school that it was a flash of insight by Christopher Columbus that taught humanity that the world was round, not flat. However, that notion is entirely erroneous. Any reasonably sophisticated pragmatic observer who notes that the higher one's viewpoint, the farther one can see, or who observes a ship pass over the horizon or the land "sink" into the sea as one's craft sails away from shore, is likely to work out that the earth's surface is curved. This conclusion might be reinforced by observations that the visible constellations and their paths' heights above the horizon were not the same at different places on Earth—that as one goes poleward the elevation of the noon sun decreases and that of the polestar increases—and that the apparent pathways of the stars are parallel in a coordinated fashion, a rotating terrestrial globe being one of the two possible logical explanations (the other being a celestial sphere rotating around a fixed earth—the actual Classical conception). The curved shadow of Earth upon the moon during lunar eclipses might also give a clue. In fact, the Greek philosopher Aristotle (384–322 BC) offered these phenomena as proofs of terrestrial sphericity, and he was followed not only by other Greeks and Romans (including Krates, discussed in chapter 1) but also by medieval Arab and European thinkers.[1] As will appear, the ancient Chinese also had formal theories about the sphericity of the globe.

Columbus, like all of his educated contemporaries, knew of the Classical Greek concepts, and it was his reading of Aristotle, Seneca, Ptolemy, Strabo, Pliny, and Captionius that formed his notion that he could sail westward from Europe directly to "the Indies." He was influenced directly by these works as well as by interpretations of them on the part of the fifteenth-century cosmographers Pierre d'Ailly and Paolo dal Pozzo Toscanelli, who, decades before 1492, supported the concept of a westward voyage to the Far East.[2] The case has even been advanced that Columbus had already heard, from an unidentified ill friend, that

friend's report of his own, slightly earlier, "prediscovery" of the New World—
a rumor discussed in the sixteenth century by the Spanish historian Gonzalo
Fernández de Oviedo y Valdés.[3]

Another myth is that Columbus, who did his own navigating in 1492, succeeded because of his use of all the most up-to-date developments in position-
finding and course-plotting. These included innovations allegedly made under
the aegis of Henry (Enrique) "the Navigator," the Portuguese prince who, well
before Columbus's first voyage, dispatched ships to explore the coast of West
Africa. Among these innovations was the use of the astrolabe and the backstaff
to determine latitude. As a navigator, however, Columbus was not, according
to J. H. Parry, "in the forefront of new developments, or even abreast of them.
He knew very little about celestial navigation; nothing, apparently, of the new
Portuguese method of measuring latitude by solar altitude. He understood the
principle of latitude-sailing, but some of his Polaris observations, which he recorded, were badly out. Even his dead-reckoning, on his outward passage, left
something to be desired."[4]

As noted, the myths about Columbus include the belief that the admiral was
the first to conclude that Earth is a globe, not a flat plane off whose edge a ship
venturing too far from land would fall. The idea that church officials espoused
the flat-earth notion and had problems with Columbus's contrary views derives
from Washington Irving's 1828 book *History of the Life and Voyages of Christopher
Columbus*, which took considerable license with fact. The notion of medieval resistance to the concept of Earth's globular nature became popular gospel. It persists to this day and is still found in influential modern books.[5] But in truth, in
Columbus's time scholars were nearly unanimous in the opinion that the earth
was spherical. Even Columbus's standard biographer, Samuel Eliot Morison—
no friend to the notion of pre-Columbian discoveries—recognized this: "of all
the vulgar errors concerned with Columbus, the most persistent and most absurd is that he had to convince people 'the world was round.'"[6]

The Spherical-Earth Theory in the Ancient West

Indeed, in the West the spherical-earth theory had been present since at least
the days of the early Pythagoreans (sixth century BC), in Greek-colonized southern Italy. The concept, perhaps originating with Pythagoras of Samos and definitely promulgated by Parmenides of Elea (flourished circa 480 BC), spread
to Greece proper, and is alluded to by the Athenian philosopher Plato (427–
347 BC) in three works. Although some did not adopt the concept, the historian
Herodotus (fifth century BC) took it seriously, and Plato's student Aristotle accepted it, stating that Earth was some 46,000 miles in circumference—almost
double the real dimension. The Alexandrian librarian Eratosthenes (circa 276 or
254–194 BC), who developed the idea of latitude and longitude, seems to have
come much closer to the true measurement, which he put at 27,967, 24,859.82,

or 24,663 miles, depending on what length stade he actually employed (and this is debated); the last and most probable figure is less than 200 miles short. Poseidonios of Apameia (circa 135–50 BC), whose ideas later influenced Marinos of Tyre, Strabo, Ptolemy, Roger Bacon, Pierre d'Ailly, and Columbus, calculated the circumference as only about 20,400 miles. This 4,263-mile underestimation is what encouraged Columbus to believe that the Atlantic was narrower than it was. This error could have likewise encouraged captains in antiquity.

The list of other classical scholars explicitly avowing terrestrial sphericity, from Empedocles (circa 500–430 BC) on, is almost endless and includes, to cite only the better known: Euclid, Archimedes, Krates, Cicero, Pliny the Elder (a copy of whose *Natural History* Columbus possessed), and the Roman poets Virgil and Ovid. Given the number of prominent adherents, it is no surprise that, according to the Harvard historian of science Stephen Jay Gould, "Greek knowledge of sphericity was never lost, and all major medieval scholars accepted the earth's roundness as an established fact of cosmology."[7] Although in Rome a handful of later thinkers rejected the idea of a terrestrial globe, for example, Lactantius (circa AD 325) and Cosmas Indicopleustes (AD 547)—and although there were, in fact, a few educated early medieval flat-earthers including Isadore of Seville, Rabanus Maurus (seventh century AD), and Boniface (Winfrid; circa AD 672–754)—the great majority of early Christian and medieval authorities appear to have espoused the spherical-earth idea (since in Latin *orbis* sometimes can mean "circle" as well as "sphere," in a few cases the opinion of the writer is ambiguous). These thinkers of the Middle Ages included Augustine of Hippo, Origen, Bede, Roger Bacon, Thomas Aquinas, and Albertus Magnus.[8]

Columbus and most of his informed contemporaries knew of all this, and Christopher's son and biographer Ferdinand stated that his father specifically cited several of the ancient authors mentioned above. Columbus's underestimate of the distance to Asia *was* (and rightly) disputed, but not the spherical-earth concept itself. This underestimate derived from Poseidonios's, as passed on by the geographer Ptolemy and by Donnus Nicolaus Germanus, Toscanelli, and others. But after Ptolemy's time, "The earth's sphericity was no longer debated by any practical navigator, cosmographer, or educated person."[9] Even in remote Dark Ages Ireland, the monk Dicuil wrote, in *The Book of the Measure of the World* (AD 825), of the *orbis terrarum*, "terrestrial globe," and some Norse also understood that the earth was spherical.

The Spherical-Earth Theory in the Early Muslim World

Medieval Arab scholars, who had retained or rediscovered much ancient Greek and other knowledge, were well aware of Earth's sphericity. During Sassanid times (circa sixth century AD), Persia's Academy of Gundishapur became a center for collecting Greek, Indian, and Chinese knowledge. After Islamicization, around AD 800, the center was moved to Baghdad by Caliph Hārūn ar-Rashīd, where translations into Arabic were accomplished. From there, diffusion carried these works and their ideas to Cairo, Córdoba, Toledo, and Sicily. Medieval Arabs such as al-Idrisi (1090–1154) espoused the globular-earth idea, having translated Ptolemy and other Greek works.

Arabs and others attempted to measure the planet's circumference in AD 830. The Kurdish geographer Abulfeda (Abū al-Fidā', 1273–1332) spoke of (hypothetical) voyages around a spherical earth. In the ninth century, the Persian astronomer Alfraganus (al-Farghānī) calculated that a degree of latitude measured the equivalent of some 66 nautical miles, and a later consortium of seventy Muslim scholars assembled by the caliph to determine the length of a latitudinal degree decided that it was equivalent to 62.3 nautical miles; the true length is about 60 nautical miles.[10]

According to the historian of Islam and Islamic science Seyyed Hossein Nasr: "Geography in Islam was also closely tied to astronomy; observatories carried out geographic measurements, such as the determination of latitudes and longitudes, and the degree of arc, for which several different methods were employed. In fact, [the eleventh-century geographer] al-Bīrūnī has often been regarded as the founder of the science of geodesy. . . . He devised a new method for measuring latitudes and longitudes, and carried out his own measurements to determine the antipodes and the roundness of the earth." Al-Bīrūnī's tenth-century predecessor al-Mas'ūdī stated that "the earth is round. . . . Most of the ancients, such as the mathematicians of the Hindus and Greeks, believe that they [the seas] are convex." Al-Mas'ūdī estimated Earth's circumference to be about 27,000 miles.[11]

With regard to Columbus, it is well to remember that his era, the Renaissance, was one of European rediscovery of Classical literature. Although this was in part from Byzantine Greeks fleeing the Turks, a good deal of the geographical knowledge involved came via the Arabs—who had occupied much of Iberia for four centuries as well as parts of Italy, occupation of Iberia ending definitively only with the Spanish Christian *Reconquista*'s final success in 1492 (thus freeing funds to finance Columbus's first voyage).[12]

The Spherical-Earth Theory in Ancient China and India

In China, the spherical-earth theory was present at least as early as the first century AD, and an orthogonal grid system was applied to maps by circa AD 100. By about the same time, the concept was present in India as well, along with a fairly accurate estimate of the orb's circumference, possibly as a result of Greco-Roman influence.[13]

Whereas a flat- and edged-earth theory might discourage distant voyaging, the spherical-earth idea would seem almost to invite exploration. But possession of the latter concept was not necessary to transoceanic movements; early Norse, for example, generally did, in fact, think of the terrestrial earth as a flat or saucer-shaped disk surrounded by monster-ridden, maelstrom-threatening ocean, but that did not prevent them from expanding their horizons empirically, and ultimately crossing the North Atlantic.

As our overall conclusion for this and the previous chapter, we may reproduce the words of the Oxford archaeologist Chris Gosden, from his "Long Term Trends in the Colonization of the Pacific": "For these people the sea was a bridge, not a barrier, and maritime movements have led to the continuous transfer of people, genes and language over large areas for a long period of time."[14]

3

Conveyor Belts of the Seas

The Prevailing Winds and Currents

[The goddess Circe sent] us . . . a favorable breeze, which sprang up from astern and filled the sail of our blue-prowed ship. All we had to do . . . was to sit still, while the wind and the helmsman kept her straight. With a taut sail she forged ahead all day . . . [and] through the darkness.

Thus she brought us to the deep-flowing River of Ocean and the frontiers of the world.

—Homer, *The Odyssey*, circa 750–700 BC

A fundamental matter to keep in mind is that measured distance is not the ultimate issue with respect to ocean crossings; rather, sailing time (along with ease) is, and in these terms effective ocean width is not the same in opposing directions, in every part, or at every season.

Traditional sailors tended to talk in terms of so many days' sail, and only secondarily (if at all) of measured distance. For example, a fifteenth-century Chinese chart of the Indian Ocean indicated degrees of separation between places by recording how many watches were involved. The Norse spoke of 12-hour sailing days rather than linear distances. To the extent that linear distances *are* given in early sources, they do not refer to situations involving the ocean's major belts of winds and currents.

The emphasis on sailing time was because "map" distance is only one of the important variables determining the time it takes to traverse an ocean. The other vital variables are the vectors, velocities, and consistencies of the winds and of the surface oceanic currents encountered, especially the winds. Among scholars concerned with questions of transoceanic interinfluences, the Norwegian experimental voyager Thor Heyerdahl was particularly prominent in stressing (even overstressing) the importance of such phenomena with respect to likely directions and routes of crossings. It is apt at this point to summarize the relevant characteristics of these large-scale air and water movements.

The prevailing wind patterns of the world are produced by regional and seasonal atmospheric pressure differences, which, in turn, reflect differences in solar insolation according to differences in latitude and times of year. The most important of the pressure zones are the enormous subtropical high-pressure cells, one of which lies over each of the major ocean basins (that is, North Atlantic, South Atlantic, North Pacific, South Pacific, and southern Indian), between roughly 20 and 40 degrees north and south latitude (figure 3.1). Winds spiral outward from these highs toward the equatorial low-pressure trough and

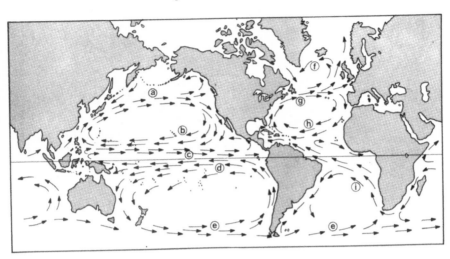

Figure 3.1. Generalized map (Mercator projection) of the principle surface ocean currents: (a) Japan/North Pacific currents, (b) California/North Equatorial currents, (c) Equatorial Countercurrent, (d) Peru/South Equatorial currents, (e) Antarctic Drift, (f) Irminger Current, (g) Gulf Stream/North Atlantic current, (h) Canary/North Equatorial currents, (i) Benguela/South Equatorial currents. Courtesy of Stephen C. Jett.

toward the subpolar low-pressure belts while being deflected according to the Coriolis effect.[1] The net result is that in the middle latitudes, on the poleward flank of each of these highs a zone of prevailing approximately westerly winds exists over each ocean basin, and that on the equatorward side of each high is a belt of approximately easterly winds—the trade winds (so called owing to their former importance to merchant shipping). On the eastern and western flanks of these high-pressure cells are zones of equatorward- and poleward-blowing winds, respectively. Further, major high-pressure cells over the poles produce the so-called polar easterlies over the boreal oceans, which extend into the sub-polar latitudes, winds that would have favored discovery of the more northerly Atlantic islands and northern America from mainland northwestern Europe and from the British Isles. These tropical trades, midlatitude westerlies, and subpolar easterlies annually shift a number of degrees northward and south-ward, following (up to a point) the 47-degree seasonal shifts in latitude of the overhead sun.

Sea Carousels: The Principal Winds and Currents

The prevailing wind systems, although not always completely consistent—espe-cially the more poleward ones—do operate most of the time. The trade winds are particularly reliable in most mid-ocean equatorial areas, at least for much of the year. The drag of the prevailing winds across the surfaces of the seas gen-erates directional drifting of the surface waters, although at a very much lower

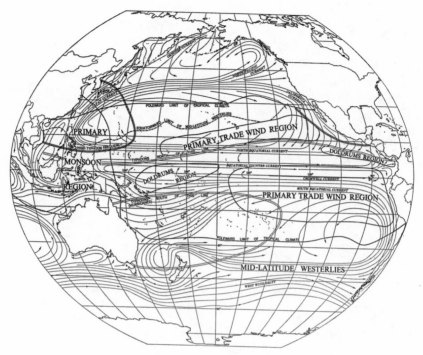

Figure 3.2. Map of the Pacific basin, showing atmospheric-circulation regions and surface ocean currents. Area ratio: 1:106,000,000. From Herman R. Friis, ed., *The Pacific Basin*, 1967, p. 12. Reprinted with permission of the American Geographical Society.

velocity than that of the winds themselves. The vectors of the resulting currents are conditioned not only by wind direction and by Coriolis deflection but also by the configurations of the ocean basins—that is, how the currents are bounded by continental landmasses. These factors result in each principal ocean basin's being characterized by a gyre: a more or less circular or oval and endlessly circulating broad "river" of surface flow running roughly parallel to the prevailing winds (figure 3.2). For any floating object in the downwind and down-current direction, the ocean is, effectively, much less "wide" than in the contrary direction or at any other latitude at which the winds and currents are flowing in a direction other than that in which the sailor wishes to travel. In fact, the eolian and hydrological gyres create what are essentially one-way streets for sailing craft, giving a "free ride" in one direction and essentially precluding the reverse, that is, travel directly upstream. It was these subtropical gyres that Columbus took advantage of and that, subsequent to improved post-Columbian Spanish and Portuguese delineation of their basic locations and functionings, allowed their routine use as round-trip "conveyor belts" across the oceans.[2] And it is these gyres that have impelled most long-distance drift voyages of disabled craft.

In the North Atlantic, during the age of sail the most used routes between Europe and the Caribbean involved the so-called Columbus Gyre. Sailing for the Americas, ships took advantage of the trade winds and the Canary Current off northwestern Africa, and the latter's westward-setting continuation, the North Equatorial Current. For the return, the prevailing westerlies and the northeastward/eastward-setting Gulf Stream/North Atlantic Drift defined the preferred route. The average speed of the Atlantic's North Equatorial Current is about 12 miles per day. The velocity of the Gulf Stream diminishes toward the north, declining from about 70 miles per day to some 10 miles per day. The average velocity of low-floating flotsam orbiting the North Atlantic gyre is 7.3 miles per day.[3] However, according to the German botanist Susanne Renner, "Because of their speed, equatorial currents [from off Africa] can transport larger floating objects with wind-exposed surfaces across the Atlantic in less than two weeks."[4]

In the North Pacific, the principally utilized route from Asia to North America —employed from 1565 to 1815 by the Spaniards' Manila galleons between the island of Luzon in the Philippines and the port of Acapulco in Mexico—was via the Japan Current (Kuro Siwo or Kuroshio, that is, 'Black Stream') and the North Pacific Drift. The latter splits off of British Columbia, and the main branch, the California Current, runs southward along the coast, with an extension to as far as southern Mexico. The return to Asia was accomplished by way of the North Equatorial Current, which was most easily accessed off West Mexico. The velocity of the Japan/North Pacific Currents range up to some 100 miles per day off Japan but drops to about 10 miles per day in the North Pacific. That ocean's North Equatorial Current moves at an average speed of about 7.2 miles per day. The fastest recorded message-in-a-bottle drift crossing from Japan to Washington State took 226 days.[5] Of course, the prevailing wind substantially increases even a sail-less vessel's velocity over that of the current alone—in the Pacific, 20 to 25 miles per day as compared to 7 to 10 miles per day for less exposed objects.

Similar current gyres exist in the South Atlantic Basin (Benguela/South Equatorial/Falkland currents/West Wind Drift) and the South Pacific Basin (Peru or Humboldt/South Equatorial/East Australian/South Pacific currents) but were less often used by Europeans. The velocity of the South Equatorial Current in the eastern Pacific is about 60 miles per day.

There is also the Irminger (Greenland) Current, which branches off from the Gulf Stream to the south of Iceland and loops back westward past Cape Farvel (Cape Farewell, the southern tip of Greenland) to the Labrador Sea, whence the Labrador Current runs southward past Labrador and Newfoundland. In spring, easterly winds favor east–west crossings from Europe; in autumn, westerlies do the opposite.

The West Wind Drift circles the globe between Antarctica and the other southern continents, but this current, with its attendant fierce weather and distance from regions possessing decent watercraft, is not usually considered a good candidate for early movements of humans.

Although western Europe and eastern Asia are suitably positioned to take advantage of these conveyors to and from America, much of sub-Saharan Africa is *not* well situated for using them to travel to the New World. Between Cape Verde and the angle of Africa, the drift is either parallel to the coast or runs *toward* Africa (Equatorial Countercurrent). In Namibia, off which runs the Benguela Current (continued northwestward by the South Equatorial Current), there were no native watercraft of note (although Indian Ocean vessels could have used the Benguela; see below). Too, sub-Saharan Africa's western coast seems to have lacked sail until late pre-Columbian times, and even then only the more northerly areas acquired it. The most promising region for origination of any sub-Saharan African-origin drifts would be the Cape Verde area of Senegambia, off which the Canary Current lies only about 50 to 100 miles.

Along Africa's eastern coast, return voyages originating in the north might appear to have been somewhat problematic to the south of Madagascar, since the strong Agulhas Current that runs from Mozambique south to the continent's tip is hard to buck and develops dangerous waves when the wind is southwesterly. Al-Bīrūnī contended that no ship that had attempted the passage had ever returned.[6] However, shipping can largely avoid these impediments by staying shoreward of the 100-meter-depth contour, and this route *was* negotiated regularly on the *Carreira da Índia* after the Portuguese pioneered the itinerary for Europeans.[7]

Any Indian Ocean vessel that *was* caught in the Agulhas Current would, by rounding Cape Agulhas and the Cape of Good Hope, find itself in the northward-flowing Benguela Current. That current (in company with the trade winds) crosses the Atlantic as the South Equatorial Current and, as the Guiana Current, runs along the northeastern coast of South America and into the Caribbean Sea and the Gulf of Mexico. This is a route that until recently was very seldom considered when thinking about ancient transoceanic contacts, but the potential certainly was there and may well have been realized.

In sum, then, many major ocean surface currents offer important assists for watercraft traveling in the directions of flow, and more often than not are augmented by approximately parallel prevailing winds pushing the vessel along. Although for these reasons the oceans are, for purposes of sailing, much "narrower" when making crossings *with* the winds and currents, and very much "wider" when going *against* them, this does not mean that it is impossible for a capable watercraft to sail readily in directions other than those of the prevailing winds and currents; in fact, most craft sail best when the wind is approximately abeam (coming from the side; see below and chapter 16).

"Breathing" In and Out: The Asiatic Monsoon System

Owing to differences in heat conductivity of oceans versus continents, over the Northern Hemisphere ones, especially over vast Eurasia, there develops each winter a subarctic dense cold-air high-pressure cell followed by a summertime midlatitude expanded warm air low, which creates highly predictable seasonal reversals in the prevailing-wind direction: outward from Asia in winter and in toward that continent from over the seas in summer. This wind reversal, or monsoon system, even reverses the direction of the northern Indian Ocean surface current gyre, from clockwise in summer to counterclockwise in winter. It was this consistent eolian pattern that facilitated the high development of relatively safe maritime exploration and trading activity in the Indian Ocean, the China seas, and Indonesia.

The southwest monsoon winds of the Indian Ocean of June through September were far more susceptible to gales and storms than were the steady, gentle northeast monsoon winds of October through April. Early Indian mariners seem to have sailed mainly with the latter, on both outward and homeward journeys, whereas Arabians did sometimes make use of the diminishing tail end of the southwest winds, in latest August and September. With stronger, larger ships and more suitable rigs, Greco-Roman traders employed the full southwest monsoon, from July on, returning from November on.

The Russian oceanographers V. I. Voitov and D. D. Tumarkin wrote of westerly winds in the equatorial Pacific "which divide the trade wind flows of both hemispheres" and which shift northward and southward with the seasons.[8] With respect to transoceanic issues, the importance of these winds and of the Asiatic monsoon system is in their (Northern Hemisphere) wintertime counteraction of the prevailing easterly trade winds far into the Pacific. The Equatorial Countercurrent—which, compensatorily, flows eastward between the westward-setting North and South Equatorial currents—is strengthened at this time of year as well. How far eastward the effects of these annual westerlies are regularly felt is not clear, although they affect all of Polynesia. In fact, in the eighteenth century Captain James Cook made the following observation: "Tup[a]ia, an islander, tells us that during the months of November, December, and January, westerly winds . . . prevail; and . . . no difficulty will arise in trading or sailing from island to island, even though they lie in an east and west direction."[9]

Early European explorers repeatedly recorded such westerly winds as far to the east as the Tuamotu Islands, often persisting for as much as two weeks and even, on occasion, for months. Rather than tack against easterlies, Polynesians waited for these seasonal winds and for storm westerlies when they wanted to sail eastward.

Prevailing winds are sometimes reduced, even reversed, or, to the contrary, reinforced, by temporary storm conditions, which can also generate strong temporary countercurrents. When a deep atmospheric depression (low-pressure system) forms over the North Atlantic—a common occurrence—easterly gales are generated in the midlatitudes and sometimes blow European sea and land birds entirely across the ocean. Watercraft, especially if disabled, would have been subject to being blown westward as well, as the Norse sagas indeed record.

The Equatorial Countercurrent and its extension northward from the Gulf of Panama, plus westerlies, must have been involved in the 1813–15 transpacific drift of the Japanese ship *Tokujō-maru* (see chapter 5).

In 1986, the experimental Polynesian double canoe *Hōkūleʻa* (see chapter 20) managed to sail eastward from Samoa to Tahiti despite the dominance of the easterly summer trades, by taking advantage of the temporary westerly winds provided by the occasional subtropical low-pressure system and lasting from a few days to a week at a time. In 1999–2000, that same craft—like many a whaling ship before it—found that northerly winds generated by wintertime lows between Mangareva and Easter Island allowed a straight cross-wind course eastward to Easter.[10]

As has been noted, winds directly from the west were not necessary to allow making progress toward the east without beating to windward (tacking)—the wind needed only to be on or abaft the beam (that is, arriving at 90° to the ship's long axis or coming from a more sternward direction). Experiments with Hōkūle'a showed, in fact, that a wind just slightly abaft the beam is more efficient for a double canoe than is a wind blowing from directly astern. Even when the wind is arriving slightly forward of the beam, some easting can be made without actually tacking if there is a good keel or leeboard(s) and/or rudder to counter leeway (off-course drift caused by the force of the wind).[11] Note, too, that in the eastern and central parts of the Pacific, and away from the equator (where the two sets of trade winds converge) the trades blow from the northeast or southeast rather than directly opposing eastward sailing by being from due east. Thus one could sail southeastward or northeastward across the wind without tacking into its teeth.

Oh, Baby! The El Niño–Southern Oscillation Phenomenon and the Countercurrents

As described, in Northern Hemisphere wintertime the monsoon effect annually reverses the prevailing easterlies of the western Pacific and, to a diminishing degree, to the east as well. Furthermore, in recent decades it has become increasingly understood that every two to nine years, and at the same season that the westerly monsoon winds have their normal impact, a reinforcing phenomenon occurs: as a consequence of a greater-than-average rise in ocean surface temperature (and, therefore, that of the air lying atop the ocean), the Pacific region experiences the El Niño–Southern Oscillation (ENSO).[12] During such episodes, the upper-atmosphere jet stream shifts to higher-than-normal latitudes; higher-than-normal atmospheric pressure develops over the western Pacific and lower pressure over the eastern Pacific; and the Pacific trade winds cease or are even reversed. Major meteorological and related consequences occur across the Indian and Pacific oceans, including drought-fostered forest fires, crop failure, and even starvation in normally seasonally wet South and Southeast Asia, sub-Saharan Africa, and Australia; drought on almost all Pacific islands; higher temperatures plus disastrously heavy rains in normally cool, arid western South America; and moist "Pineapple Express" winds from Hawaii to normally dry Southern California. Surface ocean currents, generated by the winds, respond accordingly. It has been hypothesized that periods of high El Niño frequency allowed eastward expansions of Oceanic peoples into previously uninhabited Pacific archipelagos.[13]

In the Southern Hemisphere summer season, ENSO westerlies have been recorded in the Marquesas as well as at Easter Island and far to the latter's east. During the 1982–83 El Niño, Easter experienced periods of as long as five weeks when the prevailing southeasterlies were replaced by westerlies. Under such circumstances, it was noted, a balloon (or watercraft?) would have been blown to Chile's Chiloe Island in the course of the summer.

In addition to replacement by westerly winds, the ENSO suspension of the easterly trades allows a transpacific eastward surge of Kelvin waves—pulses of the water that the easterlies had kept piled up in the western Pacific. This strengthens the Equatorial Countercurrent (see below) and extends the branches at its eastern end northward to as far as Baja California and southward to Peru, and even causes temporary cessation of the westward set of the Equatorial Currents.[14] The modern El Niño pattern began between 2500 and 1000 BC; during the previous millennium or so, such events were less frequent.[15]

All this raises the probability that the 150- to 500-mile-wide (North) Equatorial Countercurrent could, at such times, have provided a feasible route from Southeast Asia to the vicinity of the Gulf of Panama. As noted, the countercurrent forms in response to the normal pileup of water blown by the trades (in the form of the equatorial currents) to the western Pacific. A return flow, between 3 and 8 degrees north latitude, helps restore the balance. Although Thor Heyerdahl characterized that countercurrent as being "no more than a narrow belt of eddies and upwellings occurring within . . . the doldrums. . . . [and] of little use to trans-Pacific voyagers," he based his observations on a 1908 publication and on failed experimental voyages.[16] However, more recent research has required modification of earlier views. The British coastal geomorphologist Cuchlaine A. M. King termed the countercurrent as being fairly strongly developed, and measurements indicated a flow through the Marshall Islands—where it is important to native navigation—of up to 2 knots against contrary trade winds.[17] During a period when the wind was calm, natives were recorded as drifting 124 miles toward the east in less than seventy hours, that is, 1.87 miles per hour and thus in excess of 40 miles a day.[18] An empty canoe from Sulawesi in Indonesia once washed up on the shore of Pohnpei in the eastern Caroline Islands, over 2,400 miles to the east.[19] Russian research in the 1960s revealed that the westerly winds of winter, in conjunction with the eastward-setting countercurrent's 0.6 to 1 mile-per-hour velocity, encourage west–east movement along the entire length of Micronesia and do not end there.[20]

According to the University of Hawai'i anthropologist Ben Finney, in the mid-Pacific the countercurrent is normally strongest in the autumn, approaching a velocity of 1 knot,[21] and the Swedish ethnologist Kjell Åkerblom put its velocity at between 1 and 2 knots (although considering it weak and that its accompanying calms and fluky winds made "this area [eastward of the Marquesas] among the least attractive for sailing ships).[22] That the countercurrent remains reasonably strong at its eastern end is indicated by sailors' observations and by lengthy west–east drift voyages recorded for the area.[23]

Heyerdahl did admit that although experimental attempts to use the countercurrent had failed, nevertheless a voyage "in this latitude is undoubtedly feasible," even if not naturally aided (as he supposed).[24] Too, the latitudes of the countercurrent are the least subject to storms and gales in the Pacific—although, as mentioned, such disturbances are more common during the wintertime monsoon reversal of the winds than at other times of the year.[25] Despite the fact that the doldrums of the intertropical convergence zone, which lie over the countercurrents, are characterized by frequent inconvenient calms, they also produce considerable rain, enhancing chances for survival.

In 1959, Soviet scientists discovered a previously unrecognized South Equatorial Countercurrent between 2° and 5°S, running from about 95°W to 165°E. It flows at about 4.6 to 11.5 statute miles per day (0.17 to 0.42 knots) and "is powerful enough to drive a vessel toward the east."[26] Further, a South Pacific Current flows from off Australia past New Zealand's North Island, its northern margin brushing many of the main groups of Polynesian islands. So, in addition to the (North) Equatorial Countercurrent there are other east-setting currents in the southern Pacific that could have aided human movements in that direction.

Climatologists now know that an erratic pressure shifting called the Northern Annular Mode alternately weakens and strengthens the Northern Hemisphere's prevailing westerly winds. Too, oceanographers have hypothesized that the strengths of the various ocean currents have varied over time, reciprocally between the Northern and Southern hemispheres, although much more research remains to be accomplished on this matter. Some paleoclimatologists surmise that during the Medieval Warm Period (circa AD 800–1275), at least North Atlantic currents were enhanced, the reverse being the case during the subsequent Little Ice Age (circa AD 1300–1870). Such fluctuations (which likely also affected other currents), along with altered storm and sea-ice conditions, could have facilitated or inhibited transoceanic voyaging during different epochs.

Circular Reasoning: Antiquity of Knowledge of the Gyres

The notion that the prevailing winds and currents might have played an important role in the pre-Columbian dispersals of humankind has a certain age. In 1850, the American geologist/ethnologist Henry R. Schoolcraft, who studied American Indians, concluded that, "The trade winds [of earlier times] would . . . have had the same effects then as now in expediting, or in carrying out of their latitudes, an ancient voyager, whether he navigated these seas by accident or design." Schoolcraft's correspondent, the naval oceanographer Matthew F. Maury, responded that "it would have been more remarkable that America should not have been peopled from Asia [by sea] . . . than that [it] should have been."[27]

The first known map of the oceans' true current systems was not produced until the eighteenth century. Although it is certainly believable that ancient mariners were fortuitously carried away by currents and by prevailing winds and thereby crossed oceans, is it plausible that any pre-Columbian peoples discovered and purposely utilized these conveyor-belt routes centuries, perhaps millennia, prior to documented modern knowledge of them?

There is little direct evidence concerning the ancients' understandings of the patterns of the prevailing global-scale winds and currents. Obviously, knowledge of local winds and currents existed from the beginning, but a sense of the wider configurations is another matter. Knowledge of the gyres certainly gave later sailors the confidence that if they sailed across the seas, there would be feasible avenues for their return, whereas earlier absence of such knowledge would have encouraged considerable caution.

One suspects that the major winds and currents of the waters off monsoon Asia were the first to be delineated, and very anciently, at least by Neolithic times and likely well before. According to the American writer Louise Levathes, the Chinese possessed "some knowledge" of the nearer Pacific's winds and currents at least by the early centuries AD,[28] and the name of the Japan Current, *Wei Lu*, is attested around 500 BC. There is an AD 1178 account of three ocean currents: the second one runs northward off Guangdong, Fujian, and Zhejiang, and "the third [a continuation of the second] makes eastward into that boundless deep the Great Eastern Ocean." As for the farther Pacific, matters are less clear; according to an AD 285 Chinese commentator, "the Eastern Ocean is . . . vast, and we know of no one who has crossed it."[29]

Certainly, denizens of the Japanese islands as well as various other East Asians were aware of the Kuroshio Current early on, and some sailors certainly inadvertently learned of its continuation across the North Pacific to North America. As Polynesians and Micronesians spread purposefully eastward across vast stretches of the Pacific, they unquestionably became familiar with at least the equatorial currents and countercurrents as well as, less certainly, the currents on the eastern and western flanks of at least the southern gyre. They appear to have encountered the West Wind Drift as well.

On the western end of the Old World, we know that the ancient Greeks and Romans generally conceived the three continents of the inhabited world (Africa, Europe, Asia) as together being surrounded by water, not slack water but "the deep-flowing River of Ocean" (*potamós Okeanóio*) as Homer termed it in *The Odyssey* some 740 years BC. *Okeanós* referred to the great, flowing Outward Sea (Atlantic), whereas the Inward (Mediterranean) Sea was usually called *Thálassos* or *Póntos*.[30]

The Greeks apparently acquired the encircling-ocean-river concept from the Babylonians, where such a configuration appears on the earliest-known world map (circa 700 BC, on clay), as remarked upon in chapter 1. According to Homer's eighth-century BC *Iliad*, referring to an earlier age, the warrior Achilles's shield carried an image of Earth encompassed by the ocean river. The concept is depicted as well on the earliest-known Greek *mappa mundi*, that of Hecataios of Miletos (late sixth century BC). About 700 BC, the Greek poet Hesiod (Hesíodos) mentioned such an ocean river. About AD 180, Minucius Felix wrote of the British Isles being bathed by a warm flow, that is, the continuation of the Gulf Stream.

All this certainly suggests awareness—whether empirical or merely theoretical—of consistent, major ocean currents, as exist, most noticeably in the West, off the Atlantic coast of Morocco. The surrounding-ocean-river concept persisted through medieval times and into the European Renaissance (for example, Adam of Bremen, circa AD 1060, referring to the North Atlantic Drift). With such a conception, one could commit oneself to the Canary Current, for instance, with the expectation that one would eventually be carried back to one's starting point, after encircling the terrestrial world. If such confidence existed, as it seems to have done, then the idea of deliberate voyaging leading to an Atlantic crossing is anything but outrageous.

Although we will probably never know with certainty, it seems quite plausible that certain ancient peoples, at least Phoenicians/Carthaginians—contemporaries of the ancient Greeks—had much earlier become aware of some of the wider patterns of the ocean currents, via voyages by individuals such as that of the Phoenician circumnavigator of Africa circa 600 BC recorded by Herodotus; that of Himlico, the Carthaginian who probed into the North Atlantic; and that of Hanno of Carthage, who cruised the entire West African coast. One can envision such explorations, foreshadowing those of the fifteenth-century Portuguese, yielding results similar to the findings obtained by those Iberians—including the discovery of Brazil, accidentally, as by Pedro Álvares Cabral in AD 1500 (see chapter 5).

In a later era, the Norse built up a considerable body of information about the prevailing winds and currents of the North Sea and the North Atlantic. Earlier voyagers may well have done the same. If the voyages of Saint Brendan and their routes as reconstructed by the American navigator Paul Chapman are to be credited, then that seventh-century Irish abbot recognized and used the North Atlantic gyre to encircle that ocean basin.[31]

As far as the winds are concerned, it is likely that it was assumed, at least in Atlantic Europe once familiarity with a broad span of latitudes was developed (by Carthaginian times or before), that prevailing wind direction was consistent within a given range of latitude; that, therefore, one could sail westward with the tropical trades and return with the midlatitude westerlies, no matter what ocean basin one was in. In fact, the Portuguese claimed to have found the South Atlantic gyre by analogy to the familiar North Atlantic one. Such an assumption would have mitigated fear of sailing into the unknown.

4

Staying Alive While Crossing the Deep

But mine is all as hungry as the sea.
　　—William Shakespeare, Sonnet 64, 1609

It is a long, long way across the span of the Pacific Ocean, and even the width of the Atlantic is far from negligible. How could voyagers traveling in boats of limited size and cargo capacity possibly have carried with them sufficient fresh water and food to sustain them during the prolonged time needed to traverse the deep? That is the question that must next be addressed.

A Scurvy Lot? The Question of Dietary-Deficiency Diseases

Prolonged deprivation of critical nutrients produces dietary-deficiency diseases, and history relates that long voyages often led to severe suffering from such conditions. The best known of these maladies is scorbutus or scurvy. This debilitating and often lethal condition common on shipboard during the two hundred years or so following 1492 (although not on Columbus's voyages), results from an insufficiency of ascorbic acid (vitamin C), which in ordinary diets is obtained largely from fresh fruits and vegetables. Symptoms include joint swelling and pain, fatigue, swollen and bleeding gums, and tooth loss. The crews of da Gama, Magellan, Cabral, Cartier, and the Manila galleons, among many others, suffered from it—on land as well as at sea. Most famously, Captain George Anson's 1740–44 expedition lost 1,255 of its 1,955 men to the malady. There are ancient and classical mentions as well. Francis Cuppage observed, "Scurvy . . . formed a tether that held back the [European] explorations leading to world expansion. . . . Colonization, dominion of the seas, mercantilism, and scientific explorations were all delayed by this persistent scourge."[1] If scorbutus held back early modern Europeans, would it not have definitively impeded earlier, less advanced voyagers?

First, let us recollect that despite the fact that scurvy was often a severe problem on very long European voyages (it did not ordinarily become an issue for the first two or three months), such voyaging was accomplished anyway. In the British Navy, the difficulty was finally definitively overcome in the eighteenth century by ships' carrying and crews' consuming citrus fruits or juices or hard cider. Although the subtitle of Stephen R. Bown's 2004 book titled *Scurvy* calls the disease *The Greatest Mystery of the Age of Sail*, carrying cider or citrus was a practice that had some systematic precedent in Europe as least as far back as the late 1500s. Through the ages, there have been, in fact, many mentions of antiscorbutics. Gilbertus Anglicus's 1227 *Compendium Medicinae*, urged ocean travelers to carry citrus fruits and pickled vegetables, presumably to evade scurvy. When Vasco da Gama's crew was suffering from scorbutus, recoveries occurred after the captain followed the advice of experienced Arabs and issued oranges.[2] The Dutch were using citrus by 1598. In the 1500s, too, Pedro Álvares Cabral and Richard Hawkins were aware of the curative properties of citrus. Also, "scurvy grass"—spoonwort and cresses—and wild celery were employed. Royal Navy experiments demonstrated the efficacy of citrus against scurvy, but the results were ignored until a second experiment was done in 1747. Even then, the Admiralty failed to adopt citrus until 1794, and the British merchant marine did not do so until 1865—a prime example of resistance to beneficial innovation even in the face of blatant incentive in the form of the avoidability of thousands of deaths and the conservation of untold thousands of pounds sterling.

Shipboard diets varied over the centuries and in different parts of the world. How, if at all, scurvy was dealt with before the European Renaissance and in the more distant past and in other regions may not normally be ascertainable, but we may observe that some of the putative transoceanic voyaging originated in lands where citrus was available. The Arab practice of preparing and carrying lime juice on long voyages may have a long history, and the fourteenth-century Arab traveler Ibn Battutah observed Chinese sailors stowing ascorbic-acid-rich "green stuff, vegetables and ginger" on board their ships.[3] Foods that also contain significant quantities of vitamin C (at least when fresh), include brussels sprouts, cabbage, lettuce, celery, cress, carrot, onion, potato, prickly pear, annona, pineapple, currant, cranberry and various other berries, conifer twigs and bark (used in infusions), and even rats (usually all too abundant on shipboard), which synthesize their own ascorbic acid. Additional good sources of vitamin C include sweet potatoes, dried peaches, quinces, plantains, soybeans, and palm wine. Still another source is seaweed, a regular foodstuff in East Asia and present in parts of the open oceans and as growth on the undersides of watercraft. In western North America, manzanita fruits were efficacious, as were chili peppers in the tropical New World.

Several twentieth-century drift voyages are instructive in this regard. During the *Cairo III*'s five-month drift in the Pacific in 1988, the crew caught fish and turtles and "threw anything edible into the general stew—[piscine] organs, muscles, bones, membranes, gristle—and probably for this reason they suffered no serious vitamin or mineral deficiencies. Their vitamin C, for example, probably came mostly from the eyes, brain, and pancreas of the triggerfish, one of their staple foods. Every time the men sucked and swallowed one of these organs they helped heal their cuts and prevented the onset of scurvy."[4]

During Maurice and Maralyn Bailey's 117-day accidental Pacific drift in 1973, in the course of which they subsisted on similar foods, including fish eyes and turtle brains, they developed saltwater skin sores (a trial for many drift voyagers) but not scurvy.[5] On a 1982, seventy-six-day transatlantic drift, Steven Callahan survived scurvy free on raw triggerfish and dorados, including organs, eyes, roe, and spinal disks, plus barnacles and a few crustaceans and birds.[6] Similarly, in 1972 the six persons (including three children) on the thirty-eight-day, 750-mile Dougal Robinson lifeboat drift voyage from west of the Galápagos into the doldrums subsisted mainly on sea turtles and fishes, catching rainwater and obtaining liquid from dorado spinal fluid and eyes as well as turtle blood.[7] Again, although they suffered from saltwater boils, no symptoms of dietary deficiencies appeared (they were not at sea long enough to be susceptible specifically to scurvy).

In connection with all this, let us briefly mention the matter of carrying adequate preservable provisions on long voyages. Some foods, like coconut and other nuts, are essentially self-preserving inside their shells. Some, like sago flour, yams, and yam-bean root (jícama), are naturally long lasting. Others do not keep well in their unprocessed states but may be converted to preservable forms. Without going into detail, one may list general methods of processing that enhance preservation, sometimes for very long periods: cooking, drying, smoking, salting, spicing, pickling, fermenting and other culturing (for example, cheese making), rendering (of fat), sealing with fat or wax, and storing in oil, lime juice, condensed fruit juice, honey, brine, or vinegar. Foodstuffs, as well as water, could be sealed into containers such as pottery vessels or bamboo internodes. Polynesians carried along live domestic animals and living fish and shellfish. Large Pacific sailing-canoes, among other craft, had enormous cargo capacities. With preserved supplies, stores could last for weeks, even months, and were supplemented by fishing and by catching birds.[8]

Mana of the Oceans: Water and Wild Foods for Survival at Sea

Modern experimental and other small-craft voyaging have much to teach regarding the possibilities for occupants of low-sided watercraft to obtain adequate food from the ocean and air as well as water from the skies during crossings.[9]

Water is far more critical to survival than is food—two waterless weeks is the approximate maximum of human tolerance. Even in temperate climates, under shelter, and with minimal activity, after five to seven days without water the body's remaining fitness wanes rapidly until debility and then death ensue. However, in the most likely drift zones—notably, those of the trade winds and the westerlies—rainwater can be collected and consumed. Fishes can be squeezed for their juice, and fish eyes and spinal disks are edible sources of moisture. Even ingestion of one's urine can recycle moisture in service of survival.

Healthy humans are capable of living for sixty to a hundred days without food, with normal bodily and mental functioning enduring for about a month. In fact, with adequate daily fresh water hunger pangs disappear following about a week of deprivation. Still, after thirty days or so lack of food becomes increasingly debilitating, and many drifts (as well as deliberate crossings) have lasted much longer than sixty days. Thus nutrition is a real issue.

It is true that fish life and bird life are scarce in and over some areas of the oceans' surface waters, especially over the deep zones and to a greater extent in the Pacific than in the Atlantic. The centers of the subtropical gyres (see chapter 2) have a particular paucity of edible creatures, but these zones, lacking as they are in consistent winds and currents, are unlikely areas for transoceanic voyaging, either accidental or intentional. But in other parts of the oceans, vertebrate sea life—such as dorados (dolphins, mahi-mahis), bonitos, sharks, and turtles—is plenteous and catchable.

Food abundance may vary not only with location but also with time of year—for example, great during the Indian Ocean's southwest monsoon but limited during the northeast monsoon. And, especially in the Pacific, predatory fishes may consume hooked smaller fishes before they can be landed. Nevertheless, many small-boat voyagers have found potential food to be profuse and obtainable during their traverses.

A considerable number of voyagers in the trade-wind belts have experienced finding on deck, many a morning, numerous flying fishes—up to half a hundred—which are both edible and usable as bait, as well as other small (and occasionally large) fishes such as dorados and snakefish, plus, sometimes, squid and shrimp. Flying fishes flee predatory dorados and are actually attracted by the white of sails and by lamps at night; the solo circumnavigator Joshua Slocum termed these found fishes "manna of the sea."[10] As have a multitude of other small-craft sailors, Thor Heyerdahl found many flying fishes on the deck of his balsa-log raft Kon-Tiki each morning. "To starve to death would have been impossible," he asserted.[11]

With the simplest of equipment—none at all, in some cases—not only fish but also turtles and seabirds can be caught. Methods include use of baited hooks on lines, spears, gaffs, nets, and the hand. Chumming attracts fishes. If one is not too far out to sea, porpoises are another possible food resource. Some additional potential sources of nourishment are seaweed (and its associated crustaceans and small fishes) and plankton (gathered by towing fabric pouches behind the craft), both of which are rich in antiscorbutic vitamin C.

An underside mini-ecosystem of seaweed, mollusks, crustaceans, fishes, and so forth forms over time beneath watercraft, especially rafts, and can be drawn upon for food.[12] Fishes, birds, and turtles are attracted by watercraft, and several small-craft voyagers have described the "floating aquariums" beneath their boats or rafts. This may in part be a matter of piscine curiosity. In other cases, fishes seek the craft's shade to elude predators. Small fishes feed on underside gooseneck barnacles, algae, and so forth. Schools of predatory dorados or tuna and individual sharks may follow a boat for thousands of miles, feeding on these smaller fishes. On all three of Thor Heyerdahl's experimental transoceanic voyages, the sailors were able to catch as much fish as could be consumed.

There have been large numbers of very long drift voyages with survivors (see the following chapter). In some cases, we have information on acquisition of water and food. For example, some nineteenth-century Japanese transpacific drift voyagers survived on fish that they speared and birds that they caught. In a study of shipwreck survivors, the physician MacDonald Critchley reported drifters consuming seaweed, crabs, flying fish, shark meat boiled in seawater, raw albatross, barnacles, dolphins, squids, and tortoises.[13]

Some modern survival experiments are germane, here. In 1952, the French medical man Alain Bombard deliberately crossed the Atlantic from the Canaries to the Caribbean in a rubber raft, surviving without resorting to carried provisions. Although emaciated and weak on arrival, he had subsisted on fish, the occasional seabird, plankton, and rainwater mixed with seawater (modest quantities of which may be beneficially consumed). In 1957, the German physician Hannes Lindemann voluntarily drifted in a foldboat from Las Palmas in the Canary Islands to Saint Martin in the Caribbean. He hooked, speared, knifed, or grabbed dolphins, pilotfish, and triggerfish, and found crabs, shrimp, and small fishes in sargasso weed.[14]

When considering the wild-food picture as described above for the contemporary era, it is well to remember that today's sea life is highly depauperate as compared to former eras—by approximately thirty times in terms of easily catchable fish, according to an informed estimate. Survival at sea would have been notably more feasible in the past, then.[15]

Thus it appears that in many parts of the world's seas, wild food supplies were easily obtained and existed in quantities more than adequate to ensure survival on transoceanic voyages, as long as fresh water—often, acquirable from rains—was sufficient. Even without supplemental fresh water, fish fluids could supply needed moisture. Survival at sea was, then, not normally an overwhelming challenge.

5

Getting the Drift

Accidental Voyages and Discoveries

Wherein I spake of most disastrous chances,
Of moving accidents by flood. . . .
And portance in my travel's history.
— William Shakespeare, *Othello* I.iii, ca. 1604

Humans in ancient times unquestionably crossed wide waters both by design and by accident. In fact, fortuitous discovery may have played a fundamental role in expanding sailors' horizons and leading eventually to purposive crossings on a regular or episodic basis. This chapter looks at unintentional drifts impelled by maritime winds and currents. It is based on empirical observation of the phenomenon as well as on the developing science of computer simulation of oceanic drifting.

The Far Travels of Flotsam

The oceans' prevailing wind and current systems, described in chapter 3, carry along anything buoyant enough not to sink to the depths. The higher a piece of flotsam of a given density projects above the water surface, the greater the degree to which the wind pushes it along faster than the current itself; thus, tall icebergs may travel as much as 40 miles a day. Unguided materials can be, and are, conveyed many thousands of miles, to fetch up on distant—sometimes, almost unbelievably distant—shores. Columbus heard that a (presumably American) carved wooden statuette, *almadías* (canoes), and even bodies of "Chinese-looking" men (probably Native Americans) occasionally washed up on the Azores, in the Madeira Archipelago, on the Canary Islands, and in Ireland, and that (American) bamboo arrived in Madeira.[1] Columbus claimed that he himself saw two bodies washed ashore in Ireland; these were probably Eskimo (Inuit).

Many logs from northwestern North America, as well as glass and plastic fishnet floats and other items from Japanese waters, commonly wash up on Hawaiian coasts, and flotsam from South America reaches the Tuomotu Islands.[2] Southeast Asian sea beans, coconuts, bamboos, and tropical logs reach North

America's Northwest Coast. Uprooted Chinese trees have landed in Oregon and other tropical trees in Maine.[3]

According to Alice B. Kehoe, "Knowledge [that] there is land to the west has been abundantly provided to Britons for millennia by the enormous quantity of drift timber washing up on their northwestern shores: a late Neolithic building . . . in Shetland used 700 meters of dressed Labrador spruce, accepted as American-originated drift."[4] Because of its location in relation to the Gulf Stream, British littorals also receive logs from various spots in the Caribbean, and Caribbean sea beans arrive on European strands. By the same token, most driftwood on the coast of Greenland is of European origin. Logs from the Americas reach Tasmania, ones from Siberia drift to Iceland and Greenland, timber and ice-locked watercraft get carried around the Arctic Ocean perimeter, and many Asian logs wash up on British Columbia's Haida Gwaii (Queen Charlotte Islands).[5] In fact, messages in bottles (MIBs) as well as plastic toys, sneakers, and the like lost from contemporary container ships have drifted all over the world.[6] Some MIB examples: one launched in the southern Indian Ocean arrived at the tip of South America, was relaunched and then drifted back to the Indian Ocean (its rate of travel was about 6 miles a day); another floated from off Gibraltar and ended up in Maine; one from Southern California was found on the shore of Okinawa, and others were retrieved in the Philippines, at Rio de Janeiro, in Colombia, and in Japan.[7]

As reported in the oceanographer Curtis Ebbesmeyer's newsletter *Beachcombers' Alert!*, derelict boats, buoys, MIBs, and so forth have drifted from Nova Scotia to Wales, from Maine to Spain and on to the Turks and Caicos Islands, from the Cape Verde Islands to Barbados, from Japan to Washington and to California, and so forth and so forth. If unguided logs, nets, floats, bottles, and other flotsam, as well as unmanned vessels, could travel to these far-flung places, how much more so could functioning sailing-vessels whose captains selected favorable sailing seasons? R. T. Callaghan noted, "Computer simulations suggest that such [human drift-borne] contacts were feasible if not inevitable at any time period."[8]

Intact Manned Vessels Out of Control

The prominent linguist Lyle Campbell, generally skeptical regarding transoceanic influences, nevertheless had the following to say: "it should be remembered that there is really little difficulty in crossing the oceans—coconuts have done it . . . adventurers in rowboats have done it. The only trick seems to be to stay alive and afloat long enough to be carried by the ocean currents to the other side."[9] Staying alive was discussed in the preceding chapter; results of remaining afloat are addressed in this one.

Adverse weather conditions cause even intact motorless or out-of-fuel modern craft to lose full control of their movements, sometimes resulting in landfalls very different from the target ones. A Tibetan Buddhist text, for instance, describes the lion prince Simhala, en route between the Bay of Bengal and Sri Lanka, being blown off course to the Persian Gulf, where the group founded a colony.[10] Herodotus alleged (if implausibly) that the first direct Greek knowledge of the Atlantic came about when powerful winds blew one Kolaios of Samos all the way down the Mediterranean and out through the Pillars of Herakles (Strait of Gibraltar), in about 630 BC (actually, Greeks knew of the ocean even earlier).

Again, the ship in which Paul the Apostle (Saul of Tarsus) traveled en route to Rome, in the first century AD, was blown helplessly astray on the Mediterranean: "I was adrift on the open sea" (2 Corinthians 11:25), perhaps inspiring him to use, in his letter to the Ephesians (4:25), the metaphor of being "carried about with every wind."

Sailors ordinarily awaited decent weather and a fair wind to take them toward their destinations. If the wind turned foul along the way, the boat could end up being blown considerable distances in an undesired direction, even with all sail furled. The Danish historian of navigation Søren Thirslund wrote, of the Norse: "'Heaving to' [staying in place at sea, perhaps aided by a sea anchor] was probably never practised by the Viking-age seamen. When a storm came up they had to run before the weather with the consequence that they could be taken far away from their intended course."[11]

Nor are storm conditions the only circumstances under which a drift voyage might be initiated. The experimental voyager Tim Severin wrote of how a few days' calm could result in an intact junk's being caught in the Kuroshio off Japan and carried far away from land.[12] In some years, that current develops an abnormal meander that goes far out to sea, and even in normal years is continued on to America as the North Pacific Drift (see chapter 3).

Disabled Drifters

Ever since there have been watercraft, there have been accidental disablements and drifts. Disabling puts a craft and its complement at an even greater disadvantage than that of an intact vessel under adverse conditions, causing it to drift entirely according to the whims of weather and sea rather than according to the dictates of its navigator's intended route. We have, for example, these dramatic lines from Greek Ionia of the eighth century BC (describing events set half a millennium earlier), in Homer's rendering of the words of Odysseus:

> Darkness swept down on us from the sky. Our ships were driven sidelong by the wind, and the force of the gusts tore their sails to rags and tatters. . . .
>
> In an instant the tempest was upon them, carrying them headlong out to sea.
>
> Before she had run very far, a howling wind hit us with hurricane

force. The squall snapped both forestays together. As the mast fell aft, all the rigging tumbled into the bilge.[13]

The *Mahābhārata*, an Indian epic of about 500 BC referring to events of circa 1200 BC, speaks of a "tempest-tossed and damaged vessel."[14] The venerable *Arabian Nights* tale of Sindbad the Sailor—fictional but still with considerable basis in experience—mentions multiple ship disablings and blowings off course:

> One day we found ourselves in the middle of a roaring, raging sea. The captain . . . slapped his face, furled the sails, cast the anchors, plucked his beard, tore his clothes, and uttered a loud cry. . . . "O fellows, may God preserve you. The wind has prevailed against us and forced us into the middle of the sea."

> [A] violent storm suddenly blew against us, tore the sails to pieces. . . .
> "We have strayed from our course and entered a sea of which we don't know the routes" [said the captain]. . . . Then he climbed the mast, in order to loosen the sails, but a strong wind blew against the ship, driving it backward, and the rudder broke . . .
> [A] violent head wind blew suddenly. . . . [The captain] said, . . . "the wind has prevailed against us and driven us into the farthest of the seas of the world."[15]

Although ocean voyaging is not nearly as dangerous as many think it is—and the tale of Sindbad is intended to maximize drama—extreme weather, unexpected squalls, encounters with submerged rocks, collisions with whales, and other mishaps, not to mention human error, have damaged or deflected myriad boats and ships.

Factors that influence the frequencies and directions of drift voyages with survivors include the kinds and magnitudes of aquatic activity and the nature of the weather in the source areas; the seaworthiness and the cargoes of the watercraft involved; the numbers of persons on board and their knowledge and skill levels; the vectors and velocities of the winds and the sets and speeds of the relevant currents; and the nature of other aspects of the weather, the sea conditions, and the biotic richness of the waters en route.

There are many, many recorded examples of modern drift voyages up to thousands of miles in length and multiple months in duration in Indonesia and the western Pacific. Most went from east to west, but many went in the opposite direction: Luzon to Taiwan, the Ryukyu Islands to Baker Island 500 miles to the east of the Gilbert Islands (Kiribati), Indonesia to Belau (Palau), the Philippines to Tinian in the Northern Marianas, the western Carolines to the Marshalls, and numerous others.[16]

One may cite three modern examples of the many recorded drifts. During

World War II a young man from Banaba Island in the Gilbert chain of today's Republic of Kiribati, fleeing the Japanese, drifted westward in a canoe for nine months and some 1,500 miles, landing in the Ninigos in the western Admiralty Islands, staying alive by eating sharks and other fish and by drinking rainwater. "In the light of this," wrote the historian Andrew Sharp, "given a stout heart, an iron constitution, and some fishing tackle, nothing is apparently too much to believe as far as survival on a long accidental voyage is concerned."[17] In an unspecified year, Western Samoan fishermen Lafaili Tofi and Telea Pa'a spent six months drifting in a small metal boat, traveling 2,480 miles. And, in 1988, five fishermen drifted for 142 days—almost five months—some 4,500 miles from Costa Rican waters to south of Hawaii, via the North Equatorial Current. They subsisted on fish, squid, sea turtles, and rainwater. Although they did experience some water shortages, food was not a major problem, and had they not been rescued they might have survived drifting indefinitely, as long as their 29-foot boat stayed afloat.[18] Then, there is the 2006 case of the three-plus-month drift of a disabled Mexican fishing boat to near the Marshall Islands, a distance of over 5,000 miles, the crew surviving on rainwater and seabirds.[19]

None of the aforementioned drifts are of transpacific magnitude, but some involve transatlantic distances. In the Atlantic, drifts from the Canary Islands to America have been recorded. One contemporary example of a transoceanic drift is a West African boatload of economic refugees that arrived in Barbados—although the passengers were all d.o.a.[20] According to simulations by Richard Callaghan, the bulk of drift voyages from the western Canaries that pass through the Antilles end up on the shores of Honduras and Nicaragua.

In 62 BC, a Roman proconsul in Cisalpine Gaul reported having received from a Celtic king a gift of some "Indians" who had been storm-washed onto the ocean shore of Germany; other such arrivals are mentioned for the twelfth century, and a 1508 French ship reported encountering a small boat full of "Indians" off England. Inuits in kayaks may occasionally have drifted to the Orkney Islands and other places in Scotland, presumably from Greenland.[21]

There is even hard evidence for a truly ancient Native North American landing in Iceland: in 1997, the Brown University archaeologist Kevin Smith reported a microblade core (the rock that remains after small parallel flakes have been removed) of very old North American Arctic type but of Icelandic materials, found in a Norse site above a circa 7500 BC former shoreline in Iceland.[22] Lightweight, northern-style skin boats like kayaks, umiaks, and currachs, as well as bark canoes (described in chapter 17) are generally more susceptible to being blown long distances than are heavy wooden craft.

With regard to the transoceanic contacts question, the American journalist Robert Hughes observed: "The American continental coast from Tierra del Fuego to the Aleutians in the west and [to] Baffin Bay on the east coast is such a vast catchment area for the globe's wind and water currents that it is inconceivable that non-native people should not have fetched up there before Columbus."[23] "Admittedly," wrote the prominent historian of the North Atlantic Vincent

H. Cassidy, "the two banks of the Atlantic valley have always proclaimed their existence to each other."[24]

Blown Away: Off-Course Ships

The significance of all of these drift voyages is less a matter of so many water-craft and people surviving such lengthy drifts than it is that the voyages often led to unanticipated discoveries and distant contacts. J. H. Parry noted in connection with the Great Age of Discovery, "Many discoveries, including some major ones, were fortuitous, the unforeseen results of wind, current or navigational error which took ships far from their intended course."[25] Parry was thinking of mariners such as the Portuguese Pedro Álvares Cabral, who, en route for India in 1500, sailed too far westward and ended up on the Brazilian coast; Alvise da Cadamosto, who, storm driven in 1456, found the Cape Verde Islands; João Gonçalves Zarco and Tristão Vaz Teixeira, who in 1418 encountered the previously unknown (to the Portuguese) Madeira Islands while fighting contrary winds; and the Spaniard Juan de Bermúdez, who, in 1505, ran across previously unknown Bermuda.

If accidental discovery could happen in that era, it could have occurred in earlier ages as well. The Azores are more likely to have been discovered from Madeira or the Canaries than from Iberia, and these mid-Atlantic islands could have become way stations in any Carthaginian, Etruscan, or Greco-Roman traffic into the ocean, as they did later for the Spanish and Portuguese. The latter made their returns homeward from West Africa via the sweep into the Atlantic called *a volta do mar*, or from the Cape of Good Hope via the similar but longer *volta da mina*, a swing out beyond the Cape Verdes and back to Portugal, passing the Azores.

In light of the occurrence of transatlantic drift voyages from the vicinity of the Canary Islands in historic times, similar voyages almost inevitably also happened in the past to the extent that there was ancient maritime activity in these same waters—as Punic and Roman remains in the Canaries attest there was.[26] The Canary Current is confined in the 60-mile-wide channel between the Canaries and Cape Juby on the African mainland, and the result is the water's accelerating to as much as 6 knots, a velocity too strong to be rowed against; any vessel in difficulty would be rapidly carried away down current.

In the North Atlantic, medieval ships en route from Norway to Scotland and in the vicinity of the Faroes were sometimes blown to Iceland, and ships sailing from Norway to Iceland were occasionally blown off course, ending up in Greenland. The Norseman Thorhall the Hunter is said to have drifted from Newfoundland to Ireland about AD 1010, and there are modern instances of Newfoundland dories drifting to Europe.[27] Accidental discovery is documented in the first recorded Norse sightings of Iceland, Greenland, and Labrador.[28]

Australia provides a fascinating case to ponder. That continent could not have been settled from Asia except after several substantial water crossings (see chapter 15). The need for boats is therefore assumed. Theoretically, however, swimming of straits of up to 40 miles or so of water is possible—some Polynesians did it—and in modern times, a number of people have swum distances up to 112 miles (including Bering Strait, the Florida Strait, and the Strait of Gibraltar); in fact, in 2009 fifty-five-year-old Jennifer Figge swam across the Atlantic (with nightly meals and sleep on an accompanying boat). Jared Diamond has suggested that swimming effected the settling of Wallacia, since certain other animal species seem to have colonized islands that way.[29] But natation of breeding-sized populations in shark-infested waters does not seem a promising means for the human settling of Australia, much less the Americas! Drift on natural rafts of vegetation is more likely, but perhaps not by very much, as evidenced by the depauperate fauna in eastern Indonesia and beyond.

The Australian archaeologist Josephine Flood wrote, "It is possible that the earliest colonists—of 50,000 or more years ago—were tide-riders, using rafts like the Kalum, a light, triangular, mangrove wood raft of double construction . . . used until recently by four tribal groups on the northwestern coast of Australia."[30] Modern computer simulations have confirmed that, given the use of rafts along the coasts of Indonesia, the directions of the prevailing winds, and the inevitability of human error and unexpected weather events, populating of Australia by accidental drift voyages could not have failed to occur.

Japanese Junk Adrift

In considering much more remote times than those of the Norse as well as longer ocean crossings, we may ask whether postulated initial, very early transoceanic encounters between Asians and Native Americans could have happened by accident. Is it stretching the imagination to the breaking point to speculate that some conceivable combination of events could actually have sent ancient Asian craft thousands and thousands of miles across the width of the Pacific to wash up on an American shore, repeatedly and with survivors?

The answer is unquestionably that such encounters could easily have occurred and almost certainly did occur, improbable though that may sound on the face of it. This conclusion is based on two considerations. The first is a trio of independent computer simulations of drifts from northern Japan. Although many of these drifts end up in mid-Pacific (including on the Hawaiian Islands), some of those in simulations conducted by the American physical oceanographer W. James Ingraham's simulations do reach California, while a number of drifts in the University of Calgary anthropologist Richard T. Callaghan's simulations end up on North America's Northwest Coast or in California, especially concentrated in Haida Gwaii and on Vancouver Island.[31] In a third team's simulations, within 180 days 5 percent of drifts from Japan would reach northwestern North America.[32] And, of course, as noted above, Japanese flotsam such as fish-net floats regularly arrives in these areas—very much increased in volume following the March 2011 Tōhoku tsunami and including docks, sections of houses, a 164-foot ship, and a 120-foot fishing boat; thirteen of an original approximately four hundred derelict vessels earlier spotted in Japanese waters were reported during 2012 and 2013 from North America's Northwest Coast, and one from the Hawaiian Islands.[33]

Second, a considerable number of actual transpacific accidental drift voyages on the part of Japanese junks were recorded in the eighteenth and nineteenth centuries, the junk being a ship type of ancient ancestry in East Asia (see chapter 20). In Japan, the historian Richard Zumwinkle wrote, "According to the "Closed Country" edict of 1636, no Japanese might leave Japan. . . . To discourage long voyages, there were drastic limitations on the permissible sizes of vessels, and the details of ship construction were so specified by regulations as to render vessels hardly seaworthy in ocean storms. And thus the seclusion laws themselves tended, in effect, to increase the number of Japanese ships that were disabled at sea."[34]

Prior to 1636, Japan had had a flourishing maritime trade with Southeast Asia and had even maintained overseas colonies there. But under the new rules, exceedingly high sterns (among the changes required by the Closed Country edict) would help make Japanese vessels unwieldy in the open ocean.[35] In addition, according to the archaeologist George I. Quimby,

> The rudder of the junk usually dropped below the vessel's bottom and was not fixed to the sternpost. . . .
>
> Bad storms with high winds and heavy seas could easily disable coastal merchant and fishing vessels. Once a junk was helplessly adrift without masts, and usually without rudder, the Kuro Siwo (Japanese) Current, the North Pacific Current, and the prevailing westerly winds destined the vessel for a trans-Pacific voyage lasting more than a year.
>
> In historic times there were often a few survivors when the wrecks were washed ashore [on North America's Northwest Coast]. On such occasions the junks were looted by the Indians and the seamen were received as slaves.[36]

The rudders of a certain number of junks were broken during unexpected severe weather or on reefs. Once the rudder was gone, the uncontrollable craft would roll its masts out and be at the mercy of the sea. Undoubtedly, the majority of such junks foundered, but as Quimby observed, some drifted to North American waters—not without severe hardship but nevertheless with at least some crew members still alive. In fact, drift voyages were common enough that a word, hyōryūmin, came into use, to refer to persons who suffered drifts (hyōryū) following disablement of their ships.[37]

In 1876, the Japanese counsel in San Francisco, Charles Wolcott Brooks, published data on Japanese drift voyages that had come to his attention, and others also recorded such manned and derelict hulks. Some of the stories are extraordinary. Junks drifted into waters ranging from Hawaii to the Aleutians to Mexico, carrying a few survivors after very long periods at sea—nine, fourteen, seventeen, and eighteen months, in extreme cases. The *Tokujō-maru*, under Captain Jūkichi Oguri, drifted for 484 days in 1813–15, from off central Honshu southward and southeastward from Japan into equatorial waters, and subsequently across most of the Pacific and then northward to where the three survivors were rescued some 300 miles to the south-southwest of Point Conception, California. During a rainless ten months, they rigged a makeshift still by boiling seawater in a kettle, setting a rice tub atop the kettle, and running a pipe through a hole in the tub's bottom; the kettle's steam rose through the pipe, condensing in the tub and yielding 12 quarts of fresh water a day. Some of the disabled junks' cargoes were of barley, rice, salt fish, preserved roe, or seaweed, and this, along with rainwater, helped crews to survive. But there were also survivors on vessels carrying only timber, ceramics, and silks. These sailors speared fish from the sea to obtain sustenance, and also caught birds.[38]

There were almost 23,000 junks registered in Japan's coastal trade in 1875, typically carrying crews of from eight to twelve, and by that year about one hundred junks had been recorded found adrift or cast up near or on North American Pacific shores. Numbers of castaway Japanese as well as some Chinese are thought to have ended up living among the coastal Indians of British Columbia and Southeast Alaska.[39] On the basis of the six junks known to have landed on the Northwest Coast between 1782 and 1876, Quimby extrapolated that fourteen or fifteen would have arrived per century, making 187 wrecks during the period AD 500 to 1750. A few pre-European-contact (although not pre-1492) iron blades have been found in Northwest Coast sites (for example, Ozette, Washington), and Quimby believed that salvage from Japanese derelicts was the source. Too, Ming dynasty nonexport ceramic fragments of AD 1550–1650 have been found in a coastal Oregon site.[40]

It is the case that Japanese fishing vessels were given higher freeboard beginning in 1598, which may have improved chances of survival.[41] Too, one may argue that the restrictions on ship size, design details, and rudders during the isolationist period in Japan were unique and not applicable to earlier times. However, surely earlier craft were sometimes disabled at sea as well. If nothing else, the history of Tokugawa Period (1603–1867) drift voyages shows that small, rudderless, mastless craft of the general sort that have been present in East Asia for millennia can and have stayed afloat long enough to have drifted to America with survivors. In fact, the consistency of the prevailing winds and currents is such that it seems inevitable that accidental drift voyages would have led to repeated transoceanic landfalls, not just a few times but hundreds, even thousands over the millennia. Can such contacts have resulted in no significant influences? I think not.

6

No Plague in the Land?

The Alleged American Absence
of Old World Communicable Diseases

Whilst my physicians by their love are grown
Cosmographers, and I their map.
— John Donne, 1635

As mentioned in the introduction, the lethal effects of Old World diseases introduced post-1492 to the immunity-lacking native populations of the Americas were devastating.[1] Beyond human demography, however, apparent presences and absences of certain specific infectious diseases in the two hemispheres raise relevant issues. Readers routinely encounter statements to the effect that the oceans precluded interhemispheric interactions and that, therefore, Native Americans were isolated from and, accordingly, exceedingly susceptible to Old World pathogens.[2] The aim of this chapter is to assess what the history of communicable diseases may really tell us about whether interhemispheric contacts could have occurred.

A Pox upon Them: Microbial Diseases
and a "Virgin-Soil" Hemisphere

The Post-Columbian Demographic Collapse in the New World

The Old World gave rise to a much greater number of serious microbial human diseases than did the New. This reflects the larger size of the Afroeurasian land mass as well as a much longer human history there plus earlier agricultural intensification, population densification, and urbanization. In addition, importantly, it reflects the close association in the Eastern Hemisphere between people and their several species of domestic and commensal animals and the presence, in the tropics, of closely related wild primates eaten as bushmeat, many important human diseases having begun as animal maladies and having transferred to humans, a process known as zoonosis. In the Bering Strait region of the Arctic, mainland Asia and America are only some 54 miles apart, and intercontinental human contact was continuous; nevertheless, this region acted as a "cold screen" that filtered out from largely overland entry into the Americas many of the disease organisms of Eurasia that were adapted to less severe climates. In addition, insect and annelid (roundworm) vectors (nonhuman carriers) for warmer-climate human microbial diseases were unable to pass through the Arctic, excepting those whose organisms and/or vectors lived continuously in the warm microclimates of their hosts' bodies (see chapter 26).

The pre-Columbian populations of the Americas have long been considered "virgin soil" with respect to most of the important Eastern Hemisphere microbial pathogens. The American archaeodemographer Henry Dobyns, for instance, asserted that "Native Americans truly inhabited a pre-Columbian earthly paradise free of the diseases evolved in the Old World."[3] It is certainly the case that when one of the early post-Columbian European contributions to the natives of the West Indies—communicable Old World diseases such as smallpox, measles, and plague—arrived, almost none of the Indians possessed any noticeable inherent immunity to the majority of them, unlike people in Europe, who, after sickening to a lesser degree, more often than not recovered from many of these maladies, owing to a degree of intrinsic immunity.

For generations, the populations of Europe had been exposed to typhoid fever, smallpox, chicken pox, mumps, and other, lesser, infectious diseases. In warmer areas of the Old World, the inhabitants had existed in the presence of various tropical diseases. Accordingly, in zones of endemism (self-sustaining disease presence), the most susceptible individuals had been weeded out of the breeding pool over the centuries, and a certain, if incomplete, genetically inherited innate immunity obtained (varying greatly in degree according to the nature of the disease), causing symptoms to be relatively mild.[4]

However, as the Canadian geographer W. George Lovell put it, "Whoever watched as Columbus came ashore . . . witnessed the beginning of a conquest that would cause the greatest destruction of lives in history," mainly from disease plus its effects on production and reproduction.[5] By 1548, for instance, the nearly three-quarter million native Taíno inhabitants of 1492 Hispaniola had been reduced to some five hundred souls, followed by full extinction as a distinct population. As the post-Columbian occupation and colonization of the Americas continued, with immigration of both Europeans and African slaves, these introduced diseases had horrendous impact on aboriginals everywhere in the hemisphere, who expired in droves. This sometimes-literal decimation (or worse)[6] often spread well ahead of direct European contact, "softening up" the indigenes for easy subjugation and domination. It was disease far more than force of superior arms that allowed the hijacking of the hemisphere by the Spanish, Portuguese, French, and British.

Disease Susceptibility and the Pre-Columbian-Contacts Question

This supreme susceptibility to foreign infectious diseases on the part of of the Native Americans of circa AD 1500 has struck a number of scholars as irrefutable evidence of a lack of important previous contact with the Eastern Hemisphere other than across Bering Strait and, in late pre-Columbian times and briefly, in subarctic Newfoundland. Had such contact occurred, it has been argued, the New World natives would already have been exposed to such diseases, which would have remained manifest in the aboriginal populations, and the natives would also necessarily have evolved some significant degree of genetic resistance to the maladies. "In fact," wrote the American archaeologist David L. Webster, "some of the best evidence for the long separation of Old and New World populations was their differential susceptibility to infectious diseases introduced by Europeans, to which native [American] populations had no immunity."[7] Therefore, a primary question to be asked at the outset of a discussion of possible early transoceanic contacts is: Is there any way that such contacts could have occurred without the introduction and continuing presence of these insidious Old World maladies and the consequent development of indigenous innate immunities? It is odd that this question has never before been addressed in any depth.[8] Isolationists have seemingly believed that the implications are so obvious that further investigation is not necessary, while diffusionists have apparently felt that the evidence of contact is there and that, therefore, however it happened, the acute infectious disease must have been excluded, the precise reasons being irrelevant or undiscoverable.

At the outset, it should be said that there are many instances in American archaeology of demographic crashes and/or abrupt disappearances of cultures over wide areas. One of the best known is the Classic Maya collapse of about AD 900, but the circa AD 1300 Ancestral Puebloan (Anasazi) abandonment of extensive sections of the American Southwest; the disappearance of humans over large parts of southwestern Missouri, Illinois, Indiana, western Kentucky, and Tennessee between AD 1425 and 1470; as well as other depopulations, have occasionally engendered hypotheses that introduced diseases played a role. Nevertheless, these notions are unproven at the moment. Many alternative possible explanations have been offered (drought, soil impoverishment, wars of extermination, and political and economic collapse, for example), and the geographic patterns of depopulation do not always appear to be expectable ones for epidemic.

The Ages of Infectious Diseases

Like anything else, diseases have histories in time and geographic space. In considering the question of introduced diseases, we need to take account of the fact that because their organisms have quite short life cycles, rapid evolution of infectious diseases (bacterial, viral, protozoan, and fungal) is possible—witness the sudden emergence of several within my own lifetime, including—just to mention the best-known ones appearing and/or being recognized since World War II—monkey fever, Kyasanur forest disease, Lyme disease, toxic-shock syndrome, Legionnaire's disease, HIV-AIDS, and sin nombre hantavirus, plus Zika, Epstein-Barr, Ebola, Marburg, Lassa, mad cow disease, and West Nile, Hendra, La Crosse, Nipah, severe acute respiratory syndrome (SARS), and Middle East respiratory syndrome (MERS) viruses, as well as new strains of malaria and of influenza of various kinds (including avian "flu"). There is even a scientific journal, *Emerging Infectious Diseases.*[9] Therefore, we cannot simply assume that all or even most of the implicated post-Columbian maladies referred to at the beginning of this chapter, at least in their later, more virulent forms, were abroad in the Old World in early times. Many of the proposed pre-Columbian contacts may have occurred before the emergence of at least most of these virulent diseases, or prior to their arrivals in the areas initiating overseas contacts. Without documentation, it should not be assumed that any particular disease was present in any particular area or era.

To be sure, certain pestilences can be shown to have been abroad in the Eastern Hemisphere for millennia, and there exist in the ancient literature descriptions of quite-recognizable symptoms of some presently known diseases. A number of epidemics were recorded during Classical times, although most are not definitively identifiable as to the specific pathogens involved. However (despite the typhoid fever epidemic of Athens in 430 BC and the epidemic of Syracuse in 395 BC), in general the populous pre-Roman Empire Mediterranean world seems to have been relatively free of major epidemic diseases. Let us look, then, at what is known about the ages and dispersals of the more prominent complaints concerned.

One of the major modern contagious maladies, (waterborne) cholera, native to the Ganges Delta, is first recognizably mentioned in India at about 400 BC. However, devastating though it was, as far as we know it remained confined to that region for the next 2,200 years, despite the Indian subcontinent's being at the heart of the vigorous Indian Ocean maritime trade network extending from East Africa to Southeast Asia, with connections beyond. Most of cholera's spread has taken place since 1847, when the history of the disease outside South Asia commenced.

Human malaria probably goes back to Neolithic Africa and is attested in pre-Dynastic Egypt circa 3200 BC. It appears to have arrived (or at least have become common) in Greece no later than the fifth century BC, reaching Rome by the first century AD, and it is also pre-Christian Era in China and India. In contrast, influenza seems not to be very old, at least in the West. Indication of its dispersal among humans is absent in Europe prior to the Middle Ages, with no really clear evidence until the fifteenth and sixteenth centuries—although it does seem to have been in Japan by the ninth century AD. No Old World flu is definitely attested in the Americas until the importation of African slaves was underway. Although swine-introduced influenza may conceivably be implicated in Hispaniola in 1493, many set 1559 as its first firm appearance in the hemisphere.[10]

Although old in the Middle East, (louse-borne) typhus's first known severe western Mediterranean outbreak, a consequence of introduction from the Levant, did not occur (in Spain) until AD 1489–90 and the disease failed to become firmly established in Europe until the seventeenth century. The United States—continuously and intensively in touch with Europe—was not significantly affected until the early nineteenth century, although probable typhus appeared in the Carolinas in 1586 and may, in fact, be pre-Columbian in the New World (see chapter 26). Food-borne or waterborne typhoid fever is probably ancient in India and elsewhere but is difficult to distinguish in the record (although it is now identified by DNA as having been present in Athens in 430 BC).

Flea-borne bubonic plague, which may have originated in pre–Christian Era southern Asia or in North Africa, was absent in ancient Greece. The first pandemic of which we are aware involving plague—a catastrophe called the plague of Justinian—began in Egypt in AD 540. Although plague reerupted here and there for another two centuries, and although the malady never died out afterward, it had long and mysterious periods of relative quiescence, not surviving in Europe except by reintroduction from the Middle East; the next thousand years saw only two great pandemics, the devastating Black Death of Europe (AD 1340–90) that followed new emphasis on overland traffic with China, and the Great Plague of AD 1665–66. Although some think that disease outbreaks in seventh- and thirteenth/fourteenth-century China may have been plague, the first epidemic in China that we are substantially certain was plague is one that struck Yunnan in 1792. It spread from there to the coast and then by sea: "along with Australia and Eastern Africa, North and South America were infected for the first time,"[11] although some observers place plague in Mexico in AD 1545, and there is a possibility of its presence in Central America and the Andes in AD 1531.

Diseases may metamorphose not only spontaneously in place but may also change evolutionarily and/or in terms of manifestation in response to changes in ecology, as these factors alter in an area over time or as when the organism is introduced into a new physical and/or sociodemographic environment. Plague is essentially a rodent disease. It becomes seriously troublesome to humans when host animals live in close association with people. Most rodents shun humans, and transmission to people is normally accomplished only via fleas from infected rats, especially the black rat, *Rattus rattus*, a human commensal of less severe Old World climates (there is also an uncommon but virulent pneumonic form of the disease that can develop, which spreads directly from person to person via breath and sputum). Because black rats infested ships as well as homes, plague was spread by sea as well as overland; yet, although it is possible that it was present earlier, it is not documented in North America north of Mexico before AD 1899.

Plague, a bacterial infection, confers immunity on its survivors. To the extent that with respect to human infection the rat is plague's (and typhus's) definitive host, the pre-Columbian absence of *Rattus rattus* and its fleas in the New World could help explain why plague seems not to have been established in the hemisphere in pre-Columbian times—although that would still leave the question as to why the rat itself did not become naturalized then, as it did post-Conquest. But on smaller vessels, rats might have been eliminable—none was seen on the experimental *Brendan* voyage, for example—and Europeans routinely took along cats to control rats. The Chinese had rat-catching dogs on shipboard, and the Irish used stoats. It is also the case that American rodents such as native rats, prairie dogs, and ground squirrels were potential reservoirs for plague, but these are not human commensals. The minimal clothing worn among most tropical American indigenes, being less favorable to harboring fleas than ample European or East Asian garb, could also have been an inhibiting factor. Too, the black rat may not have been as common in the Old World East, where the more aggressive but not human-companionable and less susceptible brown rat (*R. norvegicus*) seems to have prevailed (ultimately spreading into Europe and largely displacing the black rat and thereby reducing the incidence of plague there).

Mumps was described by the Greek physician Hippocrates (fifth century BC) as well as during Roman times, and was recorded in Japan by the AD 900s. However, although measles (morbilli, rubeola) is thought to be very old in China, its first clear description is that by the Persian physician Rhazes (Rāzi) circa AD 900. The pre-Roman Mediterranean region is thought to have been free of measles and of rubella (German measles), and in France measles seems not to have appeared before the Middle Ages. It did not reach Australia until 1854 (some scholars feel that the ancient Greek, Roman, and Chinese epidemics may have involved measles and that it was at least pretty clearly present by the seventh century). Measles is first attested in the post-1492 New World only following about thirty-two years of contact, thereafter becoming the biggest killer after smallpox. Yellow fever (usually thought of as West African in origin, but see chapter 26) is not well documented until the seventeenth century—first in Brazil in 1643 (in Africa, not until 135 years later), although in AD 1526 Gonzalo Fernández de Oviedo implied that it had been present among Spaniards in Santo Domingo in AD 1493.

Rubella escaped description until 1619, although it may previously have been confused with measles and smallpox. Scarlet fever is a relatively modern disease, and its first clear mention is from Italy in 1553, when it was diagnostically differentiated from chicken pox, a disease of unknown but perhaps not tremendous age. According to some authorities, scarlet fever was absent in pre-AD-1500 China, although others say that it was distinguished there from smallpox, chicken pox, and measles by the sixth century. Diphtheria was first recognized as such in AD 1882 and is considered to have been a new disease in the early modern period, although a few epidemics in ancient Greece and in sixteenth- through eighteenth-century Europe involved diphtheria-like maladies, and it is said to have appeared in Mexico in AD 1601 (barely possibly, 1559) and in Peru in AD 1614. Whooping cough (pertussis) can be traced back with confidence no further than the middle of the sixteenth century, and it was almost certainly absent in the ancient world (although symptoms described in thirteenth-century Korea are consistent with whooping cough).[12]

Many microbial species manifest more than one strain and, as indicated above, populations of microorganisms may undergo significant genetic changes when introduced into a new host environment, and the result often is new and more pathogenic strains; in fact, bacteria are the planet's most evolutionarily active organisms.

Smallpox, a viral infection, has an interesting history in this connection. It could not have existed prior to population growth and nucleation (clustering together in settlements) during the Neolithic. It is definitely known from Egypt in the second millennium BC and is also attested quite early in the Indus Valley region. It may possibly be implicated in Roman-period Mediterranean epidemics (but apparently not in Classical Greece) such as that of Antoninus (AD 165–89), and it is said to have been introduced into North China by the Huns in 243 BC but could be much more ancient there. It is documented in Europe in AD 581 (although not becoming established there until the Renaissance) and in Japan in the AD 700s. Rhazes described it plainly for Mesopotamia during the AD 900s.

However, with regard to India, where the disease is thought to have originated by 1500 BC, it seems that the first Indian description of *virulent* smallpox (*Variola major*) does not occur until the sixteenth century AD, when the first notice of an epidemic is recorded—about the same time that it began its post-Columbian devastation of Native (and immigrant) Americans (it first arrived in Hispaniola about 1518—some twenty-six years after Columbus's first voyage). Less deadly *Variola minor* had been known in Europe since antiquity, and in Columbus's day infected Europeans suffered a mortality rate of only 3 to 10 percent. However, as mentioned, *Variola major* is not attested until into the 1500s, after which it became one of the chief demographic checks in Europe. In the Americas, Indians suffered a circa-95-percent mortality rate from the malady.

A fascinating fact concerning smallpox in India is that inoculation appears to have been known to Hindus as long ago as the first millennium BC: "certain classes . . . are purported to have enjoyed a certain amount of immunity from the disease . . . since ancient times"[13] (sailors are not, however, mentioned as one of these classes). Inoculation of a different sort was also known in China's southwestern Szechwan; it may have been undertaken as early as the second century AD and was widespread by the sixteenth. The practice is also recorded in Egypt by the thirteenth century AD.

Diseases and Acquired Immunity

Although epidemics—including of plague—often spread from port to port, in the case of a number of maladies (mainly, viral ones) that convey postinfection immunity, repeated exposure led to a kind of "curtain of immunity" along some coasts. Merchant sailors, who visited a variety of far-flung ports of call during their careers, would have been exposed to a range of diseases early on, and would presumably have contracted—and, if surviving, acquired immunity to—more diseases than would have the average inlander.

For millennia before the nineteenth-century development of germ theory, contagion—the passing of diseases among human beings—was recognized as a means of their spreading. For example, a circa 1700 BC letter found at Mari,

Syria, orders people to avoid all use of an ill person's possessions in order to avoid contagion. The Romans posted guards at the gates of their city to control infection. In the Middle Ages, lepers (although not highly contagious) were routinely driven off or isolated.

The influential Persian physician and polymath Avicenna of Bukhara (Pūr Sina', circa AD 980–1037) was aware of the contagious nature of certain diseases, and this led to the introduction of quarantine as a method of curtailing the spread of transmissible complaints.[14] Every medieval European port of note had its lazaretto, where visitors were confined prior to being permitted to land. Quarantine was also common among American Indians. With this in mind, we can suppose that a captain recruiting a crew would have rejected any obviously ill individuals. He might even have kept the crew in isolation prior to the voyage in order to minimize the chance of infection on board. A crew free of contagious diseases was quite likely the rule rather than the exception, at least with respect to most of the maladies under discussion. One historically known instance is that of Captain James Cook's expeditions, on which the crew appears to have been free of contagious diseases other than those picked up at Tahiti and Batavia late in the voyages.

Another consideration regarding introduction of disease to the New World is what might be called the "time-filter factor." For most infectious disease microbe populations to remain viable, they must have hosts continuously available. The lines of those germs that require transmission by an intermediate host (such as a mosquito) would die out once the territory of that vector was left behind (note, however, that some potential for shipboard mosquito larvae survival existed, as in water butts). For directly infectious diseases, a continuous chain of susceptible humans is needed to sustain transmission. With the pneumonic form of plague, the death rate is 95 to 100 percent, and demise comes after only a day or two, quickly eliminating the deceased as a source of infection. Almost no one (or any rat) initially infected with such plague would survive a prolonged ocean voyage, and if he did, by the time the ship landed he would be recovered and unable to pass on the infection to the indigenes.

In the case of infectious diseases such as the poxes and mumps that impart postinfection permanent immunity to their victims, if a voyage is relatively slow and especially if it involves a small craft carrying a small party, any of these kinds of disease organisms is likely to have run its course during the crossing. Thus, before journey's end, all personnel would either be dead or disease-free and immune, and unable to transmit the sickness to residents at the landfall.[15] The Fiji Islands, for example, were measles-free as long as sailing-vessels alone served them; however, when steamships cut the time of the voyage from India to about thirty days, measles was able to survive and to infect denizens of the archipelago.[16]

Assuming (1) a complement of ten individuals (the number needed for a schooner-sized Roman vessel, some standard-sized Roman merchantmen had crews as small as five), one of those ten persons having contracted mumps on the eve of embarkation; and (2) a fully susceptible crew, a maximum noninfectious latent period of eighteen days (other diseases have shorter periods—for example, eight to twelve days for the poxes) and a contagious period of eight days (longer for some maladies, for instance, up to a month or more for whooping cough), a pathogen could, if passing from each ill individual only at the end of the possible term of contagiousness, survive for 260 days (nearly nine months—longer, if the crew was larger, shorter if smaller) and thus would endure through any crossing of reasonable length. However, such an absolutely worst-case scenario is so highly unlikely as to be hardly worth considering even with a fully susceptible crew, because such diseases are quickly transmitted among people in close quarters; it is almost certain that within the confines of a small ship, any such disease would spread to all susceptible crew members within the initial four days of exposure, so that, as already noted, after one month or less everyone would be dead or immune and incapable of transmitting the disease when they reached the other side of the sea.

This time-filter factor would be even more effective in the case of the wide Pacific than of the much narrower Atlantic. Early post-Columbian Mexico-to-Philippines crossing times ranged from fifty-six days to as much as 172 days. On the Atlantic side, in 1492 it took Columbus but thirty-three days to travel the circa 4,250 miles between the Canary Islands and the Bahamas. In 1493, he shortened that time to twenty-nine days and in 1502 to a mere twenty-one days, but even this would have exceeded the period of infection of most of the implicated diseases. The 1497 crossing of John Cabot from Bristol to Newfoundland lasted no longer than Columbus's first traverse, although for many years most crossings took about twice as long (the *Mayflower*, for example, took sixty-four days in 1620). Only when voyaging became routinely more rapid with the multiplication of masts and sails, and involved ever-larger ships and crews and, especially, complements of passengers (particularly, of European children and young, disease-susceptible African slaves—see below), might acute infectious maladies have had a good chance of still being on shipboard at the time of landing.

Even substantial numbers of personnel hardly guarantee transoceanic disease transmission. The Norse settlement in Vínland included about 160 persons, and no serious sickness was reported. With one possible exception, there is no indication of transmission of any European disease to Native Americans at that time or during sporadic Norse contacts with northeastern North America over the next few centuries. Perhaps even more striking is that there is no evidence that the circa 70,000 Norse settlers of Greenland passed diseases on to the indigenous Inuit. Columbus's 1492 expedition was disease-free. His second, 1493, expedition to the West Indies involved seventeen ships and 1,500 colonists, yet no epidemics were initiated by personnel or rodents of this or other Columbian voyages. In the first ten years of the sixteenth century, better than two hundred ships traversed the Atlantic, carrying thousands of European settlers and their microorganisms. By 1510, about ten thousand Europeans lived on Hispaniola. At the time, epidemic plague and typhus or influenza were rampant in Spain's south, the source of most of the voyages. Yet although a few have suggested that swine-introduced flu (eight sows accompanied the 1493 voyage) may have broken out in Hispaniola, there is no documentation of any of the diseases under discussion having been contracted by the native peoples during this time. The historian Paul Kelton considered it highly unlikely that hogs introduced influenza to residents of Hispaniola and also pointed out that communicable diseases were absent on the de Soto expedition of 1538–42.[17] Likewise, although it may have occurred we have no record of disease introduction to Brazil between Cabral's landfall in 1500 and the epidemic of 1552.

Despite the aforementioned limiting factors for the acute infections, the protozoan malaria (*Plasmodium*), which is documented for Classical times and earlier in Europe and which conveys no immunity, would not have been filtered out during long voyages, being chronic and uneliminable from the body. If present among the complement, it would have been transmitted wherever its vectors, mild-climate *Anopheles* mosquitoes, were present. There have been a few murmurings about possible pre-Columbian malaria in the Americas, but current evidence is against its having been present there or in most of the Pacific. In fact, it seems not demonstrably to have been in post-Columbian North America before AD 1684.

We should also bear in mind that since some of the diseases under discussion, such as malaria, are tropical/subtropical and require particular genera of insect hosts, their apparent absence in the pre-Columbian New World in no way argues against contacts between peoples of higher latitudes or from tropical/subtropical areas historically free of these diseases, such as the Pacific islands. Further, although it seems that anophelines were present in the pre-Columbian Americas, the *Aedes* spp. vectors of yellow fever and dengue fever may not have been. For these diseases, both vector and virus would have to have been imported and to have reached human populations dense enough to maintain them. (American *Haemagogus* mosquitoes *can* carry yellow fever; see chapter 26.)

The pathologist Francis E. Cuppage asserted, with regard to eighteenth-century European ships, "Tuberculosis, smallpox, malaria, and typhus took their toll."[18] John Toohey mentioned syphilis, malaria, fluxes (dysentery), typhoid fever, tropical fevers, and various parasites but not smallpox, chicken pox, or measles.[19] Interestingly, actual records of the British and American navies of around 1800 show that respiratory ailments, including colds, influenza, pneumonia, and tuberculosis, accounted for nearly half the illnesses on board. Malaria was also important, and dysentery and liver disorders, along with syphilis and gonorrhea, are also noted as common and rheumatism and the like occasional. In the warmer climes, additional health hazards mentioned include yellow fever, typhus, cholera, and perhaps plague. *Not* mentioned in general summaries were the "childhood" acute infections mumps, measles, rubella, scarlet fever, smallpox, and chicken pox—that is, most of the major killers of Indians in the colonial Americas.[20]

When sixteenth-century Spaniards inadvertently introduced smallpox into Mexico, with catastrophic effect, it happened via an infected *Negro* that they had brought with them. The Spaniards themselves were not affected, having already had the disease in childhood; in Spain, it was rare that anyone had not contracted the infection before adulthood.

Immunity for measles settles at about 90 percent of the adult population, scarlet fever at some 86 percent, with susceptible individuals living mainly in isolated settings and not in busy ports. This means that for most communicable diseases that convey immunity, the average expectable number of non-immune individuals in a ship's crew of ten from a typical area of endemism would, at most, be one—who, if infected, would be dead or no longer infectious within a month at the maximum, too short a time for early ships to have completed the crossing. The historian Noble Cook and the geographer George Lovell flatly stated, "it would be necessary to have a group of children on board a fleet to transfer measles across the Atlantic."[21]

In contrast to noncolonial voyaging, European colonialism involved bringing still-susceptible European children along as well, plus young African slaves. Further, the contact established was essentially continuous, allowing multiple reintroductions of diseases, thus repeatedly devastating even populations too small to support endemism (see below), and, ultimately, continuing colonization plus natural increase led to foreign-derived populations large enough to support endemism (not until the nineteenth century in North America for smallpox and measles). We should not imagine that any putative pre-Columbian voyaging was for purposes of colonization on the European imperialist model, especially involving importation of slaves; there is no reason to suppose that it was, although small-scale colonizations of other types may well occasionally have occurred.

Population Size and Density, and Disease Endemism

Because they have short periods of infectiousness and are passed directly from person to person and not via nonhuman vectors, acute infections are diseases of the crowd, unable to flourish in situations involving small, scattered settlements. At least most of the first such human "herd diseases" probably arose with early Middle Eastern intensive cultivation and incipient urbanization, which led to larger, denser populations. Decades ago, it was hypothesized that such infections needed minimum host population sizes for permanent maintenance, and if these dropped below the threshold levels, the diseases would die out there.

The concept of "critical community size" is now well recognized; it is the minimum magnitude of a substantially interacting population necessary to allow infection of susceptible persons at a rate high enough for the malady to persist—a coherent human population that is sufficiently numerous and dense that a copious new crop of susceptible youngsters is available for infection by the time the malady would otherwise be on the wane owing to acquired immunity. This is especially true of the acute community infections rubella, cholera, diphtheria, mumps, measles, smallpox, and chicken pox, which spread quickly from victim to victim but are of short duration in the body. Thus islands probably did not give rise to, or provide lasting reservoirs for, these kinds of diseases, having had populations that were too small and isolated to support endemism.

In the Arctic and subarctic, population densities would have been much too low to maintain such diseases. Sparse, scattered populations may account for the fact that, like American Indians, most native Siberians had not evolved genetic immunities and were highly susceptible to diseases introduced and reintroduced in historic times by Russians, especially to smallpox and measles, suffering population reductions of from 44 to 80 percent but not achieving endemism. Although pre-Russian-conquest contact between Siberia and neighboring populous regions was not intensive, no one suggests that there was none, and in fact there was a significant fur trade.

History provides numerous examples of disappearances, reintroductions, and additional disappearances of acute infections on islands following initial introductions: for example, of measles in the Faroes, the Fijis, Greenland (first appearance, 1951), and Iceland (with a population of some 200,000). Both smallpox and measles were repeatedly reintroduced to populous medieval Japan but did not become endemic. In fact, study of disease records shows breaks in the continuity of measles in all island populations of less than 500,000.

In the 1970s, estimates of how large a coherent population would be required to produce endemism for measles ranged from a million to several million—a size found in the pre-Columbian New World probably only in highland Central Mexico. More recent empirical study of (interconnected) towns in England and Wales showed, for measles, a somewhat lower community endemic fadeout threshold, of about 800,000 persons, and a dramatic drop-off below about 315,000. The range for the several diseases in question is probably about from a quarter to a half million. The archaeodemographer Ann F. Ramenofsky asserted that, "Distribution of population and contact mechanisms in the New World simply did not permit the fixing of crowd infections." The biomedical anthropologist Charles F. Merbs concluded, "the potential for the Old World crowd infections to become established in the Americas would have been slight . . . [r]egardless of how much [transoceanic] contact had taken place."[22]

Owing to these minimum host population size and density requirements, with respect to high-density-dependent diseases (1) a "virgin-soil" population like Mexico's would have to have been far, far larger than one in, say, Europe (or than Mexico's in fact was[23]) to support endemism: because of the lack of immunity, as soon as an imported deadly disease hit, the population would quickly be reduced to levels below those necessary to sustain the disease;[24] and (2) overseas voyages originating in, and/or arriving at, uncrowded places, would have had a low likelihood of carrying persons infected with these diseases or to have engendered endemism in the contacted areas. In fact, had English connections with their North American colonies, or Spanish and Portuguese ones with theirs in South America, ceased after, say, fifty years, never to be resumed, those few infectious diseases possibly introduced by that time would likely soon have died out in those places, leaving no medical evidence that they had ever been present, not to mention that they had devastated the indigenous populations. Nor would much improvement in genetically inherited immunity have developed among American populations to protect against future reintroductions, since only one or a very few cycles of epidemic would have played out as a selective force, rather than a continuing exposure over centuries, even millennia, as was the case with Old World populations large and dense enough to support endemism. This is illustrated by the case of the Hopi of Arizona: traditionalists who contracted the disease but refused Western medicine in an 1898 epidemic suffered a 74 percent mortality rate, despite the Hopi's having experienced repeated smallpox epidemics over the previous three centuries.

While the above remarks apply to the short-duration acute crowd infections, the medical historian Aidan Cockburn observed that, in addition, "Even pathogens that can live in their hosts like commensals for months find it difficult to survive if the population is too small."[25]

Summary of Reasons for the Seeming New World Absence of Many Old World Communicable Diseases

The presence, prevalence, and effects of any communicable disease reflect a complex mix of historical, environmental, etiological, cultural, behavioral, nutritional, and demographic factors (including birth rates). The diseases that devastated aboriginal American populations following the Columbian colonization were, in several cases, not demonstrably in existence or in existence in their later virulent forms at the various times and/or places proposed as sources of pre-Columbian transoceanic influences (although the field of historical epidemiology is young and the possibility of new evidence being discovered always exists). Specifically, as far as present data indicate we can probably safely eliminate the apparent pre-Columbian absences of at least influenza, cholera, rubella, diphtheria, whooping cough, scarlet fever, the virulent *Variola major* strain of smallpox, and possibly measles and chicken pox, as relevant to most or all proposed pre-Columbian transoceanic contacts.

With regard to any acute infections remaining in consideration, these were mostly childhood diseases in their areas of endemism, and adult sailors and passengers would probably almost always already have acquired immunity and thus have become incapable of being transmitters. In cases of slow voyages and small crews, any infectious diseases that did accompany the crew would likely have run their courses and have been eliminated prior to completion of the crossings.

Last, the acute infectious diseases of the crowd were maladies of areas with large and dense populations and could not have been introduced when contacts did not originate in such areas. Too, if but small native populations were encountered upon debarkation, the critical host-abundance threshold for permanent pathogen invasion would not have been present. Even if such diseases *were* introduced and *were* decimating, receptor populations would normally or always have been too small (especially, following an epidemic) to support disease endemism and no diagnostic evidence of any epidemics would have survived, nor would significant inherited immunity have been attained.

Malaria, and to a lesser extent, plague, do remain difficulties with respect to at least some possible encounters. Nevertheless, the supposed lack, in the pre-Columbian Americas, of the Old World diseases discussed above, cannot legitimately be used as a blanket exclusionary phenomenon with respect to proposals of early transoceanic interactions.

In closing, we may repeat that none of these diseases is documentable as having ever been transmitted from Europeans or Africans to Native Americans during the initial quarter century following AD 1492. The first certain people-introduced acute infection, smallpox, did not reach the Caribbean until the end of 1518, and others did not demonstrably arrive until far later. If putative pre-Columbian absence of these Old World diseases in the Americas "proves" that no pre-Columbian contacts occurred, then (ignoring barely possible swine-introduced influenza) it also "proves" that the voyages and nonepidemiological impacts of Columbus, John Cabot, Cabral, Fernandes, Hojeda, Vespucci, Corte-Real, Coelho, and perhaps Balboa and Ponce de León, or any of Columbus's other pre-1518 successors, never took place. If, following Henry Dobyns, we provisionally accept 1545 as the first New World occurrence of plague and use this as a criterion, then the list is expanded to include Cortés, Magellan, Pizarro, Coronado, Verrazzano, Sebastian Cabot, Cabeza de Vaca, Cartier, Almagro, de Soto, Orellana, and so forth.[26] Or, using yellow fever alone, tentatively first documented for 1647 (but see chapter 26), we can similarly dismiss the reality of the sixteenth-century Spanish settling of the Caribbean, New Spain (Mexico), New Granada (northwestern South America), and Peru, as well as the English settling of Virginia in 1605 and Massachusetts in 1620! Furthermore, since measles did not strike Greenland until 1951, Eirík the Red and company—as well as the later pre-1951 Danish occupation—must be mere figments of the imagination!

The point is, of course, not that these historically known expeditions, conquests, and colonizations never occurred—they did—but that even massive transoceanic contact does not guarantee communicable disease transmission.[27]

7

Why Most Domesticated Animals and Plants Stayed Home

When something important is missing it is said to be "conspicuous by its absence." A matter that has puzzled many when considering the possibility of early transoceanic influences is the question of why, despite numerous cultural commonalities, the pre-Columbian New World nevertheless lacked many important domesticated animals, crop plants, and technologies present in the Old.

In the early 1920s, A. L. Kroeber confidently stated, "No domesticated plant or animal (except the dog) was transported from one hemisphere to the other before Columbus."[1] This seemed to him a strong argument against transoceanic contacts having taken place, as it did to other influential scholars such as the Göteborg Museum ethnologist Erland Nordenskiöld and the Harvard University plant taxonomist Elmer Drew Merrill. The noted Harvard Mayanist Herbert J. Spinden put it plainly: "The fact that no food plant is common to the two hemispheres is enough to offset any number of petty puzzles [of similarity] in arts and myths."[2] With entirely different suites of domesticates, these and other distinguished scholars concluded, the pre-Columbian cultures of the Old World and the New had to have developed separately, with minimal or no communication between them.[3]

Absent Domesticated Animals

In Eurasia and northern Africa, the following animals were domesticated in early times: horse, donkey, various kinds of cattle, two species of camel, sheep, goat, reindeer, pig, rabbit, dog, cat, chicken, mallard duck, goose, guinea fowl, pigeon, and some lesser others such as dormouse, ferret, honeybee, and silkworm. In the Americas, the list was much shorter. The dog appears to have been imported many millennia ago via Beringia (the present greater Bering Strait region); the animals domesticated within the hemisphere were the turkey and the cochineal insect in Middle America, and the llama, alpaca, guinea pig, and muscovy duck in South America. Some have attributed this relative paucity of New World domesticates to a narrow range of domesticable American fauna. Jared Diamond, the physiology and membrane biophysicist turned UCLA geographer, has asserted, "Surely, if some [other] local wild mammal species of these [non-Eurasian] continents had been domesticable, some Australian, American, and African peoples would have domesticated them and gained great advantage from them."[4] Nonetheless, there did exist many potential New World domesticates that were ignored despite their clear tamability in several cases, including a number of animals that were close or approximate equivalents of Old World domesticates: bison, musk ox, bighorn sheep, mountain goat, caribou, peccaries, hares and rabbits, pigeons, geese, mallard duck, prairie chicken, and so forth—granting that only hares, rabbits, geese (winter only), pigeon, and mallard were native to Nuclear America (Mesoamerica and the Central Andean region), the regions that possessed elaborated civilizations. Also ignored as potential domesticates were various other deer species, tapir, quail, partridges, and pronghorn.

The Andean camelids alone were used in a fashion somewhat like Old World herd animals: although smallish, llamas served as beasts of burden, and both llamas and alpacas were fiber and meat sources. Since there are hints of quite early southwestern Asian cultural influences in Peru, one must wonder to what extent llama and alpaca herding might reflect such influences, but as far as is known, neither they nor any other New World animal were milked. Like most of the world's non-Caucasoid peoples, adult American Indians cannot digestively tolerate liquid milk—the same factor that contributed to the failure of dairying to spread from the West into East and Southeast Asia and the Pacific islands and surely enough to have prevented its adoption by Native Americans. A number of cultures even consider milk to be a disgusting excretion in the context of adult consumption. Other widespread animal-food avoidances in various parts of the world—of perfectly safe, nourishing, and tasty items, including beef, pork, horsemeat, chicken, cat and dog flesh, fish, insects, eggs, and so forth—that is, "natural" things to eat, seem to be purely or largely cultural in nature, not medical, physiological, or economic.[5]

As far as bovines, equines, and to some extent certain other animals were concerned, their non-nutritional utility came mainly from their functions as pack animals, as mounts, and as providers of traction for plows and wheeled vehicles, plus, to some extent, in turning mills and threshing cultivated grain—none of which concepts other than packing existed in the pre-Columbian New World (see chapter 8). Thus draft animals would have been useful only if the entire technology of harnessing and harness making (which included metal parts), plows and/or carts, roadbuilding, and so forth, had been adopted as well. Sometimes, even when a new and useful species was introduced in Colonial times, the natives would fail to employ it for one or more important purpose that prevailed in the place from which the animal was imported. For example, when the Paiute of western North America's Great Basin obtained Spanish-introduced horses, they ate them rather than keeping them for riding or other uses.

The maintaining and raising of domesticated animals demanded, in most cases, a whole complex of knowledge: about breeding, providing for nourishment and protection, controlling, and, with some species, gentling (including by gelding), and training. There was also the need to provide feed. In Europe, for example, the raising of oats for horses consumed large acreages of land that otherwise could have been devoted to feeding humans. True, some domesticated creatures—pigs and chickens, for instance—required little care; perhaps not incidentally, the chicken is, in fact, almost certainly a pre-Columbian importation to the Americas (see chapter 26).

Despite demonstrated seaborne contacts between western South America and Middle America, guinea pigs and camelids failed to be introduced to the north, or the Mesoamerican turkey to South America. Neither, for that matter, were guinea pigs, llamas, or alpacas adopted as food or fiber sources in Europe after Columbus, despite European colonization of their homelands. Only the turkey attained a moderately significant role there—probably commencing before 1492 (see chapter 26).

Absent Cultivated Plants

The major food crops, especially, have been pointed to as items that would surely have been exchanged had contacts taken place, particularly in light of the fact that the Asian domesticates wheat and rice became important staples in many parts of the New World following their introduction by Europeans, and in light of the fact that productive varieties of American potatoes, manioc, maize, sweet potato, and so forth assumed vital roles in the Old. In the mid-twentieth century, E. D. Merrill was particularly extreme in his demand for ethnobotanical indication of significant transoceanic contacts: "Until someone can prove that other food plants than the common gourd (not a basic food plant) were of *universal distribution* in cultivation in North and South America, Africa, Asia and the Pacific Islands in pre-historic times, I remain unconvinced."[6]

In response to this supposition, we may first observe that there were excellent wild food plants in the Americas that were never, as far as we know, taken into domestication or, in some cases, even utilization, in the fashion of their Old World equivalents. A notable example is grapes and grape wine, and the list includes crab apple, cherry, plum, half a dozen species of berries, a similar number of species of nuts, wild rice, and a number of other foods in North America alone, plus any number of grasses, greens, and tuberous plants.

Regarding cultivated species, it is now clear that an impressive number of crop plants *were* exchanged between the hemispheres before Columbus (see chapters 27, 28, and 29). However, as far as is presently known, wheat, rice, potatoes, and manioc were not among them. This may be for any of several reasons. First, many contacts proposed to have occurred involved places lacking these crops. Too, in some cases, the physical environments at putative points of contact were unsuitable for the alien domesticates. For some lesser crops, efficient pollinators for them may have been missing in the new areas; for example, the honeybee was not native to the Americas.

Crop species also change over time under human selection, and in the past some were less attractive than they are today. Maize of yore, for instance, was not the superproductive hybrid, even genetically modified corn of the twenty-first century, and flavorful sweet corn seems to have arisen little earlier than the time of initial European conquest. Note that despite its presence in the Southeast in the second millennium BC and in the Midwest by 170 BC, maize is not attested in the northeastern United States until about AD 750, hardly a rapid adoption despite undoubted contacts.

Knowing that many cultural interactions have occurred without exchanges of domesticates, we may consider additional possible reasons for lack of transfer. Some plant materials, especially those propagated from cuttings, do not travel well, especially on "wet" craft such as rafts and sailing-canoes, where they can be spoiled by saltwater. The sweet potato is a case in point (although with assiduous care it can be—and was—carried across considerable pelagic distances). The oceanic introduction of a number of sensitive crops—for example, of tea from China to India and of the rubber tree from Amazonia to Malaya—awaited the invention, in the 1820s, of the Wardian case, a sort of sealed-glass terrarium.

Nonagricultural peoples would not have adopted foreign crops even when these were known to them, since they would have lacked the prerequisite practice of farming. Even farming peoples often ignored new crops offered to them. In 1786, Admiral J. F. G. de la Pérouse introduced maize, fruit trees, and other alien crops, as well as pairs of hogs, goats, and sheep, to Easter Island, but none of these was adopted at that time by native horticulturalists. Later government attempts to introduce maize growing there failed owing to the natives' unfamiliarity with observing the annual alternation of the seed-crop cycle, island agriculture being based upon vegetative propagation. People liked to eat the corn at an immature stage and also consumed the seed stock.

Earlier, the Portuguese explorer for Spain Pedro Fernandes de Queirós had tried to introduce new crops to Pacific Islanders. This effort included sowing seeds of American crops in the Marquesas Islands in 1595 and in the Santa Cruz Islands in 1606, and planting other crops in Tahiti in the late 1700s; subsequent visitors found none of these surviving on those islands.[7] In Polynesia, only Maoris adopted grain growing from Europeans, being exapted ("preadapted") because New Zealand's midlatitude climate already required them to develop winter storage of harvested crops.[8] The soybean failed to diffuse from East Asia to Europe, perhaps because of the complexity of its processing into bean curd and soy sauce.[9]

No crop plants or domesticated animals were introduced by most of the early European exploratory expeditions in North America, although hogs and other animals were often taken along. Despite millennia-long interaction with lands to the east, cotton, citrus, sugarcane, banana, rice, and eggplant were not accepted in the Mediterranean world until the Islamic conquests of about AD 900.[10] Many crops, including rice, were actually dropped as Austronesians migrated from South China southeastward into the Pacific islands.

In the case of much of the temperate-zone Americas, European conquest and, often, total or near eradication and replacement or at least deculturation of native farming peoples led to a considerable Europeanization of the agricultures of the conquered areas (although the European settlers did adopt a number of Native American crops). But conquest and replacement of this sort and on this scale have never been suggested in the context of pre-Columbian contacts, so no comparable results should be expected in that context. Interactions that *have* been suggested involved either replacement of nonfarmers, with the farming newcomers' domesticating local equivalents of the homeland crops; or contact not involving any kind of conquest or replacement; and/or contact involving only small numbers of foreigners, few if any of whom would have been farmers.

Too, it seems that once certain crops have become thoroughly integrated into native economies, playing defined roles—economic, culinary, social, religious, and so forth—it may be difficult for a foreign food plant to make inroads. If one is raising maize, for instance, the niche of a staple grain crop is filled, and wheat might be rejected. In the specific case of maize, the archaeologist David C. Batten calculated that in Mesoamerica a unit of land planted in maize could support twice as many people as a unit of land of the same size in Europe where wheat was the crop.[11] This being the case, why would wheat be of interest to the maize growers? (Wheat did catch on among natives of some temperate climate areas—for example, the southwestern United States. In these midlatitudes, wheat filled a somewhat different niche than maize because wheat matured earlier and could be grown at higher elevations. Nevertheless, initially, at least, it was planted in "hills" like maize, and not broadcast as was done in Europe.)

The celebrated Israeli domesticated-plant geneticist Daniel Zohary wrote, "the knowledge of how to grow, process and use the introduced plants, is also essential . . . this know-how is frequently so complex that only close human contacts—or even better, the co-migration of crops and people—are able to bring about long-distance diffusion and adoption of many novel crops."[12] For example, Old World wheat farming was accomplished with plowing (itself requiring draft animals and yoking) and by broadcast sowing, both alien to the potential New World recipients. Wet-rice cultivation also involved methods unfamiliar to American indigenes, including transplanting from seedbeds and inundating the transplanted seedlings, and rice is harvested with a special (usually iron) knife that did not exist in the Western Hemisphere. Typically, wet-rice-raising also involves use of water-buffalo-powered plowing, and both the animal and the instrument were lacking in America.

Not only food-raising procedures but also food-harvesting and food-processing approaches affect adoption. Wheat, for example, needed different treatment than maize. Wheat harvest was accomplished with a tool, the sickle, that was not native to the Americas, and then—again, unlike maize—the reaped wheat had to be threshed, with a flail (another nonnative tool) or with (absent) animals, and then winnowed. With a lack of turned millstones in the ancient Americas, production of wheat flour with the simple native saddle-stone and muller (metate and mano) required grinding four times as compared to only three times for maize.[13] Nor were there culinary traditions in the Americas of bake ovens, leavened bread, noodles, or dumplings. All of these factors would have been impediments to the adoption of wheat.

The British cultivated-plant geneticist and taxonomist J. G. Hawkes has observed that "a newly introduced plant would have needed to show some quite outstanding features compared with the existing ones to be easily incorporated into those [preexisting agricultural] systems."[14] Specialty plants were probably more readily adopted than staples. Plants for which there *are* no local equivalents but that are cultivated and prepared by methods similar to ones existing in the recipient culture, would likely have had a notably better chance of being adopted. For example, in post-Columbian times melons (Old World domesticates) often became appreciated crops among squash-raising American Indians, and squashes became quite popular in many parts of Europe.

Furthermore, people generally tend to distrust foods with which they are unfamiliar, and food habits are notoriously difficult to change; if one is used to rice, for example, one may be loathe to add unfamiliar maize, and vice versa. Noting the resistance of isolated South American rain-forest tribes to new foodstuffs, the American geographer and anthropologist William Smole quoted Pero Vaz de Caminha on the Portuguese experience with natives at the time of the AD 1500 discovery of Brazil: "We gave them things to eat: bread, boiled fish, comfits, sweetmeats, cakes, honey, dried figs. They would hardly eat anything of all this, and, if they tasted it, they spat it out at once."[15] Another example of rejection involving taste is Colonial West Indian slaves' initially rejecting breadfruit because they preferred the flavor of plantains.[16]

These matters of taste have much to do with culturally conditioned perceptions and with habit, although there *are* genetic tasting differences among different populations[17] and although infants do acquire something of the taste preferences of their mothers through ingestion of mother's milk—and even in utero.[18] It is also possible that differences in taste-bud densities, which can vary by as much as two-thirds, and thus differences in sensitivities to certain flavors among populations, can influence taste preferences at the population level.[19]

Not only flavor, habit, and physiology but also prestige are involved. Although exotic foods sometimes exert prestige appeal among elites, in Southeast Asia, native rice is distinctly the preferred and more prestigious grain, and maize has made inroads mainly only where the physical environment or trading possibilities do not favor wet-rice cultivation or importation. Until recently, the average Han Chinese had an aversion to maize, even becoming ill from the very odor of maize pancakes. Although now more widely popular as a longevity-promoting food, maize remains largely a staple of ethnic minorities, the very poor, and children. The South American sweet potato is widely consumed in China today but is nevertheless unappreciated and seen as essentially a food of the poor, whereas grain is preferred by the more affluent.[20]

The American psychologist and psychobiologist Paul Rozin and associates have confirmed that not only youngsters but also adult humans experience "neophobia" toward unfamiliar, especially "foreign," foods. According to Rozin and his wife, Elizabeth, a chef, "attachment to traditional flavorings seems to be as strong, if not stronger, than the attachment to traditional staple foods. Human beings are remarkably conservative in their food habits and are typically reluctant to try new foods and to abandon old familiar ones."[21] The American historian Felipe Fernández-Armesto added, cultures are "collectively hostile to new culinary influences. . . . Contempt for foreign foods and foodways was well established in antiquity."[22] The French sociologist of food Claude Fischler further pointed out that neither nutritional nor taste characteristics of a potential food is a reliable predictor of adoption and consumption.[23] The paleoethnobotanist Kristen Gremillion wrote, "Suspicion of novelty . . . [is probably adaptive, because it] guards against the risk entailed by surrendering familiar practices with well understood outcomes in favor of new and unknown crops and technologies."[24]

Given these factors and the importance of traditional cuisines in defining ethnic identities as well as those of often-despised aliens,[25] it is no surprise that many societies have refused potentially productive crops, livestock, and other food-related innovations. Just as huge areas of the Old World rejected various inventions, within the pre-Columbian New World similar rejections took place with respect to crops. The Andean potato and coca, for example, were not adopted northward of lower Central America, despite ongoing seaborne contacts between northwestern South America and Middle America. Likewise, the natives of the California culture region did not adopt maize agriculture or pottery despite the seeming great practical values of both and despite Californians' proximity to pottery-making maize farmers for at least a millennium and a half.[26] The conclusion of the American cultural geographer Frederick J. Simoons was, "Traditional foodways tend to be maintained unless modified by disruptive factors of some sort," such as outright conquest by foreigners.[27] The American food anthropologist Ellen Messer agreed: "major changes in consumption habits are usually brought on by major disruptions in ordinary routines," such as war, migration, land shortages, and the like.[28]

A case study of the Highland Kichwa of Colonial period Peru is illustrative. The Yale art historian George Kubler referred to Bernabé Cobo's observations of 1652: "his account of these various species reverts continually to the fact that many European introductions had not been adopted by the Indians," and Father Cobo's lists of crops raised by Natives for themselves includes no European ones. From the beginnings of the Colonial period, many Indians raised some

European crops such as wheat solely to satisfy Spanish demands for tribute, and the whole production might go to the Spanish in kind or be sold in order to pay tribute in cash. Certain other crops were environmentally unsuited to the Highlands and so were not adopted. As Kubler further observed, "The Quechua cultivation of maize or potatoes has a rigid, semiceremonial character . . . little affected by European tools or methods. No alien crop or harvest of marginal value could be assimilated which interfered too largely with the rituals of communal agriculture" or that would be in competition with existing crops by occupying the same environmental and/or culinary niche (for example, rye versus quinoa), that would require additional labor or unfamiliar methods or equipment to raise or process, or that did not fit into the traditional cuisine.[29]

Crops traveling in the opposite direction fared differentially as well: fifteen to twenty climatically suitable New World crops were not adopted in southern Europe (for example, the staples quinoa and grain amaranth), and others were only slowly accepted, being retarded by tastes, lack of familiarity with the appropriate cultivation and processing methods, and even folk beliefs.

Difficult though it now is to imagine Italian cuisine without the tomato and German or Irish cooking minus the potato, these American foods were initially looked upon in most of post-Columbian Europe with suspicion, being solanaceous—belonging to the nightshade family, which included poisonous and psychotropic members that were associated with witchcraft. Too, tomato fruits of the era were no larger than today's cherry tomatoes.

Unprocessed potatoes of the time *were* slightly toxic, and some people were repulsed by the potato's resemblance to a leper's extremities or to testicles. Although seed-reproduced root vegetables were raised in Europe, there was no tradition of tuberous staples there, and propagation using "eyes" was unfamiliar. In addition, until more accommodating varieties were developed through selection, the potato, a plant of the tropics, did poorly in Europe's climate of long summer days. Despite its high productivity, nutritiousness, good flavor, and ease of planting, harvesting, and preparation, and despite elites' belief that the spud was aphrodisiac, only war and famine forced the potato's widespread adoption (potatoes being productive and the crop in the ground being hard to destroy).

Maize, that delicious and nutritious Amerindian staff of life, while not totally ignored in Europe (note Italian polenta), has still never become an important human foodstuff in most of that continent. It was perceived as a Muslim and low-status crop and an animal food, and the Native American technology of niacin-releasing alkali processing was not imported with the plant.[30] The English archaeologist Warwick Bray observed that despite massive and sustained transatlantic intercourse, "all the sources agree in suggesting that the discovery of the New World made no immediate impact on the diet of Europeans. Introduced plants rarely became staple foods in Europe before the seventeenth century."[31]

Finally, introduction of crop plants and domesticated animals could take place only if the voyagers carried such plants and animals across. If colonization was not the aim, there would not have been an immigrant population sufficiently knowledgeable about the agricultures of their homelands from whom the natives could learn. In any case, on long, arduous voyages, limited cargo capacity might well limit foodstuffs to only what was needed to feed the personnel. The modest-sized craft in operation would not have had room for breeding-size populations of large livestock and their feed. The surprising thing is that early Colonial Spaniards, Englishmen, and other Europeans did ultimately manage to get viable numbers of horses, cattle, and sheep across, not that their possible precursors apparently failed to do so.

Even if domesticated plants and animals *had* been brought over by foreigners, would they have survived once the foreigners departed or were eliminated or absorbed? Certainly, if the criterion of inevitable native adoption of Old World crops and livestock is applied to the agricultural Norse's settling of Greenland and Vínland, the Norse were never present in the New World—despite the proof of history and archaeology that they (and some of their cows and pigs) were. In brief, lack of any particular cultivated plant or domesticated animal species or set of these, no matter how potentially useful, by no means precludes significant and influential contact having occurred.

8

Low Tech

The Absences of Many Old World Inventions in the New World

We often despise what is most useful to us.

—Aesop, circa 550 BC

From at least the time of the famed Columbia University anthropologist Franz Boas (1858–1942), the absence of a number of key (as well as less notable) Old World culture traits in the New World has been seen as telling. In 1961, George Kubler summed up the dominant point of view of his time (and to a great extent of today) when he wrote, "The diffusionists have never given any explanation of the absence of large-wheeled vehicles and of old world beasts of burden in America. Would these powerfully useful instruments not have survived the displacement more readily than Hindu or Buddhist symbols [proposed to have been introduced]? Between equivalent peoples of differing traditions, tools and useful items travel much more quickly than symbolic forms."[1]

What's Missing in America

The two missing-in-America items that Kubler forwarded are very far from being the only presumed pre-1492 New World material absences. The US National Museum anthropologist Herbert W. Krieger's list of 1935 included bellows, pottery glazing, the vehicular wheel, the crank handle, the potter's wheel, stringed instruments, the rudder, kiln-baked brick, and the true arch. He added, "The conclusion is obvious, namely that the high cultures of America, like the more humble Amazonian tropical woodland cultures, are products of a long period of development entirely independent of Asiatic or Oceanic influence, not to mention that of the African Negro."[2]

In addition to many of the above traits, A. L. Kroeber had (in 1923) also listed the following absences: proverbs, divination from viscera, ironworking, and oaths and ordeals. In 1945 he added philosophy, alchemy, writing, monasticism, eunuchism, and games of mental skill.[3] With respect to the wheel, the screw, and the plow, he thought that "with no diffusion in these fundamentals, evidence must be unusually complete before one can put faith in the diffusion of isolated items, especially when their occurrence is in parts of America remote from Asia."[4]

Draft animals, milking, and coined money have also been mentioned as absences, and a long list of items in the realms of traditional technology and material culture could be added, including: true outriggers on canoes, planked and framed watercraft fastened with wood or metal, pottery floats, rowing, rigid shoes, skis, ice skates, the true chimney, gem faceting, glassmaking, porcelain, the sickle, the threshing flail, the threshing sled, risen breadstuffs, both chopsticks and forks, both beam and screw presses, the aboveground oven, pickling, felt making, the crane, the well sweep (shadoof), the bucket chain, the force pump, the vacuum pump, the siphon, the buckle and the belt hook, the safety-pin fibula, shoulder straps on burden baskets, the door hinge and the door latch and the door lock, roof slates and ceramic roofing tiles, most kinds of wood joinery (including casks and cribbed-log buildings) and associated tools such as the carpenter's saw and the auger, coiled-metal springs, metal swords and knives, plate armor and chain mail, the ratchet, the pendulum, the razor, shears, certain weaving devices, soapmaking, the candle, the xylophone, the thumb piano, bagpipes, the pipe organ, multiarmed figures in art, short-term time-keeping devices, the ink pen, and acupuncture, among others.

Some allegedly absent cultural traits were, in reality, present in the ancient New World, if not always widely or in the areas of highly elaborated culture. In some cases, these have only recently been recognized, after the aforementioned diffusionism skeptics had made their lists. For example, divination from entrails, a widespread but odd Old World practice, was performed in Peru as well. In late prehistoric northern New Mexico and in parts of Mesoamerica, a crude lead glaze was used to decorate some pottery.[5] A few jars with screw tops have been found at Mayan sites. Musical bows are used in some areas. Oaths and (rarely) ordeals in connection with criminal accusations were employed by certain groups of North American Indians.[6] Hand-formed baked brick occurs widely at Maya sites in Tabasco (especially at Comalcalco), and there are a few reports from Oaxaca, Puebla, and México.[7] More or less standardized (if not coined) copper-ax money was used in northern Peru, southern Ecuador, and Oaxaca.[8] The grid-pattern city is said to have been exclusively an Old World phenomenon, but in fact the city of Teotihuacan in Central Mexico was given a rough grid layout, as was—uniquely among the Maya—Nixtun-ch'ich' in Guatemala.

The supposed absence of the sail in the Western Hemisphere was once used as an argument against overseas contacts—until its pre-Columbian use in Ecuador and Peru was recognized (it may well have been used in the Caribbean and in the Arctic, as well; see chapter 16).[9] The true chair has been considered absent in the Americas, but Tairona ceramic models from Colombia depict a kind of chair with a back and a deeply concave seat, apparently for reclining; too, figurines from the Mayan island of Jaina, Campeche, include aristocratic individuals seated on chairs with legs and a back.[10]

The jury is still out on other items. For example, there is some evidence that gunpowder, always supposed to be absent in pre-1492 America, was used for rocketry in western Mexico,[11] and distilling—ordinarily thought a sixteenth-century introduction—may have been pre-Columbian in the New World. It could well be the case that some other supposedly absent traits did actually occur in the Americas but have yet to be recovered archaeologically or ethnographically. Undoubtedly, many practices—and, potentially, oral traditions of overseas contacts—died out as a consequence of the devastating post-Columbian epidemics and other disruptions brought on by European colonization (see the introduction and chapter 6). Just as important may be the fact that certain things for one reason or another simply did not appeal sufficiently and so did not spread.[12]

In this chapter we consider closely six major alleged absences—the vehicular wheel, the plow, ironworking, the potter's wheel, the lathe, and the true arch—in the Western Hemisphere. The aim is to see what, if anything, these missing or supposedly missing items may really say about the possibility of pre-Columbian contacts between the Old World and the New, rather than reflexively excluding such a possibility on the basis of absences. Some items will be shown to have in fact existed in the New World but were largely ignored or found to be impractical, just as these same inventions failed to catch on in parts of the Old World itself for a variety of reasons both pragmatic and perceptual.

Reinventing the Wheel?

Why a Wheelless New World?

The wheel is perceived as being one of the most fundamental practical breakthroughs of human innovation—the quintessential invention. Scholars long contended that, although rotary drills, spindles, spinning tops, and log rollers existed in the pre-Columbian New World, along with roller stamps (cylinder seals), the principle of the wheel or, more broadly, axial rotation, was otherwise absent: no wheeled vehicles, cog wheels, cams, rotary querns, stone-wheel doors, wind or water mill wheels and rotating grindstones, whirligigs, water-lifting noria wheels, trip-hammers, treadmills, reels or windlasses or cranks or pulleys, screw pumps, paddlewheels, ship's wheels, dials, potter's wheels or lathes (but see below), spinning wheels, fishing reels, rotary saws, jeweler's wheels, children's hoops or yo-yos, bearings, swivels and gimbals, and so on. The argument was then made: If significant contacts between the peoples of the two hemispheres had occurred, it is inconceivable that technologies of such supreme usefulness would not have been adopted in the New World. However, as with so many matters discussed in this book, the picture proves to be not so simple, and blanket assertions are often based on inadequate information.

Although many seem to take it for granted that (outside the Arctic and subarctic) the vehicular wheel was almost ubiquitous in the premodern Old World, this was far from the case. First, wheeled vehicles, after their invention, were less used even in the wheel-using parts of the ancient Old World than is often supposed. This was true especially after the wide introduction of animal riding circa 1100 BC. (The earliest present evidence for horseback riding comes from the Pontic-Caspian steppes at about 4200 BC, but the practice seems not to have penetrated into most wheel-using areas until much later.)

The plow is likely the evolutionary precursor of the first wheeled carts and wagons (perhaps via the drawn sledge) of circa 4500–3300 BC, the plow's beam becoming the early wagon's single, central draft pole. Just where the wheeled vehicle was first invented is uncertain; some favor the desert and grassland plains of Mesopotamia, others the steppes of Eurasia to the north of the Caucasus Mountains, and some posit multiple, scattered independent inventions. In any case, these early carts were ponderous, slow-moving vehicles best suited for transporting farm produce or building supplies over relatively short distances. For a time, some Inner Asian nomads used carts in their movements on the generally even-surfaced and riverless steppes, but these were later superseded by riding and pack animals.

One reason for limited vehicle use was the lack of decent roads. This helps account for the fact that early land transport of bulk merchandise in wheel-possessing parts of the Old World was largely by trains of donkeys or mules (later, camels) and not by wagon, pack animals being better able to negotiate uneven and muddy routes and to cross rivers.[13] Also, unlike vehicles, pack animals had the advantage of breedability, obviating the need for wagon-construction skills. In ancient Rome, for instance, mules were the main land carriers of grain, three being able to transport the equivalent of a wagonload.[14]

Poor roads remained the norm, including among more advanced societies, until relatively recent times. As late as the second half of the eighteenth century, even western European roads were frequently impassible for wheeled transport. The French historian Fernand Braudel observed that in 1800 the carriage of a French inspector of roads overturned six times and bogged down in mud eleven times in going a mere 500 miles. Even in 1840, messengers in carriages took two weeks to travel from Paris to Marseilles.[15]

Other factors also operated in the Old World. Knowledge of the vehicular wheel was probably almost universal in Tibet, but the wheel was not utilized there for vehicles because, since the wheel represented Buddhist doctrine as a whole, the cycle of existence, royalty, and perfection—as well as the Buddha himself—it was too sacred a symbol to use secularly.[16] In the Southeast Asian lowlands, almost everyone and everything traveled by river, and wheels were essentially irrelevant. In mountainous areas, established human porterage continued to carry the goods, despite knowledge of the existence of the wheel; wheeled vehicles are of little utility where road-making is impractical, not only in rugged country but also in wetlands.

Owing to uneven terrain, even in the mid-twentieth century the wheel was little used in large parts of Iranian and Pakistani Baluchistan. In portions of Scotland in the late eighteenth century, wheeled vehicles were rare or absent. On their tour of the Hebrides in 1773, Samuel Johnson and James Boswell saw no tracks of cartwheels, or carts, in the roads of the islands Skye, Mull, Col, and Ulva. Even in the 1920s, there were no roads on twenty of the twenty-one Faroe Islands. This does not signify, of course, that people in these places were ignorant of wheels. The acquisition of carts and carriages was probably inhibited by a combination of general isolation, lack of manufacturing means and expertise, poverty, limited overland distances to be traveled, rough terrain, and poor or absent roads—plus the availability of the sea for travel and transport, along with the ability to use it.

Although known, the wheel was not much employed in most of ancient eastern Asia. The complete absence of wheeled vehicles in sub-Saharan Africa prevailed despite millennia of caravan traffic across the desert and receipt of a variety of significant cultural influences from the Mediterranean world and in spite of the fact that, as attested by petrographs in Saharan southern Algeria, southwestern Libya, northern Mali, and elsewhere—even in the Canary Islands—chariots were once used by the Berber-speaking Garamantes and related Saharan peoples, who controlled the transdesert caravan traffic for over a millennium beginning about 500 BC.

The most striking Old World example of the absence of the wheel is the case of its disappearance between the third and sixth centuries AD over vast areas of southwestern Asia and North Africa, leaving a largely wheel-free belt from Morocco to Southeast Asia, after the adoption of the dromedary camel (a southern Arabian domesticate) as an important pack animal, following invention of the camel saddle in the late BC period. Camels could carry 1,000-pound loads 25 to 30 miles a day, could eat even tough and thorny plants, could go weeks without drinking, and had nearly transparent eyelids that allowed them to see even during sandstorms. They were less expensive to feed and water than mules or oxen and were stronger, faster, longer-lived, and able to go where there were no roads and little water. They proved so efficient as dryland beasts of burden that, compared to expensive and temperamental wheeled vehicles and their greater number of required drivers, the testy beast won the contest hands down, and wheels became a thing of the past.[17] The abandonment of wheeled transport in the Middle East would last until the nineteenth century—longer, in some areas—and there are no references to wheeled vehicles in medieval Islamic source materials.

Granted, the New World suite of potential domesticates did not offer the alternative of full-sized camelids (only much smaller llamas, in the Andes, which could carry only about 60 pounds each). But any voyages from the aforementioned Afro-Asian zone during the relevant time period certainly could not be expected to have introduced the wheel to the Americas.

Given that for various reasons wheeled transport was never adopted or was given up in large parts of the interconnected Old World itself, it cannot be argued that its absence in the New necessarily reflects lack of contact. As the eminent British archaeologist Stuart Piggott put it, "The main reason for the absence of such transport elsewhere (the New World, for instance) seems reasonably explicable. The stimulus to the invention of a wheeled vehicle, whatever the more imponderable economic factors that might make it an acceptable technological instrument to a society, must have been the availability of [animal] power beyond human capacity."[18] The Americas lacked large domestic animals with potentially great tractive power, and use of animal traction existed only in relatively northern latitudes, involving dogs pulling travois—burden-bearing frames slung between trailing poles (Great Plains)—and sleds (Arctic and subarctic). (Although caribou and bison were domesticable and the principle of traction applicable to them, their potential remained unrealized.)

Also lacking would have been appropriate expertise. To be of much utility, wheels must be perfectly circular, balanced, and properly attached to the axle and the axle to the frame, and wheels must be sufficiently strong but not overly heavy and cumbersome. Even the earliest wheels known to archaeology, found in graves on the Ukrainian/Russian grasslands of 3300–2800 BC, were fairly complex. They were solid, some of a single piece of wood but others of three or four planks assembled using mortise and tenon joints, and each of the naves (hubs) was secured to the axle arms by a lynchpin.[19]

Although solid wheels have continued in use to the present, spoked wheels, for chariots, appeared about 2100 BC or a bit earlier. According to David W. Anthony, author of *The Horse, the Wheel, and Language*, "The earliest spoked wheels were wonders of bent-wood joinery and fine carpentry. The rim had to be a perfect circle of joined wood, firmly attached to individually carved spokes inserted into mortises in the outer wheel and a multi-socketed central nave, all carved and planed with hand tools." No untrained person could make such wheels, which require joinery (absent in the New World outside of the Northwest coast). Anthony added, "The wheel, the axle, and vehicle together made a complicated combination of load-bearing moving parts . . . [that] had to fit precisely. . . . The first wagon-wrights had to calculate the relationship between drag, axle diameter/strength, axle length/rigidity, and the width of the wagon bed."[20] In Eurasia, the specialized occupation of wheelwright came into existence to meet these exacting requirements, and there were also specialized cartwrights/wainwrights to construct the rest of the vehicle. If postulated transoceanic voyages did not include such specialists among their passengers, as is highly likely, then the probability of wheeled vehicles being introduced was probably quite small.

Even if wheels *had* been introduced, carts and so on would not have spread until and unless suitable roads had been constructed (there *were* good roads in the Maya and Inca realms and in parts of the Amazonian lowlands, and a few in the North American Southwest, but real roads were rare or absent elsewhere in the Americas). Even where roads existed, unfordable rivers might be major barriers. Vehicle-passable bridges were not built in the pre-Colonial Americas. Even in Eurasia, although there were a few ferries, prior to Roman times vehicular bridges were rare; in areas of seasonal flooding such as Egypt and Mesopotamia, they were all but nonexistent.

In addition to technological, topographical, and ideological barriers to transmission, there no doubt were often other impediments as well. In Mesoamerica, for example, because maize was twice as productive as wheat was in Europe, a city's basic food supply could be produced nearer to town, lessening the transport needs.[21] Piggott observed that wheeled vehicles seemed to be, in Mesoamerica, irrelevant since transport requirements there had been met by alternative means (human porterage).[22]

Generally, when an abundance of inexpensive labor is available, there is little incentive to adopt more labor-efficient technologies. Regarding human foot transport, the historian of technology K. D. White observed:

> In simple, undeveloped communities the cheapest and most ubiquitous form of land transport is a man or a woman with a load carried on the head, shoulders or back [maximal efficiency being attained by using a shoulder pole].
> ... where there is an abundance of cheap manpower, load-easing devices do not develop. Loads too heavy or too bulky for one man to handle are divided between two. . . . Human load-carriers have a physical advantage over their animal competitors: [although they can carry only a quarter of the weight a mule can, they are] much more versatile; and . . . [are] "self-loading and self-unloading." . . .
> Where human muscle-power is cheap and abundant, it continues to prevail over more sophisticated sources and techniques; indeed its use persists in many parts of Africa and Asia today.[23]

In fact, in Mesoamerica human porterage remained important until the mid-twentieth century, despite the continuing post-1521 presence of introduced beasts of burden and wheeled *carretas*. In Nepal, porters still routinely bear loads exceeding their body weights for many miles up and down steep, high-altitude trails.

Big Wheel, Little Wheel

Although a few authors have argued that wheeled vehicles might in fact have existed in the pre-1492 Americas, so far those contentions have not been convincing. However, in the 1940s Gordon Ekholm drew attention to true wheels in Mexican archaeology—not on practical vehicles but on "toy" (probably actually votive) ceramic animal figurines. Terra-cotta wheels had been attached to the ends of the animals' legs by wooden axles passing through holes in those legs, and the figurines could have been pushed or pulled along on any reasonably smooth surface. The Mexican figurines themselves and the attachment of their wheels are highly reminiscent of certain of those in a widespread Old World tra-

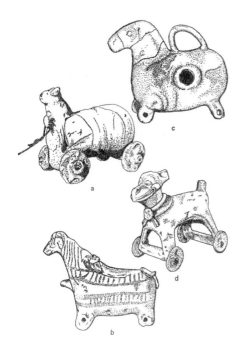

Figure 8.1. Ancient funerary wheeled-animal pottery figurines: (a) Sumerian, Ur, Iraq, circa 2000 BC; (b) Hittite, Antakya, Turkey, circa 1500 BC; (c) Phoenician, Ibiza, Spain, circa 1000 BC; (d) epi-Olmec, Tres Zapotes, Mexico, circa time of Christ. From *Early Man and the Ocean: A Search for the Beginnings of Navigation and Seaborne Civilizations* by Thor Heyerdahl, © 1978 by Thor Heyerdahl. Used by permission of Doubleday, an imprint of the Knopf Doubleday Publishing Group, a division of Random House LLC. All rights reserved.

dition: terra-cotta (as well as metal) wheeled model animals and animal-pulled vehicles were found in scattered areas throughout the ancient Eurasian ecumene (civilized world) and beyond (figure 8.1).[24] Whether or not Old World models inspired the Mexican wheeled "toys"—the *Encyclopedia of American Indian Contributions to the World* asserts independent invention[25]—the "toys" demonstrate that the principle of the wheel was present in the Americas. In fact, a few of the Mesoamerican figurines stand atop wheeled platforms, manifesting a concept little short of that of a wagon. And yet the ancient Mexicans seem never to have constructed actual vehicles. It is impossible to say why, definitively. Lack of roads is not the entire answer, at least in those regions in which excellent roads were constructed. But with the availability of human porterage and as long as no large draft animals were domesticated, vehicle use would in any case have been confined to hand carts, wheelbarrows (not present in Europe until the Middle Ages, although older in China), and, at most, dog-pulled carts, which would not have been of huge practical value in light of those animals' limited tractive strength.

As has been mentioned, the Americas lacked the plow (see below)—the presumed evolutionary predecessor of the first wheeled vehicles—and the New World also lacked knowledge of harnesses (except with northern dog teams). Old World wheeled models were derived from actual wheeled vehicles. The fact that there was no such precedent in the Americas is a point in favor of the idea that Mexican wheeled "toys" are a reflection of Old World influence, as some have indeed proposed. That the principle, though known, was seemingly never applied to practical vehicles could also have been influenced by the figurines' presumed cultic use.

Following the Plow

Like the wheel, the plow is often pointed to as something that was completely absent in ancient America but that would have been enthusiastically accepted had it been offered—as, allegedly, it would have been had any transoceanic relations occurred.

However, early plows were nothing like the efficient turners-over of the soil that modern self-polishing steel plows (which were invented only in the nineteenth century) are. Unless the soil was very loose, the primitive wooden plow (*ard* or breaking plow)—still used in many areas of the world although often not even having metal sheathing—did little more than stir the ground's surface, and in fact is commonly referred to as the "scratch plow." It is useful mainly with light, friable, alluvial soils of drier climates, which it pulverizes, thus improving moisture retention and the rising, via capillary action, of mineral nutrients from below. However, the scratch plow is not good for damper, heavier soils such as those typical of northern Europe or eastern North America. Around the time of Christ, the forerunner of the modern plow came into use north of the Alps and the Loire. It had wheels, a coulter for making a vertical cut, a plowshare for making a horizontal cut, and a moldboard for turning over the sod. The clods were then broken with a harrow and a roller, without which this plow was not terribly effective. In China, a much more efficient moldboard plow had come into use two or three centuries BC, for use in heavy soils.

Where it could be used effectively, the scratch plow did have a definite utility, expanding the area that could be cultivated by a single person, which accounts for its wide dispersion in the Old World. However, it was not as useful as many suppose.

Until modern times, the plow (like the riding of animals and the use of wheeled vehicles) never diffused into (or was reinvented in) sub-Saharan Africa, portions of Southeast Asia, or Australia and the Pacific islands. In these regions, relatively simple implements such as the hoe or even just the dibble or digging stick, sufficed, and were not replaced by the plow, even on the east coast of Africa where intensive trading relationships with plow-using societies around the Indian Ocean went on for millennia, or in the Sudan belt, which traded with the Mediterranean world for thousands of years. The overseas representatives of plow-using Indian Ocean societies were sailors and merchants, not cultivators, and the trans-Saharan traders were mainly pastoralists, not farmers, so the plow stayed home. In light of this African absence alone, the lack of the plow in the New World loses its import as an objection to the idea of contacts.

The British historian A. G. Hopkins noted, in *An Economic History of West Africa*, that draught animals are needed to work a plough effectively. Draught animals could not survive in the forest, where, in any case, the plough was ill-suited to the dominant pattern of irregular, tree-studded plots. Ploughing in the savanna could easily lead to soil erosion. . . . All the same, the plough could have been used in some parts of West Africa . . . [but] was not adopted . . . because its greater cost did not guarantee a more than proportionate increase in returns. Ploughs and draught animals were expensive to buy, and the latter were expensive to maintain. The plough can prepare more land in a shorter time than can manual labour, but this achievement often involves a fall in output per man hour, and, in some cases, in output per acre as well.[26]

Plowing may be just the thing for loosening the surface of the soil prior to broadcasting wheat or barley, but if one is deep-planting several maize seeds in a "hill," especially in a stump-studded *milpa* clearing, a hole-poking dibble may be much preferable to the scratch plow. Plowing is not relevant for such tropical staple crops as tubers and bananas or in fields where certain forms of intercropping or raised beds are involved. To the extent that Colonial Andean Indians planted the introduced crop wheat, initially they did so in holes rather than by broadcasting, and conservatively held on to their traditional tools. In any event, for deep working of the compact, turf-covered soil the spade-like indigenous Andean foot plow or *chakitakylla* was superior to the scratch plow, especially in small or narrow terrace plots, which were characteristic of the highlands, or on steep slopes.[27]

However, as in the case of wheeled vehicles, the most obvious barrier to New World adoption of the plow was the lack of large draft animals in the hemisphere. Without a horse, mule, ox, camel, or equivalent to pull a plow, the implement is useless, and no potentially suitable native beast existed south of North America's bison country. Thus, New World absence of the plow says nothing about whether or not transoceanic contacts took place.

Ironing Out the Differences: The Absence of Ferrous Metallurgy

The question of the apparent absence of iron-making in the pre-Columbian New World, where (with one late exception) putatively ancient North American iron workings have not in fact been shown to be before AD 1500, is somewhat more problematic. Iron is the most useful of metals, and its ores occur quite widely in nature. One might suppose that adoption would have been almost automatic among societies of a sufficient technological level of development, had iron-making technology been offered.

Knowledge of how to smelt iron had arisen in southwestern Asia by 2000 BC, and by 1200 BC had become fairly common among the Hittites in Anatolia. It subsequently diffused to most of Eurasia and Africa but not to pre-Columbian Australia or the Americas. Granted, it had not reached all the areas suggested as possible sources of transoceanic influence by the required dates—for example, it was absent in second millennium BC Shang China and in pre-1000 BC Egypt, but many of the source areas and times proposed did involve iron-making cultures.

There is only one definite known case of pre-Columbian iron making in the Americas, a smithy at the Norse L'Anse aux Meadows site in Newfoundland circa AD 1010. This introduction died with the departure of the Europeans, the process not having been passed on to the natives.[28]

In some cases, iron might not have appeared so supremely useful a substance in New World cultural contexts as it did in Afro-Eurasia. The MIT professor of archaeology and ancient technology Heather Lechtman looked at this question for the Andean region of South America. She first noted that bronze and then iron were pragmatically critically important in the Old World. There, they were valued because they were tough and could hold an edge. Primary uses were for swords, daggers, and armor; for fittings and tires for wheeled vehicles, including war chariots; and for tools. In the Andes, in contrast, weaponry involved slings and clubs, not swords and knives, and did not require metal; wheeled vehicles were absent. Copper and bronze tools were made, but stone blades were about as good for most purposes. For Andeans, metals' main values were symbolic, not practical. Metals were primarily visual expressions of adornment, status, and political power (as they had once been in pre-iron Eurasia, as well). Further, hardness was valued, but not at the expense of malleability, because the main use was to make metal sheets that could be pounded into repoussé designs. Finally, a main reason for the use of copper was that it could be alloyed with silver and gold and then processed by depletion gilding (*mise-en-couleur*) to yield gleaming golden- or silver-surfaced objects (also accomplishable through wash gilding). Iron did not have that capability and itself had a relatively drab and rust-susceptible surface, and for these and the reasons mentioned above it might not have had much appeal.[29]

Iron-making and ironworking involved a complex technology that in some ways differed markedly from copper smelting and copper-working, requiring, among other things, higher temperatures and closer control of atmospheric conditions than those needed for producing copper or bronze. In addition, like wheel manufacture, iron manufacture demanded specialists who were not likely to have been involved in ocean crossings. Iron production required prospecting; extraction and transport of ore; ore preparation; fuel selection and transport; charcoal making; discovery, extraction, transport, and preparation of clays for making the furnace; and construction of same. The furnace had to be loaded, bellows (unknown in the Americas) constructed and operated, the smelting supervised, the iron bloom extracted and shingled, and proper ritual observed. The technology entailed additional prerequisite tools and techniques such as air pipes, tongs, long-handled iron hammers, substantial anvils, and so on, most if not all of which were absent in the New World.[30]

Routinely, this elaborate technology and associated ritual were maintained as a set of professional secrets kept within the "guild," and only a minute portion of any population had mastery of it. In fact, ironworkers were (and in some areas still are) often perceived as dangerous warlocks who called upon occult underground forces to work iron and were thus to be avoided by others, as is especially well documented for recent centuries in Africa.[31] For that reason alone, these individuals might not have been allowed on ships. In some contexts, especially in connection with religious practice, even the *use* of iron was prohibited. In traditional India, for example, although useful and thought to be protective against evil, iron is also seen as black and ritually evil, associated with the inauspicious deity Sani (Saturn).[32] The Bible quotes, "If thou wilt make me an altar of stone, thou shalt not build it of hewn stone: for if thou lift up thy tool upon it, thou hast polluted it" (Exodus 20:25). The book makes a point of stating that no "tool of iron [was] heard in the house [of the Lord], while it was building (1 Kings 6:7; cf. Deuteronomy 27:5; Joshua 8:31).

Even if an ironsmith had been a member of an overseas expedition, he would not have passed on his skills to people outside the guild, and if he died, his knowledge of iron-making would die with him. Furthermore, unless appropriate ores were locally available the technology could not be introduced. Nor is there reason to suppose that any newcomers would have wished to encourage the indigenes to adopt something that, if kept to themselves, gave the interlopers very considerable advantage. Thus, in light of the difficult and proprietary technology and ritual knowledge involved, the small number of practitioners that existed, secrecy, and taboos associated with iron and ironsmiths, we should not be surprised by the failure of iron manufacture to be introduced into the pre-1500 New World. In fact, I know of no purely indigenous groups that adopted iron smelting even after European arrival.

Turning Things Around: The Lathe and the Potter's Wheel

The wood- or stone-turning lathe was long believed to be unknown to any ancient Americans, and all pre-Columbian pottery was thought to have been made without the potter's wheel. Until relatively recently, the nearest thing to the potter's wheel known from the pre-1492 New World (as well as in parts of China) was use of a mat or plate that could be turned manually every so often—or even as rapidly as a simple potter's wheel—to facilitate the potter's working on the in-progress vessel placed upon the mat or plate. However, in the early 1970s, at a Peruvian site called Pashash, both lathe-turned stone cups and fragments of seventy-one wheel-thrown ceramic cups were unearthed, dating to about AD 310–600.[33] These remain the only such finds in the hemisphere. It is not supposed that the items were imported. However, their very limited spatial and temporal distribution hints strongly at the possibility of localized influence from across the Pacific, with the technology never really catching on or spreading but instead dying out rather quickly.

If the knowledge was there and the technology so useful, two questions arise:

(1) whether locally invented or introduced, why was it not retained at, and diffused from, Pashash? and (2) why do many pottery-making American Indian groups continue to this day to manufacture their ceramics without a potter's wheel centuries after that device became widespread in the hemisphere following European conquest? The general answer to both questions is, as the cases of the true arch (see below) and the wheeled vehicle (see above) show, people are quite capable of rejecting something that may strike others as irresistibly practical. Adoption of alternatives almost always involves overcoming the stubborn resistance of habit, vested interests, supernatural sanction, ritual requirements, and so forth; more often than not, adoption fails to occur or to endure. Too, acceptance and spread may be inhibited by cultural filters in the society's communications network.

The potter's wheel was, in fact, hardly universal in the ceramic-making regions of the Old World. Following its invention millennia before Columbus, the device did not spread beyond the peoples of commercially oriented higher culture in the Eastern Hemisphere into more marginal areas, where the coiling and scraping and paddle and anvil methods of vessel manufacture continued to prevail. The potter's wheel was absent in sub-Saharan Africa, despite contact with societies that made turned pottery. Sri Lanka's Veddahs, surrounded by the Sinhalese, failed to copy the latter's potter's wheel. Why, then, did the device not diffuse farther than it did?

Many decades ago, the American sinologist Berthold Laufer pointed out that the potter's wheel employs a quite different technology than does hand molding of pottery. The pre-1500 geographical range of the potter's wheel corresponded quite closely to that of wheeled vehicles, and Laufer proposed—probably incorrectly—that the ceramic-forming device descended from, and spread with, the vehicular one. In China and India, at least, whereas hand forming of pots is a female task, wheel turning is a male one, and crossovers are not permitted.[34]

Different factors operated in different places. In some cases, traditional pot forms could not readily be produced with a wheel—for example, carinated bowls (made in two halves) and large pots. After the Spanish conquest, the Mam Maya of Guatemala generally rejected the production-speeding wheel, principally because women potters, precluded from "male" tasks, had an abundance of time and saw no need to accelerate output.[35] In Nigeria, to manufacture wheel-thrown ceramics the local clay would need to be laboriously refined and kilns (requiring capital investment and much firewood) used, and an assistant might be required to turn the wheel.

During the early 1940s, the Mexican government attempted to introduce the potter's wheel to the indigenous potters of Ticul, Yucatán. The attempt failed. Reasons for the failure included the cost of acquiring the device and the fear of risking one's livelihood while learning the operation of an unproven innovation. Too, there was a perception that hand molding was just as fast as wheel throwing. Once one has learned the new motor habits and developed the appropriate muscles, wheel turning is, in fact, much speedier; however, that is not the case until one has gained the requisite strength and skill. At Ticul, too, the local clay was seen as being too thick and coarse for use with the wheel: the grit in the whirling clay abraded the potters' hands; turning the device with their bare feet also resulted in irritation. The old ways prevailed and the wheel was abandoned.[36]

One efficient alternative to the potter's wheel is use of molds, which were widely employed in Mexico and Peru. The Berkeley anthropologist George M. Foster Jr. wrote of Mexican half-mold and mushroom-mold techniques, by which pots could be produced "more rapidly than by all but the best wheel-throwing potters." The resulting vessels were stronger and nicer looking than the usual wheel-made Indian pots.[37] Likewise, in a follow-up study the American anthropological-ceramics historian Louana M. Lackey noted that larger pieces and asymmetrical ones can be made with molds but not with wheels. "For these reasons rather than tradition. . . . [Mexican] potters accustomed to convex molding, will continue to do so. . . . The reasons for rejecting the wheel are valid."[38]

As the American archaeologist Keith Nicklin declared, "Unless the full potentiality of the wheel is exploited, then it has a dubious advantage over certain efficient hand techniques of forming pottery [such as use of a good turntable]."[39]

The unavoidable conclusion is that, as with wheeled vehicles, the absence of the potter's wheel adds little or nothing to arguments concerning pre-Columbian contacts.

It may also be pointed out that the pottery-firing kiln was absent in the Americas, with a single exception: small kilns appear in the archaeology of Matacapan, Veracruz, Mexico, between AD 400 and 700.[40] This is another case of a technology that was probably introduced but failed to spread.

Vaunted Vaults: The Truth about the True Arch and the True Dome

Although widely supposed to have been absent in the pre-1492 Americas, the true arch has, in fact, been reported from a limited number of sites in Mesoamerica (mainly, in the Maya region), and, as David J. Eccott wrote, "it is no longer admissible to use its supposed absence here as an unqualified cornerstone of the argument, as is often done, that the New World civilizations were completely independent from those of the Old World."[41] Too, the Eskimo snow house is a variant of the true dome (the arch rotated). Despite these constructional devices' usefulness in Old World architectural history, they failed to spread to any appreciable extent in the pre-Columbian New, indicating again that, no matter how potentially useful it may seem to be, no item's adoption is guaranteed.

Likewise, even though it was known, the true arch was not used even in many parts of the Eastern Hemisphere. The Canadian archaeologist/epigrapher David H. Kelley wrote that "it is unclear why neither the true arch nor the wheel were to be found in Egypt for more than a thousand years after Mesopotamian influences transformed Egypt from a Neolithic farming stage to a semiurban, literate society."[42] Even where employed, in both ancient Mesopotamia and Egypt the arch's use was confined largely to subterranean drainways, and it did not become a really notable feature of aboveground architecture anywhere before Roman times. The arch remained generally absent in pre-1500 sub-Saharan Africa, northern and Southeast Asia, Australia, and Oceania.

One impediment to adoption of the true arch is the requirement for centering during erection. Centering is typically a temporary wooden framework set up to support the under-construction arch's voussoirs (vaulting stones or bricks) until the keystone can be put into place. Without good timber supplies (for example, on Peru's desert coast), wooden centering would be difficult or impossible to provide. Too, in the absence of carpenter's saws (not present in the Americas), the cutting of planks would have to be accomplished with adzes, a very much more laborious process and perhaps not worth the effort. Nor, in most areas, were nails or even joinery techniques present for assembling any centering.

The diffusionist American professor of architecture Paul Shao has proposed additional reasons for a dearth of New World true arches and for why in Nuclear America corbeled arches and vaults were used instead. (Corbelling involves horizontal blocks projecting farther and farther out over the room the higher in the vault they are; the projecting stones or bricks are held in place by the weight of the overlying masonry rather than by a keystone.) "The corbel [arch/vault] does not require precise dressing of the stone, nor rigid adherence to specifications and formulas, as required in the true arch," wrote Shao,[43] and corbelling holds up better in seismically active zones such as characterize most New World civilizational centers. (Note, however, that in Europe there are plenty of true arches employing undressed [but mortared] stones, as well as abundant true arches in some Old World earthquake-prone areas such as Italy and Turkey.) Too, unlike in Europe and Southwest Asia, where large interior spaces (as in temples, churches, and mosques) were valued, New World temples (like Hindu ones) were meant for rituals undertaken by one or a few priests and did not involve large indoor assemblies.

It turns out also to have been the case that in the Old World, the dome was not just a simply utilitarian form of roofing, elicited by structural and environmental considerations, but that it had mortuary/domiciliary (cf. Latin *domus*) symbolism that, beginning in the Levant, fostered the spread of the form for tombs, churches, and the like—a symbolism not present in America.[44]

So, as in the cases of all the other technologies discussed above, the (incomplete) absence of the true arch and the true dome in America does not signify lack of overseas contacts.

9

More on the Whys of Technological Absences

Absence of evidence is not evidence of absence.
—Carl Sagan, late twentieth century

As the previous two chapters have highlighted, those skeptical of diffusion tend to make much of cultural absences, especially those involving useful organisms and technologies. For example, the British archaeologists Paul Bahn and John Flenley wrote, "The total absence and ignorance of woven textiles on Easter Island is damning evidence against any link with Peru. . . . A further argument against strong South American influence is the complete absence of the pressure-flaking technique on stone tools throughout Polynesia."[1] Of course, the lack of suitable fiber and, on many islands, of suitable stone, could have something to do with these absences, even if contact did occur.

Argumentum ex silentio or *argumentum ad ignorantiam* is a chancy matter in this context. In considering absences in the New World, it should be recollected that because of the severe depopulation of the post-Columbian Americas, many native societies disappeared or were reduced to mere vestiges of their former selves, and there was often considerable disorganization and cultural loss as a consequence. Thus at least some now-vanished nonmaterial- and even material-culture traits that *had* been present may have left no evidence of their previous existences, in which case apparent absences may be deceptive. Still, there is no question that many Old World traits were not present in the New World. What does this really say?

A number of prominent diffusionist thinkers have addressed this issue of "missing" traits. Gordon F. Ekholm, for instance, stressed that every contact situation was unique and involved many variables and that, therefore, there can be few general principles governing the process.[2]

Great differences in degree of cultural elaboration militate against cultural transfer. Historically, material innovation has been largely elite driven, through elite-employed artisans. Too, many "inventions" remained the exclusive preserve of such an elite—individuals who seldom opted to emigrate or even to travel overseas; as stay-at-homes, neither they nor their artisans would have spread their privileging traits abroad. (Egalitarian societies, lacking the drive for domi-nance and display and lacking subsidized technicians, did relatively little inno-vating outside of that involving use of plant-derived substances such as drugs, poisons, and rubber.)

The Know-How Gap: Absent Useful Technologies

In making some of the points reprised in chapter 8, the art historian Douglas Fraser argued that useful innovations often fail to spread even to adjacent societies.

> If we judge West African culture by the absence of wheeled vehicles, the plow, the true arch, draft animals and milking, then the well-documented Islamic penetration of the western Sahara cannot have taken place. For these traits are all well known in Moslem North Africa. . . . The ancient Greeks also [long] rejected [the true arch] though it was known earlier in Sumer, Babylon, and Egypt. . . . Moreover, such New World traits as the corbel arch, pyramid, and ball court, present in Meso-America, were not invariably adopted in adjacent areas to which diffusion is known to have occurred. Logically, then, the gaps in the New World inventory . . . are completely silent on the question [as to] whether or not significant con-tacts may have occurred in other sectors of human life.[3]

Many other instances of what to some seem inexplicable absences within the Old World might be forwarded. Despite contacts with those who did, sub-Saharan Africans did not ride animals or have writing before the arrival of Arabs. Coined money, employed in India, was not adopted in most of the Hinduized areas of Southeast Asia, and most of the same region completely rejected the true arch despite contacts with arch-using societies.[4] Indonesians did not em-ploy sophisticated fishhooks, in spite of their use in surrounding regions and in spite of Indonesians' engaging importantly in fishing.

Although aspects of China's technology strongly influenced some other re-gions, except in bronze metallurgy and military equipment very little effect of foreign technology on China before AD 1500 can be detected. Likewise, de-spite that country's relatively influential position, centuries were required for many highly useful Chinese technologies—for example, the wheelbarrow, the crank, the south-pointing needle, the stern rudder, the Chinese lugsail (never fully adopted), gunpowder, papermaking, and printed texts, plus other, less use-ful items such as the kite—to be adopted in the West, despite significant inter-action. The Chinese junk spread only very slowly into Indian Ocean waters de-spite its demonstrated superiority to ships already in use there, and it was much modified in the process. In the twelfth and thirteenth centuries, when Chinese maritime trade in the region was extensive, little was borrowed from China in terms of general culture or technology.

Another interesting example of nonadoption is that of kissing—of considerable currency in Western courtship and something Westerners perceive as quintessentially instinctive—but a behavior not practiced in a considerable percentage of the world's societies, and as a mark of affection (as opposed to foreplay) absent in many more. "Surely kissing is one of the most natural things in the world. . . . But this is what we think, and a whole lot of people think very differently. To them kissing is not at all natural. . . . It is a deplorable habit, unnatural, unhygienic, bordering on the nasty, and even definitely repulsive."[5]

Again, sexual imagery—reflecting a major human concern—is abundant in some cultures (for example, in Hindu India) but rare in others (for instance, those of pre-Columbian Central Mexico). As the religious precept forbidding graven images was taken to its logical limits, Sunnite Muslims even ceased production of images of the human face, flying in the face (one could say) of what one might expect in light of the fascination people generally have for physiognomies of their own species. In fact, iconoclasm against older depictions of human faces became widespread, and still goes on (for example, the 2001 Taliban destruction of the giant Buddha sculptures of Afghanistan's Bamian Valley and the "Islamic State's" 2015–16 smashing of ancient statues and temples in Iraq and Syria). There were European episodes under the seventeenth-century English Puritans and during the French Revolution.

The other side of the coin of people often not doing the "natural" is their doing the "unnatural." Genital mutilation, traditional Chinese foot-binding and fingernail-growing, Ubangi insertion of lip plates, and Kayan Lahwi Red Karen neck elongation in Myanmar, as well as contemporary tongue piercing and the like, are cases in point.

In the New World, fermented alcoholic beverages—generally considered highly appealing to humans—were prominent in many contiguous parts of South and Middle America but in other areas of the hemisphere were completely lacking. This absence has greatly puzzled a number of adherents of what can be called the obviousness-yields-invention school. At the end of the nineteenth century, noting this absence among tribes of the eastern United States, the botanist V. Harvard mused, "We may well wonder at their failure to make wine . . . nothing is easier than to make than wine, the process consisting merely in pressing out the juice and letting it ferment. It is strange indeed that they should not have stumbled upon it."[6] Presumably, some cultural impediment was in play that was not overcome. Of course, on the other side of the sea, alcoholic beverages were (with variable success) tabooed in the Muslim world and in some other religious traditions.

Here Today, Gone Tomorrow: Cultural Impoverishment

In addition to failures to adopt innovations or introductions, cultural losses have also sometimes occurred. The disappearance of wheeled vehicles in North Africa and southwestern Asia has been described in chapter 8. Another example of loss is that experienced by the (now-extinct) Canary Islanders, who must have reached their offshore home using watercraft but who possessed none when Renaissance Europeans first encountered them, despite the availability of timber.[7] Archaeology evidences that, over time, Tasmanians gave up bone tools and the gear and practice of fishing, and also implies loss of cold-weather clothing, hafted tools, boomerangs, and spears and spear throwers. Linguistics indicates that as Austronesians moved from Taiwan (as is widely supposed) into Indonesia and then out into the Pacific, a number of items dropped out of the cultural inventory that was present in Taiwan, including grain farming, the water buffalo and perhaps the dog, houses on piles, loom weaving, and knowledge of metals.

Adding outriggers to canoes was a practice abandoned following Polynesians' arrival in New Zealand, supposedly because the trees in the new land were large enough to allow construction of broad canoes. Long-distance sailing technology disappeared entirely on Easter Island and at certain other locations in the Pacific, in some cases owing to the lack or loss of trees and thus of wood and rope fiber, in others because the costs and risks of canoes and voyaging became no longer worthwhile as local self-sufficiency improved. The bow and arrow as a weapon, and likely the blowgun as well, vanished in Polynesia.[8] Pottery making (of Lapita ware) not only dropped out as the first known settlers of Polynesia spread from west to east—there was a lack of good clays in many of the eastern islands—but also ultimately became extinct in Western Polynesia, where it had been present for centuries—first devolving and then disappearing, possibly because new ways of cooking plus a lack of grains to be stored in jars made pottery unnecessary, and perhaps because its function as a widely traded prestige good declined along with long-distance trade in general.[9]

Technologies can vanish if the people with the appropriate skills die out or depart. Instances include the loss of most navigational star lore on Takú Island, when introduced disease killed the most knowledgeable captains; the Torres Islanders' loss of canoe construction, owing to the deaths of those possessing the requisite skills; and cessation of adze making on Murua (Woodlark) Island, when the relevant specialists perished. Another example is the disappearance of wheel-turned pottery manufacturing in northwestern Europe and parts of Algeria and Morocco following the withdrawal of the Romans.[10] After eight hundred years of utilization, for unknown reasons the Roman invention for bailing ships' bilge water—the rotary chain pump—dropped out of use between the seventh and fifteenth centuries AD.

Changes of fashion or loss of the rites perceived as prerequisite to the manufacture of an item can also result in the loss of technologies. Most Navajos, for instance, gave up basketmaking because of burdensome associated taboos, preferring to trade for baskets.

A prime example of loss occurred after the Portuguese had introduced matchlock firearms to Japan in AD 1543 and after these new weapons had been reproduced and used for a time. In the aftermath of a destructive battle in 1637, firearms were gradually phased out in favor of a return to the traditional and highly symbolic sword, owing to the perception of guns as unaesthetic, lower class, and part of a suite of undesirable foreign cultural imports like Christianity and Western business practices. Despite their military advantages, firearms virtually disappeared from those islands until reintroduced by Commodore Matthew C. Perry in the mid-nineteenth century.[11] It is also the case that, for both similar and different reasons, in China of the same era the Imperial court made major efforts to curtail the spread of gunnery as well as the proliferation of gunsmiths versed in the art.[12] Chinese officials were afraid that possession of guns could abet banditry and uprisings. Too, most people disdained the military, adhered to tradition, and were loathe to admit that a foreign technology could be superior. Again, in the Turkish Mamluk Kingdom the elite disdained firearms, only grudgingly allowing blacks and low-class soldiers to use them in light of the Ottoman threat.[13]

If You Build It, They Won't Come: Invention without Adoption

"History," wrote the anthropologist Ralph Linton, also "affords many examples of valuable and quite workable inventions which the inventor's society failed to accept. As we say, 'The time was not yet ripe.'"[14] A number of potentially utilitarian inventions of the Classical world, such as wind and water mills and even a sort of steam engine, were not widely used or failed to be developed to their obvious potentials. In the case of the steam engine, the reason seems to have been that the upper-class thinkers who conceived the device felt it beneath them to deal with the working- or slave-class practicalities of manufacturing and operating it.[15]

A medieval European example of laggard development is that of the very useful crank handle, which the historian Lynn White called "extraordinary not only for its late invention [in Europe], or arrival from China, but also for the almost unbelievable delay, once it was known, in its assimilation to technological thinking. . . . At the beginning of the 1400s, at least twelve centuries after it was known in China and six centuries after its first appearance in Europe, the crank was still a dormant element in technology."[16]

The imagination of that quintessential Renaissance man, Leonardo da Vinci, conceived a great variety of inventions—the bicycle, a kind of military tank, a flying machine, a crude guided missile, a parachute, a diving suit, a submersible, contact lenses, a photometer, possibly even a form of photography—that for one reason or another were not implemented or did not catch hold. In this connection, the science writer Amir Aczel noted, "It seems to be a law of nature that a technology is developed and then waits a long time for people to discover their need for it, rather than the other way around. The time and place have to be right for the implementation of a new technology."[17] A suite of impediments must be removed before adoption can take hold. If even local acceptance in the place of an innovation's inception often does not occur, such an item's being ignored by a foreign culture should not be at all astounding.

Choosing à la Carte: Diffusion as a Selective Process

It is worth emphasizing the findings of a 1953 symposium of anthropologists on the topic of acculturation: "Cultures do not meet, but people who are their carriers do. As carriers of traditions such contacting individuals never know their entire cultures and never convey all they know of them to one another. That part of their cultural inventory which they do transmit is conditioned primarily by their reasons for making the contact, that is, by the cultural concomitants of the role that they assume in dealing with an alien group. . . . Unless there is a full representation on both sides there can be opportunity for only a partial intercultural transfer."[18]

As was suggested in the previous chapter, specialized occupations such as that of wheelwright or iron-smelter may well not have been represented among the crews and passengers of early transoceanic craft, particularly if colonization was not an aim. Even when colonization *was* envisaged, it would not have been possible for one or a few ships to carry across the whole suite of occupations and the sum of a complex society's knowledge, and what is transplanted by a few people to a new area is inevitably a quite dilute version of the mother society—especially if the colonizers have emigrated because of rejection of aspects of their cultures, such as powers and symbols of rank or aspects of their religion. Thus there is a *cultural* founder effect just as there is a *genetic* one.

Cultural simplification over time with abandonment of increasingly irrelevant or difficult-to-maintain traits (a "reducing tradition") often occurred as well, especially in pioneering situations—as in the case of the pronounced simplification of European culture on the American frontier, in which a relatively small proportion of Old World traits was successfully transferred or maintained. Losses, as well as adoptions of local native ways, plus ad-hoc innovations, quickly differentiate pioneer offshoots of a culture, making tracing undocumented origins back to specific source areas sometimes difficult or impossible. Too, ships frequently carried crews composed of members of more than one ethnicity, a fact that would further differentiate the homogenizing immigrant cultural manifestation from any one particular homeland culture.

As I have suggested, some New World absences could also be a result of foreigners deliberately not sharing their advantage-conveying or esoteric knowledge with the natives, preferring to retain their "edge." In other cases, the locals might not have possessed the technological or conceptual sophistication to enable them to adopt a new technology or philosophy, or the new item might in some other way not have fit into the existing cultural or physical environment. Or, the trait might have been imperfectly understood and have been altered through reinterpretation. Diffusion in trading situations might well be limited by language barriers, security precautions, custom, monopolies, and use of middlemen or even silent barter.

In sum, it is clear that (1) cultural spreading is a highly selective process, with many traits not being offered and many of those that are offered being rejected for a variety of reasons, some obvious, some unascertainable; (2) in the processes of adoption and adaptation, accepted traits are often altered beyond ready identification as to their specific foreign sources; and (3) for the most part, scholars who have contended that absences disprove pre-Columbian contacts have not adequately thought things through, especially in light of the many absences within parts of the admittedly interconnected Old World. Absences are significant, and there are certainly reasons for them, reasons worth trying to identify, but lack of contact is not required to account for them, and failure to spread on the part of one item does not necessarily preclude spread on the part of another. In fact, lack of contact not only cannot be proven by evoking absences, lack of contact cannot be demonstrated by any means, and independence may never legitimately be assumed, only considered more or less probable on the basis of available evidence.

Separate but Unequal: Why Unbalanced Absences?

One other issue needs to be explored here: the implications of the many Old World culture traits absent in the New in contrast to the paucity of New World traits not found in the Old. Diffusionists have noted that if the peoples of the New World had been as independently inventive as the isolationist position implies, then one might expect to find among them either most of the missing Old World traits as well or, alternatively, important New World inventions that were absent or late in the Old World. As Douglas Fraser wrote,

> Apart from platinum working, there are remarkably few [exclusively New World traits]; these include the stirrup-spouted vessel, whistling jars, [the] stepped-fret pattern [in art], porcupine quill work, hammocks, certain specialized weaving processes, and a variety of natural and agricultural products [like the tobacco and rubber complexes, which depend on the native flora]. Interestingly enough, the majority of these traits appear to derive not from New World high-culture centers, as we might expect, but from the more primitive American societies. This goes in the face of [isolationist Erland] Nordenskiöld's . . . own observation that "the higher the development of a civilization, the greater the probability that new inventions will be made independently."[19]

While we may add to Fraser's list a handful of other seemingly unique New World items (for example, duck decoys in North America's Great Basin, acid etching of shell in southern Arizona, full fluting of spear points probably beginning in eastern North America, lacrosse and shinny sports equipment in North America, the gourd-and-cord "telephone" in Peru, freeze-drying in the Andes, the poncho in Nuclear America, and drawstring garments such as the hooded parka and the kayak coat in the Arctic), we may also in fact whittle down his list of exclusively New World traits. Infant hammocks are used in Indonesia,

Central Asia, and elsewhere. Stirrup-spouted vessels occur at scattered places in Africa and in the archaeology of Jōmon Japan. For centuries the stepped-fret pattern has been used as a design element in textiles among various Iranian- and Turkic-speaking Central and Southwest Asian groups, and variants are attested in the fifth-century BC Scythian Pazaryk finds of the Altai Mountains, on a pile textile fragment from Iraq of the third century BC to third century AD, in a first- to second-century carpet fragment from China's Xinjiang Province, and from Egypt circa AD 400.[20] Another variant is known from contemporary Tibeto-Burman speakers of central Nepal.

Why did Old World populations produce so many, many more innovations? Several factors may have contributed to this imbalance. First, Afroeurasia is simply vaster than the Americas, had a much larger population and a correspondingly greater number of potential and intercommunicating innovators, and was more urbanized (cities being principal centers of innovation).[21] Apart from cultivated plants, transoceanic cultural transfer seems largely to have been from the Eastern Hemisphere to the Western rather than the reverse or a more or less equal exchange. The Americas were very distant from what may well have been the world hearth of civilizational innovation in southwestern Asia as well as from the secondary hearth of North China and failed to receive many of the Old World's innovations.

This asymmetry has additional implications. Other than certain cultigens, Native Americans had little to contribute to Old World societies that the latter did not already have. Too, most New World societies lacked deepwater sailing craft, which may account for the fact that the majority if not almost all of the proposed transoceanic voyaging would have been initiated in the Old World. Arriving foreigners and their practices could be observed and copied by the Indians, but without Native Americans reciprocally arriving in numbers in Afroeurasia, people of that land mass would have had no comparable opportunity to learn from the denizens of the Americas (unless numerous Amerinds were transported back home).[22]

The Mystery of the Missing Artifacts

Truth shall spring out of the earth.
—Psalms 85:11

The wakes of watercraft are ephemeral and do not endure to give witness to their makers' passages. Thus other indications of voyaging and contacts must be sought. In this quest, we turn first to archaeology—keeping in mind, though, that, as the archaeologist Betty Meggers put it, "only a minute fraction of the archaeological residue of any culture has ever been collected, with the result that significant information about an extinct configuration may have survived but not been encountered."[1]

One archaeological genre of proof of contact, direct or indirect, is the presence of "trade goods": diagnostic artifacts—that is, distinctly characteristic ones—of the donor culture, found in the archaeology of the recipient (or reciprocal) culture. A perennial objection to the idea of early transoceanic influences in the New World—especially on the part of artifact-focused archaeologists—is the alleged absence of Old World objects in ancient American archaeological sites. If significant pre-Columbian contacts had really taken place, it is often asserted, at least a *few* objects of Old World provenience should appear in New World sites. That they do not, the argument continues, shows that such contacts are imaginary or, at very most, were minimal and had no perceptible influence. Where people go, it is contended, they go carrying objects characteristic of their cultures, inevitably trading some of these to the natives, interring certain ones with their dead, and losing others, some of which will later be discovered by archaeologists. "Show us the artifacts, and then we'll talk," seems to be the position of many. Let us consider, then, the oft-asked question: If there were contacts, then where are the artifacts?[2]

The first thing to note is, "In archaeology, you find what you seek,"[3] that if you don't look for indications of pre-Columbian foreign artifacts, there is a good chance that either you will not find them or will reject their genuineness. Similar lack of looking was long the case with respect to pre-Clovis human presence in the Western Hemisphere (see below). In addition, as the Canadian archaeologist of the Arctic Robert McGhee underlined, "The problem of archaeology is that the discoveries are of randomly preserved occurrences, and it sheds only narrow and scattered beams of light into a large and murky expanse of time and space."[4] Too, archaeological investigation, although intensive in some regions of both Old and New worlds, has barely scratched the surface, as it were, elsewhere, and some vast regions are essentially unknown from this point of view. Thus our information is incomplete, sometimes woefully so, for that reason alone. But there are other factors that limit the recoverable data and their interpretation even where thorough, high-quality excavation has been accomplished.

Rotten Luck: Bias in Preservation

An artifact in the archaeological sense is a human-made material object, formed by reduction and/or construction. In order to exist as evidence, it must have in some form survived the centuries or millennia since the moment of its deposition in the site. But every site has a subsequent history, "involving a wide assortment of organismic and physical agents seemingly bent on shuffling, sorting, scattering, or otherwise transmogrifying the past. . . . The archaeological record, of course, consists of what is left."[5]

Some materials preserve well under the majority of conditions: most notably, stone objects, fired ceramics (the archaeologists' beloved potsherds), and gold and platinum objects. Additional metals may survive in varying degree, and sometimes shell, bone, teeth, and ivory do as well. Other materials decay or otherwise break down over time unless extraordinary conditions for preservation exist—as in the desiccating sands of the virtually rainless Atacama Desert of South America or other regions possessing extremely dry climates such as those of the Sahara and Inner Asia; or in certain dry caves or in dry, safe storage rooms as in isolated Tibetan monasteries; in subaqueous anaerobic/reducing environments in marshes, swamps, bogs, and certain deep-sea situations; under anaerobic mudslides; or in permafrost or ice. These perishables include items made of most organic materials: wood, bark, leaves, fiber, horn, skin, hair, chitin, and feathers, as well as foodstuffs and so forth, and are subject to fungal and bacterial decay as well as to destruction by insects and rodents—not to mention by heat and ultraviolet light; wind abrasion; salts, acids, alkalines, and other reactive chemicals; freezing water; and various other agents of deterioration.

Although imprints of some of these perishables on other, lasting materials (for example, pottery) are found occasionally, or partial preservation occurs through charring or by incidental impregnation with a preservative substance such as a metallic salt, in the main we do not find these things present in most exposed sites, especially in humid climates. An example is the fact that we have no surviving textiles from ancient Babylonia or Assyria or, except for some cloth in a tomb in the Crimea, from the ancient Greeks or from the early Olmec, Mayan, or Mexican cultures. Had we not the literary and artistic attestation of this material's use, we would be ignorant of its importance in all these places (although in some cases we could infer its *presence* from archaeological spindle whorls, loom weights, and textile-impressed potsherds). Another instance is the blowgun/poisoned dart, Amazonia's quintessential weapon; based on archaeology alone, we would have no idea of its existence, much less it key role, in the rain forest. Too, unless they were lost or became grave goods, metal objects tended to be melted down for reuse of the material after they became worn out, broken, or obsolete. Building stones and even marble statues were often cannibalized for new construction or were calcined to produce lime.

Thus the range of kinds of artifacts likely to be found after any great lapse of time is severely restricted. Further, many sites are subject to continuing erosion, and over time even nonperishable artifacts will be removed from context and dispersed or destroyed. As the Australian archaeologist Peter Bellwood summed it up, "the problem may have more to do with sampling and survival than a true absence."[6]

Much of what we know about past Old World material culture comes from documents rather than from objects. For instance, on the basis of actual remains, we would not know that the plow and wheeled carts were present in ancient Mesopotamia. However, records of these items survive on clay tablets used for inventory keeping and the like. In the near absence of such records for the pre-Columbian Americas, a very great deal may have escaped detection.

Aside from ordinary stone tools and broken ceramics, a very significant percentage of portable human-made objects found in archaeological sites are recovered from burials. Although in some cases foreign objects, especially items of tribute, might be considered special and suitable for interment with the deceased, it might more often be the case that such objects did not fit into the ritually prescribed categories of funerary furniture and accordingly were excluded.

Additional factors play a role. Despite a historically attested vigorous ancient Mesopotamian trade with Harappan South Asia, for instance, other than a very few stone seals nothing in Indus Valley archaeology attests this, since—as we know from documents—Mesopotamian exports were mainly "invisible" goods such as foodstuffs and woolens, which leave no diagnostic trace. Similarly, during the second and third centuries AD, Roman ships reached China at least three times, and the Roman Empire had overland trade relations with that state, but Roman finds in China are very few. The eleventh- and twelfth-century Jewish records from the Cairo geniza (a repository for written materials, whose discard was prohibited by religion) indicate that invisible goods, especially plant products, also dominated the Indian Ocean trade at that much later period. Goods involved included spices, aromatics, dye products, and varnishing plants; ambergris; raw metals; textiles; pearls, beads, and cowry shells;

shoes and other leatherwork; Chinese porcelain, Yemenite stone pots, and African ivory; and coconuts and timber.[7] Of these, only two or three are both culturally diagnostic and nonperishable.

Although Ancient Classical trade and early medieval exchange between Egypt, India, Persia, and East Africa were brisk for centuries, very little in the way of pre-Islamic diagnostic artifacts has been unearthed in East Africa.[8]

All that remains of Byzantine and Sassanid overland trading expeditions to China are a few gold coins left in oases along the way. Without these, the outstanding historical importance of the Silk Road would be artifactually unattested. The sole significant import to the Roman Empire from the East seems to have been silks, and so, with the exception of a few Asian souvenirs, there is essentially no trace of the South and East Asiatic trade in intensively investigated Roman archaeology.[9] Were it not for written records, we would be ignorant of this supremely significant East–West exchange.

Also to be pointed out is the distressing fact that amateur pothunters and professional looters have removed huge quantities of otherwise surviving artifacts from sites; who knows what critically informative items may have disappeared from scholarly purview owing to this? Such digging at very least disturbs a site's stratigraphy—the layering that allows objects to be dated and that reveals the objects' association with other objects at the site (see below).

Discovery and Diagnosticity

Naturally, to be informative any foreign portable artifact that may exist must first be discovered, which, in light of the presumed rarity of such items and the low ratio between numbers of excavations and numbers of sites, may be the biggest obstacle of all. This results in what the Canadian archaeologist Paul Tolstoy has termed "the vanishingly small sampling fractions, which guarantee the absence of relatively rare items from our collections."[10]

Further, to be useful in signaling outside influences, an artifact must be diagnostic of the alien culture. As David H. Kelley observed, "Part of the solution to the problem [of lack of artifacts] may lie in incorrect assumptions about the recognizability of foreign artifacts."[11] Provenience is obvious enough if the item is as distinctive as a Mickey Mouse watch or a toy inscribed "Made in occupied Japan." However, most artifacts that a culture produces are not that characteristic. Some kinds of items are nearly ubiquitous and so tell little about possible origins. Others, even if less widely distributed in the world, have no particular qualities that link them to this or that culture; if an archaeologist found one in a site, unless the item was of a clearly foreign material or was obviously anomalous to the kind of culture represented, the excavator might have no reason to suppose that it came from anywhere else and might well simply interpret it as a previously unknown type of artifact produced by the native society that occupied that site. Even some well-known shared types of artifacts that are both distinctive and essentially identical are simply assumed by most to be of independent origin in the two areas concerned. A case in point is that of the bark-cloth beaters of Indonesia's Sulawesi and those of Mexico.[12]

Archaeologists must scramble to keep up with the literature concerning their own specialties and regions, and, understandably, in few cases are conversant with anything beyond the rudiments of the artifactual suites of neighboring regions, much less those of the hemisphere opposite that in which they work. Further, many of the Asian areas suggested as sources of transoceanic travelers are peripheral to main centers of civilizations, and their archaeologies have been little studied. In other words, unless an object's exoticity were awfully obvious, as with, say, a lapis lazuli bead in Mississippi, a multiarmed, elephant-headed Ganesh sculpture in Mexico, or a steel sword inscribed SPQR in Peru, it might well not be recognized as an import. If the average Americanist archaeologist of the eastern United States were to unearth an ancient chert projectile point made in Africa, for instance, would he or she even consider the possibility that it was of extrahemispheric origin, much less recognize its African provenience?[13] Thus mere artifactual identity is not enough; for simpler items, even if one should happen to recognize identity one can easily assume that different groups could have, and did, come up with the same form independently. The distinctiveness of an imported item might not need to be as great as the Mickey Mouse watch mentioned, but it would have to be great enough that almost anyone would agree that the probability of duplicate innovation was tiny. Further, in most archaeologists' eyes any reservation concerning the pre-1492 dating of the site being studied or concerning the stratigraphic position of the object itself would disqualify the item as evidence of pre-Columbian contact.

In sum, it is possible that a multitude of Old World artifacts *have* been excavated in impeccable pre-Columbian stratigraphic context but have simply not been recognized as such. Even so, should not at least a *few* really distinctive items left by putative foreigners have been unearthed? The answer to that depends on the factors we have mentioned as well as on others.

What kinds and quantities of items might have been involved in any transoceanic exchange? Generally speaking, the longer a journey, the fewer non-necessities will be taken along. Travel in small watercraft for thousands of miles with limited space for food and water supplies, as well as for possible cargo, would have precluded bringing a lot of extraneous objects. Nor would vital possessions or those conveying advantage readily be given or traded away. The Norse sagas, for instance, indicate that the Greenlanders were careful not to let swords, knives, and the like fall into the hands of North American natives. Even if trade were in view, only valuable and easily carried items would be transported. One would not expect a boatload of ceramics, for instance, to be prepared for a transpacific destination in ancient times. Traveling lightly, taking along (and usually taking home again) only required objects, would more likely have been the rule rather than the exception.

No serious transoceanic-contact hypotheses explicitly suggest that significant trade in diagnostic artifacts was going on. Much of any transoceanic contact might have been in the form of one-way intentional or unintentional, usually small-scale migrations. Other contacts, even if round-trip, might have involved noncommercial activities, such as religious proselytizing. If there was any trade, it was probably in materials that conformed to the principle of economic geography that states that high-value, low-bulk, easily preserved items would be the only ones worth making the trip for.

Possible trade products—all nonartifactual and most archaeologically perishable—include raw precious metals, valuable stones, showy bird feathers, and luxurious furs, as well as whale and walrus ivory, spices, drug plants, poisons, and dyestuffs. True, high-value-added items such as jewelry and luxury textiles could have been involved—although they may not have been—but again, to provide useful evidence these would still require both archaeological preservation and being distinctive enough to be recognized as alien. Would, for example, a piece of South Asian tie-dyed cotton cloth found in a thousand-year-old grave in Peru be visually distinguishable as foreign, especially since no specimens of that age have survived in Asia? Has any Oaxaca archaeologist even thought of comparing pre-Columbian Mixtec jewelry of Mexico to that of southern Asia?

Valuable Old World objects brought over (perhaps for devotional purposes) would probably in most cases have been taken home again if return voyages were involved. If their possessors instead remained in America, the objects might have been used to the point of wearing out; if the artifacts were made of valuable materials, these might well have been melted down, recarved, or otherwise recycled and thus have disappeared as forms recognizably from abroad.

Finally, even if all of the hypotheses of specific transoceanic intercultural contacts that have been proposed prove to be true—an improbable prospect—the number of preservable and distinctive artifacts likely to have been left in the opposite hemisphere is small enough that trying to find them today would indeed be looking for the proverbial needle in a haystack. If such items had existed and had entered native exchange networks, they would have been dispersed, reducing the likelihood that any one site would yield enough material to convince the excavator of its legitimacy as evidence of contact.

This notion is supported by cases, some described above, in which we know there has been contact or migration and yet there is little or no artifactual evidence. After describing a vigorous trade between the Roman Empire and India, a trade that burgeoned beginning in the first century BC and included Indian ambassadors to places in that empire as distant as Spain, the British archaeologist Sir Mortimer Wheeler noted that were it not for the impressive witness of history, the magnitude of this trade would certainly not have been guessed. Material relics of it in the West are few, very few, for the good and obvious reason that most of them were of an impermanent kind such as spices and textiles.[14] Genetics, religious practices, and oral tradition have demonstrated that Jewish male ancestors of Zimbabwe's Lemba people came there from Yemen, yet there is no artifactual indication in Lembaland of these Southwest Asian origins.[15] Genetics shows the Polynesian population of Easter Island to include a pre-Columbian American Indian component (see chapter 31), yet no corresponding artifacts have been unearthed. As for the New World, the Yale archaeologist Frank Hole wrote, "The notorious mystery of the Navaho [and Apache] intrusion into the [American] Southwest [from western Canada circa AD 1400] is a reminder that population movements can be demonstrated linguistically but are hard to track down archaeologically."[16]

A noted patron of and participant in US Southwest archaeology, Harold S. Gladwin, pointed out that we know that as recently as 1847, Brigham Young led his Mormon followers from Illinois to Utah, but if we did not have a written record of the journey and were compelled to rely solely on the material evidence left behind them, it would be impossible today, after only one hundred years, to trace their trail across the prairies or even prove that the movement had taken place (although plenty of artifactual evidence is to be found at their terminus).[17] Likewise, other than one William Clark graffito in Montana, the only archaeological evidence of the 1804–6 Lewis and Clark expedition that opened up half a continent is a handful of artifacts excavated at the Lower Portage Camp near Great Falls, Montana, a site found only after twelve years of searching; one button at Montana's Lolo Creek; plus a few possibles at Fort Clatsop, Oregon—and these at sites known in advance to exist. Too, how many artifacts left directly by the multitude of beaver-trapping mountain men of the earlier nineteenth century in the American West have been found in situ? Other than a few inscriptions, I cannot think of any.

Archaeologically recovered artifacts relating to Columbus's voyages (as opposed to settlements he established), Cortés's and Pizarro's conquests, and the Coronado expedition, as well as the wanderings of Cabeza de Vaca, are also scarce or absent, and, except for the last, we are speaking here of large expeditions with itineraries known to history, a fact that has inspired a concerted quest for their remains. Only after over two hundred years of on and off searching was the settlement called Villa de la Navidad that Columbus established in Haiti in 1492 identified, in 1977; otherwise, just a few seemingly relevant items have been found on Columbus's San Salvador (Watling Island).

The sixteenth-century Spanish conquistador Hernando de Soto and 600 men accompanied by 220 horses and a herd of hogs spent four years exploring what would become the Southeast of the United States—and discovered the Mississippi River. Only two sites have been found that can be associated with this expedition. One, near Bradenton, Florida, and thought by some to be de Soto's first winter's camp, was discovered only by accident. The other, in south-central Georgia, is an Indian village site containing a suite of early sixteenth-century European artifacts. Likewise, despite much searching only two campsites (most notably, a trove at Blanco Canyon, Texas) and two battle sites (at Hawikuh, on New Mexico's Zuni Indian Reservation, and at Piedras Marcadas Pueblo, near Santo Domingo, New Mexico) from Coronado's 1539–42 entrada into the American Southwest and Great Plains have been identified, although the Spanish army was accompanied by 1,000 Mexican Indians and 550 horses. Excavations even of well-established Spanish missions in the American Southwest, such as Hawikuh, Awatobi, and Pecos, yielded remarkably little in the way of Spanish religious artifacts, these churches having been emptied by fleeing clergy and then sacked by the Indians during the Pueblo Revolt of 1680.

The American historical archaeologist Jeffrey P. Brain has noted "the challenge of pinning down the initial European contacts and footholds, for they tended to be exceedingly fleeting and astonishingly fragile affairs which left little evidence in the archaeological record. It is a study of ephemera."[18] That statement refers not to Norse, Irish, Basque, Bristolian, Portuguese, or possible earlier European pre-Columbian contacts with the Americas, but with the early *post-Columbian* presence of Europeans of a mere half millennium or less ago. The ancient Irish presence in Iceland is known historically and from place-names, but so far no Hibernian artifacts have been unearthed. Likewise, no material evidence has been found of the ascetic Irish anchorites known to have preceded the Norse on the Faroe Islands.[19] Regarding the Anse aux Meadows, Newfoundland, site, Brain asserted, "it took an intensive search and excavation to establish the [existence of the] site. Had the site been reused, it is unlikely that its historical importance would ever have been revealed, so slender was the in-ground evidence. It is probably for this reason that no other Viking—or any other pre-Columbian European—site has ever been substantiated, never mind the ravings of an overly enthusiastic lunatic fringe."[20]

The Massachusetts avocational archaeologist James P. Whittall observed that the dry-stone structures of New England that he saw as being circa AD 600 in age and Celtic in origin have been disparaged as such owing to the lack of Celtic artifacts there and have been deemed Colonial-period root cellars and walls by critics, but Whittall also pointed out that no diagnostic *Colonial* artifacts have turned up at these sites, either. (A number of carbon-14 dates on such sites indicate considerable antiquity.)[21]

Douglas Fraser, however, made the point that, in any event, "the establishment of a relationship between two cultures hinges not on the demonstration of contact [as proved by objects] but of the impact as revealed in the cultural elements themselves. Otherwise the Buddha figures found in Scandinavian graves would be far more significant than in fact they are."[22] This is a typical diffusionist point of view; although it has much to be said for it, in part IV we will nevertheless consider the question of actual demonstration of contact, because contact is what creates opportunity for cultural transfer.

The Layered Look: Stratigraphic Context

As noted, even when clearly extrahemispheric objects *are* discovered in pre-1492 sites, they are generally rejected as evidence if they are not professionally unearthed in a clear pre-Contact stratigraphic position, that is, if they are found on the surface or appear unprovenienced, as on the market or in the hands of relic collectors. Whereas surface finds—mainly of locally produced potsherds and lithics (human-modified stone items)—are routinely utilized and accepted without question in archaeological surveys, finds of extrahemispheric objects—sometimes classed as "OOParts," out-of-place artifacts—are not; out of context means out of consideration (and a fair number have even been discarded). Thus the considerable quantity of Roman and Roman-period Hebrew coins that have turned up in and around Kentucky have generally been dismissed as having been lost by coin collectors (not notably careless with their precious possessions) or by other moderns—despite a certain consistency in dates and geographical distribution.[23] It would seem reasonable that a uniform criterion be applied to all surface finds, irrespective of expectability. However, many contend that extraordinary claims require extraordinary proofs. This higher bar placed in front of suggestions of long-distance contacts has been a frustration for diffusionists.

In some instances, the unearthing of what may prove to be genuine foreign-made objects has been thrown into confusion not only by the amateur status of the discoverers but also by postdiscovery exploitation of the finds by unscrupulous forgers who made and sold or planted copycat artifacts. This is potentially the case with the "Michigan relics" and Iowa's "Davenport relics," which have generally been dismissed in their entirety as frauds.[24]

What Kinds of Sites Might Have Been Involved?

Not all archaeological sites are equal. That is, sites are of many different kinds and may exist in a variety of different types of locations. Instances of trans-oceanic contacts naturally would have commenced along coasts, with any inland penetration most likely taking place via rivers. In general, seaside and riverside sites are less amenable to long-term preservation and/or detection than are upland sites. This is because certain geomorphic processes are commonly at work along shore or bank that do not affect, or affect to a lesser degree, places away from the water.

Waterside sites are more likely to be damp than are better-drained inland sites; thus, perishable artifacts will quickly disappear (except in anaerobic wetlands, which are not normally selected for settlement). Then, if the sites are very near the sea, coastal processes may either erode away the site, by the action of waves, including tsunamis (common around the Pacific Rim), or cover the site, by dune accretion. One instance of removal by erosion is the disappearance of most of the monuments set up along the African coast by Portuguese explorers during the AD 1400s.

Very old sites along strands have been particularly susceptible to inundation, owing to eustatic/steric sea-level rises to a bit above present levels, which occurred during the Early Holocene, peaked about 2000 BC, fell as postglacial isostatic rebound (land rise owing to removal of the weight of the Pleistocene ice sheets) was echoed by depression in northerly sea floors, and rose again during the Medieval Warm Period. During the subsequent Little Ice Age, stormy conditions caused extensive coastal erosion.[25] In parts of the Arctic and subarctic, rebound has lifted old strands, resulting in raised formerly coastal sites becoming hidden by terrestrial vegetation. In other situations—as where tectonic downwarping or deltaic sag has occurred (as in North Africa)—coastal subsidence has left former shoreline sites under water.

Regarding river-floodplain sites, if seasonal flooding does not wash away remains of any camps, the annual increment of sediment deposited by receding floodwaters will soon bury any such remains, and if they end up being below the plow zone, the likelihood of their later being unearthed by archaeologists is almost zero in most cases. Along streams in semiarid regions, cycles of alternating channel trenching and filling may leave little to be found a few centuries after a place was occupied. Of course, not all sites of foreign origin would be in such vulnerable locations. Nevertheless, on the whole, sites of overseas contacts are more likely to have been obliterated or hidden by the forces of nature than are native sites.

In consideration of all of the above, regarding potential Old World artifacts in the New World we may pose the following summarizing questions: how many such artifacts would have been brought by foreign visitors in the first place; of those brought, how many would have ended up in stratified archaeological deposits; of those, how many would have survived the forces of decay, erosion, animal and human disturbance, and so forth; of those, how many would have been found in situ by professional archaeologists; of those, how many would be distinctively diagnostic of their cultures of origin; of those, how many would actually be recognized as being of foreign origin? In pondering this, we may gain a better perspective on the low probability of our finding and identifying artifacts imported from the other hemisphere and on the hubris of those who talk as though the probability would be high. It took some 120 years from the Danish scholar C. C. Rafn's first proposal of Norse contacts with North America for a North American Norse habitation site to be found (which finally convinced doubting archaeologists), and the discovery occurred only because the discoverers believed that it should be there and therefore went and looked. But because of their presuppositions—that there *is* no locus in quo, scene of the "crime"— few archaeologists bother to look for pre-Norse overseas-contact sites.[26]

We may also wonder why *nonmaterial* cultural commonalities shared by the Old World and the New, such as unlikely beliefs or practices, should carry less weight than do material objects, other than the fact that these, being nonmaterial, cannot always be documented for pre-Columbian times. Diagnostic artifacts such as pottery may be an expectable indicator over relatively short distances, but when very long distances are involved only ideas (such as technical concepts and folklore) may travel and be transplanted.

What *Has* Been Found?

Despite their relative dearth, it is nevertheless the case that a fair number of clearly pre-1500 Old World portable artifacts (such as Chinese and Hindu figurines, European swords, Mediterranean coins, and a Tahitian breadfruit-pounder) *have* been reported in the New World, mostly as surface finds and by people other than archaeologists.[27] The problem in almost all of these cases is lack of archaeological context. As mentioned, unless an item is found by a professional archaeologist in undisturbed and datable stratigraphic context, it does not count as real evidence—at least if it is as rare and controversial as an extrahemispheric object. There is good reason for this not counting: how can anyone be sure that the artifact, unequivocally old though it may itself be, was not accidentally dropped on the site last week, carried down a hole by a pack rat, or even planted as a hoax. There are simply not enough of these reported finds to make those possibilities seem completely unlikely. Too, the question of authenticity is frequently raised: may not the object(s) in question themselves be fake(s)?

Under a Colonial chimney in Virginia, archaeologists unearthed a Paleolithic European-style stone knife, made of French chert. Although known to have been in place for three centuries, the artifact is not directly datable (see chapter 26). The larger part of an Eastern Zhou period (770–221 BC) Chinese cast-bronze buckle was found beneath a millennium-old Inupiat house site on Alaska's Seward Peninsula,[28] but transpacific carriage is not required to explain its presence, only trans–Bering Strait carriage. Some archaeological finds of iron objects, presumably of Asian origin, have been made in sites of Alaska's Old Bering Sea and Ipiutak cultures, beginning about AD 200–500 and AD 350, respectively, as well as among later pre-Columbian Inuit, all of which could reflect either trade across Bering Strait, the arrival of drifted Asian boats, and/or seaborne exchange—as could some seeming cases of pre-1492 Chinese-coin finds on the North Pacific coast.

Quite a few Norse items have been found at scattered sites in the eastern Arctic and subarctic of Canada, especially at L'Anse aux Meadows, Newfoundland, and in Baffin Island, and the archaeological community generally accepts the L'Anse site as a genuine European settlement in the pre-Columbian New World (although not according it any great influence on native peoples). Too, the Newfoundland archaeologist Patricia D. Sutherland has excavated what appears to have been a medieval Norse shore station on Baffin Island, and the Nanook site has yielded a stone crucible used to manufacture bronze. In addition, a single late eleventh-century Norwegian penny has been unearthed in a twelfth-century Indian site in coastal Maine (see below).[29]

The Toluca Valley Roman Head

The only other reasonably well known exception to the seeming general lack of diagnostic pre-Norse portable artifacts is a small, bearded ceramic head whose face looks definitely Caucasoid and which was excavated during the 1930s, under what appear to have been unexceptionable circumstances, from a pyramid burial of latest pre-Conquest age (circa AD 1476–1510) in the Toluca Valley, state of México, by the respected Mexican archaeologist José García Payón. At the 1960 International Congress of Americanists in Vienna, the diffusionist art historian of Asia Robert Heine-Geldern announced that this head was Roman, of about AD 220. If the Roman identification is correct—experts currently agree that it is, and the classicist Bernard Andreae placed it in the Severian period, AD 193–235—this object stands as the only fairly widely accepted pre-Norse Old World portable artifact found in the Americas outside of Alaska under demonstrably controlled conditions in a pre-Contact context.

Thermoluminescence (TL) dating imprecisely places the object's manufacture between about 870 BC and AD 1270, ruling out a Colonial age but not tying it firmly to the Roman epoch (although three of the four TL dates range between 449 ± 473 BC and A.D. 460 ± 333). There is one slight caveat, however. Although pre-Cortesian, the site's maximum probable date range includes eighteen years of post-1492 time, during which it is at least barely conceivable—although very highly unlikely—that such an object brought from Spain to the Caribbean as a keepsake could have been lost, stolen, or traded to Indians and, in native exchange networks, to have found its way across the Gulf and into a Central Mexican tomb.[30]

One instance is a very low number, but (were it not for the caveat) it would be sufficient to show that at least one pre-1492 non-Norse transoceanic contact occurred (it is wholly implausible that the head was carried or traded group to group overland and via Bering Strait). However, the find tells little else. In the opinion of David H. Kelley, it has almost no value either for the study of culture history or for the study of cultural process. We do not know whether the figurine head was brought by one lost Roman or whether it had passed through a hundred intermediary hands and traveled widely before being brought to America.[31] (Heine-Geldern thought that it might have come via Vietnam.) García also mentioned a few other similar finds, but their exact proveniences and present whereabouts are cloudy.

One may mention the reported 1841 finding of a New Zealand Maori *mere onewa* (war club) in a pre-Incaic grave in North Coast Peru, as well as similar (but poorly documented) finds in widely scattered locations elsewhere in western South and North America.[32] Too, in 1957 a cylinder seal was dug up at the Formative (Neolithic) site of Chiapa de Corzo in Mexico, which the noted Semiticist William F. Albright agreed carried a few degenerate Egyptian hieroglyphic cartouches.[33]

The Palos Verdes Anchors

Then there are the Palos Verdes anchor (and other) stones. They are of Chinese style, and, during the 1970s, divers found numbers of them in an area off Southern California. Anthropologists Larry J. Pierson and James R. Moriarty III thought them very old (on the basis of manganese deposits) and thought that at least two of them were of stone other than local but akin to rock occurring in South China. However, the historian Frank Frost asserted that Santa Barbara geologists had determined the objects all to be made of the local Monterey Formation shale and proposed that they represented the activity of nineteenth-century Chinese immigrant fishermen. So far, no definitive evidence of their age and provenience has been forthcoming, despite calls for full investigation.[34]

The Bat Creek Bracelet

A group of artifacts that in 1889 a worker for the Smithsonian's National Museum of Natural History found in the Bat Creek Mound in East Tennessee has generated considerable controversy. In brief, under a skull in the mound was a small fragment of siltstone on which appeared an inscription in Hebrew, reading "for Judea" or "for the Judeans"—a passage that was initially misidentified as written in the Cherokee syllabary. A study performed by a pair of twenty-first-century petrographers found that patination in the grooves of the inscription were consistent with centuries of burial in the mound. With the interment were wooden earspools impregnated with copper oxide from an adjacent pair bracelets made from heavily leaded yellow-brass. American Indians did not manufacture brass, but bracelets of the material were anciently produced in parts of the Old World, comparable ones having been manufactured in the Mediterranean world only during the first and second centuries AD. These particular objects from Bat Creek are usually explained as Colonial trade bracelets, which were common on the frontier. Then the economist J. Huston McCulloch had a carbon-14 test done on a sample from one of the copper-stained earspools, which yielded a range of highly probable dates of AD 32–769, consistent with the first- to second-century AD style of the Hebrew letters. So, pending additional tests, it appears that we have here potentially genuine Old World artifacts from a pre-Columbian archaeological site excavated by a professional (recognizing that in 1889 professional standards were not what they are today).[35]

Additional Inscribed Relics

There are many additional purported unearthings of other truly or possibly pre-Columbian foreign objects or objects made by foreigners in the New World. Among the more intriguing of these are the Bent (Silverbell) artifacts from near Tucson, a number of apparently ceremonial objects of lead carrying Latin inscriptions, some excavated under the supervision of the noted archaeologist Byron Cummings—and then abruptly dropped by him. To some—notably, the late American historian Cyclone Covey—these items reflect a ninth-century presence of Roman Jews; to others, they are post-Contact Masonic paraphernalia or outright twentieth-century fakes whose inscriptions were culled from a Latin textbook and which were cemented into the caliche in which they were found with plaster of paris.[36]

From the United States come the debated inscribed "Michigan relics"; the Davenport, Iowa, artifacts; the Hebrew-inscribed Newark, Ohio, "holy stones"; the Grave Creek and other Canaanite-inscribed portable stones from the Ohio River Valley; the Kensington Runestone; and many other writings on rocks. In

Figure 10.1. The Newport Tower, Rhode Island: medieval church or seventeenth-century mill? From Thomas Wentworth Higginson, *A Larger History of the United States of America to the Close of the Jackson Administration*, Harper and Brothers, 1885, p. 43.

South America, the collection of the late Father Carlo Crespi of Cuenca, Ecuador, includes myriad unprovenienced metal plates carrying Mediterranean written signs, and there are the not-well-sourced *fuente magna* ceramic bowl and the Pokotia Monolith from Bolivia's Titicaca basin, which carry Sumerian writing. All of these are, unsurprisingly, controversial. Their fuller evaluation awaits a second book.

Nonportable Artifacts

In addition to portable artifacts—the only ones that can actually be imported—one may also mention nonportable ones, produced on the spot in the New World. These are, for the most part, inscriptions on rock written in what a few consider to be Old World languages and alphabets—not elaborated on here. Then, there is the Newport Tower in Rhode Island (figure 10.1), which some think to be a church in medieval European style, and which others feel to have been English-built in the 1600s as a windmill. One writer has even proposed a Chinese origin.[37] Truly, investigations of transoceanic-contacts questions continue to produce a plenitude of ambiguities and controversies.

To recap, the almost complete dearth—so far—of recognized pre-Norse Old World portable artifacts found in situ (or even otherwise) in New World sites (or vice versa) raises questions worth addressing, but such a lacuna—even if real and not just apparent—by no means precludes important contacts having taken place. Still, in the absence of artifacts other kinds of evidence must be drawn upon.

Under the Carpet: Excluding and Nonreporting of Artifacts

Archaeologists demand artifacts. A catch-22 situation may arise when a seeming Old World artifact does turn up, for anomalous objects are sometimes assumed by excavators to be fakes, plants, or at very least intrusive OOPArts, and archaeologists and art historians have indeed on occasion been burned by fraudsters. As the Canadian archaeologist Grant Keddie has observed, "when North American archaeologists find porcelain, copper or iron artifacts they all too often assume that they date to the known post-contact period and eschew a careful attempt at verification."[38] Regarding a potentially Phoenician terracotta head of Caucasoid type found by an amateur along the Río Balsas in Guerrero, Mexico, the archaeologist George Vaillant wrote, "If it were of Old World origin, it must have been imported to Middle America after the Conquest of Mexico, since no contact with a high Old World culture has been established anterior to that time."[39]

Regrettably, too, the issue of failure even to report Old World materials found by archaeologists needs to be mentioned. Although it is obviously difficult to obtain information on this point, there is anecdotal indication that the occasional archaeologist will consider Old World artifacts found in his or her pre-1492 digs to be by definition physically intrusive (for example, brought down to a pre-Contact stratigraphic level by burrowing animals, deep plowing, frost turbation, or other means), because they *cannot* be pre-Columbian. Such objects are labeled intrusive or are not reported. In 1928, for example, the American Museum of Natural History archaeologist Ronald Olson found iron objects in an Indian midden on California's Santa Rosa Island, but, assuming all iron to be post-Contact, he did not mention the metal in his published report—his handwritten notes state, "A gopher must have put it there."[40]

The role of fear must also be mentioned. For instance, when the archaeologist Guy Mellgren found, in a prehistoric Indian midden, the fourteenth-century Norse billon coin mentioned above, he "refrained from publishing this find in order not to endure the inevitable scorn, disbelief, and ostracism that would have been heaped upon him by the archaeological profession. He did not wish to be accused of fraud and have his reputation besmirched. This was not the first or last time that an atypical genuine archaeological find would go unreported, for the same reason. George Carter, who knew of specific instances, told him in confidence by those involved, believed such losses have been significant."[41]

This is also true of archaeological specimens of Old World plants. For instance, in Margaret Towle's *The Ethnobotany of Pre-Columbian Peru*, there is a section titled "Excluded Species." These are Old World plants that she was convinced could not be pre-Columbian, so she rejected them as potentially real archaeological occurrences (but at least she listed them). Towle cited one report of the Southeast Asian mangosteen, but this "was brought to the New World . . . well after the period of discovery. There were two reports of the plantain, also a Southeast Asian domesticate. However, this Old World species was brought to America only after the European discovery," so the remains must have been misidentified, she asserted.[42] The Eurasian cucumber was also reported once, but Towle likewise relegated it to "Excluded Species" (see chapter 28).

In the case of tobacco leaves being discovered inside the mummy of the ancient Egyptian Pharaoh Ramses II, as described in chapter 29, the Egyptian government actually prohibited further investigation, presumably for political reasons. In the case of some possibly pre-Contact chicken bones (see chapter 26), an archaeo-orinthologist denied to George Carter that he had such bones. When the bones' existence was confirmed years later and Carter confronted him, the man explained his rationale: "I didn't want to encourage you in your madness, George," he said.[43]

Rio's Roman Wreck

Politics not infrequently plays a role in distortion and suppression of evidence. Fuller discussion must await a future book, but the case of Robert Marx and a seeming Roman wreck in Brazil is worth detailing here.

Brazil is home to many undated rock inscriptions translatable as Phoenician, Greek, Latin, or even Norse. In 1975, a diver reported retrieving ship's fragments as well as amphorae in the Rio Urumbo of Brazil's São Paulo state. They were allegedly Phoenician.

In 1976, a local diver discovered Roman-style amphorae on the bottom of the Bay of Guanabara, that marvelous harbor on whose shore lies Rio de Janeiro.[44] Over the years since the mid-1960s, fishermen had found more than fifty intact specimens of these liquid-storage jars. Beginning in 1979, Robert Marx, an American adventurer and underwater archaeological investigator, interviewed local divers and fishermen who had brought up such jars, and he examined two intact examples. He asked several oceanographers to independently examine the barnacles and other marine creatures on the containers, and the organisms were determined to be from Guanabara Bay and not from the Mediterranean and to have required centuries to develop; some of the encrustations carbon-dated to about AD 500.

In 1982, Marx dove on the site, where he found that most of the pottery fragments were cemented to the bottom rock by coral. He had experts investigate representative sherds. Radiocarbon dating put their age at around 2000 years ago, plus or minus 140 years, and thermoluminescence dating gave a nearly identical age. The leading expert on sourcing and dating amphorae, the University of Massachusetts classicist Elizabeth Lyding Will, concluded that the containers were of the second or third century AD, made at Roman Kouass, the ancient port of Zilis (present Dehar Jedid) on the Atlantic coast of Morocco to the southwest of Tangier.

Using sub-bottom-profiling sonar, the MIT electrical engineer and Jacques-Yves Cousteau collaborator Harold E. Edgerton identified two targets that were consistent with their being parts of a wreck. Later probing by Marx verified the presence of wood. "Shortly after Edgerton's report [on the sonar findings] appeared, the Portuguese and Spanish governments expressed great concern to the Brazilian government about the possibility that this discovery could displace Cabral as the discoverer of Brazil and Columbus as the discoverer of the New World"[45] and could—as claimed Italy's ambassador—give unrestricted rights of citizenship to Italian immigrants to Brazil. Soon afterward, the Brazilian government, initially calling the wreck Phoenician, declared the site to be a restricted zone and had a dredge barge dump tons of earth atop it for "protection"— protection of the reputations of the Renaissance explorers, it would seem, and to squelch any claims to Brazil that Italy might make. Following this literal cover-up, all further underwater archaeology in Brazilian waters was banned.

Ilha do Sal in the Cape Verde Islands off westernmost Africa was a major premodern salt source, and Marx found thousands of Phoenician and Roman potsherds on the beaches there. He has speculated that storm or current may have carried Mediterranean-origin ships across the Atlantic to Brazil from those islands. Fishermen around Rio claimed to have brought up life-sized legs made of marble as well as a bronze statue. The latter was broken up and sold as scrap metal. Many Classical coins and a Roman bronze fibula have also turned up.

Another alleged Roman wreck—this time found in Venezuela in 1987 and dating to about 49 BC to AD 79—has been reported as well, although details are lacking. There, again, "local tempers intervened" and caused the find to be suppressed.[46] In this context, a hoard of Roman coins (the latest struck in the fourth century AD and now at the Smithsonian) was found on a Venezuelan beach, but it seems never to have been fully written up.[47] A Spanish-style shipwreck, containing amphorae dated to the thirteenth century AD, was discovered off Honduras's Roatan Island. When the dates came in, the divers' permits were revoked, and no further investigation has been allowed.[48]

Quite a number of amateur diffusionists perceive nonreporting and the like as a conspiracy of silence and suppression on the part of professional archaeologists. There is too much fractiousness among professionals for any true conspiracy to be maintained; what is manifested is a belief system that is part of the culture of the discipline, as well as, in some cases, rampant nationalism that rejects the entire notion of foreign influences.[49]

Nonreporting is a problem that has not been confined to matters concerning transoceanic contacts. In the equally contentious area of the antiquity of humans in the Americas, "in most cases excavations never went deeper [than Clovis levels] because no site was then accepted as older than Clovis, the supposed first New World culture."[50] Worse, several pre-Clovis sites went unreported because the scientists feared for their reputations.[51] The career of at least one prominent early-humans archaeologist was wrecked because of her stance.[52] Under these kinds of circumstances, the accepted record may be badly skewed by the effects of presupposition and of fear. In such a climate, a hypothesis cannot be believed in until there is evidence for it. As it is thought that no such evidence can exist, no one looks for it or reports it or correctly interprets it if it does turn up. This is why a possibly incorrect existing paradigm can remain unassailably set in concrete.

The Supposed Silence of the Historical Record

In this distracted globe. . . .
I'll wipe away all trivial fond records,
All saws of books, all forms, all pressures past.
—William Shakespeare, *Hamlet*, 1:5, 1599–1601

While archaeologists require physical remains as evidence, for historians the written record is *the* evidence. It is through study of documents that standard history is written. Owing to a dearth of such records, many historians give up on pre-Columbian America, ignoring oral traditions, archaeology, and geographic distributions as avenues for reconstructing the past. According to the Swedo-Finnish artist and historian of ships Björn Landström, "The Egyptians and, even more so, the Phoenicians were good mariners, and their ships were seaworthy enough to have taken them over the seas with the trade winds. But even if they did actually cross the ocean, there is no record that any of them returned to tell the tale, and as long as we have no written records or other [concrete] forms of evidence, that possibility has no place in the history of exploration."[1]

As I once heard a Navajo woman say to a historian skeptical of oral tradition: "You historians think that if it isn't written, it didn't happen."

Among students of history, a common if naive assertion is: If there *had* been ancient ocean crossings, these would be reflected in the historical record, and that record is silent. The assumption is that anything as dramatic and as potentially important as crossing an uncharted ocean and coming upon a new, exotic, populated, and resource-rich continent would have received wide notice back home or would at least have been recorded.

Reality is more complicated. One must indeed acknowledge that very little in the way of unequivocal written records bearing on pre-Columbian contacts has turned up so far, but there are a number of reasons why this should not be seen as astonishing even if we posit that many such voyages took place. First of all, historians have hardly yet mined all the extant written records that might have a bearing on the issue at hand. Places such as the General Archive of the Indies in Seville and the Vatican Library in Rome continue to hold great quantities of material as yet unstudied by modern scholars.

Nonexistent, Unreadable, and Unrevealing Records

Obviously, no written record can be expected for nonliterate societies, many of which are potential source areas for contacts. Equally obviously, one-way accidental, missionary, colonizing, or other voyages would leave no records, in their areas of origin, of overseas disembarkations. Beyond this, important contact involving return voyages can and has taken place without leaving any surviving written record, even in cases of quite literate cultures. The fact that there were contacts among ancient Greece, India, and China is widely accepted (on the basis of art and archaeology), despite the near absence of historical accounts. Indeed, one may doubt that there would remain any record of the famous and influential thirteenth-century travels of the Venetian Marco Polo and his relatives had Polo not been captured and incarcerated by the Genoese upon his return to Italy from China, dictating his *Travels* to his fellow prisoner Rustichello, who, fortuitously, was a writer, while languishing in jail with nothing else to do. Of the fifteenth-century "discoverer" of continental North America John Cabot, nothing he may have written down survives; even his burial place is unknown.

As mentioned, in ancient times most parts of the world were illiterate or essentially so, and no written records are expectable. In some other areas (for example, Indianized Southeast Asia), where writing *was* practiced, ability to use it was not widespread and it was employed in restricted ways, so that very little was produced and what *was* produced is of limited value for our purposes. Then, it is the case that we cannot yet (and may never) read some writings. For example, little progress has been made on deciphering Etruscan inscriptions, which use the Greek alphabet to convey an unknown language, and the important Indus Valley script remains unreadable. Mayan writing was deciphered only during the late twentieth century, and much remains to be read.

The Years Take Their Toll: Deterioration of Records

Written documents of yesteryear have had a low rate of survival, a consequence of the many destructive forces that may act upon archaeological and historical materials. One instance was the 1875 explosion of the ship *Magenta*, which was carrying to France 2,080 Punic stelae, many inscribed, from the ruins of Carthage. Although the bulk were eventually recovered by divers, almost four hundred still rest on the bottom of the bay at Toulon.

Before the advent of printing, the majority of documents existed as unique or in only a limited number of exemplars, and so their contents were vulnerable to total loss. Written records on relatively imperishable materials such as clay tablets, potsherds (ostraca), stone, metal, and, to a lesser extent, shell, bone, and ivory, are, with the occasional important exception (such as in the library of Ashur-bani-pal), typically brief and usually involve texts that are lists of or dedications to deities, ritual formulas, formulaic proclamations of power, commemorative honorifics, king lists, records of military events, diplomatic letters, observations of nature, omen lists, or simple inventories. Historical epics have survived in fragments only.

Most longer works (as well as many letters and the like) were normally written on (expensive) papyrus or on animal-skin leather, parchment, or vellum (Mediterranean area); on paper/bark cloth (China, Mesoamerica), textiles (silk in China), or palm leaves (southern Asia) or bamboo splints, wood, or bark (various regions); or on wax tablets (Mediterranean area). Except in hyperarid desert environments and in dry caves (as in Egypt and in parts of Palestine and Inner Asia), these perishable materials seldom survived the centuries. The Jewish historian Josephus (first century AD) wrote that the Phoenicians had kept voluminous written records, including ones on geography, but beyond a few tens of thousands of mostly formulaic votive and funerary inscriptions on stone, not one original Phoenician document survives today. Even the majority of Middle Eastern records on clay tablets were destroyed or became illegible with time. Of those that have been recovered, half, an estimated 100,000, remain untranslated.

Although large numbers of documents (for example, 113 of Sophocles's plays, all of Didymus Chalcenterus's circa 3,500 books) are known about only by reference in other works, quite a few Classical Greek and Roman texts (or at least fragments of same) *are* known and are relied upon by historians. However, these are not the original documents, written in their authors' hands. In almost every case they are copies of copies, at many removes from the writers' originals, in most instances not dating to before the High Middle Ages. The books that were reproduced and whose contents were thus preserved were great works of literature, science, geography, history, and philosophy, not (with a few notable exceptions) records of individual, nonofficial voyages of exploration, trade, or colonization.

Even many of the key great works did not survive—for example, the thirty books of the Greek Ephoros's geography and Eratosthenes's *Measurement of the Earth* and *Geographica* and his innovative and highly influential map of the known world—and are revealed to moderns only through quoted passages, synopses, reconstructions, or mere references by other ancient authors. Six-sevenths of the known works of Pliny the Elder are extinct, and but a small fraction of the two thousand or so works he consulted to write his *Natural History* have survived. (Manuscript survival rates greatly increased beginning in Late Antiquity, when vellum replaced more perishable papyrus.)

The contents of most ancient libraries were destroyed, the one partial exception being that of the Assyrian king Ashur-bani-pal, whose "books" were written on clay tablets that were preserved by baking in, rather than being destroyed in, the fire that consumed the library building. Most of the perishable documents of antiquity disappeared through some combination of accidental fire, water damage, mold, earthquake, use of corrosive iron-gall inks, wear and tear, putrefaction, insect damage, or deliberate destruction or other disposal, including for the making of new paper. Many a manuscript went up in flames as fuel, was used as packing material and then discarded, was made into papier-mâché objects (cartonnage), or suffered some similar fate, especially during eras of incursions by illiterate barbarians or under the sway of zealotry on the part of adherents of scriptural religions (for example, the Roman Catholic Church's destruction of documents deemed heretical, epitomized by Savonarola's "bonfire of the vanities"), or when bitter rivals overran literate but pagan and competing civilizations and destroyed their libraries and archives—for example, in Athens, Alexandria (see below), Carthage, Jerusalem, Rome, Islamic Iberia, Christian Britain (the Viking destructions of monasteries like Lindisfarne, Iona, and Lambay, and, later, Henry VIII's burning of English monastery libraries), and Buddhist Southeast Asia. In the fifth century AD, the imperial library of Constantinople and its 100,000 or so books were destroyed by rebels and by fire. Rebuilt, it was looted and burned in 1203–4 during the vicious Fourth Crusade. Following a second restoration, in 1453 the Turks demolished it once more, and over 120,000 volumes were lost. In modern times, France's Archives Nationales burned during the reign of Napoleon III.[2]

The Great Library of Alexandria and Its Destruction(s)

The great port city of Alexandria, Egypt, provides the classic example of what destruction may befall a place and its records. After its founding by Alexander the Great in 331 BC, this eponymous city became *the* center for learning, especially geographical. The great royal research museum and library there was renowned throughout the Mediterranean world, and the institution aspired to having a global collection including every known work. Other libraries were purchased, and scrolls carried by passengers arriving in the port were taken and copied. One conservative figure given is 54,000 volumes, another 100,000; some estimates reach as high as 700,000 scrolls.

Just who or what was responsible for the destruction of the collection has been debated. Actually, it seems likely that scrolls and codices were lost in various ways over the centuries. This strategic city changed hands militarily more than once. Dio Cassius reported that in a 48 BC siege, the forces of Julius Caesar fired enemy ships in the harbor and that the fire spread to the docks and warehouses, destroying 40,000 stored books. Perhaps in compensation, it is alleged, the triumvir Marcus Antonius gave to Queen Cleopatra some 200,000 volumes taken from the Library of Pergamon in Asia Minor.

We know that troops of the Roman emperor Caracalla sacked the city in AD 215 and at least threatened to burn down the museum. During the same century, the city suffered destructive riots. Emperor Aurelian's men partially pillaged the metropolis during the 270s. A few years later, Emperor Diocletian's forces thoroughly plundered Alexandria once again, and the library must have suffered. Most of the Classic quarter of the town was demolished during the earthquakes and tsunami of AD 365, part sinking beneath the sea. Persians occupied the city for ten years in the early 600s, until driven out by the Byzantine Greeks, who were Eastern Orthodox Christians.

With some exceptions, Christians of the time sought to destroy pagan Classical writings, and the library's Greek and Roman texts were largely replaced by Christian ones. The vestiges of the library's ancient works were eliminated under Byzantine Emperor Theodosios the Great (ruled, 379–95), by order of Theophilos, the fanatical bishop of Alexandria from 385 to 412. In 640 and again in 645, Muslim Arabs conquered the metropolis, and this was apparently the definitive death knell for even the Christian writings. The conquering general, 'Amrou ibn al-As, on the orders of Caliph Umar, directed that the books be burned, because, it is told, if they were compatible with the Koran, that book was their superior source, and if they were incompatible there was no reason to preserve them. The books were used to fuel the water-heating stoves of the public baths of the city for six months. Any records the great library might still have contained were then forever lost.[3]

Much of the reason that Europe's Dark Ages are still relatively dark to historians is owing to these kinds of destructions of records. Even from the late Middle Ages, when the English city of Bristol was a key player in maritime expansion, no important records from that period survive in the city's archive. In more recent times, Napoleon I's troops seized the Vatican's priceless secret archives and sent them to Paris. On the emperor's eventual defeat, some of this material was returned to Rome. However, because of high transport costs, material considered unimportant was sold as wrapping paper and for the making of cardboard.

Virtually everything of importance written in Chinese between the advent of papermaking in about AD 100 and around the year 700, when compensatory mass-production printing began, was either reproduced in print or lost, owing to the flimsiness of the medium. Even after that, as Joseph Needham tells us, "the great interdynastic upheavals and foreign conquests destroyed even whole editions of printed books. There are tens of thousands of books of which we know only the titles. Without printing there would have been a million."[4]

Eyes Only: Deliberate Secrecy and Destruction of Records

Even when some antique historical accounts do exist (for example, Herodotus, Diodorus of Sicily, Caesar, Plutarch, Tacitus), they were incomplete from the outset. Throughout history, recorders have selected among the myriad facts, reporting only those that served their ends or the ends of their patrons or their religious ideas, and distorted or omitted those facts that did not. Further, the doings of the elite and of armies might be attended to, but mariners were generally of low status and the activities of the ordinary merchant, fisherman, or ship's captain like as not would receive no official written notice. In the case of the Norse, for instance, the exploits of chieftains were described in detail, while the doings of most less distinguished men were not recorded. (As it happens, an estimated 80 percent of the medieval Icelandic sagas have been completely lost.) For every high-profile long-distance voyage of discovery in history, there were probably several, perhaps dozens, of voyages of discovery and exploitation of discovery that went unremarked in writing. The main reason that we have records of the voyages of da Gama, Columbus, and others of the great age of European exploration, in which official possession of overseas territory was by right of first discovery—which needed to be proclaimed—is that these expeditions were state sponsored (and even then, we have precious little in some cases—for example, concerning Cabot). Private endeavors would likely have remained largely or entirely private and undocumented.

Another salient factor in the absence of documentation is secrecy. As Clement, a late-second-century-BC bishop of Alexandria, expressed it, "secret things are entrusted to speech, not to writing."[5] One must always keep in mind the ancient and strong traditions of arcane, esoteric, hermetic knowledge in magic, religion, alchemy, and profession. Geographical information was often treated as trade and/or military secrets. In fact, we may turn around the assertion that if contacts had occurred there would be records of them, by saying that if contacts had occurred it is likely that special efforts would have been made to keep secret the valuable knowledge thus acquired. Columbus had a charter from the sovereigns—Ferdinand and Isabella—to possession of all lands he discovered, and it was therefore in his interest to publicize his discoveries. Earlier voyagers to North America, lacking any such charter, would likely have hidden their hard-won information from rivals and authorities. Reported destinations might even often have been falsified.

Secrecy and the evasion of legally required trading licenses translate into a lack of written sources for both southern and northern unofficial medieval ventures into the Atlantic, whose initiators would have had nothing to gain and much to lose by revealing their overseas activities. For example, the Iceland and Greenland trade carried out by foreigners was forbidden by Danish officialdom, so that although the English of Bristol continued to engage in such trade, many voyages remained unrecorded so as not to risk confiscation of ship and cargo (as had happened, for example, to the Greek Eudoxos of Cyzicos a millennium and a half earlier, on his return to Alexandria from India). English fishermen and merchants also covertly defied a royal Norwegian trade monopoly. Similarly, merchants—effectively smugglers in many cases—who had located lucrative sources of goods or new markets would not normally have communicated this to any competitor or have risked taxation and regulation by reporting to a central authority.

At the governmental level as well, silence was often policy, illustrating seventeenth-century Cardinal Armand de Richelieu's dictum, "Secrecy is the first essential in affairs of state." When Francis Drake returned from his 1577–80 peregrinations, a state of secrecy was imposed on him and his crew, and his logs and charts sequestered. Even today, nothing is more closely guarded than a nation's strategic maps, in our time compiled with the use of high-security satellites; this is accompanied by the leaking of false geographic information to the enemy. Covert activity was equally true of past societies such as the Phoenicians, whose knowledge of such matters is lost to history in part because of their desire for secrecy. Owing to Portuguese-Spanish rivalry during the Great Age of Discovery, divulging the contents of secret royal maps depicting newly found lands was a capital crime—although informants often did leak information (and disinformation) to foreign clients. Few copies of such maps were made, and nearly all of the official Spanish maps from the period have disappeared, as has Portugal's master world map of the early 1400s.

In China, mapmaking goes back at least to the Warring States period (474–221 BC). According to the historical writer Robert Temple, a map of the third century AD was placed "in the secret archives. This was not exceptional, for throughout history, and especially in China, the possession of superior maps was the key to political and military success, analogous to having advanced strategic weapons today. . . . It is easy to understand how so many early maps [some referred to in texts] did not survive; they were not copied, and were frequently destroyed."[6]

Some destruction of maps may have been to prevent their capture by the enemy. Suggested pre-1492 arrivals in the Americas on the part of fifteenth-century Portuguese explorers were, according to Eviatar Zerubavel, "probably kept secret by the Portuguese crown for political and economic reasons. Such a deliberate policy of secrecy may in fact explain the paucity of records we have of possible pre-Columbian crossings of the Atlantic made not only by the Portuguese (as well as by the Phoenicians and Carthaginians long before them) but also by [anonymous and fanatically secretive Bristol] English [and Portuguese] (and perhaps also Basque) sailors who may have discovered the rich fishing grounds of Newfoundland some time before Columbus's first voyage to America."[7]

With all this in mind, we should approach surviving historical maps that fail to show the New World in a somewhat more skeptical mode with respect to their necessarily conveying all contemporaneous "in-group" knowledge.

Further, not only were the making of maps and the writing of history distorted for cultural, political, theological, and personal reasons, documents were sometimes destroyed to advance political aims. For example, the first-century BC Chinese historian Qian Sima asserted that in order to avert invidious comparisons with past rulers and reference to principles inconsistent with those promulgated by the then potentate, in 213 BC the first Chinese emperor, Qin Shi Huang, decreed that "the records of the historians apart from those of Qin should be burnt," except for copies kept for the use of seventy court academicians. Anyone else even merely mentioning these documents was to be executed, and Confucian scholars themselves were buried alive.[8] Then, at the end of Qin's reign, much of what remained in the imperial library was destroyed by fire.

That was not the last of the great destructions in China. In AD 23, war resulted in the burning of the palace library. In AD 190, seventy cartloads of books disappeared during a flight from the eastern capital. A sack of the capital at Loy-ang in AD 311 obliterated many more records, and the Liang dynasty's imperial collection was torched by its own emperor when he was bested by conquerors in AD 555. Books were also destroyed in China because they were judged apocryphal, threatening, of poor literary quality, or morally corrupting.[9]

According to the historical researcher Henriette Mertz, during the fifth century AD, documents had become so overwhelmingly numerous that an imperial order was issued to condense all books into a few pages each. The originals were then destroyed. In the thirteenth century, a condensation of the condensations was ordered, and the original condensations were discarded.[10]

Deliberate destruction continued to occur from time to time in China. During the mid-1400s, a new isolationist policy dictated the suppression of all records of China's earlier overseas endeavors, thus perhaps depriving us of exactly the information needed to answer our questions about early ocean crossings from the Middle Kingdom. In the early seventeenth century, Jesuit missionaries ordered the burning of books on geomancy (*feng shui*) as pagan; such books contained, among other information, descriptions of the use of lodestone south pointers and information concerning the origin of the compass.[11] In modern times, during the Great Proletarian Cultural Revolution beginning in 1966, many libraries in China were ravaged or destroyed in a campaign to obliterate everything relating to the past.

Reminiscent of the actions of China's first emperor, in late pre-Columbian times the king of the Aztecs ordered the past erased, and many texts were accordingly burned.[12]

A variation on the secrecy theme is associated with xenophobic isolationism, such as that embraced at times by Korea, Japan, China, and certain other countries. Even under ordinary conditions, the experiences of a private ship captain, much less a common sailor, would receive little or no notice among the record-keeping authorities. When isolationism prevailed, the chances of there being records of voyages were even slimmer. During the mid-1400s, for example, takeover of the Chinese state by a new, antimaritime, isolationist faction dictated not only cessation of the fabulous far-ranging voyages directed by Admiral Zheng He but also the suppression of records of his and earlier overseas endeavors.[13] In isolationist Edo-period Japan, a rigid class system precluded nobles from taking notice of information obtained by illiterate commoners, including mariners, regardless of the information's importance, especially if the sailors had been "contaminated" by contact with foreigners.[14] Under such circumstances, reports concerning transoceanic travels would very surely have arrived stillborn.

Finally, we may mention additional book burnings by religious fanatics and conflagrations countering perceived threats by rival religious groups. In 168 BC in Jerusalem, the Romans deliberately destroyed the Jewish library during the Maccabean revolt. As mentioned, some of the materials at Alexandria were destroyed for Christian and Muslim religious reasons. This kind of destruction obliterated most native written records on the American side of the Atlantic as well. At the time of the Spanish Conquest, Mesoamerican civilizations possessed multitudinous bark-paper books and maps. As the popular historian Ian Wilson recounts it, in Mexico the conqueror Cortés was

> given a map of the whole coast down to the Isthmus of Panama. Every city which they came upon had substantial archives. . . . Because the Aztecs set great store by their calendar, and are reliably believed to have kept methodical records at least as far back as the sixth century AD, their archives would almost certainly have included exact details of the arrival of "Quetzalcoatl" and any similar transoceanic visitors.
>
> The tragedy is that [Bishop Diego de Landa and] most of the [other] Spanish regarded the Aztecs' written records . . . as works of the devil, deserving only of the most thorough destruction. In barely a generation, they destroyed all the official record offices and temple libraries. . . . Any remaining documents became sold as "wrapping paper to apothecaries, shop-keepers, and rocket-makers." Today all that is left is barely a handful of totally inadequate scraps [the "codices"].[15]

Many tacitly assume that following a successful return from voyages of discovery, at least the fact of that discovery would be accepted back home. However, this is not necessarily the case, and disbelief may well have been more usual than credulity. In the fifteenth century, according to the historian of maritime expansion J. H. Parry,

> often the chance discoverer would be in no condition to explore, and when he finally reached home—if he ever did—he might be unable to give more than the roughest indication of where his discovery lay, or even to convince his hearers that he had really found land and not a deceptive cloud bank. His report might be forgotten; or the land he claimed to have found might fade into a limbo of folk recollection or legend. Many such legends were current in late medieval Europe. . . . Responsible rulers and skeptical investors . . . would not send ships out deliberately on long and possibly dangerous voyages away from the known routes of commerce merely in the hope of making chance discoveries, or in order to investigate vague and implausible reports of discoveries made in the past.[16]

Concerning Records from Antiquity

The Yale physicist and historian of science Derek de Solla Price studied the Antikythera mechanism, a complex machine involving thirty cogwheels that was found in a wreck off a Greek island and that was once a complicated calculator of the movements of heavenly bodies and of the timings of eclipses. Price stated that the surviving historical record says nothing about it or its ilk. He then made cogent observations concerning which records have and which have not come down to us from Classical Greece and Rome:

> We have but little artifactual evidence of advanced ancient science and technology. The ample scholarship on the literature might suggest that we nevertheless have adequate information, but in fact we have lost much. To survive, a text had to be seen as justifying repeated hand-copying, re-editing, and perhaps translating . . . until it could reach through the ages and reach the relative sanctuary of the printed book. Even quite important works by the most famous authors are known to us only through their listing by some biographer. And how many authors are known only by name, how many books by lesser authors have died quite unrecorded?
>
> If this be true of the works that record the genius of great philosophers, the mathematicians, and the theoreticians of astronomy, it is doubly true of the record of technology. Even for the later periods before printing there are only the rarest accidental survivals of Villard de Honnicourt (thirteenth century) and of Leonardo da Vinci (fifteenth century). From classical times there is almost nothing of this sort. What we have instead are a few books that describe the technical practices in civil and military engineering, architecture, and agriculture, and so on. In the first place these are often silent in just those places where we would wish for an exact statement of technical detail; in the second place we are dealing in all such works with what has become known as Low Technology, the . . . [mundane] crafts of daily life—[but not High Technology,] those sophisticated crafts and manufactures . . . intimately associated with the sciences, drawing on them for theories, giving to them the instruments and the techniques that enable men to observe and experiment and increase both knowledge and technical competence.[17]

The overall conclusion must be that the historical record is woefully incomplete and that secrecy often reigned concerning just those kinds of things we would wish to discover. The relative dearth of historical accounts of overseas journeys does not, then, by any means preclude such journeys' having occurred.

The "Silent" Historical Record Speaks

Documents Possibly Describing
Pre-Columbian Crossings

The palest ink is better than the most retentive memory.
—Confucius, circa 500 BC

All of the aforementioned forces leading to loss and destruction of records not-withstanding, it may still be asked whether at least *some* recorded hint of over-seas knowledge should not be expected to have survived, had such knowledge existed. Surely, some may say, absolute historical silence about something so important is completely implausible. Be that as it may, written references to *some* transoceanic voyages, whether true or fictional, *have* come down to us.

On Papyrus and Parchment:
Mediterranean and West European Records

Despite frequent assertions to the contrary, in the West there are traditions from ancient and Classical times concerning ocean voyaging and overseas lands. Ac-cording to the fourth-century AD Roman writer Rufius Festus Avienus in *Ora Maritima*, the Carthaginian Himlico (see below) claimed to have crossed the Atlantic in four months. During the reign of Augustus, Strabo suggested that a "new world" existed in the sea between Europe and India. The narrow-Atlantic concept of Krates of Mallos has been described in chapter 1, and such Roman philosophers, historians, and geographers as Lucius Annaeus Seneca, Plutarch (Loukios Mestrios Ploutarxo), Gaius Julius Solinus, and Pomponius Mela ad-vanced the notion of lands to the west of the Mediterranean. The Roman epic poet Lucan (Marcus Annaeus Lucanus, AD 35–65) averred that just prior to the conqueror's death Alexander the Great of Macedon had plans to take his forces westward into the Atlantic, to circumnavigate the globe, and to conquer new worlds, a notion also contained in epigrams collected by Seneca the Elder in the first century AD, but Alexander's counselors are said to have assured him that there was nothing beyond the sea and that in any case the ocean was too holy to be crossed by ships.[1]

Pliny the Elder spoke of a frozen sea (*mare concretum*), which was called the Cronian Sea and lay a day's sail from Thule (Iceland). In about AD 100, Plutarch, in *Moralia*, quoted the Carthaginian Sextius Sylla to the effect that "Far o'er the brine an isle Ogygian lies," five days' sail to the west of Britain, and that there were, toward the summer sunset, three other isles equidistant from Britain and from one another. The island natives told that, on one of these lands, Cronus had been confined by his father, Zeus.[2] Some have proposed that "Cronland" (sometimes spelled "Gronland"), from "Cronus," is the origin of the name "Graenland"/"Groenland" rather than Eirík the Red's having coined the "Graenland"/"Groenland" label in the tenth century. In fact, Cronland and Island are mentioned in two documents of the 830s, a century and a half before Eirík's going to Greenland.[3] Plutarch continued his account:

> Demitrius [of Tarsus] told us [circa A.D. 84] that . . . he himself, by the Emperor's command, made a voyage of inquiry and observation to the nearest of the deserted islands, which had a few inhabitants, *all sacred persons* and never molested by the Britons. . . .
>
> The "other side," and "the outermost shores of the world" are here: "To the great continent by which the ocean is fringed is a voyage of about five thousand stades [ca. 612 miles], made in row boats from Ogygia, or less from the other islands. . . ." The sea was slow of passage and full of mud . . . [from] streams the great mainland discharges, forming alluvial tracts and making the sea heavy like land [perhaps coagulated partially frozen seawater and/or Icelandic volcanic ash].
>
> There were supposedly Greeks living on the outer continent. . . . Sylla also reported that every thirty years . . . the Carthaginians outfitted an expedition to these North Atlantic islands where Cronus was a prisoner of sleep. The members of these expeditions relieved others who had sailed there thirty years before to serve the god. Many of these, however, preferred not to leave [this mild-aired place of easy living].[4]

Cyrus Gordon, a Semitic linguist and historian, collated an intriguing suite of comparable accounts in the Greek language.[5] He pointed out that Theopompus of Chios (b. ca. 380 BC) "mentions an enormous 'continent,' outside the Old World, inhabited by exotic people living according to strange life-styles," that once sent a fleet to the Eastern Hemisphere.[6] The fourth-century BC philosopher Aristotle or (more likely) a later member of his school (a Pseudo-Aristotle) noted that Carthaginians sailed for four days outside the Strait of Gibraltar to a rich tuna-fishing ground (probably, the Canary-Saharan Bank off Lanzarote):

> In the sea outside the Pillars of Hercules [Strait of Gibraltar] they say that an island was discovered by the Carthaginians, desolate [uninhabited], having wood of every kind, and navigable rivers, and admirable for its fruits besides, but distant several days' voyage from them. But when

the Carthaginians often came to this island because of its fertility, and some even dwelt there, the magistrates of the Carthaginians gave notice that they would punish with death those who should sail to it, and destroyed all the inhabitants lest they should spread a report about it, or a large number might gather together to the island in their time, get possession of the authority, and destroy the prosperity of the Carthaginians.[7]

Versions of this tale were also given in *De Mirabilibus Auscultationeibus* ([On Marvellous Reports], circa fourth century BC, author unknown), which mentioned dense forest and many fruits, and by Statius Sebosus (about 40 BC). The first-century BC historian Diodoros Sikeliotes (Diodorus Siculis, Diodoros of Sicily) wrote of a vast "island" in the ocean many days to the west of Africa, a mountainous land but nevertheless possessing beautiful plains and navigable rivers and inhabitants living in well-built homes and with irrigated groves and gardens. This country long lay undiscovered because of its great distance. But, wrote Diodorus,

> The Phoenicians, then, while exploring the coast outside the Pillars [Strait of Gibraltar] for the reasons we have stated [trade and colonization] and while sailing along the shores of Libya [Africa] were driven by strong winds a great distance out into the ocean. And after being storm-tossed for many days they were carried ashore on the island . . . and when they observed its felicity and nature they caused it to be known to all men. Consequently, the Tyrrhenians [Etruscans], at the time they were the masters of the sea [before 474 BC], intended to dispatch a colony to it; but the Carthaginians prevented their doing so, partly lest many inhabitants of Carthage should move there because of the excellence of the island, and partly to have ready in it a place in which to seek refuge against an incalculable turn of fortune, in case some total disaster should overtake Carthage. For it was their thought that, since they were masters of the sea, they would be able to move, households and all, to an island that was unknown to their conquerors.[8]

Of course, total disaster *did* overtake the Carthaginians, in the form of their eventual defeat and the utter destruction of Carthage—*Carthago delenda est*—in 146 BC, at the end of the Punic wars with an emerging Rome (Tyre, the mother city, had been destroyed some two centuries earlier by Alexander of Macedon). Some have considered the wooded island mentioned to be Madeira. However, that land lacks navigable rivers and as far as is known held no pre-Portuguese population, much less a civilized one, and, so far, has produced no Carthaginian archaeology. If a true land with great rivers is being referred to, only America can be meant.[9]

The second-century AD author Aelian also mentioned the above tale, as told in Gadir (Cádiz), and believed in Plato's continent beyond sunken Atlantis as well (see below). Strabo asserted that the Phoenicians/Carthaginians possessed far more maritime geographical knowledge than did the later Romans, and many diffusionists consider the former to be prime candidates for having made pre-Columbian voyages to the Americas.

The second-century AD Greek wit Lucian of Samosata's *A True Story* describes an eight- or eighty-day voyage to an inhabited hilly, wooded island in the Atlantic during an expedition launched to satisfy curiosity as to where the opposite shore of the ocean might lie and as to who might live there. Although a fantasy, this tale shows that some were asking these kinds of questions.

In the first century AD, Seneca the Younger mentioned a probably real (though unsuccessful) expedition of exploration in the North Atlantic: "Banished from the boundaries of the known world, boldly through the forbidden darkness they go to the limit of things and the outermost shores of the world. . . . Are we seeking people located on the other side under a different pole of the heavens, and for an unknown world free from the blast of winds? The gods call us back and they forbid mortal eyes to see the boundary of things."[10] This certainly sounds like a transatlantic attempt—unsuccessful, but nevertheless an attempt.

Around AD 100, Plutarch recounted the Roman general Quintus Sertorius's falling in with some sailors on Spain's ocean coast circa 75 BC, sailors who had recently returned from Atlantic islands some 1,000 miles away[11]—a distance that would put them in the Azores. One may also note the 1934 fisherman's find of a Romano-British storage jar from pre–AD 200 that was 898 feet down, on Porcupine Bank 150 miles to the west of Ireland,[12] keeping in mind Robert Marx's Rio Roman wreck described in chapter 10.

Strabo asserted the possibility that a circumnavigation of the world in open water was possible (see also chapter 1). Seneca the Younger wrote, "How far is it from the uttermost shores of Spain to those of India? But very few days' sail with a favoring wind." Samuel Eliot Morison recounted that Columbus "ascertained that Aristotle [Strabo?] was reported to have written that you could cross the Ocean from Spain to the Indies *paucis diebus*, in comparatively few days; and Strabo, the Roman geographer who died about A.D. 25, [quoting Eratosthenes, third century BC] hinted that it had actually been tried. 'Those who have returned from an attempt to circumnavigate the earth do not say that they have been prevented from continuing their voyage by any opposing continent, for the sea remained perfectly open, but through want of resolution and scarcity of provision.'"[13] Might others, better provisioned and with more resolution, have succeeded (unrecorded or kept secret) where those mentioned by Seneca—if the truth was being told—failed? At any rate, the concept that was involved and the attempt itself, or even just the report of the voyage and even if that report was untrue, communicates something of significance.

One should say at least a bit about Plato's story of Atlantis circa 400 BC, supposedly collected by Solon (638?–559 BC) while in Egypt: "In those days the Atlantic was navigable and there was an island in front of the straits which you call the columns of Hercules; the island was larger than Libya [Africa] and Asia put together and was the way to other islands, and from the island you might pass through the whole of the opposite continent which surrounded the true ocean."[14] The question is not whether there was an enormous, now-sunken water-surrounded continent in the Atlantic—geophysics shows otherwise—rather, what this story says about belief: whoever believed Plato (and many did) would believe in islands and a continent beyond the present Atlantic Ocean.

Then there is the tradition that in AD 714 or 734, seven Spanish bishops, with others, fled the Moors in Iberia and sailed from Oporto to the Atlantic islands of the Seven Cities and Antillia. Too, the medieval Andalusian Arab geographer al-Idrisi wrote in 1154 of eight Iberian cousins having voyaged, with several months' provisions, from Lisbon onto the "Sea of Darkness," "to discover what it was and where it ended." The explorers sailed westward, apparently reaching the area of the Azores after eleven days, followed—in fear of the storms encountered—by a dozen days more southward, to "Goat Island." They returned home via one of the Canary Islands, which were inhabited by red men with little beard and also an Arabic-speaking castaway.[15] In a somewhat similar vein, al-Mas'ūdī wrote, in AD 947, that in AD 889, "In the [Atlantic] ocean of fogs . . . adventurers . . . penetrated it on the risk of their life, some returning back safely, others perishing in the attempt. Thus a certain inhabitant of Cordoba, Khashkhash [ibn Sa'īd ibn Aswad] by name, assembled a group of young men, his co-citizens, and [from (Columbus's) port of Palos de la Frontera] went on a voyage in this ocean. After a long time he returned with booty. Every Spaniard knows this story."[16]

The ninth-century Irish *Navigatio Sancti Brendani Abbatis* and the post–AD 900 Icelandic sagas represent what appear to be largely factual histories of overseas contacts, even though parts of the *Navigatio* are thought by some to suffer from insertion of mystical elements from the book of Revelation and possibly from some conflation. Saint Brendan's *Navigatio* was well and widely known in medieval times, in numerous and increasingly embroidered versions, and true or not was widely believed, its "Promised Land" being shown on maps. It may well have inspired later voyages, even, in part, Columbus's.[17] There were, likewise, medieval tales of the Welsh bastard Prince Madoc having crossed the ocean.[18] One may also mention the debated Vinland Map, which shows Greenland and Norse Newfoundland and which, if genuine, dates to the mid-1400s AD.[19] Too, a fifteenth- or sixteenth-century copy of a map that Marco Polo allegedly sketched in the thirteenth century shows Bering Strait and Alaska and carries the word "Fusang"—a Chinese place-name that will be discussed.[20]

That belief in earlier transatlantic voyages sometimes motivated explorers is underlined by the fact that Martín Alonso Pinzón, captain of the *Pinta* on Columbus's first voyage, is said to have favored the voyage because Pinzón had seen, he claimed, in the Vatican Library, a document asserting that in the time of King Solomon (tenth century BC), Bilqis, the queen of Sheba (Saaba, in present-day Yemen), sailed down the Mediterranean and into the Atlantic and reached "Sypanso" (Cipangu—that is, Japan), "which is fertile and rich, and in size exceeds Africa and Europe"[21] (this description sounds like an echo from Plato's Atlantis tale).

A few late pre-Columbian European maps (in addition to the Vinland Map) exist that some have interpreted as showing parts of the Americas, but just what is depicted remains debatable at best. Perhaps more interesting are sixteenth-century maps that accurately depict parts of the New World that supposedly had not yet been explored.[22] Then there are certain old Chinese maps that some have seen as including representations of the Western Hemisphere.[23]

Chinese geographies of AD 1178 and 1225, apparently based on hearsay from Arab merchants or seamen, speak of a far country, which required one hundred days to reach. "Far beyond the western sea of the Arabs' countries lies the land of Mu-lan-p'i," wrote Zhou Qufei. "Its ships [the ships that sail there?] are the biggest of all. One ship carries a thousand men; on board are weaving looms and market places. If it does not encounter favorable winds it does not get back to port for years. No ship but a very big one could make such voyages." The sinologist Hui-lin Li made a plausible case that the land described and its products (including a grain with 3-inch kernels [maize?], a giant "gourd" [pumpkin?], and a "strange sheep" [llama?]) was America.[24]

Watercraft were less developed in sub-Saharan Africa than in the Mediterranean or in southern and eastern Asia, and sail seems not to have been traditionally employed. However, dugout canoes were widely used in the humid tropics of that continent and some quite large ones existed on the western coasts. Arab Muslims from Morocco may have introduced Mediterranean-style ships to Islamicized Mandinga-speaking Senegambia. In his circa 1342 *Masalik al-absar fi mamalik al-amsar*, the Syrian Shihāb al-Dīn Ahmad ibn Yahýa ibn Fadl Allāh al-'Umarī recorded that Amīr Abū l-Hassan 'Alī ibn Amīr Hajib, son of the Mamluk governor of Cairo, had been told by the Berber sultan of Mali, Mansan Musa, that about AD 1300 the monarch's predecessor

did not believe it was impossible to reach the other end of the circumambient ocean; he wanted to reach that and was determined to pursue that plan. So he equipped two hundred ships full of men, and many others with water, gold and provisions, sufficient for several years. He ordered the captains not to return until they had reached the other end of the ocean, or until they had exhausted the provisions and water. So they set out on their journey. They were absent for a long period, and at last just one ship returned. When questioned about their news, the captain replied: "O Sultan, we navigated for a long period, until we saw in the midst of the sea a great river which flowed massively. My ship was the last; others were ahead of me. When they reached that place they could not return, and they disappeared. We did not know what happened to them. As for me, I did not enter that river." But the sultan did not believe him. [In 1307 h]e ordered two thousand ships to be equipped for him and his men, and one thousand more for water and provisions. Then he con-

ferred the regency on me and departed with his men and that was the
end of his time and of those who were with him.[25]

The ocean river mentioned would seem obviously to have been the Canary/
North Equatorial Current, a conveyor belt to the Caribbean (see chapter 2).
Whether any of these (perhaps exaggeratedly) many ships actually reached the
New World is unknown, but it seems more than possible. There are cultural
hints of pre-Columbian African black presence in the greater Caribbean region, especially on the mainland (see chapter 30), as well as African and Asiatic genes (see chapter 31).

Records East of Eden

Paperwork: Chinese Archives

In his article "The Chinese Exploration of the Ocean," the historian Chiao-Min
Hsieh wrote, "Throughout most of their long history of cultural and scientific
development, the Chinese people have been but passively interested in the ocean.
Believing that no land existed beyond the Pacific, most early Chinese explorers directed their expeditions westward. . . . Apparently there have been few, if
any, planned deep penetrations of the Pacific Ocean by the Chinese during their
long history."[26] However, the picture proves to be not quite that straightforward.

There existed in ancient China a Daoist belief in five islands in the far eastern ocean, inhabited by immortals, who subsisted on the herbs of immortality.
Two of these islands eventually sank, says the story, and many attempts to find
the three remaining isles failed. But later, in 219 BC, according to the ancient
historian Qian Sima,

> the [Shandong Daoist] Xu Shi [a.k.a. Hsü Fu] of Qi and others submitted a
> memorial saying that in the sea there were three spirit mountains named
> Penglai, Fangzhang, and Yingzhou, and immortals dwelt on them.[27] They
> begged to be able to fast and purify themselves and to go off in search of
> them, together with some youths and maidens. Thereupon Xu Shi was
> commissioned to send several thousand young boys and girls out to sea
> to seek immortals. . . .
>
> Next, he [the Emperor of Qin] sent Han Zhong, Hou Gong, and Master
> Shi to search for the immortals and the elixir of everlasting life. . . . Master
> Lu, a man from Yan, returned from his mission to sea. . . .
>
> The magician Xu Shi and others had gone to sea [apparently, from
> Langye, at the southern base of the Shandong Peninsula] in search of
> spirit elixirs, but after several years had not obtained any, and the expenses
> had been heavy. . . . They made up a false story, saying: "The elixirs can
> be obtained on Penglai, but we are always harassed by huge sharks and
> so cannot go there. We would like to request that skillful archers go along

with us, so that when we see them they will shoot them with repeating crossbows."[28]

The requests for youths and maidens—and, according to Hsieh, for grain, seeds, and livestock as well as artisans in all trades, including navigators—and then for crossbowmen, suggest that colonization against native resistance was the occult aim, and the several years' voyage makes the other side of the Pacific at least a conceivable destination. Han dynasty records indicate that Xu Shi voyaged to a place "of flat plains and great lakes," remained, and made himself a king (how reports of this came back to China is not specified). One might think of Western or Central Mexico, but Hsieh presented a strong case that Xu Shi and company actually finally settled on the Japanese island of Honshu and that Xu may even be identical to the legendary Jimmu Tenno, founder of the Japanese Empire.[29] Even so, this *is* a case of major Han Chinese seaborne colonization.

The *Liang Shu* (*History of the Liang Dynasty*), written during the Tang dynasty (AD 618–907), synopsizes earlier records of a report of circa AD 499 concerning a Buddhist priest Huishan (Hwui Shan), who, after a long absence from southern China, claimed that he had made a voyage across "the great eastern sea." This work was first translated in the West by Joseph de Guignes, in 1761, engendering much discussion as to whether Huishan had gone to Mexico. The story drew the attention of Edward P. Vining, who, in 1885, reproduced and discussed it in *An Inglorious Columbus*. This work has continued to draw the attention of diffusionists, and some have interpreted the itinerary Huishan gave as including Japan, the Kurile Islands, the Aleutian Islands, Alaska, and California, the last being the land he called "Fusang." In 1953, Henriette Mertz used this material to construct what she saw as the exact itinerary of the monk, who was probably engaged in missionary activity. She even attributed to him the planting of the metaphorical seed of the Mayan rise to brilliance, a task he was, in fact, far too late to have initiated.[30] Huishan characterized Fusang as lying "twice ten thousand *li*" (Chinese units of distance) or more (circa 8,000 miles)[31] to the east of the "Great Han country," which Mertz interpreted as Alaska and which is, itself, an equal distance to the east of China.

Without worrying here about the accuracy of Mertz's reconstructed itinerary, we may nevertheless ask, could Fusang really be in America? Actually, there is nothing in Huishan's condensed account that indicates what route he took to reach Fusang. Although the 16,000-mile eastward distance mentioned would put the place well beyond the Americas, large, round numbers were often used as literary metaphors in China (cf. "I have a million things to do").

The name Fusang, said Huishan, derives from the abundance of the *fusang* tree, which has oak-colored leaves that resemble those of the tung tree (which are heart shaped) and that, when young, are eaten like bamboo shoots. It bears edible reddish, pear-shaped preservable fruits; cloth, paper, and a kind of silk can be made from the tree's bark. Mertz thought that maize (which is hardly a tree) was being referred to. Another suggestion, yucca and/or agave, is slightly more plausible. These plants, which are shrubby or small-tree-like, possess bayonet-shaped leaves vaguely like those of bamboo, edible fruits that can be dried, and bast fiber in the leaves that was used for making textiles (bark paper was also made in Mexico, but from true tree bark, not from yucca).

Wall-less cities with plank houses are described, as are writing, use of copper but not iron, markets, and processions signaled with drums and (conch shell?) horns. Most of this (excepting plank houses) could indeed fit with Mexico and seemingly nowhere else between there and China except perhaps Korea and Japan. However, also listed as present in Fusang are long-horned, burden-carrying cattle as well as horse- and deer-drawn carts/chariots, and the milking of domesticated (rein)deer for kumis-making is described—none of which actually apply to anywhere in the Western Hemisphere. Too, the people there are said to lack weapons and not to engage in warfare—quite the opposite of the actual situation in Mexico. Perhaps the *fusang* tree is the Old World paper mulberry.[32]

What are we to make of this tale, then? Most opinion seems to be that Fusang is some island to the east of China, perhaps in the Japanese chain. The titles of officials given appear to be Korean. The story could be, at least in part, mere fanciful invention (a pre-Huishan mention of Fusang says the trees are 20,000 *li* high), or might represent a conflation of reports on more than one area, occurring in the course of the condensations that Huishan's original report underwent over the centuries. We are unlikely ever to know for certain. All that may be said with confidence is that a long overseas voyage of some kind was made—a fact not without interest, regardless of destination.

Interestingly, Huishan did not claim discovery but alleged that five missionizing Buddhist monks from Kabul, Afghanistan, had preceded him to Fusang, in AD 458. The name Fusang appears in later Chinese annals as well, ultimately becoming a modern label for America.[33]

Mertz also attempted a reconstruction of itineraries relating to the overseas "Mountains of the East," in the oldest surviving geographical treatise, the *Shan hai jing* (Classic of the Mountains and Seas), dating to perhaps the tenth or eleventh century BC. One of these routes is coastal, which Mertz thought referred to the shore between Southeast Alaska and Santa Barbara, California; the others, she interpreted as referring to the Rocky Mountain chain and the Cascade Range. Although there are too many ambiguities in the surviving textual fragments to yield confidence in any such specific reconstructions,[34] it is indeed possible that the Americas are here referred to, whether as a theoretical continent or as one known of empirically.

A number of inscriptions on stone have been reported in the New World that are purportedly in Old World languages and scripts. Such inscriptions, if genuine, would constitute, on the American side of the oceans, historical records of contacts. These are not dealt with in this book.

Polynesian Traditions

In the absence of writing (ignoring Easter Island *rongorongo*), the Pacific Islanders had only oral history. However, traditions from Kiribati, the Marquesas, and Hawaii refer to a great land to the east of all the islands. Unless this land was merely imaginary, what could it have been other than the Americas? Still, none of these tales can be shown to be pre-Contact.

Oral History? Native Americans Have Their Say

There were almost as many different origin stories among aboriginal Americans as there were "tribes." Many of these tales involve supernatural happenings and fall into broad mythic categories such as the Earth Diver story, the account of the Emergence from the Underworld, and so forth. These tales may be viewed literally among believers or metaphorically or in some other fashion among nonbelievers. However, there are certain other narratives of at least a quasi-historical nature that involve American Indians' own accounts of overseas origins of certain cultural practices, clans, or whole peoples.

The Tlingit of Southeast Alaska told of two sisters who were part of a small group that was driven ashore from over the seas, landing on uninhabited Dall Island. The younger went to Haida Gwaii (the Queen Charlotte Islands) and founded the Haida Nation, while the elder stayed put and founded the Tlingit.[35]

In South America, the Tukana of interior Colombia and the Cashibo of eastern Peru both have stories of having come from across the Pacific, and on Peru's North Coast there was a tradition of overseas culture bearers.[36] In North America, according to the Native American historian Vine Deloria Jr., "Several tribes, the Hopi, nations within the Colville [Reservation of Washington State], and traditions within the Chippewa, Ottawa and Potowatomi suggest that early ancestors crossed the ocean and came up the rivers."[37] The Hopi tale describes the flooding of the "Third World" (post-Pleistocene sea-level rise?) and an island-hopping eastward ocean voyage in reed boats and on bamboo rafts to a new continent—the "Fourth World." The story involves a white god, called Bahana.[38] The legend of a white man coming from the west by water is shared by the Mandan of the Great Plains and by many other Indian groups.

The Yuchi, aboriginally from Alabama and Georgia, claim to have come to the North American continent from islands in the east (which contemporary Yuchis identify with the Bahamas), where much of the land sank beneath the sea. Other Indians of northeastern North America have traditions recounting apparently pre-Columbian visits by whites in ships.[39]

Perhaps the most interesting of these foreign-origin stories are from Mesoamerica (see also chapter 30).[40] The late sixteenth-century Nahua prince and historian Fernando de Alva Ixtlilxóchitl, drawing from written and oral Aztec sources, wrote that the Chichimecs ("barbarians" of northern Mexico) came "from western parts," from "Babylon," to "this New World" and that "the Tultecs . . . came to these parts, having first passed over great lands and seas, living in caves and passing through great hardships, until getting to this land. . . . Those who possessed this land in this third age were the Ulmecs and Xicalancas; and according to what is found in their histories, they came in ships or barques from the East from the land of Potonchan from which they began to settle."

Captain Hernán Cortés's conquest of Central Mexico was greatly facilitated by native belief that he was, or was descended from, the great leader from overseas that legend spoke of. The Aztec emperor Moctezuma said to the captain (and to his own lords) that the Mexicas (Aztecs) were of foreign origin from "very remote parts," their lineage having been "led to this land by a lord to whom we all owed allegiance." The area of origin was thought to be "where the sun rises." The great colonial chronicler Fray Bernardino de Ribera Sahagún stated in his *Historia general de las cosas de Nueva España*, "The first settlers who came to this land of Mexico . . . arrived at the port with ships, with which they [had] crossed the sea." The Franciscan brother offered a more detailed story: "The account which the old people give is that they came by sea from toward the north, and it is certain that they came in some vessels of wood, but it is not known how they were built; but it is conjectured . . . that they came out of seven caves and that the caves are the seven ships or galleys in which the first settlers of this land came. . . . The first people of this land came from toward Florida, and they came along the coast and disembarked at the port of Pánuco which they call Panco [Panotlan], which means, place where those that crossed the water arrived. These people came looking for a terrestrial paradise . . . and they settled near the highest mountains they found." Sahagún stated this slightly differently elsewhere: "It has been innumerable years since the first settlers arrived in these parts of New Spain [Mexico] which is almost another world; and they came in ships by sea landing at the port which is to the north. . . . And from that port they commenced traveling along the coast of the sea, viewing the snowy peaks of the volcanoes, until they arrived at the province of Guatemala [modern Tabasco?] . . . and they went to settle in Tamoanchan where they were for a long time."

Finally, Sahagún stated in his pre-*Historia* notes: "The Mexicans are foreigners. . . . Countless years ago before the arrival of the Spaniards the ancestors of the Mexicans arrived in boats and disembarked 'in the north' at the port named Panoaya, or Pánuco, north of the present port of Veracruz. Under the guidance of their high priest . . . they traveled inland and founded a town named Tamoanchan, where they lived peacefully for a long time."[41]

Another chronicler, Fray Juan de Torquemada, drawing upon independent native sources, wrote, "certain nations came from toward the north, who landed at the port of Pánuco. These people were well dressed, and well adorned in long clothing, after the style of the Turks. . . . It is unknown whence it [the nation] might have come." (Pánuco is some miles up the Río Pánuco from modern Tampico, the farthest-westward port on the Gulf of Mexico.)

Legends such as these were not confined to the Aztecs but were widespread in the Americas, including among the Maya. Bishop Diego de Landa, Colonial chronicler of Yucatán, stated, "Some of the old [Itzá] people of Yucatán say that they have heard from their ancestors that this land [of New Spain] was occupied by a race of people, who came from the East and whom God had delivered by opening twelve paths through the sea." Likewise, the Tzental of Chiapas had a story, collected in 1554, of the arrival of one Votan and his followers from across the ocean—from Chaldea, according to one early interpreter. Again, in highland Guatemala tales were recorded concerning overseas arrivals of the three nations of the Quiché, from "where the sun rises, a place called Pa-Tulán, Pa-Civán," which the informants thought corresponded to the Christians' Israel. In the *Annals of the Chakchiquels*, it is stated, "From the west we came to Tulán, from across the sea; and it was at Tulán where we arrived." Tulán was the legendary first American home of the peoples of Mesoamerica. It means "place of the reeds" and is often identified with the paramount Toltec site of Tula.

Thus there exist in the New World a number of native traditions of ancestors or culture bearers arriving from over the oceans. The simplest explanation for these tales is that they have some basis in historical reality.

II

Means

The Types and Availabilities
of Watercraft and Navigation

The means employed determine the nature of the ends met.
—Aldous Huxley, 1937

In part II, we turn to the means that would have been required to effect ancient ocean crossings: watercraft and navigation. In his 1994 *A History of Working Watercraft of the Western World*, Thomas Gillmer contended that, with a very few exceptions, "archaeologists, by the very nature of their discipline, are confined to the activity of land-based inhabitants. They do not understand well the workings of a ship or the ways of the sea."[1] Indeed, the quite specialized nature of maritime travel has very much limited most scholars' understandings of the relevant issues and has, in fact, led to the emergence of a number of major misconceptions about watercraft, sailing, and navigation, misconceptions that have sometimes seriously hindered reconstructions of the past. Here, we question standard suppositions such as the one that the journalist Simon Winchester repeated in his 2010 book *Atlantic*: "It took an inordinately long time for anyone to cross the ocean. It was to remain a barrier of water, terrifying and impassible, for tens of thousands of years."[2]

13
Some Nautical Myths and Issues

"The time has come," the Walrus said,
"To talk of many things:
Of shoes—and ships—and sealing-wax—
Of cabbages and kings—
And why the sea is boiling hot—
And whether pigs have wings."
                    —Lewis Carroll, 1872

Conventionally, archaeologists and historians view ships and sailing as having commenced on the Nile River, expanded to the Red Sea and Indian Ocean, passed to the Phoenicians and their Carthaginian successors and to the Minoans and Greeks, with know-how accumulated over the millennia in the Mediterranean eventually culminating in the caravels of Portugal and Spain that finally allowed humans to embark upon the open ocean. It has been typical of this mind-set to make it "not only unthinkable but impossible" that distant ocean exploration could have happened before the fifteenth century.[1]

In addition, the Eurocentrism of many historians and other scholars has led to a number of misapprehensions regarding the capabilities of non-European craft. Just one example of this point of view will suffice: "Before Magellan entered the Pacific in 1520, in what we would call a primitive sailing ship . . . there were only primitive rafts and dugout canoes; later, outrigger canoes; followed, still later, by the double canoes (catamarans) with built-up sides. There were more advanced types of ships in Japan, China, Malaysia and India, but of a type which scarcely could make very long transoceanic voyages successfully."[2]

The Columbus Myth

The words of one historian exemplify the established perception: "A number of technical changes came together to make ocean voyages possible: the compass, celestial navigation, improved shipbuilding, and guns to meet whatever challenge might appear," and only then did exploration go beyond the coasts and the less distant islands.[3] However, much of this widespread perception rests on misinformation. A way to begin dealing with these misconceptions is to address head-on the Columbus myth.

Stephen Jay Gould observed, "All defining events of history develop simplified legends as official versions—primarily, I suppose, because we commandeer such events for shorthand moral instruction, and the complex messiness of actual truth always blurs the clarity of a pithy epigram."[4] "[We] seem to need heroes, defined as courageous iconoclasts who discerned germs of modern truth through strictures of ancient superstition."[5]

Ian Wilson, in his book *The Columbus Myth*, asserted, "On both sides of the Atlantic umpteen generations of schoolchildren have been taught to regard the continent of America as having been an island effectively cut off from the rest of the world until Columbus's out-of-the-blue arrival."[6]

Even half a millennium after Columbus, just about everyone is inculcated with the proposition that until 1492, no one had ever conceived of sailing westward to Asia. "Since the earth itself was thought to be a spherical [sic; circular] disk, navigators venturing to the imaginary border of this circumferential [ocean] river would fall over the edge and never return. Not only was the sea filled with enormous whirlpools, monstrous demons, and dragons with man devouring jaws lying in wait for everyone who entered it, but the ocean and its secrets—according to religious belief—belonged to god and was not to be explored by humans."[7] Moreover, some allegedly believed that the sea boiled in the tropics.

As far as the monsters are concerned, these appear simply to have been exaggerations based upon sharks, giant squids, octopuses, whales, and marine crocodiles. The source of the monsters idea is perhaps the Bible itself, in which it is written (Psalms 104:25–26): "this great and wide sea, wherein are things creeping innumerable, both small and great beasts." Nevertheless, as the psalm goes on to state, "There go the ships."

It is further widely held that, in any case, before the inception of the astrolabe, the mariner's magnetic compass, and accurate charts for plotting courses, no one dared go far out of sight of land for fear of becoming lost, and that before the adoption of full decking, the stern rudder, multiple sails including the lateen mizzen course (triangular aft sail; see chapter 15), and other supposed late medieval and early Renaissance innovations in European marine architecture and rigging, there were no watercraft able to cross oceans.[8]

In fact, perfectly capable watercraft had existed for millennia, especially in southern and eastern Asia. Europe, too, had able ships, but sailing rigs and methods were earlier and far more highly developed in greater Southeast Asia. Even in the late eighteenth century, the sailing-canoes of Pacific Islanders could easily outpace and out-maneuver Captain Cook's flagship, the clumsy collier-bark *Endeavour*, the natives' craft literally sailing circles around it. Celestial navigation and other means of orientation and haven-finding were well developed anciently—again especially in Island Southeast Asia and the Pacific but also around mainland eastern and southern Asia, in the Mediterranean, and in Atlantic Europe (see chapters 22 and 23).

The Myth of the Superiority of Land Transport

"In the glorious Age of Discovery," wrote Donald S. Johnson in *Phantom Islands of the Atlantic*, "the . . . first sailors to venture out across the Atlantic had before them an uncharted wilderness, one that far exceeded in its dangers and its terrors that of any overland travel route."[9] This statement reflects a common perception that the sea was a far more arduous and hazardous medium of travel than was land. But in fact, as the British historian Peter Whitfield (more informed than Johnson) pointed out in his *The Charting of the Oceans*, "The idea that seas and rivers are great dividers of peoples is a myth. . . . Throughout history rivers and seas have been the means of communication, travel and trade."[10] Hear the wise words of fourth-century-AD Basil of Caesarea: "there is only one sea, as those affirm who have travelled around the earth. . . . The sea is good in the eyes of God . . . because it brings together the most distant parts of the earth and facilitates intercommunication of mariners."[11]

Most of us who live in the developed modern world, with its rapid railroads, swift highway-borne automotive traffic, and passenger aircraft that move at velocities approaching the speed of sound, tend not to be terribly aware of the historical superiority of water travel over land travel. Today, wind-propelled sailing seems a slow means of movement indeed, and many observers project this modern perception into the past, assuming that whereas lengthy human movements and long-distance interactions may have occurred overland, long-distance, especially open-water contact by boat was probably not very important earlier than the Renaissance. The truth is, however, that in those areas in which craft were available, until the nineteenth century water transport was normally far faster, safer, and cheaper than moving equivalent distances overland. The basic reason is simple. As the historian of shipping Richard W. Unger wrote, "Ships always enjoyed an advantage over land transport from the days of the first dugouts, because in the water there is less friction to overcome than on land."[12]

As observed in chapter 8, roads, if they existed at all, were normally rocky or rutted and dusty in dry times and quagmires in wet. Travel on them was slow, uncomfortable, and hazardous. Even where wagons or pack animals were available, the quantities of goods that could be transported were strictly limited. A 100-ton ship—the size of a typical Greek or Roman merchantman—can carry the equivalent of six hundred mule loads. Furthermore, beasts of burden and draft animals had to be managed, fed, and cared for, and they were susceptible to theft, disease, and disablement. In addition, man and beast had to spend some eight hours in the twenty-four at stationary rest, whereas—thanks to changes of watch—ships at sea could sail all night as well as all day. Even on the superb Roman road system, which included many paved ways, a mule cart made only about three miles an hour, a rate easily surpassed by a ship with favorable winds. K. D. White calculated that, at 3 knots (3.45 mph), a Roman merchantman would average 72 miles per day, nearly three times the estimated average for an ox-drawn wagon; it cost less to transport grain from one end of the Mediterranean to the other than to haul it 75 miles by road.[13]

In Roman times, land transport of goods using animals was fifty-eight times more expensive than sea transport.[14] In the large parts of the premodern world where pack animals were *not* used, that is, where foot travel was the sole land option, only even-smaller quantities of goods could be carried per person, at very slow rates. In contrast to the limitations of land transport, ships could move very large quantities of cargo as well as considerable numbers of passengers, and for propulsion could employ the wind, an entirely free good; nor was any road-, bridge-, or caravansary-maintenance required. In addition to dramatic superiority in terms of capacity, cost, and speed, ships had the advantage of avoiding all the other impediments of land transport: multiple jurisdictions and tolls as well as brigands and hostile peoples; topographic barriers such as deserts, jungles, swamps, unbridged and ferryless rivers, canyons, and mountain ranges; not to mention other hazards, such as avalanches and sandstorms (as on the Silk Road), ferocious beasts, and disease contagion from human contacts en route.

Accordingly, where navigable waters were present and watercraft and crews available, water was always the preferable medium for trade and travel over any great distance. Not until the coming of the railroad in the nineteenth century did land transport offer a quick viable alternative. Even today in some countries— for example, Bangladesh and Amazonian Brazil—surface travel and transport are still mostly by water.

Despite the *pax romana*, the empire's excellent roads, and the Romans' reputation as mediocre mariners, it is hardly astonishing that the *Mare Internum* (Mediterranean) and the *Pontus Euxinus* (Black Sea) were crisscrossed by sea routes and that the Egyptian wheat that fed the city of Rome was shipped by sea, not overland. According to the preeminent historian of travel in the Classical world, Lionel Casson, "Wheat from Egypt, olive oil from Spain, wine from France, elaborately carved stone coffins from Athens—these and dozens of other products were hauled back and forth across the Mediterranean by a merchant marine larger than any Europe was to know again till the eighteenth century."[15]

Most people today probably have an exaggerated sense of how great the danger of storm at sea was, based upon the post-Columbian experience of ships trying to beat round Cape Horn against contrary prevailing winds in the "Roaring Forties," upon travel in the storm belt of the northern Atlantic, and upon descriptions of Caribbean hurricanes and East Asian typhoons—all used to dramatic effect in art and in nautical fiction and film, and in news reports. But the climate in mid-ocean is actually much more uniform than on land, and the dangers of storms and unfavorable winds could be minimized by careful (if imperfect) weather watching and by selection of the empirically identified most storm-free seasons and routes for major voyages (see chapter 23), as well as by use of prevailing winds and currents (chapter 3).

As mentioned, European experience in poleward waters has colored the Western view of the dangers of the oceans. Severe storms are rare in the tropics, and the hurricane/typhoon seasons of the subtropics can be avoided. Magellan, for example, encountered *no* storms on his winter 1520/21 crossing of the aptly named Pacific. Myriad mariners, starting with Vasco Núñez de Balboa and including James Cook, have found the tropical Pacific to be calm, typically. The storm season is limited to November through March, and storms are practically nonexistent from April through October. One index of safety is the loss of only thirty ships in the 250-year history of the usually overloaded Manila galleons' annual sailing between Mexico and the Philippine Islands.

Although haze is common, there are few overcast days in the tropical Pacific, and almost no fog or mist, and the heavenly bodies are seldom obscured for more than three days running. Generally speaking, then, tropical waters—in which much of the postulated transoceanic voyaging would have taken place—have more predictable and clearer weather, fewer storms, and lower waves than more poleward seas, and the pathways of sun and stars are less seasonably variable and less oblique in passage and therefore easier to steer by, and these bodies are visible most of the time.

Granted, there existed some uniquely marine hazards in addition to unanticipated squalls and storms, including heavy seas generated by distant weather, irresistible currents, onshore winds, persistent calms, blinding fogs, uncharted reefs, occasional tsunamis affecting ports, and (toward the poles) icebergs, plus teredo "worms" (wood-boring clams) that drill holes in unprotected hulls in warmer waters (see chapter 14).

In addition to possible mutiny, there were sometimes hostile naval forces (for example, those of the Carthaginians in the western Mediterranean) and often pirates (although for many years, not in Roman waters). Pirates could be a difficulty in any traveled Old World coastal area, especially those with islands and indentations, but were an especially serious problem at "choke points" that funneled ship traffic through narrows, thus making that traffic vulnerable to attack—notably, the Straits of Gibraltar and Messina, the Bosporus and the Dardanelles, the Red Sea—particularly, the Bab el Mendab—the Strait of Hormuz (infested by Arab corsairs) and the Persian Gulf in general, and the East Indies' Strait of Melaka (Malacca), plus, in colonial times, the Mozambique channel, the Straits of Florida, and the Caribbean's Windward Passage. However, the existence of pirates implies that shipping was taking place in spite of them. Pirates were not an issue in the open ocean far from land, especially in waters not on regular trade routes, and organized piracy was, as far as we know, absent from the pre-1500 Americas.

In spite of the various real maritime hazards, people sailed widely. For instance, the record indicates that the Norse suffered heavy losses (probably owing mainly to weather), yet this did not result in a low frequency of voyages.

In earlier times, there were very lengthy overland human movements, ranging from the trans-Eurasian silk trade to the deployment of great armies (for example, that of Alexander of Macedon to India and back), to the centuries-long migrations of entire peoples (for example, Huns, Avars, Visigoths, and Tupí).

If, then, water travel is far easier than land travel, where maritime traditions existed could not humans, in numbers, have managed to travel lesser, but still transoceanic, distances by sea?

All shores on the principal seas (other than the Caspian) are connected with, and accessible to, one another by salt water—something explicitly recognized at least as far back as the days of Eratosthenes of Cyrene (later, of Alexandria).[16] Culture usually spread, often in leapfrog fashion, along coasts and around seas far faster than it spread into the interiors, creating a thin, interrupted coastal perimeter in which widely dispersed generalized maritime/mercantile culture hybridized with various specific local, land-based cultures. The Mediterranean, for example, which the Romans nicknamed *mare nostrum*, has, throughout history, served as a unifying feature far more than a separating one: for megalithic peoples, for the Phoenicians/Carthaginians, for the Greeks, and, most thoroughly, for the Romans, among others. On a larger scale, the Indian Ocean functioned somewhat similarly for millennia. There seems to be no intrinsic reason why the Atlantic and, especially, the Pacific, could not have played similar kinds of roles.

A small number of thalassophobic scholars have proposed to explain certain similarities between Asian and Mesoamerican and South American cultures by postulating some diffusion through Siberia, across the post-Pleistocene Bering Strait, and then southward overland. However, the difficulty of travel across this cold, scrub-covered country makes direct East Asia–tropical America foot travel seem less likely by far than voyaging across the Pacific, especially in light of the absence of the traits in question in the northern latitudes. The northern environment would not, of course, have permitted group-to-group transfer of agricultural crops and practices or other traits dependent upon milder climes.

The Myth of the Danger of Open-Ocean, Deepwater Voyaging

Many non-nautical writers have supposed that voyaging in the open ocean, distant from land and over profound depths, entails far more risk than does creeping along in the coastal shallows. Even some of those writing about nautical topics hold a similar perception. Thus the Canadian anthropologist Wade Davis stated, "It was the impossibility of keeping track over a long voyage of every shift in speed, current, and bearing that kept European sailors hugging the coastlines before the problem of longitude was solved with the invention of the chronometer" in the eighteenth century.[17] Yet as is well attested in the maritime literature, this perception of the security of coast hugging is exactly the opposite of the truth in most situations, at least for larger craft going substantial distances. Under normal circumstances of long-distance voyaging, and especially with deep-draft craft, in addition to avoiding coastal pirates it is the case that being in deep water and possessing plenty of sea room in which to ride out any storm or onshore wind is much to be desired, for a ship's greatest risk is being stranded: driven into shallows or onto a lee shore, and running inextricably aground and/or breaking up. Shallow water is more susceptible to steep-wave generation at any given wind velocity than is deep water. Too, in inshore waters there are tidal and long-shore currents to contend with and there is greater risk of collision with other craft. So, sailors seek to maintain good offing unless looking to make use of local land or sea breezes or coming into port or searching for shelter behind an island or headland during a storm.

Blanket pronouncements to the effect that "Sailing ships before the age of the compass tended to hug the coast and seldom ventured beyond sight of land," being fearful of the open sea,[18] are highly misleading. Granted, in AD 1154 the Andalusian Arab geographer al-Idrisi asserted: "No seafarer dares to sail out into the Atlantic sea and steer a course away from land. Men sail along the coastline and never leave it out of sight.... What lies beyond the sea is known to no man. No one has been able to discover anything that is to be trusted with regard to the ocean, this by reason of the difficulties in the way of seafaring, the lack of light [owing to cloud and fog, common off Morocco] and the numerous storms."[19] However, he stated all that as preface to observing that eight Arab cousins *did* go out onto the "Sea of Darkness" from Lisbon, as described in chapter 12.

The fact is, the seasoned long-distance mariner breathes a sigh of relief as the land sinks out of sight, and his most uneasy moments come when approaching the shore. Even in the Mediterranean, where small coastal craft involved in port-to-port trading circuits (cabotage) *were* the rule, open-sea voyaging was also anciently engaged in. The 1999 discovery of eighth-century BC Phoenician wrecks in 1,300 feet of water 38 miles to the west of Ashkalon, Israel,[20] and evidence of other ancient shipwrecks at deepwater sites many miles out of sight of land, suggest that ancient sailors of these seas had the means and inclination to traverse open waters and were by no means limited to hugging the coastline. This was certainly true in Roman times (a period yielding over four hundred known wrecks), when huge grain ships sailed directly from Alexandria, Egypt, to Ostia and Portus, the harbors of Rome.

14

The Myth of the Inadequacy
of Pre-Columbian Watercraft

Vessels large may venture more,
But little boats should keep near the shore.
—Benjamin Franklin, 1757

Another major maritime myth is that the larger the body of water crossed, the larger the vessel must be to cross it. This myth includes the contention that the watercraft available to pre-Columbian peoples were too tiny to permit long-distance voyaging, were too weak and unstable to survive ocean waves, and lacked the kinds and numbers of sails and the appropriate rigging needed for sufficiently expeditious crossings. As described in the previous chapter, in this view the Atlantic was an insuperable obstacle until the fifteenth century, when improvements in ship design, specifically the development in Portugal of the ocean-going caravel, allowed the inception of the Great Age of Discovery. Like many an author before him, in his generally well informed book *The Discovery of the Sea* the Harvard historian J. H. Parry argued that relatively large ships like the caravel and the carrack were required, to be safe enough as well as capacious enough to carry sufficient supplies to permit long-duration voyages, as did the Canadian historian Richard W. Unger in *The Ship in the Medieval Economy*: "The full-rigged ship was the great invention of European ship designers in the middle ages," involving the sternpost rudder, three masts with shortenable square sails plus, on the mizzen, an improved lateen sail for tacking, and a bowsprit sail to aid maneuvering.[1]

There are at least two kinds of response to the unsupported contention that earlier watercraft were not large enough to be suited to ocean crossings: (1) determination as to whether sizable craft did exist in the relevant time periods, and (2) determination as to whether large size actually conveys critical advantages in the realm of seaworthiness or supplies.

Sizes of Watercraft during the Great Age of Discovery

Many imagine that the ships of the great age of European exploration and early colonization were quite large, but in fact none was exceptionally so, and some were distinctly small. The Portuguese ships of Bartolomeu Dias's fleet that rounded the Cape of Good Hope in 1488 were of about 50 tons' burden. Vasco da Gama's 1497 flagship *Gabriel*, which went on across open ocean to India, had a length of about 125 feet. Columbus took three ships on his 8,000-mile first transatlantic probe. Although actual measurements no longer exist, his flagship, the two-masted *Santa María*, is thought to have been about 75 to 85 feet long and of 90 to 100 tons burden, with a crew of thirty-nine; the *Pinta*, some 69 feet long and about 60 tons; and the *"Niña"* (*Santa Clara*), approximately 55 feet or a bit more long and with a capacity of 50 to 60 tons (Columbus used *Niña* again on his second voyage; John Cabot's *Matthew* was probably about the same size). The tonnages of the principal ships of the third voyage were comparable, being circa 101, 70, and 60, but Columbus had come to conclude that smaller ships were preferable for exploration. Those on his second voyage included several Cantabrian barks, probably much smaller than the *Niña*. Later ships of the Spanish treasure fleet ran about 100 feet long.

Francis Drake, terror of the seas of Spanish America, sailed 30,000 miles with a crew of sixty+ in the *Pelican* (renamed *Golden Hind* en route), including 7,000 miles across the Pacific in 1577. The *Pelican* ran 70 to 100+ feet from stem to stern and had a capacity of from 85 to 150+ tons; the expedition's *Christopher*, which crossed the Atlantic but did not reach the Pacific, weighed in at a mere 15 tons. The even-smaller frigate *Squirrel*, in Humphrey Gilbert's 1583 fleet of transatlantic exploration of the North American northeast, was of a mere 8 tons.

Alvaro de Saavedra Cerón took the *Florida*, a vessel of perhaps 40 to 50 tons, across the Pacific in 1527–28. Henry Hudson's *Discovery* (1610) was a bark of 55 tons that crossed the Atlantic and back, carrying on explorations during arctic-winter conditions. The flagship of the 1684 expedition of Robert de la Salle, which went from France to Texas, measured only 51 by 14 feet. Even Captain James Cook's bark *Endeavour*, which explored the Pacific and encircled the globe in 1769, was no more than about 100 feet long. Captain Bligh's infamous *Bounty* had a lesser length: 87 feet.

To be compared to the magnitudes given above is the burden of an average Roman cargo ship, 100 tons, although the larger class of Classical merchantmen (for example, the Antikythera wreck of circa 90 BC) was around 300 tons and capable of carrying 10,000 amphorae. Those numbers may tellingly be put side by side with the figures for the ships of the Portuguese mariner Ferdinand Magellan on the first recorded circumnavigation of the globe, extending from September 1519 to September 1522. The *San Antonio* (which deserted at the Strait of Magellan) was 100 tons and had a length of 102 feet); the *Trinidad* (broke up in the Malukus [Moluccas]), about 92 tons, with a length of 78 feet at the waterline; the *Concepción* (burned in the Philippines, where Magellan himself was killed), 75 tons; and the *Santiago* (wrecked in Patagonia), 62 tons. Although the 71-ton *Victoria* was the sole ship completing the entire 42,000-mile east–west tour, all five ships succeeded in crossing the Atlantic and three made the additional three-month traverse of the Pacific from Chile to the Philippine Islands as well. An English emulator of Magellan, Thomas Cavendish, employed ships of 40 and 60 tons for a 1586 circumnavigation and on his 1591 transatlantic voyage used a 60-tonner plus a vessel of only 20 to 40 tons.

The explorers of the Age of Discovery, then, used relatively modest to small ships, preferring small ones to larger ones for coastal exploration because littler vessels could penetrate bays and estuaries and were less likely to run aground on uncharted coastal reefs and shoals. Even in the nineteenth century, Charles Darwin's *Beagle* was, for instance, only 90 feet in length, shorter than the *Mayflower*, which had carried English colonists to Massachusetts two centuries before.

Maximum Sizes of Pre-Columbian Watercraft

The West

As for the ancient world, long before the Romans some large, even very large ships existed. Sources such as the book of Genesis (6:15) on Noah's ark and that story's Mesopotamian predecessor, the Akkadian legend of Gilgamesh, describe vessels 438 feet and 189 feet long and with three and six decks, respectively. Although these tales cannot be taken literally, nevertheless other sources assure us of the ancient presence of very sizable craft. The Palermo Stone, an inscribed fragment of black diorite, records that the king's ship of state during the reign of Pharaoh Sneferu of Egypt (circa 2600 BC) was 100 cubits (172 feet) in length. Boats of a fleet of fourteen buried with a First Dynasty (2920–2770 BC) Egyptian pharaoh ran 60 to 80 feet in length. A royal river barge found buried next to Egyptian King Cheops's (Khufu's) pyramid (circa 2450 BC) measured 142.4 feet long and 20.4 feet in the beam and had a 54-ton displacement. The world's oldest known shipwreck story, from Egypt circa 1700 BC, reports a vessel some 180 feet long and 60 feet wide, carrying a crew of 120.[2]

These craft were modest compared to Egyptian vessels (in most cases, towed barges) of circa 1500 BC constructed to transport stone monuments down the Nile. To cite a single example, the barge ordered to carry two 350-ton obelisks for Queen Hatshepsut is variously estimated to have been from 180 by 60 feet to 207 by 82 feet—or larger than an eighteenth-century European man-of-war, which carried a load of some 1,500 tons—to as much as an almost incredible 311.7 by 105 feet, with a displacement with cargo of 7,300 tons! Even the smallest of these figures represents a burden 30 *times* that of Columbus's *Niña*. Seagoing vessels (for travel to the Levant) are depicted by about 2475 BC, and reliefs at Queen Hatshepsut's tomb at Deir el-Bahari show Red Sea merchant galleys estimated to have been up to at least 90 feet in length (see figure 20.3).

The 20-ton Bronze Age Levantine Uluburun wreck from off Turkey, dating to the end of the fourteenth century BC, measured some 49 feet in length and over 16 feet in breadth. The longest of Minoan ships are believed to have been about 115 feet from stem to stern; even 26- to 39-foot craft appear to have carried crews of from eleven to fifteen.[3] The *Elissa*, the larger of the two Ashkalon wrecks mentioned in the previous chapter, measured about 47.6 feet long and 23 wide, although such ships are thought sometimes to have exceeded 98 feet in length. Farther west, Punic (Carthaginian) warship-beaching ramps from 100 to 160 feet long and a minimum of 16.5 feet wide have been unearthed, and two small warships excavated in Sicily were 115 feet long and 16 feet in the beam.[4]

Later on, as Casson noted, "Big merchantmen were plying the Mediterranean as early as the fifth century BC. For by this time a standard Greek term for a seagoing freighter was 'ten-thousander,' and whether the figure refers to the number of amphoras or of sacks of grain that could be loaded aboard, the capacity works out to almost 400 tons. The average British East Indiaman before 1700 was no bigger than this, nor were the first packets that plied between Liverpool and New York a century later. . . . The 'ten-thousanders' or even larger craft took care of the long-distance hauls over open water."[5]

Greek and Roman cargo ships may have *averaged* some 100 tons burden, but some Roman-era ones were much larger and had two decks; 340 tons was the standard size for large merchantmen, some being of 500 tons, and the Albegna amphora-transport wreck off Liguria in Italy seems to have been of about 500 to 600 tons. Long-distance haulers sometimes even exceeded 1,000 tons. The most notable of these haulers was the second-century AD Roman grain carrier *Isis*, with a length of 180 feet, a beam of 45 feet, and an estimated capacity of 1,200 to 1,300 tons, plus a passenger capacity of some six hundred. The largest Roman merchantmen carried three masts plus a short mizzenmast.

Western antiquity's largest known seagoing ship, for grain and for royal passengers, was that commissioned by a third-century BC ruler of Syracuse, Sicily, King Hiero. A three-masted three-decker ship, it carried a 1,700-ton cargo on its maiden voyage and may have had a displacement of up to 1,900 tons—32 to 38 times the size of Columbus's *Niña*![6] It is, then, abundantly clear that lack of ability to construct and sail sufficiently large, multimasted working ships is in no way a valid issue with respect to the ancients of the Mediterranean region.

Even the collapse of the Roman Empire in the West did not put an end to the building of sizable ships in the Mediterranean. The Byzantine Marzamemi Church wreck of circa AD 550 and found off Sicily was at least 80 feet long, with a burden of 200 to 300 tons, and another Sicilian find, the Greek Patano Longarini ship of circa AD 500, attained a length of some 130 feet. By AD 800, Byzantines were using *dromon* warships of up to 165 feet in length. In AD 969, Fatimid naval transports 275 by 110 feet were arrayed against defenders in Egypt. During the High Middle Ages, Venetians and Genoese—in some ways, successors of Byzantium—built ships of up to 500 tons' displacement.[7]

Northwestern Europe, too, provides examples of fairly good-sized vessels, although nothing approaching the great Greco-Roman ships. A logboat over 71 feet long was discovered in Ireland, dating to about 1940 BC.[8] One of the circa AD 300 Nydam wooden boats unearthed in 1863 in Schleswig, Germany, was symmetrical and measured 76 feet in overall length, with a 10.5-foot beam, and was propelled by fourteen oarsmen. The circa AD 600 Sutton Hoo ship from Anglo-Saxon England was about 89 feet long.[9] The Norse sagas mention the largest warships, *draker* or dragonships, as being up to 260 feet long and capable of transporting up to four hundred warriors. If the sagas exaggerate, such ships certainly, in reality, reached at least 150 feet in length. The longest

Figure 14.1. Ship depicted in a fresco of about the sixth century AD in Cave II, Ajanta, India. Note the three masts with vertically elongate square lugsails, the *artemon*-like sail at the bow, the pair of steering oars, and the jars near the helmsman (who is not to scale with the ship). From A. L. Basham, *The Wonder That Was India*, Oxford University Press, 1959, p. 227.

archaeologically known Norse ship, *Aegir*, found near Roskilde, Denmark, was 121 feet in length.[10]

The Indian Ocean and the East Indies

In the virtual absence of underwater archaeology for most of the Indian Ocean, there is much less in the way of reliable information on ancient ship sizes there and in adjacent seas than there is for the Mediterranean and for Atlantic Europe, but there is *some*. For instance, a thirteenth-century Indonesian shipwreck found in the Java Sea had an estimated displacement of 300 tons.[11]

As long ago as the mid-second-millennium BC, Mesopotamian cuneiform texts indicate that trading ships that arrived from the Indus Valley had cargo capacities of 20 tons—rather modest, but still as large as that of the *Discovery*, which brought settlers from England to Jamestown, Virginia.[12]

The Sanskrit book *Yukti Kalpa Taru* gives detailed statistics on a large number of classes of South Asian ships and boats. The largest—four-masters—measured 176 by 22 "cubits." If these cubits are the same as Egyptian ones, the dimensions would be about 1,096 by 138 feet—undoubtedly a great exaggeration but still indicative of very large size. Other impossibly large ships—up to 4,987 feet long—are claimed in stories.[13]

A ship depicted in the Ajanta Caves to the northeast of Mumbai (circa sixth century AD) sports three masts (figure 14.1), and some vessels shown carry horses or elephants.[14] Historically known *yatra dhoni* of Sri Lanka measured up to 98 feet long. Arab-influenced Pakistani *bheddis* were up to 70 feet long. Seagoing *balams* of Bangladesh reached up to 60+ feet in length and 14 feet in the beam and carried two masts and three sails. At the commencement of the European Great Age of Discovery, the South Indian commercial crossroads boasted ships of up to 1,000 tons.[15]

There are seven two-level decked outrigger ships shown in the reliefs on the Buddhist pyramid of Borobudur, Java (circa AD 842), carrying one and two tri-

Figure 14.2. Relief carving of an outrigger ship, Borobudur, Java, circa AD 842. Note the curving mastheads on the two shear-tripod masts, the lugsails, and the *artemon*-like spritcourse. Aragorn Dick-Read from Robert Dick-Read, *The Phantom Voyagers*, 2005, p. 197. Courtesy of Robert Dick-Read.

pod masts (figure 14.2). The originals of these ships with circa 30-ton capacity are estimated to have measured about 77 by 12 feet.[16] Likewise, according to the textiles specialists R. J. Holmgren and A. E. Spertus, who studied depictions on cloth, some medieval Indonesian ships "might have reached 1000 tons," with a complement of one thousand crewmen.[17] A sixteenth-century observer in the Moluccas reported sizeable *djuangas* and heard of even larger ones, with estimated keel lengths of 108 to 120 feet, ships propelled by two hundred paddlers and carrying nearly one hundred warriors. In the eighteenth century, the measured length of a "galley" on Sulawesi was 91.5 feet.

Ships filled with warriors are depicted in ninth-century AD bas-reliefs at Angkor Wat, Cambodia. Chinese observers as early as the third century AD wrote of Southeast Asian ships that that carried six hundred to seven hundred persons plus 10,000 bushels of cargo (circa 250 to 1,000 tons). The student of Indian Ocean maritime trade Shahnaj Husne Jahan noted that antique literature indicates that the Southeast Asian Bay of Bengal *kunlunbo* transported six hundred to one thousand passengers. Records from the third through the sixteenth centuries AD indicate that 500-ton Indian ships were sailing to the Middle East.[18]

According to the sinologist Hui-lin Li, the Arabs "were at that time [the Middle Ages] leaders in maritime activity, possessing extensive geographical knowledge of many lands and capable of building the largest of seafaring ships. Their sea-going vessels were apparently ten or more times as large as those of Columbus on his first voyage to America two centuries later."[19]

The Far East

As for indications coming directly from the Far East, quantitative data are generally lacking for early periods. However, fourteenth- and fifteenth-century depictions by westerners show East Asian ships as much larger than their own ships and carrying four or five masts. Europeans' travel accounts agree. In the late 1200s, for example, Marco reported that the Polo brothers had traveled in a fleet of fourteen twelve-sail four-master junks, some with crews numbering 250 to 260 men and provisioned for two years, in anticipation of a twenty-one-month round-trip voyage from China to Hormuz. Marco described Chinese merchant ships in the India trade of late pre-Columbian times:

> They have one deck; and above this deck, in most ships, are at least sixty cabins. . . . They have one steering-oar and four masts. Often they add another two masts, which are hoisted and lowered at pleasure. The entire hull is of double thickness. . . .
>
> Some of the ships, that is the bigger ones, have also thirteen bulk-heads or partitions [so that if one compartment is breeched, the others do not flood]. . . .
>
> The crew needed to man a ship ranges from 150 to 300 according to her size. They carry a much bigger cargo than ours. One ship will take as much as five or six thousand baskets [or mat bags] of pepper. At one time their ships were even larger than those now in use; but in many places islands have been so washed away by the force of the sea that there is no longer a sufficient depth of water in the harbours to take the larger ships, so they are built with a smaller draught.[20]

The early fifteenth-century Venetian merchant Niccolò de' Conti also described supposedly Indian-built compartmented four-masters larger than Western ships, and two Chinese books from the third century AD describe craft in South China or Annam that carried four masts.[21]

Excavated East Asian shipwrecks are most scant, but archaeologists have investigated remains of a few junks of the Song dynasty (AD 960–1279). The two-masted Quanzhou ship of about AD 1277 appears to have been about 112 feet long and 36 feet wide and of about 380 tons. In earlier times junks were up to 171 feet in length (a dimension surpassed by ships in the Ming navy), carrying as many as five masts—a phenomenon that surprised Europeans in the thirteenth century. In fact, Chinese ships may be the source of the European adoption of three masts on ships, commencing in the fifteenth century, although there is Classical Mediterranean precedent.[22]

Chinese ships seem first to have reached these sizes during the Sui and Tang dynasties (sixth to tenth centuries AD). One engineer was building 98-foot-high five-deckers about AD 587, and in the eighth century the largest Chinese ships carried loads of up to 635 tons; each had several hundred sailors. A pair of 197-foot dragon boats are mentioned for circa AD 965, and an AD 759 writer alleged that during the Jin period a naval ship 984.3 feet long was constructed.

The student of Chinese ships Valentin A. Sokoloff claimed that fifteenth-century records indicate 600-foot-long junks. Many of the ships of Admiral Zheng He's spectacular fifteenth-century expeditions are said to have exceeded

1,500 tons, with one writer estimating a burden of some 2,540 tons and a displacement of 3,150, although both smaller and larger estimates have also been made. Documents tell of Zheng's sixty-two largest treasure ships being 443 feet long and almost 180 feet wide, carrying up to nine masts and crews of 450 to 500 men! Although some have dismissed these sizes as impossible,[23] in 1962 a rudderpost was discovered archaeologically that is so enormous that it implies a ship between 479 and 535 feet in length. The Ming-period Longsiang shipyard near Nanjing had 1,500-foot-long drydocks. One sinologist concluded that the largest of the "treasure ships" were three times the magnitude of Admiral Horatio Nelson's eighteenth-century flagship of the line *Victory*.[24]

Although its ships did not equal China's, Japan, too, had quite sizable vessels, to judge from first-century AD rock paintings and clay models of large, sophisticated boats of circa AD 300. Ambassadorial missions sent to China in the early 700s traveled on ships carrying about 150 passengers. A hundred-person Japanese ship is recorded as having been wrecked off the China coast in the late 1100s, and in the fourteenth century a shogun commissioned trading ships with capacities of up to three hundred persons. By the fifteenth century, merchantmen of over 1,000-*koku* (39,700-bushel) capacities were being sent to China, carrying crews of around one hundred, plus passengers. A number of Japanese ships are known to have traveled to Mexico and back during the early 1600s.[25]

Oceania

As for the Pacific itself, based on European Contact-period observations of watercraft it is thought that the double canoes in which the Polynesian diaspora is supposed to have taken place were generally some 60 to 70 feet long with circa 40-ton capacities, and carried about fifty to sixty crew and passengers. But much larger craft existed, even in the historic period when watercraft and long-distance sailing had long been on the decline. These vessels are termed "canoes" only because of the narrowness of their beams relative to their lengths. This narrowness is a function of the canoes' lashed-plank construction, which limits beam. Nevertheless, narrowness makes for speed. In terms of magnitude, capacity, possession sometimes of two masts, and partial decking, however, they may truly be considered ships, and in fact, they were so termed by Captain Cook.

Few archaeological boat remains have been found in Oceania. However, on Huahine important vestiges of a canoe estimated to have been some 80 feet long were unearthed, dating to about AD 1000. The craft had a 35-foot mast and a 12-foot steering oar, and carried outriggers.[26] The last old-time Cook Islands seagoing canoe measured 60 feet long. In the pre-Contact Fijis, the Fijian war *vaka drua* could carry up to three hundred men plus cargo, and had 45-foot-long steering oars; *ndrua* double canoes reached lengths of 120 to 150 feet and widths of 50 feet. A Samoan-built Fijian double canoe described in 1875 had a capacity of five hundred to six hundred persons, and other Fijian and Tongan ones could transport two hundred to three hundred. In the Tuamotus, double canoes ranged from 75 to 120 feet long, with a width of 27 to 33 feet, carrying one or two masts and 50 to 120 people, and in Hawaii Kamehameha I's double canoe was 108 feet long. Such canoes required some 120 to 140 paddlers.

In New Zealand, Maori war canoes ranged from 60 to 120 feet long and carried as many as 150 people. A Tahitian double war canoe measured by Captain Cook reached 108 feet. Although war canoes were paddled, not sailed, other large single canoes had capacities of up to three hundred men. The largest *voyaging* canoes, some of which carried two masts and sails, were only about 76 feet long, with maximum crews of about twenty—although tradition tells of the twelfth-century voyager to New Zealand Whatonga's canoe carrying four navigator priests and a crew of sixty-two. In the Tokelau Islands, two-masted double canoes could carry 150 to 200, and in the Tongas about 150.[27] Maori traditions speak of sailing-canoes carrying two or three masts, and voyaging *pahi* canoes could carry at least 7.5 tons, including twenty-five crew members, equipment, and supplies, and could travel six to seven weeks without reprovisioning.[28]

Although their craft were on the decline by the time of European colonization, some Melanesians also possessed two-masted single and double canoes, of up to 65.6 feet in length, as well as war canoes of even greater size. In a few places, more than two hulls—up to fourteen, yielding dimensions of 51 by 59 feet—would be fastened together and a platform created. These seagoing craft carried pottery and sago flour for trade. Micronesians also once had double canoes, but in historic times they generally voyaged in single-outrigger craft (figure 19.2), which reached at least 75 feet in length.[29]

Does Size Matter?

Having roundly disposed of the myth that vessels as large as those of the Great Age of Discovery did not come into being except in Europe and until the time of Prince Henry the Navigator and Christopher Columbus, we turn to the issue of vessel size from a different angle, that of the necessity (or lack thereof) of large size for making ocean crossings.

The carrying capacity of a hull of a given shape increases geometrically with increase in linear dimensions. Therefore, larger size does convey advantages in terms of capacity to convey people, livestock, goods, supplies, and armament, the increased numbers of crewmen required notwithstanding. Still, as the sizes of early post-Columbian European ships of exploration attest, fairly modest craft were often used for purposes of exploration and even colonization, because small size translated into shallower draft and more strength and maneuverability.[30]

Seaworthiness does not increase proportionate to size. To the contrary, the larger the size, the greater the stresses set up by wind and wave as they encounter the inertia of the heavy craft, and thus the greater the possibility of breaking up. A fairly small craft, if well built, is more likely to survive a long sea voyage, especially if it is of flexible construction—as are lashed-log rafts and sewn-plank boats. "It has been repeatedly demonstrated by modern sailors that boats under twenty-five feet in length are safest for the Pacific."[31] There are numerous examples of modern transatlantic voyages in tiny boats, several of which were 13.5 feet or less in length (see chapter 21). The record for small size seems to be that of sixty-two-year-old Hugo Vihlen's 1994 voyage from Newfoundland to England in his 5-foot 4-inch, garage-built *Father's Day*.[32]

As Thor Heyerdahl[33] and many others have attested, a principal reason for the greater safety of smaller boats has to do with the distances between the crests of the waves or swells. If the length of a vessel approaches or exceeds one sea-swell wave length, then when two swells support the two ends of the craft there is tremendous stress placed on the less supported middle portion, and the vessel risks sagging and having its back broken by its own weight. Likewise, when the craft's middle lies atop a tall wave's crest, the bow and stern of the vessel are left unsupported, and hogging may result from stress of the craft's being shoved upward amidships. The greater the amplitude of the swells, the greater are these compressive and tensional forces. Tortional stresses, when sailing at an angle to swells, cause larger vessels to wrack (twist) as well. In contrast, a short, lightweight boat is simply lifted up and down as the swells pass beneath her and experiences minimal stress.

A 25-foot boat is only about four times the length of a recumbent tall man, and it is true that really tiny watercraft can be unstable in choppy seas—as can even somewhat larger ones when extreme wave conditions are encountered. Nevertheless, empirical evidence demonstrates beyond any doubt that even boats whose lengths are less than that of one man can, under reasonably favorable circumstances, make transoceanic crossings.

As far as capacity to carry supplies is concerned, the tendency is to think in terms of the postmedieval situation involving European global exploration and colonization and the carrying on board of virtually all foodstuffs to be consumed during voyages, as well as the supplies, such as weapons, tools, seed, and livestock, needed for the establishment of colonies. However, where colonization was not an aim, or even where it was but involved low-tech populations with few goods to carry, cargo capacity need not have been so great. Further, with lesser craft like rafts and smaller sailing-canoes, unlike with high-sided European ships or large junks, fishing is easily feasible. If much of the food supply can be thus obtained en route, then the need to carry supplies is much reduced. This is shown by the great number of documented lengthy postdisablement and postmutiny voyages involving small open craft with numbers of passengers (see chapter 4). The one that immediately comes to mind is the 1789, forty-one-day, 5,850-statute-mile, storm-harried forced voyage of Captain Bligh and eighteen men ousted from the *Bounty*, originating off Tofoa in the Tonga Islands and terminating at Coupang, Timor, in a short-provisioned and severely overloaded two-masted, 23-foot, 2.5-ton-displacement ship's launch (a few stops being made in Australia).[34]

Rigidity and Rigging

Other misconceptions concerning the ability of sailors to cross the oceans involve notions concerning the strength of ships' hulls and the capabilities of their rigs. Some think that until ships came to be skeleton-built, that is, their construction commencing with a rigid, integrated frame, as opposed to being shell-built (hull planking built up prior to insertion of ribs, thwarts, and such), they lacked sufficient strength for dealing with ocean waves.[35] Skeleton building for wooden ships evolved gradually in the West but appears not to have reached full development until the thirteenth century in western Europe. East Asian junks achieved comparable strength thousands of years ago, using a system quite different from that developed in Europe (see chapter 20). It turns out that flexible watercraft possess certain advantages over rigid ones and were routinely used for long-distance ocean voyaging in the Indo-Pacific region (see chapter 19).

The notion that before the AD 1400s, ships' masts and sails were too few to provide sufficient motive power and speed, and that before the addition of a fore-and-aft-rigged lateen sail to the mizzen mast, their square rigs were inadequate for sailing into the wind, that is, tacking to make progress in an upwind direction.

In certain ways, European marine architecture did decline after the fall of Rome, and early medieval craft tended to be single-mast, single-square-sail vessels, unlike the typical two-masted Roman merchant ships of yore, which carried a mainsail plus three or four lesser sails (see chapter 16). We have seen that multimast and multisail ships were common in Chinese waters. Too, rigs permitting relatively easy tacking were ancient in Asian and Pacific seas.

Medieval European ship design and rigging *had* improved by AD 1400 over what it had been during the preceding several centuries: high, pointed bows to meet head seas; two or three masts and more than one main-mast course (a sail at a particular level) to provide greater propulsive power; and better rigs, which permitted sailing within six or seven points—67.5 or 78.75 degrees—of the wind. This permitted faster voyaging and made year-round Atlantic sailing more feasible. Still, improvements that meant easier exploration and enhanced trade, as well as the possibility of large-scale overseas colonization, do not imply that transoceanic voyaging from Europe or North Africa had previously been impossible or even extremely challenging. We need only look at the considerable transatlantic traffic—including nonstop between Greenland and Norway—of the Norse in their open, square-rigged, single-sailed, single-steering oared *knerrir* (merchant ships) to see that such voyages were more than just possible—and in rough northern waters, at that.

Giving No Quarter: Issues Concerning Rudders

To keep a sailing-vessel on course, both by steering and by limiting leeway, when sailing in a direction other than straight downwind a craft requires some means of exerting lateral resistance to the wind. On keeled craft, the keel contributes in this regard. On keel-less craft, leeboards may be installed. Up to the invention of the pintle-and-gudgeon (metal-hinged) sternpost rudder, Western ships were steered, and their leeway impeded as well, by one or a pair of heavy, broad-bladed oars suspended slantwise from each quarter (the sternward portion of one side) and operated from the deck by a tiller bar held by a single helmsman. These "quarter rudders" were rotated, not swept from side to side. According to Joseph Needham and to many others, without the invention of the stern rudder—or rather its adoption and adaptation from earlier Chinese models—the Portuguese discoveries that preceded Columbus's would not have been possible. With only steering oars, so goes the claim, ships, especially those over 50 tons, lacked maneuverability in heavy weather and thus dared not venture onto the open sea.[36] This view reflects one of the hoary contentions concerning Columbus's voyages—that the arrival of the stern rudder in Europe contributed an essential element that finally permitted sailing across the Atlantic.

The rapid replacement, in the West, of quarter rudders and of median stern sweeps by pintle-and-gudgeon stern rudders would seem to speak for itself as to their relative utilities. But although at first glance this replacement appears to have been a simple matter of a superior technology supplanting an inferior one, the story is far more complex. In *The Development of the Rudder*, the maritime historian Lawrence V. Mott observed, "The quarter rudder . . . was a very effective device . . . by the time of the Romans it had evolved into an instrument capable of controlling very large ships. . . . The quarter rudder was eventually replaced as the primary control device for ships during the [European] nautical revolution that began in the late thirteenth century with the widespread adoption of the pintle-and-gudgeon rudder by Mediterranean shipwrights. Yet this revolution did not involve the simple replacement of an older steering device with a new mechanism but entailed a profound change in hull design and rigging—to which the pintle-and-gudgeon rudder was directly related."[37]

In other words, the sternpost rudder was effective in conjunction with a particular kind of ship design and was neither necessary nor even the best system for every kind of craft.[38] In part, quarter rudders were abandoned because the oars used would have to have been too long to operate with the elevated freeboard of the high-sterned ships that Europeans had begun to build.

Further, the declared superiority of the stern rudder was true only with reference to the weak northern European single-steering-oar mounting system when applied to larger ships, and not with reference to the much better Mediterranean mounting system or those of other regions of the world. In fact, the balance and redundancy of paired quarter rudders conferred some advantages. Neither was there anything to prevent northern ships from employing two of them, as smaller Mediterranean vessels continued to do, but the stern-rudderless Norse ships that reached North America were propelled almost entirely by sail, not by rowing, and the single quarter rudder was long enough not to come completely out of the water when the ship heeled. The experimental *Brendan* voyage in an Irish skin boat, as well as Magnus Magnusson's replication of a Norse crossing, showed the single quarter rudder to function entirely satisfactorily (see chapter 21).[39] It appears, then, that the absence of the sternpost rudder did not play any critical role in inhibiting transoceanic voyaging, especially with respect to smaller craft.

Stern rudders (worked with lines rather than with a tiller) reached the Indian Ocean (from the South China Sea) before AD 985. In China, the true median rudder, set centrally at the stern transom (or at a more forward one), is earliest attested in China in a Han dynasty ceramic model. The rudder posts of Chinese rudders were sometimes in gudgeon-like fittings but did not employ the true pintle and gudgeon system. The particularly efficient form of the balanced rudder was well established by at least the eleventh century and had been anticipated by the balanced median rudder of the Han model.[40] Therefore, whatever may be contended about Western ships, it cannot be said of China from Hou Han times (first century AD) on, that lack of the device prevented that country from undertaking transoceanic voyages. Other approaches and equipment enhancing early Chinese nautical success included multiple staggered masts, which were related to bulkheads connected with watertight-compartment ship construction (by the second century AD and probably much earlier); the chain pump (first mentioned in an AD-80 work), used to evacuate bilgewater; and the magnetic compass (probably before AD 800; see chapter 22).[41]

Running Afoul: Sea Worms and Associates

In addition to ordinary fouling with barnacles, mussels, and seaweed, which reduces velocity, in many warmer regions or where warm currents penetrate cooler climes the wood of watercraft is attacked by marine boring clams—"shipworms"—and other organisms.[42] "The most common borer, *Teredo navalis*, can enter unprotected wood surfaces at a density of up to 5,000 per square foot. It has a life span of ten weeks, during which it can chew out a tube one-fourth inch in diameter and six or more inches long, with no external manifestation except for its tiny entry hole."[43] Boring clams, which are able to grow to two feet long, can be a major hazard, because as hulls become weakened by myriad holes they may leak and eventually break up. Owing to such damage, Columbus had to scuttle all four of his ships on his 1502 voyage, and Vespucci also experienced shipworm problems. After six-and-a-half months at sea, Éric de Bisschop's experimental cypress-log raft *Tahiti-Nui II* broke up owing to shipworm damage.[44] The experimental junk *Tai Ki* was destroyed by a combination of shipworm damage and rough seas.[45] All this has led some to conclude that shipworm problems would likely have prevented at least Pacific crossings in pre-Renaissance craft. Nevertheless, tests conducted in Panama indicated life-spans for wood of from two to twelve years, according to wood type, age, and seasoning, as well as to water salinity (teredos require a minimum of 12 percent salinity).[46] The tropical wood of the mandailis tree, used for shipbuilding in the East Indies and Malay Peninsula, is not attacked by shipworm,[47] and the widely used wood of southern Asia's teak tree is also rather resistant to teredos. In any event, it is indisputable that thousands of early post-1492 ships successfully traveled long distances unprotected.

Too, in some regions, hull coatings were devised to combat the clams and other fouling organisms. A number of sources on the Indian Ocean, including Marco Polo, mention *chunam*, a variable concoction involving lime, fish oil, animal fat, and other ingredients. An "ointment" coating is mentioned as long ago as the circa-1200-BC Akkadian Gilgamesh legend, and the mixture goes back to at least 5500 BC in Mesopotamia (see chapter 17). Tung oil was utilized in China.[48] Bitumen was applied in Egypt and southern Asia, conifer pitch, sea-mammal tar, arsenic, and sulfur in the Mediterranean and Atlantic Europe. Oil, clay, and charcoal were used in Polynesia. A least in New Caledonia, new hulls were soaked in seawater for three weeks, so that the salt could draw out the sap and thus convey some protection.

In addition, early infestation can be avoided by fitting craft in freshwater river mouths rather than in saltwater, where the clams are found. Tim Severin treated his experimental bamboo raft *Hsu Fu* with lacquer, a traditional and toxic sealer for Asian watercraft, and saw its first teredos only after six months at sea.[49]

To test the old-time Indian Ocean antifouling treatment, on the basis of Lakshadweep (Laccadive) Islands practice Severin started by having his experimental Arabian boom *Sohar* made out of *aini* wood from Karnataka State, India, which has a high lime content and is much longer-lived in the water than is more commonly used teakwood. Subsequent treatment consisted of painting the hull's exterior with a mixture of fish oil and sugar and then coating it with lime. After a circa 6,000-mile voyage from Oman to Canton (Guangzhou), China, "Her traditional antifouling had protected the hull effectively against shipworm, whereas unprotected timber, especially sapwood, was riddled by teredo."[50]

Other antifouling possibilities are periodic diving and scraping of the hull, or—if suitable land is encountered—careening, scraping, and hole plugging.

Sheathing ships' hulls with sheet copper or lead protects physically against sea worm and, because of the toxic cuprous or plumbous oxide produced, protects chemically against fouling by marine flora. Ancient Jewish sources mention "copper ships," and on some Carthaginian and Roman ships protective copper and lead sheathing over resin-impregnated fabric was employed.[51] The earliest known remains of lead sheathing were found on a late fifth-century-BC wreck from Italy's Strait of Messina.[52] Although a satisfactory answer to teredos, difficult-to-make and expensive metal sheathing was discontinued at the end of ancient times in the West and was not revived until the late sixteenth century. There is evidence that in the Far East application of metal sheathing is at least as old as it is in the Mediterranean region.[53] Note that sheathing was not used in Columbus's or Magellan's or Drake's day. So if even they could make return transoceanic—even around-the-world—voyages despite shipworms, then, presumably, others, in ancient times, could have as well.

After dispensing with the myths concerning the superiority of land transport, the dangers of deepwater voyaging, and the inadequacies of size and design of early watercraft, it is difficult not to agree with David H. Kelley when he asserts: "The presence of adequate watercraft for these purposes has been available in most coastal waters all around the world these past five thousand years. Watercraft and navigational techniques far superior to those of Columbus have been in use in many parts of the world for at least three thousand years. As an a priori reason for rejecting contacts, this view [of inadequacy of watercraft and navigation] has no validity at all."[54]

15

It's Earlier Than You Think

The Antiquity of Seagoing Watercraft

Surely oak and threefold brass surrounded his heart who first trusted a frail
vessel to the merciless ocean.
                                                    —Horace, first century BC

Humans are terrestrial creatures, physically structured to allow pedal land travel.
True, people also possess the structural requirements for swimming, but swim-
mable distance is strictly limited (to about 40 continuous miles for a very fit
person lacking professional training and special equipment) and many, perhaps most, people around the world, even a good percentage of sailors, never
learned to swim. In the face of this physical limitation and in view of the existence of water bodies and aquatic resources, over the millennia humans devised a remarkable variety of craft to permit themselves to travel over the face
of the deep. The watercraft developed ranged from the simplest flotation devices to boats and ships that were supreme achievements of preindustrial technical complexity and sophistication. Clearly, any discussion of possible transoceanic contacts needs to give appropriate consideration to the several solutions
to the water-transport challenge that humans have contrived in different areas
of the world, and to evaluate their respective capabilities. That is, the question
of *means* for possible early ocean crossings must continue to concern us in this
and the following few chapters.

How Old in the Old World?

Southeastern Asia and Near Oceania

Until rather recently, the consensus has been that utilization of ocean-serviceable
watercraft began relatively late in human history. However, the past few decades have witnessed a revolution in our understanding of the antiquity and
importance of their human use.[1] Coastal cultural adaptation goes back at least
165,000 years, and we now know that in some regions watercraft were well developed by peoples of paleolithic technology long prior to the end of the Pleistocene epoch, which terminated some 11,700 years ago. No physical remains
or depictions of such craft have been recognized as of yet (with one exception,

mentioned below). However, dated stone tools found on the Indonesian island of Flores suggest a presence there, some 840,000 BC, of Middle Paleolithic humans, presumably *Homo erectus*, predecessor to our species, *Homo sapiens*, which, in turn, appears to have emerged in Africa about 195,000 years ago and to have reached eastern Asia some 70,000 years ago or somewhat earlier. The pre-*sapiens* humans could have arrived on Flores from the Asian mainland only by making at least two sea crossings, the minimum width of the wider of the two straits having been some 15.5 miles at lowest sea stand. Repeated natural rafting is unlikely and watercraft use is implied—although some authorities believe that simple floats would have been adequate.

The Australian cognitive archaeologist Robert G. Bednarik has undertaken experiments with simple rafts of bamboo and rattan whose construction was based on hypothetical paleolithic models and which were built employing Lower Paleolithic types of stone tools. In 2000, Bednarik's crew of a dozen paddlers successfully negotiated the treacherous Lombok Strait in twelve hours in the raft *Nale Tasih 4*. In 1998, he and a four-man crew had traveled on 59-foot *Nale Tasih 2*—which carried a palm-fiber sail—680 miles from Timor to off Australia, in thirteen days; it took only six days to reach the edge of the continental shelf, Australia's Last Glacial Maximum shoreline. Only paleolithic-style foodstuffs, containers, and tools were utilized (see also chapter 21).[2]

Less extreme in age than the 840,000 years mentioned above—and therefore less controversial—are possibly 100,000- to 200,000-year-old stone tools from both Flores and Timor. Reaching Flores from Sundaland (Pleistocene lower-sea-level western Indonesia) at these times would have required a minimum of four water crossings, reaching Timor nine, of up to 18 miles.

Many culture historians have an image of most of pre-nineteenth-century humanity's being essentially land-bound and either technologically too primitive to have been able to traverse great distances or sedentary farmers whose horizons were extremely limited, often traveling, in their lifetimes, no farther than to surrounding villages or to the local market town. Whereas this image is undoubtedly accurate for the majority of the world's farming and urban populations of the past, there did exist, on land, wide-ranging hunters and gatherers, pastoral nomads, and peripatetic populations such as India's Banjaras and Europe's India-derived Gypsies. On the water were southern and eastern Asia's sea nomads (attested archaeologically as far back as 5000–6000 BC[3]) as well as the mobile inhabitants of the far-flung Pacific islands. And, in contrast to the essentially terrestrial agricultural portions of humanity, there was, as has been mentioned, a thin but highly significant littoral line of fishing and trading peoples possessing maritime adaptations that were quite different from the lifeways of the interior.

Early Maritime Culture

In 1986, the Italian archaeologist of Southwest Asia Maurizio Tosi proposed that maritime cultures emerged separately from those of the early centers of agrarian civilization, not in response to the latter's thirst for exotic goods. The preexistence of these maritime societies allowed rapid co-option of their skills on the part of Mesopotamians and others. Tosi saw four hearths of maritime elaboration: the North Sea, the Mediterranean, the Arabian Sea, and Island Southeast Asia. These developments would have occurred between 14,000 and 5,000 years ago, maritime connections among the emerging urbanizing centers intensifying as early as the fifth millennium BC, a millennium or more before the birth of Mesopotamia's first states.[4]

Early regular use of watercraft for interisland voyaging is thought to have emerged in a "voyaging corridor" extending from the Asian mainland to the Melanesian islands, where favorable conditions included warm waters, myriad intervisible islands, shelter from cyclones, dependable seasonally shifting monsoon winds, and a generous supply of bamboos, and this zone exhibits the earliest indication of systematic human expansion via watercraft.[5] It is likely the major fountainhead of ancient nautical development.

The evolution of watercraft no doubt began during the Lower Paleolithic, initially with simple swimming floats, followed by riding floats—of wood, bundles of dried stalks, wild gourds, or inflated animal skins—and leading, as time went on, to rafts, to basketry and skin-covered boats, and to crude sewn-bark canoes. As time rolled on, craft became increasingly waterworthy and knowledge of seamanship slowly advanced. Any very early long sea voyages were probably accidental (see chapter 5). But whether accidentally or not, in Australia human occupance (probably initially by people similar to contemporary Negrito Andaman Islanders) seems to have been firmly established by about 45,000 years ago (and very possibly began by 60,000 or more years ago) in Northern Territory, the entrants probably coming by sea from Timor. In Tasmania, people were present by about 38,000 years ago. Direct evidence of watercraft at about 20,000 years ago exists in the form of a pictograph on a rock in Western Australia. The painting shows four persons in a craft with turned-up ends,[6] perhaps a reed-bundle raft-boat—a type that survived into historic times in Tasmania (see chapter 17).

Throughout the last two million years or more, there have existed significant water gaps in Wallacia, which lies between the Southeast Asian mainland/Greater Sunda Islands/Borneo (Sundaland) zone and the low-sea-level coasts of New Guinea and Australia (Sahul), requiring a number of crossings of straits. No route to Australia had a maximum gap of less than about 55 miles, even at lowest sea stand when most of the region's areas of now shallow sea were dry land, and many of the islands involved lacked intervisibility. People have to have had watercraft to make such crossings. These early transits—even those postulated to have occurred as long ago as the Middle Paleolithic—must have been deliberate. Although sophisticated watercraft are not implied—simple paddled rafts would do—it is nevertheless extremely doubtful that accidental displacement of people of both sexes on natural rafts of vegetation or using floats would have arrived in numbers great enough to establish sustainable populations—several groups that included five to ten women of reproductive age, according to one opinion[7]—in so many areas. The depauperate faunas to the east of Wallace's Line[8] argue against the efficacy of natural rafting, and neither were modern humans' premodern predecessors rafted to the east of Flores as one would expect had natural rafting been a viable mechanism in the region.

We now have an archaeological human—probably proto-Negrito—foot bone from northern Luzon in the Philippines (to the east of Wallace's Line and so accessible only by water) dating to some 67,000 years ago. Human occupation of the Talud Islands between Mindinao and Sulawesi and some 62 miles distant, was established around 35,000 years ago. Accepted dates of the earliest known archaeological sites in Wallacia, New Guinea, and Australia generally run in the 40,000s before present, although some scholars propose substantially earlier figures. Evidence of humans in New Guinea goes back to about 53,000 (some say 54,400–65,000) calendar years ago, the ancestors probably having arrived via Indonesia's Molucca Islands. Archaeology attests to pelagic fishing at about 43,400 calendar years ago in East Timor.

Earliest radiocarbon dates for human (presumably, ancestral Papuan) occupancy of islands of Near Oceania to the north and east of New Guinea are astonishingly early: about 45,400 calendar years ago in New Britain and New Ireland, 24,000 to 43,100 years ago in Bougainville, and some 37,100 years ago in the Solomon Islands' Buka.[9] Again, watercraft would have been the only feasible means for colonizing these lands, and deep-sea fishing is evidenced in New Ireland at some 35,000 years ago.[10] Most of these islands are intervisible, but to reach Buka from New Ireland required an 87-mile ocean voyage, one-third of which was out of sight of land. Manus in the Admiralty Islands, which humans reached at some unknown date prior to 28,000 years ago, involved an open-sea crossing of either 118 or 136 miles, 35 or 53 miles of which would have been a "blind crossing," in which neither island would be in direct sight.[11]

Beginning about 24,000 calendar years ago, New Britain obsidian for tool-making was being carried to New Ireland 217 miles away and by the end of the Pleistocene was finding its way throughout the Bismarck Archipelago. By about 1000 BC (and possibly earlier), long-distance seaborne trade was taking such obsidian some 2,175 miles westward from New Britain and the Admiralty Islands to Borneo.[12]

Although at low sea stands the islands of the western Pacific were both much larger and more numerous than at present, major water gaps still existed (see chapter 23) and were crossed. The traversing of these kinds of gaps makes it likely that sail was invented during the Pleistocene, by Papuans, in the greater Indonesian region long before the arrival of Austronesians there, and was employed in these crossings (see the following chapter). It would seem probable that the craft on which it was used were bamboo and/or log rafts (see chapter 17).

Okinawa, in the Ryukyu Islands and probably always a minimum of 43 miles from Japan or Taiwan (although this has been debated), was settled by about 35,000 years ago and has yielded "Minotogawa man" skeletons dated to some 17,000 or more years ago. In Japan proper—probably settled some 40,000 years ago via the Korea Strait—obsidian was being obtained from Kozushima in the Izu Islands 34 miles off Honshu and 15.5 miles from the nearest intervening island, as early as 30,000 years ago, showing that Paleolithic voyaging was going on in East Asia as well.[13]

In sum, there can be no question that seagoing watercraft were available to Upper Paleolithic peoples in Australasia and East Asia, and that there were many millennia during which the development of craft capable of later truly transoceanic voyages could occur. In fact, greater Southeast Asian waters appear to have been the global center of the early development of watercraft, sails and rigs, navigation, and maritime travel.

The Mediterranean and the North Atlantic

The Mediterranean Sea is studded with islands, most being visible from the mainland as well as intervisible with neighboring islands. For decades it has been recognized that the Greek isle of Kefallinia was occupied in the Middle Paleolithic, requiring a water crossing of some 3.7 miles, and that Paleolithic humans had reached Crete by 10,000 BC. In Greece, obsidian from the Cycladic island of Melos was found at the Peloponnesian mainland site of Franchthi Cave 115 miles away, at late Upper Paleolithic levels, some 10,050 BC.

Mesolithic settlements occurred on Cyprus, forty miles from Anatolia (by the tenth millennium BC), on Sardinia (about ninth to eighth millennium BC), on Corsica (7000–6300 BC), and on Mallorca (fifth millennium BC). Farming became established on Cyprus, and, following a circa 38,000-year-old Paleolithic settlement in the case of Sicily, on Sicily and Crete (a minimum of 40 miles from other land) between 8200 and 6000 BC. During this last period, obsidian from the islands around Sicily was reaching northern Italy, Dalmatia, Corsica, Provence, and North Africa. Gotland in the Baltic and all the island groups around Great Britain have Neolithic remains, and settlement by farmers goes back to the mid-sixth millennium BC in some of these areas. The presence of these populations necessitated their pioneers having crossed bodies of water subject to violent weather and sea changes and, often, out of the sight of land. Tenerife in the Atlantic's Canary Islands, about 65 miles offshore and visible from the mainland, was settled by about 500 BC.

Although these are all respectable dates, until fairly recently there was little evidence of really early voyaging in the Mediterranean/North Atlantic world. That has changed. Bednarik, who has concluded that going to sea in boats may be a million or so years old and rude sails and sea anchors as much as 60,000 to 30,000 years old, determined that five Mediterranean islands were reached in Pleistocene times, including as early as 300,000 years ago in the case of Sardinia. Human remains dated to about 50,000 years ago were found on Crete, where *erectus*-type stone tools appear at pre-170,000-year-old levels (and style suggests 700,000 years). There is evidence of humans on southern Ionian islands at some 110,000 years ago. Similar Acheulian tools on both sides of the Strait of Gibraltar suggest regular crossings by hominins—probably, *Homo erectus*—as early as 1.4 million years ago. The strait, which at present is 9 miles across and exhibits strong west–east water flow, would have had an island in it 1.6 million years ago, with straits 3.1 and 1.2 miles wide. Around 20,000 BC, there was also a common Upper Paleolithic material culture on both sides of the straits.[14] One would expect bundle rafts (see chapter 17), presumably paddled, to have been the conveyances.

These and many other examples that have come to light in recent decades have drastically altered our understanding of the antiquity of human mobility over the waters and have demonstrated that for tens, even hundreds of thousands of years, watercraft have played a central role in spreading the human race across the globe, linking continents and islands. In fact, most archaeologists now think in terms of the first settling of the Americas having occurred with humans traveling coastally around the North Pacific rim by boat instead of across dry Ice Age Bering Strait.[15] If Paleolithic people could have accomplished such a movement, could not have later peoples possessing much-superior watercraft have done so?

16

Have Sail, Will Travel

The Origins, Types, and Capabilities of Sails and Rigs

And who else by the Art of Navigation have seemed to imitate Him, which
laies the beams of his chambers in the Waters, and walketh on the wings of
the wind?

—Samuel Purchas, early 1600s, referencing Psalms 104:3

The invention of the sail was one of humankind's most significant accomplishments, rivaling if not outweighing in importance the invention of the vehicular wheel. The Australian Polynesianist archaeologist Atholl Anderson considered its emergence to have been "no less significant than Neolithicization and
urbanization."[1] The sail was a tool that utilized, with minimum effort, an ongoing and gratis source of energy without diminishing the supply, and that fact
ultimately led to the ability to travel to anywhere touched by the seven seas. Just
where sails first came to be used cannot be definitively ascertained, although—
as mentioned in the previous chapter—coastal/insular greater Southeast Asia
was perhaps the earliest hearth.

Putting Wind in the Sail: Origins

Whereas accidental drift voyages could carry castaways in sail-less watercraft
for great distances, even sometimes across seas, intentional transoceanic travel,
especially if involving return voyages, almost necessarily involved the use of
sail. Although people widely propelled their craft by poling and paddling, and
in some Old World areas by sculling or rowing, and although in modern times
a number of oar-powered transatlantic, transpacific, and transindian crossings
have been made, at least in the tropics paddle power alone would not be practical for very long voyages, owing to the high food and water requirements that
such physical effort would engender—although paddling or rowing remained
an important supplement during periods of calm and of contrary winds.

The principle of using wind pressure as a source of propulsion no doubt
arose by observation of its effect on the craft alone and/or on a person in the
craft, especially if standing and even more so if holding something against which
the wind could press (or, stricltly speaking, behind which the wind could create

a propulsive vacuum). In fact, ancient depictions and modern ethnographic observations suggest that a vertically held foliated tree branch or palm frond (possibly used as camouflage while hunting) may have been the first protosail, probably followed by a crude manually maintained mat, perhaps made of two palm fronds plaited together, yielding a kind of hand-held bipod mast with sail. If the invention of the sail was later, leather or basketry shields could also have functioned as protosails. The ancient Mesopotamian Gilgamesh legend has its hero holding his garment aloft as a field-expedient sail.

The earliest true sails, which seem certainly to have preceded the loom-weaving of cloth, were presumably made of matting. These sorts of sails have survived into contemporary times in certain parts of the world. In some areas (for example, northwestern Europe), leather sails were used instead. Later, lighter-weight and more flexible cloth sails of linen, wool, and cotton came to be utilized—initially, of plain weave, later of twill weave, the latter imparting greater strength.

What most consider to be the earliest depiction of a seeming sailing craft so far discovered is from As-Sabiyah, Kuwait, where an apparent boat with a converging bipod mast is painted on an Ubaid 3-period ceramic disk dated to the late sixth millennium BC.[2] Models, pottery and fresco representations, and petroglyphs of boats with masts and rectangular sails are known from pre-Dynastic Egypt at circa 3500 BC and from circa 3400 BC in Mesopotamia.

Ships with square sails are also depicted on Minoan seals from Crete of about 2000 BC. South Asia's earliest representations of masts (some possibly bipod) and (probably square or rectangular) sails date to the Harappan period (third millennium BC). In China, direct evidence of sails goes back into the second millennium BC. On the basis of these data, many believe that use of sail did not commence until around the fifth millennium BC,[3] and around the mid-Holocene there is indeed much evidence for increased maritime mobility. The experimental voyager Dominique Görlitz has reported Neolithic rock paintings, distributed from the Algerian Sahara to Northeast Africa, that depict masts, sails, and leeboards.[4] In my opinion and that of a number of others, sail was being employed much earlier.

It's Rigged: Sail Types and Suspensions and What They Can Do

Sails may be classified on the basis of their shapes, but far more important is how they are rigged—that is, how they are disposed in relationship to the mast via their attachment to it. This matter of orientation and mounting critically affects the sailing properties of the craft. This is especially relevant with respect to making way in an upwind direction by means of tacking or shunting (two different methods of zigzagging upwind via alternating "reaches"—segments of the route—at an angle off the wind less than 90 degrees). The technicalities of sails, rigs, and vector changes are complex, and the present explanation is somewhat simplified.

At some point in time, poles would have come to be substituted for the human in holding a palm-frond or other incipient sail. On the basis of early Egyptian, Harappan, and Chinese evidence, we may suppose that bipod shear masts (two poles that converge and are lashed together at the masthead) preceded or accompanied the earliest single-pole ones. At least in Egypt, the bipod is believed to have been developed to divide the stress between the two, weak sides of the papyrus-bundle craft (see chapter 17). It is often said that on the Nile, where linen was fairly early employed, a dependable upriver wind invited use of sails to counter the downriver current, and that Egypt may have seen the West's earliest sail use, in late pre-Dynastic times, circa 3500 BC. On the other hand, the steady seasonal monsoon winds of the waters off of southern Asia might also have favored sail development, and I strongly suspect that the sail first emerged in those waters rather than on the Nile.

Square Rigs

The earliest true sails for substantial craft appear, at least in the West, to have been square rigged. With this system, each rectangular sail hangs from a horizontal yard (a single spar or a pair of spars lashed end to end, butts overlapping). The yard is hung from the head of a shear bipod mast or from the forward side(s) of the vertical monopod mast(s), at the yard's center, and extends athwart the craft while at rest (at right angles—square—both to the mast and to the craft's long axis). Half of the sail extends to starboard of the mast, half to port. With square-rigged sails, the wind always blows against the same side of the sail, the side that faces the stern when the sail is at rest.

In earlier Dynastic Egypt (and in some regions into modern times), in addition to the yard there was a boom (spar) at the foot of the tall sail,[5] a feature dropped in New Kingdom times in favor of a loose-footed, reefable (shortenable) sail. Sail shortening, useful when the wind blows strongly, seems, in the West, to have been an eastern Mediterranean innovation, and involved brails—lines rising from the after deck, passing over the yard, and descending again to the foot of the sail, along which they were attached at intervals.

Although superior for sailing down or across the wind, simple square-rigged sails were not well suited to sailing *into* the wind, being, even until the nineteenth century, incapable of sending a ship at an angle much closer to the wind than 80 degrees (that is, at an angle of 80 degrees away from the direction from which the wind was blowing). For that reason, oars were very important in the early Mediterranean, to some extent in Norse Scandinavia, and in some other Old World regions. Still, as time went on even square-rigged vessels came to be able to tack, though not efficiently, by bracing the sail at an angle of up to about 25 degrees to the ship's long axis. However, sailing with a favorable wind was still overwhelmingly preferred for longer distances. Far better for tacking were fore-and-aft-rigged sails (see below); with them, a boat could sail much closer to the wind than could a square-rigged vessel.

To the square-rigged rectangular mainsail (*velum*), about the first century

Figure 16.1. A small Roman merchantman (*corbita*), showing the mainsail, a pair of raffee sails at the masthead, and an *artemon* on the bowsprit. Note the quarter rudder and the cabin aft. From Gordon Grant and Henry B. Culver, *The Book of Old Ships*, 1935, p. 50. By permission of Roxanne Grant Lapidus.

BC the Romans added a pair of triangular topsails (*sipara*, raffee sails) and, more importantly, a smallish, rectangular foresail (*artemon*) at the bow, a device picked up in the Indian Ocean (presumably by Greeks) that somewhat improved maneuverability. Occasionally, a sail was added at the stern (figure 16.1). The supplemental foresail seems to have fallen out of use in the Mediterranean after Classical times, only to be reintroduced in the early fifteenth century. Previously, we have seen that Roman merchantmen could make excellent time—4 to 6 knots with the wind and 2 to 3 against it.[6]

Several facts suggest the possibility of an ultimate origin of a number of watercraft and rigging features in southern Asia, early spread into both the Mediterranean and Yellow Seas, and a subsequent substantial replacement in the source area by more advanced vessels and rigs as the evolution of ship, sail, and rig proceeded. These facts include: (1) the ancient Egyptian possession of the square sail with yard and boom on a shear bipod mast and the rig's continued survival in the West and in the Arabian Sea, (2) possible depiction of square sails with yard and boom and of parallel-bipod masts in Harappan art, (3) indications of the rig's early presence in China with a parallel-bipod mast, (4) shear tripod masts in Indonesia and shear bipod masts in Myanmar (Burma), and (5) Egyptian-looking boat forms from Pakistan and China.[7]

Fore-and-Aft Rigs

As mentioned, the focus of sail and rig evolution, especially that of fore-and-aft rigs, seems to have been Southeast Asia, probably around the shores of the South China Sea. With fore-and-aft rigs, at-rest sail orientation is parallel with the long axis of the craft, not parallel to the beam as in square rigging. To allow more efficient sailing against the wind, the sail's leading edge (luff) is bent (bound) to the mast, to a tilted yard, or to a stay, and trails this. A ship carrying a square-rigged sail, which is hung from a horizontal yard, can travel at only a limited angle to the wind without the sail's leading edge being taken aback—caught on the wrong side by the wind—whereas a fore-and-aft-rigged sail's attachment to mast, yard, or stay allows setting the sail at a much greater angle to the wind while minimizing the risk of being taken aback.

Although fore-and-aft rigs are less efficient than square rigs when the wind blows from abaft the beam (from any direction between directly sternward and 90 degrees to the side of the craft), fore-and-aft rigging much facilitates tacking or shunting; with such sails, the wind blows against alternate sides of the sail on alternate reaches. The most efficient (weatherly) fore-and-aft-rigged vessels can sail to within 45 degrees of the direction of the oncoming wind, as compared to the approximately 80 degrees for simple square-rigged craft.[8]

The oldest type of fore-and-aft-rigged sail seems likely to have been some form of the spritsail (figure 16.2). This may have been invented as much as 45,000 years ago for use on rafts, probably by ancestors of the Papuan denizens of present-day eastern Indonesia, some of whom very early moved eastward to New Guinea and into islands beyond. Although variant forms exist, the most usual kind, the *Oceanic spritsail* (Polynesian Oceanic rig) is typically triangular and bent to two inclined spars (sometimes called a bifid mast, one spar being the functional mast, the other the sprit) diverging from their lower ends (more or less an inverted sheer-bipod mast). This type is the characteristic sail of Polynesia. With it, Polynesian canoes could sail handily as close as about 75 degrees off wind direction (even 60 degrees, say some), and it may have been the propulsive device on single-outrigger canoes in the initial Austronesian spread into Polynesia. (The possibly older common spritsail—rectangular rather than triangular—is a Malaysian type with occurrences in China and India, which also appeared in the Mediterranean during the second and third centuries AD, presumably adopted by Greco-Roman traders active in the Indian Ocean.[9])

A lugsail is defined as a sail that is bent to a yard hung from a mast at some point along that yard, with the yard in the same vertical plane as the craft's long axis rather than as its beam, and with more of the sail area aft than forward of the mast. Over time, the Oceanic spritsail seems to have been largely replaced in Indonesia and Micronesia by the *crane spritsail* (old Micronesian rig or "Oceanic lateen sail"), a lugsail that, like the spritsail, is triangular but whose functional

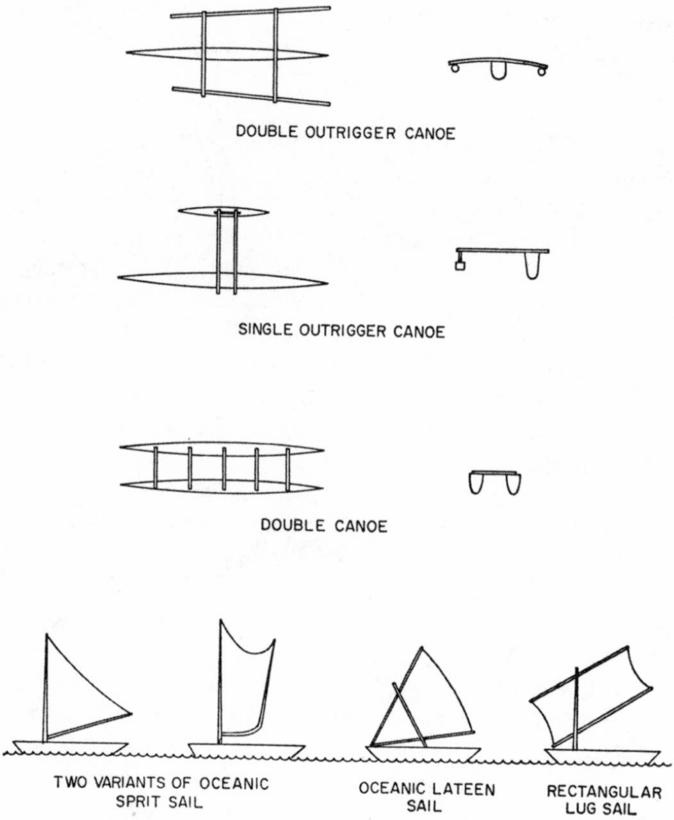

Figure 16.2. Traditional Pacific hull and sailing-rig types ("oceanic lateen sail" = crane spritsail). From Edwin Doran Jr., "Outrigger Ages." *Journal of the Polynesian Society* 16 (2) (1974): 131.

mast has been moved forward and is propped by a forward-raking pseudomast (which in some cases becomes a vertical mast); there is an angled spar along the sail's foot.[10] The type remains Micronesia's typical sail and is employed for shunting rather than for ordinary tacking; in shunting, the mast is restepped toward the canoe's opposite end and the two ends of the canoe alternate as bows on alternate reaches. This sail and rig later spread to Fiji and Tonga.

A third type of fore-and-aft-rigged sail is the *rectangular boom lugsail*. It is oblong and has canted upper and lower booms, the upper boom or yard being hung from near the masthead. It reminds one of the Old Kingdom Egyptian boomed rectangular sail, except for the fact that the yard and boom are angled and are hung fore and aft rather than square. Cave paintings from southeastern Sulawesi in Indonesia dating to about AD 1200 depict Egyptian-looking crescentic boats, each carrying a rectangular-boom lugsail hung from the head of a forward-set mast, as well as paired steering oars.[11] This sail type came largely to replace the crane spritsail in the Indonesian and Melanesian regions. The more efficient *square boom lugsail* and the even better *trapezial boom lugsail* were developed later, along the Gulf of Thailand coast and the coast of Vietnam, respectively.[12]

The early Chinese sail, as represented in the Shang dynasty (circa 1600–1028 BC) ideograph, was almost square and was supported by a parallel bipod mast (such sails and masts survive in parts of Melanesia). This sail was presumably minimally maneuverable, and it was followed, by the time of the Han dynasty (206 BC–AD 220), by the *Chinese balanced (stiffened) lugsail* (figures 17.4 and 20.1). Joseph Needham speculated that the Chinese lugsail arose from the "Indonesian canted square sail" (square boom lugsail), which in turn he thought went back to the Egyptian square sail.[13] It is rigged fore and aft, with from a sixth to a third of the sail before the mast, and is suspended at a corresponding point down the forward-slanting yard. Strengthened, stiffened, and kept flatter by means of bamboo battens; bound to vertical ropes on luff and leech (leading and trailing edges of the sail); and supported and manipulated by multiple sheets (moveable ropes) attached to the battens, the bamboo-matting lugsail was both almost impossible to tear and carry away and a very efficient instrument, one that allowed large ships to sail closer to the wind than any medieval European or Arab ship could. Matting sails, said one twelfth-century source, are useful with winds of almost any direction and "will carry men wheresoever they may wish to go."[14] The battens and the ease of lowering the elevation of the yard facilitated reefing (shortening batten by batten, from the foot) when the wind rose, precluding the necessity of furling the entire sail in a gale (however, the whole sail *could* be lowered in an instant). Many westerners have praised the efficiency and ease of handling of the Chinese lugsail.

Finally, there is the so-called Mediterranean lateen sail, a kind of virtually *triangular lugsail*, which is now characteristic of the Indian Ocean. It is good in light winds and is able to sail closer to the wind than is a square-rigged sail. It can be used for tacking, although this is not often done in the steady winds of that monsoonal sea, because it cannot be shortened, only replaced by a smaller sail. Its leading edge is bent to the single long, forward-slanting yard, and the yard is hung from a rather short vertical mast at a circa 45-degree angle.

Most presume the lateen sail to have originated in the Indian Ocean basin, a descendant of one of the easterly lugsails (although some think it possibly of Mediterranean origin).[15] Except for being loose-footed, it resembles the trapezial lugsail of Indochina, which, in turn, likely descended from the crane spritsail. A rock drawing from Gujarat in India showing a triangular sail dates to about 300 BC. The lateen sail thus seems to have come into existence by the fourth century BC or earlier; it became widely prominent after about AD 800, especially among Arabs.

Although requiring more hands and skill than a square sail, by the second century AD (and probably earlier) the lateen rig seems to have spread into the eastern Mediterranean, presumably from the Red Sea.[16] In the Mediterranean, this sail spread westward and gradually became the standard type used on smaller craft, which, in connection with their frequent enterings and leavings of ports, benefited particularly from the sail's tacking ability—despite the need (as with other lugsails) to rehang the boom when coming about (directly changing the vector of progress, with the wind on the opposite side of the sail) or jibing (looping completely around to a new tack, as was commonly done with square rigs). In late pre-Columbian times, a somewhat improved version of the lateen sail also came to be applied to the mizzenmasts of larger European ships, before being replaced in post-Columbian times by a more easily maneuvered *gaff-rigged boom sail* probably derived from Southeast Asia's common spritsail.[17]

Coming to America: Pre-Columbian Sail in the New World

As for the use of sail in the pre-1492 Americas, the only early direct indications are raft models from Arica, Chile, from about AD 200–500, which carry square matting sails. On the basis of early post-Columbian reports, pre-European-contact Ecuadorian balsa-log rafts (see chapter 17) employed both square sails and triangular fore-and-aft-rigged ones, both made from cotton cloth, on shear bipod masts, and sails were also used on dugout canoes in northern Ecuador. Pre-Columbian balsa rafts may well have reached the Galápagos Islands some 600 miles off the South American shore, where there exists disputed archaeological evidence.[18]

The Ecuadorian square sail is said to have differed from that of Europe in its masting, rigging, and utilization. As depicted in a 1618 woodcut, the triangular sail differs from any Indo-Pacific one in being loose-footed and bent to a curving mast.[19] However, the form could conceivably have derived from the simple Oceanic spritsail by elimination of the sprit, or it could represent an old type that later died out in Asia and the Pacific.

Other than this, sails are widely considered to have been absent in the pre-Columbian Americas. However, in 1577 the English explorer Martin Frobisher described skin or bladder sails on eastern Inuit (Eskimo) skin-covered umiak boats, and intestine and grass-mat sails may have been used by pre-1492 northern Alaskan Eskimos.[20] The American cultural anthropologists Harold E. Driver and William C. Massey considered Inuit sails to be aboriginal, along with others found along the Saint Lawrence River and at spots on the eastern seaboard of the United States.[21]

Suggestions of pre-Contact spritsail use in the West Indies, where settlement goes back to some 6,000 years ago, seem plausible. These are based on evidence of a high degree of mobility involving strait crossings almost impossible to make without sail, on native traditions, on early Spanish reports, and on native words for "sail."[22] Driver and Massey also accepted the sail as aboriginal among the Maya. Despite occasional speculation to the contrary, sails' pre-Columbian presence on the Northwest Coast of North America is very doubtful.

In summary, Old World sail use can be directly documented as far back as the fourth millennium BC, and indirect evidence indicates that it very likely extends back tens, possibly even hundreds of thousands of years in time. Thus the technological means of propulsion needed to make intentional transoceanic voyages has existed throughout the time period under discussion, the post-glacial Holocene.

17

Products of the Paleolithic

Rafts

Then I gathered many pieces of wood from the trees. . . . Then I found a way to twist grasses and twigs into a kind of rope, with which I bound the raft. . . .

. . . we hurried to the raft, untied it and, embarking on it, pushed it into the sea.

—Sindbad the Sailor, in *The Arabian Nights* (ca. AD 900)

Much of what we know about folk watercraft we owe to that indefatigable marine biologist James Hornell, whose *Water Transport* (1946) is the classic source, and to his collaborator, the Cambridge anthropologist A. C. Haddon. Also most worthy of mention is the nineteenth-century French Admiral Pierre Pâris's 1843 *Essai sur la construction navale des peuples extra-européens*[1] and the geographical distribution studies of the German scholar Hans Suder, in his *Von Einbaum und Floss zum Schiff* (1930). Many others have contributed since, as will be seen in these pages.

The study of nineteenth- and twentieth-century traditional craft is useful in reconstructing past vessel forms and distributions, because "we know that boatbuilders and sailors are extremely conservative in their choice of designs."[2] It cannot be known with certainty how far back in the human past and at what levels of technological attainment people began to construct and use particular kinds of watercraft, and direct archaeological evidence specific to truly ancient rafts and boats is, so far, disappointingly slim. Still, by comparing available skills that *have* been dated to particular time levels—skills such as coiled basketmaking, hut construction, and hide tanning and sewing—as well as by studying geographical distributions of historically known individual types of craft, it is possible to make educated estimates. Certainly, upper-paleolithic-level technology included the kinds of watercraft discussed in this chapter, not everywhere but in at least certain parts of the world, and some of these sorts of conveyances may even have arisen at the Lower Paleolithic level, well before the Late Pleistocene epoch, which ended a dozen millennia ago (see chapter 15).

Making a Bundle: Rafts Constructed from Clusters of Stems

Watercraft that, for flotation, depend on the natural buoyancy of the materials from which they are made rather than on the water displacement of a hollow,

air-filled hull, are termed "rafts." What appears likely to be one of the most ancient forms of raft (going back, in my view, to the African Upper Paleolithic,
possibly even the Lower Paleolithic, not just the Mesolithic as some see it) is
made, usually, from bundles of dried reeds, bulrushes, or comparable vegetal
material (for example, papyrus on the Nile, palm-leaf stalks in Bahrain, grass
in Sonora, bark in Tasmania, and so forth). Some of these craft were entirely in
the horizontal plane; others had bundles lashed along above the edges, which
made these rafts into what we may call raft-boats.

Where substantial trees are absent or rare, as in dry-climate areas, reeds,
bulrushes, or their ilk, found in the few wet spots such as the shores of exotic
streams and of sink lakes, may be the best (or only) material from which to construct craft. It is mainly in such areas that bundle raft-boats have survived into
modern times, although some have persisted in wetter-climate regions as well.
In historic times in the Old World, craft of these kinds have been described for
Botswana, much of northern Africa and the Mediterranean islands and littoral;
the Black Sea; Ireland and Hungary; around the upper Persian Gulf and Bahrain; southern Afghanistan and the northern Indian subcontinent; Sri Lanka;
Vietnam and South China; Japan; and southeastern Australia (in Tasmania,
they carried up to eighty passengers).

Archaeologically, bundle rafts were depicted well BC in many of these places.
Reed vessels are mentioned in the ancient Babylonian predecessor of the biblical Noah story, and the Babylonian origin myth involves the god Marduk creating the earth in the form of a floating reed raft. Moses (Moshe) was placed in a
bitumen-sealed papyrus-bundle boat, as described in Exodus 3:2, and his story
recalls that of an inscription that claims that Sargon of Akkad (circa 2300 BC)
was placed on the river in a basket of rushes sealed with bitumen. Reed boats
are also mentioned at Isaiah 18:2, speaking of the land beyond the rivers of
Ethiopia "that sendeth ambassadors by the sea, even in vessels of bulrushes
upon the waters."

That seagoing reed-bundle boats are ancient is directly indicated by a 5511–
5324 BC find at the Ubaid-related coastal site of As-Sabiyah, Kuwait. There, over
fifty slabs of barnacle-encrusted bitumen were found. The pieces of bitumen
(from 62 miles away), mixed with fish oil and ground coral, showed impressions
of reed bundles, ropes, and string, and are thought to be fragments of the earliest
watercraft—other than dugout canoes and one possible skin-boat fragment—yet
found archaeologically. At the same site, excavators discovered a ceramic model
of what is thought to be a bundle raft-boat. Bitumen-coated remains similar to
those at As-Sabiyah have been found at R'as al-Jinz in coastal Oman as well.
They evidence that, before coating, the raft exteriors were sheathed with reed
mats to reduce water and shipworm penetration as well as chafing.

Seaborne traffic during these times is also suggested by immediately pre-
Sumerian Ubaid potsherds from Mesopotamia found at many sites along the
Arabian side of the Persian Gulf. Sumerian records tell of Oman-bound craft of
18 tons' cargo, and circa 2000 BC writings provide the exact quantities of reed
bundles, rope, matting, fish oil, and bitumen required for a raft-boat.[3]

Figure 17.1. Crescentic craft, perhaps a bundle raft-boat, with quarter rudders and an apparent square sail bent to parallel bipod masts, depicted on a seal from Mohenjodaro, Pakistan, Harappan Civilization (2500–1500 BC). From Rhada Kumad Mookerji, *Indian Shipping*. London: Longmans, Green, 1912.

A crescent-shaped boat with a cabin and a pair of stern rudders appears on a rectangular seal discovered at the Indus Valley Harappan site of Mohenjodaro (figure 17.1); its form plus striations upon it hint strongly at the stems and bindings of a bundle craft. The third-century BC Greek mathematician Eratosthenes of Cyrene stated that reed craft with Egyptian-style sails and rigging were used for coastal voyages from the Ganges to Sri Lanka. Interestingly, some of the long, warrior-laden, quarter-rudder-steered craft depicted on bronze drums of northern Vietnam's maritime-oriented Dongson (Đông-so'n) culture that ended about AD 100 appear to be of bundle construction, and bundle raft-boats continue in use in that country. *Bufa* (bulrush rafts) were formerly used in South China, although other rafts there seem to have been of lashed-plank construction.[4]

Lashed-palm-rib rafts are known from New Guinea and the Solomon Islands. New Zealanders and denizens of its far-offshore Chatham Islands built rafts of bundles of plant stems and stalks, up to 60 feet long and capable of carrying sixty persons. Easter Islanders made reed-bundle floats and rafts, and such craft are mentioned in Hawaiian folklore.

In the western parts of the Americas, similar small craft were used from Washington State to Mexico's Sonora and from northern Ecuador to central Chile and northwestern Argentina, and they are also recorded for coastal Brazil. A bundle-raft model some 2,000 years old was found in northern Chile, and such craft, carrying platforms but no sails, are often depicted on Moche pottery from Peru of the first millennium AD (figure 17.2).[5]

There are three potential explanations for the extremely wide but disjunct

Figure 17.2. Depiction on a Moche pottery vessel of circa AD 600, Lambayeque Valley, North Coast of Peru: a sail-less seagoing double-decked bulrush-bundle raft-boat carrying three supernaturals, four prisoners, and cargo. Arm and legs symbolize the craft's "swimming" motion. From Izumi Shimeda, *Pampa Grande and the Mochica Culture,* © 1994. By permission of the University of Texas Press.

geographical distribution of these rafts: (1) multiple independent inventions; (2) a single origin and numerous subsequent dispersals to scattered places; or, most likely, (3) a very ancient single origin followed by very wide and largely continuous dissemination along coasts, with gaps developing subsequently as a consequence of replacement by later, superior forms of craft in those areas. In 1956, the historian of watercraft Richard LeBaron Bowen wrote, "It would seem that the reed raft or canoe must have reached South America by means of a coastwise diffusion from Asia by way of the Aleutian Islands, Alaska, and the west coast of America."[6] Likewise, in 1965, the geographer Clinton Edwards, a specialist in aboriginal South American watercraft, wrote, "Their distribution down the west coast of the Americas indicates a well-marked trail along a portion of a circum-Pacific route."[7]

Whatever the true story of bundle raft-boat dispersal, as far as construction is concerned the reeds or other materials are harvested, dried, and tied into bundles, and several bundles—usually two to form the floor and two to make sides—are lashed or stitched together (as in coiled basketry, which may not be as old) to form the raft. In a very few areas (especially Mesopotamia and Southern California), bitumen was applied to diminish water absorption. In most cases, the craft thus formed are/were small, propelled with pole or single or double paddle, and employed mainly for transport on rivers, lakes, marshes, or

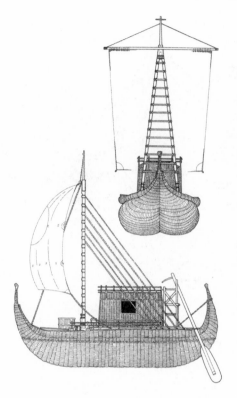

Figure 17.3. *Ra II*, a replica ancient Egyptian-style papyrus-bundle raft-boat carrying a cabin, a steering oar, and a square sail on a shear bipod mast. Note the stay supporting the high, curved stern. From *Early Man and the Ocean: A Search for the Beginnings of Navigation and Seaborne Civilizations* by Thor Heyerdahl, p. 18, © 1978 by Thor Heyerdahl. Used by permission of Doubleday, an imprint of the Knopf Doubleday Publishing Group, a division of Random House LLC. All rights reserved.

near-shore waters of the sea. Such small, paddled craft would have been quite capable of transporting humans relatively rapidly along the coasts of the world and even across not-too-broad stretches of open sea; Bering Strait, for instance, would have been no great barrier.

Beyond these little hand-propelled, often rather quickly waterlogging raft-boats, however, were some—certain of those used on the ancient Nile and probably on the Red Sea and the Bay of Bengal, some in Ethiopia, and those used on Bolivia and Peru's Lake Titicaca—that were longer lasting, employed sails on shear bipod masts, and were up to 70 feet long, as is documented from quite ancient times in a few cases (figure 17.3). Commonly, the bow and stern taper(ed) and curve(ed) upward, although other configurations have existed. The shapes of these craft suggest that they were designed to be used at sea, high bows and sterns functioning to break the waves.

The *totora* bulrushes from which Peruvian and Bolivian raft-boats are made are extremely buoyant. Tests by W. Castro in 1956 showed that after fourteen months of immersion in saltwater, a craft made of this material exhibited no hint of waterlogging, decomposition, or damage from marine organisms. Although they can break up, as long as they are intact they resist leeway owing to a "reverse keel"—that is, the groove between the two principal bundles that make up the "hull" (centerboards were employed on Lake Titicaca).[8]

The Norwegian explorer/scholar Thor Heyerdahl, particularly, suggested that the larger of these flexible craft were capable of transoceanic crossings, and in fact so demonstrated by experimental voyages (discussed in chapter 21); he even thought them capable of circumnavigation. He wrote, "A reed boat of the classic type securely lashed together . . . is beyond any doubt the safest type of watercraft ever invented," being very stable, having shallow draft, being capable of landing in surf without danger of breaking up, and not being subject to sinking by shipworm (not entirely true). It can also carry a greater weight of cargo than a wooden craft of comparable size. Its main disadvantages are a speed slower than that of wooden vessels, the lack of a hold, and a relatively short life expectancy.[9]

Balsas: Log and Bamboo Sailing-Rafts of Southern Asia and Northwest South America

Another ancient watercraft type is the raft of parallel logs or bamboos. Often, these rafts were quite simple, consisting simply of the lashed- or pegged-together parallel members plus a few cross poles, and were maneuvered and moved along with pole, paddle, or sweep, on rivers, lakes, estuaries, and lagoons. In a few places in Oceania, sails were applied to such primitive craft. The very wide but disjunct tropical and subtropical distribution of simple rafts—including among some paleolithic-level cultures—implies great age, although perhaps less than that of bundle rafts. The technology of the Middle Paleolithic would have been adequate for the construction of such craft.

Atholl Anderson has calculated that, at half-load, an 86-square-foot bamboo raft could carry almost 7,000 pounds, the equivalent of twenty to forty adults and their children plus supplies.[10] Simple rafts unquestionably much facilitated early human coastal and island-hopping movements but probably were inadequate for carrying people the widths of the great oceans, at least under normal circumstances. However, in historic times there existed traditions of sophisticated seagoing sailing-rafts in southern and eastern Asia, in Polynesia, and on the northwestern coast of South America. These rafts, which were ordinarily constructed using an odd number of logs (the middle one being longest), usually employed a steering system involving a centerboard and/or narrow "daggerboards" (most commonly, three) that could be raised and lowered between the logs or bamboos. Such rafts in Asia were fitted with rectangular spritsails or Chinese lugsails (figure 17.4).

The best educated guess for the geographical origin of efficient daggerboard sailing-rafts is the eastern or southeastern coast of China, although others have suggested northern Vietnam and even India, home of the catamaran sailing-raft. The usual construction material is rattan-lashed bamboos treated with shark

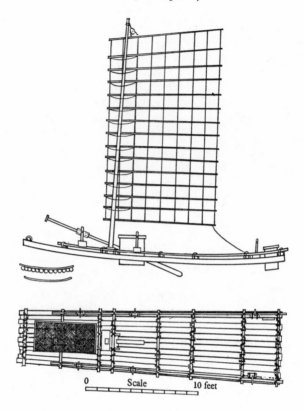

Figure 17.4. An earlier twentieth-century bamboo sailing-raft carrying a Chinese lugsail, Taiwan. From G. R. G. Worcester, "*Four Small Craft of Taiwan,*" *The Mariner's Mirror*, 1956, p. 304. Reproduced by kind permission of the Society for Nautical Research.

fat or tung oil. Although it is very likely substantially older, the sailing-raft's invention in China is traditionally attributed to the thirty-third century BC, and accounts that are more clearly historical refer to the fifth century BC.[11]

Although archaeological records of sailing-rafts are almost nonexistent, an Eighteenth Dynasty Egyptian tomb painting and a tomb relief of the 1400s BC depict rafts with both square and triangular sails in "Punt" (Puoni), probably the area around the mouth of the Red Sea, and such rafts were still in use in nineteenth-century Yemen. The first-century AD *Periplus of the Erythrean Sea* mentions large rafts of this area sailing to the Ganges and Myanmar (Burma).[12] A bas-relief of a sailing-raft is found on the circa AD-800 pyramid of Borobudur, in Java, and the craft is definitely pre-1500 in Taiwan and in China's Fujian province. At least in post-1500 times, it was found on India's Coromandel Coast, in northern Vietnam (where larger ones, up to 34 feet long, carried three masts), in Southeast China (where some rafts reached 40 feet or more in length), and

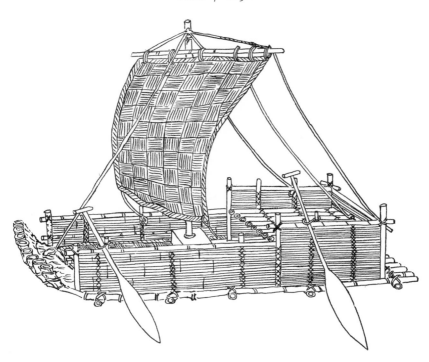

Figure 17.5. Japanese woodcut of a nine-bamboo sailing-raft from Tai-tung, Formosa (Taiwan), 1803. Note the bent-up "prow" to counter waves; steering oars serving as leeboards, fore and aft; sides built up with lashed bamboos; the aft platform; and the square-rigged matting sail. From S. N. Hata, *A Voyage to the Island of Chi-po-ran*, Formosa, 1803.

(in somewhat different form) in southern Korea. Some of the larger Taiwan rafts were fitted with a breakwater, built up sides, and a quarterdeck-like platform (figure 17.5). The sailing-raft also occurred in pre-Contact Ecuador (the *balsa*), and in Brazil (the *jangada*, possibly but not clearly pre-Columbian).[13]

Sailing-rafts of up to 50 feet long were used on the Pacific islands of Mangareva, Tonga, and Samoa and were said to have predated canoes. Marquesan traditions spoke of rafts with as many as five levels and a capacity of eighty passengers and crew.[14]

As mentioned in chapter 16, balsawood-log and possibly bamboo sailing-rafts carrying cabins were pre-Spanish-contact on the coasts of Ecuador and northern Peru (figure 17.6), and in Colonial times plied Pacific waters at least as far northward as Panama and as far southward as Lambayeque and probably La Libertad, Peru. In earlier epochs, they appear to have traded to as far southward as Chile and to as far northward as West Mexico.[15] An apparent example is depicted on a Moche vase, and many feel that large, blade-like objects found buried at Ica, Peru, which carry carved marine motifs and date to around 300 BC, are (pos-

Figure 17.6. Traditional seagoing balsa-log sailing-rafts, each carrying a cabin and a shear bipod mast with a furled square sail. *Guaras* (daggerboards) were used for steering; Guayaquil, Ecuador, by François-Edmond Pâris, circa 1840.

sibly ceremonial) daggerboards. Apparent stone anchors like those used historically on sailing-rafts have been found in pre-Columbian coastal Ecuadorean archaeology. Contact-period reports indicate two-masted Ecuadorian rafts up to about 50 feet in length and with cargo platforms and cabins, capable of carrying over fifty persons. During Colonial times, rafts reached 100 feet in length and involved up to 30 logs, and one such raft was said to have carried as many as fifty Spanish soldiers plus three horses to Ecuador's Puna Island some 40 miles offshore.[16]

These speedy Asian and South American sailing-rafts generally carry or carried fore- and aft-rigged sails. They resist(ed) leeway. Raising the stern daggerboard causes the raft to come more sharply into the wind, and lowering it causes the raft to fall off. The craft were capable of sailing close-hauled, more so than could European sailing ships.

Their extraordinarily shallow draft, which allows them to scud across the surface of the sea, as well as their flexibility, make these rafts safe in shallow coastal waters that would doom other kinds of craft. Flexibility also protects against stress-caused breakup (although flexing can result in wear and tear on the members and their lashings). Because the water surges relatively freely between the logs or bamboos, heeling, pitching, and rolling are minimized. If such a raft capsizes, it is easily righted. For the same reason, sailing-rafts are generally thought of as "wet" watercraft. Accordingly, it has been contended that cool water temperatures essentially precluded their use at sea poleward of about 40 degrees latitude. However, on larger rafts the wetness was mitigated by such devices as a large wooden tub for cargo and crew set atop the bamboos, or a high pole and thatch platform or cabin.

As Heyerdahl remarked, "to ride the towering surf and venture among the reefs and rocks . . . nothing was safer and better suited than shallow-drafted, bump-proof, wash-through rafts of buoyant balsa logs or compact bundles of *totora* reeds."[17] Early Spanish chroniclers attested this for Ecuadorian rafts. According to Clinton Edwards, large sailing-rafts "were capable of speedier and probably more comfortable passages than European ships of the first contact times."[18] The watercraft expert Edwin Doran Jr. concluded, "There seems to be no question that rafts could have crossed the Pacific, repeatedly and in appreciable numbers."[19]

On their 1525 voyage to Peru, one of the Spanish conqueror Francisco Pizarro's ships encountered a raft off that shore, steered by means of quarter rudders and daggerboards. Noting its capacity, which he placed at 36 tons in modern measure (Pizarro's own caravel had a displacement of some 40 tons), the conquistador's pilot Bartlomé Ruiz wrote, in his secret diary, "its hull and keel [*sic*] were built of bamboo canes [*vigas*; likely, balsa logs] as thick as posts and lashed together with enequén [*cabuya*] . . . and the upper parts were built of thinner canes and held together with the same ropes, and the people and the merchandise were contained here together, out of reach of the water. Its masts and booms were of fine wood, and its sails of good cotton were rigged like those of our own ships, with excellent shrouds made of enequén . . . and round stones like a barber's grindstone that they use for anchors."[20]

The raft carried silver and gold objects, pearls, beads, blankets, and clothing, and seems to have been engaged in an expedition in which textiles were being traded for seashells. Note that the craft Ruiz described carried more than one mast and sail. Most specialists believe that such rafts were the vehicles for pre-Columbian trading contacts between Ecuador and Western Mexico, a trade for which there is considerable archaeological and other evidence.

As to whether the Asian and South American sailing-rafts represent a single historical tradition, transmitted across the Pacific, opinions have differed, but it seems highly unlikely to most experts that such a sophisticated development as daggerboard sailing was duplicated independently. As Joseph Needham and Lu Gwei-Djen put it, "The similarities between the sailing-raft of the Peruvian and Ecuadorian coasts and those of South China, Taiwan and Vietnam, have been blatantly obvious for many years now; as many scholars have seen, it is almost quixotic to refuse any connection between them. . . . We would not hesitate to say that we believe the American sailing-rafts to be the direct descendants of the South-east Asian types through an influence mediated by actual trans-Pacific voyagers over many centuries, voluntary or involuntary."[21]

18

Out of the Ice Age

Skin Boats of the North

Small boats . . . covered with the skin of a slain ox. . . . In such craft, the
Venetian navigates the flooded Po and the Briton his wide ocean.
—Lucan, first century AD

Although rafts were effective in many ways, their very nature provided little
potential for further evolution. Later in time than rafts but still very anciently,
displacement-hulled craft came into existence, ultimately ramifying into a variety of kinds of vessels, including those that led up to modern wooden ships.

There are only a few major traditions of preindustrial hulled-watercraft construction, and most of these have largely coherent geographic ranges reflecting
both physical-environmental and historical factors. One of these traditions, associated largely with the far and moderately far North in both hemispheres (where
the material has a relatively long life expectancy), is that of elongate hide-covered
pole-framework boats. Simple skin boats seem to go back to Upper Paleolithic
Magdalenian times (16,000–10,000 BC) in Eurasia, although multiple-hide
ones may have awaited the Mesolithic. The oldest known depictions of seagoing watercraft—petroglyphs of boats resembling Inuit umiaks—date to about
4000 to 6000 BC or more on the Isle of Sørøya in northernmost Norway. An
ivory from far eastern Russia's Chukotka circa 1000 BC depicts whale hunting
from an umiak. The oldest archaeological possible boat remains discovered so
far are what may be a frame fragment from a skin craft, found in Schleswig-
Holstein, Germany, and dating to the ninth millennium BC.[1]

Circa 600 BC, the Carthaginian captain Himlicar mentioned Breton hide
craft voyaging to Ireland, and three centuries later the Greek traveler Pytheas
of Massalia saw such craft in the north as well. Probably based on Pytheas's account referring to around 320 BC, Pliny wrote of six-day tin-trade voyaging from
Britain to Brittany in hide boats.[2] Rufius Festus Avienus (fourth century AD)
wrote of the Cornish, in *Ora Maritima*, "They fit their vessels with united hides /
And often traverse the deep in a hide."[3] The Classical authors Lucan, Caesar,
Strabo, and Solinus also mention animal-skin craft and voyaging in them upon
the Irish Sea and the English Channel. Franks are said to have been ranging

widely and raiding their neighbors in skin "ships" during the third century AD, and the sixth-century Atlantic voyages of the Irish abbot (Saint) Brendan were undertaken in a hide-covered sailing-vessel called a currach (described below).

Skin-boat construction involves a framework of bent and lashed poles, laths, and/or wickerwork,[4] which is then covered with tanned, greased, stitched-together hides, sometimes in multiple layers (if the hides are not greased, as among Aleuts, they become waterlogged within a couple of days and begin to deteriorate if not beached and dried). Skin boats include (1) largely riverine and estuarine basket-like round coracles or "bullboats" (conceivably derived from dome-shaped skin-covered huts), apparently originating in Southwest Asia, likely in Paleolithic times and spreading with the earliest farmers of the Neolithic; and (2) framework craft longer than wide, which were perhaps influenced by bark-canoe forms and which developed in the north of Eurasia, later spreading to arctic America.

Some European seagoing hide boats were provided with keels, reached lengths of over 71 feet (about 80 feet is the theoretical maximum length), and were capable of carrying at least twelve persons (figure 18.1). The Cambridge archaeologist Grahame Clark averred, "The keeled skin-covered boat represents in effect a perfect adjustment in the sphere of sea-transport between an economy based to some extent on the pursuit of sea mammals and an ecology deficient in trees capable of providing the timber needed for solid dug-out canoes" or bark for bark canoes.[5]

Elongated skin boats, most propelled by paddling, are still used from Kamchatka to Greenland, the best-known examples being the Inuit's small, covered kayak, the eastern Siberians' equivalent called the baidarka, and the larger, open but seaworthy umiak, which linguistics implies have minimum ages of 4,000–5,000 years and archaeological attestation dates to even earlier. Umiaks range up to 60 feet in length, with even 40-foot ones having a capacity of 5 tons of cargo and sixty persons, and at least in historic times they sometimes employed a square sail. Without a load, these skin boats were fast, maneuverable, and of very shallow draft.[6] Aleuts have been known to travel up to 900 miles in skin boats.[7] In Alaska, there is archaeological indication of whale hunting at 2000 BC, and an AD 500 kayak model has been found near Point Barrow.[8]

The known ancient range of skin boats once included most of the Eurasian Arctic as well, as depicted in Neolithic and Bronze Age Scandinavian and northern Russian rock engravings. An eighth-century BC stele on Ireland's Bantry Bay depicts a seagoing currach with four oarsmen and a steering oar.

The longer-than-wide Irish seagoing currach (curraugh, curagh) and the Welsh river and bay carrack or coracle (corwgl, from coria [hide]) of the Celtic British Isles persist to the present (with canvas now substituted for greased ox hides). Formerly, skin boats were used in Italy and Spain as well. Too, there are or were round coracles in Mesopotamia, on Himalayan rivers, in Mongolia, and in the Americas.[9] Skin boats in most areas were sail-less, but in western Europe masts and small sails were often added to seagoing currachs. A circa

Figure 18.1. Conjectural reconstruction of Saint Brendan's hide-covered lathwork Irish sailing currach of the sixth century AD, by John Kollock. Note the rowing benches and the quarter rudder. From Paul H. Chapman, *The Man Who Led Columbus to America*, 1973, p. 36. Courtesy of Nancy Kollock.

200 BC gold model of a keel-less boat from Broighter, Derry, Ireland, is usually presumed to depict a skin boat of some 40 feet in length. It carried a mast with yard and originally had nine oars on each side.[10]

Although (unless provided with keels) these lightweight craft had leeway problems and thus were not suitable for windward sailing or rowing, with fair winds larger currachs were capable of traveling safely over great distances and could also be propelled swiftly by oarsmen. Western Irish fishermen preferred them as safer than wooden boats, which were ten times more expensive as well.

Like other hulled watercraft, skin boats depend for their buoyancy on the hollowness of their hulls, the air occupying those hulls being less dense than the water displaced thereby. Their intrinsic lightness of weight means that they are (1) of very shallow draft, good for inshore exploration and having no need for deepwater harbors; (2) swift when rowed or sailed; (3) easy to carry, a practical feature when beaching or for portaging over ice floes, around rapids, or between lakes; (4) unlikely to be stoved in upon impact with rock or ice, owing to their lightness and flexibility; and (5) able to ride atop the waves rather than plow through them, thus shipping relatively little water.

At sea, naught but a quarter-inch of leather between oneself and the abyss might not inspire a great sense of security in the inexperienced. However, as watercraft specialists Björn Landström, Howard Chapelle, Norbert Ohler, and others have repeatedly emphasized, high-freeboard hide boats have abundantly proved their stability in the rough seas of the North Atlantic. Indeed they have been called the most seaworthy of all primitive small craft and in this respect more than the equal of any vessel type in thousands of years of boatbuilding.

Skin boats are particularly appropriate for northern waters because, as noted above, their seemingly fragile hulls in fact tend to bounce off any skerries or floating ice encountered rather than being stoved in by them, as might an inflexible wooden hull. Capable of carrying dozens of persons and ten or more tons of cargo long distances, larger hide boats were quite suited to making migrations by sea. Like rafts, however, and unlike primitive wooden boats, skin boats offered little potential for further evolution.

Mesolithic and Neolithic Legacies

Dugouts and Lashed-Plank Watercraft

This *Kura-hau-po*
A canoe to brave the ocean winds
A canoe to dare the clouds of heaven
   —Maori prayer, New Zealand

Later in time than rafts and skin boats but still very anciently, wooden displace-ment-hulled craft, an entirely distinct tradition, came into existence. Unlike rafts and hide craft, early wooden-hulled boats possessed the potential of much fur-ther development and ultimately diversified into a variety of kinds of vessels, including those that led up to contemporary ships.

Bark Canoes: Barking up the Wrong Tree

The earliest canoes—and arguably the earliest true hulled craft, perhaps preced-ing even rafts and skin boats—seem likely to have been those consisting merely of a partial cylinder of bark stripped from a suitable tree, the ends of the half tube being plugged with clay, gathered and bound, or sewn together and sealed. Simple bark canoes are associated with Paleolithic-level technologies and have a peripheral distribution in the Old World, being found in East Africa and in northern and eastern Australia, with a few apparently residual occurrences in Malaysia. This distribution implies that in the areas lying between the eastern and western areas of modern bark-boat occurrence, such craft were replaced by more recently developed, more efficient vessels: dugout canoes. Bark canoes themselves lacked the potential for much further evolution using that material.

In the Americas, simple sewn-bark craft occurred in southern Chile, another marginal area. However, although Australian bark canoes have been shown ca-pable of crossing water gaps of significance, it is almost inconceivable that they could have reached South America across the Pacific.

Where the far more sophisticated birchbark canoe of North America's and Siberia's boreal forests comes in is unclear.[1] It may have first developed as a hy-brid between primitive bark canoes and framed skin boats. They, too, are un-likely candidates for use in transoceanic traffic, although the Beothuk of Newfoundland did paddle up to 50 miles between coastal islands in 20-foot bark canoes. Any more extensive travel seems likely ordinarily to have involved more substantial and stable craft than these.

Simple Dugout Canoes of the Shallows

The dugout canoe or logboat is very possibly a descendent of the bark-roll craft or might conceivably have been inspired by the removal of the edible pith from split sago-palm trunks. To make a primitive logboat, a downed tree would be split with wedges, with most of one of the halves then being carved out by means of ax and adze and/or fire. This hollowing made the dugout much more buoyant than a solid half log. In its early stages, at least, the craft was normally propelled by pole or paddle.

The logboat's beginnings are to be sought at the Late Pleistocene mesolithic technological level, when hafted edge-ground stone tools became available. Unlike frail bark craft, dugouts are widely known archaeologically, as far back as 7900–6500 BC in western Europe, by 6000 BC in Nigeria as well as on China's lower Yangzi River and in Korea, and by 7500–3500 BC in Japan; a 3000-BC example comes from the US Southeast. Whatever its point or points of origin, the dugout became extremely broadly distributed among neolithic-level and more elaborate cultures in forested areas of both hemispheres, sometimes reaching lengths of 70 feet or more. Although dugout manufacture and use are thousands of years old, the type's vast distribution is probably more a reflection of its relative utility and consequent rather rapid spread than it is a function of really extreme age as in the cases of primitive bark canoes and simple rafts, which are fragile in the first instance and constantly wet in the second. Too, not being streamlined, paddled rafts are relatively slow and cumbersome.

If one takes a unitary view of the dugout's origin, one would probably look to timbered and river-veined Southeast Asia as the region of emergence.[2] Dugouts were no doubt at first used mainly for moving around on streams and lakes and in calm, near-shore waters of coastal areas. Although on North America's Northwest Coast they sometimes went up to at least 40 miles out on the open sea after whales, single, round-bottomed dugouts without outriggers (see below) are not really suitable for long-distance ocean travel. Nevertheless, some may have crossed oceans under unusually favorable conditions. For example, during the Middle Ages, a non-African "red and strange" man arrived in Spain in a logboat, implying a crossing by an American Indian (see chapter 5).[3]

Sailing-Canoes of the South Sea Islands

Later, somewhere on the shores or riverbanks of Southeast Asia, expanded dugouts came to be made. The boatwrights would utilize a large whole log, hollowing it out through a narrow slit along the top of its recumbent self, soaking it with hot water or steam to impart temporary flexibility, spreading it apart, and bracing it with ribs and/or thwarts. Later, such craft began to be further enlarged by having their gunwales raised via a plank (washstrake) lashed to each of them, the gunwales first having had holes drilled to receive cording made of rattan, coir, or other fiber. On occasion, decking would be added. In many areas, additional strakes came to be appended, and circa 2,000-year-old fragments of such craft are known archaeologically from Japan. Slightly earlier depictions on pottery imply vessels 100 feet in length. This enlargement seems eventually to have led to the keeled, lashed-plank ships that came to predominate in the Indian Ocean, as well as to the capacious V-cross-section "sailing-canoes" used in the discovery and settlement of the far-flung Pacific islands. Linguistics indicates that washstrakes were in use by 4000 BC or earlier. Fragmentary remains of a number of Southeast Asian boats comprising plank sides on dugout-like keels have been found, the earliest dating to the mid-first millennium AD.[4]

Sail use very likely preceded the sailing-canoe, being first employed on rafts. In its original form, the dugout was too subject to rolling to carry sail very successfully, although canoes do have the advantage over ballast-carrying Western ships in that they do not sink when swamped and can be quickly bailed out. At some time and place, probably in South China many thousands of years ago, masts and sails were added to expanded dugouts, and the sailing-canoe was born. That single-log sailing-canoes originated in Southeast Asia, among Austronesian-speakers' linguistic ancestors, is indicated by the widespread names *bangka* and *wangka* (with variants) applied to them. Those words apparently go back to proto-Austronesian believed to have been spoken on the southeast coast of China 6,000 years ago—even to ancestral Austroasiatic—as do lexemes for "mast" and "sail."[5] Although the earliest such canoes may well have been developed in Taiwan or, more likely, on the Chinese mainland, much of the later innovation appears to have been around the Java Sea, with diffusion proceeding largely in an easterly direction into Oceania but also westward, to South India, the East African coast, and Madagascar.

Double canoes (figure 19.1) involved two parallel expanded-dugout hulls (whose sides might be built up with one or more strakes and which were often decked). These hulls were held a short distance apart by being lashed to cross-booms laid atop the hulls at right angles. A platform could be built atop the booms, for cargo and passengers, and this platform often supported a cabin of poles and palm fronds. Such canoes carried one or two masts. Captain James Cook deemed them "not only vessels of burden, but fit for distant navigation."[6] The anthropologist and experimental voyager Ben Finney wrote that "the double canoe was one of the finest ocean vessels of the ancient world."[7]

Because they are raft-like, double-hulled sailing-canoes have great stability at sea. But they are lighter in weight than are rafts and meet less water resistance, making them swifter than log rafts and able to sail closer to the wind. It is widely thought that double sailing-canoes, probably using the Oceanic sprit-sail, preceded outrigger craft (single canoes having a parallel float lashed below the ends of cross-booms on one or both sides) and came to be used before,

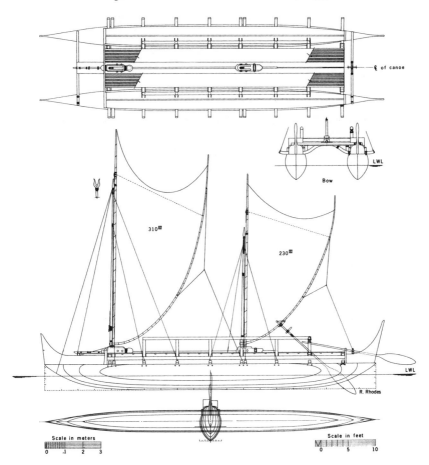

Figure 19.1. *Hōkūle'a*, the Polynesian Voyaging Society's replica traditional two-masted Polynesian double voyaging canoe built in 1975. Note the Oceanic sprit-sails of the crab-claw variety, the pair of steering oars, and the platform connecting the two hulls. From Ben R. Finney, "Voyaging Canoes and the Settlement of Polynesia." *Science* 196, no. 4296 (1977): 1279. Reprinted with permission from AAAS.

probably considerably before, 1500 BC, perhaps by 4000 BC or even earlier. In China, their invention (originally, as a river ferry) is traditionally assigned to 2687 BC. As mentioned, their design was a hybrid between the canoe and the sailing-raft, the latter of which they appear to have largely replaced. Their raft-like character is suggested by their Polynesian name, *pahi*, which, one supposes, derives from *baebae*, an old pre-Chinese, Yue name meaning 'raft' (cf. Polynesian *paepae* '[seagoing] raft').

The historically known Old World distribution of double-hulled canoes includes certain coasts and rivers in South Asia; the Mekong River and certain rivers of China; scattered coastal spots in Malaysia, New Guinea, and Melanesia; on Nanusa and Chuuk (Truk) in the Caroline Islands; in most of Polynesia; and, apparently without sails, on the Angola and Congo coasts of Africa.

The keel and the more or less V-cross-section hull of the sailing-canoe resisted—although not always very well—the making of leeway (as leeboards, daggerboards, and stern rudders did on keel-less craft farther north and as did quarter rudders wherever found). Despite being caulked with coconut fiber and breadfruit sap, such craft were often leaky and had to be constantly bailed during storms; nevertheless, they were very seaworthy.

One myth concerning watercraft is that rigidity, as obtained with pegs, nails, spikes, and heavy frames, is to be desired as imparting greater durability. However, as suggested in chapter 17, there is a contrary but effective alternative, which the sailing-canoe exemplifies. As the experimental voyager Steve Lissau observed, "The [Oceanian] hulls were naturally somewhat flexible since they were constructed of lashed pieces of wood. Inadvertently, this flexibility gave them tremendous durability as they would 'give' rather than break under rough seas. If damage did occur, lashings could be easily replaced at sea."[8]

As we have seen, it is widely thought that most of the initial Austronesian colonization of the noncontinental Pacific islands was accomplished via double sailing-canoe, whose two hulls were decked at each end.[9] According to P. Jourdain, who studied Polynesian craft, "The construction of these boats was the work of true naval architects, of master artisans and workers who were highly qualified and crowned with great social prestige. They formed a religious caste under the direction of the high priests, and every one of their acts was regulated by well defined rites."[10] It should be remembered that these amazing vessels were constructed without metal tools or fastenings and without drawn plans or templates of any kind. Nor was any cloth available to make sails, and matting had to suffice.

Late pre-Columbian and later pre-European-contact archaeological specimens of canoe parts—including planks and end pieces with holes for lashings, thwarts, outriggers, steering paddles, and woven sail fragments—have been unearthed in New Zealand and on the Society Islands' Huahine.[11]

The ordinary speed of double canoes in Oceania in a good wind was a respectable 8 or 9 knots, with an impressive maximum of around 15 to 16 knots, although these canoes could do little better than 4 knots to windward. They had a sea-keeping endurance of from three to seven weeks or more. Steve Lissau considered their range to be perhaps 3,500 miles in thirty days' sailing.[12]

At some point in time, the double canoe in Island Southeast Asia and the Pacific apparently began gradually to be to some extent replaced, or at least complemented, by the single-outrigger canoe, in which a single smaller, solid-log or bamboo float off one side of one hull replaced the other hull. On paddling canoes, the outrigger(s) served to stabilize what otherwise is a rather tippy craft; on sailing-canoes, the outrigger's function was more as a righting balance against the heeling occasioned by the force of the wind on the sail, and on single-outrigger craft it was normally kept on the windward side, where it facilitated hiking-out.[13] The outrigger booms also provided a place to construct a cargo and passenger platform—a phenomenon that linguistics hints goes back to proto-Austronesian times some 4000 BC.[14]

The early Austronesian single outrigger canoe was propelled by an Oceanic spritsail. Beginning perhaps between 1000 and 500 BC, this simple spritsail was then largely replaced to the west of Polynesia by the crane spritsail, and, for sailing upwind, tacking was replaced by shunting. Finally, the double-outrigger canoe, carrying a float on each side, propelled by a rectangular boom lugsail and returning to tacking, came to prevail in Indonesia and (derivatively) on either side of the Mozambique Channel, these last innovations perhaps being associated with the Dongson culture of northern Vietnam or the neighboring Austronesian Cham people shortly BC, but being spread largely by Indonesian Austronesians.[15]

Fijian *druas* could sail 37.75 degrees into the wind. This is to be compared with Spanish galleons, which could do no better than 27 degrees. Even more weatherly were Micronesia's "flying proas," the finest premodern sailing-canoes ever built. These were ocean-going single-outrigger craft that reached at least 40 feet in length and carried cargo platforms (figure 19.2). The flat lee side of the transversely asymmetrical hull acted as a sort of leeboard, the water pressure on the lee side controlling lateral drift by exerting pressure on the hull toward windward and also compensating for the retarding tendency of the outrigger on the weather side. These craft could sustain astounding velocities, from 17 to 28 knots. In 1686, a proa made the 1,200-mile journey from Yap to Manila in four days, averaging 14.4 knots.[16]

The geographic correlation between outrigger canoes and speakers of Austronesian is so close that we may confidently assume that all occurrences among non-Austronesians reflect Austronesian influences. Although outrigger canoes have never been recorded for the pre-Columbian Americas, observers in historic times described "log-balanced" canoes, a Southeast Asian form, on the Pacific coast of the New World, and a ceramic model of one is known from pre-Columbian Ecuador. These canoes resemble outrigger craft—they likely are riverine adaptations of the double-outrigger canoes—but the logs, bamboos, or bundles of bamboos of balanced canoes are placed just outside the gunwales and do not reach the water unless the craft lists. If listing does occur, then these buoyant sponsons counteract it. One of the more interesting facts concerning log-balanced canoes (as well as among a number of other kinds of craft) in the Americas, some carrying spritsails, is that they are often termed *panga* or *pongo*, which may be compared with the Philippine *bangka* (< proto-Austronesian *wangka* and *bangkaq* 'canoe'; see above), to Tai *'baang*, to the Dravidian Tulu *pongayi* 'canoe' and Tamil *vanka*[n] 'plank-built boat,' and to the proto-Indo-Aryan *ponga/*ponka* 'hollow.'[17]

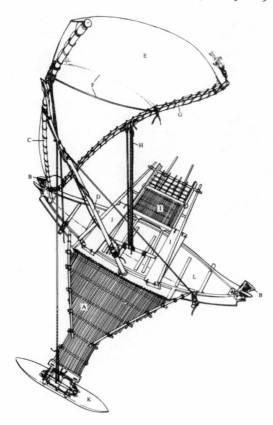

Figure 19.2. Twentieth-century Micronesian *wa serak* or outrigger voyaging canoe with a crane spritsail and platforms. *A*, outrigger platform. *B*, "eye." *C*, gaff. *D*, mast. *E*, sail. *F*, brailing lines. *G*, boom. *H*, sheet. *I*, lee platform. *J*, bench. *K*, outrigger. *L*, interior of hull. Drawing by Richard Berry. From Stephen D. Thomas, *The Last Navigator*, 1987, p. 137. Courtesy of Stephen D. Thomas.

Sindbad's Conveyance: Lashed-Plank Craft of the Indian Ocean

The typical larger craft of the Indian Ocean seem to derive ultimately from the same tradition as that from which came the big canoes of Oceania, but development went in somewhat different directions. The predominant Indian Ocean boats before AD 1500 were pointed-ended, flat-bottomed (cf. early Egyptian ships as well as junks), usually at least rudimentarily keeled craft, which developed over time into more round-bottomed keeled ships of good size, including, eventually, the lateen-rigged booms of the Arabian Sea. The strakes of their nail-less, carvel-constructed plank hulls were lashed onto the canoe-like keel and to each other, by continuous stitching through drilled holes, and sealed with pitch.[18] That such craft have a long history is indicated by the Akkadian Gilgamesh legends of circa 1200 BC, which describe the multidecked ark as having a stitched-plank hull into which a framework is inserted by lashing.[19]

As in ancient Egypt, where plank sewing is early directly attested (see chapter 20), doweling came often to be employed to hold together the edge-to-edge planks in Island Southeast Asian and Indian Ocean craft. Both doweling and

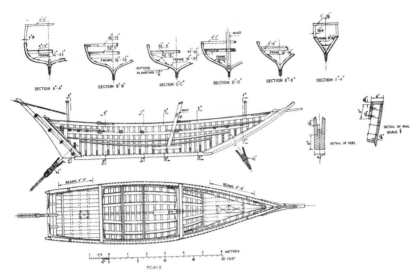

Figure 19.3. Medium-sized *bheddi* fishing boat and cargo carrier, in Karachi, Pakistan, mid-twentieth century, by Henry Magnusson. From Food and Agriculture Organization of the United Nations, 1955, Rahimullah Qureshi, Henry Magnusson, and Jan-Olof Traung, "The Fishing Boats of the World," https://archive .org/stream/fishingboatsofth034609mbp/fishingboatsofth034609mbp_djvu.txt.

lashing are attested archaeologically on a 49-foot craft found off Mindanao, dating to AD 150–650.[20]

Like the larger of the Austronesian canoes, traditional Indian Ocean craft were shell built, beginning with a dugout keel and building up the sides with adze-hewn planks and then, often, adding flexible, lashed-on internal ribs plus thwarts (figure 19.3). One, two, and perhaps sometimes more masts were stepped. These ships were rather leaky, but the developed vessels were fully capable of, and engaged in, long-distance ocean voyages.[21]

Westerners have sometimes perceived lashed-plank craft as frail. For example, the well-known historian of the Arabs G. F. Hourani wrote, "those [ships] of the Arabs were sewn with stitches of coconut fiber; they were fair-weather craft which could fall apart in heavy seas."[22] In contrast, the pioneering historian of Indian shipping Shereen Ratnagar had a different—and more accurate— view: "Sewn vessels can be very large, even up to 200 tons . . . and are competent for long voyages on the high seas. . . . Stitched boards are flexible and therefore do not break easily. It would be well not to underestimate their utility for long coastal [and even open-sea] voyages in the first millennium."[23] The American geographer Paul Wheatley agreed, writing, "The [sewn-plank] mode of construction produced a resilient ship well adapted to withstanding the stress of monsoon storms and the jarring shocks of rock and reef."[24]

Despite the fact that some Indian Ocean ships attained substantial dimensions, no iron was used in their construction. The Sanskrit book *Yukti Kalpa-taru* says that the metal was omitted from ship construction owing to the supposition that magnetic rocks in the sea would pull out any nails, a tradition repeated by Ptolemy as well as in the tale of Sindbad the Sailor. The Tangerine traveler Ibn Battutah's more prosaic explanation (in the fourteenth century AD) is more plausible: "the Indian Ocean is full of rocks [reefs;] and if a ship joined with iron bolts strikes a rock, it is broken up; but when it is fastened together with this [coir] cord it has elasticity and does not break."[25]

Unlike Austronesian canoes, which obtain stability by use of twin hulls or of outriggers, plank boats and derivative keeled ships ordinarily do so by being beamier (broader) than canoes—although sometimes single or double outriggers would be added, too, as in the case of certain Sri Lankan ships and the similar, probably Indonesian, ships depicted in reliefs from the eighth century AD at Borobudur, Java (one ship, lacking outriggers, may be Indian). The craft were steered by means of a pair of quarter rudders (see figure 14.2).[26]

The presumed Austronesian, latest tenth-century AD Cirebon cargo-ship wreck, found in the Java Sea, exhibited strakes secured with wooden pegs and lashed to frame members through pierced lugs. A number of other Southeast Asian terrestrial archaeological boat finds and shipwrecks, ranging in age from around AD 320 to AD 1300 and in length up to 105 feet, display the lashed-lug system as well. These craft were relatively light and flexible. The nautical salvor/archaeologist Michael Flecker wrote, "Overall, the lashed-lug construction technique can be viewed as a magnificent piece of engineering."[27]

The best-known lashed-plank craft are the predominately Arab-sailed dhows, which seem to have been in use from the sixth century AD on.[28] There are no western Indian Ocean (Arabian Sea) archaeological examples of earlier plank boats or ships, but we do have the ninth-century AD Belitung stitched-plank Arab wreck excavated in Indonesia.[29]

There is no question that "sewn"-plank construction has respectable antiquity in India. Although the exact structure of the craft it depicts is not apparent, a terra-cotta model from the circa 2000 BC Harappan presumed port of Lothal depicts a keeled sailing boat with upturned prow and stern. A graffito on a Harappan potsherd depicts a ship in profile. It is arcuate and pointed-ended, carrying what appears to be a tripod mast holding a furled sail with yard and boom, as well as a quarter rudder; it resembles early Egyptian "spoon-shaped" craft. Similar-looking boats existed in South and Southeast Asia into the twentieth century. A lashed-plank canoe is shown in a second-century BC bas-relief at Sanchi in central India, and a lashed-plank vessel is referred to in a Pali text (Pali is the no-longer-spoken language of the Buddhist scriptures).[30]

The first-century AD Greco-Roman *Periplus of the Erythraean Sea* also mentions such craft for Oman. A silver model of plank-boat form was unearthed at late fourth-millennium BC Ur at the head of the Persian Gulf, and a Mesopotamian origin for the ship type has been speculated—although the Indian subcontinent seems more than equally likely, with a relationship to Austronesian canoe construction. Timber would need to have been imported for desert Persian Gulf and South Arabian shipbuilding. In historic times, India has been the source of such logs there, although anciently timber was sometimes imported from Lebanon. According to al-Idrisi, Omanis constructed their ships not at home but on the Lakshadweep (Laccadive) Islands off India's Malabar Coast.

Hulled Wooden Ships East and West

The Junk and the Nao

Absolute, unvarying rigidity, rigidity!
—Rudyard Kipling, "The Ship That Found Herself," 1895

Like rafts, the smaller sailing-canoes are essentially "wet" craft on which the travelers are subject to being soaked by wave, spray, and leakage. This is acceptable in the warm tropics. However, farther poleward "dry" craft are distinctly preferable, and outrigger canoes are generally absent to the north of Vietnam's Annam, although they once were present in Taiwan. In China proper, a completely different, rigid-hull tradition emerged, that of the dry craft known as the junk.

Compartmentalization in China: The Junk

In common with Mediterranean ships, the Chinese junk (figure 20.1) was a sizable rigid wooden vessel that was carvel-constructed (the edges of its hull planks abutted rather than overlapped). The junk differed markedly from Western ships—showing that functionally similar end products can be achieved by very different specific means—and some see it as a descendant, via the small three-plank sampan, of the three-log or three-bamboo raft, the sampan being a boat supposedly first created as the raft's sides were built up to contain cargo.

First, although its plank bottom curves longitudinally, in cross-section the traditional, keel-less Chinese junk is flat-bottomed, not round- or V-bottomed, which gives it superior stability and cargo capacity. It has bluff transom (square) ends instead of the Mediterranean ship's stem- and sternposts and rounded, wedge-like, or pointed ends. Finally, instead of having a continuous, framed hold as does a European ship, the junk is divided like a bamboo into separate water-tight compartments by means of a series of transverse bulkheads built simultaneously with the addition of the side planks. This imparts unequaled strength and rigidity as well as another very significant safety feature: if the

Figure 20.1. Early twentieth-century Jiangsu freighter, a five-masted northern Chinese junk carrying Chinese lugsails with yards slightly inclined forward. Note the sheets tied to each sail's luff and leach and the means of attachment of each batten to the mast. Also note the bluff ends. There are decking, cabins, and bulkheads creating watertight compartments, and a median stern rudder. This is a type probably ancestral to many sorts of Chinese ships. From G. R. G. Worcester, *Sail and Sweep in China*, 1966, p. 36. With permission of the Science Museum Group, London.

hull is holed at one place, the leakage is confined to a single compartment. In the absence of a keel, longitudinal rigidity is achieved by application of great wales of timber along the ship's sides. That this type of construction began early is suggested by the curved ladderlike Shang dynasty (second millennium BC) written character for "ship," and there is no question that the vessel was in use before the time of Christ. A terra-cotta model of a small junk from the Han dynasty (206 BC–AD 220) has been published, and archaeologists have excavated a large ship-construction berth circa 200 BC in Guangzhou.[1] Kofun-period (AD 250–800) Japanese boat-form *haniwa* (terra-cotta funerary models) also display bulkhead-separated compartments.[2]

Geographically, the distribution of the junk is centered on coastal China, and, in a variety of forms, the craft came to be the characteristic ship of East Asia from northern Vietnam to Japan. Large and handy vessels had been outlawed in Japan in 1636 (see chapter 5), which came close to terminating a previously lively overseas trade. Although "Chinese junks were as a rule slender, seagoing vessels which could sail the oceans . . . the only large Japanese junk which still existed in this [twentieth] century was a broad, heavy and bad sailer"; interestingly, except for its rudder the Japanese junk closely resembled a Roman merchantman rather than traditional Chinese models.[3]

A fascinating fact is that flat-bottomed, high-sterned, transom-ended ships of very similar profile, dating to pre-Dynastic times, existed in ancient Egypt.[4] And in both Egypt and southern China, bipod masts were used (shear in Egypt, parallel in China), as were the antihogging truss and oculi on the bow (see below).[5] In Japan, instead of Chinese lugsails the more archaic junks there carry tall, rather Egyptian-looking square-rigged sails.[6] A west–east influence has been suggested. However, as proposed above, an Indian Ocean origin, with carriage both eastward and westward and then replacement in the intermediate area, seems to me more likely.

The standard junk's flat bottom made it well adapted to movement and exploration in shallow offshore waters (at least, in those lacking reefs). The absence of a keel allowed leeward drift, a problem dealt with by the application of leeboards and centerboards (derived from earlier raft daggerboards) and, by the first century AD or earlier, by use of the median rudder.[7] Presumably under Indonesian influence, keels, V-shaped cross-sections, and pointed ends for ocean voyaging came to characterize many junks in later pre-Columbian times, largely in the south.[8]

With its Chinese lugsail and stern rudder, the junk is highly maneuverable and well suited to voyaging on the open ocean,[9] although this is not universally recognized. Despite unequivocal evidence of early junk use at sea, after noting the scarcity of records the nautical historian Jeremy Green wrote that "it seems that, before the 8th century [AD], the Chinese did not possess ocean-going ships. Vessels operating in trans-Asiatic trade and visiting China were not local but mainly from Southeast Asia and the Indian Ocean. It seems probable that the southern Chinese evolved an ocean-going vessel that incorporated elements derived from Chinese coastal vessels and these visiting ships. This shipbuilding tradition reached its zenith in the Sung [Song] and Yüan dynasties" (960–1279 and 1279–1368).[10] In light of the evidence reviewed above, however, it seems that junks capable of, and engaging in, blue-water voyaging are ancient in China.

The Nao: Frame-Fitted Wooden Ship of the West, and Its Ancestors

Proverbs 30:18, 19 states, "There be three things which are too wonderful for me. . . . The way of an eagle in the air; the way of a serpent upon a rock; the way of a ship in the midst of the sea"; and wonderful indeed were some of the ancient seacraft of the Mediterranean world.

When westerners think of premodern ships, most think first of rigid-hulled wooden watercraft with keels along their bottoms and with attached posts at tapered stem and stern, and with sides built up of edge-to-edge planks secured to a wooden framework. This is the classic craft of the Mediterranean and adjacent communicating seas—although contrary to the popular perception, as late as the twelfth century most frames were largely or entirely installed *after* the hull was built ("shell" rather than "skeleton" construction).[11] These ships embody what is known as the "nao" tradition, employing the Spanish word, which, in turn, derives from the Latin *nav-is* 'ship' (cf. Greek and Sanskrit *nau-*). We know much more about the history of this line of ships than we do of other lines, owing to an abundance of ancient depictions and descriptions as well as to buried vessels in Egypt plus the many wrecks investigated as a result of the rise of underwater archaeology since 1950.

In 1900–1901, Greek sponge divers directed by Professor A. Economou salvaged materials from the large circa-75-BC Greco-Roman Antikythera wreck. Another investigation of an ancient wreck—the first-century-AD Greco-Roman Mahdia ship, off Tunisia (where 85 feet of keel remained)—was undertaken from 1908 to 1913. In these and other salvage operations, sponge divers did the underwater work, while the archaeologists remained at the surface, on the boat. Then, in 1943 Jacques-Yves Cousteau and Émile Gagnan developed the Aqua-Lung. When the device became generally available in 1946, treasure hunters quickly stripped almost all of the then-known Mediterranean wrecks, although in 1950 the archaeologist Nino Lamboglia undertook—still from the deck—supervision of his dredgers' lifting of material from a first-century BC Roman wreck off Albenga near Genoa; this was the first operation stressing the site's historical value, not just its works of art.

Cousteau used the Aqua-Lung and an airlift in 1952 to dive on, and dig in, two BC Roman wrecks near Marseille. During the 1950s, building on the experiences of Cousteau and of diver-excavator Philippe Talliez, increasing sophistication was introduced to underwater digs off southern France. And in 1959, the New York sailor, diver, and anthropologist Peter Throckmorton developed improved methods for excavating at the Cape Gelidonia wreck in Turkish waters, in which the archaeologist was, at last, on the seabed. As a graduate student, George Bass was a team member there, and he went on to become the premier practitioner in the field. He founded the Institute of Nautical Archaeology at the University of Pennsylvania, which later moved to Texas A&M University. With Bass, the focus shifted from the contents of wrecks to the structural characteristics of the ships.[12] Underwater archaeology is now a recognized subdivision of the larger field of archaeology and has yielded much information on the construction of ancient vessels.

One of the characteristics of Classical Western ships was their strength. The strakes of the shell were rigidly held together with myriad mortise and tenon joints; each tenon was transfixed by dowels, and then a robust frame was inserted into the hull, which was not only strong but also staunch (watertight). Masts were fitted with square-rigged sails, "designed first and foremost for safety and not for speed, and equipped with the ancients' special [brailing] system for shortening sail, which was far safer and more effective than that [subsequently] favored in the Western world until the present century."[13]

Ancient Egyptian Ships

The existence and growth of Egypt as a civilization depended on water transport. Even the souls of the dead were thought to travel westward across the Winding Waterway via boat, to join the sun god in his bark. It is not terribly surprising, then, that the ancient Egyptians were pioneers in building predecessors to the nao.[14] Despite a paucity of appropriate timber in Egypt, wooden watercraft there were numerous and often large. They generally had a sickle-shaped sheer line and were beamy and of shallow draft. The lack of timber would seem to make it unlikely that wooden watercraft evolved primarily in Egypt. As a result of this dearth, some boats had to be built up of short lengths of local acacia (*Vachellia*) wood, scarfed and joined together with mortises and tenons, butterfly cramps, and pegs.[15] But other craft came to be made from long planks of cedar wood imported from Lebanon, especially out of the Levantine port of Byblos (large-scale trade in Lebanese cedar for shipbuilding is referred to as early as circa 2600 BC).

As mentioned in chapter 16, ceremonial sailing craft were abundantly depicted on pre-Dynastic pottery. That ships were highly important at least from shortly before the beginning of the First Dynasty (2950–2775 BC) is demonstrated by the fourteen sewn-plank ships interred at a royal tomb at Abydos, unearthed in 1991 8 miles from the Nile. Petroglyphs elsewhere in Egypt indicate that the shift from dependence on papyrus-bundle raft-boats to wooden-hulled craft, probably carrying sail, took place in the mid-fourth millennium BC.[16]

Typical larger Egyptian hulled sailing craft of the Old Kingdom were shell built and horizontal bottomed in cross section, starting with (usually) three long planks. Their sides were carvel constructed, using mortises and tenons. The hull was stiffened by insertion of independent ribs and crossbeams, the latter supporting the decking. Like that of the Chinese junk, the Egyptian hull was keel-less, but the crossbeams were often connected by an internal stringer that added rigidity. The hull planks were drilled and were then lashed with cords to the ribs and to longitudinal strengthening battens that covered and sealed the seams between the strakes.

To prevent the ship's back from breaking when the middle of the ship was atop a swell, an antihogging truss was often added: a cable running between bow and stern and supported by vertical forked posts rising from the deck. Girdle trusses—horizontal ropes encircling the upper part of the hull at the deck level—were sometimes employed in early times, as well. A seagoing ship with an antihogging truss is depicted in a bas-relief circa 2450 BC.

As discussed in chapter 16, it is conventional, but very probably incorrect, to attribute the invention of sail to the pre-Dynastic Egyptians and for use in river travel. Features of Egyptian craft—such as a curved sheer line (facilitating

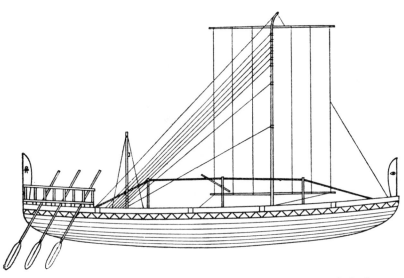

Figure 20.2. Egyptian Nile ship of before 2000 BC. Note the quarterdeck, the antihogging truss, the square-rigged sail on a forward-placed mast, and the three tillerless steering oars. From Courtland Canby, *A History of Ships and Seafaring*, 1963, p. 14.

turning) with overhangs at the ends, a high stern, the antihogging truss, and rigging details—suggest adaptation to the sea, not to a calm river,[17] supporting the notion of an Indian Ocean rather than a Nilotic origin for such craft. (Unless a boat's ends and sides are vertical, *some* sheer naturally results from the flexing of the strakes as they converge toward stem and stern.) High sterns not only protect from pooping—swamping by following seas when sailing downwind—they also act as vanes to keep a boat's bow turned *into* the wind and so meeting that wind's waves head-on when the paddler/oarsman is fishing instead of steering. An elevated stern would also improve visibility for the steersman. It has been suggested that high bows and sterns would facilitate loading and unloading at high riverbanks, but I consider that to be dubious.

The typical Egyptian ship was propelled by a single oblong sail on one mast. However, if petroglyphs are to be credited, some vessels carried up to four masts. When there was but one mast—shear-bipod on ships of the earlier period, single in the later—it was set up well forward during Old Kingdom times (figure 20.2) and stepped amidships during the New. Aft, there were pairs of steering oars—sometimes as many as five—installed on the two quarters in the earlier period, reduced to one pair or even to a single oar placed axially over the stern by New Kingdom times, as use of a tiller became usual.

Beginning in the Middle Kingdom, ship bottoms were made laterally rounded, not flat as before, but vessels continued to have high sterns. Reliefs dating to circa 1500 BC depicting an expedition to "Punt" (probably the Horn of Af-

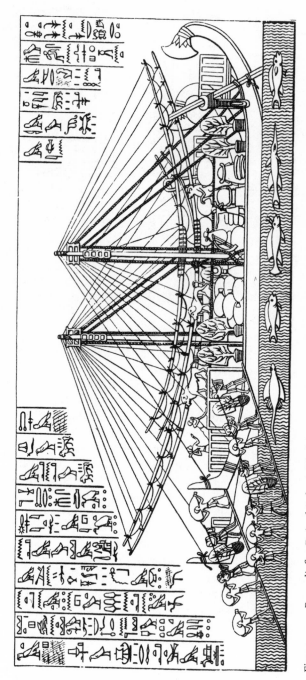

Figure 20.3. Bas-relief at Deir el-Bahari, Thebes, Egypt, depicting the loading, at Punt, of two ships sent down the Red Sea there by Queen Hatshepsut, fifteenth century BC. Note the high curved stern, the single mast set amidships, the furled square sail with a yard and a boom, and the steering oar. Cargo includes sizable live plants and large animals. Drawing by Auguste Mariette, 1912.

rica and vicinity) carved on Queen Hatshepsut's fifteenth-century BC mortuary temple near Thebes, are the best-known evidence for New Kingdom seagoing ships. These still-keel-less ships had a blade-shaped stem piece and a recurved stern (figure 20.3).[18]

Other Early Mediterranean Ships

The Mediterranean ('Between Lands') Sea, with its Aegean, Adriatic, Ionian, Tyrrhenian, Ligurian, Balearic, and Alborán subseas, has been called "the cradle of navigation." Although that might well be disputed, in certain ways the Mediterranean was indeed favorable to early shipping. The most prominent players in this development were the Greeks of the Aegean and the Phoenicians of the Levant.

Minoan Greek ships and slightly later Phoenician ships represent a tradition distinct in a number of ways from the Egyptian one, although very probably influenced by some aspects of Egyptian ship construction. Present at least by the twenty-first century BC, they are of uncertain origin but were ancestral to the subsequent post-Minoan Greek, Roman, and other Mediterranean craft. They may have begun as Indian-derived lashed-plank vessels, that form of construction being attested in the Mediterranean for Archaic times and later.[19] Unlike contemporaneous Egyptian ships, these shell-built true naos featured keels, high sternposts, and, especially, stemposts, as well as ribs. Mortise-and-tenon joinery of the strakes was incorporated and improved over the Egyptian model by the insertion of transverse pegs through the boards and tenons, yielding greater hull strength; ribs were sewn in.[20]

Crude engravings on seals from Minoan Crete as old as about 2000 BC show single-masted (sometimes, possibly, three-masted) ships with quarter rudders. However, the only period detailed depiction of Minoan ships comes from a fresco at the site of Akrotiri on the Aegean island of Thera (figure 20.4). The largest of these vessels is estimated to have had an overall length of about 78 feet, 9 inches; a beam of some 12 to 16 feet, 5 inches; and a displacement of from 19 to 24 tons. However, it is thought that Minoan ships probably ranged up to about 115 feet in length. Tapering bows and sterns curved upward.

Mediterranean cargo ships were quite tubby—broad and round hulled—and were decked. These ships initially carried a single oblong square-rigged sail with upper and lower yards on a short mast and were steered by means of a single quarter rudder. Although rowing supplemented sail, wind propulsion was paramount for extended journeys. Unlike known Egyptian sails, the Minoan sail's yard could be manipulated by braces to allow use of side winds.[21]

Some Phoenician "Tarshish"-class (big cargo) ships or *gauloi* (as well as warships) added a short raked bowsprit-like foremast with a small square spritsail, with both sails bent to yards that could be braced to the wind, a tremendous advance on the single square sail used in Egypt and Crete (figure 20.5).[22] One late sixth-century BC painting of a probably Punic ship at Tarquinia, Italy, shows a black (bitumen-painted) hull, two masts with oblong sails, and a pair of quarter rudders. In Classical times, more masts and sails were commonly added, and

Figure 20.4. Reconstruction of a ship with a steering oar depicted in a Minoan mural circa 1628 BC at Akrotiri, Thera, Greece. The original fresco depicts a captain, a navigator, a helmsman, twenty-one paddlers on each side, and passengers aboard. From Rodney Castleden, *Mycenaens*, © 2005, Routledge, reproduced by permission of Taylor and Francis Books UK.

Figure 20.5. Phoenician sailing ship carrying a single mast with a loose-footed square sail plus a quarter rudder; note the stem- and sternposts. From George Goldsmith Carter, *Sailing Ships and Sailing Craft*, 1969, p. 6.

models show that some Bronze Age Greek merchant ships were decked. Phoenician ships had quarterdecks to shelter the personnel.[23]

The oldest known remains of a seagoing wooden ship are probably Levantine, the Ulu Burun wreck of circa 1350 BC from off southern Turkey. Known Phoenician shipwrecks (1200–539 BC) are few. As noted in chapter 13, two, from the eighth century BC, were found off Israel. One was about 46 feet long, and the other 47.6 feet in length and 23 feet in the beam.[24] A mid-first-millennium Greek wreck found off Sicily measured almost 70 feet in length.[25]

Northwestern European Wooden-Hulled Watercraft

In addition to hide boats, by the Bronze Age northwestern Europe possessed wooden ones. About AD 100 the Roman historian Tacitus mentioned that the Suiones, apparently the Swedes, were "mighty in ships." Some think that the ships of Scandinavia originated by the substitution of wooden planks for the hide coverings of the northern sewn-skin boats of yore perhaps under influences emanating ultimately from the Mediterranean world, although significant similarities to southern Asian craft have also been noted.

The form of the circa-350-BC Danish Hjortspring wooden paddling boat (and similar boats shown in Bronze Age and Iron Age petroglyphs) seems clearly to have been modeled on a skin-covered prototype. Skin-boat ancestry is further hinted at by the securing of the clinker-laid planks (each strake overlapping the one beneath) to an inserted frame by drilling holes and lashing ("sewing") the lower strakes to the ribs—although this is also reminiscent of the structure of Indo-Pacific craft (see chapter 19).[26] Stitched-plank boats are archaeologically attested at about 1750–1620 BC in northern England (Kilnsea boat), 1300 BC in southern England (Dover boat), and 1600 BC in Wales (Caldicot boat), and ten altogether—up to 60 feet long—have been excavated in Britain. These may not have been true ocean-going craft, but the early Bronze Age North Ferriby boat from England, which dates to 2020–1780 BC, is believed to have been seagoing. Its estimated length is 42–62 feet.[27] Tests of a replica carrying a somewhat conjectural sail showed the craft to be capable of crossing the North Sea in three or four days.[28]

Much later in time in England—from the mid-seventh century AD—we have the spectacular clinker-built Anglo-Saxon Sutton Hoo ship, which housed a rich burial. The nailed-together vessel, in the nau tradition and not a descendant of the sewn-plank craft described above, was some 89 feet in length and propelled by 37 oars. In the same family of ships were those of early medieval Norden.[29]

There is no actual evidence for use of sail in Scandinavia before the seventh century AD. Before that, craft were apparently rowed, which would still have allowed interisland travel. When sail was adopted, the preexisting lashing of the planks to the frame afforded appropriate hull elasticity, providing "give" under the impact of seas—although medieval Norse ships came to secure their strakes with treenails and iron rivets and to depend on rigidity. Half decks were added at either end.

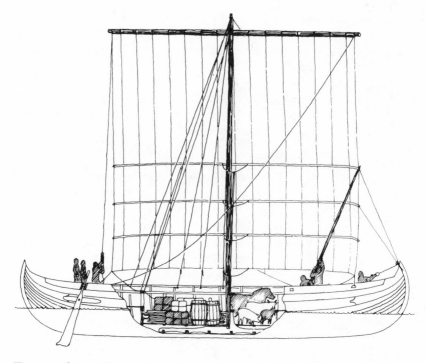

Figure 20.6. Lengthwise cutaway reconstruction of the *Skuldelev 1* wreck, a Norse seagoing cargo ship with a hold, showing the square sail and rigging (note use of the *beitáss*, or bearing-out spar). © The Viking Ship Museum, Denmark.

Several eighth- through tenth-century Norse ships have been unearthed archaeologically, the most famous being the 71.5-by-17-foot Oseberg Ship and the 76.5-by-17.5-foot Gokstad Ship. These two ships were for both traveling and going to war, and about the tenth century their type gave rise to both the true fighting longship (*långbåt*) or dragonship and the tubbier *knörr* (*knarr*), a keeled and clinker-built, one-masted cargo ship, examples of which have also been found archaeologically (figure 20.6).[30] The *knörr* of Bjarni Herjolfsson, the first recorded Norse captain to glimpse mainland North America, averaged about 150 nautical miles per day, and it was in such vessels that the Norse transatlantic movements took place.[31]

Study of the forms and histories of premodern ocean-going watercraft indicates, then, that for millennia, vessels capable of making transoceanic voyages were found in many coastal areas of the Old World and on South America's Ecuadorian littoral. The vehicles as well as the needed methods of navigation (see the following two chapters)—the *means* of crossings—were there. Having the means, would humans not have used them to the fullest?

Modern Experimental Voyages

The Empirical Approach

"Wouldst thou,"—so the helmsman answered,
"Learn the secret of the sea?
Only those who brave its dangers
Comprehend its mystery!"
  —Henry Wadsworth Longfellow, 1850

As pointed out in chapters 1 and 14, scholars doubting transoceanic contacts long contended—and many still do—that early watercraft were incapable of traversing the great seas, at least under any circumstance other than a rare fluke. If the oceans could not be crossed, they argued, then cultural similarities on the two sides of said seas had, at least for the most part, to represent evolutionary parallels and convergences, not contacts, thus proving that independent invention, even of very specific and arbitrary traits, can and does take place. In contrast, diffusionists, taking the position that the cultural similarities between the hemispheres were too numerous and detailed to be attributed to anything other than cultural transfer, felt that the existence of adequate ancient watercraft was demonstrated by these similarities, despite a lack of archaeological or other concrete evidence of suitable vessels.[1] In effect, there was an intellectual standoff. But the no-crossings or almost-no-crossings position has become increasingly challengeable owing not only to advances in underwater archaeology but also to experimental voyages in replica watercraft. Owing to the latter, observed the Danish nautical archaeologist Ole Crumlin-Pedersen, "several theories launched from writing desks have had to be scuttled following a successful voyage in one of these 'floating hypotheses.'"[2]

Kon-Tiki and Experimental Archaeology

The first empirical attempt specifically intended to break the standoff was made by the much-lauded and much-maligned Norwegian Thor Heyerdahl, who essentially created a new area of inquiry, experimental archaeology—specifically, experimental voyaging. Heyerdahl's 1947 voyage in the pre-Columbian Ecuadorian-style balsa-log raft Kon-Tiki (see chapter 17) was an effort to show empirically the capability of such craft to have transported humans from South

America to Polynesia, where he had perceived cultural evidence of American Indian contact and settlement. "In what may be his single greatest contribution to science," wrote P. J. Capelotti, "Heyerdahl demonstrated that anthropologists had better be ready to take their hypotheses to sea."[3] The *Kon-Tiki* voyage, widely covered by the media, galvanized the imaginations of many and set off a whole raft (one might say) of adventurous voyages by others.

With *Kon-Tiki*, Heyerdahl was the first substantially to break through the intellectual barrier that contended that long voyages by "primitive" watercraft—or even by developed ones—were impossible. Since "Señor *Kon-Tiki's*" first exploits, numerous experimental voyages on rafts but also in a variety of other craft have been undertaken in replica versions of early vessels. It is widely hypothesized among diffusionists that sailing-rafts, which evolved from simple, sail-less rafts, were the first craft that allowed ocean crossings, and that they may, therefore, have been the vessels that, through accidental drift or via intentional exploration, led to the first noncoastal overseas arrivals in the New World by people from the Old. As we have seen, pre-Columbian sailing-rafts were indigenous to scattered locations in southern and eastern Asia as well as to Ecuador, and may well represent the kind of vehicle that carried these arrivals, who, in turn, transplanted that vehicle to the shores of the new hemisphere.

Although a *jangada*—the Brazilian version of the sailing-raft—had sailed 2,150 miles from Recife to Rio and back in a test voyage in 1922, sailing-rafts' long-distance capabilities remained almost universally disputed.[4] Then came Heyerdahl's 1947 experiment, in which the 45-foot *Kon-Tiki* was lashed together from nine feather-weight balsa (*Ochroma*) logs and fitted with *guaras* (daggerboards), a shear-bipod mast (like those of Lake Titicaca), and a square sail. With six men on board—all inexperienced as sailors—the raft was launched into the Humboldt Current after a 58-mile tow out from the coast at Callao, Peru. *Kon-Tiki* crashed onto the reef at Raroia in the Tuamotu Islands 101 days later, having traversed some 4,300 miles of open ocean without serious mishap, averaging about 40 miles per day.[5] (Actual movement across water accounted for only about a quarter of that distance; the rest was accomplished by the moving current's carrying the raft along.)

At the time, Heyerdahl lacked a full understanding of how daggerboards functioned. However, in 1953, he had another balsa raft built and, with information supplied by local Ecuadorian fishermen, learned to tack the craft by simultaneous manipulation of sail and *guaras*, demonstrating how the natives had sailed cargo rafts for hundreds of miles against wind and current, as described in Colonial reports.[6]

Critics called *Kon-Tiki's* success a one-time stroke of luck. Experimental voyages have been extensively criticized ever since, though none more than Heyerdahl's. Indeed, snide derision of Heyerdahl's accomplishments became something of a sport in academia and elsewhere. For example, on the basis of interviews with archaeologists, the American travel writer Paul Theroux alleged, "His efforts in the Pacific greatly resemble the muddling attentions of, say, the hack writer of detective stories when faced with an actual crime scene. In a lifetime of nutty theorizing, Heyerdahl's single success was his proof, in *Kon-Tiki*, that six middle-class Scandinavians could successfully crash-land their raft on a coral atoll in the middle of nowhere."[7]

If not snide, the views of the British archaeologists Paul Bahn and John Flenley concerning Heyerdahl's first voyage are typical among professionals. After asserting that pre-Columbian South Americans lacked the sail (but see chapter 16), they pointed out that the *Kon-Tiki* was towed out to sea before beginning its self-propelled voyage and thus the trip cannot be counted as a true drift. They then complained that "the comparison of Kon-Tiki with the drift voyage of a prehistoric vessel is hardly fair; Kon-Tiki was an intentional navigated voyage with a known, if general, destination, and the crew had the benefit of radios, maps and sophisticated navigational instruments. We must conclude that Kon-Tiki showed nothing more than that, by using a post-European-contact kind of sail-raft and modern survival equipment, it is possible to survive a 101-day voyage between Peru and Polynesia."[8]

There are critics who dismiss the significance even of those experimental voyages involving vessels and navigational methods that essentially duplicated ancient ones and whose provisions were limited to traditional foodstuffs prepared and transported in traditional ways. These critics point first to any imperfections in period authenticity, as in clothing, tools, utensils, fire starting, medical supplies, or the like. They point, too, to the fact that modern researchers are advantaged by knowledge of the earth's configuration and of what to expect out there in terms of winds and currents, as well as by usually having the extra security of a radio on board with which to call for help if needed. This, contend the critics, supplies psychological and practical benefits that invalidate these experiments as far as proving ancient sailors' capabilities is concerned.

To require of contemporary voyagers a mentality and kind and degree of knowledge that duplicates those of ancient voyagers is to create criteria intrinsically impossible to meet. What cannot be gainsaid is the empirically based conclusion that limitations of the craft and of ancient navigational methods and supplies can no longer legitimately be seen as having precluded pre-Columbian transoceanic voyaging.

Granted, experimental craft and voyages have not attained perfection. Unless substantial archaeological remains of a craft type exist, the specifics of construction must be somewhat conjectural if based only on early descriptions and/or graphic evidence and modern descendant craft plus surmise. Further and very importantly, contemporary experimental voyagers lack the intensive training from childhood and the accumulated lifetimes of individual and group experience on the part of those who of old built and sailed the original vessels. These modern limitations generally work to make the experimental craft *less* well built and the voyaging *less* skilled than was true of the ancients'. The accomplishments of experimental craft and voyagers should not be thought of as surpassing the capabilities of their ancient predecessors but as representing, in most

ways, the *minimum* expectable from those predecessors. If the relatively amateur modern experimenters could be successful with their imperfect replicas,
how much more so could their practiced professional predecessors have been?

Other Experimental Log and Bamboo Sailing-Rafts

The *Kon-Tiki* traverse was not just a fluke. During the two-and-a-half decades
that followed, more than a dozen copycat manned rafts set out from South
America to cross the eastern Pacific to Polynesia, and all succeeded in accom-
plishing long-distance journeys; more were to come. The early ones included
two 7,450-mile solo voyages to Samoa by the American William Willis, in 1954
and 1964. The first voyage, on the balsa-log raft *Seven Sisters*, took 115 days. The
second, although undertaken on a nonperiod 35-foot steel-pontoon raft, is notable in that the injured seventy-year-old skipper continued on to Queensland,
Australia, an additional distance of over 3,000 miles.[9]

In 1955, the Czech musician Eduard Ingriš and crew sailed the balsa raft *La
Cantuta* from northern Peru to the Galápagos Islands. This was followed, in
1956 to 1957, by the sixty-five-year-old French adventurer Éric de Bisschop, who
made a 196-day, 7,000-mile voyage in the bamboo raft *Tahiti-Nui*, which carried two shear-bipod masts with pandanus matting sails. The route was from
the Society Islands to just short of the Juan Fernández Islands, where a collision caused the craft to break up some 300 miles to the west of South America.
A journey of this length would have been more than enough for a North Pacific
crossing from Japan to California. De Bisschop, who had also experimented with
a double canoe, concluded that sailing-rafts were easier to handle than were
such canoes. In 1958, de Bisschop made another, 124-day drift voyage, in the
log raft *Tahiti-Nui II*, from Chileto, Peru, to the Cook Islands. Near Penrhyn
Island, the raft broke up, requiring building a small emergency raft to take the
personnel on to the Cooks, for a total distance of about 5,500 miles.[10] The raft
wrecked at Rakahanga Atoll and the captain was killed.

In 1959, Ingriš and crew, in *La Cantuta II*, made a second attempt, this time
reaching the Tuamotu's Matahiva from Peru. The year 1965 saw Carlos Cara-
vado Arca and companions sail the balsa raft *Tangaroa* nearly 5,000 miles from
the central coast of Peru to Fakareva in the Tuomotus.[11]

In 1966–67, the Spaniard Vital Alsar captained the raft *Pacifica* out of Ecuador. Supposedly owing to the selection of too-sappy balsa logs, after 143 days the
raft rotted to pieces after being trapped for months in a circular current near
the Galápagos Islands. In 1970, a wiser Alsar and three crew members, employing drier logs, succeeded in sailing the new, seven-log, 42-foot *La Balsa* 8,564
miles in 160 days, from Ecuador to Australia via Samoa, averaging about 53.5
miles a day! Unlike Heyerdahl on *Kon-Tiki*, Alsar was aware of how the nine
guaras operated and found that their manipulation permitted excellent directional control. Purists have objected to the facts that, like Heyerdahl, Alsar used
a bipod mast (documented only for the Peruvian Highlands, not the coast) in-

stead of a monopod mast, treated the logs' lower sides with crude oil instead of animal or plant oil, used commercial hempen rope for lashings, and took along a sextant and nonindigenous foods. Nevertheless, the expedition was a dramatic demonstration of sailing-rafts' capabilities, including, especially, the ability to steer using *guaras*. In 1973, Alsar outdid himself and led a flotilla of three balsa rafts—*Aztlán*, *Guayaquil*, and *Mooloolaba*—for 179 days, ultimately arriving in Brisbane, Australia, via the Marquesas Islands, a distance of 9,200 miles! En route, two of the rafts became quite waterlogged, but they did arrive.[12]

The most recent balsa-raft voyage at this writing is that of Thor Heyerdahl's grandson Olav. His *Tangaroa* was equipped with ten daggerboards and a large square sail plus a topsail and carried a crew led by Torgeir Higraff. The 2006 voyage from Callao to Tahiti was accomplished in seventy days, thirty-one days fewer than the 1947 *Kon-Tiki* traverse from Callao to Raroia.[13]

Another voyage was undertaken, in 1993, by the inveterate Irish experimental voyager Tim Severin and four others, this time from Asia, in a 60-foot bamboo sailing-raft—*Hsu Fu*—modeled after those of Vietnam and carrying three masts equipped with Chinese lugsails. After proceeding from Hong Kong to Japan, the craft cruised for 105 days, traveling some 4,500 miles across the North Pacific, averaging 40 miles a day, finally falling to pieces 925 miles (or some fifteen days) short of California as a consequence of a combination of the stormiest summer in forty years and the rotting and eroding of the raft's split-rattan lashings. Severin concluded that transpacific raft voyaging was not very practicable, being too difficult and exhausting. However, he did acknowledge that if *Hsu Fu* had embarked from North China rather than Hong Kong, the 5,500 total miles it did travel would have allowed it to reach California. In fact, the raft might well have made the last 20 percent of the distance from Hong Kong to Cape Mendocino had the lashings been unsplit and tarred (as in rattan-basketry boats of northern Vietnam). In any case, the feasibility of such a craft sailing from Japan to California was essentially proven.[14]

More recently, a team led by John F. Haslett conducted intrahemispheric experiments with Ecuadorian balsa-log-raft replicas. In 1995, their first craft sailed 600 miles in thirty-eight days, from Salango, Ecuador, to Panama's Azuero Peninsula. The following year, a second raft, fitted with two lateen-rigged sails—the 60-by-20-foot *Manteño-Huancavilca*—traveled 700 miles northward in seventeen days, but had to have its logs replaced in northwestern Colombia owing to shipworm damage, despite the wood's having been treated with barbasco poison and antifouling paint. *Manteño-Huancavilca II*, instead treated with tar from Ecuadorian tar pits, then sailed northward but became both becalmed and caught in a gyre off Panama, circling for sixty-eight days and finally being abandoned off Costa Rica owing to teredo infestation. Later in the year, a fourth, abortive attempt to sail to Panama was made. Despite having failed to solve the shipworm problem—they concluded that the logs would have held up much longer had they been dried for a year or more—the team ascertained that Ecuadorian sailing-rafts were "fully capable" ocean-going craft and that they were easily maneuvered by raising and lowering the daggerboards. Even with very poor winds, the team was able to sail against a swift current.[15] In 1998–99, Haslett's raft *La Manteña* sailed from Ecuador to Colombia and, after repairs, on to Hawaii.[16]

As mentioned in chapter 15, in the East Indies Robert Bednarik's team conducted several experiments with conjectural Middle Paleolithic rafts, using only Paleolithic-type tools, methods, supplies, and so forth. The bamboo raft *Nale Tasih 2* performed outstandingly, even in storms, and made 2–3 knots under good conditions, 4–5 knots under optimum ones.[17]

These and multiple other, sometimes extremely long, experimental voyages should remove all doubt that "primitive" sailing-rafts were capable of successfully transporting humans virtually anywhere in the Pacific Basin.

Experiments with Bundle Raft-Boats

As known to the contemporary world, the ancient watercraft type called the bundle raft is rather small (see chapter 17). But after extensive study, Heyerdahl concluded that in the past such craft were often larger (as shown in Egyptian and Mesopotamian reliefs and frescos) and, as we have asserted, capable of ocean crossings. Wilferedo Castro had already sailed a Lake Titicaca raft up and down the Peruvian coast and then docked it at Callao. After fourteen months in the water, there were no signs of waterlogging, rot, or damage by marine organisms. Trials with a second *totora*-bulrush raft, *Los Incas*, confirmed that genre of watercraft's seaworthiness.[18] Accordingly, Heyerdahl decided to conduct a transatlantic experiment with as near to a replica bundle raft-boat—named *Ra*—as he was able to have constructed.

The length of *Ra*, built with papyrus stems according to sub-Saharan African methods and equipped with a shear-bipod mast, measured 50 feet by 16.4 feet. Launched in May 1969 from Safi, Morocco, with a crew of seven of assorted nationalities, after fifty-five days on the Atlantic it had deteriorated to the point that it had to be abandoned, but only after having gone some 2,720 nautical miles, to within about 400 miles of Barbados in the West Indies. A year later, a new, substantially smaller version, the 39-by-15-foot *Ra II* (see figure 17.3) that had been constructed with *totora* bulrushes according to Bolivian methods, successfully sailed, with eight on board, 3,270 miles on the Canary and North Equatorial Currents from Safi to Barbados, in fifty-seven days—despite a broken steering oar and the raft's becoming increasingly saturated because the reeds had not been cut at the correct season. All food and water carried was prepared and stored in ways appropriate to ancient times (mostly, in ceramic jars).[19] The Mexican anthropologist Santiago Genovés, a member of both of the *Ra* crews, concluded, "The Atlantic was not an impossible barrier after papyrus rafts were primitively built."[20] The *Ra* expeditions showed that bundle-raft-boat crossings could be accomplished even by people of highly diverse backgrounds and limited nautical experience, without benefit of modern provisions.

In 1969, too, the American adventurer Gene Savoy constructed a totora-bundle raft-boat and sailed it some 2,000 miles, from Peru to Panama.[21]

In the late 1970s, Heyerdahl constructed *Tigris*, a 60-foot Sumerian-style spiral-bound-reed-bundle raft-boat carrying two square-rigged cotton sails on a shear bipod mast as well as leeboards and quarter rudders. On the 143-day Tigris Expedition, he and ten other men sailed 4,300 miles from Iraq to Pakistan, with three stops and an occasional short tow, and, from there, across the Arabian Sea nonstop to Djibouti in Northeast Africa. At the end of the five months' journey, *Tigris* was still in perfectly seaworthy condition. Velocities of up to 5 or more knots were attained, and the complement found the craft uncapsizable, even in severe storms. The crew was able to supplement carried supplies with wild fish, turtle, and porpoise.[22]

In 2000, the American Phil Buck led an expedition of eight in *Viracocha I*—a two-masted, 64-foot craft similar to *Tigris*—some 2,500 miles from Arica, Chile, to Easter Island, the raft arriving in good condition. During the forty-four-day leg to Isla Sala y Gómez, the vessel averaged about 4 knots.[23] The Spanish explorer Kitín Muñoz, who had captained a seven-week voyage from Callao, Peru, to the Marquesas Islands in the five-person, 65.7-foot bundle craft *Uru* in 1988, criticized *Viracocha* for having used some synthetic rope for tying its core bundles. In 2003, Buck and a crew of eight sailed *Viracocha II* 2,850 miles from Viña del Mar, Peru, to Easter, in seventy-five days, arriving in rather waterlogged condition.[24]

These various cross-ocean bundle-raft voyages had depended on sailing with the prevailing winds and currents and had not seriously tested the rafts' abilities to sail in different directions. Then, a nine-person team under the German Dominique Görlitz had Aymara Indians build a 39.4-foot, 6-ton bundle raft, *Abora*, which they fitted with mast, sail, and leeboards as seemingly depicted on circa 2800 BC petroglyphs in Egypt. In 1999, the team sailed from Sardinia to Corsica to Tuscany, over twenty-six days. In 2002 they sailed Bolivia-made *Abora II* a total of 1,339 statute miles, from Alexandria, Egypt, to Beirut, Lebanon, in nine days, then 127 miles to Lacarna, Cyprus, in five more. The return to Alexandria involved 1,702 miles of tacking against contrary winds, on reaches 75 to 80 degrees off the wind. Usually, three leeboards were used in the bow and two on the stern, but in strong winds, up to fourteen were employed. Eighty percent of the voyage was accomplished across or against the winds, and the average rate of progress was almost 30 miles a day. Görlitz concluded that a stone-age bundle raft could sail anywhere in the Mediterranean.[25]

Not all experimental reed-bundle-raft voyages have been entirely successful. In 1997, Kitín Muñoz's 131-foot *Mata Rangi* broke up in a storm after twenty days, only 185 miles to the west of its starting point, Easter Island. In 1999, his 95-foot three-master *Mata Rangi II* stayed afloat for eighty-eight days but broke in half and had to return to port.[26] In 2005, nautical archaeologist Tom Vosmer's experimental bitumen-sealed reed-bundle framed and hulled boat *Magan*,[27] which had set off from Sur, Oman, in an attempt to reach India, swamped only

7 miles offshore. In 2008, Görliz's *Abora III* sailed from New York to within 500 nautical miles of the Azores but then was abandoned because of bad weather that had damaged the raft's stern (the crew did find that the craft could progress against unfavorable winds and across currents and that under better conditions it could probably have survived a crossing).[28] Failures do not signify as long as there is the occasional success. The successes have demonstrated at least the transatlantic capabilities of bundle rafts.

An Experiment with an Irish Skin Boat

Sizable skin-covered boats fitted with sails are known historically primarily in northwestern Europe, especially in the Celtic-speaking areas of Ireland and Wales, and among certain Inuits.

In 1963, the Ulsterman Wallace Clark undertook a voyage in a twelve-man currach to replicate the relatively short sixth-century journey of Saint Columba (Calum) from Northern Ireland's County Derry to the old monastery isle of Iona, in Scotland's Inner Hebrides.[29] However, the major experiment involving long-distance sailing of a skin boat is that of Tim Severin, reported in his 1978 book *The Brendan Voyage*.[30]

Severin followed, to the extent possible, ancient descriptions in the ninth-century *Navigatio Sancti Brendani Abbatis* and a somewhat later drawing of Brendan's boat, complemented with knowledge of currachs historically observed in Ireland's Dingle and other regions. He had forty-nine oak-tanned oxhides—impregnated with cod oil and wool grease—sewn together with waxed-flax thread over a leather-lashed ashwood frame. The seams were sealed with grease, and two masts carrying flaxen sails and rigging were added.

The 5-ton-displacement *Brendan* was 36 feet long by 8 feet wide and steered by a quarter rudder (see figure 18.1). It may have strayed from optimum authenticity by omitting a (documented) keel and instead using undocumented leeboards to counter leeway as well as in installing a bit of Styrofoam for safety, but its performance was nevertheless generally representative of that of a medieval hide craft. Without its leeboards, keel-less *Brendan* could not sail better than at right angles to the wind (as contrasted to 60 degrees off *with* the boards), and favorable winds were a requirement; when these were not forthcoming, Severin simply sailed at right angles to his route until the wind turned more favorable. Being small, when gales kicked up high waves the boat was somewhat sheltered from maximum wind buffeting by being down in troughs much of the time, and pouring whale oil in the wake damped wave crests and reduced the likelihood of being pooped. *Brendan* was very hard to capsize (although also almost impossible to right). Bailing was necessary only in rainy weather and could be accomplished in ten to twelve minutes by five men (although on the voyage, a bilge pump was employed).

Use of modern foodstuffs predominated on the first legs, but between Iceland and Newfoundland period foods such as dried/smoked/salted meat, cheese, oats, and hazelnuts were stressed and proved superior to contemporary pre-pared foods. The voyage was to test the *craft*, not medieval means of naviga-tion, and modern methods of position-finding were applied.

Although encountering some hazards, over six months' time in 1976 and 1977 Severin's four- to five-man group crossed from the Dingle Peninsula to Newfoundland in this craft, by way of the Hebrides and Faroe Islands and Ice-land. The Iceland–Newfoundland leg required but fifty days. Despite its com-promises with modernity, this experiment effectively demonstrated the trans-oceanic capabilities of an ancient type of skin sailing boat.

An Experiment with an Ancient-Style Junk

Many East Asian junks have been sailed across the Pacific and other oceans during the past 500 years,[31] and the numerous eighteenth- and nineteenth-century transpacific drift voyages by junks have been discussed in chapter 5. But as we have seen in chapter 20, ancient junks were not identical to more modern ones. In the early 1970s a team led by the Austrian journalist Kuno Knöbl (Konrad Knöbl-Katstellitz), a student of the Austrian diffusionist Robert von Heine-Geldern, had built as near a replica of a small Han dynasty junk of 2,000 years ago as was feasible. In 1974, the *Tai Ki*, as it was dubbed, was towed from Hong Kong to Taiwan, whence it sailed northeastward, weathering twelve typhoons but being done in by the thirteenth after the hull had become riddled by shipworms (despite its pretreatment with protective tung oil). The ship was abandoned to the north of Hawaii after a voyage of about four months.[32] Still, the distance traveled and the time at sea endured argue for the likelihood that ancient junks could have made successful transpacific voyages. Had the craft been outfitted while in fresh water free of shipworm larvae, the experimental voyage might well have been completed.

Experiments with Sailing-Canoes

Although generally unsuitable for long-distance ocean-going, simple sail-less single dugout canoes can, under proper circumstances, make long trips at sea. In 1955, the German doctor Hannes Lindemann made a sixty-five-day cross-ing of the Atlantic from the Canary Islands to the Caribbean's Saint Croix in a significantly modified African logboat, *Liberia*, that he had fitted with a sail.[33]

Sailing canoes of greater complexity are still widely employed in Island South-east Asia and Oceania, so their use continues to be observable. To test the com-mon assertion that these vessels would have been incapable of passing directly across the wide Indian Ocean, an experimental voyage in such a canoe—the *Sarimanok*, of traditional design and materials—was undertaken by the mari-time historian Robert James Hobman and crew, to demonstrate the feasibility of a presumed Indonesian migration route to Madagascar. Built in the Philippines, in 1985 the double outrigger craft, which had a keel length of about 45 feet, departed from Bali and, with a stop in the Cocos (Keeling) Islands to disembark an ill crewman, arrived in northern Madagascar after a circa 4,000-mile journey across the Indian Ocean that depended on "primitive" navigational methods.[34]

In 1976, New Zealander James Siers had had constructed the poorly but largely traditionally built 76-foot Kiribati two-masted single-outrigger canoe *Taratai* and captained it from Tarawa to Fiji (with stops), a distance of about 1,500 miles covered in twenty-four days at sea.[35]

After sailing the 12-ton junk *Fou Po II* from Xiamen (Amoy) to Molokai via New Guinea in 1934–35, in 1939 Éric de Bisschop built the Polynesian-style double canoe *Kaimiloa* and, with one crew member, sailed it from Hawaii to Cannes, France, via the Cape of Good Hope, taking 263 sailing days in five legs.[36] This was only partially an experimental voyage, because the craft was built with sawn planks, bolts and nails, and Chinese-style compartments, and was fitted with a Chinese lugsail. Still, the voyage showed that craft of the general double-canoe type can sail essentially anyplace.

Far more important were the voyages of the *Hōkūle'a*, built in 1975 and sailed mainly by Native Hawaiians under the sponsorship of the Polynesian Voyaging Society and the leadership of the University of Hawai'i anthropology professor Ben Finney.[37] *Hōkūle'a* tested the abilities of an ancient Polynesian-style twin-hulled canoe a little over 60 feet long (see figure 19.1), with a burden of about 12 tons and a crew of ten. Since it was not practical to construct the craft entirely from authentic materials and by neolithic techniques, a compromise was made in which fiberglass-coated plywood planks were lashed to one another (mostly with synthetic line) and to rigid laminated-wood internal components, but according to old-time design. An authentic pandanus matting sail was used. Thus the emphasis in the subsequent experimental voyages was not on craft strength or materials but rather on sailing performance and traditional navigational methods.

Hōkūle'a sailed best on a broad reach (with the wind slightly abaft the beam) and proceeded steadily in moderate trade winds and seas at 7 to 8 knots; velocity averaged 8 to 10 knots when reaching before strong winds and high seas, 4-plus knots (100 miles per day) or somewhat less during long voyages.[38]

Some years after a 1976 Maui–Tahiti trip of nearly 3,000 miles plus a thirty-two-day nonstop Oahu–Tahiti voyage in 1980 with a twenty-two-day return, *Hōkūle'a* sailed a total of another 12,000 nautical miles in six legs: Hawaii to Tahiti in thirty-four days, Tahiti to Rarotonga in the Cook Islands in sixteen days, on to New Zealand's North Island (Aotearoa) in sixteen days (all in 1985), then to Tonga and Samoa in twenty-two days, followed by a return to Tahiti via Aitutaki in the Cooks in nineteen days (both in 1986), and finally back to Oahu from Tahiti via the Tuamotu Islands in thirty-three days (in 1987). The total number of days at sea during this two-year odyssey was about 162, the average sailing speed being some 85 miles per day.

By 1996, *Hōkūle'a* had traveled 75,000 nautical miles. In 1999–2000, *Hōkūle'a* sailed from Hawaii (via Henua Enana, the Tuomotus, Mangareva, and Pitcairn) to Easter Island and back as well. By the end of 2013, the vessel had logged some 130,000 nautical miles, the equivalent of more than 4.5 times around the globe, and a 47,000-mile round-the-world voyage had been begun.[39] Finney asserted that "the overall conclusion to be drawn from the many successful crossings between distant islands is inescapable. The double-hull canoe is well adapted to long-distance voyaging, and noninstrument navigation methods are sufficiently accurate to make a landfall on distant islands and archipelagos."[40]

Hōkūle'a's voyages inspired crew member/navigator Nainoa Thompson to oversee the construction and sailing of two additional Hawaiian double canoes, Hawai'i Loa and Mauloa. When tested, Hawai'i Loa, constructed of native materials, gave results comparable to those of Hōkūle'a. In 1985, too, the Maori two-masted double canoe Hawaiki-nui, also built (by the Maori Greg Whakataka-Brightwell) from native materials and, using traditional navigational techniques and foods, sailed under the Society Islander Francis Cowan from Tahiti to Moorea, Raiatea, and Raratonga, and then on to New Zealand waters, making landfall twenty-two days out of Raratonga.[41]

From New Zealand, in 1992 the Maori double canoe Te Aurere sailed to Tahiti, the Marquesas, New Caledonia, Norfolk Island, and Hawaii. Over sixteen weeks in 2012 and in company with a second double canoe, Ngahiraka-Mai-Tawhiti, Aurere traveled to Tubuai, Mangareva, and Easter Island, depending exclusively on traditional way-finding methods.[42]

One may also record the 1980 voyage of the Ancient Pacific Cultures Research Project's Yasei-go III, a 43-foot double canoe constructed on the basis of ancient rock paintings, which, under Captain Kazunobu Funimoto, sailed 4,842 miles from Tokyo Bay to San Francisco Bay in fifty-eight days, logging up to 170 miles a day. The craft then went on to Acapulco, Guayaquil, Lima, and Valparaíso, for an overall total of well over 10,000 miles.[43]

Too, in 1965 the New Zealand sailor David Lewis navigated his modern catamaran Rehu Moana Polynesian fashion to Huahine, Raratonga, and back to New Zealand.[44] In 1997, Gene Savoy sailed his lashed-plank double-hulled Feathered Serpent III-Ophir from Callao, Peru, to Hilo, Hawai'i, in forty-two days. In addition, the French archaeologist Erik Pearthree constructed Ka Imi Ku'a, a replica of a Tahitian double canoe, and, with Anne Di Piazza, in 1997 and 1999 sailed it from Hawaii to the Phoenix and Line Islands.[45] Manuai Matawai, of Melanesia's Manus Island, built a traditional two-masted canoe and (using plastic sails) has taken it among many of the islands of Oceania, logging over 3,000 miles.[46] Finally, based on a 1769 depiction, Australia's Atholl Anderson and Hanneke Boon built (with nontraditional materials) a Maori-style double canoe with sail. Trials showed the craft to be efficient up to 90 degrees off the wind and workable up to 65–70 degrees.[47]

The foremost post-Hornell scholar of Oceanic sailing craft was Edwin Doran Jr. After both literature research and in-the-field experimentation regarding Oceanian canoes, he concluded that "there appears to be no factor of seaworthiness or sailing capacity which precludes trans-Pacific crossings by such canoes."[48]

Experiments with Southern Asian Sewn-Plank Vessels

As mentioned in chapter 19, the temples (early eighth century AD) at Borobu-dur, Java, are replete with carvings, and some of these are detailed depictions of ships carrying two masts and outriggers. In 2003, Philip Beale, an English fund manager, had an approximate replica constructed by a native boatbuilder in Indonesia's Kangean Islands. The two-masted, double-outrigger ship was adequately stable, neither pitching nor rolling, and it reached a maximum speed of about 7.5 knots. After a test run to Jakarta, from August 2003 to February 2004 Beale and his crew of about fifteen—half Indonesians—sailed 3,500 miles, first to the Seychelles Islands in twenty-six days at sea, averaging 5.3 knots, and then, via the post-Columbian "Cinnamon Route," on to Madagascar and South Africa, surviving a storm that carried away their sail. From Cape Town, they proceeded up Africa's west coast to Accra, Ghana, all in an effort to show that ancient Indonesians could have influenced culture there.[49]

In 1980, Tim Severin oversaw the construction of a traditional Indian Ocean sewn-plank boom. Its length was 80 feet and its beam 20 feet, 4 inches. The builders fitted *Sohar* with two masts and three lateen-rigged sails of handmade canvas (figure 21.1). In 1980–81, with an international crew of twenty, he sailed the vessel 6,000 miles from Muscat in Oman to Canton in China, via four other ports en route, making as much as 135 miles in a single day and employing tra-ditional celestial navigation. Provisions included both old-fashioned foodstuffs (dates, pulses, rice, and so forth) and canned goods; water was replenished dur-ing rains. A concession to contemporary times was a bilge pump to relieve the crew of hand bailing. *Sohar* attained a maximum velocity of up to 9 knots and averaged about 2 knots—consistent with known voyage speeds from the ninth and tenth centuries. She could sail to an effective 65 to 70 degrees off the wind and was found to be safe in heavy weather, surviving several severe squalls, in-cluding one that shredded her sails. Long nonstop segments were from Mus-cat to Calicut in South India, from Sri Lanka to Wei off the tip of Sumatra, and from Singapore to Guangdong, China.[50]

In 1996, Severin had a 59-foot, two-mast Kei Islands prahu—a type of In-donesian lashed-plank ship—built. He named it the *Alfred Wallace*, after the famous nineteenth-century British naturalist, and he and his crew cruised the Molucca Islands in it. Although in some respects this trip did not meet the cri-teria of an experimental voyage, Severin did confirm that the *Alfred Wallace's* rectangular boom lugsails could pick up even a light breeze; though powerful, they were difficult to handle. They could not be reefed in bad weather and had to be taken down and rehung on the opposite side of the mast when tacking. Yet for centuries, they were the principal kind of sail for the far-flung maritime trade of the East Indies.[51]

Finally, in 2010 Michael Flecker's *Jewel of Muscat*, a two-masted, square-rigged dhow built to imitate the ninth-century AD Belitung wreck and based also on historical descriptions and depictions, was loaded with traditional foodstuffs

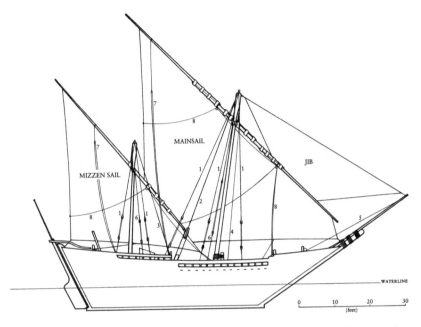

Figure 21.1. The traditional Omani sewn-plank boom *Sohar*. Note the lateen sails hung from forward-tilted yards hanging from short masts. Sail and rigging plan: *1*, shroud. *2*, main halyard. *3*, mizzen halyard. *4*, jib halyard. *5*, jib talk outhall. *6*, choke tackle. *7*, peak vang. *8*, brailing line. From Tim Severin, *The Sinbad Voyage*, 1983, p. 236.

and sailed from Oman to South India's Karnataka and on to Peninsular Malaysia and Singapore, taking 138 days and surviving a cyclone. Its square sails allowed keeping a course within an impressive 51 degrees of the apparent wind.[52]

Experiments with Ancient Mediterranean-Type Ships

A number of replicas of ancient Mediterranean ships have been constructed and tested—although not, so far, in a transoceanic context. In 2008, a 66-foot-long, 30-ton-displacement replica of an ancient Egyptian Punt ship, *Min of the Desert*, was constructed of Douglas fir, fitted with a mast and square-rigged sail, and given eighteen days of Red Sea trials. "The ship proved agile and fast. During an unexpected storm, it weathered 10-foot waves and winds over 20 knots, and the two massive steering oars trailing the ship's hull helped keep it on course. . . . At one point, the ship hit 9 knots, or about 10 miles an hour, with most of its sails furled."[53]

Tim Severin's *Argo*, intended to reflect Jason's Mycenaean craft of about 1300 BC, was a 54-foot, 20-oared Aleppo-pine-built galley with sail, constructed in the ancient mode. The crew took her from Greece to Georgia at the head of the Black Sea, a distance of about 1,500 miles, and in 1985 sailed her widely around the Aegean and Ionian seas. "Under full sail she behaves superbly" before the wind.[54]

In 2008, Philip Beale had an approximate replica of a single-masted and single-sailed, quarter-rudder-equipped Phoenician ship made and tested. Although traditional materials and pegged mortise and tenon shell-first construction were adhered to, an engine was added for entering and leaving ports. Modern navigational, communications, safety, and cooking equipment was employed, and no attempt was made to use only traditional foods. Thus only the craft itself was tested. With the ancient Egypt-sponsored circumnavigation of Africa that Herodotus described in mind, the vessel left Arwad, Syria, in August 2008, sailed through the Suez Canal and down the Red Sea, with a couple of stops, to Yemen and on to Oman. Tacking proved impractical, so the ship waited for the wind. In August 2009, the vessel sailed well out to sea southward from Salalah, Oman, to Mayotte in the Comoro Islands, a distance roughly equivalent to that from West Africa to Brazil. Then it went on to Beira, Mozambique, and, with two stops, to and around the Cape of Good Hope. The route from the Cape to Gibraltar was a blue-water one, via Saint Helena, Ascension, and Flores in the Azores. The Ascension–Azores leg alone was *twice as long* as necessary to have accomplished a transatlantic voyage; in fact, the vessel came within 400 miles of South America and passed close to the Lesser Antilles. The voyage continued up the Mediterranean, with stops, to Lebanon and Syria, arriving in October 2010. Total distance sailed: 20,000+ nautical miles. In the spring of 2012, the craft sailed from Syria to London, via Gibraltar.[55] Clearly, a ship of this kind could have traversed the entire Atlantic with ease.

The nautical archaeologists J. Richard Steffy and Michael Katzev's replica of the circa-300-BC, approximately 46-foot Kyrenia, Cyprus, wreck, *Kyrenia II*, "functioned perfectly. . . . [It] achieved remarkable speeds and weathered some severe storms without trouble." On its experimental voyage from Cyprus to Athens, its rig, based on ancient descriptions, allowed the sail to be finely controlled and the ship to sail relatively close to the wind.[56]

Experiments with Replica Norse and Anglo-Saxon Ships

What was probably the first—and for decades, the only—true experimental voyage involving a replica of a pre-Columbian craft was undertaken by the Norwegian merchant and yachtsman Magnus Anderson, on the occasion of the 1893 Columbian Exposition. His 76-foot *Vikingship*—a reproduction of the circa AD 800 Norse Gokstad ship—and its twelve-man crew crossed the Atlantic from Bergen to Newfoundland and continued on to Chicago. Although incorrectly rigged, it displayed considerable seaworthiness. The 2,625-mile voyage from Norway to Newfoundland took a mere twenty-eight days, with an average speed of about 94 miles a day.[57]

A number of full-sized replicas of Norse craft have been built and sailed here and there since. For instance, the *Imme Aros*, a 47.5-foot replica of the twelfth-century Ellingå ship, tested in 1969, proved to be very seaworthy and able to beat to within about 60 degrees off the wind. It was capable of making 8 to 9 knots' speed. The 39-foot *Imme Skinfaxe*, based on the slightly larger Danish merchantman wreck *Skuldelev 3*, could sail 55 to 60 degrees off the wind, making good 1 to 2 knots; it made 8 knots or more with the wind.[58]

The 1998 voyage in Hodding Carter's *Snorri*, a replica of the archaeological small *knörr Skuldelev 1*, went from the site of Greenland's Eastern Settlement up the Greenland coast, across to Baffin Island, and southward to the tip of Newfoundland—taking eighty-seven days, owing to weak winds. In 2016, the 115-foot longboat replica *Draken Harald Hårfagre* sailed from Norway to the Saint Lawrence River via Iceland, Greenland, and Newfoundland. More impressively, in the mid-1980s Ragnar Thorseth's circa 23-ton *Saga Siglar*, another replica of little eleventh-century *Skuldelev 1*, crossed from Norway to North America in stormy seas via Iceland and Greenland—and then sailed to and through the Panama Canal, across the Pacific and Indian Oceans, through the Suez Canal, and back to Norway, completing the first open-boat circumnavigation of the globe. Over one twenty-day period in the Pacific, it averaged 150 nautical miles a day.[59] This last voyage makes it clear that a small ship of Norse type could sail virtually anywhere on the world's oceans.

Rather similar to Norse ships were Anglo-Saxon ones, and the latter people were renowned for their competence in navigation. During the 1980s and 1990s, the civil engineer/naval architect Edwin Gifford and his geographer wife, Joyce, built and undertook sea trials with half-scale models of two archaeological Anglo-Saxon vessels from Kent and Sussex, respectively, retaining correct hull shape although making some compromises with materials. Each craft was fitted with a Roman-style square sail and a side rudder. Their model of the 44-foot-long, 5-ton tenth-century AD Graveney find, named *Ottor*, was handy at sea and maneuverable in confined waters, and trials indicated that the full-sized vessel was capable of attaining speeds of over 7 knots and making an English Channel crossing during one day's daylight. It could sail to within 70 degrees of the wind and make good 1 knot tacking in relatively smooth water. The model of the seventh-century AD 83.3-foot, 13-ton Sutton Hoo ship, *Sæ Wylfing*, proved stable and safe. The original's top speed would have exceeded 10 knots, and it would have averaged around 7, permitting a passage to France in half a day. If the breeze was not too strong and the sea not too high, by wearing this vessel, too, could make good but a paltry 1 knot against the wind.[60]

Altogether, the results of these various experiments leave little room to doubt the abilities of traditional watercraft—including log and bundle rafts, skin boats, and sailing-canoes, as well as junks, Classical naos, and wooden Norse craft—to travel over virtually any distance to almost any coastal destination.

Modern One- and Two-Person Small-Boat Crossings

The experimental voyages in replica vessels described above involved craft of at least moderate size. However, in chapter 14 the point was made that large size does not convey advantage in the realm of seaworthiness, that it in fact makes a craft more vulnerable to having her back broken. Another matter remains to be considered: Can very small craft with tiny complements really survive the seas and make ocean crossings? Again, the answer is an emphatic affirmative and comes in the form of a multitude of recorded modern one- and two-person small-boat voyages. Such crossings have been made by solitary men and women, teenagers and senior citizens, amateurs and even amputees, in craft less than 6 feet in length and in not only conventional craft but also in canvas boats, peddled boats, and many another unlikely vessel.[61] In 2012, for example, a sixteen-year-old girl sailed solo around the world. The endurance record as of this writing is 1,151 continuous days at sea without resupply.

Whereas these various contemporary voyages involved modern boats, equipment, and knowledge, plus at least the possibility of rescue, and did not replicate pre-Columbian craft, supplies, learning, or methods, they do unequivocally demonstrate that not only does it not require large and capacious craft or large personnel to cross even the widest oceans intentionally, it does not even require sail, since the Atlantic, the Pacific, and the Indian Oceans have all been crossed in rowboats—and in relative safety. Numbers of small boats have been lost at sea, but the usual cause has been serious accidents to craft resulting from their being cut down by a commercial ship, or from fire—of which the common causes are ignition of engine fuel or explosion of gases like propane—not hazards relevant to ancient voyaging.

Although holding what remains very much a minority view, the anthropologist Alice Beck Kehoe has forcefully expressed her conclusions from a study of watercraft capabilities and of the archaeological record, and we close Part II with her words: "By 4,000 years ago, the world was truly one, outriggers and junks and currachs and barques out on the planet's oceans. . . . Crossings and recrossings of great breadths of ocean are clearly proven. There can be no doubt that transoceanic contacts have been possible and probable, though not likely sustained, for at least the past 4,000 years."[62]

Asea without a Compass

Celestial Way-Finding

The navigator recalls his sea lore,
Remembers the guiding star for Ifaluk;
When one is down, another rises.
He remembers those stars
Deep within him,
Stars by which he can steer
And grows impatient to be on his way.
                    —song from Ifaluk Atoll, Caroline Islands

As has been observed in previous chapters, many scholars—ignoring the feats of the Polynesians and others—have alleged that mariners could not have found their way around the vast open oceans without charts and without the compass and other instruments of relatively modern navigation. Even as early as the seventeenth century, the poet Abraham Cowley could versify,

Our course by stars we cannot know,
Without the compass too below.

In this chapter, we shall see that this is far from being the case.

Personal Magnetism: The Navigator's Compass

In 1620, Sir Francis Bacon declared that three relatively recent but initially obscure inventions—printing, gunpowder, and the magnetic mariner's needle—all from China—"have changed the whole face and state of things throughout the world."[1] It is to the third of these that we now turn.

Knowledge of the property of certain iron-rich minerals, especially magnetite (lodestone), of attracting other fragments of those minerals or metallic iron, can be documented in the Mediterranean region back to at least the time of the sixth-century BC Greek, Thales of Miletos. The historian of mathematics Amir D. Aczel forwarded evidence of a link between lodestone divination, sixteen directions, and seafaring there going back into antiquity.[2] However, in the West the first known mention of a magnetic direction-indicating device—simply a magnetized needle inside a straw floated on water—dates from only AD 1187. "With a floating needle," claimed the historian Richard W. Unger, "skippers were still limited to following the coast and to staying in port in the winter to avoid storms and cloudy skies."[3]

Indications are that the first European appearance of the modern navigational compass was in Amalfi, Italy, around AD 1300, involving a dry-pivot rotating magnetized steel needle combined with a sixteen-point compass card put into a box. Textual evidence suggests wide use of lodestone compasses in the north somewhat earlier, by about the middle of the thirteenth century AD. The European advent of the device, along with suitable charts on which to plot courses (beginning, in Italy, about AD 1250–65), is often said to have been among the late medieval/early Renaissance developments creating conditions that made Columbus's crossing feasible. Aczel, who authored a 2001 comprehensive book on the topic, attributed supreme historical importance to the instrument:

> Within a few decades of 1280, the world saw a dramatic rise in trade, and with it, increased prosperity. . . . A single invention—the magnetic compass—made this possible. The compass was the first instrument that allowed navigators . . . to determine their direction quickly and accurately at any time of the day or night and under almost any conditions. This allowed goods to be transported efficiently and reliably across the seas and opened up the world to maritime exploration. The earth would never be seen the same way again.
>
> The compass was therefore the most important technological invention since the wheel.[4]

Such hyperbole aside, it is generally recognized that the magnetic navigator's compass was a Chinese, not a European, invention. North-and-south-pointing needles are described in an AD-1044 Chinese text, and the use of the needle at sea is solidly attested by 1090. But nautical use is thought probably to have begun not long after AD 850, and somewhat earlier dates have also been suggested; lack of early documentation likely reflects known Chinese secretiveness concerning the device.

Knowledge of the principle of ferromagnetism itself is far older in China and could conceivably have been early employed at sea. Lodestone "south-pointers" (primarily for geomancy) are mentioned in fourth- and first-century BC texts, and a third-century BC book refers to the device as ancient. It was a magnetite spoon, probably representing the Big Dipper, and was laid atop a dial-like diviner's board; it would rotate around the point at which the bowl rested upon the board. By 120 BC, a twenty-four-direction board was used. Ultimately, perhaps about AD 450, people found that an iron needle could be magnetized by rubbing it with lodestone, and this allowed much more precise readings.

An important step with respect to usefulness for navigation was the discovery and tabulation of declination, the areal variability of the directions of the lines of the Earth's magnetic field, which have to do in part with the fact that the magnetic poles are a bit equatorward of the geographic poles. In many areas, lack of knowledge of declination could result in serious miscalculations. The aforementioned step was accomplished for Chinese waters by the time of the late Tang dynasty, circa AD 880.[5]

There is a Sanskrit word for the magnetic compass, implying early Hindu use. Indian Ocean Muslims were also employing it by the thirteenth century, having borrowed it from the Chinese, and the instrument may have reached northern Europe via the Levant.[6]

The mariner's compass is certainly a highly useful device, especially during daylight and in overcast weather, when the stars are invisible, and ultimately it became virtually ubiquitous in overseas navigation. But the magnetic compass is not without its shortcomings—not only magnetic declination[7] but also deviation (caused by interference from nearby objects made of iron). Stellar navigation (examined more closely below) does not suffer from these problems, and unlike compasses the stars never malfunction. In fact, an anonymous Chinese sailor once explained that "the shipmaster to ascertain his geographical position by night looks at the stars; by day he looks at the sun; in dark weather he looks at the south-pointing needle."[8] In other words, the compass was used only when overcast skies precluded celestial methods.

The compass is, then, by no means essential for deepwater voyaging and long-distance navigation, as even Aczel acknowledged: "Navigators of antiquity managed well without the advantages afforded by the compass. . . . Navigation across the seas took place long before the compass was invented—but the compass made navigation more efficient by opening the seas to winter navigation and by extending a ship's range to regions that were previously unexplored."[9]

In *The Conquest of the North Atlantic*, the British naval historian G. J. Marcus contrasted the known facts of Norse navigation with the perceptions of various authors who have propounded the notion of the necessity of possessing the compass in order to sail out of sight of land: "The immense range and scope of the ocean navigation of the North in the Middle Ages is even today, in all likelihood, not properly appreciated outside the confines of Scandinavia. The long-continued traffic between Norway, Denmark, Ireland, the Orkneys, Shetlands, and the Sudreyjar ['southerly realms'], and the Faeroes, Iceland, and Greenland, serves as a complete and convincing refutation of the old fallacy—which is, nevertheless, an unconscionable time dying—namely, that it was not until the introduction of the magnetic compass in the later Middle Ages that European mariners dared to venture out of sight of land."[10]

If celestial and adventitious navigation was so accurate, then, why *did* use of the magnetic compass so widely and thoroughly replace it? As mentioned, the compass functions when the heavenly bodies are invisible. Yet an accurate course usually can be maintained at these times by reference to swell direction instead (see chapter 23). The compass's ultimate ascendancy appears to have been more a matter of greater efficiency than of superior accuracy: any reasonably able person can learn to use a compass and declination tables in a very short period of time, whereas the ability to navigate accurately celestially and by sea swells requires years of training and experience plus prodigious memory; as is usual with humans, ease was preferred to effort—laziness, not necessity, is the mother of invention, one might say. And it appears that with the compass's replacing earlier sophisticated means of direction-finding, the latter were largely forgotten in Europe and even navigators came to think that without the compass, ships could not find their way at sea.

Following One's Star: Noninstrumental Celestial Navigation

In Oceania, a boat's initial vector toward a known destination might be set by aligning the craft with certain terrestrial landmarks. Once a ship is out of sight of land and away from shallows, visual pilotage ends and navigation begins. Moderns have tended to follow the thinking expressed in 1625 by the English anthologist of travel accounts Samuel Purchas: "barbarous Empires [had] never grown to such glory . . . because learning had not fitted them for Sea-attempts, nor wisdome furnished them with navigation."[11] However, there were, in fact, excellent means of finding one's way that were well known to premodern sailors, collectively called "environmental navigation."

Dead Reckoning

The most basic means of navigating the sea from place to place is *dead reckoning*, in which a craft's position is estimated on the basis of direction of movement, speed, and time elapsed. Direction is ascertained either with a compass or by methods described below; speed estimated by both "feel" and use of formal or informal logs (objects that are allowed to float along the length of the craft and timed, to indicate velocity); and time elapsed, calculated simply by counting days and sometimes hours. In medieval and Renaissance Europe, a traverse board—a kind of pegboard—was used to tally these things. The greatest challenge in dead reckoning is making compensations for leeway (lateral drift in winds other than from dead astern) and for the sets (directions and velocities) of currents. Of these, the currents pose the greater difficulty, because leeway can at least be estimated on the basis of wake angle while many (not all) currents are indiscernible, especially in the dark. Still, the modern small-boat sailor David Lewis found, of contemporary motorboat fishermen in the Pacific islands, that "their knowledge of currents in all seasons is encyclopedic, far surpassing in detail and accuracy that in European hydrographic publications."[12] Oceanic (and undoubtedly many other) navigators were well able to compensate reasonably accurately for crosswinds and currents.

For dead reckoning, direction needed to be determined. The most ancient means of achieving this was, no doubt, by use of the heavenly bodies: the sun in daytime (including via shadows that the rigging casts on the sails) but particularly the stars at night. (This was done not only at sea but on open land as well, as perhaps reflected by the story of the Star of Bethlehem that guided the magi.)

The development of modern instrumental, position-based navigation was largely a post-Columbian phenomenon; earlier, traditional European methods were inferior to those of several other regions of the world. Methods of celestial navigation beyond simple determination of direction (see below) were known in Renaissance Europe, but even Columbus and his peers were more simple dead reckoners than skilled stellar and instrumental navigators—dead reckoning being an art at which many were admittedly quite accomplished, even though accuracy was constrained. The sole celestial bodies that the average southern European navigator had the knowledge to use prior to the end of the sixteenth century were Polaris (the North Star) and the sun, because most voyaging was coasting, interisland, or across open waters of fairly limited extent, as in the Mediterranean and the North Sea. Even as late as 1537, the Portuguese mathematician Pedro Nunes characterized the pilots of his day as, despite ostensible training in these matters, knowing "neither sun, moon, nor stars, nor their courses, movements or declinations; neither latitude nor longitude of the places on the globe, nor astrolabes, quadrants, cross staffs."[13] Somehow, sailors got around anyway. As the nautical historian Samuel Eliot Morison noted, "there is a certain feel for a ship and the sea, possessed . . . by thousands of humble shipmasters unknown to fame, which is as good or better than scientific navigation."[14]

Even half a century after Cabot, in a book called *Regiment of the Sea*, the English mathematician/navigator William Bourne asserted that the more conservative mariners, "them that wer auncient masters of shippes," would disparage those of their fellows who had to employ the newly available instruments and methods, such as the astrolabe and the quadrant—both used for fixing the altitude of the sun and the stars above the horizon (for determination of latitude) and for other calculations—along with declination tables.[15] As noted in connection with the compass, such instruments may have been adopted more for efficiency than for increased accuracy, thus allowing, during an era of rapid expansion of maritime exploration and trade, a plethora of men of lesser aptitude to become navigators, with greater alacrity and ease.

Certainly, not all sailors through European history were as limited as those criticized by Nunes. Granted, early instrumentation was rudimentary at best. Although the astrolabe is more than two millennia old (a second-century BC or earlier Greek invention), it is first recorded used at sea, among the Arabs, only in the eighth century AD. The astrolabic quadrant—a simpler device to measure angles, which was developed in Egypt about AD 1200—also came into use, but both of these instruments, like later sextants, were of minimal utility when a ship was rolling and pitching. Still, earlier, simpler ways of fixing solar and stellar altitudes were surprisingly effective. In fact, while the ship was in heavy seas the unaided eye could be more accurate than a hand-held instrument. As observed by the eighteenth-century Spanish explorer José Andia y Varela, for instance, Tahitian sailing masters "steer by the stars . . . and they hit it off [their destinations] with as much precision as the most expert navigator of civilized nations could achieve."[16] Orientation by means of stars was capable of greater precision than was use of the magnetic compass.

The point of observing the stars, which have fixed positions vis-à-vis each other as far as Earth observers are concerned, is that owing to the rotation of the earth, the celestial "sphere" gives the appearance of rotating through the course of the night, and each star seems to travel along a fixed arching pathway from eastern to western horizon. Thus each star "moves" along above a particular parallel of latitude, with only Polaris—the current North Star—standing nearly stationary (approximately over the North Pole, on the axis of Earth's rotation).

The Polestar System of Navigation

Two systems of stellar navigation developed and were used, both separately and simultaneously. The first employed a polestar. Stellar positions vis-à-vis the poles change a bit over time (circa 50.3 seconds of arc per year), owing to Earth's axial precession (wobble). After about 2300 BC, Polaris (Alpha Ursae Minoris) was the Northern Hemisphere polestar. Kochab (Beta Ursae Minoris) was used as well, and had been the polestar prior to Polaris. Before that, Thuban (Alpha Draconis[17]) had been. In the days of medieval Irish and Norse voyaging, Polaris was about 7 degrees off north, although a nearby fifth-magnitude star was close to the celestial pole.

The polestar system is most useful in the middle latitudes but less so for the high latitudes (where the polestar is too high in the sky) and for the equatorial latitudes (where the polestar may be too low on the hazy horizon to be visible). Polaris cannot ever be seen from beyond a little to the south of the equator—although the pointer stars of Ursa Major (Great Bear or Big Dipper) remain visible much farther southward than does Polaris itself. However, in Northern Hemisphere middle latitudes, one can easily ascertain the direction of north or south and, with reference to north or south, the other directions. By keeping the polestar at a particular "o'clock" position vis-à-vis the craft's direction of travel, one can maintain a consistent course. At least among Arabs, the duration of time traveled was approximated by observation of the relative heights above the horizon of one star directly ahead and a second star directly astern.

Further, the angular elevation of the polestar above the horizon can be used as a visual indicator of what latitude the observer is at. The medieval Portuguese employed fingerbreadths, wristbreadths, and handbreadths, one finger equaling about 2 degrees, one palm or fist about 8. The star's position vis-à-vis the rigging was also used. In the Indian Ocean and the Far East, elevation was expressed in terms of roughly standardized fingerbreadths and fractions thereof, with an accuracy to within half a degree under relatively calm conditions. Medieval Arabs roughly standardized this by employing the *kamal*, a simple tablet-and-knotted-string device for ascertaining the angular height of the polestar. When Polaris was not visible, the heights of other stars or asterisms having known relationships with Polaris were employed.[18]

The antiquity of the polestar system is unascertainable, but the Ionian poet

Homer (circa 800 BC) sang of "the Great Bear which wheeling round / Looks ever towards Orion and / Dips not into the waters of the deep."[19]

The Phoenicians are also known to have studied stellar navigation and to have used the Lesser Bear (Ursa Minor or Little Dipper) for navigating, and the Romans, too, employed star elevation for navigating.[20]

Owing to its visually large size and continuous apparent movement, the sun is not nearly as accurate an indicator of direction as are the nighttime stars. Nevertheless, solar noon altitude and points of rising and setting give some idea as to latitude. I-Kiribati (Gilbert Islanders), probably among many other Oceanian peoples, possessed a sun compass with thirty-two points of rising and setting at different times of the year.[21]

Polaris and most other stars are invisible in the high latitudes between mid-May and the beginning of August, owing to the "midnight-sun" effect. Absent Polaris in the Southern Hemisphere, the Southern Cross (Crux)—much less satisfactory—must be made to do for ascertaining south. Of course, no stars can be seen under overcast or foggy conditions or (other than the Sun) during daylight hours. It is, in fact, sometimes contended that celestial navigation would be ineffective in zones characterized by cloudy skies. This is clearly an issue during very prolonged cloudiness; the Norse, for instance, often experienced *hafvalla*, disorientation at sea. But it should not be supposed that latitude sailing (see below) requires continuous visibility of the heavens; only an occasional view is needed to verify or to correct direction. Since the navigator would have memorized the sky's basic pattern of stars, seeing just one or two that were recognizable (by magnitude, color, and neighboring stars) through some small gap in the cloud cover would have been enough for him to estimate reasonably accurately where the star he is using should be, even when it was completely obscured.

Northern voyages in the Atlantic were occasionally undertaken in winter, to take advantage of clear, dark skies. Notwithstanding, spring and early autumn were preferred despite lower visibility, because temperatures were higher, storms fewer, and seas lower but stars nevertheless visible many nights despite those nights' much shorter durations. (Late summer to mid-autumn was preferred for Greenland sailings, to avoid pack ice.)

During daylight, the sun's noon and/or midnight elevations and azimuths of rising and setting substituted for Polaris's elevation and direction. In the tropical seas, only one fully overcast day in about forty would be expectable. Under light cloud or fog, to ascertain azimuth some Norse mariners—and perhaps Romans before them—seem to have used a light-polarizing calcite crystal known as a sunstone.[22]

The Star-Path System of Navigation

The second system of stellar navigation involved the star paths or lanes themselves, and was used particularly in the tropics (the higher the latitude, the less precision there is, owing to the curvature of the earth: the apparent trajectory of a star swings increasingly equatorward as it moves toward its apogee; within 15 degrees of the equator, one can see virtually all the stars visible in both hemispheres during the course of a night). If one knows which star or sequence of stars of the same declination passes directly over a destination, one can easily ascertain when one reaches the latitude of that destination.[23] Further, by visually noting the angle that any star stands above the northern or southern horizon at its apogee, one can estimate how far (in angular degrees) one is from the latitude of that star (not that most premodern navigators possessed the concepts of an earth grid or degree distance per se). Knowledge of which stars "travel" along which latitudinal pathways also allows the navigator to ascertain his latitude en route by observing which star is directly overhead at its zenith, to an accuracy of from 1 to 2 degrees. A navigator may also obtain an idea of his latitude in terms of where the circular apparent course of a particular poleward star is tangent to the horizon.

In addition, the locations of risings and settings of the individual stars can be used as points of reference for maintaining a consistent direction of travel (again, this works best in the tropics, where the rises and sets of stars are relatively steep). In the tropical Pacific, where some two hundred stars were named and many more known and utilized, it was conceived that a sequence of stars rose from a "pit" on the eastern horizon arc and sank into another "pit" on the western one. One sailed by directing the craft's bow toward one of these horizon points and backsighting over the stern to another star 180 degrees from the first (if there happened to be a star "pit" in that direction). In practice, horizon haze was common, and rising and setting points often had to be estimated after the star had risen some distance or before it had completely set.

In historic times, from three to nine star paths were regularly utilized in the different island groups. However, Indian Ocean sailors and those of at least the western East Indies, as well as many Micronesians, used a thirty-two-point conceptual sidereal compass, which would have involved about six pathway stars for each of the thirty-two directions (see below). Headings could be checked using Orion's belt, which, being nearly above the equator, rises due east and sets due west.[24]

Drift or other circumstance sometimes puts one off course. In traveling approximately east and west (as between the two hemispheres), that fact is signaled by the craft's no longer being in line with one's fore and aft guide star "pits." One may resume the proper direction by sailing northward or southward to where the stars are once again in line, and then proceed. Unlike in modern Western navigation, the key to horizon-point sailing is in maintaining proper direction for the appropriate time duration, not in knowing the precise position (latitude and longitude) of vessel or target.[25]

For determination of more northerly and southerly directions, Caroline Islanders and probably various others have long employed the fact that as constellations in those directions "rotate" while they arc across the night sky; their different "o'clock" orientations are indicative of different azimuths.

In addition to solar and stellar elevations and pathways, another signal exists in the form of day length at any given season (other than around the equinoxes), that length varying with latitude—the higher the latitude, the greater the seasonal variation in duration of daylight. Around AD 1000, the Icelander Oddi Helgason even compiled a table of solar declinations.[26]

Getting Around: Solving the Problem of Longitude via Latitude Sailing

As this discussion has shown, *latitude* (north–south position) is relatively easy to ascertain noninstrumentally. However, *longitude* (east–west position) can only be at all accurately determined when one is able to keep correct time; dead-reckoning methods can be highly imprecise. If one is able to keep track of what the time of day is at the prime meridian (0° longitude), then by comparing clock time with solar noon at one's position—noon being determinable, among other ways, by the moment of shortest shadow cast by the mast—one can calculate by the difference between the two times how many degrees to the east or to the west of the prime meridian one is. In Classical times, that meridian was variously set as passing through Alexandria, Egypt, or through the westernmost of the Canary Islands. Today, it is designated as passing through Greenwich, outside of London, England. But only when accurate chronometers were developed in 1765 was such precision obtainable on shipboard.[27] The nighttime progression of circumpolar stars in their pathways was temporally indicative but not highly accurate; a device called a nocturnal (to note the position of the star Kochab in Ursa Minor as it rotates around Polaris), was accurate only to within 15 or 20 temporal minutes and so was of very limited use in fixing longitude. No stars other than old Sol were visible during daylight hours. The sand clocks and hour candles of somewhat earlier days in the West, time-keeping joss (incense) sticks in the East, and tallying of chant repetitions in Micronesia provided too much room for error, and water clocks were likely largely unusable at sea.[28] Counting of heartbeats or pulse—variable, anyway—could probably not be sustained for prolonged periods, although these could be used with a log for estimating velocity.

There was, however, a way around this dilemma: latitude sailing. One sailed, by dead reckoning, northward or southward to a position on the (astronomically determinable) desired latitude but well to the west or the east (normally, selecting the windward side) of the destination (say, a mid-ocean island), and then one simply sailed eastward or westward along the parallel of latitude to the destination, at the end employing haven-finding methods if need be to locate that destination (see chapter 23). G. J. Marcus asserted, "It cannot be too strongly emphasized that latitude sailing was the underlying principle of all [Western] ocean navigation down to the invention of the chronometer," and this was standard in the Indian Ocean and the China seas, as well.[29] It was a common saying among European Renaissance sea captains that all one required to find one's way around the world was the "Three Ls": latitude, lead line, and lookout.[30]

Longitude was significant in terms of knowing how many degrees farther east or west one would have to go to reach a destination, and lack of knowledge of one's longitudinal position could put a ship at risk of wrecking on a shore arrived at sooner than expected. However, with respect to simply *finding* the long north–south shores of the Americas, or any place on those shores, ascertaining longitude did not signify—contrary to the impression given by Dava Sobel's popular 1995 book *Longitude*. Thus the ability to determine latitude reasonably accurately was sufficient for almost every purpose in almost every case, even in locating small islands. This ability goes back into remote antiquity, even if not always involving the exact concepts and calculations familiar to more modern geographers and navigators. Too, since the entire European Great Age of Exploration took place without the ability to determine longitude accurately, such inability would not have been a determining inhibiting factor in navigation during earlier eras.

Ancient Knowledge of Stars and Navigation

Despite the lack of need for mariners in the east-west-trending Mediterranean to accurately ascertain latitude, not-inconsiderable celestial knowledge was present in the ancient West. Megalithic peoples of Atlantic Europe are thought to have been knowledgeable in astronomy. Phoenician navigators had celestial knowledge and also used charts—as did, in all likelihood, the ancient Greeks and Romans. The Greeks employed the stars in navigation, and Strabo credited Sidonian Phoenicians—who may have originated in the Persian Gulf region—with being the source of the first Greek rudiments of stellar science. Homer described Odysseus as steering by the Pleiades, Arcturus, and Ursa Minor, and Pliny, Strabo, and Lucan made similar references. Like the Malayo-Polynesians', the Greeks' use of the stars for navigation stressed points of rising and setting. One of Ptolemy's claims to fame was his *Mathematical Syntaxis* (*Almagest*) of circa AD 142, a compilation of facts and figures for delineating a map of all known stars (of which he cataloged 1,028), drawn in part from earlier work by Hipparchos of Nicaea (second century BC), who had listed some 850 stars plus their positions in relation to the ecliptic. In the first half of the fourth century BC, Eudoxos of Cnidos had written a textbook on the stars as well.[31]

Although not known as notable astronomers, the ancient Egyptians did have a good solar calendar, created a device to determine a star's azimuth, possessed a developed positional astronomy, and constructed tables of star culminations (zeniths) and risings. They directionally divided the sky into decans (10-degree arcs) defined by constellations. It appears to have been from them that, about 600 BC, an Ionian, Thales of Miletos, obtained knowledge of these things and of surveying methods such as triangulation, that provided much of the foundation for Classical Greek stellar navigation and position-finding.[32]

The great center of early celestial observations (and supporting mathematics) was Mesopotamia. The Semitic Babylonians (beginning about 1700 BC) and the later Chaldeans were particularly notable in this regard (perhaps with influence from India). The Babylonians, from whom we get the division of the circle into 360 degrees, were the first documented scientific astronomers, and much of their lore passed to the Greeks via the third-century BC Babylonian Berosos and others, especially following the conquests of Alexander.[33] Babylonian concepts also "took permanent root in Tamil literature" of South India, "as opposed to post-Hipparchan geometrical astronomy in north Indian Sanskrit sources. . . . There can be no doubt whatever that a great deal of this intellectual and social intercourse went on by sea."[34]

Both Greek and Indian astronomy influenced Arabian concepts, particularly those of the Sabaeans of ancient Yemen, whose remarkable knowledge of astronomy, astrology, and mathematics was renowned. This lore was carried on and refined by post-Muhammad Arabs, who, as previously mentioned, used the *kamal*.[35] Likewise, the Celts (especially, their druids) were knowledgeable about the stars and stellar movements, and the Norse, too, navigated by the sun and by star paths and used the guiding North Star.[36]

In China, calendrical and astronomical sciences, studied from earliest times, were connected with, and developed by, the sovereign and thus were "official." As early as 800 BC, jade disks with edge notches indicating various stars in the Big and Little Dippers were made, implying navigational use. By the end of the first century AD, according to Needham, there were Chinese books on astronomy for navigation: "The Chinese pilots of ancient times thus knew their stars. . . . From the earliest times their shipmasters sailed by the stars and the sun when out of sight of landmarks. The great astronomer Chang Hêng [Zhang Heng] referred in his *Ling Hsien* [*Ling Xian*] about [AD] +118 to the 'sum of 2,500 greater stars in all, not including those which the sea people observe.'"[37] Useful though the magnetic compass proved to be, even in the fifteenth century Admiral Zheng He (see chapter 14), who used the device by day, by night used the stars instead. Marco Polo reported Chinese use of the North Star to determine direction and latitude.[38]

Regarding elsewhere in Asia, in AD 1060 the *New History of the Tang* indicated that the Javanese had some knowledge of astronomy and constructed gnomons for measuring noon by changing shadow length, while in the Indian Ocean, Oceania, and other places, masts and their stays as well as stem- and sternposts were also used as gnomons for maintaining sailing direction. In Polynesia, although much navigational lore has been lost over recent centuries, scholars have been able to tease out considerable information. Like the Chinese and Babylonians, they and Micronesians utilized the rising and setting points of the stars and seem, like the Greeks, probably to have used the culminations (zeniths) of the stars as well (although this remains undocumented). They employed a sixteen- or thirty-two-point conceptual wind compass. Micronesians had a well-developed (but largely secret) system of stellar navigation, in the Caroline Islands transmitted via astronomy/navigation schools. The system

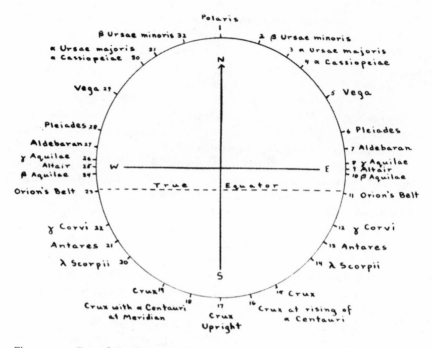

Figure 22.1. Central Caroline Islands conceptual sidereal compass. From Ward Goodenough, *Native Astronomy in the Central Carolines*, 1953, p. 6.

included use of a thirty-two-star sidereal mental compass similar to one used by Arabs and others in the Indian Ocean (figure 22.1). In the Caroline Islands, a sort of mental system of triangulation called *etak* was highly developed for sailing between known islands, using a third as a reference point. I-Kiribati navigators memorized at least 178 stars, constellations, and nebulae.

Sailors of modern Madura in Indonesia use a star compass as well. "Indeed, there is every reason to believe that what we term 'Polynesian-Micronesian' navigation was merely part of a system once practiced all through the Asian seas, and which very possibly did not even originate in Oceania at all."[39]

An indication of the extent of pre-European geographical knowledge in Oceania is the Ra'iatean navigator Tupa'ia's providing Captain Cook with the names, relative locations, and characteristics of eighty-nine islands—fifty-five of which are identifiable today—stretching from the Marquesas and the Tuomotus in the east, to the Australs and the Cooks, and to Samoa, Tonga, Fiji, and the Tokelaus in the west, a span of some 5,000 miles. Tupa'ia himself had visited eight islands in his native Society group, two in the Australs, and two in the Tonga Archipelago—all this in the mid-1700s, following a long decline in Polynesian voyaging. Likewise, the eighteenth-century Spanish explorer Domingo de Bonschea's Tuomotuan navigator Puhoro provided a list of forty-two islands, in the Tuomotus, Societies, and Cooks, along with their terrestrial and marine topographies, products, and degree of agreeableness of their inhabitants, as well as how many sailing days were required to reach them.[40]

Off Course: Navigational Error

J. H. Parry wrote, "dead reckoning, with only magnetic compass and sand-glass for measuring direction and distance sailed, was liable to cumulative error, which over a long voyage might amount to many hundreds of miles."[41] Although stellar navigation is not totally perfect, modern experiences like those of the experimental *Hōkūleʻa* project and the voyages of the New Zealand physician and seaman David Lewis have established that stellar navigational and dead reckoning errors on long voyages tend not, in fact, to accumulate but, rather, to offset each other. *Hōkūleʻa* has sailed the 2,000+ miles between Hawaii and Tahiti five times, its navigator Nainoa Thompson employing only non-instrumental means. At the end of a 1,600-mile instrumentless voyage in his *Rehu Moana*, Lewis found himself off his destination by only 70 miles. The University of Auckland archaeologist Geoffrey Irwin estimated typical Polynesian long-voyage error to have been in the neighborhood of a mere 5 percent on established routes.[42]

The overall picture among pre-Columbian maritime peoples, then, was that means existed and were employed to navigate the world's seas relatively safely and with confidence. Available noninstrumental celestial and noncelestial navigation were quite adequate for traveling to, and returning from, almost anywhere on earth without chart, compass, or astrolabe.

23

A Matter of Course

Seamarks and Haven-Finding

He [the competent navigator] knows the value of signs, both regular
accidental and abnormal, of good and bad weather; he distinguishes the
regions of the ocean by the fish, the color of the water, the nature of the
bottom, the birds, the mountains, and other indications.
—*Mu'allim* (Sanskrit: Pilot in the Arabian Sea), AD 434

The terms "way-finding" and "haven-finding" refer to the art of traveling toward
and locating the specific destinations that one is seeking and include the celestial navigation discussed in chapter 22. In the present chapter, the emphasis is
on what is known as adventitious or secondary aids—noncelestial, noninstrumental methods of ascertaining one's general location and direction when at
sea—and the methods of detecting land when approaching it but still out of
sight, by means of often-minute yet telling changes in the environment that go
unnoticed by the uninitiated. As the German historian of European watercraft
Uwe Schnall put it, like other premodern sailors, "Seamen of the Middle Ages
were trained to observe not only weather conditions . . . but also the slightest
change in their surroundings, to a degree which is unthinkable in the present
technology-dependent world."[1] The navigators of times past, with far less other
knowledge to master and with far, far fewer distractions of the types that di-
vert humans today, took a passionate interest in these matters and used much
of their capacious human memories to build enormous reservoirs of practical
marine, atmospheric, and stellar lore.

Flightiness: Following the Birds

From time immemorial, the movements of birds have been used as indicators
of the direction of land. First, the routes of seasonal terrestrial migrants give
clues that land lies in the directions from and toward which birds come and
go over the waters. For instance, various shorebirds that breed in the far north
spend their winters in Indonesia and Australia, returning to Alaska and Siberia
via Taiwan, the Ryukyus, Japan, the Kuriles, and the Aleutians, a route that has
been suggested as the itinerary of initial or otherwise early discovery and settle-

ment of America by watercraft-borne Asians. Likewise, the Belau and Caroline Islands of Micronesia are linked to Japan, the Ryukyus, and the Philippines by the Asiatic-Belau Flyway; and the Japanese-Marianan Flyway runs from Kamchatka through Japan, the Bonin, Volcano, and North Mariana Islands, and on southwestward, southward, and southeastward into the other Micronesian island groups. Additional avian migration routes crisscross the Pacific island world and on occasion were followed by Polynesians seeking new lands. Some Pacific golden plovers migrate round-trip from the Aleutians to the western islands of the Hawaiian chain, down that chain to the Big Island, and south via the Line Islands to Eastern Polynesia. Other plovers seek out islands in the Marshalls, Gilberts (Kiribati), and Ellises (Tuvalu).

Since it appears that most migrating birds orient themselves by sensing Earth's magnetic field, sailors who followed such migrants were, in a sense, employing an avian magnetic compass. The student of Polynesian sailing Edward Dodd observed, "migratory birds were . . . an indication, nay, they were a proof positive that land lay in the direction in which they flew," and pointed out that once a voyager ascertained their vector, he could correlate that vector with a star path and be able to sail in the correct direction even if the migratory stream ceased.[2]

The southward migrations of long-tailed cuckoos and bob-tailed godwits are said to have led Kupe—the founding navigator from Raratonga—to New Zealand some eight centuries ago. The return migrations of plovers and/or those of the bristle-thighed curlew may have led Tahitians to Hawaii.[3] Knowing that plovers require land, Polynesians concluded that if birds could cover a distance in a single flight, they themselves could certainly cover it in a large canoe. After their first success, they soon would have been following bird migrations in every direction, until all of the islands to which these birds migrated were found. In fact, an old Tuomotuan chant goes, "Mine is the migrating bird winging afar over remote oceans, / Ever pointing out the sea road of the Black-heron. . . . / It is the road of the winds coursed by the Sea Kings to unknown lands!"[4]

The Chinese also used migrating birds as guides.[5] In the Atlantic world, great flocks of waterfowl fly annually from Scotland, via the Shetlands and the Faroes, to Iceland and points west, showing the way. Sixth-century Irish mariners were noting the flights of birds, including Iceland- and Greenland-breeding geese and swans, four species of which winter in Ireland. Skeins on the "Swans' Way" were easy to follow back northwestward by boat, and this is what led the Irish to Iceland and other northern islands in the eighth century AD, according to the ninth-century monk Dicuil. One migration route of shorebirds connects western Ireland, western Scotland, the Faroes, and Iceland, and another links Scotland with Norway via the Shetlands—all of which may well have encouraged various European searches for land out in the Atlantic, including in prehistoric times.[6]

It is not only the vectors of migrating birds that are important but also the flights of birds that feed at sea during the day and return to their nests or roosts on the land at day's end. Such homing birds, which include boobies, noddies, fulmars, petrels, frigate birds, tropic birds, pelicans, gannets, cormorants, gulls, and terns, may be encountered far from land: brown terns up to 40 miles out, white terns up to 125. Avifauna from Iceland, such as eider ducks, are seen as much as 150 miles from that island, although few terra-firma-tied avian species regularly range more than 100 miles from land; 50 miles is more usual, globally.

Distances to land can be estimated, as early Arabs did, on the basis of which species are encountered and how numerous they are. Whether the birds are flying landward or seaward is signaled by the time of day and whether the birds' beaks are fish-full or empty. The flights of these birds can be especially valuable navigational aids in fog (including by voice), but of course they may be of use in finding (or avoiding) the land during clear weather as well. In effect, having such birds daily fly, let us say, only 50 miles out to sea expands the diurnal virtual diameter of an island—even a mere bird rock—to a minimum of 100 miles (two radii of 50 miles each)![7]

According to the sixteenth-century Spanish chronicler Bartolomé de las Casas, who summarized Columbus's journal, "The Admiral knew that most of the islands which the Portuguese held had been discovered through the flight of birds." Therefore, when approaching the Bahama Islands (previously unknown to him in 1492), he altered his course to follow the flocks. In 1500, the Portuguese captain Pedro Cabral found Brazil by following birds he knew to be terrestrial. The Portuguese discovered Flores in the Azores through observing land birds flying in its direction. Likewise, in the Pacific I-Kiribati navigators were taught to follow gulls to land.

In fact, land birds, such as sharp-eyed corvids, were often taken to sea in cages, to be released when it was supposed that land was near; upon release, the birds would fly high, sight the land, and make for it, the ship following. This practice was recorded in Babylonian times and appears not only in the form of Noah's doves (and raven) of Genesis (7:6–12) but also in the preceding Akkadian/Sumerian myth of Gilgamesh, in which a dove, a swallow, and a raven are released. In librarian of Alexandria Apollonios of Rhodes's *Argonautica* (mid-third century BC, describing the thirteenth century BC), a dove was released to "to explore the way." Use, in India and Ceylon, of captive land-finding birds is mentioned in Hindu and Buddhist texts as far back as about 500 BC (*Kevaddha Sutta of Dīghha*) as well as by Pliny (first century AD) and by Cosmas Indicopleustus (AD 535) for Sri Lanka. The Maori tradition of the discovery of New Zealand refers to release of captive land-seeking birds. Again, according to the *Hauksbók* and *Landnamabók* one of the early Norse explorers to Iceland liberated land-finding ravens.

Seabirds also have customary feeding grounds, according to where fish are abundant: over soft-bottomed shallows—for example, the Grand Banks—and in cold waters, as off the west coasts of continents between 25 and 35 degrees latitude and where currents, such as the Labrador, descend from the Arctic. Encountering such grounds, if they are known, provides a locational check. Too, different bird species are characteristic of different portions of the seas. Norse sailors on the direct voyage from Norway to Greenland knew they were passing the correct distance south of Iceland if they encountered the correct avifauna and feeding whales.

Insects are sometimes blown great distances off shore. The experimental voyagers in *Hawaiki-nui* recognized that they were approaching land when they encountered insects some 185 miles off New Zealand's North Island.[8]

Denizens of the Deep

Organisms other than birds, such as fishes, crustaceans, sea turtles, sea snakes, and sea mammals, can also provide clues for navigators.[9] Certain species of cetaceans, for example, follow distinct and lengthy migration routes and have particular feeding grounds, and certain sorts of sea mammals and fish may be absent or present, or may school, in certain waters. For instance, porpoises seldom go more than the equivalent of an hour's sail beyond land, and the presence of cod indicates continental shelf, as does that of certain kinds of flying fish. The *Periplus of the Erythraean Sea* (*Periplous Maris Erythraei*; Greco-Roman sailing directions from the first half of the first century AD) mentions the fact that, around India, the presence of sea snakes of different colors signals that one is nearing different parts of the coast.

The Way the Wind Blows: Its Direction and Character

In about 389 BC, Plato observed that "the true pilot must give his attention to the time of year, the seasons, the sky, the winds, the stars, and all that pertains to his art if he is to be a true ruler of his ship."[10] The matter of winds and currents has been examined extensively in chapter 3, but in addition to their roles in influencing direction and speed of travel the winds were also valuable for way-finding. Although at certain latitudes and at some times at all latitudes, winds may be fluky and inconsistent, in many other cases wind direction may remain steady for quite prolonged periods of time, even months on end; the trade winds and the monsoon winds are famous for this quality. If direction is consistent, then a course may be maintained by keeping the vessel at a constant angle to the wind. (Obviously, this becomes modestly more complicated when tacking against an unfavorable wind.) The Norse, for example, recognized eight directional winds, as had the Greeks before them (twelve, in some cases).[11] In addition to making use of sixteen- or thirty-two-point wind compasses, Indian Ocean and Oceanian cultures employed mast pennants of feathers, palmetto bark, and pandanus leaves to indicate wind direction; the Chinese had feather weathercocks as well.[12]

The quality of the wind can also be eloquent. According to their origins over warm or cold land or water, winds vary not only in velocity and consistency (steady versus blustery), but also in terms of temperature, humidity, and odor, thus providing locational hints. Such clues are recorded as having been employed, for example, in Polynesia, ancient Greece, and western Europe.[13]

A Swell Angle

As we have seen, contrary to the landlubber's (or even the modern electronic navigator's) notion that the oceans are not only vast but also featureless, devoid of "landmarks," the surfaces of the seas in fact vary areally in a number of ways, and these geographical differences create "seamarks" that can be used as indicators of direction and location. The sailor-archaeologist Brian Fagan averred, "The marine landscape was as decipherable and predictable as that of the land."[14] One way in which this operates has to do with the velocity, form, amplitude, wavelength, and direction of waves (within the zone of generating wind) and swells (outside that zone). The magnitude of waves/swells reflects the strength, duration, and fetch of the wind. With distance outside of the zone of generation, swells' amplitude and steepness diminish and wavelength increases.

Although use of swells for maintaining vector is best known from Oceania, where such skills survived longer than in most other areas, it is also reported widely elsewhere, including Indonesia, the Indian Ocean, and the Shetland Islands.[15]

More than one set of swells may be present in any area, creating complex patterns of superimposition as well as chaotic zones of interaction, which serve as temporary seamarks.[16] Groundswells are generated by the prevailing winds and other swells by storm winds, and in many parts of the world's seas groundswells tend to maintain very consistent direction, at least seasonally. Under these circumstances, to preserve a particular course a helmsman can simply sustain a consistent angle to the crest lines of the swells of a particular set. Experienced traditional navigators are able to maintain a vector even in the dark, by means of the feel of the craft's pitch and roll, which reflects the angle at which the swells are encountered; at sea, navigators can often best sense the movements of the vessel by positioning their testes on the rigging. In Oceania, navigators are able, blind, to distinguish by feel as many as five separate swell sets at once.

Further, the character of swells changes over shallows, the swells tending to shorten in wavelength and to steepen, even break, and this, again, can indicate one's whereabouts. Also, as swells approach an island, they "pile up"—shorten wave length and increase amplitude—against the swellward shore and even cause a reflective counterswell that reaches up to 30 miles to sea. These phenomena are obvious to the experienced traditional sailor, as documented in the Indian Ocean and Oceania. On the down-swell side of an island, the two wings of the now-curving lines of swells converge, forming a perpendicular line of occlusion turbulence that, if sailed "up" leads directly to the land. Larger landmasses and island chains create down-swell "swell shadows" as well as wind shadows. At least a dozen different kinds of swells are recognized in Micronesia, and in the Marshall Islands the specifics of the various patterns in the archipelago were taught by means of charts constructed of sticks and seashells.[17]

Sea Color, Sea Character, and Phosphorescence

The color and surface appearance of the sea also provide aids to way-finding. The "ocean blue" is indeed ultramarine in hue, at least under clear skies, in most warmer, deepwater circumstances. But shallows produce lighter-colored, usually greener-looking waters, with variations correlated with differences in the bottom materials. Temperature, salinity, sediment load, and plankton content also affect tone. For instance, cooler, more gas-charged waters normally carry abundant plankton, which imparts a greenish tint, as do cold waters diluted by ice melt. Water that is more saline is bluer than water that is less salty. Debouching rivers can color the sea with silt, which may be carried hundreds of miles by currents. Change of water color as a signal of the proximity of land is a phenomenon referred to in the *Periplus* and in India's *Jātakamālā* of circa AD 400.

Where the warm Gulf Stream borders adjacent, cooler waters, the color contrast may be marked, being bluer on one side and greener on the other; the same is the case with respect to the Pacific's Kuroshio. Water temperature itself may speak volumes, since different currents and different waters vary markedly in thermal characteristics. Occasionally, submarine hot springs create thermal seamarks, and volcanic gas vents may do similarly (for example, the Formia Banks near the Azores).

When the wind is blowing contrary to a current, it generates steeper waves and barely discernable ripples; when the wind direction is the same as that of the current, the waves are smaller and flatter and fold over gently downwind and trail foam to leeward. Smoothness of the water surface or certain kinds of waves or streaks may signal a current or an upwelling, and where two opposing currents run adjacent to each other, there may be major turbulence and especially abundant sea life (including congregations of tuna), some of which biota is stimulated to glow in the dark owing to the water disturbance. At least in Micronesia, there are deep swell movements that produce a presumably bioluminescent pulsing phosphorescence at depth, indicating land as far as 80 to 100 miles away. The direction of the flashes alternates between landward and seaward, being of shorter duration in the latter direction; the closer to the land one is, the more frequent are the flashes. General near-surface, nonpulsing bioluminescent manifestations in the water may also provide locational clues. Interactions of swell sets may be detectable in the dark owing to turbulence-stimulated bioluminescence.

Seamark reefs may be detected by water color, bioluminescence, and the presence of localized short, steep waves.[18]

Look, up in the Sky! Fogs, Clouds, and Glows

The clouds and fogs of the atmosphere reflect the temperature and moisture conditions of the lands and waters below them or over which they have passed. Therefore, if one can "read" these indications, one can make some deductions about what lies below or upwind, and this may provide vital information regarding the direction and proximity of land. Fog, for example, tends to form when moist air encounters frigid water—for example, a cold current or upwelling from depth, or cold land. The fog that characterizes the Grand Banks results from an encounter between the warm Gulf Stream and the cold Labrador Current and creates a striking seamark.

As Columbus explicitly recognized, clouds routinely form more often over islands and coasts than over water, and over highlands than over lowlands. Thus the presence of a stationary cloud in an otherwise cloudless sky or in a sky in which the other clouds are moving speaks of the presence of an island or other land, which maintains cumulus clouds generated by atmospheric convection and by orographic (mountain) lifting and cooling of winds. Such ordinary standing clouds, which commonly have summit heights of from about 1,600 to 2,500 feet above the ground, can often be seen for scores of miles at sea, long before the land itself becomes visible.[19] If, for example, the summit of such a cloud were the lesser of those heights, and if a vessel's lookout climbed the lower part of the mast to attain a modest eye elevation of 9 feet above the water's surface, from the visibility standpoint the effective detectable diameter of even a tiny island would be almost 50 miles. Often, in fact, clouds tower far, far taller; fair-weather cumulus clouds commonly peak at about 8,500 feet, swelling cumulus at perhaps 17,500 feet, and anvil-headed cumulonimbus at over 30,000 feet—even to 60,000 feet, in the tropics—and these would be visible much, much farther away. Even if there is no continuing standing cloud, if clouds form, dissipate, and reform over a discrete spot, an island or mainland mountain is indicated. The 3,000-foot-high peaks of the Faroe Islands, for example, are visible from 60 miles out to sea, and their standing summer cumulus clouds from 120 miles out.[20]

Other kinds of clouds may also signal land. Trade and other winds may generate very long, distinctive "bow-wave" clouds where they lift to cross over a high island. On the downwind side, the split winds' convergence from the two sides of a mountain may create a long ribbon of persistent line cloud; one such band regularly extends up to 60 miles beyond the Hawaiian island of Molok'ai. Long, arched orographic "foehn clouds" extend downwind off New Zealand as well.

The bottoms of standing or passing clouds may be distinctive in color, as a consequence of the reflection of light from the lighter-blue waters of a lagoon or other tones from other surfaces, and may be visible at least as far as 25 miles away. Sometimes, lightning in such clouds signals their locations even at night. When the sky is overcast, that overcast tends to be thicker over land. Too, for short-term purposes, the vector of moving clouds can be used to calibrate one's own direction of travel. Ancient navigators would have observed and utilized all of these phenomena.

As mentioned in chapter 1, in the case of glaciated areas like Greenland, even with a cloudless sky the "ice blink"—an icecap's reflection above the horizon, visible up to 60 miles away—would reveal the location in daytime. The "loom" of sunlight (or even moonlight)—a shimmering column of skyglow reflected from the coral sands or shallow lagoon of a tropical island—is a similar phenomenon. The sky above a vegetated island is darker than sky over the ocean.

Some deserts generate dust storms that evidence land far to sea. Saharan dust, for instance, blows across the entire Atlantic and into the Amazonian interior.

If the island or mainland itself has very elevated parts, then it alone (not considering standing clouds over its summit) would be visible far to sea. For example, the elevation of the summit of Hawai'i is about 13,000 feet, and from eye level would theoretically be visible in exceptionally clear weather at a distance of 135 miles. Even a 1,000-foot peak may sometimes be seen at a distance of 100 miles. These visibility-distance figures doubled represent the effective diameters of the islands, not even counting their *actual* diameters.

In addition to these phenomena that "expand" the sizes even of small islands to reliable detection diameters of 60 to 80 miles and theoretical effective diameters of 100 to 150 miles, making them much more findable, there is the fact that many of the ocean's islands lie in chains. These chains form "screens," or "blocks," *some* island of which is likely to be encountered even if the navigator initially misses his specific island target. Oceanian expeditions usually involved flotillas of twenty-five to thirty canoes, sometimes up to eighty, which fanned out in an advancing line of craft some 2.3 miles apart. This disposition would tremendously extend the fleet's aggregate visible horizon (canoes kept in touch at night by means of drum beats and the blowing of conch-shell trumpets). Knowledge of such facts and utilization of such techniques would presumably have greatly enhanced early explorers' sense of security that they would eventually find land.

Other Indicators

Following a consistent vector vis-à-vis current direction was sometimes undertaken by ancient navigators in order to maintain a course. Flotsam—for example, logs, seaweed, even human-made objects—could give indications as to proximity and direction of land as well as the geographical origins of currents. Columbus used such signs. Indian Ocean navigators would drop a ball of coal ash into the water; a current would tend to elongate the floating residue in the direction of flow.

When sailing near land—main or island—another class of seamarks would sometimes be used. On a known route, ships might maintain that route by sailing at such a distance from a particular island that, for instance, half the height of the mountains would be showing above the sea horizon (the Norse, for example, so used the Shetlands and the Faroes on their voyages from Bergen in Norway straight to Greenland).[21]

Littoral seaweed 125 miles or more miles to sea reflects land, whose direction may be deduced if the weed is moving in a current. When a craft is very near the land, the sound of breakers may signal the shore's proximity, even at night or in the fog, as can terrestrial or intertidal-zone odors wafting out on the nocturnal land breeze. Smells could sometimes be detected at great distances; one early explorer remarked that the scent of rosemary could be identified 30 miles out to sea. In Polynesia, pigs on board canoes were keener-nosed than their humans and displayed excitement when land was scented.[22]

The fact of encountering ice, and the sizes and forms of the floes and/or bergs, can reflect location. In shallower waters, sounding and taking bottom samples is another guide. Use of lead and line with sticky tallow or wax at the lead's end to bring up bits of bottom material was recorded by Herodotus and appears in a third-millennium BC Egyptian boat model.[23] Since bottom material varied from place to place, the samples obtained gave information about a ship's location.

Weather or Not: Premodern Prediction Capabilities

Sailing safely depended in part upon selecting meteorologically favorable times for voyages. This usually meant (1) times of favorable winds, and (2) seasons and moments as storm-free as possible. Some premodern peoples had developed considerable predictive capacities in this regard. An old-time English rhyme runs, "Red sky at night is a sailor's delight; / Red sky in the morning, the sailor takes warning"—one of numerous traditional sailors' meteorological maxims (red color being an indication of high humidity levels; see Saint Matthew 16:2–3).

The approaches were varied. The Greek botanist Theophrastos (early third century BC) wrote of short-term weather prediction on the basis of animal behavior, while Polynesians noted whether or not ants and crabs had closed the entrances to their burrows. In the Indian Ocean, mariners observed sea snake and bird behavior to foresee storms. Caroline Islanders used a mental sidereal almanac and calendar that allowed prediction of seasonal winds, currents, precipitation, and overcasts. In addition to observable characteristics of winds, cloud shape and color, floral responses, and faunal behaviors, variables useful for short-term forecasting include the depths to which surface-current movement extended (as ascertained by stones suspended on cords), which reflects oncoming wind velocities; water color; rainbows and lunar, solar, and stellar halos (indicating the presence of atmospheric ice crystals); low-horizon sun color; the phases of the moon; and variations in the colors of the planets owing to high-altitude atmospheric alterations, which presage sudden weather changes.[24]

Different kinds of moving clouds and their sequence of appearance indicate different kinds of coming weather, as can lightning, and there is a whole associated Polynesian vocabulary. According to *Hōkūleʻa*'s navigator Nainoa Thompson, brown clouds herald strong winds, high clouds no wind but much rain. Others pointed to black clouds as signaling rain with some wind. Clouds' movements reveal wind directions and speeds, which in turn point to sky stability, weather fronts, and the like. Traditional Indian Ocean navigators are able to predict cyclonic weather forty-eight hours in advance, based on rising winds and squalls, increased wave amplitude, water spouts, and poor fishing.

Porpoises swimming toward sheltered waters flag a coming storm, as do frigate birds coming unexpectedly to land. Frigate birds' flying seaward signals calm weather.

The eighteenth-century explorers José Andia y Varela, James Cook, and Joseph Banks all opined that Tahitian sailing masters were better at weather prediction than were European navigators, and Cook perceived Polynesian forecasting abilities to be uncannily accurate. Some Polynesians could predict the weather three days in advance, using signs such as the sound of the surf and the behaviors of sea creatures. Tahitians could foretell the advent of out-of-season westerlies a day or so in advance.[25] The Norse were able to forecast the weather a few days ahead and to plan their schedules and itineraries accordingly.[26] Apollonios's version of the oldest-known voyaging saga in Western literature, the Bronze Age *Argonautica*, characterizes the helmsman Tiphys as "an expert mariner who could sense the coming of a swell across the open sea, and learn from sun and star when storms were brewing or a ship might sail."[27]

How Important *Was* Navigational Ability?

We have explored the noninstrumental means of navigation, haven-finding, and weather prediction available to ancient navigators and have demonstrated the considerable accuracy obtainable by simple methods and ample memories. Still, this question remains: Just how important to the issue of transoceanic voyaging *is* close position-finding or other accurate navigation? Obviously, with respect to accidental voyages, it is of no relevance except with respect to attempted return journeys. Yet even with regard to intentional interhemispheric voyaging, exactitude in navigation is of little practical moment in terms of a voyage's successfully reaching land. If one's target is one of continental size, one "can't miss it," as direction givers often say. Pedro Fernandes de Queirós, Captain Álvaro de Mendaña's navigator in 1597, expressed it succinctly: "the most stupid can go in their embarkations . . . to seek a large country . . . since if they do not hit one part, they will hit another."[28] Still, navigational and haven-finding ability likely played a role in fostering maritime activity in general and in imparting confidence to prospective transoceanic voyagers. This sense of confidence is not to be underestimated. As the Latin poet Virgil—and many a motivational writer after him—put it, "They can because they think they can."[29]

III

Motives for Ocean Crossings

Objects which are usually the motives of our travels by land and by sea are often overlooked and neglected if they lie under our eye.
—Pliny the Younger, first century AD

As we have seen, accidental transoceanic drift voyages almost certainly took place and almost certainly left their marks on pre-Columbian New World cultures. However, most diffusionists propose much more than this: major cultural influences, as a consequence of intentional, likely often round-trip voyaging. Intentional voyages would be undertaken only in the presence of persuasive motivation.

Inducements of various kinds have been referred to, in passing, in previous chapters. Here, we may approach the question of motive more thoroughly and systematically by considering general reasons for travel and emigration as they existed, or are thought to have existed, before AD 1500. The kinds of motives manifested are divisible into what students of migration term "push" factors and "pull" factors, although in many cases these are simply two sides of the same coin and operate simultaneously. Movement is also conditioned by what information is available and by perceptions as to the costs of relocation.

24

Repellants

We are cast out and this boat is our country now—and the sea is our refuge.
—Joseph Conrad, 1897

Historically, human movement has often been motivated by negative phenomena, forces presenting incentives to leave a locale. These expulsive factors made life elsewhere—almost anywhere, perhaps—more attractive than remaining at home, at least for some members of the population. Fear and suffering were the basic emotions—of or from death, hurt, hardship, obligation, or shame—and reduction of physical, financial, or social insecurity was the goal. Here, we inventory some of the major classes of repellant phenomena.

Earth Force: Physical-Geographic Factors

Push factors include physical-geographic phenomena such as severe drought; soil erosion and fertility decline; and crops lost to pests or disease, to hurricanes, and to volcanic eruptions and their consequent mudflows, shade-producing airborne ash, and lowered atmospheric temperatures. As an example of volcanic disaster, the catastrophic eruption on the Aegean island of Thera about 1628 BC may not only have disrupted civilizations and precipitated migrations, it may also possibly have given rise, at least in part, to the legend of Atlantis, which Plato placed in the Atlantic (his story, attributed to Egyptians, could conceivably be a conflation of the Thera episode and some notion of a transatlantic landmass as discussed in chapter 1). On New Britain, the San Cristobal eruption of circa 1600 BC was much, much larger than Krakatau's of 1883, covering huge expanses with ash. Such catastrophic eruptions also occurred in the more distant past.

In southeastern Asia and Oceania, occasional drought-producing monsoon failures as well as great floods have repeatedly led to severe social and political disruptions and may well have triggered some overseas migrations. The periodic ENSO-associated megadroughts of southeastern Asia (see chapter 3)[1] would not only have acted as a push factor, they would simultaneously have provided westerly winds for traversing the Pacific. In the Marquesas Islands, food shortages brought on by drought led to formation of great fleets carrying hundreds of refugees and great stocks of food and water, live animals, and young plants, sailing off to search for a new place to settle.[2] Perhaps the best-known modern instance of the food-scarcity phenomenon is the flight of huge numbers of Irish from the mid-nineteenth-century potato famine.

Other physical-geographic phenomena include earthquakes and tsunamis. Among such disasters, one can point to the disappearance beneath the waves of the Peloponnese's Mycenean port of Pavlopetri circa 1000 BC, the seismic sinking of the Anatolian port of Klazomenai in the sixth century BC, the down dropping of much of Egypt's port of Alexandria and nearby Canopus and Herakleion (exacerbated by deltaic subsidence) in AD 365, and the seismic subsidence of the harbor of Roman Palestine's Caesaria, plus the post-Columbian sinkings of the Lisbon, Portugal, harbor and Port Royal in Jamaica. In a few cases, large-scale tectonic activity has caused widespread coastal inundation. For example, since antiquity the subducting African tectonic plate has resulted in roughly 13 feet of subsidence along the North African littoral, dropping some important archaeological sites under the sea.

Massive mudslides and the occasional radical shifting of the courses of great rivers (for example, China's Huang He) also occasionally triggered migrations, as did pestilence.

As seen in contemporary times, tsunamis have been highly disruptive in, and even very far from, earthquake-prone areas, especially around the Pacific. The Tōhoku region of Japan's Honshu Island has experienced large earthquakes and tsunamis every 500 to 800 years—the latest, in 2011, which carried water 8 miles inland. North America's Northwest Coast shows evidence of thirteen earthquake-tsunami impacts during the past 6,000 years. In AD 1076, a tsunami inundated up to 310 miles along the coast of South China.[3] Seawater puts salt into the soil and, for a time, damages or kills wild vegetation and prevents successful farming, and gatherers and farmers are obliged to seek sustenance elsewhere.

A Rising Tide Lifts All Boats: Eustatic and Sterical Sea-Level Changes

A potentially important push factor that has only recently been receiving significant attention has to do with the seas themselves, that is, eustatically and sterically rising sea levels. As has long been widely recognized, with the melting of the continental ice sheets at the end of the Pleistocene epoch some 12,000 years ago and with rising temperatures leading to volume expansion of the oceans' waters, sea levels rose hundreds of feet, drowning thousands of square miles of coastal plains—about half of Sundaland and Wallacia, for example (figure 24.1). Less well known is the fact that in the subsequent Holocene epoch, the ocean

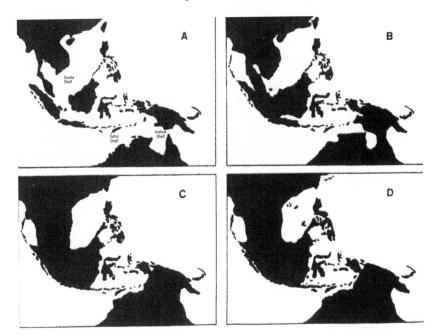

Figure 24.1. Map showing land areas of Southeast Asia and northern Australia at various Late Pleistocene–Holocene sea stands. (A) o m, ca. 6000 BC–present; (B) -50 m, ca. 12,000 BC; (C) -100 m, ca. 16,000 BC; (D) -130 m or more, ca. 22,000–18,000 BC. From John R. H. Gibbons and Fergus G. A. U. Clunie, "Sea Level Changes and Pacific Prehistory," *Journal of Pacific History* 21, no. 2 (1986): 64. With permission of Taylor and Francis Ltd., http://www.informaworld.com.

surface continued to rise (at a diminishing pace); thousands of years after the end of the Pleistocene, in at least some areas there were significant periods during which the sea rose to levels higher not only than those immediately post-Pleistocene but also higher than those of today.

These Holocene surges seem largely to have been triggered by the so-called Climatic Optimum of roughly 6500 to 3000–2500 BC, during which time atmospheric temperatures rose to some 2 degrees warmer than those pertaining during the twentieth century, leading to additional glacial melting, sea-level rise, and inundation of coastal areas, peaking globally between about 1900 and 1700 BC. In the Pacific, this inundation is documented, among other places, for much of present Micronesia, Japan, and Taiwan. In parts of eastern and southeastern China, ocean waters penetrated up to nearly 19 miles inland. The height of the sea seems to have reached its maximum in the Persian Gulf around 4000 BC. In the Atlantic, rising sea levels drowned parts of the Hebrides Islands of Scotland. In Scandinavia, levels rose from 13 to 22 feet higher than at present. In later periods, mean sea-level rises of up to 6.6 feet above present height occurred in northwestern England, peaking about 600 BC and AD 300.[4]

According to the Berkeley archaeologist of the Pacific islands Patrick Vinton Kirch, "The global rise in sea levels . . . continued in the Pacific region until about 4,000 years ago, when a high stand of between 1 and 1.5 m [3.2 and 4.9 feet] higher than the modern level was reached. . . . This high stand remained at approximately the same level for about two millennia and then fell by about 2,000 years ago—fairly rapidly by some indications—back to its modern level," thereby reexposing myriad drowned islands.[5] In the Indian Ocean Basin, such Holocene sea-surface rise is evidenced in the Gulf of Kutch and at Bahrain, having reached up to 6.6 feet above present levels. On the other side of the world, the rise in the Bahama Islands was nearly 10 feet.[6]

Exactly what effect rising sea levels might have had on population movements is not always clear. Although coastline length likely increased, land area would be reduced and coastal people's former territories would disappear. In Sundaland, for example, terminal Pleistocene/initial Holocene rising waters inundated an area larger than that of India. Moving inland into the territories of others or into radically different environments might often not have been a viable choice for victims of flooding. Probably, different populations reacted differently to rising sea levels, with at least some taking the long-distance migration option of going to sea to seek a new home.

Here and there, traditions occur that conceivably relate to Holocene rises in sea level. For instance, Marco Polo wrote of Sri Lanka that it was once 30 percent larger but that "the north wind blows so strongly in these parts that it has submerged a great part of this island under the sea."[7] There are also Indian tales of a flooded continental shelf and submerged cities.[8]

Flood legends are found globally (more than five hundred are known), particularly commonly among island Austronesians.[9] In Polynesia, Taiwan, the Philippines, and elsewhere in Southeast Asia, it is common for peoples to point to a local mountain as their place of origin or where their ancestors went to escape an enormous flood. A legend of the island of Wei ('Move'), located some miles off the northwestern tip of Sumatra, has it that the island was once attached to Sumatra but then moved out to sea. An Easter Islander tradition asserts that the reason for the inhabitants' migrating to their island was to seek a new, safe country since the rising waters of the sea were drastically diminishing their old homeland in the west. In North America, the Yuchi, formerly of Alabama and Georgia, believe themselves to have come from islands in the east, where a good deal of the land sank beneath the ocean. A Cornish legend relates that the sea took the land between Cornwall and the Scilly Islands.[10] Foremost among such tales are, of course, the Atlantis legend and the biblical and Mesopotamian flood stories, the Mesopotamian one now thought, by some (but denied by others), to relate to the Holocene inundation of the Black Sea Basin.

Not Fitting In, but Fitting Out: Societal Imperatives

Sociopolitical unrest was among the most common motives for departure: war—including invasion, conflicts between local factions, and revolutions—and, if conquest occurred, ensuing unpalatable foreign domination and taxation, even slavery and deportation. History provides a depressingly almost endless list of cases. In the Aegean, earlier Greek residents fled the invasions of Dorian Greeks, for example, and a major reason for the Ionian overseas dispersal in Archaic Greek times was the expansion of the Persian Empire into western Anatolia. Again, in face of Kirghiz invasions there was a mass migration of Uyghurs from Mongolia into Gansu and Xinjiang. Another example is post-Roman-withdrawal Britons fleeing invading Saxons, some crossing the English Channel in the fifth century to resettle in Brittany.

We may expect that the rapid expansions of empires—for example, the Assyrian, the Persian, the Roman, the Chinese, the Mongol, the Aztec, the Inca—or of militant religions (notably, Islam), were particularly engendering of flight (for example, Zoroastrians/Parsis and Manicheans fled before the expanding Muslims, to India and to Central Asia and China, respectively). In some empires, slaves or even whole tribes were forcedly moved great distances to further the aims of the state.

Interfamily struggles in demographically growing but land-poor Norway were a significant factor in the Norse Viking diaspora. Likewise, oral histories of the Pacific islands are replete with references to defeated parties fleeing to sea before their enemies. According to the early French explorer J.-S.-C. Dumont d'Urville, Samoa and the Fiji Islands were frequently intruded upon by entire populations of fugitives.[11] According to James Hornell, "The pressure of overpopulation and resultant tribal warfare were the usual impelling factors in [later Polynesian] voyages of discovery. It was traditional knowledge that other islands existed. Whenever a family or clan or tribe found their enemies too powerful, emigration, perilous though it was, offered the only alternative to slavery and death."[12] An instance was a group of Maoris involved in a dispute's fleeing New Zealand when attack was inevitable, and sailing 1,600 miles to Raratonga. The vanquished frequently embarked immediately, preferring to entrust themselves to the mercies of wind and wave rather than await certain demise from their enemies on land.[13] These were truly cases of being "caught between the devil and the deep blue sea," and the sea was often chosen as the lesser of the two evils.

An oppressive domestic regime might also inspire some to leave, if those departing had little remaining stake and few prospects in the homeland, as was the case with late-twentieth-century "boat people" from Vietnam, Cuban and Haitian refugees to Florida, and Africans and Syrians to Europe. Pre-Columbian examples include Greeks leaving to found colonies owing in part to oppression by wealthy landlords back home, and Norse fleeing to and settling Iceland in order to evade the tyranny of Norwegian King Harald. During the late Han dynasty in China, one Wang Zhong fled Shandong when a rebellion stirred things up, sailing with all his people to Korea and settling in the mountains there.[14]

Escape is the defining theme of push factors, flight from formal or informal servitude or other domination, punishment, involvement in feud killings, familial and other personal animosities, sorcery, taxes or other debts or obligations, economic privation, shame, and even boredom.[15]

Religious persecution may be added to this list. Well-known examples include the Jewish Diaspora from Roman Palestine, Roman suppression of early Christians, the expulsion of the Spanish Muslims and Jews in 1492 and the Catholic Inquisition plus later European pogroms, the martyrdom of hundreds of thousands of Japanese Christians in the sixteenth and seventeenth centuries, and the flight of Puritans to Massachusetts in 1620. Less known is the persecution of Buddhists in ninth-century China and in India, with the harassment in the latter country's causing many to flee from Coromandel to Southeast Asia. The Javanese chronicles report that around AD 603 an Indian ruler from Gujarat, forewarned of the destruction of his kingdom, sent his son with five thousand followers to Java in six large and one hundred small boats and then sent for two thousand more of his former subjects. This may relate to the collapse of the Saka Kingdom and the replacement of Buddhism by Brahmanism, accompanied by various military takeovers.[16]

One can easily imagine individuals deciding that taking one's chances sailing for little-known or merely postulated distant lands might be preferable to intolerable conditions or certain disaster at home—an approach exemplified again and again in recent centuries. Even far lesser negative incentives may have been involved on occasion; for instance, rage and shame are mentioned as motives for voyages of flight from Tikopia in the Santa Cruz Islands. As recently as 1985, a young man of the island of Anuta, after a public accusation, sailed away in a small outrigger canoe, reaching the islands of Vaniloko and Santa Ana some 600 miles distant.

Depression and Repression: Economic and Political Imperatives

Economic factors have motivated the majority of modern migrations, with flow from less prosperous to more prosperous (or potentially more prosperous) regions, and this operated in the past as well. Overpopulation (and consequent land, raw materials, food, and employment shortages) appears to have been a frequent fundamental factor. The Archaic Greeks, for instance, used their overseas colonies not only to produce food and raw materials to compensate for deficits back home but also to absorb excess population, as did western European imperial powers in a later era. In China, the ruler often dispatched male relatives southward to establish new polities in "barbarian" territory, so as to relieve demographic pressure, develop new farmland, and strengthen defense. Limited land suitable for husbandry in Norway, and then in Iceland, was a major factor inspiring westward-expanding Norse transatlantic colonization.

Sometimes, loss of established trading partners could disrupt economies and lead to explorations and movements in new directions. One example is the disruption of the Central Asian caravan trade along the Silk Road at various times, owing to Mongol and Turkic depredations. The unavailability of that route stimulated enhanced seaborne exchange between East and West via Indian Ocean trade. Later in time, the spread of Islam severed traditional overland routes to the East, and seeking a safe way to continue to tap the riches of Asia was the main stimulus for the fifteenth-century maritime expeditions of Portugal and Spain, leading directly to the Great Age of Discovery and the European colonization of much of the world.

Dissidents occasionally departed voluntarily, and sometimes criminals and other troublemakers (Eirík the Red, for example) were temporarily deported or permanently expelled (compare "transportation" of eighteenth-century British petty criminals to Australia). In one recorded instance, in 1893 a chief and nine others (including three women) were banished from Manihiki in the Cook Islands and sailed to Samoa.[17] In fact, in Oceania, according to the New Zealand Polynesianist G. S. Parsonson, "Many were set adrift in rafts or small canoes for crimes and peccadilloes of various sorts, murder, adultery, insults, breaches of etiquette, even juvenile incorrigibility or mischievousness. Men of abnormal physical strength or influence of whom people were jealous or afraid might be exiled. On occasion, a considerable number of individuals might be deported together."[18] In other cases, the state ordered ordinary people to resettle in newly established overseas colonies. Ancient Greek examples include the choosing of obligatory colonists by lot on Thera, and rebellious youths being sent away from Sparta.

In summary, a number of factors, both physical-geographic and socioeconomic, often worked to drive people from their native lands and to impel them toward distant horizons where they had a chance of escaping negative situations.

25

Attractants

[I was] leading a life of the utmost joy and happiness until one day a group
of merchants came by, showing signs of travel. . . . So I felt a longing for
travel and trade, and I resolved to undertake another voyage. . . . I found a
large ship.

— Sindbad the Sailor, in *The Arabian Nights* (ca. AD 900)

As mentioned in the previous chapter, "pull" factors are often the other side of
the "push" coin: positive expectations of attaining freedom, security, power, or
position to replace depression or oppression. Pull factors are attractants that
draw migrants from home—for example, the "God, gold, and glory" of early
modern European imperialism. Many but not all of these pull factors are economic: natural resource procurement; trade; acquisition of new land to farm,
graze, timber, or mine, or from which to exact tribute through conquest or in-
timidation; and obtaining of training and/or employment. Some occupational
categories involved peripatetic lifeways—for example, pastoral nomads, sea nomads, some mendicant and thieving castes, tinkers and Travelers, performers,
military personnel, and many masons and miners, and, of course, sailors and
merchants.

The American historical ethnographer Mary W. Helms examined in considerable detail the many motives that prompted travel in the Old World, including such categories as "adventure, curiosity, self-realization, fame and prestige,
and freedom from social constraints. . . . pilgrimage to holy places to seek personal or family help, curing, exile or penance, acquisition of ritual or other
highly valued goods [such as saints' relics], and official government business,"
plus fellowship (socializing, exchanging news), popularity (as from storytelling),
gaining songs and/or ritual knowledge, scholarly or religious study at libraries, and espionage.[1]

Better Barter: Resource Acquisition and Trade

The Bible speaks of "They that go down to the sea in ships, that do business in
great waters" (Psalms 107:23; circa 1000 BC). Human acquisitiveness seems almost boundless, and since at least the Neolithic the quest for material gain has

no doubt been the most frequently impelling reason for long-distance journeying, as modern gold rushes to California, Australia, and the Klondike exemplify.
"Greed," wrote the chronicler of the sea Tony Meisel, "can overcome an awful
lot of fear and discomfort, danger and privation."[2] Portugal's Prince Henry the
Navigator had put it somewhat more quaintly half a millennium earlier: "You
cannot find a peril so great that the hope of reward will not be greater . . . in
honour and profit." Even earlier, in the fourteenth century, the Chinese Wang
Li wrote, "By the time of [Kublai Khan] . . . for people in search of fame and
wealth . . . a journey of ten thousand li constituted just a neighborly jaunt."[3]

The quest for items of symbolic value—as of power and prestige—may operate as effectively as that for items of mundane commercial value. According
to the Cambridge cultural geographer Robin A. Donkin, "Second in order of importance [after subsistence] . . . are what people crave: the rare and the exotic.
These fuel the imagination . . . and draw men to the ends of the earth, often
with great profit, always at great personal risk. . . . The further away and more
mysterious [these exotica were,] the richer they were deemed to be."[4] Young
Norsemen, for example, seem to have gone over the sea to raid Irish monasteries at least in part to obtain exotic baubles to use back home as bride prices.[5]

Competitiveness plays a role. One theory concerning the rapid migration of
carriers of Lapita culture into western Oceania during the second and first millennia BC is that these probable proto-Polynesians were involved in competition
to discover and to appropriate occurrences of previously unowned, high-value
raw materials. Generally in history, these kinds of acquisitions were accomplished by more or less legitimate exploration, extraction, and trade, but piracy
and other brigandry were sometimes practiced as the quicker road to riches.

Maritime trade already had a long history of interlinking the lands of the Old
World by the time King David composed the psalm quoted above. Written records of such trade date from at least 3100 BC, when Egypt sent forty ships to
Byblos in search of cedar wood and came to record imports of cedar, fir, pine,
juniper, resin, and wheat. Other products that the early Egyptians sought by sea
voyages (especially, from Punt) include gold, ivory, fine and aromatic woods,
incense, slaves, and monkeys and baboons—items that remained popular for
thousands of years.

This is not the place to attempt even a highly condensed description of maritime trade in the pre-Columbian Old World, which was especially intensive in
the Indian Ocean, except to mention that archaeology indicates that during the
second millennium BC the far-western Lapita peoples of the Melanesian region
traded pottery, obsidian, chert, basalt oven stones, adzes, building stone, and
shell objects among islands, sometimes via long marine itineraries.[6] In fact,
populations on a number of resource-limited islands survived only as long as
overseas exchange with better-endowed islands continued, and they also depended on food collecting from fairly distant uninhabited isles. Trade among
distant Austronesian islands sometimes became economically and socially ritu-
alized, as in the famous kula ring of Melanesia.[7]

Quite a Trip: Travel in Pursuit of Psychoactive Substances

Among the many items traded in ancient times were drugs, for indulgent and mystical uses as well as medical ones. They represent a special category of commodity, comprising spices, many of which are not only flavorful but also have mildly psychoactive components or stimulate endorphin production, and plants that produce more striking mental effects than do spices. In Eurasia, hallucinogens such as *Amanita* mushrooms, henbane, belladonna, mandrake, harmel, water lily, and datura; the indulgents hashish, opium, betel nut, kava, kola nut, qat, ephedra, tea, and coffee; and a great variety of medicinals (including several of the above), have long been trade items. In China, Daoists had a belief in the existence of drugs and waters of immortality on what was known as the Penglai Mountain Island in the eastern ocean (see chapter 12). The island, which some have endeavored to identify with the Americas, was frequently depicted on tripod "mountain jars" (mortuary censers) whose form has been thought by some to be reflected in Teotihuacan-style lidded tripod jars from Mexico and Guatemala.[8]

Many more psychoactive drug plants, both indulgent and hallucinogenic, were used in the New World than in the Old: one hundred+ as compared to twenty-five or so Eastern Hemisphere species. These American plants include peyote and San Pedro cacti; morning glory; mushrooms; ayahuasca/caapi/yagé (*Banisteriopsis caapi*); the leguminous taxa *Piptadena* (vijó), *Anadenanthera perigrina* (willka), *Acacia niapo* (yopo), *Elizabetha*, and *Mimosa*; *Virola* (ebene), latua, jimsonweed (*Datura*), cocoa, tobacco, coca, *Ilex guayuso*, ephedra, guaraná, and yerba maté; plus frog and toad toxins. Within South America, shamans traveled great distances to obtain drugs and medicinal plants and to exchange knowledge with confreres.[9] There is good evidence that at least tobacco and coca were brought from the pre-Columbian Americas to the Old World and psychoactive hemp (*Cannabis sativa*) from Asia to South America (see chapter 29). Drugs have the advantage of being high-value, low-bulk products and thus are suitable for very long distance trade.

The Rule of One: Political Power Grabs

In addition to the lure of wealth, the simple gain of a sense of power over events, people, territory, resources, even nature, has been a driving force for many, whether involving personal or national glory, obeisance from others, or even revenge. Overseas adventures were often engendered by a seeking of power through military-backed political control—a tendency that peaked during the European Age of Imperialism.

In the early centuries AD, nonfirstborn sons (cadets) of South Indian potentates are said to have sailed to Southeast Asia to carve out for themselves new kingdoms. At any rate, Hinduized/Buddhized states came to exist in most of the present-day countries of Southeast Asia; the first known Indian colony in Java was established in AD 75.[10] In Africa, younger brothers who saw little hope of gaining prestige or social advancement at home would often leave with their followers and establish and rule migratory offshoots elsewhere. Among the Maya, disaffected kin segments would sometimes move elsewhere where they could found their own polities.[11]

Many ancient Greeks, too, left home owing in part to the primogeniture system, as, in the European Colonial era, did many aristocratic English younger sons (cavaliers) who settled in Virginia. Likewise, traditions indicate that in western Polynesia primogeniture led to younger sons seeking new islands on which to establish their own lineages and acquire new lands, achieving what is called "founder rank enhancement." In the Austronesian realm, founders, especially early ones, are typically revered, and to this day their descendants possess greater status than do others. Likewise, a chief's brother might take a following with him to seek new territory where *he* could be chief. The Australian Polynesianist archaeologist Peter Bellwood called this "urge to explore, settle, and possess new territory . . . a major factor in the spread of the Austronesians."[12]

Some sons of Tongan chiefs went to Fiji as soldiers of fortune, in order to learn the arts of war.[13] The wars of conquest and revenge that resulted were endemic in some areas of Oceania; in one recorded case, Tahitians raised an armada manned by 7,760 warriors in order to gain ascendancy in Eimeo.

Passing on Piety: The Role of Religion

On occasion, the desire for spiritual gain, rebirth into a higher form, or eternal salvation, or the urge to promulgate the faith and save souls, has impelled as much as, or more than, material acquisitiveness. Such religious motives operated in the past (and present), often involving pilgrimage (for example, to Jerusalem, to Mecca, to Varanasi [Benares]) and, sometimes, overseas crusades. Quests for Buddhist and Christian religious relics were common.

A goal for some was personal spiritual seclusion. In China, Daoists felt that an understanding of nature was prerequisite to understanding how to order human society. They retired to the forests and mountains and other remote places and tried to make sense of nature by examining it directly.[14] Similarly, during the early Middle Ages Irish hermits known as anchorites sought remote islands and other isolated places in which to pursue personal spiritual progress. In one recorded case, Irish monks set out in an oarless boat with only a week's supply of provender, determined to serve God wherever He took them (they drifted to England).[15] Irish anchorites preceded the Norse in the Faroes, Iceland, and, very probably, Greenland, and some feel that they even established themselves in mainland North America.

> They were directed by a sense of dedication which had to have been the single most important factor in their success. . . .
> If their craft foundered underneath them and the crew perished, then

they reached their divine reward doubly blessed because they had died in God's service. . . .

There can seldom have been a stronger drive to probe the unknown in the entire history of human exploration. It was the quintessential motive for exploration at almost any price, and there is no reason why it should not have brought them across the Atlantic.[16]

At times, entire peoples have removed themselves from their homelands as a reaction to changing religious values. This seems to have been the case with a group that departed Anatolia and took up residence on Cyprus around 6,500 BC in order to retain their conservative cultural practices threatened by changes proceeding apace on the mainland.[17] Much later, in the Pacific, as G. S. Parsonson related it, devotees of the deity Tane departed Tahiti rather than do obeisance to the god Oro; they settled in the outer fringes of the Cook Islands. During the nineteenth century, pagans frequently fled from Christianized islands.[18]

As wrote the underwater archaeologist Philippe Diolé, "Like copper, like tin, like poetry, like the axe of the labyrinth and the swords of Huelva, faith traveled on board ship. The God of Asine and Taenarum, the ancestor of Poseidon . . . walked on the waters before ever Jesus did."[19] However, universalizing religions such as Buddhism, Christianity, and Islam insist they are relevant to all of humanity, in contrast to basically national religions such as Hinduism, Shinto, and Judaism. Among universalizing religions, proselytizing was important and often generated distant travel and energized culture change. This was accomplished through the peregrinations of missionaries desiring to propagate the Truth and to indoctrinate others.

Change was also engendered by people from outlying areas journeying to the "heartland" to gain merit, to receive religious instruction, or to obtain sacred relics—as, for example, in the case of Buddhists from China and Java traveling to India. In contrast, to garner trade and other connections with the larger world as well as prestige and legitimization, local Southeast Asian rulers often welcomed Indian Hindu and Buddhist savants to their territories and adopted foreign ways.[20]

Christian missionaries had reached India possibly as early as the first century AD, and China by the seventh. In medieval Europe, among motives for travel the most important was spreading the Word, including to China during the Mongol era when overland travel was made possible again after centuries of closure. Such travel included the search for the "lost" Christians of "Prester John" in Africa and of Thomas (Te'oma/Didymos) the Apostle in Asia.

Proselytization was one major motive for post-Columbian Spanish conquest in the Americas. Even adherents of nonuniversalizing religions often got around. For example, there were Jews in China even before the Diaspora, but they did not set out for distant places in order to gain converts as did some members of the universalizing faiths. Buddhism is of particular interest among the proselytizers, since it is some five hundred years older than Christianity and more than a millennium older than Islam. During the early centuries of the Christian era, Bengali Buddhists are known to have proselytized in China, Korea, and Japan, and others did similarly at other places and times.[21] A strong case has, in fact, been made for Hindu/Buddhist influences on pre-Columbian Mexicans and Mayans.[22]

Food for Thought: Learning and Recruitment

As mentioned, travel was sometimes undertaken for religious instruction and to study writings. We can point to the specific example of the fifth-century Chinese Faxian (Fa-hsien), who went to Nepal, India, and Sri Lanka seeking Buddhist texts. In some instances, there were also directed efforts to acquire and import practical information and ideas from abroad—efforts ranging from espionage to open study and imitation, even apprenticeship. During China's Sui and Tang dynasties (AD 581–906) and Japan's Asuka period (AD 538–645), the Japanese ruler sent envoys to the Chinese court. This permitted Japanese artists and craftsmen to study the arts of China firsthand and to return to Japan to apply what they had learned. Chinese-trained Korean artisans were imported as well. In certain cases, societies recruited foreigners to bring in organizational skills not previously present. For example, under Chinggis (Genghis) Khan (AD 1206–27), the inexperienced Mongols of an emerging empire brought in Uyghurs and other foreigners (for example, the Polos) to fill skilled administrative positions.[23]

Other travelers set out for a variety of other reasons, ranging from the desire to seek new trading partners to a wish to visit with distant kin and friends, even to find suitable marriage partners. One notable motive in the ancient world had to do with an enormous interest in celestial observations, particularly among the peoples of Mesopotamia and of Mesoamerica. Chapter 22 has detailed the practical value of certain of such observations for navigation. In addition, prediction of the movements of heavenly bodies, including the occurrences of eclipses and the wanderings of planets, gained for the usually priestly prognosticators the perception, on the part of the uninitiated populace, of the possession of awesome supernatural powers. In addition, the workings of the heavens were widely believed to influence human affairs, and thus the very serious "science" of astrology arose and spread. Learning about certain celestial phenomena requires observations in distant parts of the world, and it would not be surprising if some specialists made global voyages to effect such observations.[24]

The Glory Road: Prestige Seeking

Often, less concrete aims operated, such as testing one's mettle. Particularly powerful was the quest for recognition, in the form of a series of "a" words: aggrandizement, admiration, adulation, adoration, acclaim, affirmation, applause, approval, approbation, appreciation, even affection. Overseas explorations and trading expeditions often yielded to their entrepreneurs more than just exotic goods and wealth or religious acquisitions; such persons also gained prestige from their accomplishments, a gain more important to many than mere affluence. A case in point is that of the commanders of the fifteenth-century Portuguese explorations sent out by Prince Henrique: these gentlemen were interested in plunder but seem to have been more motivated by a yearning to enhance their reputations and standing. Earlier in history, the Romans tell us that the terrestrial migration of the Helvetii in 58 BC resulted from an ideology of "glory-seeking young men."

In situations where potential prestige gains from voyaging were enormous and/or where failure to undertake such voyages engendered utter humiliation, reluctance to risk safety and comfort might well be overridden, particularly among young men replete with an adolescent sense of invulnerability and/or ready to accept a dare. Tongan youths, for example, are known to have voyaged "600 or 800 or even 1000 miles, being not infrequently absent a year or two . . . wandering and gadding from island to island." This is reminiscent of the more serious European tradition of the *Wanderjahre*.[25] A Tongan named Kao Mala is said to have made a 1,085-mile nonstop voyage from Fiji to Futuna, before returning to Tonga.[26] "One young blood who swaggered ashore with tales of distant adventures provoked such envy that 'it became the object of ambition with every adventurous chief to discover other islands.'"[27]

In the Oceanic islands, those who learned the esoteric skills of navigation became individuals of high renown, and this knowledge contributed to political power as well. Voyaging itself conveyed status. The British prehistorian Clive Gamble viewed Polynesian expansion as reflecting "a heroic tradition inspired by a worldview of discovery in which prestige went to those who founded colonies and made the return voyages."[28] The lures of adventure and reputation were so powerful among Polynesian men that even the failure to return on the part of many such voyagers did not deter others from setting out.

There were also other kinds of prestige seeking that engendered voyages. For instance, according to the Greek historian Diodoros Sikeliotes, the seeking of glory in battle was the motive behind Bronze Age Jason's voyage to Colchis (Caucasian Georgia) in the *Argo*, around 1250 BC. Among Polynesian men, such bellicose glory seeking was a routine activity in some archipelagos.

Over the Horizon: Curiosity and Adventure

Samuel Johnson observed in 1751, "Curiosity is one of the most permanent and certain characteristics of a vigorous intellect," and the novelist of the seas Joseph Conrad opined, "The sea . . . has been the accomplice of human restlessness."[29] The contemporary writer of historical fiction James Cowan put it nicely: "What lies beyond the margin of the world often sings to us with the voice of a siren, as if calling us into its embrace. We listen, we are lured, and finally we are seduced."[30] The British maritime historian Peter Kemp observed of Phoenician mariners that "behind their skill lay the spirit of adventure and a determination to discover what filled the great unknown spaces of the world, by daring wild waters."[31] The Vikings were motivated in part by the "spirit of restless curiosity—*aefityr.*"[32] Similar motives, including the desire to become familiar with foreign lands and peoples, stimulated countless other expeditions—and not only in the West.

As A. C. Haddon expressed it: "A restless disposition has been a fruitful cause of movements. . . . It . . . manifests itself largely as a spirit of adventure. In some such way we may account for bearers of better modes of living and of a higher socio-religious culture adventuring into the Pacific."[33]

According to J. E. Weckler Jr., Pacific Islanders, especially the Polynesians, motivated perhaps in part by the isolation of island life, manifested "a fearless and abiding desire to explore ever farther into the mysterious ocean."[34] This desire was reinforced by traditional tales about the great voyages of the past; a typical folk song from the Micronesian atoll of Ifalik goes:

Sleepless, the captain leaves his house,
He cannot lie down and rest
Beside his wife on the mat
A good wind springs up,
The captain wants to be on his way.
The gods take possession of him.
He must away.

The Captain remembers far lands
He wants to go quickly.[35]

This escaping the humdrum, this seeking of drama, of adventure (and perhaps concomitant glory) included testing one's personal resources in the face of challenges, plus what the American nature writer Sigurd Olson has termed "the heightened awareness that comes with a certain amount of danger,"[36] poetically expressed by Lord Byron as "the exalting sense—the pulse's maddening play / That thrills the wanderer of that trackless way."[37]

More prosaically, what seems to be a genetically influenced stronger than normal quest for reinforcement from the neurotransmitters adrenaline and dopamine (producing thrills and satisfactions, respectively) through adventure has been studied as psychology in Michael J. Apter's *The Dangerous Edge* and anthropologically in J. R. L. Anderson's *The Ulysses Factor: The Exploring Instinct in Man.*[38] As noted, this urge was prominent in the Pacific region. For instance, James Siers found that when he proposed to make an experimental voyage from Tarawa, a multitude of very inexperienced men volunteered to accompany him, "purely for the sake of adventure."[39] On voyages undertaken by skilled, experienced sailors, the sense of competence, the feeling of pride in one's prowess and accomplishment, the fellowship of teamwork in a mutual enterprise, these were among the rewards. Insatiable human thirst for knowledge and just casual curiosity were no doubt strong elements—the desire to see what lies beyond the known limits, around the bend, over the hills or the horizon, across the wide waters. A prime example is that of the medieval Tangerine Ibn Battutah (AD 1304–1378), who traveled some 75,000 miles, as far as East Africa, Malaysia, and China, simply to see the world.[40]

The biogeographers William Keegan and Jared Diamond wrote of a phenomenon they labeled "autocatalysis," in which initial discoveries—likely based on an *expectation* of land beyond the horizon that led to exploration—trigger a snowballing of further exploratory activity fueled by the expectancy and reinforcement afforded by further finds of previously unknown lands.[41] In this context, one may mention that in the early nineteenth century, over eight hundred people departed the Marquesas to find and settle a land of abundance they believed to exist somewhere in the west (their fate is unknown).[42]

Lines from "The Seafarer"

"The Seafarer" is a tenth-century AD Anglo-Saxon poem from western Wessex. This excerpt captures the restless spirit of the sea wanderer (presented here in contemporary prose language and form).

> Therefore my thoughts are now urging my mind to try the high seas, the tumult of the salt waves for myself. My heart's desire incessantly calls on my spirit to set forth in search of the land of another people far from here.
> . . .
> Therefore my mind is now soaring beyond the stronghold of my bosom, my spirit is moving over the sea-flood, travelling far and wide over the whale's domain, over the surface of the earth.
> It returns to me ardent and eager: the lone flier yells, impelling my soul to set forth on the road of the whale, out over the expanse of the seas.[43]

"Imaginary" Islands

Venturing into the Atlantic no doubt was also encouraged by the concept, pre-Classical in origin, of an island in or beyond the ocean river, one inhabited by famous military heroes as well as by assorted legendary and mythical people. Both Homer and Hesiod wrote about such places, in about 740 and 700 BC, respectively. Homer's Cimmerians lived on an island in the Ocean River, in a land of perpetual mists and night, which may have been Britain; Hesiod's Islands of the Blessed, "beyond glorious Ocean" and home of the heroes, may have been the Canary Islands or Madeira, which could reflect Phoenician or Carthaginian knowledge that reached the Greeks.

During the Middle Ages, the Atlantic Ocean was believed to be to be dotted with islands, such as the Celts' Avalon, Land of Youth, and Land of Women; and, as Carl Sauer put it, "Those who lived on its borders turned their attention and imagination to the west."[44] In 1994, the American maritime historian

Donald S. Johnson released *Phantom Islands of the Atlantic*, and in 1995, the American geographer Robert H. Fuson published *Legendary Islands of the Ocean Sea*, about ancient Mediterranean and medieval western European concepts of lands in and beyond the Atlantic. Whether the earliest known of these traditions reflected some dim but factual cultural memory or were purely products of the imagination, they persisted for millennia, and belief in them inspired actual voyages intended to find these lands.

The Madeira Islands appeared on two mid-fourteenth-century European maps, many years prior to the archipelago's official (and accidental) discovery in 1418), reflecting Atlantic maritime activity unrecorded in texts. Further, the molecular clock dates an archaeological Madeira mouse carrying Scandinavian genes to circa AD 1033, implying a Norse arrival.[45] During the fifteenth century, the Portuguese "were combing the Atlantic in search of the legendary islands of Antillia, Brasil, and the Seven Cities, and it is quite possible that they had actually reached America by 1424 as well as in the 1470s and 1480s," according to Eviatar Zerubavel.[46] Ships from Bristol in England also sailed westward in search of the Isle of Brazil during the 1480s.[47] (Fuson considered Antillia and Satanaze, as shown on Zuane Pizzagano's 1424 nautical chart, to represent Taiwan and Japan, respectively, but shown in the western Atlantic since the New World was not yet known to mapmakers and the Atlantic and the Pacific were conflated as one Ocean Sea.[48])

As the Canaries, Madeiras, Cape Verdes, and Azores came into Portuguese purview, "The supply of islands seemed endless. It was not unreasonable for people who knew the earth was round and who underestimated its size, to suppose that they could go westward from island to island until eventually they entered the archipelago which, they were told, lay off the east coast of Asia"[49] One wonders whether earlier peoples might have had a similar experience and response. After all, unlike the pre-Prince Enrique Portuguese, the Carthaginians and their Levantine forebears had a well-established tradition of long-distance voyaging and far-flung commerce.

As mentioned, the pre-Classical Greeks imagined the landmass of Afroeurasia to be surrounded by the flowing-river Ocean. Herakles's tenth labor was to fetch cattle from Erythia, an island far out in the Atlantic, beneath the red setting sun; his eleventh labor was to fetch the golden apples of the Hesperides, on an ocean isle in the extreme west. Likewise, the Archaic poet Hesiod wrote of Gorgons "who dwell beyond renowned ocean in the farthest parts toward the night, where are the shrill-voiced Hesperides," and of the glorious dead who "dwell in islands of the blessed by deep-eddying Ocean."[50] The reference might be to the Canary (Fortunate) Islands off northwestern Africa. The Canaries are visible from the mainland and were settled by Berber speakers by 500 BC. Punic (Carthaginian) remains have been found there.[51] In the second century AD, Ptolemy selected the westernmost of these islands to define his prime meridian, and the island of Lanzarote is the locus of a Roman settlement, dating from the first century BC to the fourth AD.[52] Plutarch mentioned Romans finding the empty "Happy Isles" in 80 BC;[53] some think that this label, as well as "Islands of the Blessed," was originally applied to the uninhabited Madeira Islands and later transferred to the populated Canaries.[54]

According to the marine writer Gardner Soule, "for centuries after Homer, Greek sailors and others searched and searched for a Utopia beyond the seas."[55] Distressed by the Roman civil war, the first-century BC poet Horace (Quintus Horatius Flaccus) urged Romans to flee: "Encircling Ocean awaits us; let us fly to the fields, the blessed, fortunate fields, and the fertile islands."[56]

Activity in the vicinity of the Canary Islands would put ships in position to drift straight to the New World if disabled, via the Canary and North Equatorial Currents. In this light, adventurer Robert F. Marx's reported discovery of a probable Morocco-laded Roman wreck in the harbor of Rio de Janeiro (see chapter 10) seems less than far-fetched.

A number of Arab sources echoed the Classical writers. The tenth-century Iraqi al-Mas'ūdī wrote that China and "the Eternal [Fortunate] Islands . . . in the Western Ocean [are] half the circumference of the earth"—some 13,500 miles —apart, which, if taken literally, would put the isles in the Caribbean or South America.[57]

Following the Signs: Oracles and Auguries

Voyaging into the *terrae*—or *mares*—*incognitae* calls for both a powerful motive and optimism about the adventure's outcome. Such optimism was in large part a matter of perception, knowledge, and skill, but also often involved belief in magical prediction of the future: reading signs and portents, consulting with seers, and sensing a destiny. For instance, the story of the Polynesian discovery of Easter Island has the king seeing it in a dream, and consequently sending out scouts to find it and then sailing to it himself with colonists.[58] In ancient Greece, oracles were routinely consulted as to what course to take, and auspices were sought in entrails and scapulae. Interestingly, the oracle of Delphi often advised her clients to emigrate.[59]

The most powerful factor impelling the Portuguese Prince Henry toward development of Portugal's overseas explorations is said by a contemporary source to have been "his horoscope, which bound him 'to engage in great and noble conquests, and above all . . . to attempt the discovery of things which were hidden from other men.'" Columbus "was much addicted to prophecies" and had a burning conviction that he was destined to fulfill Seneca's passage in *Medea* about finding land beyond the sea.[60] The case of Irish anchorites placing the drift of their boat in God's hands has been mentioned. Belief in supernatural forecasts and divine destinies may, then, have made crucially important contributions to exploration of the seas.

The Dartmouth cultural geographer Vincent H. Malmström has reminded us that, in the last analysis, "Any reconstruction of the knowledge or belief systems of a preliterate society [or of one whose records did not survive] must of necessity be at least somewhat imaginative. . . . What the stimulus or motivation or accidental discovery may have been that led to such and such . . . we oftentimes can only speculate. And in so doing, one is obliged to seek the most conservative and credible solution possible, while at the same time realizing that the true explanations for some human thoughts and/or actions may well border on the bizarre and irrational."[61]

The Friction Factor

Those of us who live pampered by the securities, comforts, and indulgences of today's First World may find it almost unimaginable what hazards and hardships many people of the past—and those of some less developed regions of the world today—accepted as a matter of course in both travel and daily life, accepted even with some cheerfulness. People were more poorly nourished than today, smaller in size, worn out at an earlier age. However, owing to unceasing labor and hard conditions, they were, in their prime, physically far fitter and more inured than most of us moderns.

Even within the last few centuries in the West, there have been numbers of examples of nonchalant acceptance of hardship. One thinks of the Mormon pioneers of 1847 pushing and pulling their worldly possessions in handcarts across the Great Plains and the Rocky Mountains and of the wiry *voyageur* fur traders of the Canadian North, canoeing thousands of miles through mazes of unmapped waterways in frail craft requiring repeated sealings of seams, carrying canoes and standard loads of 180 pounds across long portages, subsisting on a diet of flour, pemmican, dried peas, and fresh fish, sleeping on the subarctic ground beneath their canoes and a single blanket, with no protection from the black flies and mosquitoes other than smudge fires.[62]

In 1759, Samuel Johnson gave his famous opinion: "being in a ship is being in a jail, with the chance of being drowned. . . . A man in jail has more room, better food, and commonly better company." In *The First Sailor*, Rudyard Kipling called the ship "that packet of assorted miseries."[63] Indeed, to read of the hardships and boredom taken for granted by seamen of the British Royal Navy around 1800, as on blockade duty, with their alternating four-hour watches in every kind of weather, the risks of drowning and disabling or fatal falls from aloft, and the threat of scurvy, boggles the contemporary mind, as does contemplation of the seaman's miniscule hammock space; the continuous pitching and rolling of his seldom-level universe; the perpetual noise of hissing water and slapping waves, of working planks and rigging, and of the pumps; the stench below decks; the lice and rats; the Spartan, vitamin-C-deficient and vitamin-A-deficient diet of tough, maggoty salt beef and pork and weevily, raturine-impregnated biscuit plus half putrid pulses, and sometimes stinking beer plus a bit of overaged, wormy cheese (this despite the British navy's being the best fed in the world); the miserly supplies of foul water; the years away from families and the lack of concourse with women; and the severe corporal discipline to which they were subjected—as well as the hazards of being in battle—makes one wonder how and why they tolerated it.[64] Yet they did; habituation prevented many of these seamen from even *contemplating* another way of life, much less yearning for one, and even led to their feeling uncomfortable during prolonged sojourns on land. There was compensation in the security of structure, in team companionship in the crew, and in the satisfaction of competence at a highly demanding and technical job—and perhaps a portion of patriotism plus the hope of prize money. Mutiny was a great rarity, and not owing only to fear of execution.

Like harsh working and living conditions, risk was also looked upon with greater sangfroid in earlier times. As the American novelist Herman Melville put it in 1891, "fear [of death is] more prevalent in highly civilized communities than [in] those so-called barbarous ones which in all respects stand closer to unadulterate Nature."[65] On the Solomon island of Anuta, for instance, where canoes and navigational skills were not the best, men, displaying a pride in their machismo, embarked upon major interisland voyages with but minimal preparation and, it appears, with scant thought as to potential hazards.[66] In the fourteenth-century English romance *Fouke le Fitz Waryn*, Sir Fulk declares to a sailor, "Truly, it is very foolhardy of you to venture out to sea." Replies the mariner, "Why indeed, sir? Every creature shall have the death that is destined for him."[67] This point of view was also characteristic of the Viking Age in Scandinavia.[68] Peter L. Bernstein, in his book *Against the Gods: The Remarkable Story of Risk*, summed up: "The revolutionary idea that defines the boundary between modern times and the past is the mastery of risk: the notion that the future is more than a whim of the gods and that men and women are not passive before nature."[69]

The relative weights of risk and reward were different as well. Prior to modern affluence, and still in many parts of the world today, people's expectations were far lower, and relative poverty made rewards that might look paltry to westerners today merit enormous risk and effort then. Human labor and life still counted far less than most materials, and medieval European traders believed themselves fortunate if one voyage in three met with success on certain of the longer itineraries.[70] But if a man were otherwise doomed to a life of deprivation, and if a single successful long-distance trading voyage could ensure a subsequent life of honor and ease, might not a person take the risk and make the effort? This certainly happened often, at least within the Old World. In the Indian Ocean trade, "The risks of shipwreck, piracy, or simple extortion, were extremely high, but successful ventures rewarded their backers with a hundredfold or even a thousandfold return on capital."[71] The *Han Annals* of China report that Roman merchant voyages to India produced 1,000 percent profits.[72] According to Tim Severin, during the early Middle Ages a successful trip to China made a man rich for life.[73] Even in the early twentieth century, one of every ten Arab ships was lost on the Indian Ocean traverse, but success of the others made this risk sustainable for the owners.

In the case of religious endeavors, another kind of reward easily offset the risk involved. How much did putting one's life in jeopardy count when compared to the direct passage to eternal paradise (as in Islam and crusader Christianity) or to the higher plane of being (as in Buddhism) that was guaranteed to one who died in the course of a religiously meritorious enterprise? In southeastern Asia and Oceania, the potential of becoming a worshipped ancestor mitigated the fear of death.[74] In the case of Vikings, the prospect of dying on a distant foreign field imparted no fear, because fallen warriors would be carried by the Valkyries—the god Odin's maidens—directly to Odin's happy hall, Valhalla.[75] The anthropologist Raymond Firth, writing of Polynesian islanders who voyaged despite many losses, observed, "Fear of storms and shipwreck leaves them undeterred, and the reference in an ancient song to the loss of a man at sea as a 'sweet burial' expresses very well the attitude of the Tikopia" people of Melanesia.[76]

In addition, long before there was OSHA or its equivalents one's trust was placed in magic and in the gods or God at every step of the voyage, including construction of the vessel to be used. In the Caroline and Trobriand Islands, for instance, and certainly elsewhere, ritual was applied to ensure that craft being built would be safe and perform well. Also, during voyages seeds and leaves attached to arm bags were intended to ensure retention of knowledge, and carvings of deities were carried as a form of "storm insurance." Incantations were sung to control weather and to bring craft safely to port. In the Marshall Islands, learning magical chants for voyages was a prime aspect of navigational training. Consider this Tahitian navigators' prayer:

> Hearken unto us throughout our voyage.
> O gods! Lead us safely to land,
> Let our voyage be propitious, free from evil!
> Leave us not in the ocean.
> Give us a breeze. Let it follow us from behind.
> Let the weather be fine and the sky clear.
> Hearken unto us, o gods![77]

In the Bismarck Archipelago and the Amphlett Islands, weather magicians were important crew members, and some were thought to have magical power over sharks. Polynesians not only carried god images or symbols on board and made offerings to them, for protection and assistance, but they also sometimes brought along the actual head of a deceased king, priest, or skillful fisherman, to obtain favorable winds.

In China, shipwrights studded prows with coins or nails or mirrors laid out in the form of Ursa Major, to ensure safe journeys. There and elsewhere in the Old World (and on North America's Northwest Coast), carved animals' heads or eyes (ophthalmoi; oculi) were added to the prows of watercraft to enliven the vessel and to allow it to "see" any dangers it needed to avoid. This perhaps derived from an early custom of placing upon the prow the skin of a sacrificed actual animal.

In Classical times in the Mediterranean, the ship was seen as possessing its own personality. It was usually named for a deity, who would then be responsible for its protection, and it might be provided with a painted-on apotropaic bow eye and a figurehead for further protection.[78] We moderns may not consider these magical approaches to have been objectively efficacious, but they certainly would have served to engender among believers a confidence that risk would be outwitted.[79]

Neither, in the past, were most people plagued with the never-ending sense of urgency characteristic of modern existence; rather, life was lived largely in the moment. In the past, major response to time's swift arrow was, for the most part, limited to episodes of true emergency or concerted endeavor and was not an endemic condition; patience and resignation were. Ordinary people—on shipboard and elsewhere—slipped into a daily routine, which, along with a heightened awareness of the ever-repeating rhythm of the days and seasons and of the template of birth, reproduction, and death, led to a more cyclical and less linear sense of time. Such repetitive practice is worse than monotonous from the contemporary point of view, perhaps. Still, people can become used to almost any routine, even feel at loose ends when it is absent. On shipboard, routine's predictability imparted a sense of security, even under circumstances that we today might experience as most insecure. Too, although boredom, resentment of lack of privacy, as well as shipboard animosities exacerbated by forced propinquity and occupational hierarchy no doubt sometimes developed, a sense of shipboard-community bonding and mutual subjection to authority and to the exigencies of survival normally created a sense of common endeavor that contributed to a smooth functioning of the craft-complement system.

Another important effect of the limitations of the past was to allow all the human brainpower that is now so dispersed by the myriad distractions of complex contemporary life to focus on a narrow range of phenomena of immediate perceived practical importance. Thus a mariner could know and be alert to the implications of the multitude of relevant environmental, geographical, and celestial subtleties, the mental mastering of which might appear to us to be an impossible task. In Micronesia even in the mid-twentieth century, for instance, some I-Kiribati navigators had memorized 178 stars. Certain Woleai Islanders were explicitly aware of 504 star courses, and Puluwatese navigators knew by heart 650 different journey itineraries involving 325 entirely unrelated star courses (see chapter 22).[80]

Difficult though these things may be to imagine for ourselves, we are, nevertheless, obliged to accept them as realities for other persons, times, and places.

People did repeatedly undertake long-distance voyages. In the context of the transoceanic-contacts question, we need to keep these things firmly in mind. No longer can one legitimately reject the possibility that past sailors (1) would have subjected themselves to the risks and burdens of months, even years of voyaging, (2) had the capacity to accomplish such voyages, or (3) would have probed far into the unknown if they had expectation of great gain.

IV

Opportunity for Exchange

Concrete Demonstrations of Contacts

Opportunity makes a thief.
    —Sir Francis Bacon, 1598

In 1973, R. C. Padden wrote, "In spite of exhaustive research . . . there is still no proof, no hard evidence on which to predicate pre-Columbian contact and diffusion from the Old World to the new or vice versa."[1] We attempt now, in part IV of this book, to see whether Padden's assertion holds up four and a half decades later, to discover whether there may in fact be true proofs of interhemispheric encounters. If the reality of such interaction is verified, then so is the existence of *opportunities* for ancient cultural transfers, which, in turn, very much increases the likelihood that such transfers really occurred.

Although explanation of cultural commonalities is our ultimate aim, cultural phenomena have less probative value in signaling contact than do certain phenomena that are at least partially nonhuman—are, that is, human-made, human-altered, or at least human-transported materials or creations that involve unique and diagnostic natural physical, chemical, or biological characteristics coupled with limited natural geographic distribution. Thus, although these items are cultural products, at least in some degree, they are nonetheless composed of substances or include entities possessing properties that lend themselves to study and identification beyond, and, to a great degree independently of, their human-cultural aspects.

Shared Physical Materials, Domesticated Animals, and Diseases

How many goodly creatures are there here!
. . . O brave new world.
— William Shakespeare, *The Tempest* (1611), V.I.II (182)

Let's Get Physical: Natural Materials

Distantly transported natural items and substances compose one category of noncultural phenomena. A professional skeptic concerning diffusionism, the archaeologist Kenneth L. Feder, acknowledged that "a nonnative raw material found in firm archaeological context anywhere in the New World in an undisturbed stratigraphic layer dated to before Columbus's voyages would represent convincing archaeological evidence of contact between native New World people and explorers or settlers from the Old World."[1]

The instance of seeming Cape Verde Islands cowry shells found in a Mississippian mound in Alabama is an intriguing (and, as yet, unexplained), transoceanic case in point.[2]

Certain inorganic materials and fossilized organic substances (for example, amber) are particularly suitable for such study, because their different sources exhibit different suites and proportions of trace elements and/or because their natural occurrences are geographically very limited (for example, lapis lazuli). Among mineral materials is turquoise, although this striking stone has not yet received much attention in transoceanic-contact studies. Neither has obsidian, but this volcanic glass *is* very frequently used in more regional investigations; once chemical-compositional studies have been made of the various potential source deposits, one can identify the geographic origins of particular archaeological finds of the material. Obsidian analysis has demonstrated early, very long distance trading in the Indo-Pacific region (see chapter 15), and obsidian from Oklahoma's Spiro Mounds has been sourced to the state of Hidalgo in east-central Mexico.

On the basis of chemical analysis, too, archaeologists have determined that the natural occurrences of the material of some red jasper artifacts found at the circa AD 1000 Norse site at L'Anse aux Meadows, Newfoundland, are in western Greenland and Iceland. At the same time, a Labrador/Newfoundland-style arrow point made of Canadian chert was found in an old Greenland churchyard, probably brought back embedded in the flesh of an unfortunate Norseman.[3] Too, a quartz microblade core, similar to 3,000-year-old North American ones, was discovered in Iceland. A European Paleolithic-style stone knife unearthed in 1971 beneath a seventeenth-century Virginia chimney (mentioned in chapter 10) is made of northwestern French chert.[4]

One group of substances proposed for study in the context of the transoceanic-contacts controversy is jade, a highly important and revered material in both East Asia and Mesoamerica, a material charged with similar cultural meanings and practices in the two regions. An excellent example of cultural correlates, which has been noted in the introduction, is the placement of a red-painted, sometimes cicada-shaped amulet in the mouth of a corpse being prepared for burial.[5] Chemically, jades are highly variable in their compositions. Although there are a great many distinctive varieties among the different jades, the most basic distinction is between nephrite (true jade) and jadeite. Until relatively modern times, Chinese jades generally came from nephrite sources and Mesoamerican ones from jadeite sources. Still, beginning with Frederick W. Putnam in 1886,[6] it has been speculated that jade, being a low-bulk, high-value material, could have been involved in transpacific trade, and attention might profitably be paid to jade objects, especially in China, with this in mind. But to date, there has been little serious or sophisticated study of this sort, and those few results that have been obtained have been less than definitive. Should such evidence eventually be forthcoming, extracontinental specimens of this highly refractory material (6.0–7.0 on the Mohs scale) would constitute the hardest of "hard" evidence.[7]

Somewhat similar to the sourcing of stone, trace-element and lead-isotope analysis of the composition of (especially, unalloyed) metal objects can now often be employed to assign an area of origin. As has been described in chapter 10, a bracelet unearthed from the pre-Contact Bat Creek Mound in Tennessee was found to be of brass, an alloy produced, before Colonial times, only in the Old World.[8]

One may also briefly mention the puzzling very old remains of the mining of native copper in Michigan's Isle Royale and Keweenaw Peninsula, along with Old World–style copper weapons and tools, some socketed, found archaeologically in the region. Far more copper appears to have been mined than can be accounted for by Native American use, leading to speculation that the metal was being extracted under the direction of, and exported for consumption by, such copper-poor Old World Bronze Age peoples of the Mediterranean as the Minoans, possibly by their copper-specialist contemporaries, the Cypriots.[9] So far, this postulate remains to be tested scientifically, although composition studies of selected Old World copper and bronze objects could prove enlightening once an adequate database of global native copper source characterizations becomes available. We do at least have some candidates for comparative characterization:

many Bronze Age Southwest Asian bronze objects exhibit copper that does "not overlap with any known source."[10] Some ingots exhibit lead-isotope compositions not so far identified in any Mediterranean copper deposit.[11]

Domesticated Animals in the "Wrong" Hemisphere

Crying Fowl: The Turkey and the Chicken

Unlike cultivated plants, dozens of which may have been shared between the hemispheres (see chapters 27–29), only three or four domesticated animals have been mentioned as possible transoceanic transfers; animals do not travel as easily as seeds or even tubers. One potential candidate, however, is the turkey (*Meleagris gallopavo*), a Mesoamerican domesticate. A turkey bone was reported to have been found archaeologically in a fourteenth-century AD palace in Budapest (but was apparently destroyed during World War II) and another in a thirteenth-century site in Switzerland (also now missing). Seeming depictions of the bird (with wattle) appear on tenth- to thirteenth-century Hungarian signet rings, as well as unequivocal painted ones in the medieval church at Schleswig— although the latter could conceivably be the work of a nineteenth-century restorer. As the fowl has been known in Europe by variants of the name *galline d'Inde*, a South Asian immediate source (or America perceived as India) is implied.[12] Regarding the Budapest bone, however, an ornithologist who later examined the published drawing asserted that it came not from a turkey but from a pheasant.[13]

In light of the very widespread nature of early Colonial-period reports, the Swedish ethnographer Erland Nordenskiöld wrote in 1931 that the chicken (*Gallus gallus domesticus*), a Southeast Asian domesticate, spread immediately and very rapidly in the Americas after AD 1500. He did not believe it to have reached the New World before 1492, and that opinion has generally prevailed over the decades. However, not everyone interpreted Nordenskiöld's data as he did. Forty years later, George Carter, in particular, took the same information, augmented it, and concluded that the chicken, incapable of flying across an ocean, was pre-Columbian in the Americas.[14]

It turns out that indigenous American groups tend largely to keep *Asiatic* varieties of chickens, not Mediterranean ones like those found among Ibericized Latin American populations, and for ritual/medical purposes, not for eggs or for flesh as is their function in Iberia. New World natives call the birds by a variety of non-Iberian names, including an Arawakan one (*karaka*) that is similar to a name used in India (*karaknath*) and a Tarahumar one (*tori*) that duplicates the Japanese label (*tori/dori*). Many of these native chickens lay blue to olive-green eggs, as also occurs with similar chickens in Japan and Polynesia.[15]

It is of particular interest that in a reconstruction of proto-Mixe-Zoquean, thought to be ancestral to a language involved in the ancient Olmec culture of Mexico—often called America's first civilization—the Danish linguist Søren Wichmann reconstructed an ancestral lexeme for 'chicken/hen' (*ce:wE[kV']*) and, in proto-Oaxaca Mixean, a word specifically for 'cock' (*na"w-ce:wy*).[16]

George Carter also pointed out some commonalities between cultural roles of the chickens of America and Asia. The plant geographer Carl L. Johannessen and collaborators took the study of such matters much further. They found that the black-boned, black-meated chicken (an Asian type) among Native Middle and South Americans—especially the Maya—had medicinal uses strikingly like those of South China, most of which seem entirely arbitrary. One example is the dripping of chicken blood onto bark paper and then burning the paper.[17]

All of this evidence, though striking, is only circumstantial. Despite some promising leads, until 2007 no indisputable pre-1492 New World archaeological occurrence of chicken—whose bones degrade quickly—had been reported. Then, intrigued by undated archaeological *Gallus gallus* bones known about for years, an international team of scholars led by the archaeologist Alice A. Storey announced that it had identified bones from at least five chickens from the site of El Arenal-1 on south-central Chile's Arauco Peninsula, occupied between AD 700 and 1300. Analysis of mitochondrial DNA in the bones showed them to be genetically indistinguishable from contemporaneous bones from American Samoa and from Tonga, over 5,000 miles away, and slightly different from ones found in Hawaii and on Easter Island.[18] In 2011, Storey and her colleagues added thirty-three chicken-bone elements from the site as well as new archaeometric data that confirmed the bones' pre-1492 dates.[19] The chicken had come home to roost at last, one might say.

New World archaeological chicken bones had, in fact, already been reported. Wendy Teeter found some at Caracol, Belize, a Late PreClassic/Early Classic–Terminal Classic Mayan site dating to between 200 BC–AD 200 and AD 800–1000, although in her dissertation she had stated that "they [two pieces of chicken bone] were found in a looted tomb, likely the leftovers from the looters' meal."[20] However, the bird may have had pre-Columbian ceremonial functions.

Ticul Álvarez and Aurelio Ocaña had already tallied eight sites in Mexico that had yielded *Gallus gallus domesticus* bones, including a partial skeleton at the Aztec Templo Mayor in Mexico City (destroyed by the conquistadors), and eleven bones in the sacred cenote at Mayan Chichén Itzá, Yucatán (others are from México and from Michoacán). Because the chicken has been assumed to be a post-1500 introduction, the authors concluded that the strata involved were all either post-Columbian or contained intrusive chicken remains.[21] Carbon dating and ancient DNA analysis are urgently needed.

More recently, Christopher M. Götz and Travis W. Stanton reported—without comment—finding fifteen specimens of chicken bone, representing a minimum of three individuals, at the pre-Columbian Mayan Champotón site, Campeche, Mexico. Although a chicken radius at the Cerro Juan Diaz site on Panama's Azuero Peninsula (200 BC to AD 1600) was found almost 30 inches below the present surface, in association with pre-Columbian materials and exhibiting the same degree of staining as other bones there, the finders considered it likely to reflect the Colonial presence signaled by a small scatter of artifacts on the surface.[22] To me, a pre-Colonial *Gallus gallus* population seems much more probable.

Dog Food: The Culinary Canine

Canis lupus familiaris, the dog, became domesticated in Eurasia. Although standard-sized dogs entered the Americas with Early Holocene or Late Pleistocene humans, there also exist some small American breeds. Globally, small dogs (including the Chihuahua and the Chinese Crested) all exhibit the same version of gene *IGF1*.[23] Since there are no small canines in the North, this causes one to wonder whether small ancient Nuclear American breeds such as the Chihuahua reflect some overseas input.

Creatures of much potential interest in this context but ones that have been relatively little studied are the small, often hairless and barkless, culinary canines, which were bred, raised, castrated, and fattened to be eaten. In 1540, Rodrigo Rangel, personal secretary to Hernando de Soto, observed, "The Indians came forth in peace and gave them corn, although little, and [take note] many hens, and a few little dogs, which are good food. These are little dogs that do not bark, and they rear them in the house for food."

The practice of dog eating dates to before 3000 BC in China, in Mesoamerica, and in Ecuador.[24] In their book *The Natural History of the Dog*, Richard and Alice Fiennes wrote: "It is of great interest to note the strange resemblance between the little dogs kept by the Aztecs and the [small, pug-like] 'happa' dogs of China. . . . quite unlike the motley crew of dogs [of the rest of the Americas]. . . . The Aztecs and the Inca developed little dogs of high quality, which were both for sacrificial rites and for the table. These dogs had special characteristics unlike any possible canine ancestor existing wild in these areas."[25] Small, short-snouted dogs were referred to as "happa" dogs, especially in southern China, as long ago as 1000 BC. The preferred culinary dog in China was the black-tongued chow chow.

What are believed to be small culinary dogs are depicted in the form of ceramic effigy jars from South America, the earliest—painted—ones being from the Chorrera culture of Ecuador (circa 1000–300 BC). Painted and unpainted effigy jars of wrinkled, hairless dogs are known from northern Peru's Moche and Chimú cultures (circa AD 1–1470; figure 26.1), in which dog bones with butchering marks are common in the archaeology, and Spanish documents from early Colonial Peru report some local dogs being eaten. Redware pottery effigy vessels in the form of such dogs occur in both Colima, Mexico, between about 250 BC and AD 450, and in Han China (circa 205 BC to AD 220), and remains of the hairless version of the Aztec dog, the *xoloitzcuintli*, which display distinctive dentition, appear by about AD 1000 in Mexican archaeology (standard Aztec-type dog remains go back to 700–1000 BC).

Although some researchers have considered the identical-looking Chinese crested dog and the Mesoamerican hairless edible dog to be of the same breed,[26] thorough genetic studies directly comparing these have not been undertaken. A 2002 study concluded that with respect to *contemporary* dogs, "The few [mitochondrial DNA] sequences from breeds of New World origin ([including Arctic breeds and] . . . the Mexican hairless . . .) were indistinguishable from those of

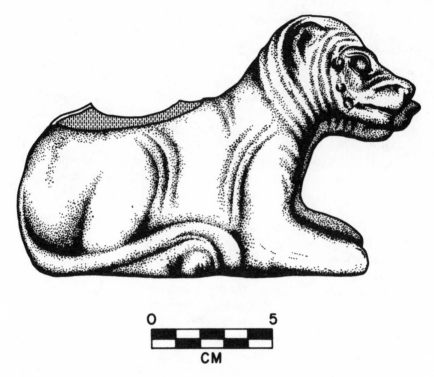

Figure 26.1. Moche V terra-cotta effigy vessel depicting a wrinkled-skinned, hairless dog, probably raised for eating, Lambayeque Valley, North Coast of Peru, circa AD 600. From *Pampa Grande and the Mochica Culture* by Izumi Shimeda, © 1994. By permission of the University of Texas Press.

Eurasian dogs. . . . [G]enetic analysis of 19 [modern] Mexican hairless dogs . . . only revealed mtDNA sequences previously observed in dogs of Eurasian origin."[27] However, most *archaeological* Latin American dogs, including hairless ones, fell into a so-far exclusively American clade (or grouping of genetically similar species that is distinct from other groupings), labeled "a." The researchers attributed loss of (female-lineage) mtDNA clade "a" to post-Columbian genetic swamping by European breeds (one wonders what [male] Y chromosome studies might show). The loss of clade "a" in the hairless animals may reflect the fact that the population of these dogs dropped almost to the point of extinction during the sixteenth century, at least in Mesoamerica (only to be revived in the mid-twentieth century by the Mexican artists Diego Rivera and Frida Kahlo, among others).

A later mtDNA study, involving a much larger sample, found that not only did the New World hairless dogs retain a majority of pre-Columbian non-European lineages but also that the Mexican one—the *xoloitzcuintli*—and the South American one—the *perro sín pelo del Perú*—exhibited an approximately 80 percent overlap in their female lineages, indicating close kinship.[28]

An international team has identified a mutation for hairlessness involving a sequence duplication within what is called the *FOX13* gene: "We found perfect concordance of the duplication with the CED [canine ectodermal dysplasia— that is, dog hairlessness] in 140 hairless dogs from the three studied breeds," the Mexican, Peruvian, and Chinese hairless dogs.[29] The authors do not speculate on how it is that all three of these hairless populations share the same mutation, but that sharing is consistent with the theory of a common origin and transfer by sea. The problem that remains, however, is that, so far, we have no archaeological remains or unambiguous graphic or literary depictions of the animal in China, and so it could conceivably have been a post–AD 1500 introduction there.

On-the-Road Hog

The domestic pig (*Sus scrofus domesticus*) is a Eurasian domesticate of considerable antiquity. Of note is that a sliver of pig bone was unearthed at the circa AD 1000 Norse site of L'Anse aux Meadows, Newfoundland.[30] Since the indigenous people did not adopt the animal, the impact of its temporary introduction was essentially nil. The Icelandic sagas tell us that the Norse also brought cattle to the New World; these had as little impact as the pigs did.

Catch This: Infectious Diseases Shared between the Hemispheres

In chapter 5, we looked at Old World diseases in the context of their assumed absences in the pre-Columbian New World. But were there any notable communicable diseases that clearly *were* shared between the hemispheres? The answer is a qualified "yes."[31]

Syphilis and Other Treponematosic Diseases

The term treponematosis encompasses four spirochete-bacteria-caused progressive diseases, some seemingly pre-Columbian in one or the other hemisphere or both. Three of these treponematosic maladies cause skeletal lesions. One, sexually and congenitally (mother-to-fetus) transmitted syphilis (*Treponema pallidum pallidum*), is a complaint whose origins and travels have long been debated. One hoary theory is that since it is not proven to have existed in the Old World before 1492, it represents one of the few important illnesses of New World origin and was brought back to Europe by Columbus's crew in 1493, as "the Indians' revenge," giving rise to more than one medical manifestation. *Virulent* venereal syphilis does appear to have first spread in Europe in the 1490s, later diffusing to Asia and Africa.[32] Closely related yaws seems to be humid-tropical African but also occurs in South America. Despite decades of debate, data gathering, and analysis, full agreement does not yet exist regarding the ages, the place or places of origin, and the early travels of these various maladies.

Compared to others, American Indians are relatively resistant to syphilis, suggesting centuries of exposure to treponematosic disease. Specifically syphilis-caused bone lesions on some pre-Columbian skeletons are clear, even judged very critically. In California's Santa Barbara Channel region, cranial lesions considered indicative of the malady go back in time as much as 4,640 years.[33]

Bruce Rothschild is an American medical professor who is a specialist in differentiating skeletal lesions of the various forms of treponematosic diseases. With the archaeologist Richard Rogers, he has identified what he believes to be bejel lesions in ten skeletons in Pacific-coastal North America and Central Mexico, most dating to from AD 500 to 1492. Bejel or nonvenereal "endemic syphilis" is an Old World complaint. The pair has proposed introduction of this Old World form having taken place via drifting Japanese junks (see chapter 5).[34] Antitreponomal antibodies have been found in Native North Americans of about AD 1240, but of what form cannot be determined.[35]

Treponemal skeletal lesions occurred on some Mediterranean skeletons as far back as Classical times, and treponematosis was widespread in the Austronesian-occupied islands, aboriginal Australia, and China. Two *possible* cases of specifically syphilitic lesions from medieval northwestern Europe were reported in 1992. However, as of 1997 the latest and most extensive skeletal studies had indicated no *clear* pre-Columbian syphilis in the Old World but its definite presence in New Mexico, Florida, and Ecuador as much as 1,600 years ago; yaws was identified in Ohio, Illinois, and Virginia and was at least 6,000 years old there.

Only relatively lately was more promising evidence for a pre-Columbian existence of venereal syphilis unearthed in Europe: one skeleton from Norwich, England, that shows clear signs of the disease, was carbon-dated to between AD 1300 and 1450, well before Columbus's famous voyage—a date that, for a time, fueled speculation that the Norse rather than Columbus were responsible for the importation. However, other, older possible examples have been reported since, suggesting syphilis's possible presence even in antiquity. One probable case of congenital syphilis from Hyères, France, dates to the third to fifth century AD and another from Austria is from between AD 1390 and 1440.[36]

Tuberculosis

The pulmonary infection known as tuberculosis (TB; *Mycobacterium tuberculosis*) is a disease that is not confined to humans and that apparently goes back at least 500,000 years, to the time of *Homo erectus*. Human-strain TB DNA is evidenced among modern humans by at least 6000 BC in the Mediterranean region and in Bronze Age populations in East Asia. Forms are found among some nonhuman animals, and TB was formerly thought to have become a human disease through close contact among people, their bovine domesticates, and milk products, and to have spread particularly in association with the crowding found in emerging Neolithic towns (but the *H. erectus* dates and later ones from Israel now preclude such a late human acquisition of TB, and genetic distance implies that human TB gave rise to bovine TB, some 113,000 years ago).

For over a century, there had been some reason to believe that TB might also have been present in the pre-Columbian New World. Indeed, in 1973 good osteological paleopathological evidence was published for a circa AD 800 mummy from Peru. Since that time, DNA, proteomic, and much more skeletal-lesion evidence has proven numerous instances. Dates of South American probable occurrences begin at 160 BC, with convincing cases commencing in that continent at about AD 290 or a bit later; at a similar date in the Mississippi Valley; and in California as far back in time as 2650 BC.[37] Known pre-1492 South American instances are mainly in the Central Andean region, with a handful in the northwest of that continent. There are very few finds in Mesoamerica, but the North American Southwest and the eastern woodlands provide quite a number of cases, some from the early centuries AD but most of a post–AD 900 date.

The implications of these findings for long-distance overseas contacts are not unambiguous. Tuberculosis being chronic and in the protective environment of the lungs, climatic factors do not influence either the risk of developing it or its subsequent course, so the Bering Strait would not have operated as a cold screen. The emergence of TB would have been density dependent, and whether Arctic human population concentration was ever sufficient to sustain endemism is very questionable. Charlotte A. Roberts and Jane E. Buikstra averred that "no cases of TB have been identified in hunting and gathering populations." Although other authors have listed this disease as a leading cause of mortality in such societies, this does not require endemism.[38] A handful of writers have even proposed a de novo emergence in the Americas, which seems highly dubious on more than one ground.

Until recently, the data supported a picture of earliest American human TB appearance in Peru followed by seaborne introduction to western Mexico, with subsequent movement to the Southwest and to eastern North America—movement opposite the pattern that a Bering Strait point of entry would produce; initial introduction to South America by sea from Asia best fit the evidence available. TB is a disease that continues in the host, so that the time-filter factor would not eliminate it on prolonged voyages. However, if the early California date is accurate, the South America–first scenario no longer holds up.

Further, TB DNA has been reported from bones of a now-extinct 17,500-year-old North American bison. This DNA is more like human TB DNA than bovine, implying that transmission via Beringia or, more likely, by boat-borne Pacific Rim movements did occur.[39] Indeed, one pair of specialists concluded that TB arrived in North America with the initial human migrants.[40] Recently, a human TB strain found in 1,000-year-old Peruvian mummies showed a close relationship with a strain that infects seals and sea lions, suggesting that sea mammals played a role in the bringing of the disease to the Americas.[41]

Typhus

Typhus (*Rickettsia typhi*), generally thought to be an Old World disease, leaves no physical markers in the archaeological record. Still, one author stated that typhus (or a similar fever) was very common in ancient Peru, and the anthropological geneticist Michael H. Crawford wrote that evidence existed suggesting that typhus was pre-Columbian in the Americas.[42]

The epidemiologist Aaron Medina-Sanchez and colleagues agreed: "the ill-ness[es] known as *cocolixtle* and *matlazahuatl* to the indigenous peoples likely were present prior to the arrival of Europeans."[43] In fact, the historian Suzanne Austin Alchon added, "One can make a very strong case for the existence of both endemic (flea-borne) and epidemic (louse-borne) typhus in the New World before 1492."[44] Thousand-year-old lice found in the hair of a Peruvian mummy are of the subtype that is the typhus vector in the Old World, and this louse may be very much older in the hemisphere.[45] The disease is likely implicated in late pre-Columbian epidemics in the Central Andean region, Mexico, and North America, and some think that *cocolixtle* may have contributed mightily to the fall of Teotihuacan and the Classic Maya collapse of AD 750–950 (but see yellow fever discussion, below). Colonial-period Peruvian populations appear to have had some degree of resistance to the disease, and there are possible de-pictions of its symptoms in Aztec pictures. Contrary to conventional supposi-tion, all this suggests an origin in the Americas; the earliest good Old World description is from Granada, Spain, in 1489. But even if the disease is of Old World origin, typhus is known especially as a disease of cold climates and so could conceivably have passed the Bering Strait. At the same time, unlike vic-tims of the acute infections, typhus survivors can be carriers, facilitating car-riage across oceans, which is certainly an alternative avenue for introduction, especially in light of low population densities in the Arctic.

Yellow Fever

In 1995, Robert L. Wilkinson presented evidence of the pre-Columbian pres-ence of mosquito-borne yellow fever in the tropical Americas, suggesting that its reservoir was American monkeys and that its vectors were the indigenous mosquitoes *Hæmagogus* spp. He noted what sounds like yellow fever symp-toms described in the Mayan epic the *Popol Vuh*, and he attributed the Clas-sic Maya collapse to an urban epidemic of the disease (but see the typhus dis-cussion, above).[46]

Yellow fever is traditionally supposed to be of African origin, but the evi-dence for this is inconclusive, and the disease could plausibly be native to South America. If African, the pathogen could possibly have crossed the At-lantic naturally in wind-blown mosquitoes or it might have been brought by human voyagers.

Conclusions Concerning Complaints

Although we have seen that syphilis, tuberculosis, typhus, and perhaps yellow fever do appear to have been on both sides of the oceans before Columbus, it cannot be shown that transfer was necessarily by sea. Introductions via Bering Strait remain a possibility, although seemingly a very unlikely one, with Pacific Rim movement at least a little more likely. At the present time, then, the infec-tious disease picture hardly proves pre-Columbian contacts. However, as out-lined in chapter 6 an understanding of some basics about disease history, eti-ology, and ecology does lead to the conclusion that the alleged pre-Columbian absence in the Americas of many Eastern Hemisphere communicable maladies by no means *disproves*—or even justifies serious objections against—the reality of the occurrence of such contacts, and certain diseases being shared between the hemispheres is at very least consistent with the notion of pre-Columbian pelagic exchanges.

Out-of-Place Parasites

If humans really arrived in the New World from overseas long before the "official" discovery, they would necessarily have brought with them any parasites that infested their digestive tracts as well as the genetic codes in their chromosomes. In addition, they would very likely have passed these on to the peoples they encountered upon arrival. Thus, some human-biological traces of such contacts should survive in the guts and genes of at least a portion of American indigenes. Here, we look into the guts, leaving the genes to chapter 31.

The Worm Turns: Intestinal Parasites

According to John Sorenson and Carl Johannessen, decisive evidence exists to show that twenty-one micropredators were exchanged between the Old and the New Worlds before 1492 (in a few cases, possibly via Bering Strait), plus many additional species that merit further investigation in this regard.[47]

About half of these shared pathogens are parasitic worms found in the intestines of human hosts. Formerly, experts thought that virtually all such parasites were confined to the Old World before 1492, that they had evolved there in tandem with domestication and urbanization, and that (with one or two exceptions) the few human intestinal parasites originating before the emergence of agriculture had been filtered out by the cold climate as Paleolithic hunters populated the Americas via arctic Beringia. As late as the 1980s, specialists generally considered the New World to have been essentially free of such pests except for pinworm. Since then that belief has changed dramatically, and it now appears that such parasitic organisms were rife within certain aboriginal American populations.

Although a few intestinal parasites are indeed ancient and turn out to be globally distributed—pinworms and the protozoan *Girardia*, for instance—and say nothing about transoceanic contacts, others are restricted to milder climes and are indeed incapable of slow passage by way of northern latitudes such as those of Bering Strait. The eggs and larvae of the hookworm *Ancylostoma duodenale*, for example, cannot survive in soils with temperatures below 59° F. Similarly, eggs of the whipworm (*Trichuris trichiura*) require warm, moist, shaded soil. Understanding this, as early as 1920 the renowned American parasitologist Samuel T. Darling observed that if Afroeurasian hookworms were found among American Indians, the Indians would have to have gotten the parasites from transoceanic "storm-tossed fishermen." Seven years later, the American physician Fred L. Soper reported *A. duodenale* infestation among the remote Lengua Indians of Paraguay and concluded that this hookworm could have gotten to South America only in one of two ways: (1) via transpacific travel or through *very* rapid migration by way of Bering Strait, or (2) by normal overland diffusion if milder climatic conditions had prevailed in the North during the late Pleistocene past (a condition for which there is only contrary evidence). In 1967, after having read of the archaeologist Betty J. Meggers's transpacific influences hypotheses, the American parasitologist Harold W. Manter suggested that *A. duodenale* had been brought to Ecuador about 3000 BC by Jōmon sailors from Japan, and that the Afroasian hookworm *Necator americanus*, found in some living populations, had been carried to the same area by the southeastern Asian founders of Bahía culture some 300 BC.

In 1970, the Brazilian Olympio da Fonseca made a major case for Asian-Pacific parasites having early been introduced to South America.[48] Only in 1974, however, was the first American archaeological find of *A. duodenale* announced, from a Tiahuanaco, Bolivia, mummy of circa AD 900. Later, a specimen dating to circa 6117 BC was excavated, in Brazil, as well as others in Chile. By 1990, many more such discoveries had been made, in both South and North America, not only of *A. duodenale* but also of *N. americanus* in pre-European-contact Brazil, the whipworm at various places in South America (at around 6670 BC in Brazil), the hairworm (*Strongyloides* spp.), and the giant roundworm (*Ascaris lumbricoides*), which is attested in Peru at about 2277 BC. The last is considered to have descended from those in pigs, which were strictly Old World.[49]

Brazilians have been particularly active in this research, citing *A. duodenale* from various places in Brazil, one early specimen, from the northeast, being from about 5300 BC, and there are also pre-Columbian dates from Peru and Chile and one from Tennessee. The Brazilians concluded that transoceanic contacts or, conceivably, very rapid coastal movements were necessary to account for these occurrences, and that the presences of various helminths among Paleoamericans placed the earliest of such contacts or movements much earlier than even most diffusionists had proposed.[50] The only conceivable alternative explanation that comes to mind is carriage via the Bering Strait area during an interglacial period, when conditions would have been warmer, although whether or not they would have been warm *enough* is uncertain. In any event, such carriage would have required a very much earlier initial entry of humans into the hemisphere than almost anyone accepts.

Bugs Abroad: Shared Insect Species

A few insect species may also be mentioned as shared or seemingly shared between the hemispheres.

Lousy Evidence

A widespread variety of the human head and body louse seems to have originated in Africa and to have spread very widely in the Old World. Formerly, it was assumed not to have reached the Americas until after the arrival of Christopher

Columbus. However, in 2008 a team of pathologists announced the discovery of such lice on the heads of mummified Chiribaya-culture bodies in Peru, dating to between AD 990 and 1350.[51]

Tobacco Chewer

The cigarette beetle (*Lasioderma serricorne*) of ancient Levantine archaeology was first described in Europe in 1798 on dried American materials, and has been thought to be of American origin. However, it was first recorded in the United States only in 1886 and I have found no archaeological reports from the Americas, so the species' pre-Columbian status in the New World is as yet undetermined. As detailed in chapter 29, archaeological specimens have been found associated with Egyptian mummies.

Boring

The supposedly South American lesser grain borer, *Rhyzopertha dominica*, has also been found in the same places and from the same times as is *L. serricorne*, as well as in a Roman site in Egypt. In addition, P. C. Buckland and Eva Panagiotakopulu noted that the beetles *Stegobium paniceum* (biscuit beetle) and *Alphitobius diaperinus* (lesser mealworm), which have been identified on bodies from Pharaonic Egypt and Roman Britain and "must therefore be of Old World origin," have also been reported from pre-Columbian Peruvian mummies and so necessarily—claim the authors—represent contamination.[52]

In short, pre-Columbian New World presence of these Old World warm-region intestinal parasites, a louse, and a few beetles provides strong evidence of actual seaborne contacts in impressively ancient times. Being biological and not cultural, their bihemispheric existence cannot be attributed to independent invention but only to human-mediated transfer.

27

Shared Cultigens

From New into Old (World)

Is there no respect of place . . . nor time in you?
—William Shakespeare, *Twelfth Night*, 2. 3. (80), 1601

In the previous chapter, we saw that there are cases—open and shut, in the instance of the chicken—to be made for the pre-Columbian presence of certain domesticated animal species in the "wrong" hemisphere, and that, being genetic entities, not man-made inventions, demonstration of any such presence suggests, more than strongly, human carriage. The present chapter and the following two look at cultivated plants in similar light and find them to be definitive "smoking guns" signaling transoceanic transfer and thus opportunity for cultural diffusion.

The Evidentiary Value of Cultivated Plants

Although no proof is absolute outside of mathematics, as noted in the previous chapter biological indications are among the clearest and least equivocal that imply early and important interhemispheric interactions. Unlike physical materials, biological ones have received considerable attention in the context of transoceanic-contact investigations. It is widely recognized that research on shared cultivated plants may go far toward finally settling the argument over whether or not influential pre-Norse transoceanic exchanges really occurred.

In chapter 7, we took note of the supposed absence of interhemispherically shared cultivated plants. This was a notion given momentum by the influential Swiss botanist Alphonse de Candolle, who in 1883 averred, "In the history of cultivated plants, I have noticed no trace of communication between the peoples of the old and new worlds before the discovery of America by Columbus."[1] This view, also loudly touted (with some grudging qualifications) by the mid-twentieth-century Harvard plant taxonomist Elmer Drew Merrill and oft repeated ever since, has been a significant reason for resistance to the notion of early transoceanic contacts. The American anthropologist and specialist in culture-trait distributions Harold E. Driver wrote in 1973,

My conclusion is that not a single case for pre-Columbian diffusion of a domesticated plant across the Pacific from the Old World to the New is tenable today. . . .

[Other than the bottlegourd, which was probably independently domesticated, a]ll other pre-Columbian domesticated species except the sweet potato were confined to only one hemisphere. The very rapid and ubiquitous exchange of domesticated plants between the hemispheres suggests that if there had been even a modest amount of communication by sea before that date more plants would have been exchanged than the record shows.[2]

An ostensible dearth of archaeological specimens of interhemispherically transferred species of cultivated plants is not surprising in view of plants' high degree of perishability under most conditions. For example, in light of a total lack of finds or depictions of tomatoes in American archaeology (the plant was first recorded by Europeans in 1519), we could not prove its pre-Columbian presence in the hemisphere (or the world) were it not for nonarchaeological botanical evidence. Despite perishability problems, indications of pre-Columbian interhemispheric sharings of cultivated plants have proliferated over the years, especially during the 1990s and 2000s, and Driver's alleged blank record has been much filled in. Indeed, as long ago as 1962 the American geographers Philip L. Wagner and Marvin W. Mikesell wrote, "The most convincing evidence of intercourse between the New World and the Old before Columbus . . . is undoubtedly the presence of certain domesticated plants (e.g., the sweet potato) on both sides of the Pacific at the time of first European contact."[3]

The modern study of human domesticates in the transoceanic context was pioneered especially by George F. Carter in the 1950s and 1960s, following earlier leads on the part of scholars such as the early twentieth-century US government botanist O. F. Cook and Carter's professor, the geographer Carl O. Sauer.[4] As these scientists pointed out, although humans may affect the evolutions of plants and animals, most notably their domesticates, none of these species can be "invented," or selected into existence as cultigens or as domesticated animals, other than where an appropriate wild ancestor exists (sometimes, more than one ancestral species has been involved, producing hybrid domesticates). Although many wild plant and some terrestrial wild animal species are shared between the hemispheres in the Arctic and subarctic, the same is not true in the Tropics and subtropics. In fact, except for strand (shoreline) plants, although sharing some genera the tropical higher-plant wild floras of the two hemispheres have almost no species in common, and none that are potential wild ancestors of cultigens.[5] If the Quaternary oceans prevented interhemispheric transfer of *wild* plant species over the hundreds of thousands, even millions, of years of their existence, they would virtually certainly have done so over the mere millennia of existence of *cultivated* plants. As the antidiffusionist Merrill himself conceded, "as a rule, even weeds, much less cultigens, do not extend their ranges from one hemisphere to another without the intervention and aid of man."[6]

Certainly, even the most remote islands possessed floras, including seed plants. Yet compared to the diversity of continental areas, at the family level these floras were usually quite impoverished, especially of seed plants, because the great bulk of wild higher plant species are incapable of successfully traveling such distances and establishing themselves. Although rafting, including of large trees undermined and carried to the sea by flooded rivers with seeds buried in the soil held by the roots, combined with long-distance drifting as described in chapter 3, can carry plant materials to very distant shores, rafts of soil and vegetation last but a few weeks at sea and the probability seems very low that seeds would escape being washed away by rain and sea spray or at least being impregnated by saltwater when making a transoceanic crossing wedged in a log or the like (pumice mats last longer but are much rarer).[7]

Certain molecular geneticists have recently asserted that a number of terrestrial plant and animal taxa *have* crossed oceans, primarily the Atlantic. However, such alleged transfers represent but a tiny percentage of the millions of *wild* species and would have occurred over tens of millions of years—not over just a few thousand as in the case of the relative handful of *domesticated* species that exist—in most cases, when the Atlantic was substantially narrower and studded with islands. Further, fossil evidence implies that that the imprecise molecular clock much underestimated the ages of the related taxa in the two hemispheres.[8]

This lack of intercontinental sharing of warm-climate wild plant species pertains because (unlike the spores of cryptogams) the seeds of the vast majority of higher plants are too heavy to be blown across oceans and lack buoyant, saltwater-resistant seeds that could float across and establish themselves on the opposite shore. Although some tiny seeds, especially if provided with down, can be carried great distances by the wind, the English plant-dispersal authority Henry N. Ridley reported that the maximum distance that even dust-sized seeds were recorded as having been transported was 700 miles.[9] Yet many scholars continue to posit hard to credit natural dispersals but refuse seriously to consider the (to me) much more plausible idea of humans crossing oceans in boats, bringing seeds and cuttings with them. It is true that, given enough time, improbable events may occur, but this applies to both natural dispersal events and human-mediated crossings.

Somewhat more likely than wind transport or rafting is transfer by bird, and the evidence of plants on remote islands supports this as having happened much more frequently. Seeds in avian intestinal tracts are usually passed through in a matter of hours—too little time for wide-ocean crossings—although the botanist Sherwin Carlquist did note that if a shorebird like a killdeer, which can retain an ingested seed for up to 120 hours, were (implausibly) to fly nonstop at its maximum speed of 50–74 miles per hour, it could carry the seed some 5,000 miles. Another, more possible means of avian transoceanic land-plant-seed dispersal is adherence to bird feathers or to muddy bird feet, the birds making the crossings and then shedding the seeds, although only quite small and/or adherent seeds (not characteristic of most of the relevant domesticates) could travel this way.[10] Still, migrating birds, with the exception of some high-latitude waterfowl and shorebirds and certain Asiatic land species that visit Pacific islands, remain within one hemisphere or the other and do not go far to sea except accidentally, nor do bats. Even seabirds do not normally traverse entire oceans, although this *can* happen during North Atlantic storms, even, on occasion, in the case of land birds.[11]

Even if a wild-plant seed did somehow arrive in a distant new area, chances are that, not being adapted to the local ecosystem, it could not survive the climate, the soil, or the competition. Unaided interhemispheric sharing is substantially less likely for domesticates than for wild species, because under cultivation domesticates have evolved a dependency on human care. Cultigens of the great majority of species are largely or wholly incapable of surviving for any prolonged period in the absence of that intervention. Many of these plants have lost their competitive abilities, their defenses against pests, and/or their capabilities of propagating themselves. Agreed Merrill, "most cultigens . . . are . . . absolutely dependent on man for their very existence."[12]

A classic case in this regard is maize, domesticated in Mexico (and considered in more detail below). Both the cob and the husk of this Mesoamerican domesticate represent mutations that occurred sometime after initial domestication. The grains' envelopment by the husk, plus the imbeddedness of the kernels in the cob, hinders seed dispersal and rooting; left to itself, without human propagation, maize does not survive in the wild and therefore cannot have established itself naturally in the Old World, even in the highly unlikely event that its large seeds could have been transported there by natural means. Other examples of the dependence of cultigens on humans are domesticated bananas and plantains (genus *Musa*; see chapter 28), which, under cultivation, have completely lost the ability to produce viable seed and are reproduced only by humans, exclusively from cuttings. Similarly, the breadfruit tree of Oceania is entirely dependent on humans for its propagation.

Thus if it is shown that any of these or other non-self-perpetuating species were present in both the Old and the New Worlds before Columbus, the only reasonable conclusion would be that humans carried them (rather quickly) across the oceans and planted them (northerly climes were too cold to permit agriculture, thus preventing gradual, largely overland diffusion of crops between the hemispheres). This conclusion would be reinforced if names of these plants, and/or beliefs and ritual practices concerning them, turned out also to be shared. Such a showing is made in the remainder of this chapter, and it will become clear that the oft-expressed perception that there were no interhemispheric introductions of domesticates—a cornerstone of most scholars' rejection of the notion of transoceanic contacts—can no longer legitimately be sustained.

Food for Thought: Domesticated Plant Species in the "Wrong" Hemisphere

How may one potentially demonstrate pre-Columbian presence of any particular species of cultivated plant in an area? In approximate descending order of reliability are the following kinds of evidence: (1) actual and identifiable macroscopic archaeological remains of the plants or their parts in demonstrably pre-Columbian contexts; (2) datable pre-1492 preserved pollen grains of the crop species; (3) datable diagnostic breakdown products of such species, including xylem cells, opal phytoliths, and residues of crop starches;[13] (4) exotic genetic components of the species; (5) chemical residues from the domesticates; (6) taxonomically identifiable depictions of the plants in period sculptures, paintings, and so forth; (7) clear descriptions of such species in pre-1492 literary works and/or uses of their modern names in early literature (however, words' meanings sometimes shift over time); (8) recognizable descriptions of the plants in early post-Columbian European reports, especially when the reports are multiple and geographically widespread; (9) local folklore concerning use of the species from time immemorial, and full integration of them into the culture, especially in religion. Here, we present a selection of examples of Old World domesticates for which the evidence of their pre-Columbian presence in the New World is particularly convincing.[14]

Peanut Peregrinations

One of the most astounding instances of the putative pre-Columbian Old World occurrence of a New World crop species in Asia is that of the peanut (*Arachis hypogaea*) in Neolithic eastern China. The species, apparently domesticated in eastern Bolivia some 8,000 years ago, has generally been thought to have been absent in Asia until the Portuguese brought it to Guangzhou, where they established a presence in 1516—although, a century ago, it *was* noticed that the variety grown in China was a Peruvian one that seemed, at the time, to have gone out of currency in Peru by the moment of Spanish arrival there. Then in the early 1960s findings of fruits were reported, initially in the Chinese literature, from two archaeological sites calibrated to about 3579 BC in the southeastern coastal province of Zhejiang and in adjacent Jiangxi, and were brought to the attention of the Western world by the Yale University archaeologist of China Kwang-Chih Chang.[15] Chang drew no diffusionist conclusions from these finds, but certain other scholars began pointing to these peanuts as evidence of very early overseas contacts; skeptics derisively dismissed them as misidentified or intrusive. In the 1990s, Carl Johannessen reexamined the specimens and considered the archaeological contexts, accepting their genuineness in terms of both identification and provenience.[16]

One archaeological find alone would, naturally, seem suspect. Two are very considerably more persuasive. A third came in 1994 when the Chinese archaeologist Chen Wenhua reported finding at least ten peanuts in the tomb of a western Han emperor in Shaanxi, a northern interior province.[17] Further, there is a description in a circa AD 300 work titled *Flora of the South*, in which the multiple fruits of a certain plant are stated to occur buried in the soil and to have surfaces like woven fibers—quite an apt description for peanuts.

The Venezuelan botanist León Croizat, among others, pointed out that a specific hairy variety of peanut is found in Peru (the presumed area of origin), in Mexico, and in Jiangxi and Zhejiang in China, and Johannessen considered the Chinese archaeological specimens to be comparable to those occurring prehistorically at Ancón, Peru.[18] Although it has gone largely unnoticed, in 1977 another archaeological peanut find was reported for Asia, this time from East Timor in the East Indies. At the time, the excavator—the now-notable British archaeologist of Southeast Asia Ian C. Glover—thought that this and other American plants at the site reflected intrusion by agriculturalist immigrants coming from the north or west and settling in Timor during the third millennium BC.[19] With the total number of eastern Asian sites reporting the peanut having reached five, it would now be most imprudent to dismiss it all as a suite of excavator mistakes.

Sweet Potatoes Can't Swim

The Mexico- or South America–domesticated sweet potato (*Ipomea batatas*) has, over the years, been the most written-about putative transoceanic plant transfer. As the Harvard anthropologist Roland B. Dixon pointed out in 1932, the sweet potato was found in some of the farthest corners of Polynesia at the time of European exploration and first contact, was embedded in local horticulture there, and was of paramount economic importance; it existed in Polynesia in more than a hundred varieties (implying antiquity to allow differentiation via vegetative mutation) and everywhere carried variants of the name *kumara*, a term also found in northern Kichwa (Quechua) and in Chibchan tongues ranging from central Peru to Columbia.[20] As the cautious Dixon acknowledged, someone must have taken the sweet potato into the islands centuries before Columbus. Even E. D. Merrill also came to agree that the plant had been essentially ubiquitous in the Pacific before the arrival of Europeans (although he thought that it might be African in origin) and added that "it would be foolish to assert that there were no communications across the Pacific in pre-Magellan times."[21] He pointed out that the first European explorers in the Mariana Islands and in the Philippines saw *batatas* (sweet potatoes) on Guam and Cebu, respectively, as well as in the Maluku Islands and probably New Guinea.

Still, although quite persuasive the case for pre-Columbian presence of the plant in the Pacific islands was, until fairly recently, only circumstantial. In fact, in the 1930s Erland Nordenskiöld averred that the evidence "definitely proved that the sweet potato . . . spread from America in a westward direction . . . not until the post-Columbian era."[22] As late as 1971, the geographer Donald D. Brand contrived a scenario that allowed the Portuguese to obtain the tuber in Brazil about AD 1500, rush it to Goa and hand it to Indians who in turn passed it, relay-race style, to Indonesians, whence it was given to Polynesians, who managed to disperse the plant throughout the Pacific in time for Captain Cook to observe it in the late eighteenth century in every part of Polynesia to which he went.[23] That would be hyperdiffusion, indeed!

Meantime, however, evidence for the plant's genuine antiquity in the islands continued to accumulate. Presumed sweet-potato-field walls plus storage pits of a type known historically to have held sweet potatoes showed up in New Zealand archaeology at circa AD 1300s levels, and AD 1425–1605/AD 1545–1725 remains of tubers were excavated on Hawai'i, as well as AD 1358–1626 ones on Easter Island—in both these latter cases, probably post–AD 1492 but still pre-Cookian.[24] Although these dates were most suggestive, the actual tubers recovered still could not be absolutely demonstrated to be earlier than the earliest recorded European transpacific voyages.

Finally, in the 1980s, despite the plant's particularly poor preservation potential, archaeologists Jon Hather and P. V. Kirch unearthed unequivocally pre-Columbian carbonized sweet potato specimens, of circa AD 1000, on Mangaia, in Central Polynesia's southern Cook Islands.[25] More recently, archaeologists have found charred fragments from an apparently fourteenth-century sweet potato on Hawai'i, and starch grains from a second site came in at AD 1310–1480. Pre-European-contact *Ipomea* starch residues and xylem-vessel elements have also been identified in far northern New Zealand, the earliest occurrence being AD 1379 ± 55. Apparent charred sweet potato fragments from Hawai'i have been dated to AD 1200–1320, and a number of other early finds come from Hawai'i, both islands of New Zealand, and Easter Island; the earliest date from the last is circa AD 1300.[26] The wide pre-Columbian presence of *Ipomea batatas* in Polynesia seems no longer to be doubted.

Molecular-genetic studies have shown that most traditional Oceanian varieties of sweet potato have their roots in Ecuador/Peru, although the plants from the Hawaiian Islands show some Central American/northern Colombian input as well, which fits with the linguistics.[27]

Some scholars have at least considered the remote possibility that golden plovers or other birds might have carried sweet potato seeds to Polynesia, despite the fact that seabirds do not eat seeds (although shorebirds sometimes do) and that land birds do not cross to the Pacific islands from tropical America. In any event, the domesticated sweet potato never grows wild under conditions of competition and so would not have established itself on new shores, even had it been a strand plant, which it was not. In fact, it is usually propagated vegetatively (by stem cuttings) and in many areas only rarely sets viable seed (not once, in a test of eighty-eight Polynesian sweet potato plants), and such seeds that *are* produced sink in water—although the seed capsules do float and the seeds themselves are impervious to salt water. Even if seeds had arrived (as is oceanographically possible[28]), Polynesians would not likely have planted them, especially in light of their practice of relying on cuttings rather than on seeds for propagating their crops (except for the bottle gourd—possibly introduced from South America—and the coconut, whose seeds are tuber sized).

Too, to germinate, sweet potato seeds require scarification. In addition, seeds of a single sweet potato plant are self-incompatible, that is, plants deriving from them cannot fertilize one another. In short, the sweet potato does not leap oceans and establish itself on its own but, rather, requires considerable care (for example, the cutting being carried in soil, watered, and protected from seawater) to be successfully transported long distances by humans, and then must be planted and cared for upon arrival.

There are two plausible alternative explanations for the crop's and the crop's name's pre-Columbian presence in the Pacific islands. Northwest South American Indians, who had seagoing sailing-rafts, could have carried the sweet potato and its local label to the Pacific islands—the scenario that I slightly favor.[29] However, Polynesians, in their systematic explorations from west to east, undoubtedly ultimately reached South America (see chapters 26 and 27), where they could have acquired the plant and the name and then carried it back into the islands, among which it would have spread via interisland contacts. As mentioned, very careful conservation of the tubers, in soil, would have been required for seedless varieties.

The Hawaiian ethnobotanist Douglas E. Yen, the most assiduous student of the Pacific spread of the species, concluded that the plant had reached Polynesia from South America between AD 400 and 700,[30] and the archaeologist Patricia O'Brien estimated that it may have reached Samoa by the time of Christ, probably owing to a drift voyage. Linguistics reconstructs the proto-Polynesian term as *kumala, perhaps initially found in Fiji by about 500 BC or possibly a millennium later in the Marquesas.[31]

A number of authorities have suggested that the sweet potato was also introduced into New Guinea, Indonesia, China, and even Africa (by Indonesians) before 1492, partly on the basis of early post-Columbian European reports. In addition there are the facts that (1) certain Old World parasitic weevils have evolved to become specific to the sweet potato (which suggests the tuber's long presence); (2) the pre-Columbian use of the present Chinese name for the plant; and (3) paleoenvironmental evidence of forest clearing in New Guinea that may reflect sweet potato introduction around AD 800.

Although all this evidence for an Asian presence is very suggestive, it is less than definitive, and many of the plant's Asian names imply post-1500 European introduction.[32] Nevertheless, the case of the sweet potato shows unequivocally that humans traversed at least most of the South Pacific long before Columbus's Bahamian landfall. In fact, as George Carter put it, "Had cross-Pacific voyages been long and arduous, the sweet potato tubers would either have spoiled or been eaten. Neither was the case, and it is clearly inferable that man made deliberate and relatively easy voyages across the greatest expanses of the Pacific."[33]

Maize Amazes

The belief persists that before Columbus, the Old World had no maize (corn), squashes, tomatoes, potatoes, or peppers.[34] However, for all of these except the potato, good cases can be made for their pre-Columbian introduction to the Old World. There is, for example, a very considerable literature bearing on the question of a pre-Columbian presence of the supreme Mesoamerican domesticate, maize (*Zea mays* ssp. *mays*), in Eurasia and Africa.

Maize appears to have been domesticated from wild teosinte (*Z. mays* ssp. *parviglumis*) in the Río Balsas drainage of western Mexico, around 7000 BC. It ultimately spread northward into what is now the United States as well as rapidly southward into Central and South America, becoming the staple and deified crop over much of those regions. In 1949 the British botanist/anthropologist C. R. Stonor of the Assam Rifles and the noted botanist Edgar Anderson suggested that maize may early have been present in Asia as well, on the basis of the fact that isolated hill peoples in northeastern India's Assam State raised very primitive varieties and claimed maize to have been one of their crops from earliest times. However, in 1951 the preeminent Harvard maize specialist Paul C. Mangelsdorf, with an anthropologist of the same university, Douglas L. Oliver, vigorously rebutted their cohorts' hypothesis of overseas transfer, partly on the basis of there seemingly being no actual physical or written record of pre-1492 maize in the Old World. Likewise, their colleague E. D. Merrill averred that maize had to have been introduced exclusively by the Portuguese and after AD 1500, and that the case against pre-Columbian maize was so open and shut that "additional field work would be a waste of time, effort, and money."[35]

Meanwhile, others entered the lists on the side of late pre-Columbian introduction of the American grain to Eurasia and West Africa, but because there was no archaeological evidence, their ecological, literary, and linguistic arguments did not convince most specialists.[36] Some alleged ancient maize pollen from Kashmir was forwarded, but others thought it to be questionable (the specimen has since been lost). Then the Indian plant geneticists D. Gupta and H. K. Jain found considerable genetic distance between primitive Himalayan varieties of maize and morphologically similar primitive varieties from the Americas, implying a long period of separation.[37] Still, in 1989 the German Argentinian botanist Heinz Brücher expressed continuing mainstream opinion when he wrote, "Maize was totally unknown outside of America before the arrival of Columbus. All reports [to the contrary are] . . . sheer phantasy."[38]

In the 1970s, while undertaking research for a chapter on pre-Columbian contacts, I came across a published photograph of a Hoysala-period (circa AD 1000–1346) Hindu temple carving in South India, depicting a female figure holding what appeared clearly to be an ear of maize.[39] At about the same time that I published this observation, a couple of other scholars, including the botanist Don B. Lawrence and the anthropologist Thomas J. Maxwell, also took note of such carvings from Karnataka State (Maxwell asserted that maize was

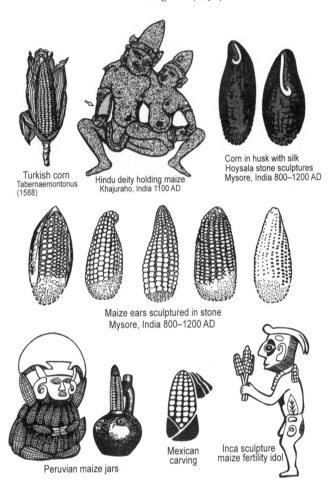

Turkish corn
Tabernaemontonus
(1588)

Hindu deity holding maize
Khajuraho, India 1100 AD

Corn in husk with silk
Hoysala stone sculptures
Mysore, India 800–1200 AD

Maize ears sculptured in stone
Mysore, India 800–1200 AD

Peruvian maize jars

Mexican
carving

Inca sculpture
maize fertility idol

Figure 27.1. Maize ears held by female figures sculpted in stone on Hindu
temples, Karnataka, India, late pre-Columbian Hoysala period, compared with
less realistic but accepted Nuclear American carvings representing maize. From
Gunnar Thompson, *American Discovery*, 1992, p. 240. With permission of the
New World Discovery Institute, marcopoloinseattle.com.

impossible for the era involved and suggested that the rather dissimilar noni
[*Morinda citrofolia*] fruit was what was depicted).[40] But it was Carl Johannessen who showed conclusively that these depictions were executed in late pre-
Columbian times and were, in many cases, actual portraits of individual ears
of maize, most huskless but some with the husk still on and the silks depicted
(figure 27.1). Johannessen noted that the varied carvings displayed over forty
anatomical traits that supported this finding; all maize breeders who had been
shown photographs of the carvings agreed.[41] Most of the sculptures are more re-

alistically maize-ear-like than are quite a number of depictions in pre-Columbian American art that are confidently identified as maize by the experts.

Subsequent investigation by Johannessen's student Gregory G. Howard and by others has shown that there are thousands of maize representations, at a minimum of 126 of these medieval temples, as well as at pre-Hoysala late Chalukyan and other Hindu and Jain temples dating back to as far as the first century AD. The superabundance of carved corn ears, almost all held in the hand with a characteristic *mudrā* (hand position), suggests a very high degree of importance of this plant in medieval Karnataka, at least iconographically and perhaps economically, which in turn implies some antiquity to allow time for such wide acceptance, especially in light of the conservatism of Indian temple art. Indian botanists and archaeologists now generally concur on the identifications of American food plants in Indian sculptures. One of these, Shakti M. Gupta, has written: "The common [current] belief is that maize originated in Mexico and came to India by the 11th–12th century. By the time these temples were constructed, maize would have been fairly common in India."[42]

Why, then, did it take so long for the corn carvings to be recognized as such by archaeologists and iconographers of India? The answer appears to be that it never occurred to them that anything represented in India in pre-Columbian times *could* be maize, and so the sculptures were never seen as such. As Louis Pasteur famously pointed out, in 1854, "Where observation is concerned, chance favours only the prepared mind."[43]

Interestingly, in 1935 the art historian Alfred De Prez had published a photograph of another Asian carving of maize, said to be on a Buddhist structure of circa AD 800 at Borobudur, to the west of Yogyakarta, Java—this was forty-three years before first publication of the Karnataka carvings as maize ears—but this revelation was apparently totally ignored. There are unmistakable maize and chili plants carved on a pre-tenth-century AD building in the Prambanan temple complex to the east of Yogyakarta.[44] In addition to the various sculptures, a potsherd of circa AD 1435 bearing an impression of a maize ear was reported from Maharashtra State, India, in 1998.[45]

Johannessen subsequently extended his work to China, where he examined a ceramic figurine of a bird from a tomb of the Han dynasty (221 BC–AD 220), whose hollow interior showed impressions of a maize-ear armature, and he has brought to light pre-Columbian use of contemporary Chinese names for the crop.[46] So far, however, actual archaeological specimens of maize have been reported from only two Old World sites, both in East Timor. A confidently identified cob and a cob fragment of ten-row maize came from horizon VII at one site, seemingly dating to just slightly BC. At a second site, the uppermost horizon (dated to about AD 1235–1420) yielded three good specimens of maize-cob parts. Despite these dates, Glover wrote of "*Annona* (custard apple/soursop) . . . and maize in the top levels; the last almost certainly a Portuguese introduction of the 16th century AD."[47] But even were there not a single such find, the other indications of maize's human-mediated presence in southern and eastern Asia

Figure 27.2. Pre-Columbian sculptures purportedly depicting pineapples in southern Asia: (1) Angkor, Cambodia, fifteenth century AD; (2) Karnataka state, India, fifteenth century AD; (3) Sanchi, India, first century AD; (4) Theodor de Bry's sixteenth-century illustration of the pineapple grown in India. From Gunnar Thompson, *American Discovery*, 1992, p. 23. With permission of the New World Discovery Institute, marcopoloinseattle.com.

seem wholly adequate, especially since *Zea mays* is one of the cultivated plants least capable of traveling and establishing itself without human help.

What has the broader world of science made of all this evidence? The authoritative *The Cultural History of Plants*, published in 2005, assures us, "Although many claims have been made for pre-Columbian dispersal of corn in the Old World, these are firmly contradicted by the complete absence of corn in the Old World archaeological record before 1492."[48]

The Pineapple: Turning Things Upside Down

The cultivated pineapple (*Ananas comosus*) is a domesticate of central South America and in pre-Columbian times was well distributed in most of the agricultural tropical New World, with the possible exception of the west coast of South America. Although capable of cross-fertilizing with other varieties and producing seed, no single variety can fertilize itself. Thus each uncrossed variety is seedless and requires human-aided propagation using suckers growing from the fruit's base, slips growing from the fruit's sides, or crowns (leafy tops). Because of a seeming lack of evidence and because seedless plants cannot establish themselves across oceans (or anywhere else) unaided, the pineapple was believed to be unknown outside of the Americas prior to 1492.[49]

Certain varieties of pineapple are naturalized (as well as cultivated) in Hawaii, and some Native Hawaiians considered them to have been present pre-Contact. In addition, many years ago ancient Assyrian relief carvings at Nineveh were interpreted as pineapples, and there is also a questionable, nineteenth-century report of ceramic pineapple models from an even older Egyptian tomb. In the 1950s, the Italian pomologist Domenico Casella published details of three Roman murals from a single house in Pompeii, plus of a separate mosaic, showing plants that he identified as pineapples. Unaware of the transoceanic-contacts controversy, Casella simply supposed that the Romans had obtained pineapples from tropical Africa or Asia (the first, an area in which there is no present evidence for them before 1492), and he gave no thought to the tropical Americas as a source.[50]

There is a multitude of depictions of somewhat pineapple-like young date palms in Pompeiian art, but unlike these, one of Casella's mural paintings shows the object in question sitting next to grapes and other fruits and with a few slim leaves sprouting from the item's side—as pineapples sometimes exhibit—plus what appears to be a tufted sucker growing from its base—common in pineapples. In the case of the mosaic, a date and a fig flank the object, and a rooster seems to have pecked the object, revealing a light-colored interior. Merrill accepted identification of these depictions as pineapples but proposed that they must, therefore, be the work of modern restorers[51]—a contention that Casella refuted.

No archaeological remains of actual plants have shown up so far, and the Pompeian identifications stood essentially alone for decades, until the late 1990s, when pineapples were reported as being "clearly depicted" in the Udayagiri cave temple (c. fifth century AD) in Madhya Pradesh and elsewhere in India (figure 27.2).[52] This identification fits well with the idea that Roman knowledge of the plant came from the Empire's well-documented activities in the South Asian subcontinent. South Asians, in turn, may have obtained the crop in tropical America.

Amaranths: Overseas Seeds

Distinct species of genus *Amaranthus* are found in each of the hemispheres, some wild, some cultivated. Grain amaranths were highly important food, ornamental, and ceremonial plants in pre-Columbian Mexico and elsewhere in the Americas. Records indicate that a plant carrying the present name for amaranth was used in China's Szechuan province in the tenth century AD. Likewise, amaranth is listed as a medicinal plant in pre-1492 Arab sources, which recognize seven varieties. However, it is not clear which species are implicated.

The plant geographer Jonathan D. Sauer, although generally cautious concerning possible transoceanic transfers, did note that both Mexican and Andean cultivated species of *Amaranthus* (Prince of Wales feather, *A. hypochondriacus*, and love-lies-bleeding, *A. caudatus*) occurred very widely in Asia and Africa but almost entirely among relatively simpler, marginal groups, not among more elaborate coastal cultures, and were deeply entrenched there, suggesting great age. He found preparation methods to be shared between the hemispheres, including popping and making balls of popped seeds with a syrup binder, as well as grinding and stirring into a drink or baking into small cakes. He viewed natural introduction of the plant to be impossible and considered pre-Columbian transfer likely but not definitive in the absence of archaeological evidence.[53]

The cause of Sauer's reservation appears now to have been, in part, removed.

In 1994, Indian archaeologists and paleoethnobotanists reported that at the Nahran site (circa 1300 BC to 350 AD) in India's Uttar Pradesh, five carbonized amaranth seeds, of the Andean *A. caudatus* and perhaps also of the Old World species *A. viridis*, had been excavated, along with seed of the New World weeds *Argemone Mexicana* (the Mexican prickly poppy) and *Amaranthus spinosis*, at 1060–1100 BC levels.[54]

Sunflower State

Sunflowers seem to have been domesticated in Mexico by 2700 BC. In his research on American plants depicted in Indian temple carvings, especially in Karnataka State, Carl Johannessen discovered what certainly appear to be depictions of sunflowers (*Helianthus annuus*). Although the blooms present fewer diagnostic anatomical traits than do maize ears, the anatomy does fit that of real sunflowers, and the carvings have solar associations in the temples.[55]

Sugar-Apple of My Eye

In addition to the pineapples mentioned above, Domenico Casella also identified certain depictions on Pompeian walls as showing fruits of the annona known as sweetsop or sugar apple (*Annona squamosa*, not a pome; called "custard apple" in South Asia). As with the pineapple, Casella concluded that the sweetsop must be of Old World origin rather than American as generally thought.[56] However, this option has not been accepted (the plant is common in American archaeology), and annona continues to be considered an American domesticate and so would have to have been imported to be present in ancient Italy or India.

Many years after Casella's announcement, Johannessen found, among the thirteenth-century temple carvings of South India as well as at tenth-century Aihole, depictions that he interpreted as fruits of the *Annona*, which is now a naturalized species in Maharashtra State. Shakti Gupta wrote that the sugar apple fruit is depicted in carvings on Hindu and Buddhist temples in Karnataka, Madhya Pradesh, Andhra Pradesh, Bengal, and other states. The earliest recorded image is from the mid-second century BC, at Bharhut, Madhya Pradesh, and the fruit is mentioned in the ancient epic *Rāmāyanam* as associated with Rama's wife Sita.[57] The fact that an archaeologist, General Alexander Cunningham, identified *Annona* in carvings on the Bharhut stupa during the nineteenth century shows how long acceptance of perceived anomalies can take (Cunningham's identification was affirmed in 1976 by the archaeobotanist R. V. Sitholey).

Even *more* recently, large carbonized pieces of sugar apple were excavated at circa AD 100–300 Sanghol in Punjab and in 1999 were identified by the Indian archaeobotanists A. K. Pokharia and K. S. Saraswat. Saraswat and Pokharia also identified seeds of *A. squamosa* from Raja-Nal-Ka-Tila, Uttar Pradesh, dating to about 700 BC. In 2008, Pokharia and others reported Neolithic sugar apple seed remains from Tokwa, Uttar Pradesh, dating to the third to second millennium BC.[58] Too, decades earlier, Ian Glover had reported *Annona* remains from the third millennium BC in East Timor. He later clarified that many *Annona* seeds had been recovered from the uppermost horizon, VII (?–2000 BP), at Lie Siri.[59] Thus the remarkably early existence of this plant in Asia seems established, yet this fact remains outside the ken of the very great majority of scholars.

I Say, Old Bean

On the basis of fairly slight circumstantial evidence, the pre-Columbian Old World presence of various American species of beans has long been argued. However, in 1986 Vishnu-Mittre, A. Sharma, and S. Chanchala reported actual specimens of three bean species from protohistoric India: the kidney bean (*Phaseolus vulgaris*), from second-millennium BC levels in Gujarat, Maharashstra, and Karnataka; and the lima bean (*P. lunatus*) and the phasey bean (*Macroptilum lathyroides*) at comparable levels in Maharashstra, as well as at about AD 100–300 in Punjab. In addition, Chen Wenhua has reported archaeological lima beans in China, from Zhejiang province, so we now have several Asian occurrences.[60]

Chili Today—and Yesterday

A common supposition is that before Columbus, chili peppers were unknown in the Old World. If so, it is puzzling that chilis (*Capsicum* spp.)—all of ultimate Mexican origin—are so embedded in Indian and Korean cooking, in several regional western and southwestern Chinese and Southeast Asian cuisines, in Turkey and Hungary (as paprika), and so forth. In fact, the Chinese character referring to the chili goes back to before Columbus. More definitive is the existence of clear depictions of chili plants in carvings on a pre-tenth-century AD temple at Prambanan, Java. Shakti Gupta found chili carvings in India as well; these were post-Columbian, but she noted that the chili pepper is mentioned in the *Shiva* and *Vāmana* puranas of circa sixth to eighth century AD.[61]

In the latter half of the fifteenth century, beginning before 1492, malaguetta peppers (chilis) were reported as an important export from sub-Saharan Africa to Europe, via North African traders. One writer of the period reported, "This pepper is called by us [the Portuguese] *de rabo* (long tailed)—because the stem on which it grows comes away with it—to distinguish it from that obtained from India."[62]

Agave: Taking a Leaf from America

The list of interhemispherically shared cultivated plants goes on and includes a number of nonfood species. The agave (*Agave* spp.) is a fibrous Middle American succulent of drier lands that has a number of uses. It grows both wild and planted and is now naturalized in the Mediterranean region. Very unexpectedly, traces of woven agave leaves saturated in pitch were found between the hull planks and the lead sheathing of the fourth-century BC Kyrenia ship, a small Rhodian-Greek Mediterranean wreck. These fibers were independently identified by experts at the US Department of Agriculture and at Kew Gardens, as well as by a third specialist, and other such finds are said to have been made.[63]

It is interesting to note that Shakti Gupta, who has published many of the carvings of American plants hiding in plain sight in India, is not a student—much less a proponent—of transoceanic contacts but has assumed that all of the crop species she has identified as pre-Columbian—including American maize, pineapple, annona, chili pepper, cashew, split-leaf philodendron, and naga lingam—must be indigenous to India rather than being imports from the New World, pre-Columbian or otherwise. But her Indian archaeobotanical colleagues A. K. Pokharia and K. S. Saraswat, in writing about the various archaeological discoveries in India, asserted, "The astounding finds of *American* beans, maize, Mexican-poppy and custard apple in India during pre-Columbian times, may therefore, be viewed as a reality" (emphasis added).[64]

The list of additional American food-crop plants for which there has, for some time, been at least a bit of evidence for pre-Columbian interhemispheric transfer is quite long. These include the tomato, squashes, the yam bean, and the cashew. Truly, the notion of the cultivated food plants domesticated in the Americas all being confined to the Western Hemisphere before 1492 has been irretrievably shattered. The same can be said, if less emphatically, for transfers in the opposite direction, as the following chapter explores.

28

Cultivated Plants

Old World Cropping Up in the New

The plant must spring again from its seed.
—Percy Bysshe Shelly, 1821

As seen in the previous chapter, an impressive number of New World species of cultivated plants were taken to the Old World before the Great Age of Discovery. We now look at the evidence for such exchange in the reciprocal direction and shall find, perhaps surprisingly, that fewer species are involved.

Additional Domesticated Plant Species in the "Wrong" Hemisphere

Planting Plantains

The cultivated plantain is a seedless, starchy, nonsweet vegetable-banana hybrid (*Musa x paradisiaca*) and apparently was anciently domesticated in the Assam-Burma-Thailand area of Asia. It is propagated via cuttings. The plantain is a strong candidate for pre-Columbian carriage to the Americas.

Most scholars have taken the position that genus *Musa*—plantains and bananas—were unknown in the New World before Columbus. Based on a statement of the Spanish Colonial chronicler Gonzalo Fernández de Oviedo y Valdés, a Spanish priest is supposed to have been the first to introduce the plantain to the Americas, from the Canary Islands in 1516. However, as Carl Sauer early pointed out, followed by others—especially, by the American cultural geographer/anthropologist William J. Smole and the Australian historian Robert Langdon—strong circumstantial evidence exists for the plant's New World antiquity.[1] These include a plethora of native names for plantains, at least two of which appear to have been widely adopted into American Spanish and Portuguese, respectively (Arawakan *plátano* and Tupian *pacova*). Further, there are many sixteenth-century reports of the fruit's indigenous use, often intensive, from Mexico's Jalisco to Brazil, too early for post-1516 diffusion plausibly to account for the existence of several early noted varieties, especially in light of the plant's clonal nature, slow maturation, and difficulty of transporting and propagating. Its becoming thoroughly integrated into native horticulture on Cuba and Hispaniola as well as in Central America in seven or eight years' time—as the early reports would require—would be the envy of modern agricultural-aid workers and was probably a cultural, physical, and biological impossibility.

Too, the plantain is a ritually embedded staple among certain isolated groups in Venezuela, Ecuador, and northern Brazil that are extremely hostile to outside influences, including foodstuffs. In fact, the plant is generally associated primarily with American Indian, not Euro-American, subsistence agriculture and especially with remote, marginal peoples. It even appears to be in some sense naturalized in places in northwest South America. These facts imply that plantain-based horticulture preceded other types of farming such as that stressing bitter manioc, which characterize less remote tropical American societies.

Nevertheless, direct archaeological evidence of pre-Columbian plantain is equivocal, as a result of incomplete documentation and possible confusion concerning the identification of plant remains.[2] If the plantain is, indeed, pre-1492 in tropical America, its ancient introduction seems most likely to be accounted for by pre-Christian Era migrations from Malaysia that I have hypothesized, although other southern Asian possibilities certainly exist.[3] Africa is also a potential source, since *Musa* phytoliths cultivated circa 500 BC have been found in Cameroon, suggesting much earlier Indonesian influence in West Africa than previously proposed. Dried plantain suckers can be conserved in viable condition for many months and then be replanted, so transoceanic transport of carefully protected cuttings is far from inconceivable.

World Traveler: The Bottle Gourd

Despite the general rule that cultivated plants do not cross oceans without being carried by humans, two sorts of plants shared by the two hemispheres since great antiquity, the bottle gourd and the New World cottons, plus a possible third of uncertain pre-Columbian age in America, the coconut, are somewhat more ambiguous in this regard.

The domesticated bottle gourd vine produces fruits that have a variety of nonfood uses. Gourds are buoyant, and they resist saltwater. Whereas the species, almost certainly of African origin, is not a strand plant, if one of its large, hollow, spherical, seed-filled fruits fell into a river, that fruit could be carried to the sea and be transported by ocean currents to far, far shores. The question is, did these plants survive marine organisms and manage to establish themselves on the other sides of the oceans, or at least to be tossed up on beaches there, then to be picked up and taken into local cultivation?

In the 1950s, Thomas W. Whitaker and George F. Carter performed tests that indicated that gourds not only float but also that the fruits can survive in salt water for 347 days or more with no decrease in seed viability, and that the seeds themselves remain able to germinate after long exposure to salt water.[4] Although this experiment did not test for conditions in tropical waters, the potential does seem to exist for transoceanic drift carriage of viable seed. Still, according to Whitaker, "the initiation of bottle gourd cultivation from this source implies a sophisticated agriculture of reasonably high level which probably did not exist at the time the first bottle gourds were reported from the Americas."[5] Whitaker, a US Department of Agriculture botanist, thought that fruits found on the shore and then thrown onto a kitchen midden might result in establishment of *Lagenaria*, allowing later, independent domestication. However, the human-utilized gourd seems not to occur in the wild and requires human intervention for its existence. Consequently, unless someone ashore picked up an in-drifted gourd, recognized its potential utility, extracted the seeds, carried them inland, planted them, and cared for the plants, the species would not have become established no matter how often fruits were washed up on the beach and tossed onto a midden.

The bottle gourd is one of the earliest known cultivated plants in Africa, Asia, and the Americas. In northern Thailand, gourds from 10,000 to 6000 BC come from Spirit Cave, a site containing archaeological remains. Dates as early as 13,000–10,000 BC have been reported from Peru's Ayacucho region, and other early Peruvian sites have also yielded gourd remains.[6] The plant is widely attested in South America by 6000 BC. In Mexico, the earliest dates so far identified are from about 8000–6000 BC, from the state of Oaxaca. If this distribution implies human carriage, then very early long-distance human movements by boat are also implied.

One thought is that ancient fisherfolk used the gourds as net floats. However, skeptics feel that the plant's American dates are far too early to be explicable by transoceanic human carriage, and they continue to adhere to Whitaker's hypothesis of early natural dispersal and later independent domestication(s). Among various problems with this concept is the fact that the rind of the only known wild-gourd species, from Zimbabwe (which is *not* the domestic gourd's ancestor but a cousin) is too delicate to make transoceanic drift at all plausible—especially in light of the fact that the utilitarian species did not establish itself in America before the end of the Pleistocene epoch and then only as a cultigen.

On the basis of fruit morphology and of geographical proximity, it was long confidently assumed that American gourds had arrived directly from Africa. However, genetic work published in 2005 indicated that American calabashes were more closely related to an Asian (*L. siceraria asiatica*) rather than to an African (*L. siceraria siceraria*) variety. Thus they would have to have survived drifting across the whole Pacific rather than via the much narrower Atlantic if flotation is how they reached the Americas; viability after all that distance and time is quite questionable. The authors suggested that coastwise human carriage by boat-possessing early Asian migrants could account for the early New World dates.[7]

The British ethnobotanist Andrew Clarke speculated that the aforementioned DNA evidence may be faulty. One may also take note of the American botanist Charles B. Heiser Jr.'s statement that elongate-fruited gourds of highland New Guinea, widely worn on that island as penis sheaths, are taxonomically more akin to those of Africa and the Americas than they are to the Asian subspecies. Too, in both southwestern and east-central Africa and in indigenous Venezuela, elongate gourds are used as phallocrypts. However, pre-Columbian timing for human transfer of the elongate-fruited variety and its use is only inferable, not demonstrable at this time.[8]

These inconsistencies seem now to have been resolved by use of higher-resolution genetic techniques, which show that ancient American gourds are, after all, affiliated with the African, not the Asian variety. The level of genetic diversity among American specimens implies several separate arrivals, whether naturally drifted or human mediated.[9]

Because the bottle gourd appears to have been absent in pre-Contact Western Polynesia, the ethnobotanists Arthur W. Whistler and Andrew Clarke and the archaeologist Roger Green concluded that it had reached Eastern Polynesia, where it *was* present before European arrival, from South America.[10]

Some Kind of a Nut: Can the Coconut Cross Oceans?

The coconut (*Cocos nucifera*) is almost certainly a native of the Indo-Pacific littoral and is documented for South Asia as early as the time of Christ. *Cocos* pollen has been dated at circa 5800 BC in the Mariana Islands. The tree grows along tropical shorelines, and in the wild its fruits disperse largely by flotation. Nevertheless, because of destructive organisms and other barriers it has been unsuccessful in establishing itself along a number of tropical strands, including those of the Moluccas, Australia, and the Galápagos Islands, onto which nuts wash up.[11] In fact, in most areas of its present range domesticated coconut seedlings require planting, watering, and other human care. Yet on the basis of early Spanish Colonial mentions (beginning in about 1514, for Panama), the cultivated coconut palm appears clearly to have been pre-Columbian on the Pacific (but not Atlantic) shore of lower Central America.[12] Even Merrill conceded that the species was pre-1492 in the New World.[13]

Archaeologically, there are a few, mostly nineteenth-century New World reports, all of which are equivocal. Thor Heyerdahl referred to mentions of coconut leaves and fiber from pre-Columbian Peruvian graves as well as to an effigy jar apparently depicting a coconut, but the leaves may have been misidentified and Heyerdahl's source provides no picture of the pot.[14] The coconut has also been reported archaeologically from Urías, Guatemala (circa AD 700), and from Copán, Honduras (circa AD 400), but no details have been offered.[15]

The North and South Equatorial Currents in the Pacific flow away from the Americas, not toward them. It is unlikely that natural drift dispersal from Oceania via the east-flowing Equatorial Countercurrent can account for the establishment of the coconut on parts of the Pacific coast of tropical America by the time of the Spanish conquest. Heyerdahl found that about halfway along the distance between Peru and Polynesia, nuts stored between his raft's logs had been killed by saltwater and by microorganisms entering through the eyes,[16] and he mentioned a 1941 test off Hawaii in which entering bacteria ended viability after four to six weeks.[17] In an independent 116-day test of thirty-six-plus wild-type nuts, the longest period of viability in saltwater obtained was 110 days. In another, 214-day test of one hundred domestic-type nuts, seventy-four days was the maximum for viability.[18] Computer simulations were undertaken to test whether the countercurrent would take coconuts from Polynesia to Panama. When wind was included as a factor, after 245 days—far surpassing proven length of maximum viability—no nuts had reached mainland America. The authors, R. Gerard Ward and Muriel Brookfield, concluded, "it is extremely unlikely that coconuts could have crossed the central Pacific . . . as unaided voyagers while remaining viable."[19]

In addition to the hazards of natural predators such as crabs and rats, as well as to coastal barriers such as mangrove swamps, the eastern Pacific itself has been a major impediment to natural plant dispersal, even from east to west, the direction of the main tropical currents, and there is no indication of any wild terrestrial vascular plant species' being carried eastward from the Pacific islands to the Americas by the Equatorial Countercurrent.[20] In any case, unlike Oceanian ones, contemporary Central American coconut palms are genetically diverse, suggesting multiple introductions of nuts as a result of multiple contacts.[21]

Although the evidence remains very slightly equivocal, then, it is far more likely that humans introduced the coconut to the Western Hemisphere from Asia than it is that natural dispersal did. The sweet potato's presence in Polynesia and the chicken's in Chile show that humans crossed the gap between Oceania and South America, rendering the conundrum of the pre-Columbian coconut less impenetrable—although the oldest published (if equivocal) American archaeological dates for the plant are somewhat early for Polynesian arrival and—especially in light of their genetic diversity—may reflect previous Malaysian and/or other Southeast Asian inputs.[22]

Cottoning to Natural Crossings

A brief word about cultivated cotton (*Gossypium* spp.) is needed. After sweet potato, cotton has, historically, been the cultivated plant most often forwarded in arguments favoring early transoceanic contacts.[23]

Distinct wild cotton species are native to the frost-free zones of both hemispheres. The earliest Old World archaeological appearance of domesticated cotton is from the fourth millennium BC in the Indus Valley region of South Asia, although the ancestral plant, *G. herbaceum*, appears to be of earlier, African origin.

There are also two prominent ancient species of New World cultivated cottons, *G. hirsutum* of Middle America and *G. barbadense* of northwestern South America. In 1947, the plant geneticists Joseph Hutchison, R. A. Silow, and Stanley J. Stephens made known a surprising discovery. Their cytogenetic studies had revealed that each of the two New World domesticated cottons was a tetraploid, that is, a hybrid carrying four sets of chromosomes rather than the usual two—two sets from each of two ancestral species, one a New World wild cotton and the other an African cotton (which proved to be *G. herbaceum* v. *africanum*). In other words, each of the two domesticated New World cotton species represents a cross between one or more American wild species and an African one—each has one ancestor from one of the hemispheres and one from the opposite hemisphere.[24] This discovery was a major one in terms of stimulating talk of pre-Columbian transoceanic voyages, especially on the part of George Carter, while E. D. Merrill clung to the notion that the hybridizations had taken place after AD 1500 and were of Portuguese instigation (later, thoroughly disproved by archaeobotanical studies).

Without going into details here, we may—only slightly provisionally—now retire this particular candidate for human transoceanic carriage. Contemporary molecular-genetic research in combination with the study of mechanisms of dispersal of species of the genus *Gossypium* have led to the conclusion that the hybridization took place hundreds of thousands of years ago, well before the emergence of modern humans, much less of their being farmers and capable of making ocean crossings, and that natural dispersal of tiny cottonseeds—by bird and by water—is entirely plausible.[25]

In their amazing 2013 compilation, Carl Johannessen and John L. Sorenson listed *ninety-eight* cultivated and wild plants and twenty-five other organisms for which they considered the evidence to be decisive for pre-Columbian transoceanic transfer (including from America to Polynesia), embracing three species of amaranth, cashew, pineapple, three species of annona, peanut, three species of beans, three species of chili pepper, papaya, ceiba, quinoa, coconut, naga lingam, three species of squash, coca, sunflower, sweet potato, bottle gourd, mango, *Monstrera deliciosa*, two species of plantain/banana, tobacco, *Polygonum acuminatum*, soapberry, two species of bulrush, and maize. They list over sixty additional species as *possible* pre-1492 interhemispheric sharings.[26] Thus, in this and the previous and succeeding chapters we have merely skimmed the surface of the evidence for human-aided pre-Colonial transoceanic transfer of organisms.

29

Tobacco, Coca, and Cannabis

The Mummies Speak, but the Scientists Stand Mute

O what may man within him hide . . . !
—William Shakespeare, *Measure for Measure*, 3. 2. 271–72

In the previous two chapters, we surveyed cultivated plant species whose pre-Columbian presences in both hemispheres evidence transoceanic contacts. This chapter examines the particularly intriguing cases of three psychoactive drug plants. These are tobacco, coca, and cannabis.[1]

Nicotiana is a genus whose numerous wild species are native to the Western Hemisphere (subgenera *Rustica*, *Tabacum*, and *Petunioides*) and to Australia, New Caledonia (presumably reflecting a pre-continental-drift unity of these land masses), Tonga, and the Marquesas Islands (subgenus *Petunioides*). Two domesticated species, *Nicotiana rustica* and *N. tabacum*, ultimately came into being in the Americas, and cultivated tobacco is known archaeologically from North and Middle America. Cultivated and some semicultivated tobaccos have seed pods that have lost the ability to open on their own, resulting in the plant's being dependent on people for propagation and survival,[2] and, therefore, for their geographic spread. All domesticated and most wild tobaccos contain the psychotropic alkaloid nicotine.

All tobacco species have generally been thought to have been confined to the Western Hemisphere and to Australia and the Pacific islands until 1492 or after. However, certain species of wild American tobaccos are now naturalized in Taiwan, Timor, Bengal, and elsewhere, and some observers have suggested a pre-Columbian presence in Asia, perhaps owing to transport of tobacco's tiny seeds by birds.

Traditions imply pre-Columbian chewing/medicinal use of tobacco in Java, Malaya, and Nias, and, possibly, cigar smoking in New Guinea. In addition, there are indications of pre-Columbian tobacco use in India, for medicinal purposes, perfume making, and smoking. The present Hindi word for tobacco, *tambak(u)*, is also found in Sanskrit, Persian, and Arabic, and (with variations such as *tanbak[u]*, *tamak*, and *tavak*) in literature at least as far back as AD 200–

700.[3] All this evidence is suggestive but falls well short of absolute proof, and there is no mention of the plant in known ancient Egyptian texts.

As for a second, archaeologically well-known South American sacred and indulgent domesticated drug plant, coca (*Erythroxylum coca* and *E. novogranatense*), no one has so far proposed that it ever dispersed by natural means from its homeland on the eastern slope of the Andes to the Old World; it did not even diffuse beyond Honduras in tropical Middle America, either naturally or through human introduction. Presumably, its complicated cultivation and specialized environmental requirements inhibited the species' spread.

Cover-Up: Enwrapping a Defunct Pharaoh's Secret

The evidentiary picture regarding possible pre-Columbian transfer of tobacco changed dramatically beginning in 1976, when the government of Egypt asked scientists in France to study and conserve the second-millennium BC mummy of Pharaoh Ramesses II ("the Great"). The French team was surprised to discover that the deceased potentate's thoracic cavity had been packed with shredded tobacco leaves, of an undetermined species, and that the mummy's wrappings contained nicotine as well as an imago of an adult supposedly American dried-tobacco-eating cigarette beetle (*Lasioderma serricorne*; see also chapter 26). In 1931 this same insect species, it turned out, had also been reported in considerable numbers from fourteenth-century BC Pharaoh Tutankhamun's tomb—the inner spaces of which had been sealed until 1922. Most of the beetle specimens were inextricably embedded in the once-liquid contents of alabaster jars in the anteroom and seemed clearly contemporary with the entombment. The beetle has now also been reported from the Late Bronze Age Minoan town of Akrotiri on the Greek island of Thera and identified at several additional ancient Egyptian sites. These early Eastern Hemisphere archaeological occurrences and lack of any in America have caused some to conclude that the insect is of Old World, not American, origin as previously supposed, despite its closest relatives being New World species and its having evolved a unique tolerance for nicotine.[4]

The original June 8, 1977, press release by Agence France-Presse stated unequivocally, "The ancient Egyptians had tobacco . . . [and] use[d] it to stuff mummies." An early, semipopular report in the French magazine *Archéologia* by one of the researchers, Lionel Balout, cited the parasitic beetle as well as the presence of tobacco in the lowest parts of Ramses's thoracic cavity plus the extreme adherence of leaf fragments to the resins of mummification, and stressed the likelihood that the tobacco was original to the mummy.[5] At this point the findings were suddenly suppressed. The Egyptians refused to allow carbon-14 dating of the tobacco and did not permit proposed examination of other mummies from the same site for possible tobacco, and the scientific reports published drew no geographical conclusions. The report of Michèle Lescot, the researcher who first described the tobacco, was truncated before publication.[6] The specimen is said to have since disappeared.[7]

For a long time, little more was heard of these discoveries in scholarly circles. Some workers who *had* learned about the mummy's stuffing suggested that the tobacco had been introduced into Ramesses's cadaver in modern times. A few, however, accepted the tobacco as being part of the original embalming material (functioning as an insecticide and antiputrifactant), but, like the French researchers, they cautiously drew no geographical inferences from that acceptance.

Finally, in 2001 two skeptics, the archaeologist P. C. Buckland and the paleoecologist Eva Panagiotakopulu, undertook a more extensive effort to lay to rest the overseas-origin hypothesis for Ramses's tobacco. Although acknowledging that there was no recorded curational history to the effect, they concluded that late nineteenth/early twentieth-century packing of tobacco into the mummy, as an insect deterrent, was much more likely than was ancient use for the same purpose. They did not speak to the seeming physical impossibility of postmummification insertion but *were* influenced by the simultaneous presence, in the mummy, of considerable pollen from some composite, observing that beginning in 1828 the ground flowers of two composite species (but not necessarily those represented in Ramsses) came to be exported from Dalmatia and the Caucasus as insecticides. Still, other composites were present in ancient Egypt and could have been used in mummification.

The Cocaine Mummies: Making the Scientists Dance

Buckland and Panagiotakopulu did not address findings developed during the early 1990s by a team of German forensic pathologists led by Bulgaria-born Svetlana Balabanova of the Institute of Forensic Medicine, University of Ulm, Austria. Balabanova's team analyzed samples from nine other Egyptian mummies, from the Munich Egyptian Museum, of ages ranging from 1070 BC to AD 395, and, in a 1992 issue of the prestigious journal *Naturwissenschaften* reported residues and metabolized products of nicotine in the hair, bone, and soft tissues of eight of them, and of cocaine—as well as the alkaloid delta-9-tetrahydrocannabinol (THC)—in all of them. The concentrations were reminiscent of those in German drug addicts.[8] Although THC derives from the Old World genus *Cannabis*, nicotine comes, of course, notably from tobacco. As far as was known to most scholars, the native tobaccos nearest to Egypt grew wild in Australia and certain Pacific islands, as mentioned above, and cocas are South American wet-tropical-forest species. Coca relatives known from South Africa, Madagascar, Mauritius, Sri Lanka, and India do not contain the relevant alkaloid, and in any case are distant from Egypt. Other Old World species of plants are not known to contain cocaine.

These startling findings produced a negative reaction in academia. A number of scientists averred that if tobacco and coca were indigenous to America (they ignored the Pacific occurrences), these plants could not have been anciently present in Egypt since there was no contact between Egypt and the New World during the period from which the mummies dated. The 1997 television special *Curse of the Cocaine Mummies* did draw popular attention to the matter. On camera, Egyptologists pointed out that there were no ancient Egyptian records of trade in tobacco or coca, or any known depictions in Egyptian art. The Oxford Egyptologist John Baines pronounced, "The idea that the Egyptians were traveling to America is, overall, absurd. I don't know of anyone who is professionally employed as an Egyptologist, anthropologist, or archaeologist who seriously believes in any of these possibilities." The Natural History Museum of London's solanaceous-plant taxonomist Sandra Knapp added, "It is very unlikely that tobacco has an alternate history, because I think we would have heard about it. Drugs like tobacco rarely disappear or are kept secret for long."

Meanwhile, a member of the original Austro-German research team reported more fully on tests of one mummy of circa 950 BC, finding nicotine and its metabolite cotinine, which showed that this was not a matter of postmortem contamination from insecticides or technicians' tobacco smoke, as had been suggested by several commentators; rather, it signaled in vivo ingestion, also supported by the alkaloid's being concentrated in the cadaver's stomach, intestines, and liver rather than in surface tissues.[9] An Oklahoma pathologist, Larry W. Cartmell, tested additional mummies. He found no cocaine, but about three-quarters of his samples did show nicotine, as well as cotinine.[10]

According to Bob Brier's 1998 *The Encyclopedia of Mummies*, which epitomized the opinion of the fields,

> At first it was believed that the traces of the drugs were the result of contamination—perhaps the nineteenth-century Egyptologists who first examined the mummies had been smoking and had dropped ash onto them, for example. . . .
>
> One extreme view, held by only a few archaeologists, is that the ancient Egyptians obtained cocaine and tobacco from the Americas via a previously unknown trade route. The more conservative and widely accepted belief is that other plants that were known to the Egyptians and that contain traces of cocaine and nicotine (for example, belladonna, henbane, and mandrake) were the source.[11]

However, none of these—or other—plants present in ancient Egypt or within Egypt's accepted geographical orbit in fact contains enough nicotine (or *any* cocaine) to account for the quantities found in the cadavers.

Other experts on mummies, wedded to the notion that tobacco and coca came from the New World only after Columbus, continued to insist that the mummies had been contaminated by nineteenth-century smokers or, astonishingly, that the original chemicals used in mummification had "broken down" and that their products could be mistaken for the residues of nicotine, THC, and cocaine—a chemical impossibility.

No evidence whatsoever was adduced for these suppositions, and yet they were widely endorsed. In one of the most recent discussions of the issue, it was proposed that the nicotine in the Munich mummies derived from unrecorded use of a mixture of tobacco and water applied in the nineteenth century to control insect infestations. It was also suggested that the presence of cocaine derived from the personal use of that drug by nineteenth-century archaeologists and conservators in Egypt and in Europe—at a time when taking cocaine was entirely legal. This conclusion was reached despite the fact that the presence of the drugs in the hair of the naturally mummified Egyptians showed that utilization was antemortem, since it requires about a month for the substances to be transferred to the hair of the user.

Once again, since it was hardly conceivable to these commentators that American tobacco and coca could have reached ancient Egypt, they concluded, despite zero documentation, that contamination was the only reasonable hypothesis.

Most observers were unaware that in 1975 it had been announced that a previously unrecognized wild species of tobacco, *N. africana, does* occur in Africa, though at the other end of the continent, in central Namibia. This plant appears to be most closely related to the wild southwestern Pacific species *N. fragrans* and to the wild South American species *N. noctiflora* and crosses readily with domesticated *N. tabacum*. It also turns out that this species is completely irrelevant to the Egyptian data, because not only is it from far away, it also contains almost no nicotine.

The authoritative 1997 compendium *Codex of Ancient Egyptian Plant Remains* includes only two lines under the heading "*Nicotiana*": "Nicotiana: Not [domesticated] 'tobacco' (*N. tabacum* L), but a wild *Nicotiana* like *N. plumbaginifolia* Viv. or *N. glauca* R. C. Grah., both species present in the Nile valley today, the latter common."[12] From this, one might infer that the mummifiers of Ramses utilized tobacco that was growing wild in the Egypt of their time. Nothing is said in the *Codex* about the fact that these wild species are native to South America or about when and how they might have reached the Nile Valley. (Both cultivated and wild tobaccos *were* reported there as long ago as 1762. Another historical source mentions tobacco in Egypt no later than 1517.[13])

It is also the case that the "cocaine tree" (*E. coca*) seems today to be a naturalized species in the rain forests of Xishuangbanna, Yunnan, where that Chinese province meets the borders of Burma and Laos and where coca is a traditional medicinal plant, although since what date is unknown. Perhaps Southeast Asia could have been the immediate source for Egyptian coca (and, possibly, of tobacco as well), although that would simply move the area of transoceanic exchange to a point farther eastward. (Since coca seeds die of desiccation after two postharvest weeks,[14] very special care would have been needed to transfer the species across the ocean.)

Another, also entirely speculative, scenario has been proposed: that plants containing the alkaloids in question once existed in Egypt but that they were collected into extinction or were extirpated by some imported malady. And then, one may mention a final explanation forwarded to account for the mummies' drug residues: that in response to the European mania for displaying mummies in nineteenth-century museums and private cabinets of curiosities, unscrupulous Egyptians stole corpses of Cairo drug addicts and created fake ancient mummies from them, for sale to unsuspecting foreigners. This economic explanation is hardly economical, however, requiring a large number of superbly deceptive fake mummies whose tissues contained all three drugs, plus the gullibility of both early and contemporary museum curators, none of whom appears so far to have agreed that any mummy assayed was anything but genuine.

Another Balabanova-led team has since tested a considerable number of additional ancient and medieval artificially and naturally mummified cadavers as well as numerous skeletons. Nicotine and its metabolite cotinine were found to occur in 115 of 134 naturally mummified bodies of Christians from AD 600–1000 Sayala in Egyptian Nubia; in one body from a Late Roman cemetery in Austria (AD 300–400); in 34 percent of the skeletons from an Austrian burial site of AD 800–1000 (particularly among infants); from numerous Alemannic burials of fifth- to seventh-century AD Germany; and from a prehistoric south Chinese skeleton, although mostly in lesser concentrations than in the artificially mummified corpses first studied. Additionally, cocaine was found in fifty-six of seventy-one naturally mummified bodies from Sayala (but from nowhere outside of Egypt), dating from between AD 600 and 1100; concentrations were highest in young children, with a lesser peak among twenty-three- to twenty-nine-year-olds.[15] That these nicotine and cocaine residues cannot have resulted from the so-called chemical cocktail of mummification is obvious, since these more recently tested bodies had not been artificially mummified. Laboratory and storage protocols essentially precluded postexcavation contamination.

With respect to true mummies, Balabanova concluded, "The results suggest that nicotiana plants were known and used since antiquity [in the Old World]. The plants have antiputrifactive and repulsive effects on insects and bacteria. Probably therefore, they were used at the embalming procedure. The nicotiana also [was likely used] ante mortem as [a] stimulant and as a 'domestical remedy' too, but not as a strong medicinal agent. . . . Cocaine . . . use may be related to the cocaine['s] effects as [a] tranquilizer and/or as [a] stimulant."[16]

According to the team that studied the Alemannic occurrences, "Currently, the general conclusion seems to be acceptable that Columbus in fact only brought with him the idea of cigar and pipe smoking to Europe, whereas Nicotiana and nicotine had long been known and used for various purposes and in various other applications."[17]

Interestingly, significant residues of nicotine and its metabolite cotinine were also identified in five of eight naturally preserved cadavers from Guangxi province in southern China, dating to some 3750 BC, thus, significantly earlier than the oldest Egyptian mummies tested. The cotinine indicated antemortem use of the source of the alkaloid, not external contamination. Nicotiana is known to have been used medicinally in China during at least the last few centuries.[18]

Balabanova and colleagues in 1997 found that among these various populations, nicotine concentrations were highest in artificially mummified Egyptians but that these mummies averaged a cotinine/nicotine ratio of only 3.4 percent; in other words, in most cases the nicotine had not been metabolized to any great degree. The authors concluded that *Nicotiana* had been employed in the mummification process, nicotine then spreading into the tissue, with a small percentage of the alkaloid oxidizing to cotinine. Naturally mummified bodies from Egypt, in contrast, displayed a cotinine:nicotine ratio of 40.3 percent, a proportion inconsistent not only with mummification but also with smoking or regular indulgent consumption, but, rather, consistent with medicinal ingestion.

The almost inescapable implication of all this is that somehow the ancient and early medieval Egyptian elite had access to drug plants native to South America. Natural carriage of these plants to Egypt (or Asia) by birds is so unlikely as to be dismissible. In any event, the climate would have been unsuitable for the growing of coca. Whether these plants would, then, have been harvested in the Americas and imported as goods (perhaps with their fellow-traveling parasitic beetles), or have intentionally been introduced in the form of seed (at least, in the case of tobacco) and become established at some tropical site accessible to Egypt (for example, in southeastern Asia via Indian Ocean trade) or, at least for *Nicotiana*, in the Nile Valley itself, is not yet clear.

Certainly, additional research on the topic should be helpful. Do mummies other than that of Ramsses II contain tobacco leaves? Can nicotine/cotinine or TCH undergo chemical change in mummies to become cocaine? Is there any pollen or phytolith evidence of pre-Columbian tobacco or coca in the Eastern Hemisphere? For the present, the evidence and arguments that Balabanova and colleagues have presented must stand.

Hashish High in Peru?

Cannabis sativa ssp. *Indica*, which is a native of western Asia, carries THC and other cannabinoids. The plant (commonly called marijuana), which has long been popular in the Middle East for its psychoactive effects, is generally assumed to have been a post-Columbian introduction to the milder-climate parts of the New World. However, in 1994 the Austrian researchers mentioned above reported finding THC (along with cocaine and nicotine) in the tissues, teeth, and hair of ancient naturally mummified bodies from both the North Coast and the South Coast of Peru—in thirty-nine of the sixty cadavers tested and with a corporal distribution indicating antemortem use. These mummies ranged in date from about AD 115 to AD 1500, pointing to many centuries of cannabis use.[19] Thus on the face of things it would appear that pre-Columbian drug trafficking—or at least, exchange of drug-plant materials—between the Old and New Worlds was a two-way street (or, rather, seaway).

We have clear evidence of ancient Egyptians' importing living plants by sea. The reliefs at Queen Hatshepsut's temple at Deir el-Bahari (fourteenth century

BC) that depict an expedition to Punt show a ship loaded with thirty-one potted myrrh trees (see figure 20.3).

On the Pre-Columbian Exchange

Although a great deal of the information concerning crops and animals in this and the two preceding chapters has come to the fore only relatively recently, a fair amount of it has been available for some time, decades, in certain cases. Acceptance has been held up by certain specialists' stout resistance, especially on the part of the authoritarian botanist Merrill in the 1950s, who attributed most South American domesticates and weeds now found in Southeast Asia to Portuguese voyages to Goa in India via Brazil's Bahia and the Cape of Good Hope, the route pioneered in 1500 by Pedro Álvares Cabral. This, declared Merrill, involved "thousands of ships" and represented the "perfect set-up for transmission of Brazil[ian] economic plants and weeds to the Orient."[20] But not only is it the case that pre-1500 Asiatic presence can now be demonstrated for a surprising number of these plants, Merrill was badly misinformed about the frequency of use of the Bahia-Goa route. According to the eminent geographer Peter Haggett, "The evidence of the 16th century annals suggest[s] that almost all Portuguese ships by-passed Brazil." Records support only two Portuguese vessels approaching that country in the 1510s and only two stopping at Bahia during the following decade, with none doing so again until 1556; "Since only 20 ships appear to have used the Bahia–Goa route between 1500 and 1730 it is difficult to ascribe to it the important role in American plant introduction proposed by Merrill."[21]

Nevertheless, statements like the following, which comes from a 1994 Cambridge University Press textbook on South American archaeology, continue to characterize the dominant thinking in the field: "Manioc, sweet potatoes, and yams are staple tropical crops around the world; chocolate, peanuts, and tobacco (along with pineapples) are among the most important cash crops of many countries. Yet all of these crops [as well as peppers and tomatoes] can be shown to have been introduced to non-American countries in the terminal fifteenth century or later. None is a precolumbian traveler. . . . The lack of any evidence of precolumbian exchange anywhere is telling."[22] Even in 2013, we heard from a very prominent archaeologist of human migrations: "the bottom line remains—no crops or domesticated animals were transferred between the Asian mainland and the Americas in prehistory, or indeed the other way, apart from dogs."[23]

A cornerstone of the inventionist view when it comes to agriculture is the concept that farming itself arose independently in at least three centers around the world and perhaps in more than three. Most people in the field would agree. However, a number of authorities, including Carl Sauer and George Carter, have entertained the notion of a unitary origin. Here are the thoughts of the great American historian of mediaeval European technology Lynn White Jr., who in

1976 rejected the possibility that agriculture emerged independently in separate centers, on the most basic of grounds:

> All three of the major centers of domestication [Southeast Asia, Southwest Asia, and Nuclear America] began to tame and exploit animals and plants within the time span of roughly 8,000 to 3,000 B.C. [later, pushed a few millennia farther back in time]: one percent of the minimal estimate of human existence. The mathematics of chance thus rules out independent invention of domestication in three discrete centers. We are left with the assumption of a single invention that—despite great distances and barriers—diffused the *idea* of domestication even though in the early stages not many domesticates got from one center to another.[24]

White's views are shared by very few other scholars but seem cogent to me.

Old World Faces in New World Places

A man finds room in the few square inches of his face for the traits of all his ancestors.

—Ralph Waldo Emerson, 1860

Genes carry the chemical codes that control an organism's basic nature, development, and functioning. Human beings, as biological entities, carry their genes with them as they migrate, and they introduce those genes when they mate with humans of the groups they encounter (studies of genetics have shown that males have done much more migrating than have females). Therefore, human biological comparisons among populations are particularly germane to considerations of transoceanic movements.

Deoxyribonucleic acid (DNA) is genetic material in the cells of all forms of nonmicrobial life, including humans, and has spawned the vigorous and growing field of DNA research. Since about 1985, DNA has increasingly been used to trace historical relationships among human populations. Although such inquiry is still in its early stages, it is evolving rapidly, and whole-genome studies are revealing a great deal beyond the results of the initially emphasized mitochondrial and Y chromosome DNA studies (see chapter 31).

When assessing the matter of human differences, it is important to keep in mind a key finding of molecular genetics. What may strike the eye as major physical differences among various groups of human beings is put into perspective by the overwhelming percentage of their genetic material that is shared by all of them (99.9 percent). The Australian anthropologist Matthew Spriggs has summarized the situation:

When objective criteria for assessing biological differences became available with the discovery of DNA, the vast majority of genetic variation was found to occur between individuals within local populations (some 85.4 per cent). Only small amounts (8.3 per cent) occur between related local populations such as nations or tribes . . . and even less between conventionally defined "racial" groups such as Asians and Africans. Conspicuous variants such as skin colour may be controlled by as few as four genetic loci.

These minor differences are useful, however, in disentangling the effects of population movements . . . as possible agents of cultural change from those generated from forces internal to the region, be they social or environmental. Cultures are carried about by populations. If these populations are sufficiently different from each other as defined by rare marker genes or subtle difference in head shape then the effects of migration as opposed to [expansion] diffusion or independent invention in culture change can be assessed.[1]

Understanding genetically controlled variable aspects of human biology can be highly helpful, then, in gaining insights regarding possible past human movements.

This chapter looks at visible, measurable phenotypic (manifest) physical human characteristics. In the following chapter, what the genes themselves tell us is examined.

Body of Evidence: Traditional Physical-Anthropological Criteria

In contemporary times, "race" among humans has been defined by constellations of physical characteristics: skin color, head form, nose form, lip form, hair form and color, and so forth. Sometimes, one or more such trait(s) is (are) especially diagnostic of one of the "races." An example is the inner epicanthic eyefold, which is a hallmark of East and Northeast Asians and which lends their eyes that "Oriental" look. Although the epicanthic fold is far from universal among American Indians, it occurs among Itzá Mayan women, and outsiders have sometimes, at least briefly, mistaken them for Chinese. Does this suggest a past East Asian demographic input to the Yucatán? Perhaps, but while phenotypic physical characteristics reflect genetic makeup, they do so in interaction with environmental factors, and their usefulness for showing historical contacts between separated populations is in many ways problematic. As the paleontologist Stephen Jay Gould put it, "Homology can often be recovered from morphology, but the forms of organisms often include an inextricable mixture of similarities retained by history (homology) and independently evolved in the light of common function (analogy). Morphology is not the best source of data for unraveling history."[2]

For example, one's stature is responsive not only to one's genes but also reflects one's nutrition during development; head form, although basically genetically controlled, is nevertheless also susceptible to alteration via intentional or incidental cradleboard or other cranial deformation; jawbone development might reflect, in part, what one chewed upon while growing up; skin color might evolve divergently fairly rapidly under different conditions of exposure to solar radiation over time[3] (and of course responds temporarily to immediate exposure), as might body size and proportions, nose form, and hirsuteness under different conditions of temperature and humidity. Further, a number of visible traits (for example, skin, hair, and eye color) are controlled by several, not just one, gene, in complex interactions with one another and with the environment.

Nowadays the significance of traditional "racial" categories, based on physical phenotypic manifestations, is questioned, owing to (1) the merely moderate to low correlation between these categories and variations in the tens of thousands of human genes other than those controlling "race," or, for that matter, even a number of the visible individual phenotypic characteristics; (2) the fact that many of the individual human genes do not, themselves, sort well into distinct geographic constellations; and (3) the fact that typically there is more genetic variation *within* populations than *between* averages of different populations. In the New World, at least, "With few exceptions, anthropometrics [bodily dimensions] and geography provide relatively high correlations, [suggesting environmental influences on physical type]. It is . . . ontological impermanence of measurements under changing environmental conditions that render anthropometrics unsuitable for tracing long-term genetic relationships between the races. . . . By the 1950s and 1960s, many American biological anthropologists had stopped using anthropometric measurements in their studies of human population relationships."[4]

Too, interbreeding between populations in contact, including during distant visits, has blurred distinctions, leading to the commonly heard assertion that there are no races, only clines (gradual transitions over geographic space). The importance of "race" is also questioned because, as mentioned, all human beings share the great majority of their genes (in fact, we humans share perhaps 95 percent of our genes with chimpanzees, as well[5]); genetic variation among individuals is much less than 1 percent, far less than the percentage used in biology to define separation at the race level.

Still, in pre-DNA-testing days visible, measurable phenotypic physical characteristics (plus a few strictly genetic traits manifested in blood, and so forth; see chapter 31) were all that workers had to go on. Although not much in fashion today, such comparisons are not to be ignored. When constellations of physical traits, many of which lack overt adaptive value and which, therefore, are unlikely to change rapidly under natural selection, are shared between populations, then some historical connection can be considered to be the most likely explanation, especially if we are dealing with fairly shallow temporal depths, periods too recent to have allowed enough time for significant organic evolution in these characteristics.

About Face

Despite the twilight of general anthropometrics, still receiving significant attention in physical anthropology are craniofacial traits, useful in comparing skeletal material found in archaeological sites. As one study put it: "Morphogenetic variation of the craniofacial skeleton has been used extensively by biological anthropologists to assess . . . genetic relatedness among human populations. Although measurement values for metric traits are a product of both heredity and environmental factors, research . . . indicates a significant degree of genetic control for most cranial measurements. . . . Although disease and nutrition affect the size of many craniofacial traits, the shape[s] of these traits are relatively unaffected by these environmental factors."[6] Further, most cranio-facial variables seem not to involve any selective advantages.

Native American peoples in the twentieth century did not generally exhibit much specific physical resemblance to extrahemispheric populations outside of Inner Asia and, especially, northeast Asia, or, if some did, those resemblances seemingly were attributable to post-Columbian admixture with foreign inter-lopers. The famous University of Pennsylvania physical anthropologist (and onetime spy) Carleton Coon once stated, "If people other than the Norse vis-ited America before Columbus, as they may well have, they left no visible im-print on the racial composition of the inhabitants of these two continents. . . . Hence we find a dilemma: if people visited America from elsewhere, they were transients, and transients have little effect on local cultures."[7]

Some scholars have, however, disagreed. In 2010, the archaeologists Elizabeth Matisoo-Smith and José-Miguel Ramírez-Aliaga published data showing that three skulls from Moche Island off Chile's Arauco Province (where the authors had identified late pre-Columbian chicken bones whose mitochondrial DNA was identical to that of Western Polynesian chickens; see chapter 26), most closely resembled Polynesian crania (but lying, morphologically, between Poly-nesians and Southeast Asians).

Other researchers had previously pointed to indications of foreign sources for some early skeletons. But although there was some not-so-easy-to-interpret prehistoric skeletal evidence, from Formative (Neolithic) Mexico, of Negroids, Mediterranean Caucasoids, and possibly Chinese,[8] the main basis for contem-plating a possible onetime presence of such exotic intruders was based upon (1) native "white-god" legends; (2) early colonial mentions of "blacks" in Central and South America and among the Zuni (a Puebloan people in New Mexico); and (3) archaeological occurrences, especially in Mexico and Peru, of depictions of faces that looked more European or sub-Saharan African or East Asian than Amerindian.[9]

White-God Tales

Legends of white gods/culture-bearers, often bearded, from over the water were first discussed in a scholarly fashion by the great early nineteenth-century Prus-sian explorer-geographer Alexander von Humboldt, who thought that these stories must refer to East Asian (encompassing Ainu) visitors, not Europeans.[10] White-god tales were widespread in the Americas and have been briefly dis-cussed in chapter 12. Those of Mesoamerica were so much believed in by the natives that when Cortés and his conquistadors arrived on Mexico's eastern coast in 1519, the indigenous people thought that the prophecy of the white gods' re-turn was being fulfilled and welcomed the newcomers. This was an important factor in a handful of Spaniards' quick takeover of much of Central Mexico.

The conqueror of Peru's Inka Empire beginning in 1532, Francisco Pizarro, was similarly received, for a similar reason: the people thought that he and his men were the returning legendary Kon-Tiki-Viracocha with his party of tall, white, bearded foreigners who had left Tiwanaku and had sailed away into the Pacific from Manta, Ecuador.[11]

Foreign Physiognomies of Pre-Columbian Peru

The half-native Peruvian historian Garcilaso de la Vega (1539–1616), himself of the royal line, stated that the eighth ruler of the Inka dynasty had been white and bearded. The early sixteenth-century conquistador Pedro Pizarro, first cousin of Francisco, reported that "the ruling class in the kingdom of Peru was fair-skinned and blond, like ripe wheat. The lords and ladies were mostly white, like the Spaniards."[12]

A minority of realistic portrait vases of elites of Peru's pre-Inka Moche culture of circa AD 1–750 look Caucasoid or largely Caucasoid rather than fully Indian (figures 30.1 and 30.2), often displaying narrow, convex noses, thin lips, low cheekbones, and eyes of Caucasian rather than typical Indian appearance. No facial hair is evident on many of the portraits, so if the men portrayed were whites, they must have plucked their beards. However, the visages of some vases display large mustaches and chin beards. A few physiognomies appear to reflect Negroid admixture.[13]

Faces of actual Moche skulls have narrower, more Europoid noses than those typical of American Indians.[14] The Harvard physical anthropologist William W. Howells, discussing "racial" classification of archaeological skulls, stated that "a certified Peruvian, #1435, refuses to be recognized as anything but European."[15] Howells wrote that although American Indians had Asian-type teeth, their elevated, narrow nasal regions are not of Asiatic form, with Peruvian skulls "in particular cozying up to Europeans." Although he considered this to be a "striking convergence" and did not propose that actual Caucasoid inputs had been involved, he may have been too cautious.[16] The American chemist James L. Guthrie took note of two studies of skull morphology that showed essential identity between samples from Peru, from Egypt, and from Crete.[17]

Thor Heyerdahl, in 1953, stressed the finding, in South Coast Peru, of many mummies possessing European-looking wavy, reddish, and fine hair quite unlike typical straight, black, and coarse Amerind hair. At Paracas Necropolis, mummies' hair was rusty brown, and two cadavers had wavy locks. Nasca (Nazca) has also yielded burials displaying fine, red hair. Skeletons manifested greater stature than previously reported among Peruvian Indians and had unusually narrow facial features. Three elite burials found more recently at Dos Cabezas were also of very unusually tall men.[18] All these are characteristics associated with some Caucasoid groups but not with typical South American Indians.

In addition, an Inka tradition spoke of a people of northeastern Peru called the Chachas as being white skinned and blue eyed. Although at the time discounting an Old World origin, in the mid-twentieth century the explorer Gene

Figure 30.1. Portrait pot displaying one-eyed male ruler with Caucasoid-appearing features, North Coast of Peru, Moche culture, 100 BC to AD 500. Ceramic and pigment, 28.9 x 21.6 cm, three-quarter view; Kate MS. Buckingham Endowment, 1955.2339, © 2000 The Art Institute of Chicago, all rights reserved.

Fig 30.2. Portrait pot displaying Caucasoid-appearing features, North Coast of Peru, Chimu culture, first half of the second millennium AD. From Hermann Leicht, *Tonplastik im reifem Stil der Chimu*, 1944, plate 25.

Figure 30.3. Plumbate ceramic incense burner depicting the face of the deity Quetzalcoatl/Kukulkan, exhibiting a generally Caucasoid appearance, from Iximché, Chimaltenango, Guatemala, circa AD 300. Collection of the Musée de l'Homme. Photo © 2015, Scala, Florence.

Savoy found, in an archaeological site of the Chacha culture, a carved stone head sporting a prominent Armenoid nose and a beard, and he visited a nearby zone inhabited by tall, light-skinned, blue-eyed Natives.[19]

Mesoamerican Rainbow

In Mexico, Guatemala, and elsewhere in Middle America, certain carvings and effigy figurines display Caucasoid-looking physical features such as hooked noses displaying nostility as well as beards, including seemingly curly ones (figure 30.3), and some depict physiognomies and that look very Negroid (figure 30.4). A few comparisons may be pointed out. One has to do with stone carvings made by the Olmec people of a millennium or so BC, in Veracruz and Tabasco states, Mexico. The eminent French anthropologist Claude Lévi-Strauss was struck by these: "there were plump, smooth-faced Orientals, and bearded individuals with aquiline profiles reminiscent of Renaissance portraits . . . it must be admitted after the voyage of the *Kon-Tiki*, that trans-Pacific contacts may have taken place."[20]

A relief scene on the Olmec stone carving called La Venta Stela 3 (and sometimes dubbed "Uncle Sam") shows what the Mexican artist Miguel Covarrubias characterized as a "fully bearded man with an enormous aquiline nose . . . a personage with surprisingly pronounced Semitic features" (figure 30.5a).[21] Some Olmec colossal basalt-carved heads, on the other hand, possess a collation of

Figure 30.4. Pre-Columbian terra-cotta portrait head displaying Negroid features, Veracruz, Mexico. With permission of bpk/Ethnologisches Museum, Staatliche Museen zu Berlin.

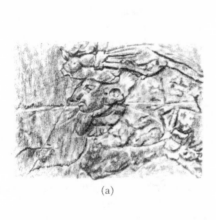

(a)

(b)

Figure 30.5. Depictions of what appear to be Old World physiognomies in Olmec sculptures of Mexico's Theocratic Formative period. (a) Detail of Stele 3, La Venta, Tabasco, ca. 1000–800 BC, relief displaying a personage with eastern Mediterranean appearance. (b) Monument 1, San Lorenzo Tenochtitlán, Veracruz, ca. 1150–950 BC, colossal head of basalt displaying sub-Saharan African appearance. Drawings by Rulon Nielson. Courtesy of Stephen C. Jett.

traits that many be seen as sub-Saharan African (figure 30.5b).[22] The Olmec specialist David C. Grove wrote of a typical colossal head that "the face . . . is well modeled and heavy featured. The eyes are normally heavily lidded, the nose is broad and flaring, while the lips are frequently thick and everted. The first [of the heads] was found in 1862 at Tres Zapotes and described as 'Negroid.' While descriptive of the general facial features, this identification has been taken too literally by some authors, for such characteristics are common among Indian groups on the Gulf coast and elsewhere in Mesoamerica, and are not indicative of transatlantic contacts."[23]

Four decades earlier, Matthew Stirling, a pioneering archaeologist of the Olmec, had observed that the Tres Zapotes colossal head "is remarkable for its realistic treatment. The features are amazingly Negroid in character,"[24] an impression later repeated by many others.[25] Stirling also appears to have been the first to articulate that this facial configuration was found, in natives, over a considerable area of contemporary Middle America, and in addition to Grove, various later archaeologists have repeated this, seemingly thinking that this should put to rest any need to evoke ancient sub-Saharan African input.[26]

No one has presented physical-anthropological data to actually demonstrate, among the area's Indians, a concatenation of such traits as a broad, flat, low-rooted nose with flaring alae and forward-directed nostrils, plus thick, everted, membranous lips with ridged seams and slight prognathism as well as low upper eyelids carrying fatty pads, which are associated with Negroid Africans, or the African-style multibraided hair as depicted on Tres Zapotes Head 2.[27] The Harvard physical anthropologist Ernest Albert Hooton specifically denied that lips of the aforementioned type occur among American Indians.[28] Beatrice de la Fuente, Mexico's foremost historian of pre-Columbian art, saw the colossal heads as Negroid and "most remote in physiognomy from our indigenous ancestors."[29]

However, even if such features do in fact exist among some present-day people of the region, would this prove, or even imply, that the traits in question are "indigenous" and not from Africa? Hardly. The features could reflect either partial descent from Negroids who were present among the ancient Olmec, or Colonial and post-Colonial gene flow from black slaves and their descendants of the Caribbean region, which has a long history of interaction with the port of Veracruz (in fact, in post-Columbian times Negroes were brought to Veracruz's Papaloapan Valley).

Neither do Caucasoid and Negroid features exhaust the list of Old World–looking facial features among the Formative peoples of Mexico. Many Olmec and Olmecoid sculptures, especially hollow ceramic figures, display eye forms that would pass muster in Chinese art.[30] As R. Buckminster Fuller observed, "You will find in Mexico every shape of face, eye, and lips, every shape of head, and you will find any and every one of these shapes and faces in every grade of color, from very dark to very light. The people of Mexico constitute a highly crossbred man of yesterday."[31]

In a 1975 book titled *Unexpected Faces in Ancient America* and in other works, the German Mexican pre-Columbian art historian Alexander von Wuthenau illustrated scores of Mesoamerican facial depictions in terra-cotta figurines that he saw as displaying East Asian, Negroid, or Caucasoid features, including beards. These figurines come from various regions, with a concentration in Gulf-coastal Veracruz state, and are especially numerous from the Preclassic period (approximately, the first millennium BC). Although many feel that he overreached in some of his identifications, a certain number of the heads do seem unequivocally to display extrahemispheric physiognomies. Unfortunately, the picture is complicated by the fact that the large majority of the pieces shown do not have good archaeological provenience, and one antidiffusionist historian of pre-Columbian art who examined von Wuthenau's collection went away convinced—rightly or wrongly—that a substantial percentage were fakes and that the collector was racist; a second archaeologist agreed, although a third archaeologist, while concurring that the collection included fakes, nevertheless stated that the heads in question were not among them.

The depiction of beards (including false ones) in Nuclear American art has received a good deal of attention.[32] Few contemporary Native Americans are able grow long beards or luxuriant mustaches, so when these are depicted they can engender thoughts of Caucasoid Old World visitors or migrants. In 1979, Kirk A. Magleby cataloged over 250 instances of beards depicted in Mesoamerican art, with Veracruz, Guatemala, Oaxaca, and Tabasco displaying the greatest numbers, the highest frequency being in Preclassic times and diminishing thereafter. Such traditions may have spawned the wearing of false beards, which are also depicted in art, or that tradition could have been derived from Egyptian use of false beards. As in Egypt, in Mesoamerica beards and false beards appear to be associated with elite personages.

Although, as mentioned, most depictions of apparent foreigners are early, some do appear in later periods. For example, in the Regional Museum of Tabasco in Villahermosa, there is a very realistic stucco portrait head of a very Caucasoid-looking individual, found at the ninth-century Maya site of Palenque. Certain Mayan murals also depict battles between dark-skinned and light-skinned antagonists.[33] At Chipal, on Guatemala's Pacific coast near the Mexican border, archaeologists unearthed plumbate pottery, including at least a couple of effigy lids, depicting a bearded man with a prominent aquiline nose (see figure 30.2). The ceramics—dating to circa AD 900–1200—from this small area are the only known vitrified pottery in Mesoamerica and probably the New World (such wares were common in Eurasia at the time).[34]

Indonesians in America?

In 1968, I published compilations of comparisons of the whole gamut of the external traits treated by physical anthropology at the time, between Carib- and Arawak-speaking peoples of tropical South America on the one hand and the denizens of interior Borneo (proto-Malays) on the other. In all features recorded, these two groups of populations corresponded closely—in average stature and sexual dimorphism in stature, body build, head form, face form, nose form, eye form and color, hair form and color, and quantity and quality of beard and body hair. Blood type O predominated in both populations, and frequencies of the M and R₁ (but not Lewis) blood factors were similar (see chapter 31). The most striking thing was that the two sets of samples resembled each other more closely than either resembled those of neighboring populations of different ethnicities.

This close comparability struck me as being more than the consequence of similar environments causing the evolution of similar physical types. Most of the traits described bear no obvious advantageous relationship to the climate, vegetation, diet, and so forth. Further, if equatorial rain-forest habitats encourage the natural selection of this constellation of characteristics, then why do quite different autochthonous human physical traits distinguish such environments elsewhere—for example, Pygmies/Negritos in tropical Africa, the Malay Peninsula, and northern Luzon, and Papuans in eastern Indonesia and Papua New Guinea? All these resemblances, plus possession of closely similar cultures (including the blowgun complex), convinced me that transpacific migration was the most plausible explanation for the resemblances between Borneo and the Amazon Basin.[35] There is now some linguistic support for the proposition as well.[36]

Sinking In One's Teeth: Dental Morphology

Interesting and suggestive though the approach may be, use of phenotypic morphological/anthropometric bases for reconstruction of human movements and relationships has faded as the direct study of the human genome and its variations among populations has progressed. Nevertheless, certain phenotypic manifestations thought to be less susceptible to evolutionarily and environmentally exogenous influences than, say, skin color or bodily dimensions, continue to be widely used. Among these is dentition. Although somewhat susceptible to selective forces, the genetically controlled shapes of human teeth have nevertheless been usefully employed to help reconstruct migrations. Sinodonty— the possession of East/Northeast Asian tooth form—seems to dominate in the North American continent. However, in South America Sundadonty—the possession of Southeast Asian–type teeth—prevails outside of the northwestern part of the continent—and in Paleoamericans and Preceramic peoples even in the northwest.[37] South American Sundadonty may essentially reflect very early human entry via rapid coastal migration, although later Southeast Asian inputs may well also have occurred—one thinks of the postulated Indonesian and Indochinese increments referred to above.

Overall, then, the Native American physical-anthropological data include some seeming anomalies in cranial, facial, dental, and certain other physical characteristics that appear to be most readily explicable, at least in large part, by significant in-migration from overseas.

Incongruous Genes in America

Examine well your blood.
—William Shakespeare, *A Midsummer Night's Dream*, 1.1, 1595

As suggested in the previous chapter, the study of human genetics, including biochemical and, especially, molecular genetics, is technical and fast developing and seems to offer critical evidence relevant to transoceanic investigations. According to the American anthropologist Kenneth Tankersley, "genome variation is rapidly becoming a powerful tool that is leading toward a quantum leap in our knowledge of human migrations and origins. . . . It is becoming increasingly evident that genetics in the twenty-first century will have as a profound effect on American archaeology as radiocarbon dating did during the twentieth century."[1] What gives molecular genetic studies the advantage over traditional physical-anthropological investigations is that, as Stephen Jay Gould wrote, "the items of a DNA program are sufficiently numerous and independent to ensure that degrees of simple matching accurately measure homology."[2] The biological scientist Austin L. Hughes concluded, "Molecular-biology data offer the promise of at last unlocking the prehistories of our own and other species."[3]

The further back in time one goes, the more problematic is the interpretation of genetic comparisons, since phenomena such as demographic bottlenecks, founder effects, genetic drift, and natural selection all work toward increasing genetic differences among populations over time. Another point is that to the extent that cladistic trees (cladograms) assume permanent separation among diverging populations, such diagrams—of proximity of relationship constructed on the basis of genetic distances among those populations—are of limited usefulness for historical reconstructions in instances in which there may have been genetic inputs from one or more outside source into selected geographic areas.[4]

In these situations, distinctive *genetic markers*, polymorphisms (variants) with no apparent evolutionary function and of restricted geographic distribution, may be particularly revealing of contacts, just as in the cultural realm minor but distinctive shared nonadaptive traits may signal contact and introduction. It is the presence of such markers, not populations' overall gene-frequency averages, that count in this context. As the physician and Oxford genetic anthropologist Stephen Oppenheimer has reminded us, "The number of people who took a major cultural advance across a sea by trade routes or otherwise may appear quite small when measured as a proportion of the indigenous people that received it. The modern traces of those seminal transfers when measured as genetic or linguistic markers may thus be quite faint."[5] Whether or not Oppenheimer is punning here, sailors are notorious for being generous with their genes.

Blood Will Tell

Scientists study a number of genetically controlled phenotypic phenomena in humans that display polymorphisms. Among these are the chemical compositions of various bodily secretions (for example, enzymes, earwax), chemical-tasting ability, and dermatoglyphics (fingerprints). As far as I know, none of these has yielded, or seems likely to yield, information particularly suggestive in the area of transoceanic interactions. Blood, however, is another matter. Although the subject is dauntingly technical even in the simplified form presented here, it constitutes a highly significant body of evidence regarding contacts.

The ABO System

Today, we are all familiar with the fact that human blood exists in four genetically controlled types with respect to what is called the ABO system. ABO blood group substances are protein and sugar compounds on the surfaces of red blood cells. During the mid-twentieth century, the differences in frequencies of the A, B, AB, and O types began to be considered useful genetic indicators of human affiliations and migrations, especially following the 1956 publication of the British geneticist A. E. Mourant's *The Distribution of Blood Groups in Animals and Humans.*

O appears to have been the original human blood type. Other things being equal, O is also selected for over A, B, and AB because of occasional A/B fetal loss owing to blood-type incompatibility with O-type mothers. Presumed-later type A is commonest in the Near East and Europe, and later-still B in Asia and Africa. It was once thought that, except for difficult-to-account-for high levels of the A1 subtype among the Blackfoot in the Montana-Alberta border country and lesser levels among neighboring peoples, American Indians were almost exclusively of type O and that this was proof that there had not been any significant contacts from the Eastern Hemisphere following initial Late Pleistocene settlement of the Americas (with the exception of the Eskimo/Inuit, among whom B was present). Small percentages of B that did show up in other Western Hemisphere aboriginals were considered to be a consequence of post-Columbian European admixture or, possibly, of parallel mutations.

Two things have come to interfere with this conclusion. One is the recognition that people with one or another of the ABO blood types possess a greater or lesser susceptibility to certain diseases (including cholera and bubonic plague) and that any advantage-carrying type may have become common in any area, owing to natural selection, only within the last few thousand years, subsequent to the appearances of the relevant diseases. Thus, type B, which may afford some protection against malaria (as may O), could have arisen and become frequent in its Old World homeland (it is genetically dominant over O) but not in the presumably malaria-free Western Hemisphere and Pacific islands. B and O convey greater resistance to smallpox than does A. Occurrence of presumed-American syphilis is more common among A and B people than among Os and could have operated in favor of O in the New World. O seems also to protect against spontaneous abortion and early infant death. However, Os may get ulcers more frequently and are susceptible to attack by antibodies against bubonic plague. Pernicious anemia is more common among carriers of type A blood than among those manifesting other types. A individuals also seem more prone to stomach cancer and diabetes than Bs and ABs and to be especially susceptible to attack by antibodies against smallpox and, if present, would have been selected against during post-1492 epidemics in the Americas.

In general, according to the physical anthropologist Stanley M. Garn, "there has been selection against . . . both A and B in favor of O, at least in Europeans. For these reasons, present gene frequencies do not provide a perfect indication of what they were in the past. . . . Blood groups are of limited value in solving ancient ties between races, but so are the conventional morphological traits."[6] Again, as Garn observed, "It is not necessary to assume that ancestral Amerindians were derived from a B-free population . . . they may have lost it in transit [for example, through bottlenecks and founder effects]. But it is equally likely that B had adaptive value in Asia but none in America."[7] Even so, if Holocene Asian transoceanic contacts have been significant, we might expect still to find at least *some* B in blood-group samples from Western Hemisphere natives.

The second and newer finding concerning the post-Columbian admixture question addresses just this issue and has to do with archaeological investigations. As of the 1960s, it was stated that researchers had not detected blood group B in any living "unmixed" American Indian, nor in pre-Columbian skeletal remains.[8] However, since that time it has been determined that *all* of the ABO types occur in pre-1492 Peruvian mummies—interestingly, particularly at earlier levels, having become quite rare as time progressed. Further, a 1974 study of 662 Zuni Indians revealed a 10.7 percent incidence of type B blood[9]— an occurrence that the anthropologist Nancy Yaw Davis attributed to a postulated thirteenth-century AD Japanese increment.[10] Too, the Quinault Indians of northwestern North America measured 13 percent A and 6 percent B.[11] In fact, "The B allele [variant gene at a particular chromosomal location] is present in more than 240 of the approximately 436 samples of indigenous American groups listed in Mourant's [1956] and CS's [Cavalli-Sforza, Menozzi, and Piazza's 1994] ABO tables. . . . More than 58 samples . . . display over 2 percent B," and some Native groups in Central and South America display frequencies of up to 8.8 percent.[12] Although the origins of A and B among these populations could be post-Columbian, they—especially B—should not be assumed to be so since the presence of A and B is also consistent with pre-Columbian introductions and B is uncommon in Iberia.

The Diego Factor

In the mid-twentieth century, a number of other genetically controlled serological systems came to be identified, including those called the MNS-U, Pp, Rhesus, Duffy, Diego, Kidd, Kell, Lutheran, and Lewis factors. Certain of them are most important to our investigation, for reasons that will become apparent. Some of these factors are either simply present or absent. Others occur in two or more genetic variants. Of these, beginning in the 1950s one blood-factor system, called the Diego (Di^a), especially intrigued migrationists, because the frequency of Diego positive was highest among South American Indians (up to 29 percent), irregular and lower over most of North America (2 to 6 percent), nearly absent in Beringia (0 percent among Inuit), but rather common among East Asians and also present in Indonesia.[13] According to Garn, "This suggests, quite reasonably, an Asiatic source of Diego in the Americas,"[14] but not overland via Alaska. A better option is migration by sea. This could perhaps have occurred via the Pacific Rim during the Late Pleistocene, but the factor's absence among more marginal peoples (presumed to be earlier than more culturally elaborated populations)[15] would argue against this, leaving later open-ocean voyaging as more likely. A third possibility is one or more later, Diego-free Holocene migrations from Siberia's having populated previously empty lands in the North or having genetically swamped small preexisting populations there.

The American organic chemist James L. Guthrie has collated a great deal of data on various additional serological and other genetically controlled characters and is the main source for the discussions that follow.[16]

The Rhesus Factor

The well-known Rhesus (Rh) factor makes red blood cells adhere to one another. The different Rhesus blood groups are thought not to possess differential adaptive values but to be neutral alternative versions. The d-negative haplotypes (variant specific lineages) of the Rhesus system provide data of interest. In the Old World, haplotype CdE (RY) occurs with above 1 percent frequency only among Dravidians in South India. In the Americas, it is found in Mexico, where pre-Columbian South Asian cultural influence has been suggested, and among northeastern North America's Micmac, where such influence has *not* been proposed (note, however, traces among the Basques, who also exhibit a high incidence of cde [R], which is also frequent among Indians of northeastern North

America[17]). *RH*R* (*cde*) and a second haplotype, *cdE* (*r"*), are common among eastern and southern Asians and are also found among the relatively late arriving Athapaskan Indians of North America as well as in the Andean region but not in most of Middle America. The areal distributions of the South American occurrences look suspiciously like artifacts of overseas inputs.

When associated with *cDe* (*Ro*), the rare V antigen (a substance that triggers an immune response) is considered to be African, but *cDeV* also occurs in a tight cluster in Central America and nearby areas—which suggests an African input, although not necessarily pre-Columbian.

The Kell System

The sub-Saharan African allele of the Kell antigen system in the blood that is designated Jsa is found at high levels (circa 25 percent) in the blood of two Native nations of the lower Amazon, and at lower frequencies around the Caribbean and in the Central Andean area but not among most South American groups. These findings fit with suggestions of pre-Colonial African admixture in the Caribbean region as well as with the existence of a few rather Negroid-looking Moche portrait vases (see chapter 30).

Transferrins

A transferrin (Tf) is a beta-globulin protein in blood plasma that can combine with and transport iron ions through the body to the bone marrow. At least twenty-nine genetic variants have been identified. In 1964, the observation was made that whereas only transferrin C was found in Native Alaskans, farther south in indigenous North America transferrin B_{0-1} occurred, and in South America phenotypes C, CD_{Chi}, and D_{Chi} showed up. Tf D_{Chi} reached levels of 58 percent among Yupa Indians of Venezuela, while electrophoretically indistinguishable Tf DChi' had previously been found only in Guangdong, China.[18] Today, tf D_{chi} is also well documented in South and Southeast Asia and in the Pacific islands. In the Americas, Chibchan Paez speakers as well as Caribs display this variant. The data are consistent with suggested pre-Columbian Asian influences in the region. TF D1, an Australoid variant that is also found in southern and eastern Asia and sub-Saharan Africa, occurs in Native northwest South America as well. Geneticists have recorded another, otherwise Old World variant, TFB2, among central Andean Indians but nowhere else in the Native Western Hemisphere.

Immunoglobins

An immunoglobin (Ig; antibody) is a protective serum protein that occurs in a number of varieties. One isotype is IgM. Data are incomplete, but a few are suggestive. A "Caucasian" variant, f;b, is also widespread in Native Amazonian, Andean, and southern South America but is nearly absent in North America. It may have been brought by early Asian migrants to the hemisphere but not by later ones, who may have swamped earlier entrants in the North.[19]

Alpha Globins

In 1995, Marco A. Zago and colleagues published a study of the serology of groups of the middle and lower Amazon drainage. Of the alpha-haplotypes of globins (serum proteins) that they found there, the one designated Ia occurs also among Indo-Europeans, Southeast Asians, and Oceanians. Haplotype IIIa is particularly common in New Guinea and Oceania. Haplotype IIe has its highest levels in the Amazon Basin but also occurs in Oceania and Southeast Asia; in South America, it is associated with an unusually large pseudo-zeta allele, this being associated with haplotypes IIa and IId in Southeast Asia and Oceania. The team concluded that "the similarities between South American Indians and Southeast Asians and Oceanic populations suggests substantial genetic affinity between these populations." The authors attribute this to common origins predating the human settling of America and Oceania, because certain Oceanian genes are missing in America.[20] They did not consider my 1968 proposal that Indonesians settled Amazonia.

The Human Leucocyte Antigen System

Human leucocyte (leukocyte, lymphocyte) antigens (HLAs) compose the human major histocompatibility complex, relating to the immune system. Among other functions, the system's genes encode cell-surface antibody-presenting proteins against pathogens. Being perhaps the most polymorphic of human genes—that is, being extremely variable among individuals and populations (over 6,400 alleles have been identified)—HLAs make excellent genetic markers. As far as I am aware, no particular HLA polymorphism has been shown to be selected for by any particular pathogen.[21]

Afro-Asiatic HLAs. Among modern American Indians are found several HLAs whose origins appear clearly to be in discrete areas of the Old World. The following HLAs, which Guthrie termed "Afro-Asiatic" because their major occurrences are in northern Africa and southwestern Asia, also occur in the Western Hemisphere: A*1, A*29, A*30, A*32, B*14, B*17, B*18, B*21, and B*37; they do not to any degree appear to be artifacts of post-1500 European or sub-Saharan African gene flow. Although information is lacking for many Native American groups, what we do know of the details of the distributions of certain of these HLAs is particularly notable.

In Afroeurasia, HLA B*21 is closely associated with Berbers and with Arabs and Arab-influenced populations. In America, its highest occurrences are among Uto-Aztecan speakers (who also display B*17 and B*37), especially those of the US Southwest and Northwest Mexico. Traces of B*21 also occur in southerly South America (Mapuche/Araucano) and Venezuela (Yupa). The Mapuche have the highest known total of Afro-Asiatic HLAs in the hemisphere and also display A*32, as do Tupians of the Caribbean and the lower Amazon; A*32 is characteristic of the Mediterranean region and of northern India. B*14 is basically a Mediterranean variety, but it also occurs at high levels in the Andean region and, with lesser frequencies, in Mesoamerica. In addition, another antigen, A*1, seems to be essentially from the Mediterranean and other Caucasoid areas but shows up once again in the Andean region but not (so far) elsewhere in Native South America (as it ought to if it were of post-1492 Iberian origin).

What is particularly striking about the above distributions is that more than one Afro-Asiatic HLA variety coexists in certain regions, greatly strengthening the probability of overseas input. Most notably implicated are (1) northerly Uto-Aztecans and (2) Andeans of Chile, Peru, and Bolivia. Further, the African Rhesus V antigen, Duffy FY*0, and Kell *Jsa* alleles, plus immunoglobin Za;bc35, also occur among these American groups, and there are others. In light of the fact that these variants have no proven adaptive value, the co-occurrence of several Afro-Asiatic polymorphisms among Uto-Aztecans and in the Andean region seems well beyond the possibility of chance convergence. All this is even more notable when correlated with suggestions of Semitic and Egyptian elements in the Uto-Aztecan languages and Kichwa's being in a proposed linguistic phylum with the Afro-Asiatic language family.[22] Something, it may be said, has gone on here: almost certainly, ancient transoceanic inputs.

Southern-Asian HLAs. Another set of HLAs—A*10, A*11, A*33, B*13, and B*22—may be termed southern Asian, being especially common in the Indian subcontinent, Southeast Asia, China, and the Pacific islands. HLA A*33 peaks in New Guinea and Southeast Asia, although it is also found to some degree in Africa and the Near East. It shows up in the Americas as well, and could have come in from any of the aforementioned areas. Again, the Uto-Aztecans figure prominently, along with the eastern Maya and the Cherokee (Iroquoian speakers, but in some genetic characteristics hard to distinguish from the Uto-Aztecan Nahua) as well as the Kichwa. B*22, whose hearth seems to be Australia, New Guinea, and Oceania, occurs also among the Inuit/Eskimo and Central Mexico's Uto-Aztecan Nahua. A*11, an allele of southern Asia (as well as among the Ainu) and Oceania, is found in samples from Mesoamerica and from Chile. A*10, common in Australia, parts of Asia, and the Pacific, is also notable among Chile's Araucano, in Mesoamerica, and among the Cherokee. Finally, occurrences of southern Asian B*13 are, as far as is now known, restricted in the Americas to the Nahua, three Andean groups, and the southern Brazilian Kaingáng. Taken as a whole, these alleles strongly suggest Southeast Asian and/or Oceanian inputs, possibly including from Ainu-Australoids, who seem to have been among the early settlers of the New World as well as later immigrants.

European HLAs. One other geographic category of HLAs remains to be discussed: the apparently European A*3, B*7, B*8, and B*12. In America, B*7 occurs most prominently among the Inuit, especially of the eastern Arctic, not only where Norse interaction took place but also where much earlier inputs from Europe have been suggested. However, B*7 appears once again among Uto-Aztecans and the Cherokee and in the Andean region. The center of HLA B*12 is the Basque zone of Spain and France. American occurrences are among the western Eskimo but also, importantly, among Uto-Aztecans, the Cherokee, and the Araucano/Mapuche. The distributions of B*8 and A*3 are similar. One might remember, in this context and that of the Afroasiatic HLAs, the Caucasoid-looking faces depicted in the plastic arts of pre-Columbian Mesoamerica and the Peruvian coast, as discussed in the previous chapter.

Glucose-6-Phosphate Dehydrogenase Deficiency Mutation

In a broad tropical/subtropical Old World belt, many people possess the glucose-6-phosphate dehydrogenase deficiency mutation (G6PD), an X chromosome disorder affecting red blood cells, mostly in males. It confers protection against malaria, a disease originating in the Old World. G6PD was also found among four of twenty-three American samples, two in the lower Amazon region and two in the Central Andes.

It is difficult to deny the strong probability that the prevalence of these and other "foreign" genetic expressions in the Andean and greater Mesoamerican regions—the same general regions where multifarious foreign influences are most suggested by cultural and linguistic evidence—reflects significant pre-Columbian intrusions from the Eastern Hemisphere, since in light of the patterns not conforming to those of the hemisphere's Colonial conquerors there appears to be no plausible alternative explanation.

Double Helix: DNA Studies

Mitochondrial DNA

DNA is a macromolecule consisting of a pair of strands joined in a double-helix configuration. DNA is organized into *chromosomes*, which encode the genetic instructions for the development and functioning of an organism. A *gene* is a stretch of a chromosome that controls an aspect of heredity via proteins. Parts of chromosomes do not code for proteins but seem to regulate gene expression.

As mentioned above, studies of DNA can be most productive. These are undertaken by examining individuals' sequences of base pairs, the building blocks of DNA. Especially used by molecular geneticists for historical reconstructions of human populations is uniparental mitochondrial DNA (mtDNA), which exists outside of cell nuclei and which is passed down exclusively in the female line, so that lineages can be traced; it preserves relatively well in ancient remains. To a lesser degree, the nonrecombinant portion of nuclear Y chromosome DNA—(formerly dubbed NRY, now termed the male-specific region, MSR)—found only in males and passed down from father to son, is used as well. However, not only is MSR more difficult to sequence than is mtDNA, it also exhibits fewer polymorphisms and therefore has less potential to be revealing. The polymorphisms involved have been supposed to be adaptively neutral. Still, some caution is called for in light of accumulating evidence that at least mtDNA haplogroups (Hgs; large-scale branches) A, C, D, and G and H offer selective advantage in colder climates.[23]

The human genome exhibits various structural variations, such as duplications, deletions, and insertions of sequences. Study of these is at a fairly early stage, but it may be that they influence gene function; they also give clues concerning past human geographic movements. mtDNA evolves these variations spontaneously and relatively quickly, at an approximately known rate, which allows rough calculation of ages of separation (times to coalescence) of lineages (the rate for MSR is more problematic).

Analysis of mtDNA variation among contemporary Native Americans commenced in 1985, and about 98 percent of these peoples have turned out to be assignable to one of four mtDNA haplogroups, labeled A, B, C, and D—all of which, plus M (ancestral to C and D), have been identified in ancient American samples. A, C, and D, but not B, are also common in Siberia and central eastern Asia. Comparison of evolution rates of mtDNA with degree of haplotype diversity implies that these haplogroups split apart (and entered the hemisphere or at least Beringia, if a single migration is posited) between 20,000 and 40,000 years ago assuming no new genetic input to the Americas other than Eskimo-Aleut circa 2000 BC following the entry of the ancestors of Na-Dené-speaking people (that is, post-7,000–10,000 years ago; see below).

It is standard for molecular geneticists, whose focus is the early populating of the Western Hemisphere, to eliminate from their analysis haplogroups other than A, B, C, D, and X (the last also present in North America; see below) as being later "contaminants." This creates a problem for those of us looking for possible signs of post-Paleoamerican but still pre-Columbian genetic inputs.

Too, it needs to be kept in mind that the directions in which the young field of molecular genetics points are not yet all definitive. Sample sizes are often small and geographically uneven, and opinions differ as to interpretation of some of the results as well as to the calibration of the molecular clock (mutation rate). My conclusion as of 2007 was that several genetically and/or cranio-facially definable movements from Asia into northern North America, plus one from Europe, had taken place, beginning with a Pacific Rim littoral influx 24,000 to 18,250 calendar years ago, involving a mtDNA-B-lacking population. Haplogroup X (see below) would have arrived in northeastern North America from western Europe, via the sea-ice edge, perhaps around 16,000 years ago (see below). The primary ancestors of present American Indians would have entered Beringia around 14,000–10,000 years ago and expanded very widely some 7,000 years ago but still without mtDNA Hg B, which, I hypothesized, might have been brought to Central America about 6,300 years ago by boat-borne migrants of family groups from the southeast of what is now China, re-inforced around 3,350 years ago by people from East China and, during the final three BC millennia, by Malayo-Polynesians from the region of Indonesia's Celebes Sea.[24] Central Americans are the Amerinds genetically most similar to the south Chinese; not only do they share mtDNA Hg B, but also Diego blood types, transferrin Hg D (see above), and certain *Alu*-element (a type of short stretch of DNA) insertions.[25] All this gains interest in light of Bede Fahey's case for Mayan being related to archaic Chinese.[26]

Concerning transoceanic contacts, one view was flippantly expressed by the science writer Steve Olson: "If any Africans, Australians, Europeans, or extraterrestrials made it to the Americas before Columbus, they didn't have much luck breeding with the locals. No mitochondrial DNA from haplotypes of people living anyplace other than Asia have been found in the Americas, with one exception [see below]."[27] However, Olson did not take note of the fact that only *women* pass on mtDNA, whereas the vast majority of history's adventurers, explorers, sailors, merchants, missionaries, and so forth have been *men*. Therefore, we would not expect any transfer of mtDNA in most overseas-contact situations. The picture is less simple in additional ways, as well. Among other things, the geographical distributions of the basic Native American haplogroups raise certain questions.

Using Joseph Greenberg's linguistic categories, one team of geneticists ascertained that all of the four aforementioned haplogroups (A, B, C, and D), each representing a separate female founder, occurred among so-called Amerind speakers (all Native Americans other than Eskimo-Aleuts and Na-Dené speakers). However, like most Native Siberians, Na-Dené speakers, who dominated Alaska and western Canada, manifested virtually 100 percent haplogroup A, raising the question as to how the ancestral Amerind founders carrying groups B, C, and D could have entered the Americas without leaving a trace of B, C, or D in the North.

A team of geneticists observed, "The presence of group B [9-base-pair] deletion [9-bp COII-tRNA^{Lys}-deletion] haplotypes in [Southeast and] East Asian and Native American populations but their absence in Siberians raises the possibility that haplogroup B could represent a migratory event distinct from the one(s) which brought group A, C, and D mtDNAs to the Americas," with an early coastal migration from East Asia being a plausible explanation for that event (see above).[28] (The 9-bp deletion is also characteristic of Oceania.)

In 1998, the geneticist Michael D. Brown and colleagues caused a stir when they announced finding a fifth "founding" mtDNA haplogroup in the aboriginal Americas, which they dubbed "X" and which appeared to represent only about 3 percent of Native Americans, a percentage so low as to raise doubts as to its having entered with the other American haplogroups. Globally, X appears to have originated in Anatolia or the Levant and to have spread, at low frequencies, through much of Europe, perhaps carried by the ancestors of the Basques, who may have been the first to carry farming westward. X's geographical distribution suggested to these workers carriage into the Americas circa 17,000–12,000 years ago, "raising the possibility that some Native American founders were of Caucasian ancestry."[29] X in Europe and X (X2A) in America are quite distinct, and no immediate ancestor of X2A is known from the Eastern Hemisphere. X2A occurs exclusively among northern North American groups: the Ojibwa (Chippewa; 25 percent), Lakota (Sioux; 15 percent), Nuu-Choh-Nulth (Nootka; 12 percent), Diné (Navajo, relatively recent migrants to the Southwest from western Canada; 6 percent), and Yakima (5 percent). In 1999, David Glenn Smith and colleagues added the Pomo, the Blackfoot, the Cheyenne/Arapaho, the Kiowa, the linguistically Kiowa-related Jemez Puebloans (one possible source of X among the Navajo), and the Micmac to this list, the Ojibwa, Kiowa, and Micmac displaying the highest concentrations. The Cherokee have since been included, and X2A has been identified in skeletons as old as Washington State's 8,500-year-old Kennewick Man. Of these eleven groups, four (including the Chippewa and the Micmac) are of Algonkian speech, and a plausible inference is that X spread with (and beyond) the Algonkians as they dispersed from southern Ontario about the first millennium BC. Interestingly, in Colonial-period portraits many eastern Algonkians look part Caucasoid. (Note that other characteristic European mtDNA haplogroups appear to be largely absent among most unmixed American Indians; see below.)

Whereas Michael Brown's team and fellow geneticist Antonio Torroni thought only in terms of X's spread from Eurasia via Beringia—despite the haplogroup's absence in most of Siberia and in East Asia—others soon linked these findings with the suggestions of the sort that Emerson Greenman had made decades previously concerning possible Pleistocene movements to northeastern North America via the edges of the frozen North Atlantic ice.[30] The Smithsonian archaeologist Dennis Stanford and the British archaeologist Bruce Bradley have proposed that the homeland of the ancestors of the carriers of the early North American Clovis culture, always believed to have been Siberia, was, in reality, to be sought in the territories of the Upper Paleolithic Solutrean culture of Spain and France and that Solutreans may have brought X to America.[31] However, Hg X likely did not reach western Europe in time to be carried to the New World by Solutreans,[32] and most scholars continue to attribute X to founding migrations of people carrying Caucasian genes eastward from middle Eurasia through Beringia. At one time, it seemed possible that Bronze Age eastern Mediterraneans ascending the Saint Lawrence River and the Great Lakes seeking Lake Superior copper could have brought in X some six millennia ago, but the Kennewick occurrence is substantially older than that.[33] The degree of sequence differences between the known American and European versions of X preclude Native America's X2A's being simply the result of post-Columbian or late pre-Columbian European admixture to the Indians.[34]

Finally, we may mention the discovery of Eurasian Hg U in the Norris Farm, Illinois, burial circa AD 1400 (on U, see below).[35]

Y Chromosome DNA

So far, Y (male) chromosome DNA (MSR-DNA) studies have contributed rather less than have mtDNA studies to answering questions regarding early human movements, especially those concerning transoceanic contacts. In terms of percentages of populations, but one major, two minor, and around eight very minor lineages have been identified among Native Americans. Two—haplogroups Q (circa 75 percent) and C (circa 2.3 percent)—are believed to be early founding ones; a third, R (circa 5.7 percent; around 12 percent in North America), is widely presumed largely to represent post-1492 European admixture (but see below) and the eight others mostly to reflect Eurasian and African inputs, for a hefty total foreign male input of 22.7 percent or slightly less. The frequency of Hg Q is highest in Native Central America, somewhat less in Native South America, and notably lower in Native North America, although dominant in all three regions.

Haplogroup C is found from northeast Asia to Australia. Apart from a few incidences in Native South America, rare C is entirely North American in occurrence in the hemisphere, with half of the eight populations in which it has been identified being Na-Denéan—Na-Denéans, thus appearing to be likely conveyers of C to the New World.[36] The haplogroup's presence in South Americans could represent a separate and later Asian input.

The geneticists Lutz Roewar and colleagues "identified a cluster of Native American founding lineages of Y chromosomes, called C-M217 (C3*), within a restricted area of Ecuador.... The same haplogroup occurs at high frequency in Central, East, and North East Asia [at 15 percent among the Ainu, and in Oceania], but is virtually absent from North (except Alaska) and Central America. Possible scenarios for the introduction of C-M217 (C3*) into Ecuador may thus include a coastal or trans-Pacific route, an idea also supported by occasional archaeological evidence and the recent coalescence of the C3* haplotypes."[37] Subclade C3b appears to be confined to North America, and the ancestral C3* is found only in four cases from northwest South America (among lowland Kichwas and the adjacent Waorani) and one (of a slightly different haplotype than the Ecuadorians') from an Alaskan Tlingit (in whose territory Japanese junks washed up in the past).

No C lineages at all have so far been identified from Central America. Ecuador's C3*s were genetically sufficiently distant from current Asian ones that the split must have predated the settling of the Americas. The Kichwas' two haplotypes related most closely to a Koryak haplotype from Kamchatka, whereas the Waoranis' haplotype was closest to a Mongolian one. "The putative C3* haplotypes of the Colombian Wayuu were only distantly related to the Ecuadorians['']." Assuming a generation length of thirty years, the time to most recent common ancestor of the South American C3*s was estimated to be 5127–3862 BC, far too late to reflect differentiation beginning with the initial settlers but quite compatible with postulated Jōmon input from Japan between 4400 and 3300 BC (see below).

mtDNA Hg U and MSR-DNA Hg R have now been identified as present circa 24,000 years ago at Mal'ta, in south-central Siberia. Thus, this may reflect an ancient population ancestral to some U and R among Native Americans, who share 14–38 percent of their ancestry with Mal'ta folks, a population that appears also to be genetically basal to Europeans.[38] Too, U, R, and other genetic elements could have entered North America via the LGM Atlantic ice and/or via later transatlantic inputs.[39] Among the later would have been Norsemen—Greenland Inuit carry Native America's highest percentages of R.

Intriguing is the presence of African-type MSR-DNA M haplotypes in several Native American populations, including Mexico's Mixe.[40] Although any or all of these occurrences might be entirely the result of post-1500 admixture from African-derived slaves, still the Negroid-looking Olmec and other portrait sculptures discussed in chapter 30 should be remembered; like today's Mixe, the Olmec are thought to have been Mixe-Zoquean speakers.

Pathogenic Human T-Lymphotropic Viruses

Human T-lymphotropic viruses (HTLVs) cause an uncommon human T-cell leukemia, the incidences of whose type I's Cosmopolitan group's subtypes A, B, and C have been studied here and there around the world. Although sexually transmissible, the retrovirus is passed on largely not by ordinary contagion but vertically, that is, from mother to nursing child, and therefore has potential in the tracing of human movements. In 1994, Tomoyuki Miura and colleagues reported that, globally, the highest seropositivity against HTLV-I existed in Japan's Ryukyu Islands and on nearby Kyushu. In 1990, it was also reported that HTLV-I antibodies had been detected among members of isolated South American indigenous populations in Andean and Amazonian Colombia,[41] and that the Transcontinental, A, subtype antibody had also been found in a 1,500-year-old Chilean mummy.[42]

Unlike elsewhere in Native America, there turned out to be high concentrations specifically of subtype A in the southwest of Colombia and in northwestern Ecuador, especially among the Noanama/Wanama. These occurrences, as well as some Caribbean instances, grouped cladistically most closely with occurrences in Japan. In Japan and the Russian Federation, subtype A is concentrated in Ryukuan Okinawa, Ainu Hokkaido, and Nivkhian Sakhalin, all areas whose populations are believed to have in part descended from ancient Jōmon people.[43] With regard to HTLV-I, Miura and coauthors wrote: "Subtype A implies a close connection of the Caribbean and South American native with the Japanese and thereby a possible migration of the lineage to the American continent via Beringia in the Paleolithic era. Subtype C consists of the West African and other Caribbean isolates, indicating that not all but part of the Caribbean strains directly originated from West Africa probably during the period of slave trade."[44]

By two years later, Masahiro Yamashita and colleagues had identified subtype A much more widely in the world, concluding that it had originated in South Asia, whence it spread to Iran and (probably with modern migration) to South Africa. They believed that the ancestors of the early Ainu had carried it to Japan, probably before the closing of the Beringian land bridge. An additional find of the HTLV-I Cosmopolitan group (subtype unspecified) among Aleuts reinforced their conclusion of the virus's entry with the first settlers some 12,000 years ago.[45] However, it is likely that the ancestral Eskimo-Aleut arrived in Alaska long after 12,000 years ago and are irrelevant to the South American situation; further, it is now clear that humans had settled in the Americas notably earlier than 12,000 years ago.

Although any such Ainu link could conceivably have been a consequence of Late Pleistocene/Early Holocene Ainu-Australoid Pacific Rim migrations,[46] HTLV-I's apparent virtual absence in North America argues against this (the very few, North Pacific coast instances found might conceivably have resulted from nineteenth-century far eastern Russian whalers' activity). But instead of reflecting the initial or other quite-early movement of humans into the New World, the link could instead or in addition be the Kyushu Jōmon Japanese contacts with northwest South America in the fourth millennium BC, proposed in 1962 by the archaeologists Emilio Estrada, Betty Meggers, and Clifford Evans, on the basis of ceramic resemblances, with subsequent limited spread.[47] In fact, a study of thirteen genetic markers indicated that the Noanama of Colombia closely resembled the Samoans (who carry some Papuan genes) and the people of Japan, especially the Ainu.[48] Investigations of genetic markers specifically related to HLAs (see above) also tie South Americans to Japan, whereas these markers seem to be absent in Central and North America. Certain other researchers in Japan had similar ideas regarding HTLV-Is. "These data support our suggestion and that of Cerna et al. [1993] that ancient trans-Pacific arrival to South America could have occurred through Oceania and perhaps from [Japan] directly."[49] Noanama Territory, it turns out, lies along the logical route between Valdivia, Ecuador, and San Jacinto, Colombia, both of which, on archaeological grounds, have been suggested to have Jōmon connections, although from different parts of the Japanese archipelago.

In addition, as has been noted above, the mtDNA 9-bp deletion (characteristic of haplogroup B), considered an Asian/Native American marker, is not present among the Jōmon or in ancient Peru and Chile (or in northern Siberia or northern North America). These distributions imply a transoceanic rather than a Pacific Rim movement. Likewise, although the West African link of HTLV-I subtype C could well have resulted from post-Columbian importation of slaves from Africa, one must also consider proposals (alluded to above) concerning pre-1492 blacks in the Caribbean region (study of the degree of difference between the African and New World versions of this virus might provide clues as to the time depth of introduction).

Some Case Studies

The Cherokee

A rare example of a molecular-genetic examination of a single Native American nation in the context of the question of pre-1492-foreign-inputs question is a study concerning the Cherokee undertaken by the part-Cherokee DNA consultant Donald N. Yates and collaborators. He characterized the mtDNA of fifty-two individuals of partial Cherokee ancestry who did not display any of the usual Native American mtDNA haplogroups A through D, identifying (in order of frequency) haplogroups T, U, X, J, H, L, and K. T, X, and J are essentially Levantine (eastern Mediterranean) in origin, with from a little to a great deal of ancient expansion into Europe.

Hg T seems to have emerged in Mesopotamia and later spread into Europe. This Hg occurred in nearly 27 percent of Yates's sample. None of the Cherokee Ts exactly matched any other known T haplotype, and the Cherokee percentage of T was three times as high as that of the general US population. Cherokee/ Melungeon-associated J haplotypes are not precisely duplicated elsewhere, either, suggesting the passage of much time to allow differentiation. H is also common in the Near East but is most frequent in France and Spain. Although it is very abundant among current white Americans, it was the least common (four instances) among these non-A, -B, -C, or -D Cherokee descendants; the Hts represented appear to be confined to North America. Hg U is largely European, North African, and South Asian and is generally absent among Native Americans. However, it reached a level of approximately 25 percent among these Cherokee descendants, whose Hts turned out to be very diverse and to include some mutations unique to American Indians, again implying considerable elapsed time since introduction. Haplogroup X occurred at levels much higher (13.5 percent) than among either other American Indian groups or Euro-Americans and comparable in frequency only to that of the Druze of Lebanon and Israel, with whom it shared certain mutations. J, apparently of ultimate Levantine origin, occurs in Europe at levels comparable to those among the Cherokee as well as in the Near East; the Cherokee descendants studied shared some haplotypes with Jews. Too, the Jewish "Cohen gene" has been traced back within the Cherokee to no later than about AD 1640.

Yates's genetically remarkably diverse Cherokee sample, the unique haplotypes represented therein, and the frequencies of the haplogroups found— quite different from those of the larger US population—are striking: "Similar proportions of these haplogroups are noted in the populations of Egypt, Israel and other parts of the East Mediterranean. . . . No such mix could result from post-1492 European gene flow into the Cherokee Nation. To dismiss the evidence as admixture would mean that there was a large influx of Middle Eastern women selectively marrying Cherokee men in historical times, something not even suggested by historical records."[50] On the frontier, miscegenation was, in fact, very largely a European-male/Native-female proposition, resulting in little or no transfer of mtDNA.

In a second phase of the study, fifty-six of a total of sixty-seven additional Cherokee-descended individuals were found to display non-A-through-D or X mtDNA Hgs, with 19.4 percent Ts (comparable to the percentage among Jews of Iraq and Iran), 16.4 percent Hs, 14.9 percent Us, 9 percent Js (common among Jews), and 9 percent Ls. Five mtDNA Hg-H participants had unique haplotypes. Additional Hgs identified were I, N, V, and W, each composing 3 percent or less of the sample; one of the I Hgs was unique. Fifty-five unique, rare, or otherwise unrecorded single nucleotide polymorphisms on hypervariable region 1 and HVR2 were identified—once again, indicative of antiquity among the Cherokee. Yates's hypothesis is that immigrants, including women, from Ptolemaic Egypt in the third century BC formed the nucleus of what was to become the Cherokee, the input not necessarily taking place in historical Cherokee territory.[51]

Haplogroups H, T, and X occur among the Micmac of Canada's Maritimes as well. In light of indigenous New World X's seemingly being confined to North America, particularly toward the north—including the Great Lakes region and the Saint Lawrence River zone—Yates suggested consideration of the thought that Mediterraneans were anciently active in the region. This again brings to mind the unexplained intensive prehistoric copper-mining activity of the Upper Great Lakes region alluded to in chapter 26.

The Kaingáng

Uniparental DNA has so far been the main basis of genetic comparisons among populations. However, Y chromosome and mtDNA tell us nothing about the genetics of one's mother's father's lineage or one's father's mother's. As molecular-genetic technology rapidly advances, we may anticipate the increasing and increasingly revelatory use of biparental, autosomal genetic systems, even whole-genome comparisons, to provide clearer pictures of historical relationships and geographic origins. Meanwhile, chemical genetics continues to offer some clues.

James Guthrie has taken note of a genetically peculiar picture among the Kaingáng people of southern Brazil. This group displays a very high frequency (47 percent) of the MS haplotype in the MSNs antigen system of the human blood (in which polymorphisms do not seem to convey differential selective advantage). The MS phenotype is characteristic of Southwest Asia and North Africa, but its distribution in Native South America is limited; it peaks in frequency (5 to 72 percent) in the upper Paraguay River drainage. Too, the Kaingáng—uniquely in South America, so far—manifest a significant frequency of HLA A*29, which in the Old World is high in Spain but also in Lebanon and in Central Africa, and they also present 1.3 percent HLA B*14, whose highest frequencies are in Portugal but which also occurs in Sardinia, North Africa, and Iraq (these HLAs appear, too, among west coast South America's Atacama and Mapuche). Haplotype B*13 occurs among the Kaingáng, as well. Elsewhere, it is most common in Oceania and South Asia but is also not unusual in Lebanon. Guthrie tentatively tied this genetic picture to Canaanite (Phoenician) inscriptions reported from the region.[52]

Additional Discoveries

Some years ago, a research team ascertained that some Polynesians and certain Indians of Chile and Argentina share four unusual mtDNA lineage markers and considered that to be evidence of contact.[53] However, another group of workers esteemed those shared lineages to reflect only a common Asiatic ancestry.[54] Neither group saw any support for Thor Heyerdahl's hypothesis of massive migrations into Polynesia from the Americas; both teams found that genetics indicates that basic Polynesian settlement was accomplished from the west, including two distinct populations—southeastern Asian and "Melanesian" (Papuan). Still, a study of HLAs as well as a whole-genome investigation have revealed pre-Columbian South American Indian genetic inputs to the population of Easter Island, despite a dearth of uniparental-DNA evidence.[55]

More surprising is the discovery of the mtDNA-haplogroup-B "Polynesian motif"—prominent in Oceania and on Madagascar—among the Botocudo, a formerly coastal people now in eastern Brazil's Minas Gerais state. "In all of the positions examined by us," wrote the researchers, "the sequences of the Botocudos had exact matches to the common haplotypes observed in Polynesians, particularly in the control region."[56] The researchers thought it likely that inputs from Madagascan slaves account for this motif in Brazil. However, the Malagasy motif differs by two mutations from the Polynesian version, and a pre-Columbian transatlantic contact from Polynesia—amazing as that would be—must be considered a possibility.

Summary

Certain genes relating to the human serological (blood) system exist in multiple variants, none of which (other than ABO) has any so-far demonstrable selective advantage. Many independent geographically restricted (and, in some cases, rare) Old World human genetic polymorphisms also exist among certain American Indian groups, clustering especially in Mesoamerica and in the central Andean region. In most cases, these genetic variants do not mirror the genetic profiles of post-1492 European or African Colonial immigrants and their descendants. The only reasonable conclusion seems to be that most or all of these genes that are "anomalous" in Native America reflect a series of significant contacts, involving gene flow, from overseas, particularly from the Afro-Asiatic (Mediterranean/Middle Eastern) and southern (South and Southeast) Asian zones but also from East Asia and sub-Saharan Africa and, probably, Europe. Asian mitochondrial-DNA haplogroup B is common among southerly Amerinds but is absent in northern North America and Siberia, suggesting seaborne arrival (or later genetic swamping in the North), a conclusion reinforced by the similar distributions of a number of blood factors.

V

Conclusions

What we know is little. What we are ignorant of is immense.
—last words of Pierre-Simon Laplace, 1825

In the course of our explorations of the human past in this volume, we have challenged the standard notion that the peoples of the New World were hermetically sealed off from those of the Old World until Christopher Columbus planted his sovereigns' flag on a Bahamian island, or at least until Leif Eiríksson and associates set up camp in Newfoundland a few centuries earlier. In the process, we have come to recognize that this notion (although also influenced by nonevidentiary factors not delved into here) rests, to a considerable extent, upon overly simple, insufficiently tested suppositions and incompletely thought-through conclusions concerning both physical geography and human capabilities. It manifests as a lack of awareness of various facts and concepts critical to making fully informed judgments regarding what really happened in earlier times.

This lack of awareness reflects the relative recency of many of the relevant findings as well as the challenging range of academic disciplines in which these findings have been reported. However, it also follows from the fact that the great majority of scholars simply accept that significant pre-Columbian, pre-Norse transoceanic interactions not only remain unattested but were, in fact, impossible, rendering any full-fledged effort to investigate the matter an unproductive allocation of valuable time. I believe that this book has shown, however, that such a perception now cries out for very serious revision. The last chapter provides a concluding overview of what we have learned about this issue and where we need next to go.

32

Mission Possible

Crossings Occurred

The real voyage of discovery consists not in seeking new lands, but in seeing with new eyes.

—Marcel Proust, 1925

In 1993, the American historian Jerry H. Bentley wrote, "The lack of solid, substantial information will make it impossible, probably forever, to develop definitive proofs either for or against theories of intercontinental diffusion."[1] However, the sum of the evidence discussed in chapters 26 through 31 seems definitive in demonstrating the reality of important transoceanic interactions, and, therefore, opportunity for diffusion of culture. Demonstration of opportunity for cultural exchange does not prove that such exchange actually occurred beyond the realm of the proof of contact itself. Still, it does mean that—at least in areas between which encounter is demonstrable—every explicit cultural similarity is a candidate for explanation in terms of overseas introduction, and such introduction may, in fact, be the most parsimonious explanation.

Come the Revolution(s)

Although many of the pertinent data and diffusionist explanatory models have been around and readily available for over half a century, there *have* been some dramatic developments in recent decades that throw much new light on the issue and that make the present synthesis most timely. I see six major evidentiary revolutions that have taken place largely since 1980. Two of these—in linguistics/epigraphy and in calendrical/cosmological studies—do not figure in this book, but the others do, have been given major treatment earlier in the work, and are summarized here.

Watercraft and Navigation

It was once widely agreed that, before the Renaissance, humans had not yet developed the *means* of effecting interhemispheric contacts: neither vessels capable of crossing oceans nor requisite navigational skills (never mind the feats of the Polynesians and the Norse). However, the development of nautical archaeology during recent decades, added to the study of historically observed traditional watercraft and sailing rigs as well as to long-distance experimental voyaging in a variety of replica craft, has vastly increased our knowledge of and respect for premodern maritime conveyances, their temporally deep roots, and their considerable capabilities. Ethnographic and historical investigations and at-sea experiments have done likewise for traditional noninstrumental navigation and haven-finding.

Archaeology has demonstrated modern human presence not only in Australia but also on islands of Near Oceania, the Mediterranean, and East Asia at least 40,000 to 50,000 years ago. Reaching these bits of land required traversing substantial and sometimes multiple water gaps and, therefore, presupposes possession of adequate aquatic craft.

These various research discoveries have made clear that watercraft and way-finding methods quite serviceable for crossing great expanses of open ocean existed far earlier than formerly imagined. In addition, advances in oceanography, climatology, and computer modeling of accidental drift and other voyages have underlined both intentional nautical possibilities and, for disabled craft, the truly impelling quality of nature's winds and currents.

Pathogens

We have noted a number of kinds of "hard," mostly biological, evidence that testify to contacts. Pathogens are among the relevant organisms.

Once thought of as an edenic "virgin-soil" hemisphere with respect to almost all Old World human pathogens, the New World, we now know, anciently harbored at least tuberculosis and perhaps one or more other Afroeurasian maladies. Both of the hemispheres possessed treponematosic diseases as well, although the sources, routes of entry, and timings of transfers remain uncertain. Less equivocal than these microbial diseases are human intestinal parasites. Since the 1980s, paleopathological investigations have revealed that four species of tropical/subtropical Old World intestinal worms that cannot endure cold climates like those of Siberia and Alaska were widespread in the pre-1492 Americas—from remarkably early times—and must have been introduced by ocean voyagers. A species of head louse was also shared.

Domesticates

The great majority of cultivated plants and domesticated animals cannot cross oceans—or even survive—without human intervention. Although there has long been circumstantial evidence of the presences of a plethora of domesticates in the hemisphere opposite that of their origins, in recent decades the archaeological discovery of datable physical/chemical remains of numbers of such cultigens and the chicken have come to attest, in material fashion, the pre-Columbian human-mediated transfer of a score or more of domesticated plants and animals. Because the establishment of novel domesticates is seldom easily accomplished, the interhemispheric sharing of so many species implies that pre-1492 transoceanic contacts were intensive.

Human Genetics

Although for over a century now observers have made comparisons between the physiognomies of certain ancient Americans and images of them in art on the one hand and certain Old World facial types on the other hand, the much more recent and very rapid development of chemical and, especially, molecular genetics has provided powerful tools for assessing historical relationships among populations globally. The geographic patterns of uniparental DNA to some extent, and of blood factors such as human leucocyte antigens to a much greater extent, appear explicable only in terms of early New World introductions by voyagers originating in various parts of the Old World.

Consilience

The issue of ancient interhemispheric intercourse is highly complex, involving myriad kinds of evidence, only some of which has been presented here. Until now, most who have addressed this topic have looked at one class of indicators or another, often coming to conclusions that are, on their own, legitimately debatable. But what a comprehensive, transdisciplinary approach such as the present one highlights is the fact that multiple, unrelated lines of both biological and cultural evidence all point to a consistent conclusion: pre-Columbian, pre-Norse interactions not only occurred but were important. This finding alone calls for a major rewriting of traditional history and prehistory. It also calls for archaeologists, geneticists, and other professionals to eschew isolationist presuppositions and thus to avoid assuming that an "out-of-place" artifact or an unexpected haplogroup necessarily reflects post-Columbian intrusion, investigative error, admixture, or fraud. In fact, instead of reflexive rejection we should begin *looking for* such seeming anomalies and testing them for possible pre-Columbian proveniences.

Most significantly, the ultimate purpose of investigating these various maritime and biological phenomena has been, all along, to weigh not only the likelihood that substantial transoceanic interactions took place in the pre-Columbian past but also, beyond that, the probability that many of the specific and detailed cultural commonalities among certain societies of the two hemispheres derive not largely from independent parallel or convergent evolution from a shared Upper Paleolithic heritage but, rather, from historical cultural transfer long after the initial peopling of the New World.

Certainly, this book has shown that the means, motives, and opportunities for such relocation existed. Our future tasks are to pinpoint more specifically what technologies, practices, beliefs, languages, and so on are likely to represent interhemispheric transfers and hybridizations, and to identify what the implications of potentially fundamental and massive exchanges may be for our understandings of both the true culture history of our species and the nature of cultural development itself.

Notes

Preface

1. Ekholm 1955, 95.
2. Quoted in Chase 1971, 7.
3. Gold 1999, 37.
4. Much of the previous text also appears in Jett 2000b, by permission of David Robinson for the Conference of Latin Americanist Geographers.

Introduction

1. On his fourth voyage in 1504, Columbus encountered, in a Native's dwelling on Guadeloupe, an iron pot and the stern post of a European ship (not of his earlier abandoned *Santa María*); the party thought it was from the Canary Islands, "proof," wrote Columbus biographer John Dyson (1991, 188), "that at least one ship had made it across the Atlantic before Columbus."
2. Zerubavel 1992, 2.
3. See Jett 2000c.
4. Haslip-Viera, Ortiz de Montellano, and Barbour 1997, 437.
5. Whitfield 1996, 5; cf. Meltzer 1999, 56; Diamond 1997, 370.
6. Also old, however, were contrary notions of a foreign origin for New World cultures, e.g., that the American Indians derived from the "lost" tribes of Israel or from a variety of other Old World nations.
7. Stengel 2000, 44.
8. The great majority of the school's literary production is available only in German. An exception is the translation Schmidt 1939.
9. Ratzel's works and Ratzel student Alfred Hettner's 1929 *Der Gang der Kultur über die Erde* influenced the thinking of the German American cultural geographer Carl O. Sauer and his many students; see Williams 2014; Speth 1999.
10. Herskovitz 1948, 505. On this school, see, e.g., Lucas 1978.
11. Carter 1988, 4; on Carter, see Jett 2007b; on the school, see Hunka 1972; Smith 2011; Crook 2011.

12. See Jett 1983, 351–53. For overviews of the entire topic, see Jett 1993, 1998b, 2014.

13. Frost 1993, 46.

14. Ekholm 1955, 96.

15. Driver 1973, 166.

16. Sociologists and some others, following more strictly the term's utilization in physics, confine use of the term "diffusion" to situations in which the innovation spreads *throughout* the originating or receiving society. Of course, today dispersal of ideas is frequently effected, very rapidly, via electronic and other media.

17. Parry 1981, 184.

18. See, e.g., Welch 1999.

19. Kahler 1965, 42; cf. Wood 2008, 10, also 92.

20. Geertz 1965, 93.

21. *Poetics* 25, 350 BC.

22. Meacham 1984–85, 91.

23. Terrell 1981, 251.

24. This would seem intuitively obvious (cf. Kroeber 1948, 413). Empirical support comes from psychological research: "Social learning (learning through observation or interaction with other individuals) is widespread in nature and is central to the remarkable success of humanity." A test of subjects' selection of social learning versus asocial trial and error and other innovative learning during problem-solving found that, "The winning strategy . . . relied nearly exclusively on social learning" (Rendell et al. 2010, 208).

25. Needham 1970, 70.

26. Bellwood 1997, 127.

27. Darjes, quoted in Piggott 1983, 4.

Part I

1. Kehoe 2010, 205; Bricker 2009, 69–70.

Chapter 1

1. Zerubavel 1992, 28.

2. Strabo mentioned that 120 ships sailed annually from the upper Red Sea port of Myos Hormos to India. The open-ocean passage from the Red Sea to the Malabar Coast took about forty days (see Fagan 2012, 125–26).

3. Lewis and Wigen 1997, ix.

4. Sarton 1993, 427. See also Sherner 2011, 281.

5. Zerubavel 1992, 74. An extremely rare exception, Johan Ruysch's map of 1507, split the world in the middle of Asia, whose eastern part was depicted at the map's left-hand (western) end. South America was shown as being to the east of Asia, with an ocean in between.

6. Lewis and Wigen 1997, 26.

7. Quoted in Sobel 1995, 165.

8. See MacDonald 1971, 14–15; Thirslund 1997, 61; Rafnsson 1997, 115; Wallace 2000, 228; Mowat 2000, 192.

9. During glacial periods, the environment of the Aleutians would have been less different from that of the present than would other areas of Beringia.

10. Speck 1970, 8. Certain other authors differ.

11. See McCartney 1984, 122–23, 135.

12. See Sawatzky and Lehn 1976; Gardner 1986, 63; Mowat 1965, 62.

13. Parry 1981, 250.

14. Lewis 1994, 12–13.

15. See Dodd 1972, 33, 59–61; Heyen 1963, 70, 72; Lissau 1978; Irwin 1992, 44, 56. See also chapter 19.

16. See McGrail 1987, 262–64; Hyde 1947, 316–17. An estimate of the average velocity of Minoan ships with fair wind is higher: 9.7 knots; see Reynolds 1996, 331.

17. On the ancients' geographical ideas mentioned in this section, see Horowitz 1998, 29, 30, 40, 42, 325, 332; Soule 1976, 213; Hyde 1947, 159–60; Thomson 1965, 98, 116, 119, 163, 202–4, 327, 331; Dilke 1985, 36; Sarton 1993, 413; and Harley and Woodard 1987, 131–60.

18. Roller 2006, 51.

19. Quoted in Romm 1992, 139–40, and Cassidy 1968, 31–32.

20. Strabo, quoted in Hyde 1947, 159, 310.

Chapter 2

1. See Russell 1991, 19; Dilke 1985, 27–28; Soule 1976, 117.

2. See Nebenzahl 1990, 2.

3. See Manzano Manzano 1976.

4. Parry 1981, 195.

5. See, e.g., Boorstin 1983, 107.

6. Morison 1942, 33. Note the interesting statement made by Columbus in his report to the Crown upon his return from his third voyage: "The earth . . . is not round . . . but is . . . in the shape of a pear" (quoted in Niederland 1989, 112).

7. Gould 1994, 12. The misapprehension that medieval thinkers were all flat-earthers seems to have been promoted by scientists engaged in the mid-nineteenth-century science-versus-religion wars (16).

8. See, especially, Russell 1991; Dilke 1985; Cassidy 1968; Thomson 1965; Nicastro 2008.

9. Fuson 1995, 18.

10. See Hyde 1947, 304–5; Miquel 1996, 796–97; Davidson 1970, 74; Vincent-Barwood 1992, 8.

11. Nasr 1968, 99.

12. See Freely 2009.

13. See Needham 1959, 498, 537; Temple 1986, 30; Basham 1959, 488.

14. Gosden 1991, 334.

Chapter 3

1. The Coriolis effect is the apparent downwind deflection of winds that results from the interaction between Earth's rotation and the planet's surface curvature. In the Northern Hemisphere, the veering is to the right when looking downwind, and in the Southern Hemisphere it is to the left.

2. The simple conveyor-belt model has recently been modified owing to recognition of the effects of eddy and of wind fields: the progress of a current is not necessarily straight but may include meanders and swirls. This somewhat dampens but does not negate the practical effects described in this chapter.

3. See King and Bird 1976, 128; Ebbesmeyer 2007.

4. Renner 2004, S31.

5. See Stokes 1934, 2782; de Laubenfels 1950, 256; Ebbesmeyer 2008b.

6. al-Bīrūnī, quoted in Dick-Read 2005, 73.

7. See Spate 1979, endpapers; Winchester 1985, 66–67.

8. See Voitov and Tumarkin 1967, 92.

9. Cook quoted in Lewis 1980, 69.

10. See Finney et al. 1989; Finney 2001. The significance of these storm-wind reversals was noted by Ferdon in 1963, 504–5.

11. See Finney 1996a, 42; Ronan 1986, 184.

12. The average of every four years, as seen since 1950, differs from that prevailing in the late nineteenth century, which was about every ten to fifteen years (see Dunbar 2000).

13. See Anderson et al. 2006.

14. See Suplee 1999, 83, 86; Caviedes 2001, 5, 13–14, 60; Philander 1990, 9, 11.

15. See Carrée et al. 2014.

16. Heyerdahl 1978, 55.

17. See King 1963, 138; also Goetzfridt 1992, 233; Lewis 1994, 144.

18. See de Laubenfels 1950, 259.

19. See Riesenberg 1965, 167.

20. See Voitov and Tumarkin 1967, 91, 94.

21. See Finney 1994, 212.

22. Åkerblom 1968, 57, 89.

23. See Butler and Butler 1991; Pidgeon 1950, 195; Robinson 1973.

24. Heyerdahl 1963, 487.

25. See Ferdon 1963, 502–5; Finney et al. 1989, 271; also Åkerblom 1968, 51.

26. Voitov and Tumarkin 1967, 91.

27. Pearce and Pearce 2010 provides additional data and thought concerning climate and current fluctuations and utilization but was obtained too late to incorporate here. Schoolcraft and Maury are both quoted in Lewthwaite 1970, 129.

28. Levathes 1994, 31.

29. Needham, Lin, and Lu 1971, 550.

30. Could the term *Okeanós*, generally thought to derive from the name of an eponymous water god (son of Uranus and Gaia), relate to *okeos* "swiftly" and *naus* "ship"? The classicist James S. Romm (1992, 13) stated that *Okeanos* is not of Greek derivation but may relate to Phoenician *ma'uk* or Sanskrit *a-çayana* "that which encircles."

31. See Chapman 1973.

Chapter 4

1. Cuppage 1994, 2, 14.

2. See Cuppage 1994, 9; Bergreen 2003, 215.

3. Norbert Ohler 1989, 50.

4. Arias 1989, 143.

5. See Bailey and Bailey 1974.

6. See Callahan 1996.

7. See Robinson 1973.

8. See Banack 1991.

9. This section is a condensation of Jett 2005–7a. Used with the permission of the Pre-Columbian Overseas Contacts Organization's *Pre-Columbiana: A Journal of Long-Distance Contacts.*

10. Slocum 1962, 344, 350.
11. Heyerdahl 1986, 34.
12. See, e.g., MacIntyre, Noji, and Estep 1998, 109.
13. Critchley 1943, 43–44.
14. See Bombard 1986; Lindemann 1998.
15. See MacIntyre, Noji, and Estep 1998, 107, 109.

Chapter 5

1. See Castlereach 1971, 81; Firstbrook 1997, 37; Seaver 1996, 208; Forbes 1993, 8. On *The American Discovery of Europe*, see Forbes 2007.
2. See Stokes 1934, 2792; Danielsson 1956, 69.
3. See Moody 2006, 70–71, 73; Emmons 1990, 10.
4. Kehoe 1998, 201.
5. See Keddie 1990, 10.
6. See Ebbesmeyer 2009b. Ongoing reports of drifts appear in Ebbesmeyer's newsletter *Beachcombers' Alert!* See also the Drifters newsletter, *The Drifting Seed*.
7. See Moody 2006, 84–85, 89–90.
8. Callaghan 2005, 109.
9. Campbell 1997, 99.
10. See Mookerji 1962, 50.
11. Thirslund 1997, 62.
12. See Severin 1994, 105, 139–40.
13. *Odyssey*, Books IX, X, and XII.
14. Mookerji 1962, 40.
15. Haddawy 1995, 19, 24, 40, 45. The Arabic title is *Kitāb Alf Laylah Wah Layla* (*Thousand-Nights, One-Night Book*).
16. See Nelson 1963, 124–28; Goetzfridt 1992, 206, 208, 234, 239, 242–43; Miles, Barratt, and McFall 2006, 187.
17. Sharp 1957, 68–69.
18. See Arias 1989.
19. Agence France-Presse 2006.
20. On transatlantic drifting, see Richardson 1985, 44, 48; Ebbesmeyer 2008a, 2009a, 2009b.
21. See Hyde 1947, 161–62; Cassidy 1968, 78; Thomson 1965, 226; Marcus 1981, 6, 25, 125, 155, 175; Forbes 2007.
22. See Anonymous 1997, 7.
23. Hughes 1991.
24. Cassidy 1968, 78.
25. Parry 1981, 42; see also, 95, 96.
26. See Alcina Franch 1955, 878; Atoche Peña at al. 1995; de Balbín Behrman et al. 1995. Pliny recorded that in 25 BC King Juba II of ancient Mauritania (Morocco) sent an expedition down Africa's west coast to the Canaries, where sailors spotted an old temple (see Babcock 1918, 65; Hyde 1947, 152–53).
27. See Mowat 1965, 228, 230; Chapman 1981, 39–40.
28. See Sauer 1968, 86–89, 100, 110.
29. Diamond 2004.
30. Flood 1990, 37.
31. On Japanese drift voyaging and related matters, see Jett 1999a, 1999b, 1999c, 2003/4, 2005–7a. Callaghan (2005) calculated that during Japan's Edict Period (AD 1603–

1867), twenty-five drifting junks would have reached Haida Gwaii and thirty Vancouver Island, the most likely sources being the central east coast of Honshu, succeeded by Hokkaido; northern Honshu and Kyushu followed (see also Callaghan 2003).

32. Too, 2–3 percent of those from northwest Europe would reach Iceland or Greenland, and 13 percent of those from southern Africa and 4 percent of those from West Africa would reach northern South America. See Montenegro, Hetherington, et al. 2006.

33. See Associated Press 2012; Eriksen 2012; Morton 2013; Ebbesmeyer 2014.

34. Zumwinkle 1970, 11.

35. See Plummer 1991, 9.

36. Quimby 1985, 7.

37. See Plummer 1991, xiii. In 1916 a disabled fishing boat from Shimoda fetched up in Haida Gwaii (see Emmons 1990, 10).

38. See Quimby 1985; Plummer 1991, 77, 80, 82, 163; also Jett 1999b, 1999c.

39. See Gibbs 1968, 17.

40. See Quimby 1985; Stenger 2005.

41. See Stokes 1934, 2800.

Chapter 6

1. Introduced livestock diseases also had indirect human-demographic effects, causing declines in some native game species, such as bighorn sheep.

2. See, e.g., Lewis and Wigen 1997, 142–43; Alchon 2003, 31.

3. Dobyns 1980, 275.

4. Native American demographic decline was particularly dramatic in part because the Indians were impacted by a *variety* of exotic diseases within a mere century or two, sometimes simultaneously. In their weakened condition, they were susceptible to additional infections. See Ramenofsky 1987, 162.

5. Lovell 1992, 426.

6. We must recognize, however, that demographic figures for this time period can be only very roughly estimated.

7. Webster 2002, 248. For a statement by one physician and medical historian, see Settipane 1995, 3.

8. At least, until Jett 2004 (q.v. for full documentation), which this chapter synopsizes and augments; permission from Christine Pellach, Odyssey-Verlag. See also Haggett 1992; Kehoe 1998, 21.

9. All this despite the over-sanguine late-1960s US Surgeon General William H. Steward's statement that "we can close the books on infectious diseases" (quoted in Hand 2014, 199).

10. However, a good case can be made for pre-Columbian American forms of influenza. Its source could be ducks.

11. Kiple, 1993, 355, 630; emphasis added. Note that the Justinian strain of plague died out completely following the pandemic.

12. See Kiple 1993, 1095.

13. Kiple 1993, 414. See also Hopkins 2002, 13–29.

14. Tschanz 1997, 31.

15. Alfred W. Crosby Jr. (1997, 96–97) recognized this as an explanation for the tardy arrival of smallpox in the Caribbean and added, "Consider that moist heat and strong sunlight, characteristic of a tropical sea voyage, are particularly deadly to the smallpox virus." (The smallpox virus can, however, survive in clothing and bedding; Ramenofsky 1987, 146, 148.)

16. Haggett 1992, 395.
17. See Kelton 2007, 56, 63.
18. Cuppage 1994, 6.
19. See Toohey 2000, 86.
20. See Estes 1995.
21. Cook and Lovell 1991, 221.
22. Ramenofsky 1987, 169; also, 148–49; Merbs 1992, 36.
23. The 1519 population of the Central Mexican Symbiotic Region is estimated to have been between 2,600,000 and 3,100,000. Mexico as a whole may have held some 17,200,000 souls, the Andean region perhaps 14,000,000.
24. The numbers of susceptibles would decline rapidly mainly because of the large numbers of disease deaths plus those caused by disruption of the food supply, but also because all survivors of the infection would be immune. Note that in indigenous North America, until the end of the 1600s European diseases did not spread widely beyond their points of introduction; see Jones 2014, 502.
25. Cockburn 1963, 81.
26. Despite a number of European voyages to northeastern North America during the 1500s, indications are "that there were *no* sixteenth-century epidemics of consequence in the Northeast" (Snow and Lamphear 1988, 28).
27. The case of the Zuni Puebloans of New Mexico is of interest. Despite ninety years of intermittent Spanish contact beginning in 1539, no epidemic seems to have affected Zuni until the establishment of a Catholic mission there in 1629 (Eckert 2005).

Chapter 7

1. Kroeber 1923, 7.
2. Spinden 1933.
3. See Nordenskiöld 1931, 24; Merrill 1954, 245.
4. Diamond 1997, 164; also, 168–74.
5. See Kiple 1993, 813–17; Simoons 1970, 1994.
6. Merrill 1954, 258.
7. See Merrill 1954, 249, 262.
8. See Yen 1974, 266.
9. See White 1976, 26.
10. See Lewis and Runyan 1990, 46; Zohary 1998, 123; Watson 2008.
11. Batten 1999, 99.
12. Zohary 1998, 132.
13. See Bailey 1940, 275.
14. Hawkes 1998, 147.
15. See Smole 2002, 287.
16. See Rutter 1936, 158–71.
17. See Nabhan 2004.
18. See Beckman 2004, 26; Vanderbilt 2013, 107.
19. See Miller and Reedy 1990.
20. See Simoons 1991, 77, 122–23; personal observations in China, 2010.
21. Rozin and Rozin 1981, 6.
22. Fernández-Armesto 2002, 135, 137.
23. See Fischler 1988, 193.
24. Gremillion 2011, 116.
25. See, e.g., Mintz and Du Bois 2002; Simoons 1994, 320, 323.
26. Some scholars believe that the region's wild foods were so abundant that there

was no incentive to develop agriculture. Some of these wild species *were* managed, up to a point.

27. Simoons 1994, 323.

28. Messer 1997, 102–3.

29. Kubler 1947, 356–57; also, 354.

30. See Brandes 1992, 1999; Gremillion 2011, 118

31. Bray 1993, 301. See also Hawkes 1998, 147–54.

Chapter 8

1. Kubler 1961, 34; see also 1984, 36, 474.

2. Krieger 1935, 42.

3. See Kroeber 1946, 19.

4. Kroeber 1923, 7; see also 1948, 776; 1953, 60.

5. See Obayashi 1959; Shepard 1942; Davis 2000, 208–11.

6. See Hoebel 1949, 373.

7. See Thomsen 1960.

8. See Hosler 1994.

9. See Edwards 1965a, 351; also Doran 2002.

10. See Labbé 1999, 47, 52–53; Kahler 1965, 41.

11. George F. Carter Jr., personal communication.

12. See, for example, Baumer 2012, 90.

13. See Hodges 1970, 167; Ratnagar 1981, 177.

14. See Casson 1994b, 25–26, 47, 52; White 1984, 52.

15. See Braudel 1988, 114–15.

16. This reminds one of the prolonged medieval European rejection of the very practical Arabic numerals, including the supremely useful zero—try calculating in Roman numerals—because Arabic numerals were perceived as infidel numbers. (Before the later Middle Ages, use of a zero symbol was confined to South and Southeast Asia and the Maya country.)

17. See Bulliet 1975, 1983; Wiet 1969, 352–53.

18. Piggott 1983, 14.

19. On early wheel technology, see Spruytte 2010.

20. Anthony 2007, 397.

21. Batten 1999, 99.

22. Piggott 1983, 16.

23. White 1984, 127–28.

24. See Ekholm 1946; De Borhegyi 1970; Sorenson 1981.

25. See Keoke and Porterfield 2002, 299–300.

26. Hopkins 1973, 37.

27. See Gade and Rios 1971, 5, 13.

28. See Ingstad and Ingstad 2001.

29. See Lechtman 1984, 8–9, 35–36.

30. See de Barros 1997, 136–37, 141; Forbes 1950, 145, 263; see also Ottaway and Roberts 2008.

31. "Activities and tools connected with iron almost everywhere seem to be symbolically loaded. . . . Smelting . . . is hedged in by restrictions—taboos and protection against the evil eye—that serve to surround it with secrecy or separateness" (Haaland, Haaland, and Rijal 2002, 35, 53). See also de Barros 1997, 145; Blakely 2006, 171–72.

32. See Abbott 1974, 213, 217, 219, 221.

33. See Grieder 1978, 96, 101, 104–9.
34. See Laufer 1917, 148–77.
35. See Reina 1966, 67–68.
36. See Arnold, Wilson, and Nieves 2007, 67–71, 76, 82–83.
37. Foster 1959, 114.
38. Lackey 1982, 148.
39. Nicklin 1971, 42; also, 37, 44, 48.
40. See Santley, Arnold, and Pool 1989, 110–12, 119.
41. Eccott 2003; see also Sorenson and Raish 1996, 15, 55, 151, 308, 380, 435. In 1780, the priest Francisco Javier Clavijero, expelled from Mexico in 1767, illustrated his book with an image of what appears to be a Native masonry-dome sudatory (see Loyaza 2005, 56).
42. Kelley 1971, 62. The earliest known true vaulting is from Tepe Gawra, Iraq, late fourth millennium BC.
43. Shao 1983, vi–vii. The earliest known corbelling is from Tell Razuk, Iraq, ca. 2900 B.C.
44. See Smith 1950, vii.

Chapter 9

1. Bahn and Flenley 1992, 53.
2. See Ekholm 1964, 501.
3. Fraser 1965 460–61.
4. See Heine-Geldern 1960, 278–79.
5. E. Royston Pike 1976, 89; see also Ford and Beach 1951, 58; Blue 1997, 35, 38; Kirshenbaum 2011, 55–59. Jankowiak, Volsche, and Garcia 2015 found the romantic/ sexual kiss in only 46 percent of the cultures they sampled.
6. Quoted in Bruman 2000, 7.
7. Another possibility is that the ancestral Guanches were brought to the archipelago by Carthaginians or others.
8. See Heinrich 2004; Blust 1996, 31, 34; Finney 1996a, 49–50; Rivers 1912, 111–16; Weckler 1943, 37.
9. See Joel 1981, 27; Irwin 1981, 486–88; Le Moine 1987; Spriggs 1997, 156–57. Yet note a survival, revival, or reintroduction of pottery in Samoa, where non-Lapita-style ceramics dating from the fifteenth to seventeenth centuries AD have been found (see Clark, Sheppard, and Jones 1997). Likewise, around the fourteenth century Tongans (re)adopted, from Fiji, where the making of pottery had survived (see Blust 1996, 34).
10. See Moyle 2003; Rivers 1912, 110, 120; Barnett 1953, 61; White 1978, 12.
11. See Perrin 1979.
12. See Cipolla 1965, 117–21.
13. See Ayalon 1978.
14. Linton 1936, 311.
15. See, e.g., Casson 1977.
16. White 1962 110–11.
17. Aczel 2001, 158.
18. Social Science Research Council 1954, 980.
19. Fraser 1965, 475; see also Jett 1971, 49.
20. See Rudenko 1970 307, plate 157; Weiming and Guohua 1989, 14; Schoeser 2003, 46; Sakamoto 1985, 15.
21. Jared Diamond (1997) suggested that, as opposed to the north–south orienta-

tion of the American continents, cutting across ecological zones, east–west oriented Eurasia provided long continuous ecological zones favoring long-distance diffusion and cross-cultural fertilization. However, this perception omits consideration of the role of intensive water travel (e.g., extending along America's Pacific coast from Chile to Western Mexico and beyond) as a vehicle of diffusion.

22. That some few Indians and Inuits did arrive in Europe is the theme of Forbes 2007.

Chapter 10

1. Meggers 1975, 18.
2. Feder (2014; 2010, 85–88) explores this theme at some length.
3. Blench 2010, 246.
4. McGhee 2005, 41–42.
5. DeBoer 1996, 139.
6. Bellwood 1997, 227.
7. See Goitein 1963, 196.
8. See Brian Fagan 2012, 139–40.
9. See Weisgerber 1986, 136–37.
10. Tolstoy 1986, 9.
11. Kelley 1998b, 27–28.
12. See Tolstoy 1963; Cameron 2008.
13. One independent scholar has recognized bifaces of styles (Arterian and Lupemban) characteristic of parts of Africa 20,000–30,000 years ago that were found on the surface in the US Southeast and in Panama (see Hranicky 2011, 20–21).
14. See Wheeler 1971, 130–35.
15. See Parfitt 2008, 3.
16. Hole 1983, 10.
17. See Gladwin 1947, 253.
18. Brain 1996, 1.
19. But pre-Norse cereal pollen *has* been identified (see Barrett 2010, 297).
20. Brain ibid.
21. See Whittall 1989, 140; also, 1991.
22. Fraser 1965, 462.
23. See Epstein 1980; Pennington 2009; Sferrazza 2010. Inscriptions in Hebrew have been reported from Tennessee, West Virginia, and Ohio, as well. In 1994, a metal detector reportedly located a cache of fourth-century Roman coins on the Wisconsin River (Joseph 2013).
24. See Guthrie 2005, 2011–14a. On the "Burrows Cave," Illinois, fraud, see Wilson 2012.
25. See Fagan 1999, 183, 185.
26. See Kelley 1995, 107; Hristov and Sorenson 2011–14.
27. See, e.g., Jett 1971; Jett 1983, 364–65; Marx and Marx 1992; Joseph 2014; Labbé 1998.
28. See Jett 2011–14a.
29. See, e.g., Schledermann and McCullough 2003; Keddie 1990; Callaghan 2005, 111; Ingstad and Ingstad 2001; Wallace 2000; Totten 2008; Pringle 2012; Stewart 2012–13; Sutherland, Thompson, and Hunt 2015.
30. See García Payón 1961; Heine-Geldern 1967; Hristov and Genovés 1999, 2000, 2001; Schaaf and Wagner 2001.

31. See Kelley 1971, 60.

32. See Imbelloni 1930; Menghin 1962; Ramírez-Aliaga 2011, 99–103.

33. See Carter 1978.

34. See Pierson and Moriarty 1980; Frost 1982; Stickel 1983.

35. On the Bat Creek controversy, see McCulloch 2011–14.

36. See Covey 1975, 2004; Williams 1991, 239–51; Payn 1996; Burgess and Marshall 2009; Feder 2010, 257–59. Donald Yates is currently reexamining the evidence and finding it persuasive.

37. See Carlson and Dranchak 2006.

38. Keddie 1990, 20; also, Callaghan 2005, 110.

39. Vaillant 1931, 244–45; testing has since shown the head to be post-Columbian in age.

40. Quoted in Davis 2000, 81. Although not relating to the transoceanic question, Cyrus Gordon's experience on a pre–World War II dig in Palestine is instructive. If hired local workers brought in expectable objects, they were monetarily rewarded; if they presented *un*expected items, they were fired for attempted fraud (Shanks 2000, 56).

41. Totten 2008, 160.

42. Towle 1961, 97.

43. Quoted in Jett 2007b. The bones turned out to be post-Columbian.

44. Based largely on Marx and Marx 1992, 306–25, also 2004; Marx 1984.

45. Marx and Marx 2004, 31–32.

46. See Pellegrino 2004, 300.

47. See Gordon 1971, 68. The analysis was being undertaken by curator Mendel L. Peterson, who died in 2003.

48. See Morris n.d.

49. See, e.g., Jett 2006.

50. Rose 1999.

51. See Begley and Muir 1999, 56.

52. See Hardaker 2007.

Chapter 11

1. Landström 1966, 18.

2. On book destruction, see Highet 1962, 94; Polastron 2007; Baez 2008.

3. For a comprehensive account of the library, see Canfora 1990. Also Baez 2008, 43–54.

4. Needham 1970, 24.

5. Clement quoted in Roberts, Donaldson, and Coxe 2007, 302.

6. Temple 1986, 32.

7. Zerubavel 1992, 26–27, 80; see also Seaver 1996, 263–64.

8. Qian 1994, 77.

9. See Dudbridge 2000, 6–9.

10. See Mertz 1972, 122.

11. See Aczel 2001, 89.

12. See Baez 2008, 134.

13. See Menzies 2002, 8, 54–56. Note, however, that Menzies exaggerates the degree of obliteration of records and makes numerous other factual errors (see Jett 2003).

14. See Plummer 1991, vii, xv, xvi.

15. Wilson 1991, 16. For iconoclasm and the destruction of records in the ancient Near East, see May 2012.

16. Parry 1981, 42.

17. Price 1974, 52. In reality, Cicero and one other Classical source refer to machines similar to the Antikythera device, as does a Byzantine source. Technological advances have permitted a fuller understanding of the device since Price wrote; see Freeth et al. 2006.

Chapter 12

1. See Romm 1992, 21, 25, 26, 138; Africa 1969, 266; Nebenzahl 1990, 9; Cassidy 1968, 40.

2. Cassidy 1968, 33.

3. See Cassidy 1968, 74.

4. *Moralia*, quoted in Cassidy 1968, 33–35.

5. Gordon 1971, 38–49; quote on 38.

6. See also Cassidy 1968, 25, 29.

7. Quoted in Cassidy 1968, 30–31.

8. Quoted in Gordon 1971, 39–40.

9. Walter Woodburn Hyde (1947, 153–54) indicated that Pseudo-Aristotle and Diodoros probably both got this story from Timaeus (Timaios of Taoromenion), a Sicilian Greek (Sicily is just across the strait from Carthage). See also Fuson 1995, 60.

10. Quoted in Cassidy 1968, 11. Albinovanus Pedo (first century AD) is said also to have described a transatlantic attempt; see Cassidy 1978, 9.

11. See Cassidy 1968, 6; Fuson 1995, 59.

12. See Breen and Forsythe 2004, 40.

13. Morison 1942, 33. The Oxford archaeologist Barry Cunliffe (2010, 272) offered an alternative translation and asked, "Did some eventually reach land? We may never know . . . but the evidence is such that we should no longer underestimate the ingenuity and daring of those who faced the sea."

14. Quoted in Babcock 1918, 63; also, Thomson 1965, 90–91, 115.

15. See Hamdani 2006, 207–9, 211, who suggested that the Canary Island population of the time derived from American Indian castaways.

16. Hephaestus Books n.d.

17. See Chapman 1973.

18. See Williams 1997.

19. See Lamprecht 2000.

20. See Olshin 2013.

21. Quoted in Landström 1966, 50.

22. See, e.g., Thompson 1996, 2007; Vargas Martínez 1996; Hapgood 1966; Trager 2006/7.

23. E.g., Rees 2014. See also Lee 2012.

24. See Li 1961.

25. Quoted in Hamdani 2006, 212–13.

26. Hsieh 1967, 87.

27. These "Isles of the Blest" were perceived as riding upon the backs of turtles (Sanders 1980 18). Interestingly, many North American Indian groups conceived of the terrestrial earth as an island sitting atop a turtle.

28. Qian 1994, 71, 74, 84.

29. See Hsieh 1967, 88–90.

30. See Mertz 1972; also, Watson 1935, and Keddie 1990, 4; Paul Shao (1976, 5–10) provides a critique.

31. This is in terms of contemporary li, at 0.4 mile; Watson (1935, 55–5) indicated that the li of earlier times was shorter.

32. Most texts explain the *fusang* tree as a giant mulberry tree (heart-shaped leaves, reddish fruits, silkworms, and bark cloth), an *axis mundi* that connects earth with Heaven, or as the "Tree of the Sun" on which one of the ten former suns rested at night. The earliest known appearance of the *fusang* pattern is on a Shang bronze sculpture from Sichuan (see Zhao 1998, 99).

33. Two European maps of the later eighteenth century located "Fou Sang" in the approximate location of Vancouver Island (Keddie 1990, 4, 5), but this may simply reflect the then-recent publication of de Guignes's translation.

34. An attempt to verify one of the itineraries is Rees 2013.

35. See Emmons 1990, 9–10. It is unclear who the husbands were.

36. See Fulop 1954; Rowe 1948, 28.

37. Deloria 1998, 15; see also Morgan 2008; May 2010.

38. See Waters 1963, 24–26. The oldest Navajo clans claim an origin on the Pacific coast. The Navajo also have a deity, Begochidi, who is "a blond or red-haired god with blue eyes" (Reichard 1963, 387).

39. See Banks 1966, 51–52; Mahan 1983, 4, 30; Boutet and Monard 1996, 57, 59, 62, 73, 75; Totten 2010.

40. See Sorenson 1955; Heyerdahl 1952; Marx and Marx 1992.

41. Summarized by Zelia Nuttall; Xtlilxóchitl, Sahagún, Torquemada, and Diego de Landa quoted in Sorenson 1955.

Part II

1. Gillmer 1994, 5. Gillmer excepted the Texas A&M underwater archaeologist George Bass and his colleagues, and there are now numbers of others.

2. Winchester 2010, 60.

Chapter 13

1. Castlereach 1971, 9.

2. Merrill 1954, 189.

3. Whitfield 1996, 1.

4. Gould 1997b, 20.

5. Gould 2000b, 76.

6. Wilson 1991, 1–2.

7. Niederland 1989, 105–6. Similar views are promulgated in the *Encyclopedia of Exploration* (MacDonald 1971, 9) and in Sandler 2008, 2.

8. See, e.g., Jacobson 1991, 8; Ohler 1989, xiv.

9. Johnson 1994, xv.

10. Whitfield 1996, 5.

11. Cassidy 1968, 47, 49–50.

12. Unger 1980, 22.

13. White 1984, 131.

14. See Selkirk 1995, 61, 144.

15. Casson 1994b: 129, 149–51.

16. See Hyde 1947, 15.

17. Davis 2010, 35. See also Unger 1980, 21; Johnson 1994, 14; Fagan 2012, 269.

18. Everitt 2003, 10.

19. Al-Idrisi quoted by Landström 1964, 85–86.
20. See Ballard et al. 2002; Pollini 2005.

Chapter 14

1. See Parry 1981, 14, 102; Unger 1980, 216, also, 212, 214, 217, 219, 228.
2. On sizes of Egyptian and other ancient craft, see Jones 1995, 62, 65, 71; Casson 1994a, 17, 19, 21–22; Jenkins 1980, 108; Lipke 1984, 97; Grimes 2003; Pulak 2008; Ward, Zazzaro, and Abdel-Maguid 2010.
3. See Reynolds 1996, 331.
4. See Soren, Ben Khader, and Slim 1990, 86.
5. Casson 1994a, 121.
6. For more information on these and other very large Mediterranean ships, see Casson 1971, 189–90; 1994b, 66; 1994a, 85–88, 121–22, 134–40; 1996, 44, 46–47; Sarton 1993, 120–25; Landström 1961, 46–51; White 1984, 212; Rickman 1980, 123–24; Hyde 1947, 313–14; Pomey and Tchernia 1978; Unger 1980, 35.
7. See Scandurra 1972, 207; Van Doorninck 1972, 136, 139, 144–46; Aczel 2001, 1050–6.
8. See Robinson, Shimwell, and Cribben 1999.
9. See Christensen 1996, 77–78; Fagan 2012, 193.
10. See Vesilind and Brimberg 2000, 11.
11. See Flecker 2003, 392.
12. See Bhacker and Bhacker 1997, 49.
13. See Basham 1959, 148–49, 157, 226.
14. See Mookerji 1962, 18, plate; Swamy 1997, 82–86.
15. See Green 1996b; Greenhill 1971, 114; Mookerji 1962, 93.
16. See Horridge 1978, 4, 7; Swamy 1997, 138–70; Peterson 2006.
17. Holmgren and Spertus 1980, 166–67; also Manguin 1993, 266.
18. See Horridge 1978, 10, 12; Jahan 2006, 124–25; also Manguin 1993, 266; Adelaar 2009, 158.
19. Li 1961, 125.
20. Polo 1958, 213–14.
21. See Mookerji 1964, 32; Basham 1964, 158; Ronan 1986, 193–94.
22. See Barnes 1993, 265; Green 1996a, 160–62.
23. See Church 2005.
24. See Ronan 1986, 73–75, 108–9, 123–24, 140, 240, 259; Sokoloff 1982, 5; see also Levathes 1994; Menzies 2002; Dryer 2006.
25. See Sansome 1943, 87; Davis 2000, 94, 96–97.
26. See Gorley 1983, 29.
27. On canoe sizes, see Haddon and Hornell 1975, 1: 19, 80–81, 116–17, 132, 134, 140, 171, 187, 200, 248, 266, 307, 326; Lissau 1978, 48; Goetzfridt 1992, 62, 67, 78; Jourdain 1970, 10–11; Lewis 1980, 73–74; Ling 1969, 266; Thompson and Taylor 1980, 1, 4, 9, 13; Barrow 1964, 42–43; Parsonson 1963, 36–37; and Lewthwaite 1967, 78.
28. See Goetzfridt 1992, 62, 78.
29. See Haddon and Hornell 1975, 62, 78.
30. See Meyers 1985, 111; Parry 1981, 144.
31. See, e.g., Merrien 1954, 10–11; Borden 1967, 25, 163; Jett 1971, 17–18; Kehoe 2008, 155–57.
32. See Klinkenberg 1994.
33. See Heyerdahl 1978, 32.

34. See Toohey 2000.

35. See Greenhill 1976, 288ff.

36. Examples of such contentions by well-known authorities include Needham 1970, 261; Ronan 1986, 212, 217–18, 232; Temple 1986, 185; and Casson 1994a, 152.

37. Mott 1997, 3.

38. Sea trials with the replica dhow *Jewel of Muscat*, which was fitted with both kinds of rudders, found the stern rudder more effective in very light winds but the quarter rudder superior in light to moderate winds; see Jackson 2012, 32.

39. See Severin 1978, 281; Jones 1986, 7.

40. On rudders, see Ronan 1986, 225–31, 269; Temple 1986, 185–86; Needham 1970, 68–69, 25–60, fig. 81; Needham, Wang, and Lu 1971, 639; Worcester 1966, 22–24; Terrell 2001, 121, 124.

41. See Temple 1986, 56, 190–91.

42. See Bass 1983, 7.

43. Van Dorn 1974, 45.

44. See Danielsson 1960, 152–53, 169.

45. See Knöbl and Dennig 1976.

46. See Steinmayer and Turfa 1996, 105.

47. Flecker 2003, 392.

48. See Polo 1958, 37, 214; Knöbl and Dennig 1976, 215.

49. See Severin 1994, 51–52, 267–58, 292–93.

50. Severin 1983, 35, 41–42, 339.

51. See Patai 1998, 43; Soren, Ben Khader, and Slim 1990, 86; Edey et al. 1974, 34–35; Casson 1996, 45.

52. See Steffy 1985, 83–84; 1994, 56; Swiny and Katzev 1973, 351; Throckmorton 1996, 20, 55, 58.

53. See Ronan 1986, 256.

54. Kelley 1995, 106.

Chapter 15

1. See, e.g., Erlandson 2001, 2010; O'Connor 2010; O'Connell, Allen, and Hawkes 2010; Fagan 2012; Bellwood 2013.

2. Bednarik 1997; 1999, 561; 2001, 236–38; Morwood et al. 1999, 286.

3. See Chen 2002, 51.

4. Tosi 1986, 94, 99.

5. See Anderson 2010, 6–7, 12; Irwin 2010, 131–32.

6. See Toyne 1999; O'Connor 2010.

7. See O'Connell, Allen, and Hawkes 2010, 59. One demographer reckoned that three young couples would have a 50 percent chance of establishing a permanent population (Bellwood 2013, 74–75). Still, no exact figure is possible, owing to variations in marriage rules, resource availabilities, perceptions, and so forth.

8. Wallace's Line is the farthest-eastward limit of ancient Sundaland, the area fringing Southeast Asia that was exposed at lowest Pleistocene sea levels and across which animals could travel on dry land. Wallacia lies to the east of the line.

9. Note that some of these dates approach the time-depth limits of ^{14}C dating, and that minute contamination can produce falsely younger dates; so, these dates are minimal. Luminescence daters' maximum figures are in the 50,000–60,000-year-ago range. The Luzon metatarsal was dated using U-series ablation.

10. See Fagan 2012, 31–32.

11. The above dates are largely from Gamble 1994, 228; 2013; Flood 1996, 3, 5; Gibbons 1995; Kirch 1997, 32; 2000, 68–71; Smith 1995, 370–71; Spriggs 1997, 23, 25, 35–37; Irwin 1992, 18; Lilley 2008; Erlandson 2010; Nijares et al. 2010; O'Connell, Allen, and Hawkes 2010; O'Connor, Ono, and Clarkson 2011; also, Peter Bellwood 2013. On the spread of modern humans out of Africa and across Asia to as far as Australia between roughly 71,500 to 60,000 years ago, see Oppenheimer 2012.

12. See Fredericksen 1997; Service 1996.

13. See Gamble 1994, 228, 230, 236–37; Ikawa-Smith 1986, 204; Erlandson 2010, 22; Bellwood 2013, 82–83; Habu 2010, 161–62.

14. See Keegan and Diamond 1987, 52; Borrell 2010; Bower 2010; Bednarik 1997, 361; 1999, 560; 2001, 223, 229, 233, 235, 560 (many archaeologists retain a more conservative view, e.g., ca. 15,000 years ago or less for earliest Mediterranean island colonization, and, owing to tectonic activity, it is not always clear whether some present islands were part of the mainland at lowest sea levels); Gilbert, Gilbert, and Iglesias 2003; McCall and Fleming 1999, 242–43; Broodbank 2013; Farr 2010, 179–82; Simmons 2012.

15. See, e.g., Erlandson and Braje 2011; Graf, Ketron, and Waters 2013.

Chapter 16

1. Anderson 2010, 12.

2. The sherd's original painted design was modified by scraping, to yield the boat form. See Carter 2010, 91.

3. See Lawler 2002; McGrail 1987, 225; 1997. 309; 2010, 102–3; Heyerdahl 1978, 5–8; Barnett 1958, 221–22; Casson 1996, 40; Reynolds 1996, 230; Hutchinson 1962, 93–96; Swamy 1997, 53, 181–82; Needham, Lin, and Lu 1971, 599–603; Anderson 2010, 7.

4. See Görlitz 2000, 21ff.; 2001, 81.

5. See David Fabre 2004/5, 114–17.

6. See also Jurisic 2000, 7.

7. Waruno Mashdi (1999, 145) made a similar observation.

8. Note that bottom fouling reduces this weatherliness.

9. Casson 1994a, 115–17, 130–33.

10. My interpretations are based on Doran 1974; 1981. For alternative interpretations, see Kirch 2000, 9; Horridge 1986, 92–93; 2008, 102; and Ronan 1986, 182. See also Anderson 2000.

11. See Rianti 2014.

12. See Doran 1974; 1981, 44–45, 82–84.

13. Needham 1970, 68.

14. Quoted in Ronan 1986, 185–92, 194–95.

15. See Anderson 2010, 8–9; Fagan 2012, 42, 128–29.

16. McGrail 2010, 103; Whitewright 2009.

17. See Doran 1981, 41–43; Swamy 1997, 65–66; Howarth 1977, 83; Unger 1980, 49–50, 217–19; Casson 1994a, 117–18.

18. See Heyerdahl and Skjølsvold 1956.

19. See McGrail 2010, 103; Anderson 2010, 9.

20. See Edwards 1965a. The Alaskan sails were not described until the nineteenth century but were not of European form (see Fitzhugh and Kennett 2010, 77–78).

21. See Driver and Massey 1957, 292–93.

22. See Doran et al. 2000; Doran 2002.

Chapter 17

1. See Alliot-Duchesne and Fortis 2010.

2. Horridge 1986, 97. Boatbuilders preferred not to risk significant design innovations for fear the craft would be rejected by potential users/buyers skeptical of anything not time tested.

3. See Lawler 2010; Carter 2002, 2010; Vosmer 2000.

4. See Horridge 1978, 4–5; Nishimura 1925, 123–24.

5. See Bawden 1996, 50.

6. Bowen 1956, 290.

7. Edwards 1965b, 112; see also 1972, 876–77.

8. That the buoyancy of reeds harvested at the appropriate season (August, in Iraq) is great is shown by Marsh Arabs living on artificial reed-bundle islands, as also do the Uru of Bolivia's Lake Titicaca (Heyerdahl 1978, 24, 203; 1980, 16, 45).

9. Heyerdahl 1978, 23, 32.

10. See Anderson 2010, 6.

11. See Ling 1956: 27–28, 49, 51.

12. See Bowen 1956, 287, 289.

13. Vietnamese sailing-rafts are called *ghe be*. They can make nearly 4 knots against the wind (see Burningham 1994, 229–32). The Korean word *palson* (raft-boat) (see Nishimura 1925, 59; Ling 1956, 45) has been suggested as a source of the Spanish lexeme *balsa* (raft), which had been speculated to have derived from some aboriginal term in Ecuador; however, *balsa* is first attested in Spain at the end of the 1200s (see Anonymous 1980, 480). The word *jangada* is Konkani and may have come from Goa via the Portuguese.

14. See Suggs 1960, 78.

15. See Dewan and Hosler 2008; Fagan 2012, 260–64.

16. For more on sailing-rafts, see Edwards 1965b, 1969, 1972; Buse de la Guerra 1986; Hornell 1946a, 81; and Heyerdahl 1978, 189, 207.

17. Heyerdahl 1968, 108–9; see also Worcester 1956, 305.

18. Edwards 1969, 8.

19. Doran 1971, 135; see also Edwards 1972.

20. Quoted in Gartelmann 1986, 247.

21. Needham and Lu 1985, 48–49.

Chapter 18

1. See Ellmers 1996, 112, 17–18; Stölting 1997; Powell 2009. The only nearer-complete archaeological specimen, from northern Greenland, dates from the fourteenth to fifteenth century AD (see McGrail 2010, 100).

2. See Cassidy 1968, 79; Cunliffe 2001; 2002, 67; 2010, 286; Mac Cárthaigh 2008.

3. Avienus quoted in Hornell 1936, 6–9.

4. Round craft evolved in two directions: by covering the light frame with a hide and by developing the frame into an exclusively basketry vessel such as Mesopotamia's *quffa* (the ark described in one version of Babylonia's Gilgamesh legend seems to have been a 38,750-square-foot *quffa*; see Finkel 2014).

5. Clark 1952, 283.

6. On skin boats, see Chapelle 1964; Suder 1930; McGrail 1987; Durham 1960; Hornell 1936; and Zimmerly and Gardiner 2000.

7. See Fitzhugh and Kennett 2010, 73.

8. See Leshikar 1988, 13.

9. In North America, bullboats were found all over the Great Plains and in much of the Rocky Mountains region, with outliers in the Southeast and the Great Lakes region. They were also known in Brazil and in Patagonia (see Driver and Massey 1957, 288–89).

10. See Landström 1961, 52; Soule 1976, 200, plate; Evans 1996, 108; Hyde 1947, 118; Mac Cárthaigh 2008, 423–24.

Chapter 19

1. In the Americas, such canoes were doubtless introduced from Siberia and in North America are confined mostly to Algonkian speakers and Athapaskan speakers (see Driver and Massey 1957, 288–90).

2. Driver and Massey (1957, 290, 291) identified two zones of logboat occurrence in the Western Hemisphere. They saw the canoes of eastern North America and those of eastern South America as a historically unitary phenomenon and that of the Northwest Coast a separate one, related to the Asian logboat tradition.

3. For possible Native American voyages to Europe, see Forbes 2007.

4. See Manguin 1993, 258–60; Habu 2010, 166.

5. See Kirch 2000, 92–93; Jett 1998a; 2011–14c.

6. Quoted in Lewthwaite 1967, 67.

7. Finney 1996b, 367.

8. Lissau 1978, 49.

9. On the basis of linguistics and other considerations, Atholl Anderson (2003) and some others, in contrast, considered it likely that initial Austronesian occupation of Western Polynesia was accomplished using single-outrigger canoes, with double canoes being a later invention in the islands, one that facilitated the settling of islands to the east.

10. Jourdain 1970, 14. For the complex operative chain of canoe construction, see Guiot 2001.

11. See Irwin 2010, 137; Johns, Irwin, and Sung 2014.

12. See Lissau 1978.

13. "Their outriggers or double hulls could produce a *righting moment* to resist the *heeling moment* from the driving force of the sail, and they had steering paddles that could resist the *yawing moment* generated when side forces on sail and hull were not directly above each other" (Irwin 2010, 137).

14. See Kirch 2000, 93. A possible single outrigger was associated with a circa 6000 BC dugout canoe found on the lower Yangzi River in China (Jiang and Liu 2005).

15. See Doran 1974; 1981, 29–30, 76–80, 89–92; Landström 1961, 222; Mahdi 1999.

16. See Haddon and Hornell 1975, 1; Parsonson 1963, 38–39; Goetzfridt 1992, 39, 46, 236, 239, 245.

17. Kelley 1998a; Jett 1998a; 2015; Swamy 1997, 36, 40.

18. From Hainan and the Philippines through western Indonesia, plank fastening (with sugar-palm fiber) was instead accomplished by discontinuous lashing through holes in bosses left on the planks. On the Mindanao craft, see Bacus 2004, 267. On types and distributions of plank lashing, see Prins 1986.

19. See Pedersen 2004.

20. See Bacus 2004.

21. See Doran 1973, 18–21; Horridge 1978, 1, 7; Bowen 1952; 1956, 284–85; Green 1996b; Jahan 2006, 119, 121, 123.

22. Hourani 1963, 28.
23. Ratnagar 1981, 164.
24. Wheatley 1975, 261. Various others have made similar observations.
25. Ibn Battutah quoted in Green 1996b, 93.
26. See Green 1996b, 152. The thirteenth-century AD Java Sea wreck appears to have been a lashed-lug Indonesian craft; see Flecker 2003.
27. Flecker 2012, 16. Chinese historical sources indicate lengths of 164 feet.
28. See Green 1996b, 93–94; Horridge 1978, 6–7; Swamy 1997, 138–70.
29. See Flecker 2000.
30. See Mookerji 1962, 21, 23.

Chapter 20

1. See Needham 1970, 64–65; Worcester 1966, 2, 8; Temple 1986, 185–86; Knöbl 1976, plate; Carter 1978, 12.
2. See Habu 2010, 166–67.
3. Landström 1961, 233; see also Posdneeff 1929.
4. Cf., too, the flood-escaping ship in the Gilgamesh legend, which had nine interior compartments (see Heyerdahl 1980, 25).
5. See Jones 1995; Ronan 1986, 98–99.
6. See Pintet 2010.
7. See Needham 1970, 66, 68–69.
8. See Barnes 1993, 264; Levathes 1996, 78; Flecker 2007.
9. See Alan Villiers 1973, 52, 54; Horridge 1978, 4.
10. Green 1996a, 158.
11. Skeleton construction is first documented archaeologically in the United Kingdom, from the second to fourth century AD. A different system came into use in the eastern Mediterranean during the fifth to sixth century AD (see McGrail 2010, 101–2). On Western watercraft, see McGrail 2014.
12. See Blot 1996, 31–32, 35, 45–50, 61–62; Throckmorton 1970, 113–63; 1996; Diolé 1954, 20–39; Marx and Marx 1992, 25–27.
13. Casson 1991, 10. A tenon is a length of wood that serves to join together two larger pieces of wood by fitting into mortises—holes cut into the larger pieces of wood to receive the tenon. Brailing involves a system of lines passing from aft over the yard to the foot of the sail (see chapter 16).
14. On Egyptian watercraft, see Jones 1995; Fabre 2004/5, chap. 3.
15. A scarf is a joining of two adjacent plank ends by reciprocally notching the two ends and fitting them together. A butterfly cramp is a flat hourglass-shaped piece of wood that fits into corresponding notches cut into two timbers to be joined together.
16. See Ward 2006; Casson 1971, 20.
17. See Heyerdahl 1978, 373; King-Webster 1960.
18. See Fabre 2004/5, 114–17, 119–21; Jones 1995; Peacock and Blue 2006, 18. Fragments of such ships have been found at Mersa Gawasis, on the Red Sea; see Ward, Zazzaro, and Abdel-Maguid 2010.
19. See Pomey 1985; Steffy 1994, 39, 41.
20. See I. Negueruela et al. 1995, 195.
21. See Hutchinson 1962, 93–96; Reynolds 1996, 331–33; Gillmer 1994, 2–7; Doran 1973, 29–33; Edey et al. 1974, 34, 39, 42–43, 45.
22. See Kemp 1978, 18–19, 23.
23. See Lancel 1995, 125; Hutchinson 1962, 97; Bartoloni 1999, 86–88.
24. See Gould 2002, 117–30, 143, 145; Ballard et al. 2002, 151, 157.

25. See Valsecchi 2010.

26. A connection with the latter region may seem hard to credit, and sewn-plank craft in northwestern Europe long preceded known Viking Age Swedish travel to Iraq. However, the existence of other cultural commonalities between Scandinavia and Southeast Asia raises some puzzling questions.

27. See McGrail 1996, 31–34, 36; Wright et al. 2001, 733; Van de Noort et al. 1999; Parfitt 2000; Clark 2004; Fagan 2012, 173–75.

28. See Gifford, Gifford, and Coates 2006.

29. See Fagan 2012, 193. Fagan noted that there was no mast step, but a reconstruction drawing shows one, holding a mast.

30. See Bill 1997; Christensen 2000; Greenhill 1976, 214.

31. See Ingstad 1969, 62.

Chapter 21

1. See, e.g., Meggers 1955, 117; Tolstoy 1972, 339.

2. Crumlin-Pedersen 1996, 110.

3. Capelotti 1997, 15.

4. See Nelson 1963, 117.

5. See Heyerdahl 1950.

6. See Heyerdahl 1978, 218–28.

7. Quoted in Thorpe 2002, 220–21.

8. Bahn and Flenley 1992, 46. Similarly, Kenneth L. Feder (2010, 156) gratuitously contended that, "Without these amenities [a solar still and modern navigational equipment], the *Kon-Tiki* voyage would not have achieved whatever success it did."

9. See Capelotti 2001.

10. See Bisschop 1959; Danielsson 1960.

11. See Savoy 1974.

12. See Alsar and Lopez 1973. Waterlogging can be inhibited by application of oil, wax, gum, or resin (see Hornell 1945, 182).

13. See Mairson 2007; Higraff 2007.

14. See Severin 1994.

15. See Haslett and Smith 2002; Haslett 2006.

16. See Sorenson 1998.

17. See Bednarik 1999.

18. See Knudson 1963, 44; Heyerdahl 1971b.

19. See Heyerdahl 1978.

20. Genovés 1971, 543. See also Genovés 1972; 1980.

21. See Savoy 1974.

22. See Heyerdahl 1980.

23. See Thorpe 2002.

24. In 1999, Colonel John Blatchford-Snell took the 44-foot *totora Kota Mama II* 2,770 miles downriver from the Bolivian Andes to Buenos Aires; see Allen n.d.

25. See Görlitz 2000; 2001, 81, 84; 2002. In another experiment, five or six paddlers took a 20-foot bundle craft from Attica to the island of Milos, at a velocity of 9 to 12 miles per day (see Broodbank 2000 102).

26. See Allen n.d.

27. See Vosmer 2003.

28. See *Explorers Club Members Only E-Newsletter*, April 8, 2008. See also Görlitz, 2006.

29. In 1991–92, Clark also undertook a voyage from Ireland to Scotland in the replica sixteen-oar medieval-style galley *Aileach*; see Clark 1993.

30. See Severin 1978; also, Mudie 1986.

31. Hans Van Tilburg (2007) analyzed ten twentieth-century Chinese junks and their long-distance Pacific voyages, showing that these craft could sail virtually anywhere.

32. See Knöbl with Denning 1976.

33. See Lindemann 1998.

34. See Crook 1990.

35. See Siers 1977.

36. See Bisschop 1939.

37. See, especially, Finney 1979; 1994; 2003.

38. Finney 1997, 42; 6–7 knots, according to Finney 1996b, 367. Atholl Anderson (2003) has contended that Finney overestimated the sizes of Polynesian sails and that the craft is a mishmash of elements of different Polynesian canoe types. Note that virtually all sailboats achieve their maximum speeds when reaching between 90 and 120 degrees off the wind rather than straight downwind.

39. See Barcarse 2014.

40. Finney 1991, 391; see also Finney et al. 1986, 50, 76; Finney 1979, 1994, 1996, 1997, 2001; Kyselka 1987; Davis 2000. In 1982–83, Marvin Creamer circumnavigated the globe without instruments, using only nature's clues (see Gooley 2012, 161).

41. See Bowman 1994; Finney 1997, 41; Babayan et al. 1987, 194–95; Whakataka-Brightwell 1998.

42. See Mulrooney 2013.

43. See Campbell 1989, 358; Davis 2000, 84–86; Jett 2008–10.

44. See Lewis 1967.

45. See *Journal of the Polynesian Society* 110 (3): 119 (2001).

46. See Matawai 2013.

47. See Anderson and Boon 2011.

48. Doran 1970, 584.

49. See James 2003; Beale 2004; on sailing routes from Indonesia to Madagascar, see Fitzpatrick and Callaghan 2008; http://www.pioneerexpeditions.com/borobudur/index.htm (accessed November 7, 2014). On possible Indonesian influences in West Africa, see Dick-Read 2005.

50. See Severin 1983.

51. See Severin 1997.

52. See Vosmer 2010; Jackson 2012.

53. Curry 2011, 66.

54. Severin 1985.

55. Beale and Taylor 2013.

56. Casson 1996, 42–43; also, Throckmorton 1996, 34, 59; Katzev 2008. A second replica was constructed and sailed, as well.

57. See McGrail 1997, 321–22; Fagan 2012, 203–4.

58. See Vadslrup 1986, 86–87, 90.

59. See Carter 2000; Jones 1986, 7; Ohler 1989, 98; Hornbostel 1997; Blumenfeld 2016; Crumlin-Pederson 1996, 111–13, 117, 119.

60. See Gifford and Gifford 1996.

61. On small-boat voyages, see, especially, Merrien 1954; Borden 1967; Jett 1971; Kehoe 1971, 2008.

62. Kehoe 1998, 19.

Chapter 22

1. Quoted in Partington 1992, 45. There are indications of a pulse of Chinese imports to Europe in the later twelfth century: the compass, the sternpost rudder, the windmill, and certain astronomical and cosmological knowledge. A second wave is manifest in the first quarter of the 1300s (see Needham 1970, 545); gunpowder had arrived a little before.

2. See Aczel 2001, 47–52.

3. Unger 1980, 130.

4. Aczel 2001, xi–xii, 158. Analysis of the oldest extant portolan chart (1290–1350), of the Mediterranean and Britain, as well as of later portolans, has shown that they were based on hundreds of contemporary magnetic readings (uncorrected for declination), implying rapid access to a multitude of information sources and widespread compass use earlier than formerly supposed.

5. See Needham 1970, 44, 240–48; Temple 1986, 149–51.

6. See Mookerji 1964, 33; Wiet 1969, 356; Temple 1986, 149; Jahan 2006, 152.

7. Declinations of up to 30 degrees occur close to Greenland, for instance, and as much as 40 degrees in the Labrador Sea; see Johnson 1994, 47.

8. Quoted in Franck and Brownstone 1984, 416.

9. Aczel 2001, 27–28.

10. Marcus 1981, 106.

11. Quoted in Parsonson 1963, 11.

12. Lewis 1994, 145, 158.

13. Quoted in Morison 1974, 175.

14. Morison 1971, 142.

15. Bourne quoted in Marcus 1980, 172.

16. Andia quoted in Haddon and Hornell 1975, 1: 145.

17. Somewhat dim, Thuban was a bit off the pole. During the third millennium BC, an imaginary vertical line connecting the brighter Mizar (Zeta-Ursae-Minoris) to Kochab (Beta-Ursae-Minoris) passed almost through the north celestial pole, and north could be determined with a plumb bob when it aligned with that line (see Spence 2000).

18. See Taylor 1956, 128–29; Severin 1983, 92–94; Arunachalam 1996; Huth 2013. On Arab navigation, see Facey and Constable 2013, especially chapters 2 and 4.

19. *The Odyssey*, book 5.

20. See Taylor 1956, 43, 48; Bartoloni 1999: 84; Gooley 2012, 245–46.

21. See Åkerblom 1968, 137.

22. Ropars et al. 2012.

23. Although the same stars always pass over the same parallels of latitude, during the year's course the suite of stars and constellations visible will change, owing to their rising four minutes earlier each day (see Gooley 2012, 108; Huth 2013).

24. According to the astronomer Louis Winkler (personal communication), in modern mathematical terms the equation relating parameters on the horizon is $\sin \delta = \cos \phi \cos A$, where d = the declination of the star (measured above and below the plane of the equator, like latitude), ϕ = the geographic latitude of the observer, and A = the azimuth of travel (heading measured in the observer's horizon plane, expressed as degrees east of north). A thirty-two-point stellar compass would imply knowing 200+ stars.

25. On star-path navigation, see Kursh and Kreps 1974, 334–35; also Lewis 1967, 307; 1978; 1994; Gladwin 1970; Goodenough 1953; Dodd 1972, 42–43, 48–50, 54;

Jahan 2006, 150–51; Arunachalam 1996; Gooley 2012, 246–47; Constable and Facey 2013, 21–25, 66.

26. See Ramskou 2000, 43.

27. Nevertheless, in the second century BC, Hipparchus of Nicaea ascertained the length of a year with an error of only six minutes, and a day to within one second of its correct length (see Hyde 1947, 13).

28. See Sarton 1993, 344–46, 349. The modern sailor Tim Severin (1997, 22) observed, however, that Sulawesi sailors used a pierced half coconut shell floated in a container of water; the shell would fill and sink within one minute of an hour each time used. Presumably, accuracy would decline during heavy seas. But note that gimbals had been invented by the second century BC and were present in both Byzantium and China. There *is* a method of determining longitude on land, but the method is not useful for navigating (see Thomson 1965; Payn 2002; Menzies 2002). This method could explain the accuracy of some early post-Columbian European maps such as the Portuguese Canerio world map of 1503–5. Rick Sanders (2003) has suggested that the Greek Antikythera device (see chapter 11) could have been used to determine longitude in lieu of tables.

29. Marcus 1980, 118.

30. See Howarth 1977, 126; also Unger 1980, 215; Constable and Facey 2013, 26–31.

31. See Dilke 1985, 14, 37; Barnett 1958, 230; Taylor 1956, 55–57; McGrail 1987, 276; Needham and Lin 1959, 229–30; Thomson 1965, 115–16.

32. See Hodges 1970, 183; Aczel 2001, 18–19; Ronan 1986, 160.

33. See Snow 1985, 36–38, 46; Sarton 1970, 77–78, 119–21, 179, 444–45, 511.

34. Needham 1970, 40.

35. See Nasr 1968, 26; Ramskou 2000, 43; Christensen 2000, 95–96.

36. See McGrail 1989, 26; Ramskou 2000, 43; Christensen 2000, 95–96

37. Needham 1970, 43, 260.

38. See Hsieh 1968, 129; Aczel 2001, 23–24, 118.

39. Lewis 1994, 84, 90, 117. On Pacific navigation, see Chamberlain, Finney, and Passey 1986; Goodenough 1953; Johnson and Mahelona 1975; Halpern 1986; Åkerblom 1963, 103–8; Finney et al. 1986, 42–43; Goetzfridt 1992, 227; also Thomas 1987; Kyselka 1987.

40. See Salmond 2008, 29–30; Fagan 2012, 67–68.

41. Parry 1981, 145.

42. See Finney 1994; 1997, 45; Lewis 1994, 144–45; Irwin 1992, 48.

Chapter 23

1. Schnall 1996, 127. On these matters, see Huth 2013.

2. Dodd 1972, 163.

3. On Pacific migratory flyways and human response to them, see Allen Keast 1957, 12; Baker 1951, 34–36; Percival 1957, 40; Goetzfridt 1992, 195, 196; Lewthwaite 1967, 67; Evans 1998, 30.

4. Quoted in Kirch 2000, 1.

5. See Needham 1970, 43.

6. See Marcus 1981, 30; Ohler 1989, 42; McGrail 1987, 279; Jones 1986, 11, 158; Taylor 1956, 74; Cassidy 1968, 89; Hornell 1946b, 146–47.

7. Concerning these matters, see Marcus 1981, 114–15; Feinberg 1995, 189; Nunn 1934, 619–20; Taylor 1956, 77–78; Cassidy 1968, 80; Severin 1983, 102; Davis 2010, 30–31; Evans 1998, 69; Jahan 2006, 150–51.

8. See Whakataka-Brightwell 1998, 120.

9. On use of organisms, see, especially, Hornell 1946a; Marcus 1981, 114–15; Landström 1966, 61–63; Bill 1997, 198; Taylor 1956, 59, 77–78; Sanderson 1956. The Arab navigator Ahmad bin Mājid al-Najdī, mentioned such practice circa AD 1460.

10. Plato, *The Republic*, 6.488d.

11. See Taylor 1956, 80; Evans 1998, 30; Whitfield 1996, 6–7.

12. See Goetzfridt 1997; Åkerblom 1968, 51–54; Haddon and Hornell 1975, 1: 145, 2: 30; Lewis 1994, 113, 133–34, 139–66; Ronan 1986, 194. Indian Ocean sailors sometimes expanded the compass to 64 points and also used current roses (see Arunachalam 1996).

13. See Taylor 1956, 37; Whitfield 1996, 6–7; Cunliffe 2001, 81; Gatty 1958, 78, 83; Davis 2010, 34.

14. Fagan 2012, 125.

15. See Ammarell 1999, 2, 146–47, 150; Arunachalam 1996; McGrail 1989, 30–31; Evans 1998, 63–65.

16. On many of these matters, see, e.g., Pretor-Pinney 2010, 14, 25–30. Less steep waves assume the form of a sine (continuous curve), steeper waves a trochoidal (crested) cross section.

17. See Davenport 1967; Haddon and Hornell 1975, 1: 372–74; Lewis 1994; Åkerblom 1968, 117–30, 141; Feinberg 1988, 113–17; Gooley 2012, 168–69, 175, 183–84.

18. See, e.g., Gooley 2012, 173, 189. For Polynesian use of these phenomena, see D'Arcy 2006, 72–73; Evans 1998, 66, 70.

19. Conventionally, a low Pacific island is conservatively considered to be directly detectable at about 34.5 miles out to sea (see Di Piazza, Di Piazza, and Pearthree 2007). To calculate theoretical visibility distance, add the square root of the height of the island or cloud to the square root of the height of the observer's eye above the sea surface. Thus, from the deck a person can see the tops of the 70-foot-high coconut palms on a low island at a distance of up to 11 miles, the top of a 400-foot-high island at 25 miles, the top of a 1,400-foot mountain at 40 miles, or the top of a 10,000-foot mountain at 100 miles (Lewis 1967, 220, 231). Climbing to a 25-foot masthead adds 6.6 miles to the distance of visibility. In practice, this formula overestimates somewhat the distance at which a high island can be seen and underestimates that at which a low one can be discerned (Åkerblom 1968, 61–62; Hilder 1972, 89, 91; McGrail 1997, 300).

20. See Mowat 2000, 31.

21. See Ramskou 2000, 43.

22. On sound and odor, see Gatty 1958, 78, 83–84. See also Evans 1998, 71.

23. See McGrail 2010, 98.

24. See Jahan 2006, 151; Goodenough 1953, 3; Goetzfridt 1992, 52, 225, 239, 244, 261, 262, 269.

25. See Haddon and Hornell 1975, 1: 145; Arunachalam 1996, 270; Lewthwaite 1967, 67; Dening 1972, 117; Bahn and Flenley 1992, 780; Evans 1998, 71–72.

26. See Bill 1997, 198; also, McGrail 1987, 260.

27. Apollonios quoted in Severin 1985, 20.

28. Queiros quoted in Parsonson 1963, 12.

29. Virgil, quoted in Spiess 1981, 51.

Chapter 24

1. See Edward R. Cook et al. 2010.

2. See Parsonson 1963, 30–31.

3. See Normile 2011, 1343.

4. See Hainline 1964, 64; Barnes 1993, 76; Edwards and Mithen 1995, 350; Fischer 1995, 37; Jiao 2007, 39–40; Lawler 2011; Tooley 1974, 32, 34, 37.

5. Kirch 1997, 163–65.

6. See Rao 1986, 380–81; Crawford 1998, 8–9; Lind 1969, 27, 137, 149–50.

7. Polo 1958, 231.

8. See Oppenheimer 1998, 274; BBC News online, January 19, 2002, and April 11, 2002, reported two apparent sunken cities off India.

9. See British physician and Oxford anthropologist Oppenheimer 1998, 228, 238, 279–95, who considers Austronesian flood legends; these, the author believed, relate to post-Pleistocene sea-level rises. See also Schoch and McNally 2003.

10. See Ferrell 1969, 185–86; Barthel 1974; Jett 1991, 98; Dixon 1996, 133–34, who mentioned three such tales; Joseph Mahan 1983, 4, 30; Cunliffe 2001, 7. The author collected the Wei and Yuchi traditions from natives.

11. See Parsonson 1963, 32.

12. Haddon and Hornell 1975, 1: 45.

13. See Goetzfridt 1992, 175; Lang 1834, 7, 64.

14. See Hyde 1947, 97; Jones 1986, 47; Ronan 1986, 165.

15. See, e.g., S. D. Goitein 1967, 42, 50, 57–58.

16. Mookerji 1962, 102, 104–7.

17. See Goetzfridt 1992, 96, 131, 193–94.

18. Parsonson 1963, 31. See also D'Arcy 2006, 58, 61–63.

Chapter 25

1. Helms 1988, 67–79; see also Goetein 1967, 51–57, 274–75, 352; Casson 1984; 1994b, 76, 84–85, 92, 94, 130, 147, 219, 300, 304.

2. Meisel 2000, 16.

3. Wang quoted in Bentley 1993, 111, 165.

4. Donkin 1997, 250; see also Carter and Crawford 2010, 211.

5. See Barrett 2010, 292.

6. See Kirch 1997, 243–45; Bahn and Flenley 1992, 71. For example, six or seven hundred years ago, axes made from Samoan basalt were distributed across a 3,100-mile swath of the island Pacific; see Petchey, Addison, and McAllister 2010, 166.

7. On kula, see Malinowski 1922; Fagan 2012, 49–52.

8. See Ekholm 1964.

9. See Helms 1988, 69–72.

10. See Sarkar 1970; Mookerji 1962, 103; although most contemporary historians dismiss the importance—or even the existence—of such conquests and the implied attendant migrations (Bentley 1993, 52), genetics indicates that 12 percent of the Balinese male Y chromosomes derive from India; Karafet et al. 2005.

11. See Anthony 1997, 23.

12. Bellwood 1984–85, 113; also Bellwood 1997; see also Kirch 1997, 65–66.

13. See Weckler 1943, 16.

14. See Needham 1970, 73.

15. See McGhee and Tuck 1977, 69.

16. Severin 1978, 259–60.

17. See Ronan 2000.

18. See Parsonson 1963, 31.

19. Diolé 1954, 165.

20. See Bentley 1993, 10, 52–53.

21. See Ohler 1989, 128; Parry 1981, xv, 48–50; Mookerji 1962, 108, 122.

22. See, e.g., Ekholm 1953; Heine-Geldern and Ekholm 1951; Kirchoff 1964; Kearsley 2001.

23. See Helms 1988, 73–74; Ragué 1976, 5; Phoebe Phillips Editions 1984, 74; Schuetz-Miller 2012, 401; Rossabi 1997, 14.

24. Cf. the global observations of the 1769 transit of Venus across the sun, which is one reason that Captain James Cook was sent to the South Pacific (Fernández-Armesto 1991, 177).

25. William Diapea, quoted in Lewthwaite 1967, 80.

26. See Sharp 1957, 68.

27. Lewthwaite 1967, 80, quoting John Williams.

28. Gamble 1994, 232; see also Haddon and Hornell 1975, 1: 45; Goetzfridt 1992, 206, 208; D'Arcy 2006, 62–63.

29. Quoted in Andrews 1993, 813.

30. Cowan 1996, 5.

31. Kemp 1978, 23.

32. Fagan 2012, 206.

33. Haddon 1934, 82.

34. Weckler 1943, 12.

35. Quoted in Burrows 1963, 105.

36. Olson 1961, 20.

37. Quoted in Lundy 2000, 81.

38. See Apter 1992; Anderson 1970.

39. Siers 1977, 190.

40. See Hyde 1947, 305; Miquel 1996, 812.

41. See Keegan and Diamond 1987, 67.

42. See Dening 1963, 109.

43. In Anderson 1970, 35–36.

44. Sauer 1968, 1; also Seaver 1996, 213.

45. See Johnson 1994, 175–77; Rando, Pieper, and Alcover 2014.

46. Zerubavel 1992, 12.

47. See Seaver 1996, 220–22, 257, 259; Marcus 1981, 164–68; Wilson 1991.

48. See Fuson 1995, 185–205.

49. Parry 1981, 45–46, 80.

50. Hesiod quoted in Cunliffe 2002, 2–3.

51. See Balbín Behrmann et al. 1995.

52. See Atoche Peña et al. 1995.

53. See Gamble 1994, 238.

54. See Fuson 1995, 60, 84.

55. Soule 1976, 78.

56. Quoted in Romm 1992, 163.

57. Quoted in Nasr 1968, 106.

58. See Barthel 1974.

59. See Boardman 1980, 202.

60. See Parry 1981, 91, 185.

61. Malmström 1997, xi.

62. See Olson 1961, 29, 33, 44.

63. Quoted in Aebi and Brennan 1989.

64. For more on shipboard conditions, see Cuppage 1994, 4–5; Milton-Thompson 1974, 21.

65. Melville 1984, 121.

66. Feinberg 1988, 149, 153.
67. Quoted in Cawthorne 2010, 110.
68. See Barrett 2010, 296–97.
69. Bernstein 1996, 1. The disproportionate numbers of contemporary small-boat accidents among American amateur yachtsmen as compared to professional mariners are instructive in considering the matter of risk. "Of these [accidents], the Coast Guard attributes the majority to bad seamanship, leading to capsize as a result of overloading, ignoring weather warnings, and venturing into sea conditions that exceed the skipper's training or experience" (Van Dorn 1974, 256). Bad seamanship would seldom have been an issue in societies in which maritime training began in childhood.
70. See Kursh and Kreps 1974, 336.
71. Williamson 1974, 78.
72. See Wheeler 1971, 174.
73. Severin 1983, 18.
74. See Dodd 1972, 27.
75. MacDonald 1971, 21–22.
76. Quoted in Åkerblom 1968, 95; regarding Chuuk islanders' low concern about death, see p. 156.
77. Quoted in Jourdain 1970, 18.
78. See Rougé 1981, 196–97.
79. Cf. Fagan 2012, 25, 44–46.
80. See Goetzfridt 1992, 217.

Part IV

1. Padden 1973, 998.

Chapter 26

1. Feder 2010, 2.
2. Moore 1915; Carter 1976; 1988, 5. Use of the site may have extended into Protohistoric times, so a Colonial European source is a possibility.
3. Fitzhugh and Ward 2000, 217, 239, 275; Ingstad and Ingstad 2001, 147; Mowat 2000, 124.
4. Anonymous 2012; Dennis Stanford, personal communication, 2013.
5. Jett 1983, 351–52; Needham and Lu 1985, 10; Goette 1936, 227–33; Balser 1988.
6. See Beck 1966, 12–13; Kinle 1962.
7. In 2012, George E. Harlow et al. reported analysis of a jade gouge from a Lapita site in the Bismarck Archipelago that was, as far as could be ascertained, chemically similar only to jade from Baja California Sur. At this writing, the celt was being compared to a jade specimen collected in 1898 in northern Irian Jaya.
8. See McCulloch 1988; 1993; 2011–14. Nevertheless, a lively debate continues.
9. See Guthrie 1996; Grimes 2001. For a recent exploration of this idea, see Menzies 2011.
10. El-Morr et al. 2013, 4302–3.
11. Stos 2009, 176.
12. See Bökönyi and Jánossy 1959.
13. See Schorger 1966, 472.
14. See Carter 1971; also Carter 1988, 10–11; 2008–10.
15. See Langdon 1989.

16. See Wichmann 1995, 276.

17. See Johannessen 1981; Johannessen and Fogg 1982; Johannessen, Fogg, and Fogg 1984. Storey et al. 2011 have raised some cogent but nondefinitive reservations concerning the circumstantial evidence, proposing that Asian-type Amerind practices could date only to Colonial times.

18. See Storey et al. 2007; Storey, Quiróz, and Matisoo-Smith 2011. The genetic and chronological conclusions were questioned, rather unconvincingly, by Gongora et al. 2008 and Thomson et al. 2014.

19. See Storey, Clarke, and Matisoo-Smith 2011; Storey, Quiróz, Beavan, and Matisoo-Smith 2001.

20. Teeter 2004, 182; quote from 2001, 140.

21. See Álvarez and Ocaña 1999, 100–102.

22. See Götz and Stanton 2013, 204; Cooke et al. 2013, 484, 494, 508–9, 516.

23. See Sutter et al. 2007; Gray et al. 2010.

24. See Schwartz 1997, 60–92; Valadez Azúa 2000, 197.

25. Fiennes and Fiennes 1968, 53–54. In terms of mitochondrial DNA, all American breeds descend from Eurasian, not New World, wolves.

26. E.g., Taylor 1990, 8.

27. Leonard et al. 2002, 1614.

28. See Van Asch et al. 2013.

29. Drögemüller et al. 2008.

30. See Ingstad and Ingstad 2001, 147.

31. For much fuller treatment, see Jett 2004. Some additional material has been added here.

32. Thornton 1987, 45. In the absence (so far) of infant cases in American archaeology, despite immunological and DNA tests demonstrating the presence of treponemal disease, experts Mary Lucas Powell and Della Collins Cook (2005, 457, 477, 582–84) felt that the presence of venereal syphilis had not been clinched.

33. See Walker and Thornton 2002, 514; Harper et al. 2011. Still, the skeletal manifestations of the different treponematosic syndromes overlap, so they cannot always be differentiated.

34. See Lawler 2011: 417.

35. See Aufderheide and Rodríguez-Martín 1998, 171.

36. See Aufderheide and Rodríguez-Martín 1998, 170; Gaul et al. 2015.

37. See Walker and Thornton 2002, 514; Gomes i Prat and Mendonça de Souza 2003.

38. Roberts and Buikstra 2003, 184, 193–94; see Alchon 2003, 45. Ramenofsky (1987, 144) stated that TB "can persist in small isolated populations."

39. See Ramenofsky, Wilbur, and Stone 2003. Note, however, that DNA breaks down over time, especially under warm and/or wet conditions, and that contamination can be a problem in ancient DNA recovery.

40. See Gomes i Prat and Mendonça de Souza 2003, 1157.

41. Bos et al. 2014.

42. See Crawford 1998, 56.

43. Medina-Sanchez et al. 2005, 327.

44. Alchon 2003, 54. Not everyone agrees that the devastating *cocolixtle* was typhus.

45. See Burton 2008.

46. See Acuña-Soto et al. 2005. The geographic pattern of abandonment is not an expectable one for epidemic, however; see Ebert et al. 2014.

47. See Sorenson and Johannessen 2013.

48. See Darling 1920; Soper 1927; Manter 1967, 3–4; da Fonseca 1970.

49. See Fernando Ferreira, Araúto, and Confalonieri 1988, 65–67; Allison et al. 1974; Horne 1985; Reinhard 1990, 159; Carvalho Gonçalves, Araùjo, and Fernando Ferreira 2003.

50. See Fernando Ferreira, Araùjo, and Confalonieri 1988, 20–23, 37, 65–67, 120–37, 144–51; Confalonieri, Fernando Ferreira, and Araùjo 1991, 864–65; also Reinhard 1992, 231–35; Verano 1997, 244–55; Montenegro et al. 2006. There are also BC occurrences in France and the Czech Republic. Two researchers attempted to account for *A. duodenale* by speculating that it had developed a cold-season hypobiosis (quiescent stage), allowing passage through the Arctic in the warm microenvironments of dwellings and transmission not only in fecal matter but also via mother's milk (Hawdon and Johnston 1996). But if so, why is it absent in that region today?

51. See Raoult et al. 2008.

52. Buckland and Panagiotakopulu 2001, 554. For more on Old World archaeological occurrences of *R. dominica* and *S. paniceum*, see King et al. 2014, 4–6.

Chapter 27

1. Candolle 1885, 461.

2. Driver 1973, 164, 166; see also Riley et al. 1971.

3. Wagner and Mikesell 1962, 15.

4. See Cook 1901, 1904; Sauer 1952; Newcomb 1963; Carter 1950, 1953, 1963, 2001.

5. See Campbell 1926, 26.

6. Merrill 1954, 236.

7. See Nunn 2009, 59.

8. See De Queiroz 2014; Will and Escapa 2014.

9. See Ridley 1930, 15, 242, 443, 446, 543–45.

10. See Carlquist 1981, 509–12.

11. Many such crossings have been recorded in the north, and the tropical/subtropical African cattle egret established itself in Brazil during the mid-twentieth century.

12. Merrill 1954, 243.

13. Xylem is woody tissue, which can be morphologically diagnostic. Phytoliths are microscopic bits of silica in higher-plant tissues, each species or genus possessing ones of unique form. Certain plants contain starches that are produced only by that species and that manifest morphologically distinctive grains.

14. Note the great font of evidential material in Sorenson and Johannessen 2013; also, Johannessen 2016.

15. See Chang 1963, 419–21; 1973, 527.

16. See Johannessen and Siming 1998, 22–25.

17. See Chen 1994, 59.

18. See Croizat 1981, 26–30.

19. See Glover 1977, 43, 46.

20. See Dixon 1932; also, Yen 1974, 13–19; Kelley 1998a, 733. Rensch (1991, 108) saw two imports of *kumara/'uala* into Polynesia: from the northern Kichwa via Easter Island and from northern Colombia to Hawaii. The fact that *kumāra* (child, son) designates Brahma's four offspring as well as a South Indian god is likely coincidental. Possibly more relevant is the fact that *kumad* is Sanskrit for a lotus (*Nymphaea esculenta* [*Nymphaea pubescens*]) whose rhizome is edible (Christian 1897, 126). The Egyptian lotus (*Nymphaea lotus*) is *kumada* in Sanskrit.

21. Merrill 1954, 274, 307.

22. Nordenskiöld 1931, 27.

23. See Brand 1971. Peter Haggett (1959) has shown that, contrary to the suppositions of Merrill, Brand, and various others, few Portuguese ships called in Brazil en route to India during the period concerned; see chapter 29.

24. See Rosendahl and Yen 1971; Yen 1974, 26–28; Skjölsvold 1961 297, 303; Higham 2001.

25. See Hather and Kirch 1991.

26. See Ladefoged, Graves, and Coil 2005; Horrocks and Barber 2005, 106; Barber 2010; Horrocks and Rechtman 2009; Pearthree 2003; Horrocks et al. 2011. Kirch (1998, 67–70) also dated charred tubers from another Hawaiian site at AD 1680–1740.

27. See Roullier et al. 2013.

28. Montenegro, Avis, and Weaver 2008.

29. See Langdon 2001. Genetic studies have indicated a pre-Contact American Indian genetic input into the Easter Island population (see chapter 31).

30. See Yen 1974, 329. Scholars have, in the meantime, moved the date forward some centuries.

31. See O'Brien 1972, 342, 361.

32. This may, however, reflect post-Columbian Spanish and Portuguese introduction of more productive Middle American *camote* varieties.

33. Carter 1963, 9.

34. See, e.g., Alden 2000, 115.

35. Merrill 1954, 261.

36. See Sauer 1962; Jeffreys 1971, 1975; Marszewski 1978, 1987.

37. Gupta and Jain 1973. "Multi-eared Sikkim primitive popcorn shows a distinct constitutive heterochromatic phenomenon similar to that found in South American maize" (Pokharia 2008, 253), pointing to a continent of origin of the variety.

38. Brücher 1985, 62. As an aside, Brücher, serving in Nazi Germany's SS during World War II, refused an order to destroy Russian botanical research facilities.

39. See Jett 1978, 635–36.

40. See Maxwell 1983.

41. See Johannessen and Parker 1989; Johannessen 1998a, 1998b, 2003, 304–10; Johannessen and Wang 1998; Sorenson and Johannessen 2013, 249–60.

42. Gupta 1996, 176.

43. Quoted in Partington 1992, 509. Marshall McLuhan's meaning was more ambiguous: "I wouldn't have seen it if I hadn't believed it" (quoted in David J. Hand 2014: 174).

44. See Johannessen and Wang 1998, 27–28.

45. See Pokharia and Saraswat 1998–99, 100. Gunnar Thompson (2010) has also published images of what he considers to be Old World maize representations, in Egypt and elsewhere.

46. See Johannessen and Wang 1998, 18–20.

47. Glover 1979, 18, 21.

48. Mark Nesbit 2005, 54.

49. See Collins 1949, 335; 1951, 143; 1948: 372.

50. See Casella 1950, 1956, 1957; Pohl 1973, 31–35.

51. See Merrill 1954, 367–69.

52. Gupta 1996, 18.

53. See Sauer 1950, 1968; Fahd 1996, 836.

54. See Saraswat, Sharma, and Saini 1994, 259, 282, 284, 331. The Mexican prickly poppy also appeared at Sanghol in Punjab, at around AD 100–300, as did a fragment of the American weed *Datura innoxia* (Pokharia and Saraswat 1998/99, 90, 100).

55. See Johannessen 1998b; Johannessen and Wang 1998, 14–16.

56. See Casella 1950, 1956, 1957.

57. See Johannessen and Wang 1998, 16–17; Gupta 1996, 18–19; Sorenson and Johannessen 2013.

58. Sitholey 1976, 20–22; Cunningham 1962, plates 33, 47; Pokharia and Saraswat 1998/99: 97–99; Pokharia 2008.

59. See Glover 1977, 43, 46; 1986, 55, 229–30.

60. See Vishnu-Mittre, Sharma, and Chanchala 1986; also, Pokharia and Saraswat 1998/99, 99; Chen 1994, 59.

61. See Johannessen and Wang 1998, 27; Gupta 1996.

62. Quoted in Crone 1967, xii, 17, 124.

63. See Steffy 1985, 84; 1994: 56; Sorenson 2002, 356. The Israeli archaeobotanist Nili Liphschitz identified another sample of the hull's vegetal material as grass, perhaps reed, not agave (personal communication, August 5, 2009).

64. Pokharia and Saraswat 1998/99, 102.

Chapter 28

1. See Smole 2002; Langdon 1993. On Old World antiquity, see Jett 2005; 2007a.

2. For details, see Jett 2002a.

3. See Jett 1968.

4. See Whitaker and Carter 1954.

5. Whitaker 1971, 324.

6. See Heiser 1973, 312; Richardson 1972, 267; Sandweiss et al. 1998, 1381.

7. See Erickson et al. 2005.

8. See Clarke 2009; Heiser 1973.

9. See Kistler et al. 2014.

10. See Whistler 1990, 48; Clarke 2009, 164, 166, 205; Green 2000.

11. See Cook 1901, 279.

12. See Ward and Brookfield 1992, 468.

13. See Merrill 1954 241, 265–56, 274.

14. See Heyerdahl 1952, 458.

15. See Robinson et al. 2000, 843.

16. See Heyerdahl 1950, 104, 136, 204; 1952, 460; 1978, 281.

17. See Görlitz 2001, 89.

18. See Edmondson 1941.

19. Ward and Brookfield 1992, 478; also 471.

20. See Dennis and Gunn 1971, 411–12.

21. See Baudouin and Lebrun 2008.

22. Cf. Jett 1968; Estrada and Meggers 1961.

23. This material is also treated in Jett 2011–14b.

24. See Hutchinson, Silow, and Stephens 1947; Johnson 1975.

25. See Jett 2011–14a, b, c.

26. See Sorenson and Johannessen 2013 (earlier versions appeared); also, Johannessen 2016.

Chapter 29

1. This material, with additional documentation, appeared in Jett 2002b, 2003/4; reproduced with the permission of Christine Pellach, for Odyssee Verlag Wien.

2. Winter 1999, 227; see also Winter 2000, 93, 99, 118.
3. See, e.g., Ashraf 1985.
4. See Alfieri 1976, 82; also Huchet 1995; Görlitz 2011.
5. Balout 1978, 40.
6. See Castello 1983, 40, 42.
7. See Görlitz 2011.
8. See Balabanova, Parsche, and Pirsig 1992; Balabanova et al. 1993; Balabanova et al. 1996.
9. See Parsche and Nerlich 1995; Nerlich et al. 1995, 423, 426, 428.
10. See Cartmell and Weems 2001.
11. Brier 1998, 30.
12. Vartavan and Amorós 1997, 180.
13. See Balabanova et al. 1993, 93; Pollmer 2000: 243–44.
14. See Plowman 1984, 155; Collins, Sayer, and Whitmore 1991, 123.
15. See Balabanova et al. 1995, 1997, 1997; Balabanova 1997; Balabanova et al. 2001.
16. Balabanova 2000, 6.
17. Balabanova et al. 2001, 72–73.
18. See Balabanova, Wei, and Krämer 1995, 68, 70, 73–74.
19. See Parsche, Balabanova, and Pirsig 1994.
20. Merrill 1954, 229.
21. Haggett 1959, 267.
22. Bruhns 1994, 362.
23. Bellwood 2013, 211.
24. White 1976, 23.

Chapter 30

1. Spriggs 1997, 10.
2. Gould 1986, 68.
3. This has to do with melanin's protection against ultraviolet radiation and its inhibiting of vitamin D production. Note, however, that whereas among Old World populations' degree of skin darkness correlates rather well with ultraviolet insolation, the complexions of New World indigenes generally differ from what one would predict on the basis of UV radiation, presumably owing to Amerinds' relative recency in the Western Hemisphere plus, in some cases, their use of clothing (see Jablonski 2004). For example, the distribution of ultraviolet-light exposure predicts black skins in the central Andean region and white skins in indigenous Siberia and Native Canada (see Swerdlow 2002, 47), but neither case conforms to this prediction, suggesting insufficient length of exposure of these populations to these environments for selection to have yielded skin color that is in permanent natural equilibrium with the relevant environmental factors.
4. Crawford 1998, 194, 233.
5. "Most of the big differences between human and chimpanzee DNA lie in regions that do not code for genes. . . . Instead, they may contain DNA sequences that control how gene-coding regions are activated and read." Said one researcher, "The differences between chimps and humans are not in our proteins, but in how we use them" (Anonymous 2007).
6. Schillaci, Ozolins, and Windes 2001, 135.
7. Coon 1962, 352–53.

8. See Comas 1973; Wiercínski 1972a, 1972b.

9. See Van Sertima 1995, 67–68.

10. See Humboldt 1814, 29–30.

11. See Heyerdahl 1952; 1971a; 1978, 93–125, 192; 385–86; 1980, 43–44.

12. Knobloch 1970, 192.

13. See, e.g., Donnan 2004, 34, 92, 117–21, 140–55.

14. See Verano 1994, 314.

15. Howells 1995, 102.

16. Howells 1989, 72, 79.

17. See Guthrie 1990.

18. See Heyerdahl 1952, 315–25; 1971a, 215; Trotter 1943, 69; Stewart 1943; Hall and Clark 2010, 76–77; Donnan and Klein 2001, 64.

19. See Savoy 1974, 3–4, 9–11.

20. Lévi-Strauss 1973, 55, 254–55.

21. Covarrubias 1946, 90.

22. See Melgar 1871; Van Sertima 1976, 1995, 1998. For illustrations and analysis of Olmec colossal heads, see Clewlow et al. 1967, especially plate 18a.

23. Grove 1984, 129.

24. Stirling 1939, 209.

25. E.g., the heads "do indeed have strangely African looking features" (Blench 2006, 178).

26. See, e.g., Sabloff 1989, 145. Feder (2010, 3–4; also, 1–2, 201–3) found the Negroid idea "fundamentally flawed and . . . just silly. . . . the [heads are the] weakest evidence possible."

27. Although ancient Egyptians were essentially Caucasoid in their physical features, ridged lip seams are depicted in some Egyptian portrait sculptures, including from the Amarna period (see Schuster and Carpenter 1996, 64). This is interesting in light of suggestions by the cultural historian R. A. Jairazbhoy (1974, 1981) and a few others that Egyptian influence is to be seen in early Olmec times, as manifested particularly in pantheon, sculpture, and language.

28. See Hooton 1933, 138.

29. de la Fuente quoted in Van Sertima 1995, 74.

30. See Guthrie 1995, 130–41, 154, 314; Campbell 1989, 266.

31. Fuller 1966, 211.

32. E.g., Heyerdahl 1978, 37.

33. On the murals, see Heyerdahl 1952, plates 29–32.

34. NA11451, University of Pennsylvania Museum of Archaeology and Anthropology. For a published example, see Miller 2001, 175, who writes of the "reputedly fair and bearded" Toltec ruler Topíltzin Quetzalcoatl (p. 176).

35. See Jett 1968, 1970, 1991.

36. See Key 1998.

37. See Sutter 2009.

Chapter 31

1. Tankersley 2000, 75.

2. Gould 1986, 68.

3. Hughes 2002.

4. Genetic bottlenecks are historical situations, such as epidemics, that extinguish some of the genetic variation within a population. The founder effect relates to the

fact that the portion of a population that emigrates and settles a new area will include only a part of the genetic variability of the parent population. Genetic drift is the accumulation over time of adaptively neutral genetic variations, leading to increasingly greater genetic differences between separated populations. Cladograms are tree diagrams showing relationships based on degree of similarity and (if no intermixing is assumed) suggest evolutionary histories.

5. Oppenheimer 1998, 224.

6. Garn 1965, 51, also 220; see also Hulse 1963, 299, 301; Diamond 1993, 18, 21.

7. Garn 1957, 222.

8. In reality, a 1937 report of an analysis of 196 Basketmaker (US Southwest) and Peruvian mummies had indicated that 2 percent tested A, 3.6 percent B, and 1 percent AB (Peru), and earlier reports of A and B among living American Indians are cited, including high levels of B among Tierra del Fuegians, in proportions not consistent with historic European admixture (see Boyd and Boyd 1937, 314). In addition, as early as 1943 the B antigen had seemingly been demonstrated in a few 8,000-year-old skeletons from Coahuila, Mexico (see Matson et al. 1967, 188).

9. See Workman et al. 1974.

10. See Davis 2000, 118.

11. See Hulse 1963, 283–84.

12. Guthrie 2000/2001: 131.

13. Miguel Layrisse and Tulio Arends (1956) reported Diego as fairly common among Venezuelan Caribs and Arawaks as well as among Cantonese and Japanese. Marion Lewis, Hiroko Ayukawa, and Bruce Chown (1956) confirmed the finding for the Japanese and also identified the factor among Minnesota Chippewa but not among Caucasoids (also, Hulse 1963, 313, 315). Matson et al. (1967, 181) identified Diego among Chile's Mapuche and Atacameño but not in samples from Polynesians and from Chile's Alacaluf. Robert L. Kirk (1979, 212–13) found some American Indian populations with up to 40 percent *Dia.* and noted important percentages among Canada's Chippewa and Cree, Venezuela's Guahibo and Piaroa, Brazil's Kaingáng, and Peru's Kichwa and Aymara, plus traces among the Mapuche and the Maya. He added to Asian cases, with examples in Thailand and China, instances among Ainu, Ryukyuan, and Mongoloid Japanese, and in Chomorros of the Mariana Islands but not otherwise in Oceania, Australia, or New Guinea.

14. Garn 1965, 45–46; see also Crawford 1998, 104.

15. Layrisse and Wilbert 1961.

16. See Guthrie 2000/2001.

17. See Crawford 1998, 101–2.

18. See Arends and Gallango 1964, 367.

19. See Jett 2007a.

20. Zago et al. 1995, 542.

21. It has been hypothesized that this extreme variability must function to afford any population potential variants with selective advantage in the face of newly arising pathogens. Alicia Sanchez-Mazas, Jean-François Lemaître, and Mathias Currat (2012) found that there *is* a weak correlation between numbers of polymorphisms in some loci and pathogen richness (a correlation that disappears when the Americas and Taiwan are removed from the calculations) but concluded that HLAs are nevertheless useful for understanding human migrations. Fernandez-Vina et al. (2012) have cautioned against the possibility of convergent independent mutations.

22. On language, see Stubbs 1998, 2014; Foster 1998.

23. See Zegura, Karafet, and Hammer 2009, 135.

24. See Jett 2007a, 114–16. I later refined my ideas concerning the Late Pleistocene entrants (see Jett 2009), but these are unpublished. On a likely overseas origin of B, see also Cann 1994, 10. Note that ancient DNA studies at the Paisley Caves, Oregon, have identified mtDNA B, at around 13,000 BC.

25. On the last, see Novick et al. 1998.

26. See Fahey 2004, 2005–7.

27. Olson 2002, 204. The exception is mtDNA Hg X.

28. Torroni et al. 1993, 591, 603–4; see also Shields et al. 1993, 558; Wallace 1993; Smith et al. 1999; Malhi et al. 2003, 119.

29. Brown et al. 1998, 1852.

30. See Greenman 1963.

31. See Stanford and Bradley 2012.

32. See Torroni 2000, 84–85; Olson 2002, 203–4.

33. See Brandt et al. 2013.

34. See Menzies 2011.

35. See Sykes 2012, 50.

36. See Zegura, Karafet, and Hammer 2009.

37. Roewar et al. 2013.

38. See Raghavan 2014.

39. See Stanford and Bradley 2012; Guthrie 2014.

40. See Schurr 2004, 198.

41. See Zamora et al. 1990. See also León-S, Ariza-Deleón, and Ariza-Deleón Caicedo 1995, 348; 1994.

42. See Meggers 2005, 25.

43. See Miura et al. 1994.

44. Miura et al. 1994, 1124.

45. See Yamashita et al. 1996. See also Jett 2015.

46. See Jett 2007a.

47. See Estrada, Meggers, and Evans 1962; Meggers, Evans, and Estrada 1965; also Meggers 2005.

48. See León, Ariza-Deleón, and Ariza-Deleón 1994, 133–34.

49. Meggers 1998, 20.

50. Yates 2012, 55–56. Also, Yates 2010; Yates and Yates 2014, 56–72. Note that although the sample was from diverse sources, this was not a peer-reviewed, formally randomized, or large-sample study. Interestingly, mtDNA Hg X is also recorded from Papua New Guinea. The Melungeons are a distinct Appalachian population whose ancestry includes both Native American and Mediterranean regional elements.

51. See Yates and Yates 2014, 97–129.

52. See Guthrie 2011–14b. Cf. Gordon 1968.

53. See Sykes et al. 1995.

54. See Bonetto et al. 1996.

55. See Thorsby 2012; Moreno-Mayar et al. 2014. American Indian input is also supported by dental morphology (see Swindler et al. 1998).

56. Faria Gonçalves et al. 2013, 6467.

Chapter 32

1. Bentley 1993, 21.

Works Cited

Abbott, J. 1974. *The Keys of Power: A Study of Indian Ritual and Belief.* Secaucus, NJ: University Books.

Acuña-Soto, Rudolfo, David W. Stahle, Matthew D. Therrell, Sergio Gomez Chavez, and Malcolm K. Cleaveland. 2005. "Drought, Epidemic Disease, and the Fall of the Classic Period Culture in Mesoamerica (AD 750–950): Hemorraghagic Fevers as a Cause of Massive Population Loss." *Medical Hypotheses* 65 (2): 405–9.

Aczel, Amir D. 2001. *The Riddle of the Compass: The Invention That Changed the World.* New York: Harcourt.

Adams, William Y., Dennis P. Van Gerven, and Richard S. Levy. 1978. "The Retreat from Migrationism." *Annual Review of Anthropology* 7: 483–532.

Adelaar, Alexander. 2009. "Towards an Integrated Theory about the Indonesian Migrations to Madagascar." In *Ancient Human Migrations: A Multidisciplinary Approach,* edited by Peter L. Peregrine, Ilia Peiros, and Marcus Feldman, 149–72. Salt Lake City: University of Utah Press.

Aebi, Tania, with Bernadette Brennan. 1989. *Maiden Voyage.* New York: Ballantine Books.

Africa, Thomas W. 1969. *The Ancient World.* Boston: Houghton Mifflin.

Agence France-Presse. 2006. "Marshall Islands: 3 Adrift for Three Months." *New York Times,* national ed., 155, no. 53, 673, A7.

Åkerblom, Kjell. 1968. *Astronomy and Navigation in Polynesia and Micronesia: A Survey.* Monograph Series, Publication 14. Stockholm: Ethnographical Museum (Etnografiska Museet).

Alchon, Suzanne Austin. 2003. *A Pest in the Land: New World Epidemics in a Global Perspective.* Albuquerque: University of New Mexico Press.

Alcina Franch, José. 1955. "El Neolítico americano y su problemática." *International Congress of Americanists* 31 (2): 871–82.

Alden, John R. 2000. Review of *A Mediterranean Feast* (Clifford A. Wright). *Smithsonian* 30 (10): 115–16.

Alfieri, Anastase. 1976. *The Coleoptera of Egypt.* Mémoires de la Société Entomologique d'Égypte 5. Cairo: Atlas Press.

Allen, J. M. N.d. "History of Reed Ships." Accessed November 12, 2014. http://www
.atlantisbolivia.org/areedboathistory.htm.

Alliot-Duchesne, Virginie, and Isabelle Fortis, eds. Designed by Panni Demeter. 2010.
Tous les bateaux du monde. Grenoble: Éditions Glénat / (Paris): Musée National de
la Marine.

Allison, Marvin J., Alejandro Pezzio, Ichiro Hasagawa, and Enrique Gerszten. 1974.
"A Case of Hookworm Infestation in a Precolumbian American." *American Journal of Physical Anthropology* 41 (1): 103–6.

Alsar, Vital, with Enrique Hank Lopez. 1973. *La Balsa: The Longest Raft Voyage in History.* New York: Reader's Digest Press / E. P. Dutton.

Álvarez, Ticul, and Aurelio Ocaña. 1999. *Sinopsis de restos arqueozoológicos de vertebra-
dos terrestres: Basada en informes del Laboritorio de Paleozoología del INAH (Collección
Científica).* Mexico City: Instituto Nacional de Antropología e Historia.

Ammarell, Gene. 1999. *Bugis Navigation.* Yale Southeast Asia Studies, Monograph 48.
New Haven, CT: Yale University Southeast Asia Studies.

Anderson, Atholl. 2000. "Slow Boats from China: Issues in the Prehistory of Indo-
Pacific Seafaring." In *East of Wallace's Line: Studies of Past and Present Maritime
Cultures of the Indo-Pacific Region,* edited by Sue O'Connor and Peter Veth, 13–50.
Modern Quaternary Research in Southeast Asia 16. Rotterdam: A. A. Balkema.

———. 2003. "Entering Uncharted Waters: Models of Initial Colonization in Polynesia." In *The Colonization of Unfamiliar Landscapes: The Archaeology of Adaptation,*
edited by Marcy Rockman and James Steele, 169–89. London: Routledge.

———. 2010. "The Origins and Development of Seafaring: Towards a Global Approach."
In *The Global Origins and Development of Seafaring,* edited by Atholl Anderson,
James H. Barrett, and Katherine V. Boyle, 3–16. McDonald Institute Monographs.
Cambridge, UK: McDonald Institute for Archaeological Research.

Anderson, Atholl, and Hanneke Boon. 2011. "East Polynesian Sailing Rigs: The *Anuta Iti* Experiment." *Journal of Pacific Archaeology* 22 (2): 109–13.

Anderson, Atholl, John Chappell, Michael Gagan, and Richard Grove. 2006. "Prehistoric Maritime Migration in the Pacific Islands: An Hypothesis of ENSO Forcing."
Holocene 16 (1): 1–6.

Anderson, J. R. L. 1992. *The Ulysses Factor: The Exploring Instinct in Man.* New York:
Harcourt Brace Jovanovich.

Anderson, O. S. 1970. *The Seafarer: An Introduction.* [Folcroft, PA]: Folcroft Editions.
(Originally published 1938.)

Anderson, R. M., and R. M. May. 1991. *Infectious Diseases of Humans: Dynamics and
Control.* New York: Oxford University Press.

Andrews, Robert, comp. 1993. *The Columbia Dictionary of Quotations.* New York: Columbia University Press.

Anonymous. 1980. *Diccionario critico etimológico castellano e hispanico: A–Ca.* Madrid:
Editorial Gredos.

———. 1997. "In the News." *American Archaeology* 1 (4): 6–7.

———. 2007. "Discoveries." *UC Davis Magazine* 24 (2): 7.

———. 2012. "New Evidence Suggests Stone Age Hunters from Europe Discovered
America." *Independent,* February 29, London.

Anthony, David W. 1990. "Migration in Anthropology: The Baby and the Bathwater."
American Anthropologist 92 (4): 895–914.

———. 1997. "Prehistoric Migration as Social Process." In *Migrations and Invasions in
Archaeological Explanation,* edited by John Chapman and Helena Hamerow, 21–32.
BAR International Series 664. Oxford: British Archaeological Reports.

———. 2007. *The Horse, the Wheel, and Language: How Bronze-Age Riders from the Eurasian Steppes Shaped the Modern World.* Princeton, NJ: Princeton University Press.

Apter, Michael J. 1992. *The Dangerous Edge: The Psychology of Excitement.* New York: Free Press.

Arends, Tulio, and M. L. Gallango. 1964. "Transferrins in Venezuelan Indians: High Frequency of a Slow-Moving Variant." *Science* 143 (3604): 367–68.

Arias, Ron. 1989. *Five against the Sea: A True Story of Courage and Survival.* New York: New American Library.

Arnold, Dean E., Jill Hutter Wilson, and Alvaro L. Nieves. 2007. "Why Was the Potter's Wheel Rejected? Social Choice and Technological Change in Ticul, Yucatán, Mexico." In *Pottery Economics in Mesoamerica,* edited by Christopher A. Pool and George J. Bey III, 59–85. Tucson: University of Arizona Press.

Arunachalam, B. 1996. "Traditional Sea and Sky Wisdom in Indian Seamen and Their Practical Application." In *Tradition and Archaeology: Early Maritime Contacts in the Indian Ocean. Proceedings of the International Seminar Techno-Archaeological Perspectives of Seafaring in the Indian Ocean 4th cent. B.C.–15th cent. A.D., New Delhi, February 28–March 4, 1994,* edited by Himanshu Prabha Ray and Jean-François Salles, 261–82. New Delhi: Ajay Kumar Jain for Manohar Publishers and Distributors.

Ashraf, Jaweed. 1985. "The Antiquity of Tobacco (*Nicotiana tabacum*) in India." *Indica* 22 (2): 91–101.

Associated Press. 2012. "The End of the Line: Coast Guard Cannon Fire Sinks Abandoned Japanese Ghost Ship." *Bristol Herald Courier* 141, April 6, A4. Bristol, VA.

Atoche Peña, Pablo, Juan Ángel Paz Peralta, Ma[ría] Ángeles Ramírez Rodríguez, and Esperanza Ortiz Palomar. 1995. *Evidencias arqueológicas del mundo romano en Lanzarote (Islas Canarias).* Arrecife, Spain: Servicio de Publicaciones del Excmo, Cabildo Insular de Lanzarote.

Aufderheide, Arthur C., and Conrado Rodríguez-Martín. 1998. *The Cambridge Encyclopedia of Human Paleopathology.* Cambridge: Cambridge University Press.

Ayalon, David. 1978. *Gunpowder and Firearms in the Mamluk Kingdom: A Challenge to a Medieval Society.* 2nd ed. London: F. Cass.

Babayan, Chad, Ben Finney, Bernard Kilonsky, and Nainona Thompson. 1987. "Voyage to Aotearoa." *Journal of the Polynesian Society* 96 (2): 161–200.

Babcock, W. H. 1918. "Certain Pre-Columbian Notices of the Inhabitants of the Atlantic Islands." *American Anthropologist* 20 (1): 62–78.

Bacus, Elizabeth A. 2004. "The Archaeology of the Philippine Archipelago." In *Southeast Asia: From Prehistory to History,* edited by Ian Glover and Peter Bellwood, 257–81. Abingdon, UK: RoutledgeCurzon.

Baez, Fernando. 2008. *A Universal History of the Destruction of Books: From Ancient Sumer to Modern Iraq.* New York: Atlas.

Bahn, Paul. 1996. *The Cambridge Illustrated History of Archaeology.* Cambridge: Cambridge University Press.

Bahn, Paul, and John Flenley. 1992. *Easter Island, Earth Island.* New York: Thames and Hudson.

Bailey, Flora L. 1940. "Navaho Foods and Cooking Methods." *American Anthropologist* 42 (2, part 1): 270–90.

Bailey, Maurice, and Maralyn Bailey. 1974. *Staying Alive!* New York: David McKay. (Reprint 1988 as *117 Days Adrift,* Nautical Books, London.)

Baker, Rollin H. 1951. *The Avifauna of Micronesia: Its Origin, Evolution, and Distribution.* Lawrence: University of Kansas Publications, Museum of Natural History 3, no. 1.

Balabanova, Svetlana. 1997. *Die Geschicte der Tabakpflanze vor Columbus aufserhalb*

Amerikas sowie das Rauchen im Spiegel der Zeiten. Seeheim, Germany: Innovations-Verlags-Gesellschaft.

————. 2000. "Detection of Nicotine and Cocaine in Ancient Human Remains from Different Locations out of America and an Archaeological Period Spans a Range from 9000 BC to 700 AD." *Migration and Diffusion: An International Journal* 1 (2): 110–24.

Balabanova, Svetlana, F. Parsche, G. Bühler, and W. Pirsig. 1993. "Was Nicotine Known in Ancient Egypt?" *Homo: Journal of Comparative Human Biology* 44 (1): 92–94.

Balabanova, Svetlana, F. Parsche, and W. Pirsig. 1992. "First Indication of Drugs in Egyptian Mummies." *Naturwissenschaften* 79 (38): 358.

Balabanova, Svetlana, F. W. Rösing, G. Bühler, S. Hauser, and J. Rosenthal. 2001. "Nicotine Use in Early Medieval Kirchheim / Teck, Germany." *Homo: Journal of Comparative Human Biology* 52 (1): 72–76.

Balabanova, Svetlana, F. W. Rösing, G. Bühler, W. Schoetz, G. Scherer, and J. Rosenthal. 1997. "Nicotine and Cotinine in Prehistoric and Recent Bones from Africa and Europe and the Origin of These Alkaloids." *Homo: Journal of Comparative Human Biology* 48 (1): 72–77.

Balabanova, Svetlana, F. W. Rösing, G. Bühler, M. Teschler-Nicola, E. Strouhal, and J. Rosenthal. 1997. "Evidence of Cocaine in Ancient Pre-Columbian Populations from Christian Sayala (Egyptian Nubia)." *Journal of Paleopathology* 9 (1): 15–21.

Balabanova, Svetlana, F. W. Rösing, M. Teschler-Nicola, E. Strouhal, G. Bühler, C. Michael, and J. Rosenthal. 1996. "Was Nicotine Used as a Stimulant Already in the VI Century A.D. from the Christian Sayala Population?" *Journal of Paleopathology* 8 (1): 43–50.

Balabanova, Svetlana, H. Schneider, M. Teschler-Nicola, and G. Scherer. 1995. "Detection of Nicotine in Ancient European Populations." *Journal of Paleopathology* 7 (1): 43–50.

Balabanova, Svetlana, Boyuan Wei, and M. Krämer. 1995. "First Detection of Nicotine in Ancient Population of Southern China." *Homo: Journal of Comparative Human Biology* 46 (1): 68–75.

Balbín Behrmann, Rodrigo, de, Primitiva Bueno Ramírez, Rafael González Antón, and María Carmen del Arco Aguilar. 1995. "Datos sobre la colonización púnica de las Islas Canarias." *Eres (Arqueología)* 6 (1): 7–28.

Ballard, Robert D., Lawrence E. Stager, Daniel Master, Dana Yoerger, David Mindell, Louis L. Whitcomb, Hanumant Singh, and Dennis Piechota. 2002. "Iron Age Shipwrecks in Deep Water off Ashkelon, Israel." *American Journal of Nautical Archaeology* 106 (2): 151–68.

Balout, Lionel. 1978. "La momie de Ramses II." *Archéologia* 115 (February): 1, 5, 32–46.

Balser, Carlos. 1988. "Jade de América Central con un possible influencia china." *China Libre Magazine* 6 (6): 14–21.

Banack, Sandra Anne. 1991. "Plants and Polynesian Voyaging." In *Islands, Plants, and Polynesians: An Introduction to Polynesian Voyaging,* edited by Paul Alan Cox and Sandra Anne Banack, 25–39. Portland, OR: Dioscorides Press.

Banks, Charles Edward. 1966. *The History of Martha's Vineyard, Dukes County, Massachusetts,* vol. 1, *General History.* (Originally published 1911.)

Barber, Ian. 2010. "Diffusion or Innovation? Explaining Lithic Agronomy in the Southern Polynesian Margins." *World Archaeology* 42 (1): 74–89.

Barcarse, Kaimana. 2014. "A Voyage around the World—In a Canoe." *Cultural Survival Quarterly* 38 (1): 20–21.

Barnes, Gina L. 1993. *China, Korea, and Japan: The Rise of Civilization in East Asia.* New York: Thames and Hudson.

Barnett, H. G. 1953. *Innovation: The Basis of Culture Change.* New York: McGraw-Hill.

Barnett, R. D. 1958. "Early Shipping in the Near East." *Antiquity: A Quarterly Review of World Archaeology* 32 (128): 220–30, plates 21–24.

Barrett, James H. 2010. "Rounding Up the Usual Suspects: Causation and the Viking Age Diaspora." In *The Global Origins and Development of Seafaring,* edited by Atholl Anderson, James H. Barrett, and Katherine V. Boyle, 289–302. McDonald Institute Monographs. Cambridge, UK: McDonald Institute for Archaeological Research.

Barrow, T. 1964. *The Decorative Arts of the New Zealand Maori.* Wellington, NZ: A. H. and A. W. Reed.

Barthel, Thomas S. 1974. *The Eighth Land: The Polynesian Discovery and Settlement of Easter Island.* Honolulu: University of Hawai'i Press.

Bartlett, John. 1955. *Familiar Quotations.* 13th ed. Boston: Little, Brown.

Bartoloni, Piero. 1999. "Ships and Navigation." In *The Phoenicians,* edited by Sabatino Moscati, 84–91. New York: Rizzoli International Publications.

Basham, A. L. 1959. *The Wonder That Was India: A Survey of the Culture of the Indian Sub-Continent before the Coming of the Muslims.* New York: Grove Press.

Bass, George F. 1983. "Shipwreck Archaeology in the Eastern United States." In *Historical Archaeology of the Eastern United States: Papers from the R. J. Russell Symposium.* Geoscience and Man, Louisiana State University, Baton Rouge, vol. 23: 5–15.

Batten, David C. 1999. "Horse Power: Wheat, Oats, Maize, and the Supply of Cities." *Ancient Mesoamerica* 10 (1): 99–103.

Baudouin, L[uc], and P[atricia] Lebrun. 2008. "Coconut (*Cocos nucifera* L.) DNA Studies Support the Hypothesis of an Ancient Austronesian Migration from Southeast Asia to America." *Genetic Resources and Crop Development* 56 (2): 257–62.

Baumer, Christoph. 2012. *The History of Central Asia,* vol. 1, *The Age of the Steppe Warriors.* London: I. B. Tauris.

Bawden, Garth. 1996. *The Moche.* Cambridge, MA: Blackwell.

Beale, Philip (interviewed by Mike Pitts). 2004. "The Seas Were Quite Big." *British Archaeology* 77: 1–2.

Beale, Philip, and Sarah Taylor. 2013. *Sailing Close to the Wind.* Leamington Spa, Warwickshire, UK: Lulworth Cove Press.

Beck, Louis. 1966. "Jade." *Anthropological Journal of Canada* 4 (1): 12–22.

Beckman, Mary. 2004. "A Matter of Taste." *Smithsonian* 35 (5): 24, 26.

Bednarik, Robert G. 1997. "The Initial Peopling of Wallacia and Sahul." *Anthropos* 92 (4/6): 355–67.

———. 1999. "Maritime Navigation in the Lower and Middle Paleolithic." *Comptes Rendus de l'Académie de Science Paris* 328 (8): 559–63.

———. 2001. "Replicating the First Known Sea Travel by Humans: The Lower Pleistocene Crossing of Lombok Strait." *Human Evolution* 16 (3–4): 229–42.

Beeson, Chris. 2003. *The Handbook of Survival at Sea.* Hoo, nr. Rochester, Kent, UK: Grange Books: Lewis International.

Begley, Sharon, and Andrew Muir. 1999. "The First Americans." *Newsweek* 133 (17): 50–57.

Bellwood, Peter. 1984–85. "A Hypothesis for Austronesian Origins." *Asian Perspectives* 26 (1): 107–17.

———. 1997. *Prehistory of the Indo-Malaysian Archipelago.* Rev. ed. Honolulu: University of Hawai'i Press.

———. 2013. *First Migrants: Ancient Migration in Global Perspective.* Malden, MA: Wiley Blackwell.

Bentley, Jerry H. 1993. *Old World Encounters: Cross-Cultural Contacts and Exchanges in Pre-Modern Times.* New York: Oxford University Press.

Bergreen, Laurence. 2003. *Over the Edge of the World: Magellan's Terrifying Circumnavigation.* New York: William Morrow.

Bernstein, Peter L. 1996. *Against the Gods: The Remarkable Story of Risk.* New York: John Wiley and Sons.

Best, Elsdon. 1954. *Polynesian Voyagers: The Maori as a Deep-Sea Navigator, Explorer, and Colonizer.* Monograph 5. Wellington, NZ: Dominion Museum. (Originally published 1923.)

Bhacker, M. Redha, and Bernadette Bhacker. 1997. "Digging in the Land of Magan." *Archaeology* 50 (3): 48–49.

Bill, Jan. 1997. "Ships and Seamanship." In *The Oxford Illustrated History of the Vikings,* edited by Peter Sawyer, 182–201. Oxford: Oxford University Press.

Bisschop, Éric de. 1939. *Kaimiloa: D'Honolulu à Cannes par l'Australie et le Cap à bord d'une double pirogue polynésienne.* Paris: Librairie Plon.

———. 1959. *Tahiti-Nui.* New York: McDowell, Obolensky.

Blakely, Sandra. 2006. *Myth, Ritual, and Metallurgy in Ancient Greece and Recent Africa.* New York: Cambridge University Press.

Blench, Roger. 2006. *Archaeology, Language, and the African Past.* Lanham, MD: AltaMira Press.

———. 2010. "Evidence for the Austronesian Voyages in the Indian Ocean." In *The Global Origins and Development of Seafaring,* edited by Atholl Anderson, James H. Barrett, and Katherine V. Boyle, 239–48. McDonald Institute Monographs. Cambridge: McDonald Institute for Archaeological Research.

Blot, Jean-Yves. 1996. *Underwater Archaeology: Exploring the World beneath the Sea.* Translated by Alexandra Campbell. Discoveries. New York: Harry N. Abrams / London: Thames and Hudson.

Blue, Adrianne. 1997. *On Kissing: Travels in an Intimate Landscape.* New York: Kodansha America.

Blumenfeld, Jeff. 2016. "Exploration News." *Explorers Journal* 94 (2): 8–11.

Blust, Robert. 1996. "Austronesian Culture History: The Windows of Language." In *Prehistoric Settlement of the Pacific,* edited by Ward H. Goodenough, 28–35. Philadelphia: American Philosophical Society.

Boardman, John. 1980. *The Greeks Overseas: Their Early Colonies and Trade.* New York: Thames and Hudson.

Bökönyi, Sándor, and Dénes Jánossy. 1959. "Adotok a pulyka kolumbuz ellötti Európai elöfordulás ához / Data about the Occurrence of the Turkey in Europe before the Time of Columbus." *Aquila: A Magyar Ornithologiai Központ Folyóirata* 65: 265–69.

Bombard, Alain. 1986. *The Bombard Story.* London: Grafton Books. (Originally published in French, 1953.)

Bonetto, Sandro L., Allen J. Redd, Francisco M. Salzano, and Mark Stoneking. 1996. "Lack of Ancient Polynesian-Amerindian Contact." *American Journal of Human Genetics* 59 (1): 253–56.

Boorstin, Daniel J. 1983. *The Discoverers.* New York: Random House.

Borden, Charles A. 1967. *Sea Quest: Global Blue-Water Adventuring in Small Craft.* Philadelphia: Macrae Smith.

Borrell, Brendan. 2010. "Bon Voyage, Caveman." *Archaeology* 63 (3): 9, 54.

Bos, Kirsten I., et al. 2014. "Pre-Columbian Mycobacterial Genomes Reveal Seals as a Source of New World Human Tuberculosis." *Nature* 54 (7523): 494–97.

Boutet, Michel-Gérald, and J. Monard. 1996. "Amerindian Oghams, the Celtic Connection." In *The Celtic Connection*, edited by Michel-Gérald Boutet. *Stonehenge Viewpoint* 107: 41–86.

Bowen, Richard LeBaron Jr. 1952. "Primitive Watercraft of Arabia." *American Neptune* 12 (3): 186–221.

———. 1956. "Boats of the Indus Civilization." *Mariner's Mirror* 42 (4): 279–90.

Bower, Bruce. 2010. "Ancient Hominids May Have Been Seafarers: Hand Axes Excavated on Crete Suggest Hominids Made Sea Crossings to Go 'Out of Africa.'" *ScienceNews: Magazine for the Society for Science and the Public* 177 (3): 14. Accessed June 25, 2016. http://www.sciencenews.org/article/ancient-hominids-may-have-been-seafarers.

Bowman, Sally-Jo. 1994. "Finding the Way." *Pacific Discovery* 47 (1): 36–43.

Bown, Stephen R. 2004. *Scurvy: How a Surgeon, a Mariner, and a Gentleman Solved the Greatest Medical Mystery of the Age of Sail.* New York: Thomas Dunn Books.

Boyd, William C., and Lyle G. Boyd. 1937. "Blood Grouping Tests on 300 Mummies: With Notes on the Precipitin-test." *Journal of Immunology* 32 (4): 307–19.

Brain, Jeffrey P. 1996. "Introductory Remarks." *Review of Archaeology* 17 (2): 1–5.

Brand, Donald D. 1971. "The Sweet Potato: An Exercise in Methodology." In *Man across the Sea: Problems of Pre-Columbian Contacts*, edited by Carroll L. Riley, J. Charles Kelley, Campbell W. Pennington, and Robert L. Rands, 343–65. Austin: University of Texas Press.

Brandes, Stanley. 1992. "Maize as a Culinary Mystery." *Ethnology* 31 (4): 331–36.

———. 1999. "The Perilous Potato and the Terrifying Tomato." In *Consequences of Cultivar Diffusion*, edited by Leonard Plotnicov and Richard Scaglion, 85–96. Ethnology Monographs 17. Pittsburgh: Department of Anthropology, University of Pittsburgh.

Brandt, Guido, et al. 2013. "Ancient DNA Reveals Key Stages in the Formation of Central European Mitochondrial Genetic Diversity." *Science* 342 (6155): 257–61.

Braudel, Fernand. 1988. *The Identity of France*, vol. 1, *History and Environment*. New York: Harper and Row.

Bray, Warwick. 1993. "Crop Plants and Cannibals: Early European Impressions of the New World." In *The Meeting of Two Worlds: Europe and the Americas, 1492–1650*, edited by Warwick Bray, 289–326. Proceedings of the British Academy 81. Oxford: British Academy.

Breen, Colin, and Wes Forsythe. 2004. *Boats and Shipwrecks of Ireland*. Brimscombe Port Stroud, Gloucestershire: Tempus Publishing.

Bricker, Victoria R. 2009. Review of *An Encyclopedia of Ancient Archaeoastronomy* (David H. Kelley and Eugene F. Malone). *Review of Archaeology* 27: 66–71.

Brier, Bob. 1998. *The Encyclopedia of Mummies*. New York: Facts on File.

Broodbank, Cyprian. 2000. *An Island Archaeology of the Early Cyclades*. Cambridge: Cambridge University Press.

———. 2013. *The Making of the Middle Sea: A History of the Mediterranean World from the Beginning to the Emergence of the Classical World*. Oxford: Oxford University Press / London: Thames and Hudson.

Brooks, Charles Wolcott. 1876. *Report of Japanese Vessels Wrecked in the North Pacific Ocean, from the Earliest Records to the Present Time.* Proceedings of the California Academy of Sciences 6. San Francisco. (Reprint 1964, Ye Galleon Press, Fairfield, WA; 1971, Amerasia Resources, New York.)

Brown, Michael D, Seyed H. Hosseini, Antonio Torroni, Hans-Jürgen Bandelt, Jon C. Allen, Theodore G. Schurr, Rosaria Scozzari, Fulvio Cruciani, and Douglas C. Wallace. 1998. "mtDNA Haplogroup X: An Ancient Link between Europe / Western Asia and North America?" *American Journal of Human Genetics* 63 (6): 1852–61.

Brücher, Heinz. 1985. *Useful Plants of Neotropical Origin and Their Wild Relatives*. Berlin: Springer-Verlag.

Bruhns, Karen Olsen. 1994. *Ancient South America*. Cambridge: Cambridge University Press.

Bruman. Henry J. 2000. *Alcohol in Ancient Mexico*. Salt Lake City: University of Utah Press.

Buckland, P. C., and E. Panagiotakopulu. 2001. "Ramses II and the Tobacco Beetle." *Antiquity: A Quarterly Review of World Archaeology* 75 (289): 549–56.

Bulliet, Richard W. 1975. *The Camel and the Wheel*. Cambridge, MA: Harvard University Press.

———. 1983. "How the Camel Got Its Saddle." *Natural History* 92 (7): 52–59.

Burgess, Don, and Wes Marshall. 2009. "Romans in Tucson? The Story of an Archaeological Hoax." *Journal of the Southwest* 51 (1): 3–135.

Burningham, Nick. 1994. "Notes on the Watercraft of Thanh Hoa Province, Northern Vietnam." *International Journal of Nautical Archaeology* 23 (3): 229–38.

Burrows, Edwin Grant. 1963. *Flower in My Ear: Arts and Ethos of Ifaluk Atoll*. Seattle: University of Washington Press.

Burton, Kelli Whitlock. 2008. "Random Samples." *Science* 319 (5866): 1019.

Buse de la Guerra, Hermann. 1986. *Historia maritima del Perú: Época prehistórica*. 3rd ed. 1, no. 2, pt. 2. Lima: Comisión para Escribir la Historia Maritima del Perú (Instituto de estudios Historico-Maritimos del Perú).

Butler, Bill, and Simonne Butler. 1991. *Our Last Chance: Sixty-Six Deadly Days Adrift*. Miami: Exmart Press.

Callaghan, Richard T. 2003. "The Use of Simulation Models to Estimate Frequency and Location of Japanese Edo Period Wrecks along the Canadian Pacific Coast." *Canadian Journal of Archaeology / Journal Canadien d'Archéologie* 27 (1): 74–94.

———. 2005. "Pre-Columbian Contacts between the Asian Far East and the Northwest Coast of North America: A Computer Simulation." *Archaeology, Ethnology, and Anthropology of Eurasia* 3 (23): 109–19.

Callahan, Steven. 1996. *Adrift: Seventy-Six Days Lost at Sea*. New York: Ballantine Books.

Cameron, Judith. 2008. "Trans-Oceanic Transfer of Bark-Cloth Technology from South China—Southeast Asia to Mesoamerica? In *Islands of Inquiry: Colonisation, Seafaring, and the Archaeology of Maritime Landscapes*, edited by Atholl Anderson, Geoffrey R. Clark, Foss Leach, and Sue O'Connor, 203–10. Terra Australis 29. Canberra: ANU E Press.

Campbell, Douglas Houghton. 1926. *An Outline of Plant Geography*. New York: Macmillan.

Campbell, Joseph. 1989. *Historical Atlas of World Mythology* 2, *The Way of the Seeded Earth* 3, *Mythologies of the Primitive Planters: The Middle and Southern Americas*. New York: Harper and Row.

Campbell, Lyle. 1997. *American Indian Languages: The Historical Linguistics of Native America*. New York: Oxford University Press.

Canby, Courtland. 1963. *A History of Ships and Seafaring*. New Illustrated Library of Science and Invention 2. New York: Hawthorn Books.

Candolle, Alphonse de. 1885. *Origin of Cultivated Plants*. International Scientific Series. London: Kegan Paul, Trench. (Originally published 1883, as *Origine des plantes cultivées* [Geneva: G. Balière, 1883]). Accessed March 23, 2013. http://books.google.com/books/about/Origin_of_cultivated_plants.html?id=kqcMAAAAYAAJ.

Canfora, Luciano. 1990. *The Vanished Library: A Wonder of the Ancient World*. Berkeley: University of California Press.

Cann, Rebecca. 1994. "mtDNA and Native Americans: A Southern Perspective." *American Journal of Human Genetics* 55 (1): 7–11.

Capelotti, P. J. 1997. "The Elusive Island." *Explorers Journal* 75 (1): 19–21.

———. 2001. *Sea Drift: Rafting Adventures in the Wake of* Kon-Tiki. New Brunswick, NJ: Rutgers University Press.

Carlquist, Sherwin. 1981. "Chance Dispersal." *American Scientist* 69 (5): 509–16.

Carlson, Suzanne O., comp., and John Dranchak, ed. 2006. *The Newport Tower: Arnold to Zeno*. NEARA Monograph. Edgecomb, ME: New England Antiquities Research Association.

Carré, Matthieu, Julian P. Sachs, Sara Purca, Andrew J. Schaur, Pascale Braconnot, Rommel Angeles Falcón, Michèle Julien, and Danièle Lavallée. 2014. "Holocene History of ENSO Variance and Asymmetry in the Eastern Tropical Pacific." *Science* 345 (6200): 1045–48.

Carter, George F. 1950. "Plant Evidence for Early Contacts with the Americas." *Southwestern Journal of Anthropology* 6 (2): 161–82.

———. 1953. "Plants across the Pacific." In *Transpacific Contacts*, edited by Marion W. Smith. Society for American Archaeology, Memoir 9, *American Antiquity* 18 (3, part 2): 62–71.

———. 1963. "Movement of People and Ideas across the Pacific." In *Plants and the Migration of Pacific Peoples, A Symposium*, edited by Jacques Barrau, 7–22. Tenth Pacific Science Congress. Honolulu: Bishop Museum Press.

———. 1971. "Pre-Columbian Chickens in America." In *Man across the Sea: Problems of Pre-Columbian Contacts*, edited by Carroll L. Riley, J. Charles Kelly, Campbell W. Pennington, and Robert L. Rands, 178–218. Austin: University of Texas Press.

———. 1976. "Shells as Evidence of Migrations of Early Cultures." *New Diffusionist* 6 (23): 50–57.

———. 1978. "Mexican Sellos: Writing in America, or the Growth of an Idea." In *Diffusion and Migration: Their Roles in Cultural Development*, edited by P. G. Duke, J. Ebert, G. Langemann, and A. P. Buchner, 186–201. Calgary: University of Calgary Archaeological Association.

———. 1988. "Culture Historical Diffusion." In *The Transfer and Transformation of Ideas and Material Culture*, edited by Peter J. Hugill and D. Bruce Dickson, 3–22. College Station: Texas A&M University Press.

———. 1998. "The Chicken in America: Spanish Introduction or Pre-Spanish?" In *Across before Columbus? Evidence for Transoceanic Contact with the Americas prior to 1492*, edited by Don Y. Gilmore and Linda S. McElroy, 150–60. Edgecomb, ME: New England Antiquities Research Association, NEARA Publications.

———. 2001. "O. F. Cook, Pioneer in the Use of Plants as Evidence of Transoceanic Movements: A Centenary Appreciation." *Pre-Columbiana: A Journal of Long-Distance Contacts* 2 (4): 252–68.

———. 2008–10. "The Chicken in Pre-Columbian America." *Pre-Columbiana: A Journal of Long-Distance Contacts* 4 (3 and 4) 5 (1): 34–38.

Carter, Hodding. 2000. *A Viking Voyage: In Which an Unlikely Crew Attempts an Epic Journey to the New World*. New York: Ballantine Books.

Carter, Robert. 2002. "Ubaid-Period Boat Remains from As-Sabiyah: Excavations by the British Archaeological Expedition to Kuwait." *Proceedings of the Seminar for Arabian Studies* 32: 13–30.

———. 2010. "Boat-Related Finds." In *Maritime Interactions in the Arabian Neolithic: Evidence from H3, As-Sabiyah, an Ubaid-related Site in Kuwait,* edited by Robert Carter and Harriet Crawford, 89–104. Leiden: Brill.

Carter, Robert, and Harriet Crawford, eds. 2010. *Maritime Interactions in the Arabian Neolithic: Evidence from H3, As-Sabiyah, an Ubaid-Related Site in Kuwait.* Leiden: Brill.

Carvalho, Gonçalves, Marcelo Luiz, Aduato Araújo, and Luiz Fernando Ferreira. 2003. "Human Intestinal Parasites in the Past: New Findings and a Review." *Memórias do Instituto Oswaldo Cruz* 98, supplement 1: 103–18.

Casella, Domenico. 1950. "La frutta nelle pitture pompeiane." In *Pompeiana: Raccolta di studi per il secondo centenario degli scavi di Pompei.* Biblioteca della Parola del Passato 4, 355–86. Naples: Gaetano Macchiaroli Editore. (Excerpt pub. 2002 as "The Annona and the Pineapple Depicted at Pompeii." *Pre-Columbiana: A Journal of Long-Distance Contacts* 2 [4]: 322–23.)

———. 1956. "A proposito di raffigurazione di ananas, mango e Annona squamosa in dipinti pompeianii." *Revista della Ortoflorofrutticoltura Italiana* 40 (3–4): 3–19. (Excerpt pub. 2002 as "Concerning the Depiction of Pineapple and *Annona squamosa* in Pompeian Paintings." *Pre-Columbiana: A Journal of Long-Distance Contacts* 2 [4]: 326–33.)

———. 1957. "Ancora a proposito di raffigurazione di ananas, mango e Annona squamosa in dipinti pompeianii." *Revista della Ortoflorofrutticoltura Italiana* 41 (9–10): 3–11. (Excerpt pub. 2002 as "More Concerning the Depictions of Pineapple, Mango, and *Annona squamosa* in Pompeian Paintings." *Pre-Columbiana: A Journal of Long-Distance Contacts* 2 [4]: 337–41.)

Cassidy, Vincent H. 1968. *The Sea around Them: The Atlantic Ocean, A.D. 1250.* Baton Rouge: Louisiana State University Press.

———. 1978. "New Worlds and Everyman: Some Thoughts on Logic and Logistics of Pre-Columbian Discovery." *Terrae Incognitae: The Annals of the Society for the History of Discovery* 10: 7–13.

Casson, Lionel. 1971. *Ships and Seamanship in the Ancient World.* Princeton, NJ: Princeton University Press.

———. 1977. "Why Did the Ancients Not Develop Machinery?" In *Mysteries of the Past,* edited by Lionel Casson, Robert Claiborne, Brian Fagan, and Walter Karp, 139–54. New York: American Heritage.

———. 1984. *Ancient Trade and Society.* Detroit: Wayne State University Press.

———. 1991. "Ancient Naval Technology and the Route to India." In *Rome and India: The Ancient Sea Trade,* edited by Vinala Begley and Richard Daniel De Puma, 8–11. Madison: University of Wisconsin Press.

———. 1994a. *Ships and Seafaring in Ancient Times.* Austin: University of Texas Press.

———. 1994b. *Travel in the Ancient World.* Baltimore: Johns Hopkins University Press.

———. 1996. "Sailing Ships of the Ancient Mediterranean." In *The Earliest Ships: The Evolution of Boats into Ships,* edited by Robert Gardiner, 39–51. Annapolis, MD: Naval Institute Press.

Castello, Martine. 1983. "L'affaire Ramses II." *Science et Avenir* 441: 38–42.

Castleden, Rodney. 2001. *Atlantis Destroyed.* London: Routledge.

———. 2005. *Mycenaeans.* New York: Routledge.

Castlereach, Duncan. 1971. *Encyclopedia of Discovery and Exploration*, vol. 3, *The Great Age of Exploration*. London: Aldus Books.

Cavalli-Sforza, L. Luca, Paolo Menozzi, and Alberto Piazza. 1994. *History and Geography of Human Genes*. Princeton, NJ: Princeton University Press.

Caviedes, César N. 2001. *El Niño in History: Storming through the Ages*. Gainesville: University Press of Florida.

Cawthorne, Nigel. 2010. *A Brief History of Robin Hood*. Philadelphia: Running Press.

Chamberlain, Von Del, Ben R. Finney, and Neil Passey. 1986. *Islands in the Sky*. Salt Lake City: Hansen Planetarium.

Chandler, Tertius. 1960. "Duplicate Inventions?" *American Anthropologist* 62 (3): 495–98.

Chang, Kwang-chih. 1963. *The Archaeology of Ancient China*. New Haven, CT: Yale University Press. (Rev. and enl. ed., 1968; 4th ed. 1986).

———. 1973. "Radiocarbon Dates from China: Some Initial Interpretations." *Current Anthropology* 14 (5): 525–28.

Chapman, Paul H. 1973. *The Man Who Led Columbus to America*. Atlanta: Judson Press.

———. 1981. *The Norse Discovery of America*. Atlanta: One Candle Press.

Chappelle, Howard I. 1964. "Arctic Skin Boats." In *The Bark Canoes and Skin Boats of North America*, by Edwin Tappan Adney and Howard I. Chapelle, 174–211. U.S. National Museum Bulletin 230. Washington, DC: Smithsonian Institution.

Chase, Laurence B. 1971. "Upheaval in Geology: An Explosion in Knowledge Has Generated New Interest among Students and Sent Seismic Tremors through a Once-Tranquil Study." *Princeton Alumni Weekly* 72 (6): 6–8.

Chen, Jonas Chung-yu. 2002. "Sea Nomads in Prehistory on the Southeast Coast of China." *Bulletin of the Indo-Pacific Prehistory Association* 22: 51–54.

Chen, Wenhua. 1994. *Zhongguo nongye kaogu tu lu* (Archaeological Picture of Chinese Agriculture). Nanchang, China: Jiangxi Kexue Jushu Chubanshe.

Christensen, Arne Emil. 1996. "Proto-Viking, Viking and Norse Craft." In *The Earliest Ships: The Evolution of Boats into Ships*, edited by Robert Gardiner, 72–88. Annapolis, MD: Naval Institute Press.

———. 2000. "Ships and Navigation." In *Vikings: The North Atlantic Saga*, edited by William W. Fitzhugh and Elisabeth I. Ward, 86–97. Washington, DC: Smithsonian Institution Press.

Christian, F. W. 1897. "On the Distribution and Origin of Some Plant- and Tree-Names in Polynesia and Micronesia." *Journal of the Polynesian Society* 6 (3): 123–40.

Church, Sally K. 2005. "Zhang He: An Investigation into the Plausibility of 450-ft Treasure Ships." *Monumenta Serica* 53: 1–43.

Cipolla, Carlo M. 1965. *Guns and Sails in the Early Phases of European Expansion, 1400–1700*. London: Collins.

Clark, Grahame. 1952. *Prehistoric Europe: The Economic Basis*. London: Methuen.

Clark, Jeffrey T., Peter Sheppard, and Martin Jones. 1997. "Late Ceramics in Samoa: A Test Using Hydration-Rim Measurements." *Current Anthropology* 38 (5): 898–904.

Clark, Peter, ed. 2004. *The Dover Bronze Age Boat in Context: Society and Water Transport in Prehistoric Europe*. Oxford: Oxbow Books.

Clarke, Andrew C. 2009. "Origins and Dispersal of the Sweet Potato and Bottle Gourd in Oceania: Implications for Prehistoric Human Mobility." PhD diss., Massey University, Palmerston North, New Zealand. Accessed August 20, 2014. http://mro .massey.ac.nz/bitstream/handle/10179/1727/02whole.pdf?sequence=3.

Clewlow, C. William, Richard A. Cowan, James F. O'Connell, and Carlos Bennemann. 1967. *Colossal Heads of the Olmec Culture*. Contributions of the University of California Archaeological Research Facility 4. Berkeley.

Cockburn, T. Aidan. 1963. *The Evolution and Eradication of Infectious Diseases*. Baltimore: Johns Hopkins University Press.

———. 1971. "Infectious Diseases in Ancient Populations." *Current Anthropology* 12 (1): 45–62.

Collins, J. L. 1948. "Pineapples in Ancient America." *Scientific Monthly* 67 (November): 372–77.

———. 1949. "History, Taxonomy, and Culture of the Pineapple." *Economic Botany* 3 (4): 335–59.

———. 1951. "Antiquity of the Pineapple in America." *Southwestern Journal of Anthropology* 7 (2): 145–55.

Collins, N. Mark, Jeffrey A. Sayer, and Timothy C. Whitmore. 1991. *The Conservation Atlas of Tropical Forests: Asia and the Pacific*. London: Macmillan.

Comas, Juan. 1973. "Transatlantic Hypothesis on the Peopling of America: Caucasoids and Negroids." *Journal of Human Evolution* 2 (2): 75–92.

Confalonieri, Ulisses Eugênio, Luiz Fernando Ferreira, and Adauto Araújo. 1991. "Intestinal Helminths in Lowland South American Indians: Some Evolutionary Interpretations." *Human Biology: The International Journal of Population Genetics and Anthropology* 63 (6): 863–73.

Conniff, Richard. 2012. "When the Earth Moved." *Smithsonian* 43 (3): 36, 38.

Cook, Edward R., Kevin J. Anchukaitis, Brendan M. Buckley, Rosanne D. D'Arrigo, Gordon C. Jacoby, and William E. Wright. 2010. "Asian Monsoon Failure and Megadrought during the Last Millennium." *Science* 328 (5977): 486–89.

Cook, Noble David, and W. George Lovell, eds. 1991. *Secret Judgments of God: Old World Disease in Colonial Spanish America*. Norman: University of Oklahoma Press.

Cook, O. F. 1901. "The Origin and Distribution of the Coconut Palm." *Smithsonian Institution, United States National Museum, Contributions from the United States National Herbarium* 7: 257–94.

———. 1904. "Food Plants of Ancient America." *Annual Report, 1903*, 481–97. Washington, DC: Smithsonian Institution.

Cooke, Richard G., David W. Steadman, Máximo Jiménez, and Ilean Isaza Aizpurúa. 2013. "Pre-Columbian Exploitation of Birds around Panama Bay." In *The Archaeology of Mesoamerican Animals*, edited by Christopher M. Götz and Kitty F. Emery, 479–530. Archaeobiology 1. Atlanta: Lockwood Press. Accessed May 5, 2016, at *Open Context*. http://opencontext.org/projects/4c9d2f6b-98d5-46bf-8871-85b106b96d5d.

Coon, Carleton S. 1962. *The Story of Man*. 2nd ed. New York: Alfred A. Knopf.

Covarrubias, Miguel. 1946. *Mexico South: The Isthmus of Tehuantepec*. New York: Alfred A. Knopf.

Covey, Cyclone. 1975. *Calalus: A Roman Jewish Colony in America from the Time of Charlemagne through Alfred the Great*. New York: Vantage Press.

———. 2004. "Calalus Reopened." *Migration & Diffusion: An International Journal* 5 (19): 107–12.

Cowan, James. 1996. *A Mapmaker's Dream: The Meditations of Fra Mauro, Cartographer to the Court of Venice*. Boston: Shambala Publications.

Crawford, Harriet. 1998. *Dilmun and Its Gulf Neighbours*. Cambridge: Cambridge University Press.

Crawford, Michael H. 1998. *The Origins of Native Americans: Evidence from Anthropological Genetics*. Cambridge: Cambridge University Press.

Critchley, Macdonald. 1943. *Shipwreck-Survivors: A Medical Study*. London: J. and Churchill.

Croizat, León. 1981. *El Océano Pacífico en la prehistoria de las Américas*. Caracas: I. P. Publicaciones.

Crook, Paul. 2011. *Grafton Elliot Smith, Egyptology, and the Diffusion of Culture: A Biographical Perspective.* Eastbourne, UK: Sussex Academic Press.

Crook, Sally. 1990. *Distant Shores: By Traditional Canoe from Asia to Madagascar.* London: Impact Books.

Crosby, Alfred W. 1972. *The Columbian Exchange: Biological and Cultural Consequences of 1492.* Westport, CT: Greenwood Press.

Crosby, Alfred W., Jr. 1997. "Conquistador y Pestilencia: The First New World Pandemic and the Fall of the Great Empires." In *Biological Consequences of European Expansion, 1450–1800,* edited by Kenneth F. Kiple, 91–108. An Expanding World: The European Impact on World History, 1450–1800, 26. Aldershot, UK: Varorium, Ashgate Publishing. (Originally published 1967.)

Crumlin-Pedersen, Ole. 1996. "Problems of Reconstruction and the Estimation of Performance." In *The Earliest Ships: The Evolution of Boats into Ships,* edited by Robert Gardiner, 110–19. Annapolis, MD: Naval Institute Press.

Cunliffe, Barry. 2001. *Facing the Ocean: The Atlantic and Its Peoples, 8000 B.C.–A.D. 1500.* Oxford: Oxford University Press.

———. 2002. *The Extraordinary Voyage of Pytheas the Greek.* New York: Walker.

———. 2010. "Seafaring on the Atlantic Seabord." In *The Global Origins and Development of Seafaring,* edited by Atholl Anderson, James H. Barrett, and Katherine V. Boyle, 265–74. McDonald Institute Monographs. Cambridge, UK: McDonald Institute for Archaeological Research.

Cunningham, Alexander. 1962. *The Stûpa of Bharhut: A Buddhist Monument Ornamented with Numerous Sculptures Illustrated of Buddhist Legend and History in the Third Century B.C.* 2nd ed. Varanasi, India: Indological Book House. (Originally published 1879.)

Cuppage, Francis E. 1994. *James Cook and the Conquest of Scurvy.* Contributions in Medical Studies 40. Westport, CT: Greenwood Press.

Curry, Andrew. 2011. "Egypt's Lost Fleet." *Discover: Science, Technology, and the Future* (June): 60–66, 68, 70.

Da Fonseca, Olympio. 1970. "Parasitismo e migraçõnes humanas pré-históricas." In *Contribuicões da parasitologia para o conhecimento das origens do homem americano.* Estudos de Pre-história Geral e Brasileira. São Paulo: Instituto de Pré-historia da Universidade de São Paulo.

Danielsson, Bengt. 1956. *Work and Life on Raroia.* London: George Allen and Unwin.

Danielsson, Bengt, from narrative of Alain Brun. 1960. *From Raft to Raft.* Translated by F. H. Lyon. Garden City, NY: Doubleday.

D'Arcy, Paul. 2006. *The People of the Sea: Environment, Identity, and History in Oceania.* Honolulu: University of Hawai'i Press.

Darling, S. T. 1920. "Observations on the Geographical and Ethnological Distribution of Hookworms." *Parasitology* 12 (3): 217–33.

Davenport, William. 1967. "Marshall Island Navigational Charts." *Imago Mundi* 15: 1.

Davidson, Basil. 1970. *The Lost Cities of Africa.* Boston: Little, Brown.

Davis, Nancy Yaw. 2000. *The Zuni Enigma.* New York: W. W. Norton.

Davis, Wade. 2010. "Requiem for a Wayfinder." *Explorer's Journal* 88 (3): 28–35.

De Barros, Philip. 1997. "Ironworking in Its Cultural Context." In *Encyclopedia of Precolonial Africa: Archaeology, History, Languages, Cultures, and Environments,* edited by Joseph O. Vogel, 135–49. Walnut Creek, CA: AltaMira Press.

DeBoer, Warren R. 1996. *Traces behind the Esmeraldas Shore: Prehistory of the Santiago-Cayapas Region, Ecuador.* Tuscaloosa: University of Alabama Press.

De Borhegyi, Stephan F. 1970. "Wheels and Man." *Archaeology* 23 (1): 18–25.

De Laubenfels, M. W. 1950. "Ocean Currents in the Marshall Islands." *Geographical Review* 40 (2): 254–59.

Deloria, Vine, Jr. 1998. "Introduction: A World in Transition." *Journal of the West* 37 (4): 6–10.

Dening, G. M. 1972. "The Geographical Knowledge of the Polynesians and the Nature of Inter-Island Contact." In *Polynesian Navigation: A Symposium on Andrew Sharp's Theory of Accidental Voyages*. Rev. ed., edited by Jack Golson, 102–53. Wellington, NZ: A. H. and A. W. Reed.

Dennis, John V., and R. Gunn. 1971. "The Case against Trans-Pacific Dispersal of the Coconut by Ocean Currents." *Economic Botany* 25 (4): 407–13.

De Prez, Alfred S. 1935. "Observations sur la flore et la faune répresentés sur les bas-reliefs de quelques monuments indo-javanais." *Révue des Arts Asiatiques* 9 (2): 57–62.

De Queiroz, Alan. 2014. *The Monkey's Voyage: How Improbable Journeys Shaped the History of Life*. New York: Basic Books.

Dewan, Lesley, and Dorothy Hosler. 2008. "Ancient Maritime Trade on Balsa Rafts." *Journal of Anthropological Research* 64 (1): 19–40.

Diamond, Jared. 1993. "Who Are the Jews?" *Natural History* 102 (11): 12, 14, 16, 18–19.

———. 1997. *Guns, Germs, and Steel: The Fates of Human Societies*. New York: W. W. Norton.

———. 2004. "The Astonishing Micropygmies." *Science* 306 (5704): 2047–48.

Dick-Read, Robert. 2005. *The Phantom Voyagers: Evidence of Indonesian Settlement in Africa in Ancient Times*. Winchester, UK: Thurlton.

Dilke, O. A. W. 1985. *Greek and Roman Maps*. London: Thames and Hudson.

Diolé, Philippe. 1954. *4000 Years under the Sea*. New York: Julian Messner.

Di Piazza, Anne, Philippe Di Piazza, and Erik Pearthree. 2007. "Sailing Virtual Canoes across Oceania: Revisiting Island Accessibility." *Journal of Archaeological Science* 4 (8): 1219–25.

Dixon, R. M. W. 1996. "Origin Legends and Linguistic Relationships." *Oceania* 67 (2): 127–39.

Dixon, Roland B. 1932. "The Problem of the Sweet Potato in Polynesia." *American Anthropologist* 34 (1): 40–66.

Dobyns, Henry F. 1980. "On Microbes, Viruses, Culture, and Demography." *Current Anthropology* 21 (2): 275–76.

———. 1983. *Their Number Become Thinned: Native American Population Dynamics in Eastern North America*. Knoxville: University of Tennessee Press.

Dodd, Edward. 1972. *Polynesian Seafaring*. New York: Dodd, Mead.

Donnan, Christopher B. 2004. *Moche Portraits from Ancient Peru*. Austin: University of Texas Press.

Donnan, Christopher B., and Christopher A. Klein. 2001. "Moche Burials Uncovered." *National Geographic Magazine* 199 (3): 58–73.

Doran, Edwin, Jr. 1970. "Sailing Characteristics of Primitive Pacific Craft." *American Philosophical Society, Yearbook 1970*: 582–84. Philadelphia.

———. 1971. "The Sailing Raft as a Great Tradition." In *Man across the Sea: Problems of Pre-Columbian Contacts*, edited by Carroll L. Riley, J. Charles Kelley, Campbell W. Pennington, and Robert L. Rands, 115–38. Austin: University of Texas Press.

———. 1973. "Nao, Junk, and Vaka: Boats and Culture History." University Lecture Series. College Station: Texas A&M University.

———. 1974. "Outrigger Ages." *Journal of the Polynesian Society* 83 (2): 130–40.

———. 1978. "The Junk." *Oceans* 11 (3): 13–20.

——. 1981. *Wangka: Austronesian Canoe Origins*. College Station: Texas A&M University Press.

Doran, Michael F. 2002. "The West Indian Sailing Canoe." *Mariner's Mirror* 88 (4): 437–46.

Doran, Michael F., Joan Andrew Smith, Christina West, and Michelle T. Made. 2000. "The Question of Pre-Columbian Carib Sailing Canoes." *American Neptune* 61 (2): 153–62.

Driver, Harold E. 1973. "Cultural Diffusion." In *Main Currents in Cultural Anthropology*, edited by Raoul Naroll and Fradd Naroll, 157–83. New York: Appleton-Century-Crofts.

Driver, Harold E., and William C. Massey. 1957. *Comparative Studies of North American Indians*. Transactions, NS 47, pt. 2. Philadelphia: American Philosphical Society.

Drögemüller, Cort, Elinor K. Karsson, Marjo K. Hytönen, Michele Perloski, Gaudenz Dolf, Kirsi Sainio, Hannes Lohi, Kerstin Lindblad-Toh, and Tosso Leeb. 2008. "A Mutation in Hairless Dogs Implicates *FOX13* in Ectodermal Development." *Science* 321 (5895): 1462.

Dryer, Edward. 2006. *Zheng He: China and the Oceans in the Early Ming Dynasty*. New York: Pearson Education (Longman).

Dudbridge, Glen. 2000. *Lost Books of Medieval China*. Panizzi Lectures. London: British Library.

Dumas, Vito. 1960. *Alone through the Roaring Forties: The Voyage of Lehi II Round the World*. London: Adlard Coles. (Reprint 2001, McGraw-Hill Education—Europe, Maidenhead, UK.)

Dunbar, Robert B. 2000. "Clues from the Corals." *Nature* 407 (6807): 956–57, 959.

Durham, Bill. 1960. *Canoes and Kayaks of Western America*. Seattle: Copper Canoe Press.

Dyson, John. 1991. *Columbus: For Gold, God, and Glory*. New York: Simon and Schuster / Madison Press.

Ebbesmeyer, Curtis C. 2007. "From Russia to America—The Sea of Okhotsk Sends Drifters to North America." *Beachcombers' Alert!* 12 (1): 2–3, 5.

——. 2008a. "African Coffin Boats." *Beachcombers' Alert!* 12 (3): 1, 4.

——. 2008b. "The Buoy from Ginoza." *Beachcombers' Alert!* 13 (1): 1–4.

——. 2009a. "Cayman Flip Flops." *Beachcombers' Alert!* 13 (3): 9.

——. 2009b. *Flotsametrics and the Floating World: How One Man's Obsession with Runaway Sneakers and Rubber Ducks Revolutionized Ocean Science*. New York: Smithsonian Books / Collins.

——. 2014. "Tsunami Derelicts from Canada to California." *Beachcombers' Alert!* 18 (3): 7.

Ebert, Claire E., Keith M. Prufer, Martha J. Macri, Bruce Winterhalder, and Douglas J. Kennett. 2014. "Terminal Long Count Dates and the Disintegration of Classic Period Maya Polities." *Ancient Mesoamerica* 25 (2): 337–58.

Eccott, David J. 2003. "The True Arch—An Absent Trait in Precolumbian America?" *Migration and Diffusion: An International Journal* 4 (13): 41–63. Accessed November 12, 2014. http://www.migration-diffusion.info/article.php?subject=archaeology.

Eckert, Suzanne L. 2005. "Zuni Demographic Structure, A.D. 1300–1680: A Case Study in Spanish Contact and Native Population Dynamics." *Kiva* 70 (3): 207–26.

Edey, Maitland A., and the editors of Time-Life Books. 1974. *The Sea Traders*. New York: Time-Life Books.

Edmondson, C. H. 1941. "Viability of Coconut after Floating in Sea." *Occasional Papers* 16: 293–304. Honolulu: B. P. Bishop Museum.

Edwards, Clinton R. 1965a. "Aboriginal Sail in the New World." *Southwestern Journal of Anthropology* 21 (4): 351–57.

———. 1965b. *Aboriginal Watercraft on the Pacific Coast of South America.* Ibero-Americana 47. Berkeley: University of California Press.

———. 1969. "Possibilities of Pre-Columbian Maritime Contacts among New World Civilizations." In *Pre-Columbian Contact within Nuclear America*, edited by J. Charles Kelley and Carroll L. Riley, 3–10. Mesoamerican Studies 4, University Museum Research Record. Carbondale: Southern Illinois University.

———. 1972. "New World Perspectives on Pre-European Voyaging in the Pacific." In *Early Chinese Art and Its Possible Influence in the Pacific Basin* 3, *Oceania and the Americas*, edited by Noel Barnard, 843–87. New York: Intercultural Arts Press.

Edwards, Kevin J., and Steven Mithen. 1995. "The Colonization of the Hebridean Islands of Western Scotland: Evidence from the Palynological and Archaeological Records." *World Archaeology* 26 (3): 348–65.

Ekholm, Gordon F. 1946. "Wheeled Toys in Mexico." *American Antiquity* 11 (4): 222–28.

———. 1953. "A Possible Focus of Asiatic Influence in the Late Classic Cultures of Mesoamerica." In *Asia and North America: Trans-Pacific Contacts*, assembled by Marian W. Smith, 72–89. Memoirs 9. Salt Lake City: Society for American Archaeology.

———. 1955. "The New Orientation toward Problems of Asiatic-American Relationships." In *New Interpretations of Aboriginal American Culture History*, edited by Betty J. Meggers and Clifford Evans, 95–109. Washington, DC: Anthropological Society of Washington.

———. 1964. "Trans-Pacific Contacts." In *Prehistoric Man in the New World*, edited by Jesse D. Jennings and Edward Norbeck, 489–510. Chicago: University of Chicago Press.

Eliot, Margaret, and P. G. Smith, comps. 1988. *Dr Johnson said . . .* London: Trustees of Dr Johnson's House.

Ellmers, Detlev. 1996. "The Beginnings of Boatbuilding in Central Europe." In *The Earliest Ships: The Evolution of Boats into Ships*, edited by Robert Gardiner, 11–23. Annapolis, MD: Naval Institute Press.

El-Morr, Zaid, Florence Cattin, David Bourgarit, Yannik Lefrais, and Patrick Degryse. 2013. "Copper Quality and Provenance in Middle Bronze Age I Byblos and Tell Arqa (Lebanon)." *Journal of Archaeological Science* 40 (12): 4291–305.

Emmons, George. 1990. *Tlingit Indians*, edited by Frederica de Laguna. Anthropological Papers 70. New York: American Museum of Natural History.

Epstein, Jeremiah F., and commentators. 1980. "Pre-Columbian Old World Coins in America: An Examination of the Evidence." *Current Anthropology* 21 (1): 1–20.

Erickson, David Lee, Bruce D. Smith, Andrew C. Clarke, Daniel H. Sandweiss, and Noreen Tuross. 2005. "An Asian Origin for a 10,000-Year-Old Domesticated Plant in the Americas." *Proceedings of the National Academy of Sciences USA* 102 (51): 18, 315–20.

Eriksen, Marcus. 2012. "Tracking Tsunami Flotsam: Wind and Currents Determine Where Debris from the Japanese Catastrophe Has Floated." *Natural History* 120 (7): 18–23.

Erlandson, Jon McVey. 2001. "The Archaeology of Aquatic Adaptations: Paradigms for a New Millennium." *Journal of Archaeological Research* 9 (4): 287–350.

———. 2010. "Neptune's Children: The Evolution of Human Seafaring." In *The Global Origins and Development of Seafaring*, edited by Atholl Anderson, James H. Barrett, and Katherine V. Boyle, 18–27. McDonald Institute Monographs. Cambridge, UK: McDonald Institute for Archaeological Research.

Erlandson, Jon McVey, and Todd J. Braje. 2011. "From Asia to America by Boat? Paleo-geography, Paleoecology, and Stemmed Points of the Northwest Pacific." *Quaternary International* 239 (1–2): 28–37.

Estes, J. Worth. 1995. "Stephen Maturin and Naval Medicine in the Age of Sail." In *A Sea of Words: A Lexicon and Companion for Patrick O'Brian's Seafaring Tales*, by Dean King, 37–56. New York: Henry Holt.

Estrada, Emilio, and Betty J. Meggers. 1961. "A Complex of Traits of Probable Transpacific Origin on the Coast of Ecuador." *American Anthropologist* 63 (5): 913–39.

Estrada, Emilio, Betty J. Meggers, and Clifford Evans. 1962. "Possible Transpacific Contact on the Coast of Ecuador." *Science* 135 (3501): 371–72.

Evans, Angela. 1996. "Saints and Skinboats." In *The Sea Remembers: Shipwrecks and Archaeology*, edited by Peter Throckmorton, 108–11, 229. New York: Barnes and Noble Books.

Evans, James. 1998. *The History and Practice of Ancient Astronomy*. New York: Oxford University Press.

Evans, Jeff. 1998. *The Discovery of Aotearoa*. Auckland: Reed Books.

Everitt, Anthony. 2003. *Cicero: The Life and Times of Rome's Greatest Politician*. New York: Random House.

Fabre, David. 2004/5. *Seafaring in Ancient Egypt*. London: Periplus.

Facey, William, and Anthony R. Constable, eds. 2013. *The Principles of Arab Navigation*. London: Arabian Publishing.

Fagan, Brian. 1999. *Floods, Famines, and Emperors: El Niño and the Fate of Civilizations*. New York: Basic Books.

———. 2012. *Beyond the Blue Horizon: How the Earliest Mariners Unlocked the Secrets of the Oceans*. New York: Bloomsbury Press.

Fahd, Toufic. 1996. "Botany and Agriculture." In *Encyclopedia of the History of Arabic Science* 3, edited by Roshdi Rashed, 813–52. London: Routledge.

Fahey, Bede. 2004. *Mayan: A Sino-Tibetan Language?* Sino-Platonic Papers 130. Philadelphia: Department of East Asian Languages and Civilizations, University of Pennsylvania.

———. 2005–7. "A Summary of *Mayan: A Sino-tibetan Language?*" *Pre-Columbiana: A Journal of Long-Distance Contacts* 3 (4/4, nos. 1 and 2): 225–35.

Faria Gonçalves, Vanessa, Jesper Stenderup, Cláudia Rodrigues-Carvalho, Hilton P. Silva, Higgor Gonçalves-Dornelas, Anderson Líryo, Toomas Kivisild, Anna-Sapfo Malaspinas, Paula F. Campos, Morten Rasmussem, Eske Willerslev, and Sergio Danillo J. Pena. 2013. "Identification of Polynesian mtDNA Haplogroups in Remains of Botocudo Amerindians from Brazil." *Proceedings of the National Academy of Sciences, USA* 110 (16): 6465–69.

Farmer, Malcolm F. 1969. "Origin and Development of Watercraft." *Anthropological Journal of Canada* 7 (2): 22–25.

Farr, R. Helen. 2010. "Island Colonization and Trade in the Mediterranean." In *The Global Origins and Development of Seafaring*, edited by Atholl Anderson, James H. Barrett, and Katherine V. Boyle, 179–89. McDonald Institute Monographs. Cambridge, UK: McDonald Institute for Archaeological Research.

Feder, Kenneth L. 2010. *Encyclopedia of Dubious Archaeology, from Atlantis to the Wallam Olum*. Santa Barbara, CA: Greenwood Press.

———. 2014. *Frauds, Myths, and Mysteries: Science and Pseudoscience in Archaeology*. 8th ed. New York: McGraw-Hill.

Feinberg, Richard. 1988. *Polynesian Seafaring and Navigation: Ocean Travel in Anutan Culture and Society*. Kent, OH: Kent State University Press.

———. 1995. "Continuity and Change in Nukumanu Maritime Technology and Practice." In *Seafaring in the Contemporary Pacific Islands*, edited by Richard Feinberg, 159–95. De Kalb: Northern Illinois University Press.

Ferdon, Edwin N., Jr. 1963. "Polynesian Origins." *Science* 141 (3580): 499–505.

Ferguson, Niall, ed. 1997. *Virtual History: Alternatives and Counterfactuals.* London: Picador.

Fernández-Armesto, Felipe, ed. 1991. *The Times Atlas of World Exploration: 3000 Years of Exploring, Explorers, and Mapmaking.* New York: Times Books/HarperCollins.

———. 2002. *Near a Thousand Tables: A History of Food.* New York: Free Press.

Fernandez-Vina, Marcello A., Jill A. Hollenbach, Kirsten E. Lyke, Marcelo B. Sztein, Martin Maiers, William Klitz, Pedro Cano, Steven Mack, Richard Single, Chaim Brautbar, Shosahna Israel, Eduardo Raimondi, Evelyne Khoriaty, Adlette Inati, Marco Andreani, Manuela Testi, Maria Elisa Moraes, Glenys Thomson, Peter Stastny, and Kai Cao. 2012. "Tracking Human Migrations by the Analysis of the Distribution of HLA Alleles, Lineages and Haplotypes in Closed and Open Populations." *Philosophical Transactions of the Royal Society B: Biological Sciences* 367 (1590): 820–29.

Fernando Ferreira, Luiz, Adauto Araújo, and Ulisses Confalonieri. 1988. *Paleoparasitologia no Brasil.* Rio de Janeiro: Programa de Educação Publica (Escola Nacional de Saúde Pública).

Ferrell, Raleigh. 1969. "Paiwanic Ethnolinguistic Groups of the West-Central Taiwan 'Black Pottery' Culture Area." *Zhongyang yanjiuyuan minzuxue yanjiuso qikan / Bulletin of the Institute of Ethnology, Academia Sinica* 28: 159–96.

Fiennes, Richard, and Alice Fiennes. 1968. *The Natural History of Dogs.* London: Weidenfeld and Nicholson.

Fingerhut, Eugene R. 1994. *Explorers of Pre-Columbian America? The Diffusionist-Inventionist Controversy.* Claremont, CA: Regina Books.

Finkel, Irving. 2014. *The Ark before Noah: Decoding the Story of the Flood.* London: Hodder and Stoughton / New York: Nan A. Talese.

Finney, Ben R. 1979. Hokule'a: *The Way to Tahiti.* New York: Dodd, Mead.

———. 1991. "Myth, Experiment, and the Rediscovery of Polynesian Voyaging." *American Anthropologist* 93 (2): 383–404.

———. 1994. *Voyage of Rediscovery: A Cultural Odyssey through Polynesia.* Berkeley: University of California Press.

———. 1996a. "Experimental Voyaging, Oral Traditions and Long-Distance Interaction in Polynesia." In *Prehistoric Long-Distance Interaction in Oceania: An Interdisciplinary Approach*, ed. Marshall I. Weisler, 38–52. New Zealand Archaeological Association Monograph 21. Auckland.

———. 1996b. "Putting Voyaging Back into Polynesian Prehistory." In *Oceanic Culture History: Essays in Honour of Roger Green*, edited by Janet Davidson, Geoffrey Irwin, Foss Leach, Andrew Pawley, and Dorothy Brown, 365–76. Dunedin: New Zealand Journal of Archaeology Special Publication.

———. 1997. "Experimental Voyaging, Oral Traditions and Long-Distance Interaction in Polynesia." In *Prehistoric Long-Distance Interaction in Oceania: An Interdisciplinary Approach*, edited by Marshall I. Weisler, 38–52. Monograph 21. Aukland: New Zealand Archaeological Association.

———. 2001. "Voyage to Polynesia's Land's End." *Antiquity: A Quarterly Review of World Archaeology* 75 (287): 172–81.

———. 2003. *Sailing in the Wake of the Ancestors: Reviving Polynesian Voyaging.* Honolulu: Bishop Museum Press.

Finney, Ben R., Paul Frost, Richard Rhodes, and Nainoa Thompson. 1989. "Wait for the West Wind." *Journal of the Polynesian Society* 98 (3): 261–302.

Finney, Ben R., Bernard J. Kilonsky, Stephen Somsen, and Edward D. Stroup. 1986. "Re-Learning a Vanishing Art." *Journal of the Polynesian Society* 95 (1): 41–90.

Firstbrook, Peter. 1997. *The Voyage of the* Matthew: *John Cabot and the Discovery of North America*. San Francisco: KQED Books and Tapes.

Fischer, Anders, ed. 1995. *Man and Sea in the Mesolithic: Coastal Settlement above and below Present Sea Level: Proceedings of the International Symposium, Kalundborg, Denmark, 1993*. Oxbow Monographs 53. Oxford: Oxford Monographs.

Fischler, Claude. 1988. "Cuisines and Food Selection." In *Food Acceptability*, edited by David M. H. Thompson, 193–206. London: Elsevier Applied Science.

Fisher, H. A. L. 1935. *A History of Europe*. Boston: Houghton Mifflin.

Fitzhugh, Ben, and Douglas J. Kennett. 2010. "Seafaring Intensity and Island-Mainland Interaction along the Pacific Coast of North America." In *The Global Origins and Development of Seafaring*, edited by Atholl Anderson, James H. Barrett, and Katherine V. Boyle, 69–80. McDonald Institute Monographs. Cambridge, UK: McDonald Institute for Archaeological Research.

Fitzhugh, William W., and Elisabeth I. Ward, eds. 2000. *Vikings: The North Atlantic Saga*. Washington, DC: Smithsonian Institution Press.

Fitzpatrick, Scott M., and Richard Callaghan. 2008. "Seafaring Simulations and the Origin of Prehistoric Settlers to Madagascar." In *Islands of Inquiry: Colonisation, Seafaring, and the Archaeology of Maritime Landscapes*, edited by Atholl Anderson, Geoffrey R. Clark, Foss Leach, and Sue O'Connor, 56–66. Terra Australis 29. Canberra: ANU E Press.

Flecker, Michael. 2000. "A 9th-Century Arab or Indian Shipwreck in Indonesian Waters." *International Journal of Nautical Archaeology* 29 (2): 199–217. Accessed November 12, 2014. http://www.maritime-explorations.com.

———. 2003. "The Thirteenth Century *Java Sea Wreck*: A Chinese Cargo in an Indonesian Ship." *Mariner's Mirror* 89 (4): 388–404. Accessed November 12, 2014. http://www.maritime-explorations.com.

———. 2007. "The South-China-Sea Tradition: The Hybrid Hulls of South-East Asia." *International Journal of Nautical Archaeology* 36 (1): 75–90.

———. 2012. "The Jade Dragon Wreck: Sabah, East Malaysia." *Mariner's Mirror* 98 (1): 9–29.

Flood, Josephine. 1990. *Archaeology of the Dreamtime*. New Haven, CT: Yale University Press.

———. 1996. "Culture and Early Aboriginal Australia." *Cambridge Archaeological Journal* 6 (1): 3–36.

Forbes, Jack. 1993. *Africans and Native Americans: The Language of Race and the Evolution of Red-Black Peoples*. 2nd ed. Urbana: University of Illinois Press.

———. 2007. *The American Discovery of Europe*. Urbana: University of Illinois Press.

Forbes, R. J. 1950. *Metallurgy in Antiquity: A Notebook for Archaeologists and Technologists*. Leiden: Brill.

Ford, Clellan S., and Frank A. Beach. 1951. *Patterns of Sexual Behavior*. New York: Ace Books.

Foster, George M. 1959. "The Potter's Wheel: An Analysis of Idea and Artifact in Innovation." *Southwestern Journal of Anthropology* 15 (2): 99–117.

Foster, Mary LeCron. 1998. "The Transoceanic Trail: The Proto-Pelagian Language Phylum." *Pre-Columbiana: A Journal of Long-Distance Contacts* 1 (1 and 2): 88–114.

Franck, Irene M., and David M. Brownstone. 1984. *To the Ends of the Earth: The Great Travel and Trade Routes of Human History.* New York: Facts on File.

Fraser, Douglas. 1965. "Theoretical Issues in the Transpacific Diffusion Controversy." *Social Research* 32 (4): 452–77. (Reprint 1999, *Pre-Columbiana: A Journal of Long-Distance Contacts* 1 [3 and 4]: 219–35.)

Fredericksen, Clayton. 1997. "The Maritime Distribution of Bismarck Archipelago Obsidian and Island Melanesian Prehistory." *Journal of the Polynesian Society* 106 (4): 375–93.

Freely, John. 2009. *Aladdin's Lamp: How Greek Science Came to Europe through the Islamic World.* New York: Alfred A. Knopf.

Freeth, T., Y. Bitsakis, X. Moussas, J. H. Seiradakis, A. Tselikas, H. Mangou, M. Zafeiropoulo, R. Hadland, D. Bate, A. Ramsey, M. Allen, A. Crawley, P. Hockley, T. Malzbender, D. Gelb, W. Ambrisco, and M. G. Edmunds. 2006. "Decoding the Ancient Greek Astronomical Calculator Known as the Antikythera Mechanism." *Nature* 444 (7119): 587–91.

Frost, Frank J. 1982. "The Palos Verdes Chinese Anchor Mystery." *Archaeology* 35 (1): 22–28.

———. 1993. "Voyages of the Imagination." *Archaeology* 46 (2): 44–51.

Fuller, R. Buckminster. 1966. *Utopia or Oblivion: The Prospects for Humanity.* New York: Overlook Press.

Fulop, Marcos. 1954. "Aspectos de la cultura Tukana: Cosmología." *Revista Colombiana de Antropología* 3: 97–137.

Fuson, Robert H. 1995. *Legendary Islands of the Ocean Sea.* Sarasota, FL: Pineapple Press.

Gade, Daniel W., and Roberto Rios. 1971. "Chaquitaclla: The Native Footplough and Its Persistence in Central Andean Agriculture." *Tools and Tillage* 2 (1): 3–15.

Gamble, Clive. 1994. *Timewalkers: The Prehistory of Global Colonization.* Cambridge, MA: Harvard University Press.

———. 2013. *Settling the Earth: The Archaeology of Deep History.* New York: Cambridge University Press.

García Payón, José. 1961. "Un cabecita de barro de extraña fisinomía." *Boletín, Instituto Nacional de Antropología e Historia* 6 (October): 1–2.

Gardiner, Robert, ed., Arne Emil Christensen, consulting ed. 1996. *Earliest Ships: The Evolution of Boats into Ships.* Annapolis, MD: Naval Institute Press. (Reprint Edison, NJ: Chartwell Books, 2001.)

Gardner, Joseph L., ed. 1986. *Mysteries of the Ancient Americas: The New World before Columbus.* Pleasantville, NY: Reader's Digest Association.

Garn, Stanley M. 1957. "Race and Evolution." *American Anthropologist* 59 (2): 218–24.

———. 1965. *Human Races.* 2nd ed. Springfield, IL: Charles C. Thomas Publisher.

Gartelmann, Karl Dieter. 1986. *Digging up Prehistory: The Archaeology of Ecuador.* Quito: Ediciones Libri Mundi.

Gatty, Harold. 1958. *Nature Is Your Guide: How to Find Your Way on Land or Sea by Observing Nature.* New York: E. P. Dutton.

Gaul, Johanna Sophia, Karl Grossshmidt, Christian Gusenbauer, and Fabian Kanz. 2015. "A Probable Case of Congenital Syphilis from Pre-Columbian Austria." *Anthropologische Anzeiger / Journal of Biological and Clinical Anthropology* 72 (4): 451–72.

Gavrilets, Sergey, and Jonathan B. Losos. 2009. "Adaptive Radiation: Contrasting Theory with Data." *Science* 323 (5915): 732–37.

Geertz, Clifford. 1965. "The Impact of the Concept of Culture on the Concept of Man."

In *New Views of the Nature of Man*, edited by John R. Platt, 93–118. Chicago: University of Chicago Press.

Genovés, Santiago. 1971. *RA I and RA II: Twice across the Atlantic on a Papyrus Raft as an Anthropological and Behavioral Experiment*. Chicago: University of Chicago Press.

———. 1972. *RA: Una balsa de papyrus a través del Atlántico*. Cuadernos: Serie Antropológica 25. Mexico City: Universidad Nacional Autónoma de México, Instituto de Investigaciones Históricas.

———. 1979. *The Acali Experiment: Five Men and Six Women on a Raft across the Atlantic for 101 Days*. New York: Times Books.

Gibbons, Ann. 1995. "The First Pacific Islanders?" *Science* 268 (5209): 365.

Gibbons, John R. H., and Fergus G. A. U. Clunie. 1986. "Sea Level Changes and Pacific Prehistory." *Journal of Pacific History* 21 (2): 58–82.

———. 1986. "Sea Level Changes and Pacific Prehistory: New Insight into Early Human Settlement of Oceania." *Journal of Pacific History* 21 (1): 38–82.

Gibbs, James A. 1968. *Shipwrecks off Juan de Fuca*. Portland, OR: Binfords and Mort.

Gifford, Edwin, and Joyce Gifford. 1995. "The Sailing Characteristics of the Saxon Ships as Derived from Half-Scale Working Models with Special Reference to the Sutton Hoo Ship." *International Journal of Nautical Archaeology* 24 (2): 121–31.

———. 1996. "The Sailing Performance of Anglo-Saxon Ships as Derived from the Building and Trials of Half-Scale Models of the Sutten Hoo and Graveney Ship Finds." *Mariner's Mirror* 82 (2): 131–53.

Gifford, Edwin, Joyce Gifford, and John Coates. 2006. "The Construction and Trials of a Half-scale Model of the Early Bronze Age Ship, Ferriby 1, to Assess the Capability of the Full-size Ship." In *Connected by Sea: Proceedings of the 10th International Symposium on Boat and Ship Archaeology, Roskilde, 2003*, edited by Lucy Blue, Fred Hocker, and Anton Englert, 57–62. Oxford: Oxbow Books.

Gilbert, J., L. Gilbert, and A. Iglesias. 2003. "The Gibraltar Strait: A Pleistocene Door of Europe?" *Human Evolution* 18 (3–4): 147–60.

Gillmer, Thomas C. 1994. *A History of Working Watercraft of the Western World*. Camden, ME: International Marine.

Gladwin, Harold S. 1947. *Men Out of Asia*. New York: McGraw-Hill.

Gladwin, Thomas. 1970. *East Is a Big Bird: Navigation and Logic on Puluwat Atoll*. Cambridge, MA: Harvard University Press.

Gleick, James. 1987. *Chaos: Making a New Science*. New York: Viking Books.

Glover, Ian C. 1977. "The Late Stone Age in Eastern Indonesia." *World Archaeology* 9 (1): 42–61.

———. 1979. "Prehistoric Plant Remains from Southeast Asia, with Special Reference to Rice." In *South Asian Archaeology 1977*, vol. 1, edited by Maurizio Taddei, 7–37. Instituto Universitario Orientale, Seminario di Studi Asiatici, Series Minor 6. Naples: Instituto Universitario Orientale.

Goette, John Andrew. 1936. *Jade Lore*. Shanghai: Kelly and Walsh.

Goetzfridt, Nicholas J., comp. 1992. *Indigenous Navigation and Voyaging in the Pacific: A Reference Guide*. Bibliographies and Indexes in Anthropology 6. Westport, CT: Greenwood Press.

Goitein, S. D. 1963. "Letters and Documents on the India Trade in Medieval Times." *Islamic Culture* 37: 188–205.

———. 1967. *A Mediterranean Society: The Jewish Communities of the Arab World as Portrayed in the Documents of the Cairo Geniza*, vol. 1, *Economic Foundations*. Berkeley: University of California Press.

Gold, Thomas. 1999. *The Deep Hot Biosphere*. New York: Copernicus Books.

Gomes i Prat, Jordi, and Sheila M. F. Mendonça de Souza. 2003. "Prehistoric Tuberculosis in America: Adding Comments to a Literature Review." *Memorias del Instituto Oswaldo Cruz* 98 (supplement 1): 151–59.

Gongora, Jaime, Nicolas J. Rawlence, Victor A. Mobegi, Han Jianlin, Jose A. Alcalde, Jose T. Matus, Olivier Hanotte, Chris Moran, Jeremy J. Austin, Sean Ulm, Atholl J. Anderson, Gregor Larson, and Alan Cooper. 2008. "Indo-European and Asian Origins for Chilean and Pacific Chickens Revealed by mtDNA." *Proceedings of the National Academy of Sciences USA* 105 (30): 1030–13.

Goodenough, Ward H. 1953. *Native Astronomy in the Central Carolines*. Philadelphia: University of Pennsylvania Press.

Gooley, Tristan. 2012. *The Natural Navigator: The Rediscovered Art of Letting Nature Be Your Guide*. New York: The Experiment.

Gordon, Cyrus H. 1968. "The Canaanite Inscription from Brazil." *Orientalia* 37 (4): 425–36.

———. 1971. *Before Columbus: Links between the Old World and Ancient America*. New York: Crown Publishers.

Gorley, Rita. 1983. "Discovery: The Polynesian Pompeii." *Aloha* 6 (2): 26–33.

Görlitz, Dominique. 2000. *Schilfboot Abora—Segein gegen den Wind im Mittelmer*. Hamburg: DSV Hamburg.

———. 2001. "Study of the Drift Capacity of Selected Cultivated Plants for the Assessment of Transatlantic Contacts in the Early Years." *Migration and Diffusion: An International Journal* 1 (6): 70–99.

———. 2002. "Pre-Egyptian Reed Boat *Abora* 2 Crosses the Mediterranean Sea on Footsteps of the Famous Navigator Thor Heyerdahl." *Migration and Diffusion: An International Journal* 3 (12): 44–61.

———. 2006. *Mit dem Schilfboot durch das Sternenmeer Abora-II-Expedition: "1000 Meilen vorwärts–6000 Jahre zurück"; Auf den Spuren vorägyptischer Seefahrer über die Ozeane*. Chemnitz, Germany: D. Görlitz.

———. 2011. "The Tobacco Beetle in Egyptian Mummies." *Migration and Diffusion*. Accessed November 12, 2014. http://www.migration-diffusion.info/article.php?id=239.

Gosden, Chris. 1991. "Long Term Trends in the Colonization of the Pacific: Putting Lapita in Its Place." *Bulletin of the Indo-Pacific Prehistory Association* 11: 333–38.

Götz, Christopher M., and Travis W. Stanton. 2013. "The Use of Animals by the Pre-Hispanic Maya of the Northern Lowlands." In *The Archaeology of Mesoamerican Animals*, edited by Christopher M. Götz and Kitty F. Emery, 191–32. Archaeobiology 1. Atlanta: Lockwood Press.

Gould, Richard A. 2002. *Archaeology and the Social History of Ships*. Cambridge: Cambridge University Press.

Gould, Stephen Jay. 1985. "Red Wings in the Sunset." *Natural History* 94 (5): 12, 14, 18, 20, 22–24.

———. 1986. "Evolution and the Triumph of Homology, or Why History Matters." *American Scientist* 74 (1): 60–69.

———. 1989. *Wonderful Life: The Burgess Shale and the Nature of History*. New York: W. W. Norton.

———. 1994. "The Persistently Flat Earth." *Natural History* 103 (3): 12, 14–19.

———. 1995a. "Age-Old Fallacies of Thinking and Stinking." *Natural History* 104 (6): 6, 8, 10–13.

———. 1995b. "The *Great Western* and the *Fighting Temeraire*." *Natural History* 104 (10): 16, 18–19, 62, 64–65.

————. 1995c. "Spin Doctoring Darwin." *Natural History* 104 (7): 6–9, 70–71.

————. 1996a. "Microcosmos." *Natural History* 105 (3): 21–23, 66–68.

————. 1996b. "Up against a Wall." *Natural History* 105 (7): 16–17, 22, 70–73.

————. 1997a. "Seeing Eye to Eye." *Natural History* 106 (6): 14–18, 60–62.

————. 1997b. "A Tale of Two Worksites." *Natural History* 106 (9): 18–20, 22, 29, 62, 64–68.

————. 1997/98. "The Paradox of the Visually Irrelevant." *Natural History* 106 (11): 12, 14–18, 60–62, 64, 66.

————. 1998. "Second-Guessing the Future." *Natural History* 107 (7): 20–24, 26–29, 64, 66.

————. 1999. "Lyell's Pillars of Wisdom." *Natural History* 108 (3): 28–34, 87–89.

————. 2000a. "The Narthex of San Marco and the Pangenetic Paradigm." *Natural History* 109 (6): 24, 26, 30, 32–34, 36–37.

————. 2000b. "Syphilis and the Shepherd of Atlantis." *Natural History* 109 (8): 38, 40–42, 74–78, 82.

————. 2002. *The Structure of Evolutionary Theory*. Cambridge, MA: Belknap Press of Harvard University Press.

Gould, Stephen Jay, and Niles Eldredge. 1977. "Punctuated Equilibria: The Tempo and Mode of Evolution Reconsidered." *Paleobiology* 3 (2): 115–51.

Graf, Kelly C., Caroline V. Ketron, and Michael R. Waters, eds. 2013. *Paleoamerican Odyssey*. College Station: Texas A&M University Press.

Grant, Gordon, and Henry B. Culver. 1935. *The Book of Old Ships, and Something of Their Evolution and Romance*. Garden City, NY: Garden City Publishing Company. (Originally published 1928.)

Gravilets, Sergey, and Jonathan B. Losos. 2009. "Adaptive Radiation: Contrasting Theory with Data." *Science* 323 (5915): 732–37.

Gray, Melissa M., Nathan B. Sutter, Elaine A. Ostrander, and Robert K. Wayne. 2010. "The IGF1 Small Dog Haplotype Is Derived from Middle Eastern Grey Wolves." *BMC Biology* 8 (16). Accessed May 5, 2016. http://bmcbiol.biomedcentral.com/articles/10.1186/1741-7007-8-16.

Green, Jeremy. 1996a. "Chinese Ocean-Going Ships." In *The Sea Remembers: Shipwrecks and Archaeology*, edited by Peter Throckmorton, 158–65, 230. New York: Barnes and Noble Books.

————. 1996b. "Eastern Horizons / Introduction." In *The Sea Remembers: Shipwrecks and Archaeology*, edited by Peter Throckmorton, 152–54, 230. New York: Barnes and Noble Books.

Green, R[oger]. 2000. "A Range of Disciplines Support a Dual Origin for the Bottle-Gourd in the Pacific." *Journal of the Polynesian Society* 109 (3): 191–97.

Greenhill, Basil. 1971. *Boats and Boatmen of Pakistan*. Newton Abbot, England: David and Charles.

————. 1976. *The Archaeology of the Boat*. Middletown, CT: Wesleyan University Press.

Gremillion, Kristen J. 2011. *Ancestral Appetites: Food in Prehistory*. New York: Cambridge University Press.

Grieder, Terence. 1978. *The Art and Archaeology of Pashash*. Austin: University of Texas Press.

————. 1982. *Origins of Pre-Columbian Art*. Austin: University of Texas Press.

Grimes, James P. 2001. "1500 BC Copper Trading between Michigan, USA and Minoa." *Migration and Diffusion: An International Journal* 1 (7): 19–28.

————. 2003. "The Pre-Columbian Connection: Ancient Transatlantic Ships." *Ancient American* 8 (50): 6–9.

Grimes, W. F. 1976. "Introduction." In *The Archaeology of the Boat*, by Basil Greenhill, 15–16. Middletown, CT: Wesleyan University Press.

Guiot, Hélène. 2001. "La construction navale polynésienne traditionnelle: Dimension culturelle d'un processus technique / Naval Construction in Polynesia: Cultural Approach of the Technical Process / La construcción naval en Polinesia: Dimensión cultural de un proceso técnico." *Techniques and Culture* 35–36: 445–78.

Gupta, D., and H. K. Jain. 1973. "Genetic Differentiation of Two Himalayan Varieties of Maize." *Indian Journal of Genetics and Plant Breeding* 33 (3): 401–15.

Gupta, Shakti M. 1996. *Plants in Indian Temple Art*. Delhi: B. R. Publishing.

Guthrie, James L. 1990. "Peruvian Skulls." *Epigraphic Society Occasional Papers* 19: 106–9.

———. 1996. "Great Lakes Copper—Still Missing." *NEARA Journal* 30 (3 and 4): 57–70.

———. 2000/2001. "Human Lymphocyte Antigens: Apparent Afro-Asiatic, Southern Asian, and European HLAs in Indigenous American Populations." *Pre-Columbiana: A Journal of Long-Distance Contacts* 2 (2 and 3): 90–163.

———. 2005. *The Blind Man and the Elephants: The Davenport Relics Reconsidered*. NEARA Monograph. Edgecomb, ME: NEARA Publications.

———. 2011–14a. "The Fraudulent 'Michigan Relics': Were They Based on Authentic Models?" *Pre-Columbiana: A Journal of Long-Distance Contacts* 5 (2–4/6, no. 1).

———. 2011–14b. "Phoenician Inscriptions in Southeastern Brazil and Native-Brazilian Genetics." *Pre-Columbiana: A Journal of Long-Distance Contacts* 5 (2–4/6, no. 1).

———. 2014. "European Genes in Early America." *NEARA Journal* 47 (2): 28–30.

Guthrie, Jill, ed. 1995. *The Olmec World*. Princeton, NJ: Princeton University Art Museum.

Haaland, Gunnar, Randi Haaland, and Suman Rijal. 2002. "The Social Life of Iron: A Cross-Cultural Study of Technological, Symbolic, and Social Aspects of Iron Making." *Anthropos* 97 (1): 35–54.

Habu, Junko. 2010. "Seafaring and the Development of Cultural Complexity in Northeast Asia: Evidence from the Japanese Islands." In *The Global Origins and Development of Seafaring*, edited by Atholl Anderson, James H. Barrett, and Katherine V. Boyle, 159–70. McDonald Institute Monographs. Cambridge, UK: McDonald Institute for Archaeological Research.

Haddawy, Husain, trans. 1995. *The Arabian Nights II: Sindbad and Other Popular Stories*. New York: W. W. Norton.

Haddon, A. C., and James Hornell. 1975. *Canoes of Oceania*. 3 vols. Bernice P. Bishop Museum Special Publications 27, 28, and 29. Honolulu: Bernice P. Bishop Museum. (Originally published 1936–37, in 2 vols.)

Haggett, Peter. 1959. "The Bahia-Goa Route in the Dispersal of Brazilian Plants to Asia." *American Antiquity* 25 (2): 267–68.

———. 1992. "Sauer's 'Origins and Dispersals': Its Implications for the Geography of Disease." *Transactions of the Institute of British Geographers* new series 17: 387–98.

Hainline, Lydia Jane. 1964. "Human Ecology in Micronesia: Determinants of Population Size, Structure and Dynamics." Dissertation 64–7350. Ann Arbor, MI: University Microfilms.

Hall, Stephen S., and Robert Clark. 2010. "Spirits in the Sand: The Ancient Nasca Lines of Peru Shed Their Secrets." *National Geographic* 217 (3): 56–79.

Halpern, Michael. 1986. "Sideral Compasses: A Case for Carolinian-Arab Links." *Journal of the Polynesian Society* 95 (4): 441–60.

Hamdani, Abbas. 2006. "Arabic Sources for the Pre-Columbian Voyages of Discovery." *Maghreb Review* 31 (3–4): 203–21.

Hand, David J. 2014. *The Improbability Principle: Why Coincidences, Miracles, and Rare Events Happen Every Day*. New York: Farrar, Straus and Giroux.

Hapgood, Charles H. 1966. *Maps of the Ancient Sea Kings: Evidence of Advanced Civilization in the Ice Age*. Philadelphia: Chilton Book.

Hardaker, Christopher. 2007. *The First American: The Supressed Story of the People Who Discovered the New World*. Franklin Lakes, NJ: New Page Books.

Harley, J. B., and David Woodward. 1987. *The History of Cartography*, vol. 1, *Cartography in Prehistoric, Ancient, and Medieval Europe and the Mediterranean*. Chicago: University of Chicago Press.

Harlow, George E., Glenn R. Summerhayes, Hugh L. Davies, and Lisa Matisoo-Smith. 2012. "A Jade Gouge from Emirau Island, Papua New Guinea (Early Lapita context, 3300 BP): A Unique Jadeitite." *European Journal of Mineralogy* 24 (2): 391–99.

Harper, Kristin N., Molly K. Zuckerman, Megan L. Harper, John D. Kingston, and George J. Armelagos. 2011. "The Origin and Antiquity of Syphilis Revisited: An Appraisal of Old World Pre-Columbian Evidence for Treponemal Infection." Yearbook of Physical Anthropology. *American Journal of Physical Anthropology* 146 (S53): 99–133.

Haslett, John F. 2006. *Voyage of the* Manteño: *The Education of a Modern-Day Expeditioner*. New York: St. Martin's Press.

Haslett, John F., and Cameron M. Smith. 2002. "In the Wake of Ancient Mariners." *Archaeology* 55 (2): 48–52.

Haslip-Viera, Gabriel, Bernard Ortiz de Montellano, Warren Barbour, and commentators. 1997. "Robbing Native American Cultures: Van Sertima's Afrocentricity and the Olmecs." *Current Anthropology* 38 (3): 419–44.

Hather, Jon, and P. V. Kirch. 1991. "Prehistoric Sweet Potato (*Ipomea batatas*) from Mangaia Island, Central Polynesia." *Antiquity: A Quarterly Review of World Archaeology* 65 (249): 887–89.

Hawdon, J. M., and S. A. Johnston. 1996. "Hookworms in the Americas: An Alternative to Trans-Pacific Contact." *Parasitology Today* 12 (2): 72–74.

Hawkes, J. G. 1998. "The Introduction of New World Crops into Europe after 1492." In *Plants for Food and Medicine: Proceedings of the Joint Conference for Economic Botany and the International Society for Ethnopharmacology, London, 1–6 July 1996*, edited by H. D. V. Prendergast, N. L. Etkin, D. R. Harris, and P. J. Houghton, 147–59. London: Royal Botanical Gardens, Kew.

Heine-Geldern, Robert. 1960. "Theoretical Considerations concerning the Problem of Pre-Columbian Contacts between the Old World and the New." In *Men and Cultures: Selected Papers of the Fifth International Congress of Anthropological and Ethnological Sciences, Philadelphia, September 1–9, 1956*, edited by Anthony F. C. Wallace, 277–81. Philadelphia: University of Pennsylvania Press.

———. 1967. "A Roman Find from Pre-Columbian Mexico." *Anthropological Journal of Canada* 5 (4): 20–22. (Translation of "Ein römischer Fund aus dem vorkolumbischen Mexiko." *Anzeiger der philosophischehistorische Klasse der Oestreichischen Akademie der Wissenschaften* 16, *Philosophischen-historischen Klasse* 98 [16]: 117–19; 1961.)

Heine-Geldern, Robert, and Gordon F. Ekholm. 1951. "Significant Parallels in the Symbolic Arts of Southern Asia and Middle America." In *The Civilizations of Ancient America*, vol. 1, edited by Sol Tax, 299–309. Papers of the International Congress of Americanists 29. Chicago: University of Chicago Press.

Heinrich, Joseph. 2004. "Demography and Cultural Evolution: How Adaptive Cultural Processes Can Produce Maladaptive Losses—The Tasmanian Case." *American Antiquity* 69 (2): 197–214.

Heiser, Charles B. 1973. "The Penis Gourd in New Guinea." *Economic Botany* 63 (3): 312–18.

Helms, Mary V. 1988. *Ulysses' Sail: An Ethnographic Odyssey of Power, Knowledge, and Geographic Distance.* Princeton, NJ: Princeton University Press.

Hephaestus Books. N.d. (ca. 2013). *Pre-Columbian Trans-Oceanic Contact, Including: Book of Mormon, Thor Heyerdahl, Kennewick Man, Sung Document, Leif Ericson, Richard Amerike, Helge Ingstad, America's Stonehenge, Melungeon, Norse Colonization of the Americas, Brendan, Kon-Tiki, Zichmni.* N.p.: Hephaestus Books.

Herskovitz, Melville J. 1948. *Man and His Works: The Science of Cultural Anthropology.* New York: Alfred A. Knopf.

Heyen, G. H. 1963. "Polynesia: Distance Tables." In *Polynesian Navigation: A Symposium on Andrew Sharp's Theory of Accidental Voyages,* rev. ed., edited by Jack Golson, 9–10. Memoir 34. Wellington, NZ: Polynesian Society.

Heyerdahl, Thor. 1950. *Kon-Tiki: Across the Pacific by Raft.* New York: Rand McNally.

———. 1952. *American Indians in the Pacific: The Theory behind the Kon-Tiki Expedition.* London: George Allen and Unwin.

———. 1963. "Feasible Ocean Routes to and from the Americas in Pre-Columbian Times." *American Antiquity* 28 (4): 482–88. (Reprinted 1964 in *Congreso Internacional de Americanistas* 35 [1]: 133–42; and in Heyerdahl 1978, 151–84.)

———. 1968. *Sea Routes to Polynesia.* Chicago: Rand McNally.

———. 1971a. "The Bearded Gods Speak." In *The Quest for America,* edited by Geoffrey Ashe, 198–238. New York: Praeger.

———. 1971b. *The Ra Expeditions.* Garden City, NY: Doubleday.

———. 1978. *Early Man and the Ocean: A Search for the Beginnings of Navigation and Seaborne Civilizations.* Garden City, NY: Doubleday.

———. 1980. *The Tigris Expedition: In Search of Our Beginnings.* Garden City, NY: Doubleday.

———. 1986. *The Maldive Mystery.* Bethesda, MD: Adler and Adler.

Heyerdahl, Thor, and Arne Skjølsvold. 1956. *Archaeological Evidence of Pre-Spanish Visits to the Galápagos Islands.* Memoirs 12. Washington, DC: Society for American Archaeology.

Higginson, Thomas Wentworth. 1885. *A Larger History of the United States of America to the Close of the Jackson Administration.* New York: Harper and Brothers.

Higham, T. F. G. 2001. "Early Preserved Polynesian *Kumara* Cultivations in New Zealand." *Antiquity: A Quarterly Review of World Archaeology* 75 (289): 511–12.

Highet, Gilbert. 1962. "The Wondrous Survival of Records." *Horizon: A Magazine of the Arts* 5 (2): 74–95.

Higraff, Torgeir Sæverud. 2007. *Tangaroa—Havets Hersker: Et Eventyr i Kon-Tikis Kjølvann (Tangaroa—The Lord of the Seas: An Adventure in Kon-Tiki's Wake).* Oslo: Bazar Forlag.

Hilder, Brett. 1964. "On Sailing Native Canoes to Windward." *Journal of the Polynesian Society* 73 (1): 74–77.

———. 1972. Primitive Navigation in the Pacific—2. *Polynesian Navigation: A Symposium on Andrew Sharp's Theory of Accidental Voyages,* 3rd. ed., edited by Jack Golson, 81–97. Wellington, NZ: A. H. and A. Reed.

Hodges, Henry. 1970. *Technology in the Ancient World.* New York: Alfred A. Knopf.

Hoebel, E. Adamson. 1949. *Man in the Primitive World.* New York: McGraw-Hill.

Hole, Frank. 1983. "Changing Directions in Archaeological Thought." In *Ancient North Americans,* edited by Jesse D. Jennings, 1–23. San Francisco: W. H. Freeman.

Holmgren, Robert J., and Anita E. Spertus. 1980. "Tampan Pasisir: Pictorial Documents of an Ancient Indonesian Coastal Culture." In *Indonesian Textiles*, edited by Matibelle Gittinger, 157–98. Washington, DC: Textile Museum.

Homer. 1946. *The Odyssey*. Translated by E. V. Rieu. London: Penguin Books.

Honigsheim, Paul. 1942. "The Problem of Diffusion and Parallel Evolution with Special Reference to American Indians." *Papers of the Michigan Academy of Science, Arts and Letters* 27: 515–24.

Hooton, Earnest A. 1933. "Racial Types in America and Their Relation to Old World Types." In *The American Aborigines: Their Origin and Antiquity: A Collection of Papers by Ten Authors*, edited by Diamond Jenness, 131–64. Toronto: University of Toronto Press.

Hopkins, A. G. 1973. *An Economic History of West Africa*. London: Longman.

Hopkins, Donald R. 2002. *The Greatest Killer: Smallpox in History*. Chicago: University of Chicago Press.

Hornbostel, Lloyd. 1997. "Strange Saga of the Viking Ship." *Ancient American* 3 (18): 2.

Horne, Patrick D. 1985. "A Review of the Evidence of Human Endoparasitism in the Pre-Columbian New World through the Study of Coprolites." *Journal of Archaeological Science* 12 (4): 299–310.

Hornell, James. 1936. "British Coracles (Part 1)." *Mariner's Mirror* 22 (1): 5–41.

———. 1945. "Was There Pre-Columbian Contact between the Peoples of Oceania and South America?" *Journal of the Polynesian Society* 54 (4): 167–91.

———. 1946a. "The Role of Birds in Early Navigation." *Antiquity: A Quarterly Review of World Archaeology* 20 (79): 14–49.

———. 1946b. *Water Transport: Origins and Early Evolution*. Cambridge: The University Press. (Reprint 1970, by David and Charles (Publishers), Newton Abbot, England.)

Horowitz, Wayne. 1998. *Mesopotamian Cosmic Geography*. Winona Lake, IN: Eisenbrauns.

Horridge, G. Adrian. 1978. *The Design of Planked Boats of the Moluccas*. Maritime Monographs and Reports 38. London: Trustees of the National Maritime Museum.

———. 1986. "Evolution of Pacific Canoe Rigs." *Journal of Pacific History* 21 (1): 83–99.

———. 2008. *Origins and Relationships of Pacific Canoes and Rigs*. BAR International Series 1802. Oxford: British Archaeological Reports.

Horrocks, Mark, and Ian Barber. 2005. "Microfossils of Introduced Starch Cultigens from an Early Wetland Ditch in New Zealand." *Archaeology in Oceania* 40 (3): 106–14.

Horrocks, Mark, and Robert B. Rechtman. 2009. "Sweet Potato (*Ipomea batatas*) and Banana (*Musa* sp.) Microfossils in Deposits from the Kona Field System, Island of Hawaii." *Journal of Archaeological Science* 36 (5): 1115–26.

Horrocks, Mark, I. W. G. Smith, R. Walter, and S. L. Nichol. 2011. "Stratigraphic and Plant Microfossil Investigations at Cook's Cove, North Island, New Zealand: Reinterpretation of Holocene Deposits and Evidence of Polynesian-introduced Crops. *Journal of the Royal Society of New Zealand* 41 (3): 237–58.

Hosler, Dorothy. 1994. *The Sounds and Colors of Power: The Sacred Metallurgy of Ancient West Mexico*. Cambridge, MA: MIT Press.

Hourani, George Faldo. 1963. *Arab Seafaring in the Indian Ocean in Ancient and Early Medieval Times*. Beirut: Khayats Oriental Reprints 3. (Originally published 1951, Princeton, NJ: Princeton Oriental Studies 13.)

Howarth, David. 1977. *Dhows*. London: Quartet Books.

Howells, William W. 1989. *Skull Shapes and the Map*. Papers of Peabody Museum of Archaeology and Ethnology, Harvard University 79. Cambridge, MA: Peabody Museum of Archaeology and Ethnology, Harvard University.

———. 1995. *Who's Who in Skulls: Ethnic Identification of Crania from Measurements*.

Papers of Peabody Museum of Archaeology and Ethnology, Harvard University 82. Cambridge, MA: Peabody Museum of Archaeology and Ethnology, Harvard University.

Hranicky, William Jack. 2011. *Prehistoric Projectile Points Found along the Atlantic Coastal Plain*. 3rd ed. Boca Raton, FL: Universal Publishers.

Hristov, Romeo, and Santiago Genovés. 1999. "Mesoamerican Evidence of Pre-Columbian Transoceanic Contacts." *Ancient Mesoamerica* 10 (2): 207–13.

———. 2000. "Reply to Peter Schaaf and Günther A. Wagner's 'Comments on Mesoamerican Evidence of Pre-Columbian Transoceanic Contacts.'" *Ancient Mesoamerica* 12 (1): 83–86.

———. 2001. "Mesoamerican Evidence of Pre-Columbian Transoceanic Contacts." *Migration and Diffusion* 1 (7): 59–78. (Revised reprinting of Hristov and Genovés 1999.)

Hristov, Romeo, and John L. Sorenson. 2011–14. "Works by Romeo H. Hristov on Foreign Objects Found in Mexico and on Other Diffusionist Topics, through 2014." *Pre-Columbiana: A Journal of Long-Distance Contacts* 5 (2–4/6, no. 1): 404–5.

Hsieh, Chiao-Min. 1967. "Geographical Exploration by the Chinese." In *The Pacific Basin: A History of Its Geographical Exploration*, edited by Herman R. Friis, 87–95. New York: American Geographical Society. (Reprinted in 1968 as "The Chinese Exploration of the Ocean—A Study in Historical Geography." *Chinese Culture* 9 [3]: 123–31.)

Huchet, J.-B. 1995. "Insects et momies égyptiennes." *Bulletin de la Société Linéenne de Bordeaux* 23: 29–39.

Hughes, Austin L. 2002. "Genetic Markers: Strength in Numbers." *Nature* 417 (6891): 795.

Hughes, Robert. 1991. "Just Who Was That Man?" *Time* 138 (14): 58–59.

Hulse, Frederick S. 1963. *The Human Species: An Introduction to Physical Anthropology.* New York: Random House.

Humboldt, Alexander von. 1814. *Researches concerning the Institutions and Monuments of the Ancient Inhabitants of America with Descriptions and Views of Some of the Most Striking Scenes in the Cordilleras*, vol. 1. London: Longman, Hurst, Rees, Orme and Brown, J. Murray and H. Colburn.

Hunka, Ronald A. 1972. "The Heliolithic Theory of Grafton Elliot Smith and W. J. Perry." Master's thesis, University of Texas, Austin.

Hutchinson, R. W. 1962. *Prehistoric Crete*. Baltimore: Penguin Books.

Hutchison, Joseph, R. A. Silow, and S. G. Stephens. 1947. *The Evolution of Gossypium and the Differentiation of the Cultivated Cottons*. New York: Oxford University Press.

Huth, John Edward. 2013. *The Lost Art of Finding Our Way*. Cambridge, MA: Harvard University Press.

Hyde, Walter Woodburn. 1947. *Ancient Greek Mariners*. New York: Oxford University Press.

Ikawa-Smith, Fumiko. 1986. "Late Pleistocene and Early Holocene Technologies." In *Windows on the Japanese Past*, edited by R. Pearson, 199–218. Ann Arbor: Center for Japanese Studies, University of Michigan.

Imbelloni, J. 1930. "On the Diffusion in America of *Patu Onewa, Okewa, Patu Paroa, Miti*, and Other Relatives of the *Mere* Family." *Journal of the Polynesian Society* 39 (156): 322–45.

Ingstad, Helge. 1969. *Westward to Vinland: The Discovery of Pre-Columbian Norse House-Sites in North America*. Translated by Erik J. Friis. New York: St. Martin's Press.

Ingstad, Helge, and Ann Stine Ingstad. 2001. *The Viking Discovery of America: The Excavation of a Norse Settlement in L'Anse aux Meadows, Newfoundland*. Translated by Elizabeth S. Seeberg. New York: Checkmark Books / Saint John's, NF: Breakwater Books.

Irwin, Geoffrey. 1981. "How Lapita Lost Its Pots: The Question of Continuity in the Colonization of Polynesia." *Journal of the Polynesian Society* 90 (4): 481–94.

———. 1992. *The Prehistoric Exploration and Colonization of the Pacific.* Cambridge: Cambridge University Press.

———. 2010. "Pacific Voyaging and Settlement: Issues of Biogeography and Archaeology, Canoe Performance, and Computer Simulation." In *The Global Origins and Development of Seafaring*, edited by Atholl Anderson, James H. Barrett, and Katherine V. Boyle, 131–41. McDonald Institute Monographs. Cambridge, UK: McDonald Institute for Archaeological Research.

Jablonski, Nina G. 2004. "The Evolution of Human Skin and Skin Color." *Annual Review of Anthropology* 33: 585–623.

Jackson, Robert. 2012. "Sailing through Time: *Jewel of Muscat*." *Saudi Aramco World* 63 (3): 1, 24–33.

Jacobson, Timothy. 1991. *Discovering America: Journeys in Search of the New World.* Toronto: Key Porter Books.

Jahan, Shanaj Husne. 2006. *Excavating Waves and Winds of (Ex)change: A Study of Maritime Trade in Early Bengal.* BAR International Series 1533. Oxford: British Archaeological Reports.

Jairazbhoy, R. A. 1974. *Ancient Egyptians and Chinese in America.* London: Prior.

———. 1981. *Ancient Egyptians in Middle and South America.* London: Ra Publications.

James, Jamie. 2003. "Sailing in History's Wake." *Time*, September 1. Accessed September 29, 2012. time.com/time/magazine/article/0,9171,480337,00.html.

Jankowiak, William, Shelly L. Volsche, and Justin R. Garcia. 2015. "Is the Romantic-Sexual Kiss a Near Human Universal?" *American Anthropologist* 116 (3): 535–39.

Jeffreys, M. D. W. 1971. "Pre-Columbian Maize in Asia." In *Man across the Sea: Problems of Pre-Columbian Contacts*, edited by Carroll L. Riley, J. Charles Kelly, Campbell W. Pennington, and Robert L. Rands, 376–400. Austin: University of Texas Press.

———. 1975. "Pre-Columbian Maize in the Old World: An Examination of the Portuguese Sources." In *Gastronomy: The Anthropology of Food and Food Habits*, edited by Margaret L. Arnott, 23–66. The Hague: Mouton.

Jenkins, Nancy. 1980. *The Boat beneath the Pyramid.* New York: Holt, Rinehart and Winston.

Jett, Stephen C. 1968. "Malaysia and Tropical America: Some Racial, Cultural, and Ethnobotanical Comparisons." *International Congress of Americanists* 37 (4): 133–77.

———. 1970. "The Development and Distribution of the Blowgun." *Annals of the Association of American Geographers* 60 (4): 662–88.

———. 1971. "Diffusion versus Independent Development: The Bases of Controversy." In *Man across the Sea: Problems of Pre-Columbian Contacts*, edited by Carroll L. Riley, J. Charles Kelly, Campbell W. Pennington, and Robert L. Rands, 5–53. Austin: University of Texas Press.

———. 1978. "Pre-Columbian Transoceanic Contacts." In *Ancient Native Americans*, edited by Jesse D. Jennings, 592–650. San Francisco: W. H. Freeman and Company.

———. 1983. "Pre-Columbian Transoceanic Contacts." In *Ancient North Americans*, edited by Jesse D. Jennings, 556–613. San Francisco: W. H. Freeman.

———. 1991 "Further Information on the Geography of the Blowgun and Its Implications for Early Transoceanic Contacts." *Annals of the Association of American Geographers* 81 (1): 89–102.

———. 1993. "Before Columbus: The Question of Early Transoceanic Interinfluences." *BYU Studies* 33 (2): 245–71.

———. 1998a. "More on Proto-Malayo-Polynesian *Wangkang and *Kumadjang, the Americas, and India." *Pre-Columbiana* 1 (1 and 2): 78–87.

———. 1998b. "Pre-Columbian Transoceanic Contacts: What Is the Evidence?" *Journal of the West* 37 (4): 1–18.

———. 1999a. "Additional Observations on Japanese Drift Voyaging." *Pre-Columbiana: A Journal of Long-Distance Contacts* 1 (3 and 4): 249–50.

———. 1999b. "A Bibliography of Works Pertaining to Japanese Drift Voyages in the North Pacific." *Pre-Columbiana: A Journal of Long-Distance Contacts* 1 (3 and 4): 251–52.

———. 1999c."The Jōmon of Neolithic Japan: Early Ocean-Goers." *Pre-Columbiana: A Journal of Long-Distance Contacts* 1 (3 and 4): 159–68.

———. 2000. "Confessions of a Cultural Diffusionist." *Yearbook, Conference of Latin Americanist Geographers* 26: 171–78.

———. 2002a. "Archaeological Hints of Pre-Columbian Plantains in the Americas." *Pre-Columbiana: A Journal of Long-Distance Contacts* 2 (4): 314–16.

———. 2002b. "Nicotine and Cocaine in Egyptian Mummies and THC in Peruvian Mummies: A Review of the Evidence and of Scholarly Reaction." *Pre-Columbiana: A Journal of Long-Distance Contacts* 2 (4): 297–313.

———. 2003/4. "More on Nicotine and Cocaine in Egyptian Mummies: A Précis of Recent Articles." *Pre-Columbiana: A Journal of Long-Distance Contacts* 3 (1–3): 45–49.

———. 2004. "No Plague in the Land? Infectious Diseases and Their Implications for the Pre-Columbian-Transoceanic-Contacts Controversy." *Migration and Diffusion: An International Journal* 5 (19): 6–31.

———. 2006. "Qui a découvert l'Amérique? Interdits scientifiques et 'politiquement correct': Politique et hypothèses des influences trans-océaniques précolombiennes." *Diplomatie: Affaires Stratégiques et Cultures Internationales* 24: 74–81.

———. 2005–7a. "Availability of Wild Foods and Water during Ocean Voyages: A Bibliographic Essay on Modern Small-Craft Experience." *Pre-Columbiana: A Journal of Long-Distance Contacts* 3 (4/4, nos. 1 and 2): 313–20.

———. 2005–7b. "Phytolith and Other Evidence of the Antiquity of *Musa* in Asia, Africa, and America: A Review of Recent Literature." *Pre-Columbiana: A Journal of Long-Distance Contacts* 3 (4/4, nos. 1 and 2): 221–24.

———. 2007a. "Genesis, Genes, Germs, and Geography: The Implications of Genetics and Human-Disease Distributions for Founding and Later Old World Entries into the Americas." In *Proceedings of the International Science Conference, Science in Archaeology*, cochairs Alison T. Stenger and Alan L. Schneider, edited by Brian F. Harrison, 100–33. [Portland, OR]: Institute for Archaeological Studies.

———. 2007b. "George F. Carter, 1912–2004." *Geographers Biobibliographic Studies* 26: 27–49.

———. 2008–10. "Gene Savoy (1927–2007)." *Pre-Columbiana: A Journal of Long-Distance Contacts* 4 (3 and 4) (1): 367–68.

———. 2009. "Genetics Geography Implies a Minimum of Four Major Late Pleistocene Movements and Four Major Early to Middle Holocene Movements of Modern Humans into the Americas." Unpublished paper presented at the International Science Conference, Los Angeles; periodically updated.

———. 2011–14a. "Early Observations on an Eastern Zhou Chinese Bronze Belt Buckle Found in Western Alaska." *Pre-Columbiana: A Journal of Long-Distance Contacts* 5 (2–4): 172.

———. 2011–14b. "Evidence for the Natural Transoceanic Dispersal of Cottons (*Gossypium*): A Review." *Pre-Columbiana: A Journal of Long-Distance Contacts* 5 (2–4) (1): 251–54.

———. 2011–14c. "Virologic and Genetic Evidence of a Connection between Jōmon Japan and Ecuador/Columbia: A Brief Review." *Pre-Columbiana: A Journal of Long-Distance Contacts* 5 (2–4) (1): 263–65.

———. 2014. "Pre-Columbian Transoceanic Influences: Far-Out Fantasy, Unproven Possibility, or Undeniable Reality?" *Journal of Scientific Exploration* 28 (1): 35–74.

———. 2015. "More on *Pongo/Panga/Banka* as Boat Names in Asia and America." *Pre-Columbiana: A Journal of Long-Distance Contacts* 6 (2): in preparation.

Jiang, Leping, and Li Liu. 2005. "The Discovery of an 8,000-Year-Old Dugout Canoe at Kuahuqiao in the Lower Yangzi River, China." *Antiquity: A Quarterly Review of World Archaeology* 79 (305): project gallery. Accessed November 13, 2014. http://www.antiquity.ac.uk/projgall/liu/index.html.

Jiao, Tianlong. 2007. *The Neolithic of Southeast China: Cultural Transformation and Regional Interaction on the Coast.* Youngstown, NY: Cambria Press.

Joel, C. E. 1981. "Neolithic D.I.Y. Societies Megaliths—Did They Do It Themselves? A Postscript to PYRAMID & MEGALITH." *Historical Diffusionism* 32: 25–44.

Johannessen, Carl L. 1981. "Folk Medicine Uses of Melanotic Asiatic Chickens as Evidence of Early Diffusion in the New World." *Social Science and Medicine* 15D (4): 427–34.

———. 1998a. "Maize Diffused to India before Columbus." In *Across before Columbus? Evidence for Transoceanic Contact with the Americas prior to 1492*, edited by Don Y. Gilmore and Linda S. McElroy, 111–24. Edgecomb, ME: New England Antiquities Research Association, NEARA Publications.

———. 1998b. "Pre-Columbian American Sunflower and Maize Images in Indian Temples: Evidence of Contact between Civilizations in India and America." *NEARA Journal* 32 (1): 4–18.

———. 2003. "Early Maize in India: A Case for 'Multiple Working Hypotheses.'" In *Culture, Land, and Legacy: Perspectives on Carl O. Sauer and Berkeley School Geography*, edited by Kent Mathewson and Martin S. Kenzer, 299–314. Geosciences and Man 37. Baton Rouge: Geosciences Publications, Department of Geography and Anthropology, Louisiana State University.

———. 2016. *Pre-Columbian Sailors Changed World History.* [Eugene, OR: author].

Johannessen, Carl L., and May Chen Fogg. 1982. "Melanotic Chicken Use and Chinese Traits in Guatemala." *Revista de Historia de América* 93: 73–89.

Johannessen, Carl L., Wayne Fogg, and May Chen Fogg. 1984. "Distribution and Medicinal Use of the Black-Boned and Black-Meated Chicken in Mexico, Guatemala, and South America." *National Geographic Society Research Reports* 17: 493–95.

Johannessen, Carl L., and Anne Z. Parker. 1989. "Maize Ears Sculptured in 12th and 13th Century A.D. India as Indicators of Pre-Columbian Diffusion." *Economic Botany* 43 (2): 164–80.

Johannessen, Carl L., with Wang Siming. 1998. "American Crop Plants in Asia before A.D. 1500." *Pre-Columbiana: A Journal of Long-Distance Contacts* 1 (1 and 2): 9–36.

Johns, Dylis A., Geoffrey J. Irwin, and Yun K. Sung. 2014. "An Early Sophisticated East Polynesian Voyaging Canoe Discovered on New Zealand's Coast." *Proceedings of the National Academy of Sciences, USA* 111 (41): 14, 728–33.

Johnson, B. L. 1975. "*Gossypium palmeri* and a Polyphyletic Origin of the New World Cottons." *Bulletin of the Torrey Botanical Club* 102 (6): 340–49.

Johnson, Donald S. 1994. *Phantom Islands of the Atlantic: The Legends of Seven Lands That Never Were.* New York: Walker.

Johnson, Rubellite, and John Mahelona. 1975. *Na Inoa Hoku: A Catelogue of Hawaiian and Pacific Stars.* Honolulu: Topgallant.

Jones, Dilwyn. 1995. *Egyptian Bookshelf: Boats.* Austin: University of Texas Press.

Jones, Eric E. 2014. "Spatiotemporal Analysis of Old World Diseases in North America, A.D. 1519–1807." *American Antiquity* 79 (3): 487–504.

Jones, Gwyn. 1986. *The Norse Atlantic Saga.* Oxford: Oxford University Press.

Jones, Terry L., Alice A. Storey, Elizabeth A. Matisoo-Smith, and José Miguel Ramírez-Aliaga, eds. 2011. *Polynesians in America: Pre-Columbian Contacts with the New World.* Lanham, MD: AltaMira Press.

Joseph, Frank. 2013. "Imperial Roman Artifacts Found in Wisconsin." *Ancient American* 17 (98): 2–3.

———. 2014. *The Lost Colonies of Ancient America: A Comprehensive Guide to the Pre-Columbian Visitors That Really Discovered America.* Pompton Plains, NJ: New Page Books.

Jourdain, P. 1970. *Ancient Tahitian Canoes.* Paris: Société des Océanistes, Dossier 4 / Baltimore: Johns Hopkins University Press.

Jurisic, Mario. 2000. "Ancient Shipwrecks of the Adriatic: Maritime Transport during the First and Second Centuries AD." BAR International Series 828. Oxford: Archaeopress.

Kahler, Erich. 1965. "What History Is and Is Not." *Princeton Alumni Weekly* (June 8): 39–42.

Karafet, T. M., J. S. Lansing, A. J. Redd, S. Reznikova, J. C. Watkins, S. P. Surata, W. A. Arthawiguna, L. Mayer, M. Bamshad, L. B. Jorde, and M. F. Hammer. 2005. "Balinese Y-Chromosome Perspective on the Peopling of Indonesia: Genetic Contributions from Pre-Neolithic Hunter-Gatherers, Austronesian Farmers, and Indian Traders." *Human Biology: The International Journal of Population Genetics and Anthropology* 77 (1): 93–114.

Katzev, Susan. 2008. "The Kyrenia Ship: Her Recent Journey." *Near Eastern Archaeology* 71 (1–2): 76–81.

Kearsley, Graeme R. 2001. *Mayan Genesis: South Asian Myths, Migrations and Iconography in Mesoamerica.* London: Yelsraek.

Keast, Allen. 1957. "Over the Sea and Far Away: The Story of Bird Migration." *Walkabout* 23 (3): 10–14.

Keddie, Grant. 1990. *The Question of Asiatic Objects on the North Pacific Coast of America: Historic or Prehistoric?* Contributions to Human History 3. Victoria: Royal British Columbia Museum.

Keegan, William F., and Jared Diamond. 1987. "Colonization of Islands: A Biogeography." *Advances in Archaeological Method and Theory* 10: 49–92.

Kehoe, Alice Beck. 1971. "Small Boats upon the North Atlantic." In *Man across the Sea: Problems of Pre-Columbian Contacts,* edited by Carroll L. Riley, J. Charles Kelly, Campbell W. Pennington, and Robert L. Rands, 275–92. Austin: University of Texas Press.

———. 1998. *The Land of Prehistory: A Critical History of American Archaeology.* New York: Routledge.

———. 2008. *Controversies in Archaeology.* Walnut Creek, CA: Left Coast Press.

———. 2010. "Consensus and the Fringe in American Archaeology." *Archaeologies: Journal of the World Archaeological Congress* 6 (2): 197–214.

———. 2016. *Traveling Prehistoric Seas: Critical Thinking on Ancient Transoceanic Voy-*

ages, ed. Jerrid M. Wolflick, Kathleen Wheeler, and Paul McCartney. Walnut Creek, CA: Left Coast Press.

Kelley, David H. 1971. "Diffusion: Evidence and Process." In *Man across the Sea: Problems of Pre-Columbian Contacts*, edited by Carroll L. Riley, J. Charles Kelly, Campbell W. Pennington, and Robert L. Rands, 60–65. Austin: University of Texas Press.

———. 1995. "Essay on Pre-Columbian Contacts between the Americas and Other Areas, with Special Reference to the Work of Ivan Van Sertima." In *Race, Discourse, and the Origins of the Americas: A New World View*, edited by Vera Lawrence Hyatt and Rex Nettleford, 103–22. Washington, DC: Smithsonian Institution Press.

———. 1998a. "*Wangkang, *Kumadjang, and *Longo." *Pre-Columbiana: A Journal of Long-Distance Contacts* 1 (1–2): 72–77.

———. 1998b. "Writing in the Americas." *Journal of the West* 37 (4): 25–30.

Kelton, Paul. 2007. *Epidemics and Enslavement: Biological Catastrophe in the Native Southeast*. Lincoln: University of Nebraska Press.

Kemp, Peter, ed. 1976. *The Oxford Companion to Ships and the Sea*. Oxford: Oxford University Press.

———. 1978. *The History of Ships*. London: Orbis Publishing.

Keoke, Emory Dean, and Kay Marie Porterfield. 2002. *Encyclopedia of American Indian Contributions to the World: 15,000 Years of Innovations and Inventions*. New York: Facts on File.

Kerber, Jordan E. 1991. *Coastal and Maritime Archaeology: A Bibliography*. Metuchen, NJ: Scarecrow Press.

Key, Mary Ritchie. 1998. "Linguistic Similarities between Austronesian and South American Indian Languages." *Pre-Columbiana: A Journal of Long-Distance Contacts* 1 (1 and 2): 59–71.

King, Cuchlaine A. M. 1963. *An Introduction to Oceanography*. New York: McGraw-Hill.

King, Derek, and Peter Bird. 1976. *Small Boat against the Sea: The Story of the First Trans-World Rowing Attempt*. London: Paul Elek.

King, Gary A., Harry Kenward , Edith Schmidt, and David Smith. 2014. "Six-Legged Hitchhikers: An Archaeobiogeographical Account of the Early Dispersal of Grain Beetles." *Journal of the North Atlantic* 23: 1–18.

King-Webster, W. A. 1960. "Experimental Nautical Research: Third Millennium B.C. Egyptian Sails." *Mariner's Mirror* 46 (2): 150–52.

Kinle, Jan. 1962. "Jadeite—Its Importance for the Problems of Asia-Ameica Precolumbian Relationships." *Folia Orientalia* 4: 231–42.

Kiple, Kenneth F., ed. 1993. *The Cambridge World History of Human Disease*. New York: Cambridge University Press. (Individual articles not separately analyzed herein.)

Kirch, Patrick Vinton. 1997. *The Lapita Peoples: Ancestors of the Oceanic World*. London: Blackwell.

———. 1998. "Landscapes of Power: Late Prehistoric Settlement and Land Use of Marginal Environments in the Hawaiian Islands." In *Easter Island and East Polynesian Prehistory: Proceedings of the II International Congress on Easter Island and East Polynesian Archaeology*, edited by Patricia Vargas Casanova, 59–72. Santiago: Instituto de Estudios Isla de Pascua, Faculdad de Arquitectura y Urbanismo, Universidad de Chile.

———. 2000. *On the Road of the Winds: An Archaeological History of the Pacific Islands before European Contact*. Berkeley: University of California Press.

Kirchoff, Paul. 1964. "The Diffusion of a Great Religious System from India to Mexico." *International Congress of Americanists* 35 (1): 73–100.

Kirk, Robert L. 1979. "Genetic Differentiation in Australia and Its Bearing on the Origin of the First Americans." In *The First Americans: Origins, Affinities, and Adaptations*, edited by William S. Laughlin, and Albert B. Harper, 211–37. New York: Gustav Fischer.

Kirshenbaum, Sheril. 2011. *The Science of Kissing: What Our Lips Are Telling Us*. New York: Grand Central Publishing.

Kistler, Logan, Álvaro Montenegro, Bruce D. Smith, John A. Gifford, Richard E. Green, Lee A. Newsom, and Beth Shapiro. 2014. "Transoceanic Drift and the Domestication of African Bottle Gourds in the Americas." *Proceedings of the National Academy of Sciences, USA* 111 (8): 2937–41.

Klinkenberg, Jeff. 1994. "Call of Adventure and of the Sea Prove Too Strong to Ignore for Aging Sailor." *Milwaukee Journal*, January 13, 1, 4.

Knöbl, Kuno, with Arno Dennig. 1976. *Tai Ki: To the Point of No Return*. Boston: Little, Brown.

Knobloch, Francis J. 1970. "The Aharaibu Indians: A 'White' Tribe in the Amazon." *Mankind Quarterly* 10 (4): 185–98.

Knudsen, Ruth. 1963. "Traces of Reed Boats in the Pacific." *American Neptune* 23 (1): 41–45 + plates.

Kroeber, A. L. 1923. "American Culture and the Northwest Coast." *American Anthropologist* 25 (1): 1–20.

———. 1948. *Anthropology: Race, Language, Culture, Psychology, Prehistory*. New ed. New York: Harcourt, Brace.

———. 1953. "Problems of the Historical Approach: Results." In *An Appraisal of Anthropology Today*, edited by Sol Tax, 44–66. Chicago: University of Chicago Press.

Kubler, George. 1947. "The Quechua in the Colonial World." In *Handbook of South American Indians*, edited by Julian Steward. Bureau of American Ethnology bulletin 143 (2): 331–410.

———. 1961. "On the Colonial Extinction of the Motifs of Precolumbian Art." In *Essays in Pre-Columbian Art and Archaeology*, edited by S. K. Lothrop, D. Z. Stone, J. B. Bird, G. F. Ekholm, and G. R. Willey, 14–34. Cambridge, MA: Harvard University Press.

———. 1984. *The Art and Architecture of Ancient America*. New York: Penguin Books.

Kursh, Charlotte O., and Theodora C. Kreps. 1974. "Starpaths: Linear Constellations in Tropical Navigation." *Current Anthropology* 15 (3): 334–37.

Kyselka, Will. 1987. *An Ocean in Mind*. Honolulu: University of Hawai'i Press.

L[ium], A[lice Fussell]. 1992. "How Syphilis Came to Europe—Maybe." *Johns Hopkins Magazine* 44 (2): 46–47.

Labbé, Armand J. 1998. "A Southern California Enigma." *Pre-Columbiana: A Journal of Long-Distance Contacts* 1 (1 and 2): 115–16.

———. 1999. *Shamans, Gods, and Mythic Beasts: Colombian Gold and Ceramics*. New York: American Federation of Arts / Seattle: University of Washington Press.

Lackey, Louana M. 1982. *The Pottery of Acatlán: A Changing Mexican Tradition*. Norman: University of Oklahoma Press.

Ladefoged, Thegn N., Michael W. Graves, and James H. Coil. 2005. "The Introduction of Sweet Potato in Polynesia: Early Remains in Hawai'i." *Journal of the Polynesian Society* 114 (4): 359–73.

Lamprecht, Sandra J. 2000. "The Vinland Map: A Comprehensive Annotated Bibliography of Works in English, 1965–2000." *Pre-Columbiana: A Journal of Long-Distance Contacts* 2 (1): 57–84.

Lancel, Serge. 1995. *Carthage: A History*. Translated by Antonia Nevill. Cambridge, UK: Blackwell.

Landström, Björn. 1961. *The Ship: An Illustrated History*. Garden City, NY: Doubleday.

———. 1964. *Bold Voyages and Great Explorers*. Garden City, NY: Doubleday.

———. 1966. *Columbus*. New York: Macmillan.

Lang, John Dunmore. 1834. *View of the Origin and Migrations of the Polynesian Nation: Demonstrating Their Ancient Discovery and Progressive Settlement of the Continent of America*. London: Cochrane and M'Crone.

Langdon, Robert. 1989. "When the Blue-Egg Chickens Come Home to Roost: New Thoughts on the Prehistory of the Domestic Fowl in Asia, America and the Pacific Islands." *Journal of Pacific History* 24 (2): 164–92.

———. 1993. "The Banana as a Key to Early American and Polynesian History." *Journal of Pacific History* 28 (1): 15–35.

———. 2001. "The Bamboo Raft as a Key to the Introduction of the Sweet Potato in Prehistoric Polynesia." *Journal of Pacific History* 36 (1): 51–76.

Laufer, Beethold. 1917. *The Beginnings of Porcelain in China*. Anthropological Series 15, no. 2. Chicago: Field Museum of Natural History.

Lawler, Andrew. 2002. "Report of Oldest Boat Hints at Early Trade Routes." *Science* 296 (5574): 1791–92.

———. 2010. "A Forgotten Corridor Rediscovered." *Science* 328 (5982): cover, 1092–97.

———. 2011. "Did the First Cities Grow from Marshes?" *Science* 331 (6014): 141.

Layrisse, Miguel, and Tulio Arends. 1956. "The Diego Blood Factor in Chinese and Japanese." *Nature* 177 (4519): 1083–84.

Lechtman, Heather. 1984. "Andean Value Systems and the Development of Prehistoric Metallurgy." *Technology and Culture* 25 (1): 1–36.

Lee, Siu-Leung. 2012. *Kun Yu Wan Guo Quan Tu* (Deciphering the Entire Map of the Ten Thousand Countries of the Earth). Taipei: Linking Publisher.

Leicht, Hermann. 1944. *Tonplastik im reifem Stil der Chimu*. Zurich: Orell Füssli Verlag.

Le Moine, Genevieve. 1987. "The Loss of Pottery in Polynesia." *New Zealand Journal of Archaeology* 9: 25–32.

León-S., Fideas E., Amparo Ariza-Deleón, and Adriana Ariza-Deleón Caicedo. 1994. "El viaje transpacífico del virus de la leukemia de células T del adulto tipo I." *Acta Neurologica Colombiana* 10 (3): 132–36.

———. 1995. "HLA, Trans-Pacific Contacts, and Retrovirus." *Human Immunology* 42 (4): 348–50.

Leonard, Jennifer A., Robert K. Wayne, Jane Wheeler, Raúl Valadez, Sonia Guillén, and Carles Vilà. 2002. "Ancient DNA Evidence for Old World Origin of New World Dogs." *Science* 298 (5598): 1613–16.

Leshikar, Margaret E. 1988. "The Earliest Watercraft: From Rafts to Viking Ships." In *Ships and Shipwrecks of the Americas: A History Based on Underwater Archaeology*, edited by George S. Bass, 13–32. London: Thames and Hudson.

Levathes, Louise. 1994. *When China Ruled the Seas: The Treasure Fleet of the Dragon Throne, 1405–1433*. New York: Simon and Schuster.

Lévi-Strauss, Claude. 1973. *Tristes Tropiques*. Translated by John Weightman and Doreen Weightman. London: Jonathan Cape. (Originally published in French, 1955.)

Lewis, Archibald, and Timothy J. Runyan. 1990. *European Naval and Maritime History, 300–1500*. Bloomington: Indiana University Press. (Originally published 1985.)

Lewis, David. 1967. *Daughters of the Wind*. Wellington, NZ: A. H. and A. W. Reed.

———. 1976. *Ice Bird*. New York: W. W. Norton.

———. 1978. *The Voyaging Stars: Secrets of the Pacific Island Navigators*. New York: W. W. Norton.

———. 1980. "The Great Canoes of the Pacific." *Hemisphere* 25 (2): 66–76.

————. 1994. *We, the Navigators: The Ancient Art of Landfinding in the Pacific*. 2nd ed. Honolulu: University of Hawai'i Press. (1st ed. 1972.)

Lewis, Marion, Hiroko Ayukawa, and Bruce Chown. 1956. "The Blood Group Antigen Diego in North American Indians and in Japanese." *Nature* 177 (4519): 1084.

Lewis, Martin W., and Kären E. Wigen. 1997. *The Myth of Continents: A Critique of Metageography*. Berkeley: University of California Press.

Lewthwaite, Gordon R. 1967. "Geographical Knowledge of the Pacific Peoples." In *The Pacific Basin: A History of Its Geographical Exploration*, edited by Herman R. Friis, 57–86. New York: American Geographical Society.

————. 1970. "Maury to Schoolcraft: Correspondence on Ocean Currents and Pacific Migrations." *Professional Geographer* 22 (3): 128–31.

Li, Hui-lin. 1961. "Mu-lan-p'i: A Case for Pre-Columbian Transatlantic Travel by Arab Ships." *Harvard Journal of Asiatic Studies* 23: 114–26.

Lilley, Ian. 2008. "Pacific." In *Encyclopedia of Archaeology*, 2, *B–M*, edited by Deborah Pearsall, 1632–43. Amsterdam: Elsevier.

Lind, Aulis O. 1969. *Coastal Landforms of Cat Island, Bahamas*. Research Paper 122. Chicago: University of Chicago, Department of Geography.

Lindemann, Hannes. 1998. *Alone at Sea: A Doctor's Survival Experiments during Two Transatlantic Crossings in a Dugout Canoe and a Folding Kayak*. Oberschleissheim, Germany: Pollner Verlag.

Ling, Shun-sheng. 1956. "Formosan Sea-Going Raft and Its Origin in Ancient China." *Chung yang yen chiu yuan min tsu hsueh yen chiu so chi k'an / Bulletin of the Institute of Ethnology, Academia Sinica* 1 (March): 1–54. (In Chinese and English.)

————. 1969. "Zhongguo gudai yu taipingyangqu di fangzhou / The Double Canoe and Deck Canoe in Ancient China and Indian Ocean." *Chung yang yen chiu yuan min tsu hsueh yen chiu so chi k'an / Bulletin of the Institute of Ethnology, Academia Sinica* 28: 233–72. (In Chinese, English abridgement.)

Linton, Ralph. 1936. *The Study of Man: An Introduction*. Student's ed. New York: Appleton-Century-Crofts.

Lipke, Paul. 1984. *The Royal Ship of Cheops: A Retrospective Account of the Discovery, Restoration, and Reconstruction*. Archaeological Series 9, BAR International Series 225. London: National Maritime Museum, Greenwich.

Lissau, Steve. 1978. "Canoes of the Pacific." *Oceans* 11 (2): 46–52.

Lovell, W. George. 1992. "Heavy Shadows and Black Night: Disease and Depopulation in Colonial Spanish America." *Annals of the Association of American Geographers* 82 (3): 426–43.

Loyaza, Xavier. 2005. "Spa: Salute per Aqua, el temazcalli." *Arqueología Mexicana* 13 (74): 54–57.

Lucas, Jack A. 1978. "The Significance of Diffusion in German and Austrian Historical Ethnography." In *Diffusion and Migration: Their Roles in Cultural Development*, edited by P. G. Duke, J. Ebert, G. Langemann, and A. P. Buchner, 30–44. Calgary: University of Calgary Archaeological Association [Chacmool].

Lundy, Derek. 2000. *Godforsaken Sea: Sailing Alone through the World's Most Dangerous Waters*. New York: Anchor Books. (Originally published 1999.)

Mac Cárthaigh, Críostóir. 2008. Introduction to *Traditional Boats of Ireland: History, Folklore, and Construction*, edited by Críostóir Mac Cárthaigh, 418–27. Wilton, Cork, Ireland: Collins Press.

MacDonald, Malcolm Ross. 1971. *Encyclopedia of Discovery and Exploration*, vol. 2, *Beyond the Horizon*. London: Aldus Books.

MacIntyre, Ferren, Thomas Naji, and Kenneth W. Estep. 1998. "Shifts in Marine Biomass and the Provisioning of Voyages before AD 1500." In *Easter Island in Pacific Context. South Seas Symposium: Proceedings of the Fourth International Conference on Easter Island and East Polynesia, University of New Mexico, Albuquerque, 5–10 August 1997*, 107–12. Los Osos, CA: Bearsville and Cloud Mountain Presses, Easter Island Foundation.

Magleby, Kirk A. 1979. *A Survey of Mesoamerican Bearded Figures*. Provo, UT: Foundation for Ancient Research and Mormon Studies.

Mahan, Joseph. 1983. *The Secret: America in World History before Columbus*. Columbus, GA: J. B. Mahan.

Mahdi, Waruno. 1999. "The Dispersal of Austronesian Boat Forms in the Indian Ocean." In *Archaeology and Language III: Artefacts, Languages, and Texts*, edited by Roger Blench and Matthew Spriggs, 144–79. London: Routledge.

Mairson, Alan. 2007. "Kon-Tiki: The Sequel." *National Geographic* 212 (92): 27.

Malhi, Ripan S., Holly M. Mortensen, Jason A. Eshleman, Brian M. Kemp, Joseph G. Lorenz, Frederika A. Kaestle, John R. Johnson, Clara Gorodezky, and David Glenn Smith. 2003. "Native American mtDNA Prehistory in the American Southwest." *American Journal of Physical Anthropology* 120 (2): 108–24.

Malinowski, Bronislaw. 1922. *Argonauts of the Western Pacific*. London: Routledge and Kegan Paul.

———. 1945. *The Dynamics of Culture Change: An Inquiry into Race Relations in Africa*. New Haven, CT: Yale University Press.

Malmström, Vincent. 1997. *Cycles of the Sun, Mysteries of the Moon: The Calendar in Mesoamerican Civilization*. Austin: University of Texas Press.

Manglesdorf, Paul, and Douglas L. Oliver. 1951. "Whence Came Maize to Asia?" *Harvard University Botanical Museum Leaflets* 14 (10): 263–91.

Manguin, Pierre-Yves. 1993. "Trading Ships of the South China Sea: Shipbuilding Techniques and Their Role in the History of the Development of Asian Trade Networks." *Journal of Economic and Social History of the Orient* 36 (3): 253–80.

Manter, Harold W. 1967. "Some Aspects of the Geographical Distribution of Parasites." *Journal of Parasitology* 53 (1): 1–9.

Manzano Manzano, Juan. 1976. *Colón y su secreto*. Madrid: Ediciones Cultura Hispánica.

Marcus, G. J. 1981. *Conquest of the North Atlantic*. New York: Oxford University Press.

Marinatos, Spyridōn. 1974. *Excavations at Thera VI: 1972 Season*. Vivliothēkē tēs en Athēnais Archaiologikēs Hetaireias 64. Athens: Typographeion tōn Adelphōn Perrē.

Marszewski, Tomasz. 1978. "The Problem of the Introduction of 'Primitive' Maize into South-East Asia, Part II." *Folia Orientalia* 19: 127–63.

———. 1987. "Some Implications of the Comparative Studies of the Vernacular Names of Maize and other Cultigens from South-East Asia, Parts 1 and 2." *Sprawozdania z Posied-zen Komisji Naukowych, Polska Akademia Nauk, Oddzial w Krakowie* 28 (1–2), *Styczengrudzien:* 101–5.

Marx, Robert. 1984. "Romans in Rio? Ancient Amphorae Found in Brazil." *Oceans* 17 (4): 18–21.

Marx, Robert, with Jenifer G. Marx. 1992. *In Quest of the Great White Gods: Contact between the Old World and New World from the Dawn of History*. New York: Crown.

———. 2004. *Treasure Lost at Sea: Diving to the World's Great Shipwrecks*. Buffalo: Firefly Books.

Matawai, Manuai. 2013. "Uncharted Waters." *Nature Conservancy* (November/December): 22–23.

Matisoo-Smith, Elizabeth, and José-Miguel Ramírez-Aliaga. 2010. "Human Skeletal

Evidence of Polynesian Presence in South America? Metric Analyses of Six Crania from Mocha Island, Chile." *Journal of Pacific Archaeology* 1 (1): 76–88.

Matson, G. Albin, H. Eldon Sutton, Raul Etcheverry B., Jane Swanson, and Abner Robinson. 1967. "Distribution of Hereditary Blood Groups among Indians in South America, IV: In Chile, with Inferences concerning Genetic Connections between Polynesia and America." *American Journal of Physical Anthropology* new series, 27 (2): 157–93.

Maxwell, Thomas J. 1979. "Maize in India, 1141 A.D.?" *Stonehenge Viewpoint* 30: 3–7.

May, Natalie N. 2012. *Iconoclasm and Text Destruction in the Ancient Near East and Beyond*. Oriental Institute Seminars 8. Chicago: Oriental Institute of the University of Chicago.

May, Wayne N. 2010. "They Came from the EAST!" *Ancient American* 14 (86): 33–36.

McCall, Daniel, and Harold C. Fleming. 1999. "The Pre-Classical Circum-Mediterranean World: Who Spoke Which Languages?" In *Archaeology and Language III: Artefacts, Languages, and Texts*, edited by Roger Blench and Matthew Spriggs, 231–48. London: Routledge.

McCartney, Allen P. 1984. "Prehistory of the Aleutian Region." In *Handbook of North American Indians 5, Arctic and Subarctic*, edited by D. Damas, 19–35. Washington, DC: Smithsonian Institution.

McCulloch, J. Huston. 1988. "The Bat Creek Inscription: Cherokee or Hebrew?" *Tennessee Anthropologist* 13 (2): 79–123.

———. 1993. "The Bat Creek Inscription: Did Judean Refugees Escape to Tennessee?" *Biblical Archaeology Review* 19 (4): 46–53, 83.

———. 2011–14. "The Bat Creek Stone Revisited: A Reply to Mainfort and Kwas in *American Antiquity*." *Pre-Columbiana: A Journal of Long-Distance Contacts* 5 (2–4) (1): 142–53.

McGhee, Robert. 2005. *The Last Imaginary Place: A Human History of the Arctic World*. New York: Oxford University Press / Toronto: Key Porter Books.

McGhee, Robert, and James A. Tuck. 1977. "Did the Medieval Irish Visit Newfoundland?" *Canadian Geographical Journal* 94 (3): 66–73.

McGrail, Seán. 1987. *Ancient Boats in N.W. Europe: The Archaeology of Water Transport to AD 1500*. Harlow, UK: Longman Group.

———. 1989. "Pilotage and Navigation in the Times of St. Brendan." In *Atlantic Vision*, edited by John de Courcy Ireland and David C. Sheehy, 25–35. Dún Laoghair, Ireland: Boole Press.

———. 1996. "The Bronze Age in Northwest Europe." In *The Earliest Ships: The Evolution of Boats into Ships*, edited by Robert Gardiner. Annapolis, MD: Naval Institute Press.

———. 1997. *Studies in Maritime Archaeology*. BAR British Series 256. Oxford: John and Erica Hedges.

———. 2002. *Boats of the World: From the Stone Age to Medieval Times*. New York: Oxford University Press.

———. 2010. "The Ma'agan Mikhael Ship 3: A Reconstruction of the Hull—By Adina Ben Zeev, Ya'acov Kahanov, John Tresman, and Michal Artzy." Review. *International Journal of Nautical Achaeology* 39 (2): 446.

———. 2014. *Early Ships and Seafaring: European Water Transport*. Barnsley, UK: Pen and Sword Archaeology.

Meacham, William. 1984–85. "On the Improbability of Austronesian Origins in South China." *Asian Perspectives* 26 (1): 89–106.

Medina-Sanchez, Aaron, Donald H. Bouyer, Virginia Alcantara-Rodriguez, Claudio

Mafra, Jorge Zavala-Castro, Ted Whitworth, Vsevolod Popov, Ildefonso Fernández-Salas, and David H. Walker. 2005. "Detection of Typhus Group *Rikettsia* in *Amblyomma* Ticks in the State of Nuevo Leon, Mexico." *Annals of the New York Academy of Sciences* 1063: 327–32.

Meggers, Betty J. 1955. "The Coming of Age of American Anthropology." In *New Interpretations of Aboriginal American Culture History*, edited by Betty J. Meggers and Clifford Evans, 116–29+. Washington, DC: Anthropological Society of Washington.

———. 1975. "The Transpacific Origin of Mesoamerican Civilization: A Preliminary Review of the Evidence and Its Theoretical Implications." *American Anthropologist* 77 (1): 1–27.

———. 1998. *Enfoques teóricos para la investigación arqueológica*, vol. 1, *Evolución y difusión cultural*. Biblioteca Abya-Yala 57. Quito: Ediciones Abya-Yala.

———. 2005. "The Subversive Significance of Transpacific Contact." *NEARA Journal* 39 (2): 22–29.

Meggers, Betty J., Clifford Evans, and Emilio Estrada. 1965. *Early Formative Period of Coastal Ecuador: The Valdivia and Machalilla Phases*. Smithsonian Contributions to Anthropology 1. Washington, DC: Smithsonian Institution.

Meisel, Tony. 2000. *To the Sea: Sagas of Survival and Tales of Epic Challenge on the Seven Seas*. New York: Black Dog and Leventhal.

Melgar, José M. 1871. "Estudio sobre la antigüidad y el origen de la cabeza colossal de tipo etiopico." *Boletín de la Sociedad Mexicana de Geografía y Estadistica* 3: 104–7, 109, 118.

Meltzer, David J. 1999. "North America's Vast Legacy." *Archaeology* 52 (1): 50–59.

Melville, Herman. 1984. *Moby Dick*, and, *Billy Budd*. London: Octopus. (*Budd* orig. pub. 1891.)

Menghin, Osvaldo F. A. 1962. "Relaciones transpacificos de la cultura araucana." In *La arqueología y etnografía y sus correlaciones continentales y extracontinentales*, 90–95 and plates. Jornadas Internacionales de Arqueología y Etnografía 2. Buenos Aires: Comisión Nacional de la Revolución de Mayo.

Menzies, Gavin. 2002. *1491: The Year China Discovered America*. New York: William Morrow.

———. 2011. *The Lost Empire of Atlantis: History's Greatest Mystery Revealed*. New York: William Morrow.

Merbs, Charles F. 1992. "A New World of Disease." *Yearbook of Physical Anthropology* 35: 3–24.

Merrien, Jean [René Marie de la Poix de Freminville]. 1954. *Lonely Voyages*. Translated by J. H. Watkins. New York: G. P. Putnam's Sons.

Merrill, Elmer Drew. 1954. "The Botany of Cook's Voyages and Its Unexpected Significance in Relation to Anthropology, Biogeography, and History." *Chronica Botanica* 14 (5/6): i–iv, 161–384.

Mertz, Henriette. 1972. *Gods from the Far East: How the Chinese Discovered America*. New York: Ballantine Books. (1st ed. privately published as *Pale Ink*, Chicago, 1953.)

Messer, Ellen. 1997. "Three Centuries of Changing European Tatses for the Potato." In *Food Preferences and Taste: Continuity and Change*, edited by Helen Macbeth, 101–13. Providence, RI: Berghahn Books.

Meyers, Mark. 1985. "The Ships of Exploration and Discovery." In *Proceedings of the Sixteenth Conference on Underwater Archaeology*, edited by Paul Forsythe Johnston, 110–11. Special Publication Series 4. Glassboro, NJ: Society for Historical Archaeology.

Miles, Rebecca, Judy Barratt, and Sally McFall, eds. 2006. *Ripley's Believe It or Not!* Orlando, FL: Ripley Publishing.

Miller, Inglis J., and Frank E. Reedy Jr. 1990. "Variations in Human Taste Bud Density and Taste Intensity Perception." *Physiology and Behavior* 47 (6): 1213–19.

Miller, Mary Ellen. 2001. *The Art of Mesoamerica: From Olmec to Aztec.* 3rd ed. London: Thames and Hudson.

Milton-Thompson, G. J. 1974. "The Changing Character of the Sailor's Diet and Its Influence on Disease." In *Problems of Medicine at Sea*, 20–27. Maritime Monographs and Reports 12. Greenwich: National Maritime Museum.

Mintz, Sidney W., and Christine M. Du Bois. 2002. "The Anthropology of Food and Eating." *Annual Review of Anthropology* 31: 99–119.

Miquel, André. 1996. "Geography." In *Encyclopedia of the History of Arabic Science*, vol. 3, edited by Roshdi Rashed, 796–812. London: Routledge.

Miura, T., T Fukunaga, T. Igarashi, M. Yamashita, E. Ido, S. Funahashi, T. Ishida, K. Washio, S. Ueda, K. Hashimoto, et al. 1994. "Phylogenetic Subtypes of Human T-lymphotropic Virus Type I and Their Relations to the Anthropological Background." *Proceedings of the National Academy of Sciences U.S.A.* 91 (3): 1124–27.

Montenegro, Álvaro, Aduato Araújo, Michael Eby, Luiz Fernando Ferreira, Renée Hetherington, and Andrew J. Weaver. 2006. "Parasites, Paleoclimate, and the Peopling of the Americas." *Current Anthropology* 47 (1): 193–200.

Montenegro, Álvaro, Chris Avis, and Andrew Weaver. 2008. "Modeling the Prehistoric Arrival of the Sweet Potato in Polynesia." *Journal of Archaeological Science* 35 (2): 355–67.

Montenegro, Álvaro, Renée Hetherington, Michael Eby, and Andrew J. Weaver. 2006. "Modelling Pre-Historic Transoceanic Crossings into the Americas." *Quaternary Science Reviews: The Multidisciplinary Research and Review Journal* 25 (11–12): 1323–38.

Moody, Skye. 2006. *Washed Up: The Curious Journeys of Flotsam and Jetsam.* Seattle: Sasquatch Books.

Mookerji, Radha Kumud. 1962. *Indian Shipping: A History of the Sea-Borne Trade and Maritime Activity from the Earliest Times.* Allahabad: Kitab Mahal. (Originally published 1912.)

Moore, Clarence B. 1915. *Aboriginal Sites on Tennessee River.* Philadelphia: Academy of Natural Sciences of Philadephia.

Moreno-Mayar, J. Victor, Simon Rasmussen, Andaine Seguin-Orlando, Morten Rasmussen, Mason Liang, Siri Tennebø Flåm, Benedicte Alexandra Lie, Gregor Duncan Gilfillan, Rasmus Nielson, Erik Thorsby, Eske Willerslev, and Anna-Sapfo Maslaspinas. 2014. "Genome-Wide Ancestry Patterns in Rapanui Suggest Pre-European Admixture with Native Americans." *Current Biology* 24 (21): 2518–25.

Morgan, Pat. 2008. "Algonquin Linguistic Group and Traditions. Part II." *Ancient American* 13 (80): 6–9.

Morison, Samuel Eliot. 1942. *Admiral of the Ocean Sea: The Life of Christopher Columbus.* Boston: Little, Brown.

———. 1971. *The European Discovery of America: The Northern Voyages.* New York: Oxford University Press.

———. 1974. *The European Discovery of America: The Southern Voyages.* New York: Oxford University Press.

Morris, John. N.d. "Roatan's Ancient Underwater Secret." *Bay Islands Voice.* Accessed November 13, 2014. http://www.bayislandsvoice.com/201006.htm.

Morton, Mary Caperton. 2013. "Setting Sail on Unknown Seas." *Earth: The Science behind the Headlines* 58 (3): 30–39.

Morwood, M. J., F. Aziz, P. O'Sullivan, Nasruddin, D. R. Hobbs, and A. Raza. 1999. "Archaeological and Palaeontological Research in Central Flores, East Indonesia:

Results of Fieldwork 1997–98." *Antiquity: A Quarterly Review of World Archaeology* 73 (280): 273–86.

Mott, Lawrence V. 1997. *The Development of the Rudder: A Technological Tale.* College Station: Texas A&M University Press / London: Chatham Publishing.

Mourant, A. E. 1956. *The Distribution of Blood Groups in Animals and Humans.* Springfield, IL: Charles C. Thomas.

Mowat, Farley. 1965. *Westviking: The Ancient Norse in Greenland and North America.* Boston: Little, Brown.

———. 2000. *The Farfarers: Before the Norse.* South Royalton, VT: Steerforth Press.

Moyle, Richard. 2003. "Waning Stars—Changes to Takā's Star Knowledge." *Journal of the Polynesian Society* 112 (1): 7–31.

Mudie, Colin. 1986. "Designing Replica Boats: The Boats of St. Brendan, Sindbad and Jason." In *Sailing into the Past: Proceedings of the International Seminar on Replicas of Ancient and Medieval Vessels, Roskilde, 1984*, edited by Ole Crumlin-Pedersen and Max Vinner, 38–59. Roskilde, Denmark: Viking Ship Museum.

Mulrooney, Mara. 2013. "The Voyage of *Waka Tapu* to Rapa Nui." *Rapa Nui Journal* 27 (1): 87–89.

Nabhan, Gary Paul. 2004. *Why Some Like It Hot: Food, Genes, and Cultural Diversity.* Washington, DC: Island Press / Shearwater Books.

Nasr, Seyyed Hossein. 1968. *Science and Civilization in Islam.* Cambridge, MA: Harvard University Press.

Nebenzahl, Kenneth. 1990. *Atlas of Columbus and the Great Discoveries.* Chicago: Rand McNally.

Needham, Joseph. 1970. *Clerks and Craftsmen in China and the West: Lectures and Addresses on the History of Science and Technology.* Cambridge: Cambridge University Press.

Needham, Joseph, with Wang Lin. 1959. *Science and Civilisation in China*, vol. 3, *Mathematics and the Sciences of the Heavens and the Earth.* Cambridge: Cambridge University Press.

Needham, Joseph, Wang Lin, and Lu Gwei-djen. 1971. *Science and Civilisation in China*, vol. 4, *Physics and Physical Technology*; vol. 3, *Civil Engineering and Nautics.* Cambridge: Cambridge University Press.

Needham, Joseph, and Lu Gwei-djen. 1985. *Transpacific Echoes and Resonances: Listening Once Again.* Singapore: World Scientific.

Negueruela, I., J. Pinedo, A. Miñano, I. Arelleano, and J. S. Barba. 1995. "Seventh-Century BC Phoenician Vessel Discovered at Playa de la Isla, Mazarron, Spain." *International Journal of Nautical Archaeology* 24 (3): 189–97.

Nelson, J. G. 1963. "Drift Voyages in the Pacific." *American Neptune* 23 (2): 113–30.

Nerlich, Andreas G., Franz Parsche, Irmgard Wiest, Peter Schramel, and Udo Löhrs. 1995. "Extensive Pulmonary Hemorrhage in an Egyptian Mummy." *Virchow's Archiv* 127 (4): 423–29.

Nesbit, Mark. 2005. "Grains." In *The Cultural History of Plants*, edited by Ghillean Prance and Mark Nesbit, 45–60. New York: Routledge.

Newcomb, Robert M. 1963. *Plant and Animal Exchanges between the Old and New Worlds: Notes from a Seminar Presented by Carl Ortwin Sauer.* Los Angeles: Robert Newcomb.

Nicastro, Nicholas. 2008. *Circumference: Eratosthenes and the Ancient Quest to Measure the Globe.* New York: St. Martin's Press.

Nicklin, Keith. 1971. "Stability and Innovation in Pottery Manufacture." *World Archaeology* 3 (1): 13–48.

Niederland, William G. 1989. "Part Two." In *Maps from the Mind: Readings in Psycho-*

geography, edited by Howard F. Stein and William G. Niederland, 15–113. Norman: University of Oklahoma Press.

Nijares, Armand Salvador, Florent Détroit, Philip Piper, Rainer Grün, Peter Bellwood, Maxime Aubert, Guillaume Champion, Nida Cuevas, Alexandra De Leon, and Eusebio Dizon. 2010. "New Evidence for a 67,000-Year-Old Human Presence at Callao Cave, Luzon, Philippines." *Journal of Human Evolution* 59 (1): 123–32.

Nishimura, Shinji. 1925. *Ancient Rafts of Japan*. Tokyo: Society of Naval Architects.

Nordenskiöld, Erland. 1931. *The Origin of the Indian Civilization in South America*. Comparative Ethnological Studies 9. Gothenburg, Sweden: Elanders Boktryckeri Aktiebolag.

Normile, Dennis. 2011. "Tohoku Inundation Spurs Hunt for Ancient Tsunamis." *Science* 334 (6061): 1341–43.

Novick, Gabriel E., Corina C. Novick, Juan Yunis, Emilio Yunis, et al. 1998. "Polymorphic *Alu* Insertions and the Asian Origin of Native American Population." *Human Biology: The International Journal of Population Genetics and Anthropology* 70 (1): 23–39.

Nunn, George E. 1934. "The Mappemonde of Juan de la Cosa: A Critical Investigation of Its Date." Jenkintown, PA: George H. Beans Library.

Nunn, Patrick D. 2009. *Vanished Islands and Hidden Continents of the Pacific*. Honolulu: University of Hawai'i Press.

Obayashi, Taryo. 1959. "Divintion from Entrails among the Ancient Inca and Its Relation to Practices in Southeast Asia." *Proceedings of the International Congress of Americanists* 33: 327–32.

O'Brien, Patricia. 1972. "The Sweet Potato: Its Origin and Dispersal." *American Anthropologist* 74 (3): 342–65.

O'Connell, James F., Jim Allen, and Kristen Hawkes. 2010. "Pleistocene Sahul and the Orgins of Seafaring." In *The Global Origins and Development of Seafaring*, edited by Atholl Anderson, James H. Barrett, and Katherine V. Boyle, 57–68. McDonald Institute Monographs. Cambridge, UK: McDonald Institute for Archaeological Research.

O'Connor, Sue. 2010. "Pleistocene Migration and Colonization in the Indo-Pacific Region." In *The Global Origins and Development of Seafaring*, edited by Atholl Anderson, James H. Barrett, and Katherine V. Boyle, 41–55. McDonald Institute Monographs. Cambridge, UK: McDonald Institute for Archaeological Research.

O'Connor, Sue, Rintaro Ono, and Chris Clarkson. 2011. "Pelagic Fishing at 42,000 Years before the Present and the Maritime Skills of Modern Humans." *Science* 334 (6059): 1117–21.

Ohler, Norbert. 1989. *The Medieval Traveller*. Translated by Caroline Hillier. Woodbridge, UK: Boydell Press.

Olsen, Olaf, and Ole Crumlin-Petersen. 1969. *Fem vikingeskibe fra Roskilde Fjord (Five Viking Ships from Roskilde Fjord)*. Roskilde, Denmark: Vikingeskibshallen i Roskilde (The Viking Ship Museum in Roskilde).

Olshin, Benjamin B. 2013. *The Mysteries of the Marco Polo Maps*. Chicago: University of Chicago Press.

Olson, Sigurd F. 1961. *The Lonely Land*. New York: Alfred A. Knopf.

Olson, Steve. 2002. *Mapping Human History: Discovering the Past through Our Genes*. Boston: Houghton Mifflin.

Oppenheimer, Stephen. 1998. *Eden in the East: The Drowned Continent of Southeast Asia*. London: Weidenfeld and Nicolson.

———. 2012. "Out-of-Africa, the Peopling of Continents and Islands: Tracing Uniparental Gene Trees across the Map." *Philosophical Transactions of the Royal Society B, Biological Sciences* 367 (1590): 770–84.

Oreskes, Naomi. 1999. *The Rejection of Continental Drift: Theory and Method in American Earth Science.* New York: Oxford University Press.

Ottaway, B[arbara] S., and Ben Roberts. 2008. "The Emergence of Metalworking." In *Prehistoric Europe: Theory and Practice*, edited by Andrew James, 193–225. Oxford: Blackwell.

Padden, R. C. 1973. "On Diffusionism and Historicity." *American Historical Review* 78 (4): 987–1004.

Parfitt, Keith. 2000. "The Dover Boat." *Current Archaeology* 7 (1): 4–8.

Parfitt, Tudor. 2008. *The Lost Ark of the Covenant: Solving the 2,500-Year-Old Mystery of the Fabled Biblical Ark.* New York: HarperCollins.

Pâris, Edmond. 1843. *Essai sur la construction navale des peuples extra-européens.* Paris: A. Bertrand.

Parry, J. H. 1981. *The Discovery of the Sea.* 2nd ed. Berkeley: University of California Press.

Parsche, Franz, Svetlana Balabanova, and Wolfgang Pirsig. 1994. "Evidence of the Alkaloids Cocaine, Nicotine, Tetrahydrocannibinol and Their Metabolites in Pre-Columbian Peruvian Mummies." *Eres (Serie de Arqueología)* 5 (1): 109–16.

Parsche, Franz, and Andreas Nerlich. 1995. "Presence of Drugs in Different Tissues of an Egyptian Mummy." *Fresenius Journal of Analytic Chemistry* 352 (3–4): 380–84.

Parsonson, G. S. 1963. "The Settlement of Oceania: An Examination of the Accidental Voyage Theory." In *Polynesian Navigation: A Symposium on Andrew Sharp's Theory of Accidental Voyages*, edited by Jack Golson, 11–63. Rev. ed. Memoir 34. Wellington, NZ: Polynesian Society.

Partington, Angela, ed. 1992. *The Oxford Dictionary of Quotations.* 4th ed. Oxford: Oxford University Press.

Patai, Raphael. 1998. *The Children of Noah: Jewish Seafaring in Ancient Times.* Princeton, NJ: Princeton University Press.

Payn, Marshall. 1996. "The Tucson Artifacts: Case Closed." *NEARA Journal* 30 (3–4): 79–80.

———. 2002. "Ancients and Longitude: Did They Know It?" *NEARA Journal* 36 (1): 25–26.

Peacock, David, and Lucy Blue, eds. 2006. *Myos Hormos—Qusair al-Qudím: Roman and Islamic Ports on the Red Sea*, vol. 1, *Survey and Excavation, 1999–2003.* Oxford: Oxbow Books.

Pearce, Charles E. M., and Frances M. Pearce. 2010. *Oceanic Migration: Paths, Sequence, Timing, and Range of Prehistoric Migration in the Pacific and Indian Oceans.* Dordrecht, Netherlands: Springer.

Pearthree, Erik. 2003. "Identification de restes carbonisées de plantes non-ligneuses découvertes sur trois sites d'habitat à l'Île de Pâques." In *Archéologies en Océanie insulaire: Peuplement, sociétés et paysages*, edited by Catherine Orliac, 172–83. Paris: Éditions Artcom.

Pedersen, Ralph K. 2004. "Traditional Arabian Watercraft and the Ark of the Gilgamesh Epic: Interpretations and Realizations." *Proceedings of the Seminar for Arabian Studies* 34: 231–38.

Pellegrino, Charles. 2004. *Ghosts of Vesuvius: A New Look at the Last Days of Pompeii, How Towers Fall, and Other Strange Connections.* New York: William Morrow.

Pennington, Lee. 2009. "New Hoard of Roman Coins Found on Ohio River Near Louisville, KY." *Ancient American* 13 (83): 46–47.

Percival, W. H. 1957. "Vikings of the South Seas." *Walkabout* 23 (4): 40–41.

Perrin, Noel. 1979. *Giving up the Gun: Japan's Reversion to the Sword, 1543–1879.* Boston: D. R. Godine.

Petchey, Fiona, David J. Addison, and Andrew McAllister. 2010. "Re-interpreting Old Dates: Radiocarbon Determinations from the Tokelau Islands (South Pacific)." *Journal of Pacific Archaeology* 1 (2): 161–67.

Peterson, Erik. 2006. "Reconstruction of the Large Borobudur Outrigger Sailing Craft." In *Connected by Sea: Proceedings of the 10th International Symposium on Boat and Ship Archaeology, Roskilde, 2003,* edited by Lucy Blue, Fred Hocker, and Anton Englert, 50–56. Oxford: Oxbow Books.

Philander, S. George. 1990. *El Niño, La Niña, and the Southern Oscillation.* San Diego: Academic Press.

Phoebe Phillips Editions. 1984. *Lacquer: An International History and Illustrated Survey.* New York: Harry N. Abrams.

Pidgeon, Harry. 1950. *Around the World Single-Handed: The Cruise of the "Islander."* London: Rupert Hart-Davis. (Originally published 1930.)

Pierson, Larry J., and James R. Moriarty. 1980. "Stone Anchors: Asiatic Shipwrecks off the California Coast." *Anthropological Journal of Canada* 18 (3): 17–23.

Piggott, Stuart. 1983. *The Earliest Wheeled Transport from the Atlantic Coast to the Caspian Sea.* London: Thames and Hudson.

Pike, E. Royston. 1976. "The Natural History of a Kiss." In *Custom-Made: Introductory Readings for Cultural Anthropology,* edited by Charles C. Hughes, 89–93. 2nd ed. Chicago: Rand McNally College Publishing.

Pintet, Roland. 2010. "Japon." In *Tous les bateaux du monde,* edited by Virginie Tromparent-de Seynes and Isabelle Fortis. Grenoble: Éditions Glénat / [Paris]: Musée National de la Marine.

Plowman, Timothy. 1984. "The Origin, Evolution, and Diffusion of Coca, *Erythroxylon* spp., in South and Central America." In *Pre-Columbian Plant Migration: Papers Presented at the Pre-Columbian Plant Migration Symposium, 44th International Congress of Americanists, Manchester, England,* edited by Doris Stone, 125–63. Papers of the Peabody Museum of Archaeology and Ethnology, Harvard University 76. Cambridge, MA.

Plummer, Katherine. 1991. *The Shogun's Reluctant Ambassadors: Sea Drifters in the North Pacific.* North Pacific Studies Series 17. Portland: Oregon Historical Society.

Pohl, Frederick. 1973. "Did Ancient Romans Reach America?" *New Diffusionist* 3 (10): 23–37.

Pokharia, Anil K. 2008. "Palaeoethnobotanical Record of Cultivated Crops and Associated Weeds and Wild Taxa from Neolithic Site, Tokwa, Uttar Pradesh, India." *Current Science* [Bangalore] 94 (2): 248–55.

Pokharia, Anil K., and K. S. Saraswat. 1998/99. "Plant Economy during Kushana Period (100–300 A.D.) at Ancient Sanghol, Punjab." *Prāgdhārā: Journal of the U[ttar] P[radesh] State Archaeological Organisation* 9: 75–104.

Polastron, Lucien X. 2007. *Books on Fire: The Destruction of Libraries throughout History.* Rochester, VT: Inner Traditions.

Pollini, John, ed. 2005. *Terra Marique: Studies in Art History and Marine Archaeology.* Oxford: Oxbow Books.

Pollmer, Udo. 2000. "Chemische Nachweise von Suchtmitteleln des Altertums." In *Tagungsberichte Robert Freiherr von Heine-Geldern: Tagung anlässlich des 30. Todestages, 30. April–3 Mai 1998,* edited by Christine Pellech, 235–51. Acta Ethnologica et Linguistica 12. Vienna: Föhrenau.

Polo, Marco. 1958. *The Travels of Marco Polo.* Translated by Ronald Latham. Harmondsworth, UK: Penguin Books.

Pomey, Patrice. 1985. "Mediterranean Sewn Boats in Antiquity." In *Sewn Plank Boats: Archaeological and Ethnographic Papers Based on Those Presented to a Conference at Greenwich in November, 1984,* edited by Seán McGrail and Eric Kentley, 35–48. National Maritime Museum, Greenwich, Archaeological Series 10, BAR International Series 276. Oxford: [British Archaeological Reports].

Pomey, Patrice, and André Tchernia. 1978. "Le tonnage maximum des navires de commerce romains." *Archaeonautica* 2: 233–51.

Porter, Eliot, and James Gleick. 1990. *Nature's Chaos.* New York: Viking Penguin.

Posdneeff, V. 1929. "The Wanderings of the Japanese beyond the Seas." *Transactions of the Asiatic Society of Japan* 2nd ser. 6: 20–51.

Powell, Eric A. 2009. "Origins of Whaling: Chukotka Peninsula, Russia." *Archaeology* 62 (1): 27.

Powell, Mary Lucas, and Della Collins Cook, eds. 2005. *The Myth of Syphilis: The Natural History of Treponematosis in North America.* Florida Museum of Natural History, Ripley P. Bullen Series. Gainesville: University Press of Florida.

Pretor-Pinney, Gavin. 2010. *The Wavewatcher's Companion.* London: Bloomsbury.

Price, Derek de Solla. 1974. *Gears from the Greeks: The Antikythera Mechanism—A Calendar Computer from ca. 80 B.C.* Transactions of the American Philosophical Society 64, no. 7. Philadelphia: American Philosophical Society.

Pringle, Heather. 2012. "Vikings and Native Americans." *National Geographic* 222 (5): 80–93.

Prins, A. H. J. 1986. *A Handbook of Sewn Boats: The Ethnography and Archaeology of Archaic Plank-Built Craft.* Maritime Monographs and Reports 59. Greenwich: National Maritime Museum.

Pulak, Cemal. 2008. "The Uluburun Shipwreck and Late Bronze Age Trade." In *Beyond Babylon: Art, Trade, and Diplomacy in the Second Millennium B.C.,* edited by Joan Aruz, Kim Benzel, and Jean M. Evans, 288–310. New York: Metropolitan Museum of Art / New Haven, CT: Yale University Press.

Qian, Sima. 1994. *Historical Records,* 25–50. Translated by Raymond Dawson. Oxford: Oxford University Press.

Quereshi, Rahimullah, Henry Magnusson, and Jan-Olof Traung. 1955. "West Pakistan Fishing Craft." In *Fishing Boats of the World.* London: The Fishing News—Arthur J. Heighway Publications.

Quimby, George I. 1985. "Japanese Wrecks, Iron Tools, and Prehistoric Indians on the Northwest Coast." *Arctic Anthropology* 22 (2): 7–15.

Raff, Jennifer A., and Deborah A. Bolnik. 2015. "Does Mitochondrial Haplogroup X Indicate Ancient Trans-Atlantic Migration to the Americas? A Critical Re-Evaluation." *Paleoamerica: A Journal of Early Human Migration and Dispersal* 1 (4): 297–304.

Rafnsson, Sveinbjörn. 1997 "The Atlantic Islands." In *The Oxford Illustrated History of the Vikings,* edited by Peter Sawyer, 110–33. Oxford: Oxford University Press.

Raghavan, Maanasa. 2014. "Two Ancient Human Genomes Reveal Polynesian Ancestry among the Indigenous Botocudos of Brazil." *Currrent Biology* 24 (21): R1035–37.

Ragué, Beatrix von. 1976. *A History of Japanese Lacquerware.* Toronto: University of Toronto Press.

Ramenofsky, Ann F. 1987. *Vectors of Death: The Archaeology of European Contact.* Albuquerque: University of New Mexico Press.

Ramenofsky, Ann F., Alicia K. Wilbur, and Anne C. Stone. 2003. "Native American Disease History: Past, Present and Future Directions." *World Archaeology* 35 (2): 241–57.

Ramírez-Aliaga, José Miguel. 2011. "The Mapuche Connection." In *Polynesians in America: Pre-Columbian Contacts with the New World*, edited by Terry L. Jones, Alice A. Storey, Elizabeth A. Matisoo-Smith, and José Miguel Ramírez-Aliaga, 95–109. Lanham, MD: AltaMira Press.

Ramskou, Thorkild. 2000. "Early Navigation of the Vikings." *Pre-Columbiana: A Journal of Long-Distance Contacts* 2 (1): 42–48. (Translated from "La navigation primitive des Vikings." In *Les Vikings et leur civilisation: problèmes actuels*, edited by Régis Boyer. Bibliothèque Arctique et Antarctique 5: 41–48. Paris: Centre d'Études Arctiques.)

Rando, Juan Carlos, Harald Pieper, and Josep Antoni Alcover. 2014. "Radiocarbon Evidence for the Presence of Mice on Madeira Island (North Atlantic) One Millennium Ago." *Proceedings of the Royal Society B, Biological Sciences* 281 (1780): 20133126.

Rao, S. R. 1986. "Trade and Cultural Contacts between Bahrain and India in the Third and Second Millennium B.C." In *Bahrain through the Ages: The Archaeology*, edited by Haya Ali Al Khalifa and Michael Rice, 376–81. London: KPI.

Raoult, Didier, David L. Reed, Katharina Dittmar, Jeremy J. Kirchman, Jean-Marc Rolain, Sonia Guillen, and Jessica E. Light. 2008. "Molecular Identification of Lice from Pre-Columbian Mummies." *Journal of Infectious Diseases* 197 (11): 535–43.

Ratnagar, Shereen. 1981. *Encounters: The Westerly Trade of the Harappa Civilization*. New Delhi: Oxford University Press.

Reader's Digest. 1978. *The World's Last Mysteries*. Pleasantville, NY: Reader's Digest Association.

Rees, Charlotte Harris. 2013. *Did Ancient Chinese Explore America?* Durham, NC: Torchflame Books.

———. 2014. *New World Secrets on Ancient Asian Maps*. Durham, NC: Torchflame Books.

Reichard, Gladys A. 1963. *Navaho Religion: A Study of Symbolism*. Bollingen Series 18. New York: Bollingen Foundation / Pantheon Books.

Reina, Ruben E. 1966. *The Law of the Saints*. Indianapolis: Bobbs-Merrill.

Reinhard, Karl J. 1990. "Archaeoparasitology in North America." *American Journal of Physical Anthropology* 82 (2): 145–63.

———. 1992. "Parasitology as an Interpretive Tool in Archaeology." *American Antiquity* 57 (2): 231–45.

Rendell, L., R. Boyd, D. Cownden, M. Enquist, M. Eriksson, M. W. Feldman, L. Fogarty, S. Ghirlanda, T. Lillicrap, and K. N. Laland. 2010. "Why Copy Others? Insights from the Social Learning Strategies Tournement." *Science* 328 (5975): 208–13.

Renner, Susanne. 2004. "Plant Dispersal across the Tropical Atlantic by Wind and Sea Currents." *International Journal of Plant Sciences* 165 (4) Supplement: S23–S33.

Rensch, Karl H. 1991. "Polynesian Plant Names: Linguistic Analysis and Ethnobotany, Expectations and Limitations." In *Islands, Plants, and Polynesians: An Introduction to Polynesian Ethnobotany*, edited by Paul Alan Cox and Sandra A. Banack, 97–111. Portland, OR: Dioscorides Press.

Reynolds, Clark G. 1996. "The Maritime Character of Minoan Civilization." *American Neptune* 56. (4): cover, 315–51.

Reynolds, Gretchen. 2000. "Tori Murden: Head-to-Head with the High Seas." *National Geographic Adventure* 2 (1): 114–16.

Rianti, Puji. 2014. Untitled photograph. *Antiquity: A Quarterly Review of World Archaeology* 88 (339): 6.

Richardson, James B., III. 1972. "The Pre-Columbian Distribution of the Bottle Gourd (*Lagenaria siceraria*): A Re-evaluation." *Economic Botany* 26 (4): 265–73.

Richardson, Philip L. 1985. "Derelicts and Drifters." *Natural History* 94 (6): 42–49, 96.

Rickman, Geoffrey. 1980. *The Corn Supply of Ancient Rome*. Oxford: Clarendon Press of Oxford University Press.

Ridley, Henry N. 1930. *The Dispersal of Plants throughout the World*. Ashford, UK: L. Reeve.

Riesenberg, S. H. 1965. "Table of Voyages Affecting Micronesian Islands." *Oceania* 36 (2): 155–70.

Riley, Carroll L., J. Charles Kelly, Campbell W. Pennington, and Robert L. Rands, eds. 1971. *Man across the Sea: Problems of Pre-Columbian Contacts*. Austin: University of Texas Press.

Rivers, W. H. R. 1912. "The Disappearance of Useful Arts." In *Festkriff tillegnad Edvard Westermarck i Anledning av hans Femtioårsdag den 20 November 1912*, edited by Ola Castrén, Yrjö Hirn, Rolf Lagerborg, and A. Wallenskiöld, 109–30. Helsinki: J. Simelii Aringars Boktryckeriaktiebolag.

Roberts, Alexander, James Donaldson, and Arthur Cleveland Coxe, eds. 2007. *The Ante-Nicene Fathers*, vol. 2. Cosimo Classics, Religion and Spirituality. New York: Cosimo. (Originally published 1885.)

Roberts, Charlotte A., and Jane E. Buikstra. 2003. *The Bioarchaeology of Tuberculosis: A Global View on a Reemerging Disease*. Gainesville: University Press of Florida.

Robinson, Dougal. 1973. *Survive the Savage Sea*. Harmondsworth, UK: Penguin.

Robinson, Eugenia, J. Marlen Garnica, Patricia Farrell, Dorothy Freidel, Kitty Emery, Marilyn Beaudry-Corbett, and David Lentz. 2000. "El Preclásico en Urías: Una adaptación ambiental y cultural en el Valle de Antigua." In *Simposio de investigaciones arqueológicas en Guatemala, 1999*, edited by Juan Pedro Laporte and Hector Escobedo, 841–48. Guatemala City: Instituto de Antropología e Historia, Museo Nacional de Antropología y Etnología / Asociación Tikal.

Robinson, M. E., D. W. Shimwell, and G. Cribbin. 1999. "Re-assessing the Logboat from Lurgan Townland, Co. Galway, Ireland." *Antiquity: A Quarterly Review of World Archaeology* 73 (282): 903–8.

Roewar, Lutz, Michael Nothnagel, Leonor Gusmão, Veronica Gomes, Miguel González, Daniel Corach, Andrea Sala, Evguenia Alechine, Teresinha Palha, Ney Santos, Andrea Ribeiro-dos-Santos, Maria Geppert, Sascha Willuweit, et al. 2013. "Continent-Wide Decoupling of Y-Chromosomal Genetic Variation from Language and Geography in Native South Americans." *PLoS Genetics* 9 (4): e1003460; doi:10.1371/journal.pgen.1003460.

Roller, Duane W. 2006. *Through the Pillars of Herakles: Greco-Roman Exploration of the Atlantic*. New York: Routledge.

Romm, James S. 1992. *The Edges of the Earth in Ancient Thought*. Princeton, NJ: Princeton University Press. (Reprint 2001, DIANE Publishing, Collingdale, PA.)

Ronan, Avraham. 2000. "Besieged by Technology." *Scientific American Discovering Archaeology* 2 (1): 92–97.

Ronan, Colin A. 1986. *The Shorter Science and Civilisation in China: An Abridgement of Joseph Needham's Original Text*, vol. 3. Cambridge: Cambridge University Press.

Ropars, Guy, Gabriel Gorre, Albert Le Floch, Jay Enoch, and Vasudevan Lakshminarayanan. 2012. "A Depolarizer as a Possible Precise Sunstone for Viking Navigation by Polarized Skylight." *Proceedings of the Royal Society A: Mathematical and Physical Sciences* 468 (2139): 671–84.

Rose, Mark. 1999. "Pre-Clovis Surprise." *Archaeology* 52 (4): 18.

Rosendahl, Paul, and D. E. Yen. 1971. "Fossil Sweet Potato Remains from Hawaii." *Journal of the Polynesian Society* 80 (3): 378–85.

Rossabi, Morris. 1997. "The Silk Trade and Central Asia." In *When Silk Was Gold: Central Asian and Chinese Textiles*, edited by James C. Y. Watt and Anne E. Wardwell, 7–19. New York: Metropolitan Museum of Art.

Rougé, Jean. 1981. *Ships and Fleets of the Ancient Mediterranean*. Translated by Susan Fraser. Middletown, CT: Wesleyan University Press.

Roullier, Caroline, Laure Benoit, Doyle B. McKey, and Vincent Lebot. 2013. "Historical Collections Reveal Patterns of Diffusion of Sweet Potato in Oceania Obscured by Modern Plant Movements and Recombination." *Proceedings of the National Academy of Sciences USA* 110 (6): 2205–10.

Rowe, John Howland. 1948. "The Kingdom of Chimor." *Acta Americana* 6 (1–2): 26–59.

———. 1966. "Diffusionism in Archaeology." *American Antiquity* 31 (3, pt. 1): 334–37.

Rozin, Elizabeth, and Paul Rozin. 1981. "Culinary Themes and Variations." *Natural History* 90 (2): 6, 8, 12, 64.

Rudenko, Sergei I. 1970. *Frozen Tombs of Siberia: The Pazyryk Burials of Iron Age Horsemen*. Berkeley: University of California Press.

Russell, Jeffrey Burton. 1991. *Inventing the Flat Earth: Columbus and Modern Historians*. New York: Praeger.

Rutter, Owen. 1936. *Turbulent Journey*. London: Ivor Nicholson and Watson.

Sabloff, Jeremy A. 1989. *The Cities of Ancient Mexico: Reconstructing a Lost World*. New York: Thames and Hudson.

Sakamoto, Kazuko. 1985. "Ancient Pile Textiles from the At-Tar Caves in Iraq." In *Oriental Carpet and Textile Studies I*, edited by Robert Pinner and Walter Denny, 9–17. London: Published in association with Hali magazine.

Salmond, Anne. 2008. "Voyaging Exchanges: Tahitian Pilots and European Navigators." In *Canoes of the Grand Ocean*, edited by Anne Di Piazza and Erik Pearthree, 23–46. BAR International Series 1802. Oxford: Archaeopress.

Sanchez-Mazas, Alicia, Jean-François Lemaître, and Mathias Currat. 2012. "Distinct Evolutionary Strategies of Human Leucocyte Antigen Loci in Pathogen-Rich Environments." *Philosophical Transactions of the Royal Society B: Biological Sciences* 367 (1590): 830–39.

Sanders, Rick. 2003. "Was the *Antikythera* an Ancient Instrument for Longitude Determination?" *21st Century Science and Technology Magazine* (Spring). Accessed November 13, 2014. http://www.21stcenturysciencetech.com/articles/Spring03/Antikythera .html.

Sanders, Tao Tao Liu. 1980. *Dragons, Gods, and Spirits from Chinese Mythology*. Rotterdam: Peter Lowe.

Sanderson, Ivar T. 1956. *Follow the Whale*. Boston: Little, Brown.

Sandler, Martin W. 2008. *Atlantic Ocean: The Illustrated History of the Ocean That Changed the World*. New York: Sterling.

Sandweiss, Daniel H., Heather McGinnis, Richard L. Burger, Asunción Cano, Bernardino Ojeda, Rolando Paredes, María del Carmen Sandweiss, and Michael D. Glassock. 1998. "Quebrada Jaguay: Early South American Maritime Adaptations." *Science* 281 (5384): 1830–32.

Sansome, G. B. 1943. *Japan: A Short Cultural History*. Rev. ed. New York: D. Appleton-Century.

Santley, Robert S., Phillip J. Arnold III, and Christopher A. Pool. 1989. "The Ceramics Production System at Matacapan, Veracruz, Mexico." *Journal of Field Archaeology* 16 (1): 107–32.

Saraswat, K. S., N. K. Sharma, and D. C. Saini. 1994. "Plant Economy at Ancient Narhan (Ca. 1,300 B.C.–300/400 A.D.)." In *Excavations at Narhan (1984–89)*, by

Purushottam Singh, 255–337. Varanasi, India: Department of Ancient Indian History, Culture, and Archaeology, Banares Hindu University / Delhi: B. R. Publishing.

Sarkar, Himansu Bhusan. 1970. *Some Contribution[s] of India to the Ancient Civilization of Indonesia and Malaya*. Calcutta: Punthi Pustak.

Sarton, George. 1970. *A History of Science*, vol. 1, *Ancient Science through the Golden Age of Greece*. New York: W. W. Norton. (Originally published 1953.)

———. 1993. *A History of Science*, vol. 2, *Hellenistic Science and Culture in the Last Three Centuries B.C.* New York: Dover. (Originally published 1959.)

Sauer, Carl O. 1952. *Agricultural Origins and Dispersals: The Domestication of Animals and Foodstuffs*. Bowman Memorial Lectures. New York: American Geographical Society. (Reprint as *Seeds, Spades, Hearths, and Herds: The Domestication of Animals and Foodstuffs*, Cambridge, MA: MIT Press, 1972.)

———. 1962. "Maize into Europe." *Proceedings, International Congress of Americanists* 34: 777–88.

———. 1968. *Northern Mists*. Berkeley: University of California Press.

Sauer, Jonathan D. 1950. "The Grain Amaranths: A Survey of Their History and Classification." *Annals of the Missouri Botanical Garden* 37: 561–632.

———. 1968. "The Problem of the Introduction of New World Grain Amaranths to the Old World (Resumé)." *International Congress of Americanists* 37 (4): 127–28.

Savoy, Gene. 1974. *On the Trail of the Feathered Serpent*. Indianapolis: Bobbs-Merrill.

Sawatzky, H. L., and W. H. Lehn. 1976. "The Arctic Mirage and the Early North Atlantic." *Science* 192 (4246): 1300–1305.

Scandurra, Enrico. 1972. "The Maritime Republics: Medieval and Renaissance Ships in Italy." In *A History of Seafaring Based on Underwater Archaeology*, edited by George F. Bass, 205–24. New York: Walker.

Schaaf, Peter, and Günther A. Wagner. 2001. "Comments on 'Mesoamerican Evidence of Pre-Columbian Contacts' by Hristov and Genovés, in *Ancient Mesoamerica* 10: 207–213, 1999." *Ancient Mesoamerica* 12 (1): 79–81.

Schillaci, Michael A., Erik G. Ozolins, and Thomas C. Windes. 2001. "Multivariate Assessment of Biological Relationships among Prehistoric Southwest Amerindian Populations." In *Following Through: Papers in Honor of Phyllis S. Davis*, edited by Regge N. Wiseman, Thomas C. O'Laughlin, and Cordelia T. Snow, 133–49. Archaeological Society of New Mexico 27. Albuquerque: Archaeological Society of New Mexico.

Schledermann, P., and K. M. McCullough. 2003. "Inuit-Norse Contact in the Smith Sound Region." In *Contact, Continuity, and Collapse: The Norse Colonization of the North Atlantic*, edited by James H. Barrett, 183–205. Studies in the Early Middle Ages 5. Turnhout, Belgium: Brepols.

Schlesinger, Victoria. 2013. "An Extreme Life." *Archaeology* 66 (5): 37–41.

Schmidt, Wilhelm. 1939. *The Culture Historical Method of Ethnology: The Scientific Approach to the Racial Question*. Translated by S. A. Sieber. New York: Fortuny's.

Schnall, Uwe. 1996. "Early Shiphandling and Navigation in Northern Europe." In *The Earliest Ships: The Evolution of Boats into Ships*, edited by Robert Gardiner, 120–28. Annapolis, MD: Naval Institute Press.

Schneider, Harold K. 1977. "Prehistoric Transpacific Contact and the Theory of Culture Change." *American Anthropologist* 79 (1): 9–25.

Schoch, Robert M., with Robert Aquinas McNally. 2003. *Voyages of the Pyramid Builders: The True Origins of the Pyramids from Lost Egypt to Ancient America*. New York: Jeremy P. Tarcher / Putnam.

Schoeser, Mary. 2003. *World Textiles: A Concise History*. New York: Thames and Hudson.

Schorger, A. W. 1966. *The Wild Turkey: Its History and Domestication.* Norman: University of Oklahoma Press.

Schuetz-Miller, Mardith K. 2012. "New World Sacred Architecture." *Journal of the Southwest* 54 (2): entire issue.

Schurr, Theodore G. 2004b. "Molecular Genetic Diversity in Siberians and Native Americans Suggests an Early Colonization of the New World." In *Entering America: Northeast Asia and Beringia before the Last Glacial Maximum,* edited by D. B. Madsen, 187–238+. Salt Lake City: University of Utah Press.

Schuster, Carl, and Edmund Carpenter. 1996. *Patterns That Connect: Social Symbolism in Ancient and Tribal Art.* New York: Harry N. Abrams.

Schwartz, Marion. 1997. *A History of Dogs in the Early Americas.* New Haven, CT: Yale University Press.

Seaver, Kirsten A. 1996. *The Frozen Echo: Greenland and the Exploration of North America, ca. A.D. 1000–1500.* Stanford, CA: Stanford University Press.

Selkirk, Raymond. 1995. *On the Trail of the Legions.* Ipswich, UK: Anglia Publishing.

Service, Robert F. 1996. "Rock Chemistry Traces Early Traders." *Science* 274 (5295): 2012.

Settipane, Guy A., ed. 1995. *Columbus and the New World Medical Implications.* Providence, RI: OceanSide Publications.

Severin, Tim. 1978. *The Brendan Voyage.* New York: McGraw-Hill.

———. 1983. *The Sindbad Voyage.* New York: G. P. Putnam's Sons.

———. 1985. *The Jason Voyage: The Quest for the Golden Fleece.* New York: Simon and Schuster.

———. 1994. *The China Voyage: Across the Pacific by Bamboo Raft.* Reading, MA: Addison-Wesley.

———. 1997. *The Spice Islands Voyage: The Quest of Alfred Wallace, the Man Who Shared Darwin's Discovery of Evolution.* New York: Carroll and Graf.

Sferrazza, Agostino. 2010. "The American Denarius." *Epigraphic Society Occasional Papers* 28: 98–109. (Translated from "Le denier américain." *Bulletin du Cercle Numismatique Liègeois.*)

Shanks, Herschel. 2000. "Against the Tide: An Interview wih Maverick Scholar Cyrus Gordon." *Biblical Archaeology Review* 26 (6): 52–63.

Shao, Paul. 1976. *Asiatic Influences in Pre-Columbian American Art.* Ames: Iowa State University Press.

———. 1983. *The Origin of Ancient American Cultures.* Ames: Iowa State University Press.

Sharp, Andrew. 1957. *Ancient Voyagers in the Pacific.* Harmondsworth, UK: Penguin.

Shepard, Anna O. 1942. "Rio Grande Glaze Paint Ware: A Study Illustrating the Place of Ceramic Technological Analysis in Archaeological Research." *Carnegie Institution Contributions to American Anthropology and History* 7 (39): 129–262.

Sherner, Michael. 2011. *The Believing Brain: From Ghosts and Gods to Politics and Conspiracies—How We Construct Beliefs and Reinforce Them as Truths.* New York: Henry Holt.

Shields, Gerald F., Andrea M. Schmiechen, Barbara L. Frazier, Alan Redd, Michail I. Voevoda, Judy K. Reed, and R. H. Ward. 1993. "mtDNA Sequences Suggest a Recent Evolutionary Divergence for Beringian and Northern North American Populations." *American Journal of Human Genetics* 53 (3): 549–62.

Shimeda, Izumi. 1994. *Pampa Grande and the Mochica Culture.* Austin: University of Texas Press.

Siers, James. 1977. *Taratai: A Pacific Adventure.* Wellington, NZ: Millwood Press.

Simmons, Alan. 2012. "Mediterranean Island Voyages." *Science* 338 (6109): 895–97.

Simoons, Frederick J. 1970. "The Traditional Limits of Milking and Milk Use in Southern Asia." *Anthropos* 65: 547–93.

———. 1991. *Food in China: A Cultural and Historical Inquiry.* Boca Raton, FL: CRC Press.

———. 1994. *Eat Not This Flesh: Food Avoidances from Prehistory to the Present.* 2nd ed. Madison: University of Wisconsin Press.

Sitholey, R. V. 1976. "Plants Represented in Ancient Indian Sculpture." *Geophytology: An International Journal of Paleobotany, Palynology and Allied Sciences* 6 (1): 15–26.

Skjölsvold, A. 1961. "Site E-2, a Circular Stone Dwelling, Anakena." In *Norwegian Archaeological Expedition to Easter Island and the East Pacific (1955–1956)*, vol. 1, *Archaeology of Easter Island*, edited by Thor Heyerdahl and Edwin N. Ferdon, 295–303. Monographs of the School of American Research and the Museum of New Mexico 24. Stockholm: Forum Publishing House / Santa Fe: School of American Research / London: George Allen and Unwin.

Slocum, Joshua. 1962. *Sailing Alone around the World* and *Voyage of the Liberdade.* New York: Collier Books. (Originally published 1900 and 1890, respectively.)

Smith, Anita. 1995. "The Need for Lapita: Explaining Change in the Late Holocene Pacific Archaeological Record." *World Archaeology* 26 (3): 366–79.

Smith, David Glenn, Ripan S. Malhi, Jason Eshleman, Joseph G. Lorenz, and Frederika A. Kaestle. 1999. "Distribution of mtDNA Haplotype X among Native North Americans." *American Journal of Physical Anthropology* 110 (3): 271–84.

Smith, E. Baldwin. 1950. *The Dome: A Study in the History of Ideas.* Princeton Monographs in Art and Archaeology 25. Princeton, NJ: Princeton University Press.

Smith, Joshua D. 2011. *Egypt and the Origin of Civilization: The British School of Culture Diffusion, 1890s–1940s* 1. Charleston, SC: Vindication Press.

Smole, William J. 2002. "Plantain (*Musa*) Cultivation in Pre-Columbian South America: An Overview of the Circumstantial Evidence." *Pre-Columbiana: A Journal of Long-Distance Contacts* 2 (4): 269–96.

Snow, Dean, and Kim M. Lamphear. 1988. "European Contact and Indian Depopulation in the Northeast: The Timing of the First Epidemics." *Ethnohistory* 35, (1): 5–33.

Snow, Theodor P. 1985. *The Dynamic Universe: An Introduction to Astronomy.* St. Paul, MN: West Publishing.

Sobel, Dava. 1995. *Longitude: The True Story of a Lone Genius Who Solved the Greatest Scientific Problem of His Time.* London: Fourth Estate.

Social Science Research Council Summer Seminar on Acculturation. 1954. "Acculturation: An Exploratory Formulation." *American Anthropologist* 56 (6): 973–1002.

Sokoloff, Valentin A. 1982. *Ships of China.* San Bruno, CA: V. A. Sokoloff.

Soper, F. L. 1920. "The Report of a Nearly Pure Ancylostoma Duodenale Infestation in Native South American Indians and a Discussion of Its Ethnological Significance." *American Journal of Hygiene* 7 (2): 174–84.

Soren, David, Aïcha Ben Abed Ben Khader, and Hédi Slim. 1990. *Carthage: Uncovering the Mysteries and Splendors of Ancient Tunisia.* New York: Simon and Schuster.

Sorenson, John L. 1955. "Some Mesoamerican Traditions of Immigration by Sea." *El México Antiguo* 8: 425–37. (Reprinted as SOR-55, Foundation for Ancient Research and Mormon Studies. Provo, UT.)

———. 1981. *Wheeled Figurines in the Ancient World.* Preliminary Report SOR-81. Provo, UT: Foundation for Ancient Research and Mormon Studies.

———. 1998. "Bibliographica Pre-Columbiana." *Pre-Columbiana: A Journal of Long-Distance Contacts* 1 (1 and 2): 143–54.

———. 2002. "Bibliographica Pre-Columbiana." *Pre-Columbiana: A Journal of Long-Distance Contacts* 2 (4): 349–58.

Sorenson, John L., and Carl L. Johannessen. 2009. *World Trade and Biological Exchanges before 1492*. New York: iUniverse.

———. 2013. *World Trade and Biological Exchanges before 1492*, rev. and exp. ed. Eugene, OR: John Sorenson and Carl Johannessen.

Sorenson, John L., and Martin H. Raish. 1996. *Pre-Columbian Contact with the Americas across the Oceans: An Annotated Bibliography*. 2nd rev. ed. Provo, UT: Research Press.

Soule, Gardner. 1976. *Men Who Dared the Sea: The Ocean Adventures of the Ancient Mariners*. New York: Thomas Y. Crowell.

Spate, O. H. K. 1979. *The Spanish Lake*. Minneapolis: University of Minnesota Press.

Speck, Gordon. 1970. *Northwest Explorations*. Edited by L. K. Phillips. Portland, OR: Binford and Mort.

Spence, Kate. 2000. "Ancient Egyptian Chronology and the Astronomical Orientation of the Pyramids." *Nature* 408 (6810): 320–24.

Speth, William W. 1987. "Historicism: The Disciplinary World View of Carl O. Sauer." In *Carl O. Sauer: A Tribute*, edited by Martin S. Kenzer, 11–39. Corvallis: Oregon State University Press.

———. 1999. *How It Came to Be: Carl O. Sauer, Franz Boas, and the Meanings of Anthropogeography*. Ellensburg, WA: Ephemera Press.

Spiess, Gerry, with Marlin Bree. 1981. *Alone against the Atlantic*. Minneapolis: Control Data Publishing.

Spinden, Herbert J. 1933. "Origins of the Civilizations in Central America and Mexico." In *The American Aborigines: Their Origin and Antiquity, A Collection of Papers by Ten Authors*, edited by Diamond Jenness, 217–46. Toronto: University of Toronto Press.

Spriggs, Matthew. 1997. *The Island Melanesians*. Cambridge, MA: Blackwell.

Spruytte, Jean. 2010. "La roue pleine et ses dérivés." *Techniques and Culture* 54–55: 473–83.

Stanford, Dennis J., and Bruce A. Bradley. 2012. *Across Atlantic Ice: The Origin of America's Clovis Culture*. Berkeley: University of California Press.

Steffy, J. Richard. 1985. "The Kyrenia Ship: An Interim Report on Its Hull Construction." *American Journal of Archaeology* 89 (1): 71–101.

———. 1994. *Wooden Ship Building and the Interpretation of Shipwrecks*. College Station: Texas A&M University Press.

Steinmayer, Alwin G., Jr., and Jean MacIntosh Turfa. 1996. "Effects of Shipworm on the Performance of Ancient Mediterranean Ships." *International Journal of Nautical Archaeology* 25 (2): 104–21.

Stengel, Mark K. 2000. "The Diffusionists Have Landed." *Atlantic Monthly* 285 (1): cover, 35–39, 42–44, 46–48.

Stenger, Alison. 2005. "Physical Evidence of Shipwrecks on the Oregon Coast in Prehistory." *Current Archaeological Happenings in Oregon* 30 (1): 9–13.

Stewart, T. D. 1943. "Skeletal Remains from Paracas, Peru." *American Journal of Physical Anthropology* new series 1 (1): 47–63.

Stewart, Tamara. 2012–13. "Evidence of Norse in Arctic Canada." *American Archaeology* 16 (4): 7.

Stickel, E. Gary. 1983. "The Mystery of the Prehistoric 'Chinese Anchors': Toward Research Designs for Underwater Archaeology." In *Shipwreck Anthropology*, edited by Richard A. Gould, 219–44+. Albuquerque: University of New Mexico Press.

Stirling, Matthew W. 1939. "Discovering the New World's Oldest Dated Work of Man." *National Geographic Magazine* 76 (2): 183–218.

Stokes, John F. G. 1934. "Japanese Cultural Influences in Hawaii." *Pacific Science Congress, Proceedings* 5 (4): 2791–803. (Reprint *Pre-Columbiana: A Journal of Long-Distance Contacts* 1 [3 and 4]: 236–47.)

Stölting, Siegfried. 1997. "The Boats of Slettnes: Sources of Stone Age Shipbuilding in Northern Scandinavia." *International Journal of Nautical Archaeology* 26 (1): 17–25.

Stonor, C. R., and Edgar Anderson. 1949. "Maize among the Hill Peoples of Assam." *Annals of the Missouri Botanical Garden* 36: 355–404.

Storey, Alice A., Andrew C. Clarke, and Elizabeth A. Matisoo-Smith. 2011. "Identifying Contact with the Americas: A Commensal-Based Approach." In *Polynesians in America: Pre-Columbian Contacts with the New World*, edited by Terry L. Jones, Alice A. Storey, Elizabeth A. Matisoo-Smith, and José Miguel Ramírez-Aliaga, 111–38. Lanham, MD: AltaMira Press.

Storey, Alice A., Daniel Quiróz, Nancy Beavan, and Elizabeth A. Matisoo-Smith. 2011. "Pre-Columbian Chickens of the Americas: A Critical Review of the Hypotheses and Evidence for Their Origins." *Rapa Nui Journal* 25 (2): 5–19.

Storey, Alice A., Daniel Quiróz, and Elizabeth A. Mattisoo-Smith. 2011. "A Reappraisal of the Evidence for Pre-Columbian Introduction of Chickens to the Americas." In *Polynesians in America: Pre-Columbian Contacts with the New World*, edited by Terry L. Jones, Alice A. Storey, Elizabeth A. Matisoo-Smith, and José Miguel Ramírez-Aliaga, 139–70. Lanham, MD: AltaMira Press.

Storey, Alice A., José Miguel Ramírez, Daniel Quiroz, David B. Burley, David J. Addison, Richard Walter, Atholl J. Anderson, Terry L. Hunt, J. Stephen Athens, Leon Huynen, and Elizabeth A. Mattisoo-Smith. 2007. "Radiocarbon and DNA Evidence for a Pre-Columbian Introduction of Polynesian Chickens to Chile." *Proceedings of the National Academy of Sciences USA* 104 (25): 10, 335–39.

Stos, Z[ofie] A. 2009. "Arcoss the Wine Dark Seas. . . Sailor Tinkers and Royal Cargoes in the Late Bronze Age Eastern Mediterranean." In *From Mine to Microscope: Advances in the Study of Ancient Technology*, edited by Andrew J. Shortland, Ian C. Freestone, and Thilo Reher, 163–80. Oxford: Oxbow Books.

Stubbs, Brian Darrel. 1998. "A Curious Element in Uto-Aztecan Linguistics." *Epigraphic Society Occasional Papers* 23: 109–40.

———. 2014. *Exploring the Explanatory Power of Egyptian and Semitic in Uto-Aztecan.* Provo, UT: Jerry D. Glover.

Suder, Hans. 1930. *Von Einbaum und Floss zum Schiff: Die primitiven Wasserfahrzeuge.* Veröffentlichungen des Instituts für Meerskunde N.S. B, Historisch-volks-wirt-schaftliche Reihe 7. Berlin.

Suggs, Robert C. 1960. *The Island Civilizations of Polynesia.* New York: Mentor Books, New American Library.

Suplee, Curt. 1999. "El Niño / La Niña: Nature's Vicious Cycle." *National Geographic Magazine* 195 (3): 72–95.

Sutherland, Patricia D., Peter H. Thompson, and Patricia A. Hunt. 2015. "Evidence of Early Metalworking in Arctic Canada." *Geoarchaeology* 30 (1): 74–78.

Sutter, Nathan B., Carlos D. Bustamante, Kevin Chase, Melissa M. Gray, Keyan Zhao, Lan Zhu, Badri Padhukasahasram, Eric Karlins, Sean Davis, Paul G. Jones, Pascale Quignon, Gary S. Johnson, Heidi G. Parker, Neale Fretwell, Dana S. Mosher, Dennis F. Lawler, Ebenezer Satyaraj, Magnus Nordborg, K. Gordon Lark, Robert K. Wayne, and Elaine A. Ostrander. 2007. "A Single *IGF1* Allele Is a Major Determinant of Small Size in Dogs." *Science* 316 (5821): 112–15.

Sutter, Richard. 2009, "Prehistoric Population Dynamics in the Andes." In *Andean*

Civilization: A Tribute to Michael E. Moseley, edited by Joyce Marcus and Patrick Ryan Williams, 9–38. Monograph 63. Los Angeles: Costen Institute of Archaeology.

Swamy, L. N. 1997. *Boats and Ships in Indian Art.* New Delhi: Harman.

Swerdlow, Joel L. 2002. "Unmasking Skin." *National Geographic Magazine* 202 (5): cover, 36–63.

Swindler, Daris R., Andrea G. Drusini, Claudio Cristino, and Cristina Ranzato. 1998. "Molar Crown Morphology of Pre-Contact Easter Islanders Compared with Molars from Other Islands." In *Easter Island in Pacific Context, South Seas Symposium: Proceedings of the Fourth International Conference on Easter Island and East Polynesiaa, University of New Mexico, Albuquerque, 5–10 August 1997,* edited by Christopher M. Stevenson, Georgia Lee, and F. J. Morin, 163–68. Los Osos, CA: Bearsville and Cloud Mountain Presses, Easter Island Foundation.

Swiny, Helena Wylde, and Michael L. Katzev. 1973. "The Kyrenia Shipwreck: A Fourth-Century B.C. Greek Merchant Ship." In *Marine Archaeology,* edited by D. J. Blackman, 339–55. Colston Papers 23. London: Butterworth.

Sykes, Bryan. 2012. *DNA USA.* New York: Liveright.

Sykes, Bryan, Andrew Leiboff, Jacob Low-Beer, Susannah Tetzner, and Martin Richards. 1995. "The Origins of the Polynesians: An Interpretation from Mitochondrial Lineage Analysis." *American Journal of Human Genetics* 57 (6): 1463–75.

Tankersley, Kenneth. 2000. "Who Were the First Americans?" *Archaeology* 53 (5): 72–75.

Taylor, David. 1990. *The Ultimate Dog Book.* New York: Simon and Schuster.

Taylor, E. G. R. 1956. *The Haven-Finding Art.* London: Hollis and Carter.

Teeter, Wendy Giddens. 2001. "Maya Animal Utilization in a Growing City: Vertebrate Exploitation at Caracol, Belize." PhD diss., University of California, Los Angeles.

———. 2004. "Animal Utilization in a Growing City: Vertebrate Exploitation at Caracol, Belize." In *Maya Zooarchaeology: New Directions in Method and Theory,* edited by Kitty F. Emery, 177–91. Monograph 51. Los Angeles: Cotsen Institute of Archaeology, University of California.

Temple, Robert. 1986. *The Genius of China: 3,000 Years of Science, Discovery, and Invention.* New York: Simon and Schuster.

Terrell, John Edward. 1981. "Linguistics and the Peopling of the Pacific Islands." *Journal of the Polynesian Society* 90 (2): 225–58.

———. 2001. "Review of 'On the Road of the Winds' by Kirch." *Journal of Anthropological Research* 57 (2): 235–36.

Thirslund, Søren. 1997. "Sailing Directions of the North Atlantic Viking Age (from about the Year 860 to 1400)." *Journal of Navigation* 50 (1): 55–64.

Thomas, Stephen D. 1987. *The Last Navigator.* New York: Henry Holt.

Thomas, William L. 1967. "The Pacific Basin: An Introduction." In *The Pacific Basin: A History of Its Geographical Exploration,* edited by Herman R. Friis,. 1–17. New York: American Geographical Society

Thompson, Gunnar. 1992. *American Discovery: The Real Story.* Seattle: Argonauts Misty Isles Press.

———. 1996. *The Friar's Map of Ancient North America, 1360 AD.* Bellevue, WA: Laura Lee Productions.

———. 2007. *Secret Voyages: True Adventure Stories from the Forbidden Chronicles of American Discovery.* Seattle: Misty Isles Press.

———. 2010. *Ancient Egyptian Maize.* Seattle: Misty Isles Bookstore@www.Lulu.com.

Thompson, Judi, and Alan Taylor. 1980. *Polynesian Canoes and Navigation.* Laie, HI: Institute for Polynesian Studies, Brigham Young University, Hawaii Campus.

Thompson, Raymond H. 1956. "The Archaeological Approach to the Study of Cultural Stability." In *Seminars in Archaeology: 1955.* Society for American Archaeology, Memoirs 11. *American Antiquity* 22 (2, pt. 2): 31–57.

Thomsen, Harriette H. 1960. "Occurrence of Fired Bricks in Pre-Conquest Mexico." *Southwestern Journal of Anthropology* 16 (4): 428–41.

Thomson, J. Oliver. 1965. *A History of Ancient Geography.* New York: Biblo and Tannen. (Originally published 1948, Cambridge University Press, Cambridge, UK.)

Thomson, Vicki A., Ophélie Lebrasseur, Jeremy J. Austin, Terry L. Hunt, David A. Burney, Tim Denham, Nicolas J. Rawlence, Jamie R. Wood, Jaime Gongora, Linus Girdland Flink, Anna Linderholm, Keith Dobney, Greger Larson, and Alan Cooper. 2014. "Using Ancient DNA to Study the Origins and Dispersal of Ancestral Polynesian Chickens across the Pacific." *Proceedings of the National Academy of Sciences, USA* 111 (13): 4826–31, doi:10.1073/pnas.1320412111.

Thornton, Russell. 1987. *American Indian Holocaust and Survival: A Population History since 1492.* Civilization of the American Indian 186. Norman: University of Oklahoma Press.

Thorpe, Nick. 2002. *8 Men and a Duck: An Improbable Voyage by Reed Boat to Easter Island.* New York: Free Press.

Thorsby, Erik. 2012. "The Polynesian Gene Pool: An Early Contribution by Amerindians to Easter Island." *Philosophical Transactions of the Royal Society B* 367 (1590): 812–19.

Throckmorton, Peter. 1996. *The Sea Remembers: Shipwrecks and Archaeology.* New York: Barnes and Noble Books.

Throckmorton, Peter, ed. 1970. *Shipwrecks and Archaeology: The Unharvested Sea.* Boston: Little, Brown.

Tolstoy, Paul. 1963. "Cultural Parallels between Southeast Asia and Mesoamerica in the Manufacture of Bark Cloth." *Transactions, New York Academy of Sciences* series 2, 25 (6): 646–62.

———. 1972. "Diffusion: As Explanation and Event." In *Early Chinese Art and Its Possible Influences in the Pacific Basin,* vol. 3, *Oceania and the Americas,* edited by Noel Barnard, 823–41. New York: Intercultural Arts Press.

———. 1986. "Trans-Pacific Contacts: What, Where and When?" *Quarterly Review of Archaeology* 7 (2–3): 6–9.

Tong, Weiming, and Lin Guohua. 1989. "A Comparison of Xinjiang and Beijing Carpets." *Oriental Rug Review* 9 (3): 12–14, 16–18.

Toohey, John. 2000. *Captain Bligh's Portable Nightmare.* New York: HarperCollins.

Tooley, M. J. 1974. "Sea-Level Changes during the Last 9000 Years in North-West England." *Geographical Journal* 140 (1): 18–42.

Torroni, Antonio. 2000. "Mitochondrial DNA and the Origin of Native Americans." In *America Past, America Present: Genes and Languages in the Americas and Beyond,* edited by Colin Renfrew, 77–87. Papers in the Prehistory of Language. Cambridge, UK: McDonald Institute for Archaeological Research.

Torroni, Antonio, Rem I. Sukernik, Theodore G. Schurr, Yelena B. Starikovskaya, Margaret F. Cabell, Michael H. Crawford, Anthony G. Comuzzi, and Douglas C. Wallace. 1993. "mtDNA Variation of Aboriginal Siberians Reveals Distinct Genetic Affinities with Native Americans." *American Journal of Human Genetics* 53 (3): 591–608.

Tosi, Maurizio. 1986. "Early Maritime Cultures of the Arabian Gulf and the Indian Ocean." In *Bahrain through the Ages: The Archaeology,* edited by Haya Ali Al Khalifa and Michael Rice, 96–107. London: KPI.

Totten, Norman. 2008. "All about a Worn-Out Coin." *Epigraphic Society Occasional Papers* 26: 160–61.

———. 2010. "The Last Word: A Description of New Netherland Including a Memory of Vikings in New York and New England?" *Epigraphic Society Occasional Papers* 28: 148–49.

Towle, Margaret. 1961. *The Ethnobotany of Pre-Columbian Peru.* Viking Fund Publications in Anthropology 30. New York: Wenner-Gren Foundation for Anthropological Research.

Toyne, Sarah. 1999. "Aborigines Were First Americans." London *Sunday Times*, August 22, 1, 8.

Trager, Leslie. 2006/7. "Mysterious Mapmakers: Exploring the Impossibly Accurate 16th-Century Maps of Antarctica and Greenland." *Explorers Journal* 84 (4): 36–41.

Trotter, Mildred. 1943. "Hair from Paracas Indian Mummies." *American Journal of Physical Anthropology* new series 1 (1): 69–75.

Tschanz, David W. 1997. "The Arab Roots of European Medicine." *Saudi Aramco World* 48 (3): front cover, inside front cover, 1, 20–31.

Unger, Richard W. 1980. *The Ship in the Medieval Economy, 600–1600.* Montreal: McGill-Queen's University Press.

Vadslrup, Søren. 1986. "Experience with Danish Viking Ship Copies." In *Sailing into the Past: Proceedings of the International Seminar on Replicas of Ancient and Medieval Vessels, Roskilde, 1984*, edited by Ole Crumlin-Pedersen and Max Vinner, 84–93. Roskilde, Denmark: Viking Ship Museum.

Vaillant, George C. 1931. "A Bearded Mystery." *Natural History* 31 (3): 243–52.

Valadez Azúa, Raúl. 2000. "Prehispanic Dog Types in Middle America." In *Dogs through Time: An Archaeological Perspective*, edited by S. J. Crockford, 193–204. BAR International Series 889. Oxford: [British Archaeological Reports].

Valsecchi, Maria Cristina. 2010. "2,500-Year-Old Greek Ship Raised off Sicilian Coast." *National Geographic News.* Accessed May 6, 2016. http://news.nationalgeographic.com/news/2008/08/080811-greek-ship.html.

Van Asch, Barbara, Ai-bing Zhang, Mattias C. R. Oskarsson, Cornelya F. C. Klütsch, António Amorin, and Peter Savolainen. 2013. "Pre-Columbian Origins of Native American Dog Breeds, with Only Limited Replacement by European Dogs, Confirmed by mtDNA Analysis." *Proceedings of the Royal Society B* 280 (1766): 1–9; 20131142 doi:10.1098/rspb.2013.1142.

Van de Noort, Robert, Richard Middleton, A. Foxon, and Alex Bayliss. 1999. "The 'Kilnsea-Boat,' and Some Implications from the Discovery of England's Oldest Plank Boat Remains." *Antiquity: A Quarterly Review of World Archaeology* 73 (279): 131–35.

Vanderbilt, Tom. 2013. "Accounting for Taste." *Smithsonian* 44 (3): 60–65, 104, 107.

Van Doorninck, Frederick. 1972. "Byzantium: Mistress of the Sea: 330–641." In *A History of Seafaring Based on Underwater Archaeology*, edited by George F. Bass, 133–58. New York: Walker.

Van Dorn, William G. 1974. *Oceanography and Seamanship.* New York: Dodd, Mead.

Van Sertima, Ivan. 1976. *They Came before Columbus.* New York: Random House.

———. 1995. "African Presence in Early America." In *Race, Discourse, and the Origin of the Americas: A New World View*, edited by Vera Lawrence Hyatt and Rex Nettleford, 66–102. Washington, DC: Smithsonian Institution Press.

———. 1998. *Early America Revisited.* New Brunswick, NJ: Transaction Publishers.

Van Tilburg, Hans K. 2007. *Chinese Junks in the Pacific.* Gainesville: University Press of Florida.

Vargas Martínez, Gustavo. 1996. *América en un mapa de 1489*. Mexico City: Taller Abierto.

Vartavan, Christian de, and Victoria Aseni Amorós. 1997. *Codex of Ancient Egyptian Plant Remains / Codex des restes végétaux de l'Égypte ancienne*. London: Triade Exploration.

Verano, John W. 1994. "Características fisicas y biolología osteológica de los Moche." In *Moche: Propuestas y perspectives*, edited by Santiago Uceda and Elías Mujica, 307–26. Traveaux de l'Institut Français d'Études Andines 79. Trujillo, Peru: Universidad Nacional de la Libertad; Instituto Francés de Estudios Andinos; Asociación Peruana para el Fomento de las Ciencias Sociales.

———. 1997. "Advances in the Paleopathology of Andean South America." *Journal of World Prehistory* 11 (2): 237–68.

Vesilind, Priit, and Sisse Brimberg. 2000. "In Search of Vikings." *National Geographic Magazine* 197 (5): cover, 2–35.

Villiers, Alan. 1973. *Men, Ships, and the Sea*. New ed. Washington, DC: National Geographic Society.

Vincent-Barwood, Aileen. 1992. "Columbus: What If?" *Saudi Aramco World* 43 (1): 2–9.

Vining, Edward P. 1885. *An Inglorious Columbus; or, Evidence That Hwui Shan and a Party of Buddhist Monks from Afghanistan Discovered America in the Fifth Century, A.D.* New York: D. Appleton.

Vishnu-Mittre, Aruna Sharma, and Chanchala. 1986. "Ancient Plant Economy at Daimabad." In *Daimabad, 1976–79*, 588–627. S. A. Sali. MASI 83. New Delhi: Archaeological Survey of India.

Voitov, V. I., and D. D. Tumarkin. 1967. "Navigational Conditions of Sea Routes to Polynesia." In *Archaeology at the Eleventh Pacific Science Congress: Papers Presented at the XI Pacific Science Congress, Tokyo, August–September 1966*, edited by William G. Solheim II, 88–100. Asian and Pacific Archaeology Series 1. Honolulu: Social Science Research Institute, University of Hawai'i.

Vosmer, Tom. 2000. "Model of a Third Millennium BC Reed Boat Based on Evidence from Ra's al-Jinz." *Journal of Oman Studies* 11: 149–52 + plate.

———. 2003. "The Magan Boat Project: A Process of Discovery, a Discovery of Process." *Proceedings of the Seminar for Arabian Studies* 33: 49–58.

———. 2010. "The Jewel of Muscat: Reconstructing a Ninth-Century Sewn-Plank Boat." In *Shipwrecked: Tang Treasures and Monsoon Winds*, edited by Regina Krahl, John Guy, J. Keith Wilson, and Julian Raby, 120–35. Washington, DC: Arthur M. Sackler Gallery, Smithsonian Institution / Singapore: National Heritage Board / Singapore Tourism Board.

Wagner, Philip L., and Marvin W. Mikesell, eds. *Readings in Cultural Geography*. Chicago: University of Chicago Press.

Walker, Phillip L., and Russell Thornton. 2002. "Health, Nutrition, and Demographic Change in Native California." In *The Backbone of History: Health and Nutrition in the Western Hemisphere*, edited by Richard H. Steckel and Jerome Carl Rose, 506–23. New York: Cambridge University Press.

Wallace, Birgitta Linderoth. 2000. "The Viking Settlement at L'Anse aux Meadows." In *Vikings: The North Atlantic Saga*, edited by William W. Fitzhugh and Elisabeth I. Ward, 208–16. Washington, DC: Smithsonian Institution Press.

Wallace, Douglas C. 1993. "American Indian Prehistory as Written in the Mitochondrial DNA: A Review." *Human Biology* 64 (3): 403–16.

Ward, Cheryl. 2006. "Boat-Building and Its Social Context in Early Egypt: Interpretations from the First Dynasty Boat-Grave Cemetery at Abydos." *Antiquity: A Quarterly Review of World Archaeology* 80 (307): 119–29.

Ward, Cheryl, Chiara Zazzaro, and Mohamed Abdel-Maguid. 2010. "Super-Sized Egyptian Ships." *International Journal of Nautical Archaeology* 39 (2): 387–89.

Ward, R. Gerard, and Muriel Brookfield. 1992. "The Dispersal of the Coconut: Did It Float or Was It Carried to Panama?" *Journal of Biogeography* 19 (5): 467–80.

Waters, Frank. 1963. *Book of the Hopi*. New York: Ballantine Books.

Watson, Andrew M. 2008. *Agricultural Innovation in the Early Islamic World: The Diffusion of Crops and Farming Techniques*. Cambridge: Cambridge University Press.

Watson, Douglas S. 1935. "Did the Chinese Discover America? A Critical Examination of the Buddhist Priest Hui Shên's Account of Fu Sang, and the Apocryphal Voyage of the Chinese Navigator Hee-Li." *California Historical Quarterly* 14 (1): 47–58.

Webster, David L. 1999. "American 'Adam' Left a Genetic Marker." *National Geographic Magazine* 196 (4): n.p.

———. 2002. *The Fall of the Ancient Maya: Solving the Mystery of the Maya Collapse*. New York: Thames and Hudson.

Weckler, J. E., Jr. 1943. *Polynesians: Explorers of the Pacific*. War Background Studies 6. Washington, DC: Smithsonian Institution.

Weisgerber, Gerd. 1986. "Dilmun—A Trading Entrepôt: Evidence from Historical and Archaeological Sources." In *Bahrain through the Ages: The Archaeology*, edited by Haya Ali Al Khalifa and Michael Rice, 135–42. London: KPI.

Welch, John W. 1999. "Dulling Occam's Razor." *Insights: An Ancient Window, the Newsletter of the Foundation for Ancient Research and Mormon Studies* 19 (4). Accessed May 7, 2016. http://publications.mi.byu.edu/publications/insights/19/4/19-4%20April%201999.pdf.

Whakataka-Brightwell, Greg. 1998. "In the Wake of Kupe." In *The Discovery of Aotearoa*, by Jeff Evans, 75–124. Auckland: Reed Books.

Wheatley, Paul. 1975. "Satyānrta in Suvarnadvīpa: From Reciprocity to Redistribution in Ancient Southeast Asia." In *Ancient Civilization and Trade*, edited by Jeremy A. Sabloff and C. C. Lamberg-Karlovsky, 227–83. Santa Fe: School of American Research.

Wheeler, Mortimer. 1954. *Archaeology from the Earth*. Oxford: Clarendon Press.

———. 1971. *Rome beyond the Imperial Frontiers*. Westport, CT: Greenwood Press. (Originally published 1954.)

Whistler, W. Arthur. 1990. "The Other Polynesian Gourd." *Pacific Science* 44 (2): 115–22.

Whitacker, Thomas W. 1971. "Endemism and Pre-Columbian Migration of the Bottle Gourd, *Lagenaria siceraria* (Mol.) Standl." In *Man across the Sea: Problems of Pre-Columbian Contacts*, edited by Carroll L. Riley, J. Charles Kelly, Campbell W. Pennington, and Robert L. Rands, 320–27. Austin: University of Texas Press.

Whitacker, Thomas W., and George F. Carter. 1954. "Oceanic Drift of Gourds—Experimental Observations." *American Journal of Botany* 41 (9): 697–700.

White, J. Peter. 1993. "The First Pacific Islanders, 30,000 Years Ago–10,000 Years Ago, Pioneers of the Ocean." In *The First Humans: Human Origins and History to 10,000 BC*, edited by Gören Burenhult, 170–74. San Francisco: HarperSan Francisco.

White, K. D. 1984. *Greek and Roman Technology*. Ithaca, NY: Cornell University Press.

White, Lynn, Jr. 1962. *Medieval Technology and Social Change*. Oxford: Oxford University Press.

———. 1976. "Food and History." In *Food, Man, and Society*, edited by Dwain N. Walcher, Norman Kretchmer, and Henry L. Barnett, 12–30. New York: Plenum.

———. 1978. *Medieval Religion and Technology: Collected Essays*. Publications of the

Center for Medieval and Renaissance Studies, UCLA 13. Berkeley: University of California Press.

Whitehouse, Harvey. 2007. "The Evolution and History of Religion." In *Holistic Anthropology: Emergence and Convergence*, edited by David J. Parkin and Stanley J. Wijaszek, 212–30. New York: Berghahn Books.

Whitewright, Julian. 2009. "The Mediterranean Lateen Sail in Late Antiquity." *International Journal of Nautical Archaeology* 38 (1): 97–104.

Whitfield, Peter. 1996. *The Charting of the Oceans: Ten Centuries of Maritime Maps*. London: British Library.

Whittall, James P., Jr. 1989. "Architecture and Epigraphic Evidence for Christian Celts in Connecticut, circa 500–700 A.D." In *Atlantic Visions*, edited by John de Courcy Ireland and David C. Sheehy, 133–42. Dún Laoghair, Ireland: Boole Press.

———. 1991. "Radiocarbon Dates Associated with Stonework in New England." *Early Sites Research Society Bulletin* 18 (1): 63–65.

Wichmann, Søren. 1995. *The Relationship among the Mixe-Zoquean Languages of Mexico*. Studies in Indigenous Languages of the Americas. Salt Lake City: University of Utah Press.

Wiercínski, Andrzej. 1972a. "An Anthropological Study on the Origin of 'Olmecs.'" *Swiatowit* 33: 143–74.

———. 1972b. "Inter- and Intrapopulational Racial Differentiation of Tlatilco, Cerro de las Mesas, Teotihuacan, Monte Alban and Yucatan Maya." *International Congress of Americanists, Proceedings* 39 (1): 231–48. (Also 1972 in *Swiatowit* 33: 175–97.)

Wiet, Gaston. 1969. "The Moslem World (Seventh to Thirteenth Centuries)." In *A History of Technology and Invention: Progress through the Ages*, vol. 1, *The Origins of Technological Civilization*, edited by Maurice Daumas, translated by Eileen B. Hennessy, 336–72. New York: Crown.

Wilkinson, R. L. 1995. "Yellow Fever: Ecology, Epidemiology, and Role in the Collapse of the Classic Lowland Maya Civilization." *Medical Anthropology* 16 (3): 269–94.

Will, Peter, and Ignacio H. Escapa. 2014. "Green Web or Megabiased Clock? Plant Fossils from Gondwanan Patagonia Speak on Evolutionary Radiations." *New Phytologist*. doi:10.1111/nph.13114.

Williams, Glyndwr. 1997. *The Great South Sea: English Voyages and Encounters, 1570–1750*. New Haven, CT: Yale University Press.

Williams, Michael, with David Lowenthal and William M. Denevan. 2014. *To Pass on a Good Earth: The Life and Work of Carl O. Sauer*. Charlottesville: University of Virginia Press.

Williams, Stephen. 1991. *Fantastic Archaeology: The Wild Side of North American Prehistory*. Philadelphia: University of Pennsylvania Press.

Williamson, Andrew. 1974. "Harvard Archaeological Survey in Oman, 1973: III—Sohar and the Sea Trade of Oman in the Tenth Century A.D." *Proceedings of the Seminar for Arabian Studies* 4: 78–96.

Wilson, Ian. 1991. *The Columbus Myth: Did Men of Bristol Reach America before Columbus?* London: Simon and Schuster.

Wilson, Joseph A. P. 2012. "The Cave Who Never Was: Outsider Archaeology and Failed Collaboration in the USA." *Public Archaeology* 11 (2): 73–95.

Winchester, Simon. 1985. *Outposts: Journeys to the Surviving Relics of the British Empire*. London: Scepter.

———. 2010. *Atlantic: Great Sea Battles, Heroic Discoveries, Titanic Storms, and a Vast Ocean of a Million Stories*. New York: HarperCollins.

Winter, Joseph C. 1999. "Feeding the Ancestors—The Role of Tobacco in the Evolution of Southwestern Agriculture and Religion." In *La Frontera: Papers in Honor of Patrick H. Beckett*, edited by Meliha S. Duran and David T. Kirkpatrick, 215–30. Archaeological Society of New Mexico Papers 25. Albuquerque: Archaeological Society of New Mexico.

———. 2000. "Botanical Description of the North American Tobacco Species." In *Tobacco Use by Native North Americans: Sacred Smoke and Silent Killer*, edited by Joseph C. Winter, 87–127. Norman: University of Oklahoma Press.

Wood, Gordon S. 2008. *The Purpose of the Past: Reflections on the Uses of History*. New York: Penguin Press.

Worcester, G. R. G. 1956. "Four Small Craft of T'ai-wan." *Mariner's Mirror* 42 (4): 302–12.

———. 1966. *Sail and Sweep in China: The History and Development of the Chinese Junk as Illustrated by the Collection of Junk Models in the Science Museum*. London: Her Majesty's Stationery Office.

Workman, P. L., J. D. Niswander, K. S. Brown, and W. C. Leyshon. 1974. "Population Studies on Southwestern Indian Tribes: IV; The Zuni." *American Journal of Physical Anthropology* 41 (1): 119–32.

Wright, Edward V., Robert E. M. Hedges, Alex Bayliss, and Robert Van de Noort. 2001. "New AMS Radiocarbon Dates for the North Ferriby Boats—A Contribution to Dating Prehistoric Seafaring in Northwestern Europe." *Antiquity: A Quarterly Review of World Archaeology* 75 (290): 726–34.

Wuthenau, Alexander von. 1975. *Unexpected Faces in Ancient America, 1500 B.C.–A.D. 1500: The Historical Testimony of Pre-Columbian Artists*. New York: Crown.

Yamashita, Masahiro, Eiji Ido, Tomoyuki Miura, and Masanori Hayami. 1996. "Molecular Epidemiology of HTLV-I in the World." *Journal of Acquired Immune Deficiency Syndromes and Human Retrovirology* 13 (supplement 1): S124–31.

Yates, Donald N. 2010. "News Flash!!!! Central Band of Cherokee / Brock Cherokee DNA Projects." *Ancient American* 14 (86): 53.

———. 2012. *Old World Roots of the Cherokee: How DNA, Ancient Alphabets, and Religion Explain the Origins of America's Largest Indian Nation*. Jefferson, NC: McFarland.

Yates, Donald N., and Teresa A. Yates. 2014. *Cherokee DNA Studies: Real People Who Proved the Geneticists Wrong*. Phoenix: Panther's Lodge Publishers.

Yen, Douglas E. 1974. *The Sweet Potato and Oceania: An Essay in Ethnobotany*. Bishop Museum Bulletin 236. Honolulu: Bishop Museum Press.

Zago, Marco A., Eduardo J. Melo Santos, J. B. Cleg, João F. Gerreiro, Jeremy I. Martinson, Jemma Norwich, and Mauro S. Figueiredo. 1995. "α-Globin Gene Haplotypes in South American Indians." *Human Biology: The International Journal of Population Genetics and Anthropology* 67 (4): 535–46.

Zamora, Tomas, Vladimir Zaninovic, Masaharu Kajiwara, Haruko Komoda, Masanori Hayami, and Kazuo Tajima. 1990. "Antibody to HTLV-I in Indigenous Inhabitants of the Andes and Amazon Regions in Colombia." *Japanese Journal of Cancer Research* 81 (8): 715–19.

Zegura, Stephen L., Tatiana M. Karafet, and Michael F. Hammer. 2009. "The Peopling of the Americas as Viewed from the Y Chromosome." In *Ancient Human Migrations: A Multidisciplinary Approach*, edited by Peter L. Peregrine, Ilia Peiros, and Marcus Feldman, 127–36. Foundations of Archaeological Inquiry. Salt Lake City: University of Utah Press.

Zerubavel, Eviatar. 1992. *Terra Cognita: The Mental Discovery of America*. New Brunswick, NJ: Rutgers University Press.

Zhao, Feng. 1998. "Art of Silk and Art on Silk in China." In *China 5,000 Years: Inno-*

vation and Transformation in the Arts, selected by Sherman Lee, 98–102. New York: Guggenheim Museum.

Zimmerley, David W., and Paul Gardiner. 2000. *Qayaq: Kayaks of Alaska and Siberia.* Fairbanks: University of Alaska Press.

Zohary, Daniel. 1998. "The Diffusion of South and East Asian and of African Crops into the Belt of Mediterranean Agriculture." In *Plants for Food and Medicine: Proceedings of the Joint Conference for Economic Botany and the International Society for Ethnopharmacology, London, 1–6 July 1996,* edited by H. D. V. Prendergast, N. L. Etkin, D. R. Harris, and P. J. Houghton, 123–34. Richmond, UK: Royal Botanical Gardens, Kew.

Zumwinkle, Richard, ed. and trans. 1970. *Kaigai Ibun.* Los Angeles: Dawson's Book Shop.

Index